Wordsworth

THE SENSE OF HISTORY

One wants to grant literature its autonomy, but one certainly doesn't want to cut it loose from the rest of the world, which in a thousand different ways it is constantly reflecting. What is the relation of literature to other things, the other things that men make and the other things that men do and think?

Cleanth Brooks

Wordsworth

THE SENSE OF HISTORY

ALAN LIU

STANFORD UNIVERSITY PRESS
Stanford, California

Published with the assistance of the
National Endowment for the Humanities
and with the assistance of a special
grant from the Stanford University
Faculty Publication Fund to help
support nonfaculty work originating at Stanford

Stanford University Press
Stanford, California
© 1989 by the Board of Trustees
of the Leland Stanford Junior University
Printed in the United States of America

CIP data appear at the end of the book

For my parents

Contents

Illustrations

FIGURES

Abbreviations

WORKS NOT LISTED HERE are cited in the text and notes in short form (author's surname, short form of title if appropriate, and page number). Complete information for such works can be found in References, pp. 645–75.

AR   *The Annual Register, or a View of the History, Politics, and Literature, for the Year. . . .* London.

B   Wordsworth, William. *The Borderers.* Ed. Robert Osborn. The Cornell Wordsworth. Ithaca, N.Y., 1982.

CEY   Reed, Mark L. *Wordsworth: The Chronology of the Early Years, 1770–1799.* Cambridge, Mass., 1967.

CMY   Reed, Mark L. *Wordsworth: The Chronology of the Middle Years, 1800–1815.* Cambridge, Mass., 1975.

DNB   *Dictionary of National Biography: From the Earliest Times to 1900.* Ed. Leslie Stephen and Sidney Lee. Rpt. Oxford, 1921–22.

DS   Wordsworth, William. *Descriptive Sketches.* Ed. Eric Birdsall with Paul M. Zall. The Cornell Wordsworth. Ithaca, N.Y., 1984.

DSFR   Stewart, John Hall. *A Documentary Survey of the French Revolution.* New York, 1951.

DWJ   Wordsworth, Dorothy. *Journals of Dorothy Wordsworth: The Alfoxden Journal 1798; The Grasmere Journals 1800–1803.* 2d ed. Ed. Mary Moorman. Oxford, 1971.

EM   *European Magazine, and London Review.* London.

EW   Wordsworth, William. *An Evening Walk*. Ed. James Averill. The Cornell Wordsworth. Ithaca, N.Y., 1984.

GM   *Gentleman's Magazine*. London.

Lakes   Gilpin, William. *Observations, Relative Chiefly to Picturesque Beauty, Made in the Year 1772, On Several Parts of England; Particularly the Mountains, and Lakes of Cumberland, and Westmoreland*. 2 vols. 1786. Rpt. as *Observations on the Mountains and Lakes of Cumberland and Westmorland*. Richmond, Eng., 1973.

LC1   Bouch, C. M. L., and G. P. Jones. *A Short Economic and Social History of the Lake Counties, 1500–1830*. Manchester, 1961.

LC2   Marshall, J. D., and John K. Walton. *The Lake Counties from 1830 to the Mid-Twentieth Century: A Study in Regional Change*. Manchester, 1981.

Letters   *The Letters of William and Dorothy Wordsworth*. Ed. Ernest de Selincourt. 2d ed. Vol 1: *The Early Years, 1787–1805*. Rev. Chester L. Shaver. Oxford, 1967. Vol 2: *The Middle Years, Part I, 1806–1811*. Rev. Mary Moorman. Oxford, 1969. Vol. 3: *The Middle Years, Part II, 1812–1820*. Rev. Mary Moorman and Alan G. Hill. Oxford, 1970. Vol 5: *The Later Years, Part II, 1829–1834*. Rev. Alan G. Hill. Oxford, 1979. Vol. 6: *The Later Years, Part III, 1835–1839*. Rev. Alan G. Hill. Oxford, 1982.

LY   *The Letters of William and Dorothy Wordsworth: The Later Years*. Ed. Ernest de Selincourt. Vol. 3: *1841–50*. Oxford, 1939.

MC   *Morning Chronicle*. London.

MM   Moorman, Mary. *William Wordsworth: A Biography*. 2 vols. Vol. 1: *The Early Years, 1770–1803*. Oxford, 1957. Vol. 2: *The Later Years, 1803–1850*. Oxford, 1965.

MP   *Morning Post, and Gazetteer*. London.

Prel.   Wordsworth, William. *The Prelude, or Growth of a Poet's Mind (Text of 1805)*. Ed. Ernest de Selincourt. 2d ed., rev. Stephen Gill. Oxford, 1970.

1850 Prel. Wordsworth, William. *The Prelude*, 1850 version. In *The Prelude, or Growth of a Poet's Mind*. Ed. Ernest de Selincourt. 2d ed., rev. Helen Darbishire. Oxford, 1959.

Prose   Wordsworth, William. *The Prose Works of William Wordsworth*. Ed. W. J. B. Owen and Jane Worthington Smyser. 3 vols. Oxford, 1974.

P2V   Wordsworth, William. *"Poems, in Two Volumes," and Other Poems, 1800–1807*. Ed. Jared Curtis. The Cornell Wordsworth. Ithaca, N.Y., 1983.

PW   Wordsworth, William. *The Poetical Works of William Words-worth*. Eds. Ernest de Selincourt and Helen Darbishire. Vols. 1, 3–5. Oxford, 1940–49. Vol. 2, 2d ed., rev. Helen Darbishire. Oxford, 1952.

RC   Wordsworth, William. *"The Ruined Cottage" and "The Ped-lar."* Ed. James Butler. The Cornell Wordsworth. Ithaca, N.Y., 1979.

SP   Wordsworth, William. *The Salisbury Plain Poems of William Wordsworth: "Salisbury Plain," or "A Night on Salisbury Plain," "Adventures on Salisbury Plain" (including "The Female Va-grant"), "Guilt and Sorrow; or, Incidents upon Salisbury Plain."* Ed. Stephen Gill. The Cornell Wordsworth. Ithaca, N.Y., 1975.

STCE   Coleridge, Samuel Taylor. *Essays on His Times in "The Morning Post" and "The Courier."* Ed. David V. Erdman. Vols. 1–2. Collected Works of Samuel Taylor Coleridge, no. 3. Princeton, N.J., 1978. Unless otherwise noted, page citations are to vol. 1.

T   *The Times*. London.

WAG   Wordsworth, Jonathan, M. H. Abrams, and Stephen Gill, eds. *"The Prelude": 1799, 1805, 1850: Authoritative Texts, Con-text and Reception, Recent Critical Essays*. Norton Critical Edition. New York, 1979.

WP   Hartman, Geoffrey H. *Wordsworth's Poetry, 1787–1814*. New Haven, Conn., 1975.

Acknowledgments

I WISH TO THANK the following for reading and commenting on parts of my manuscript; their critical enthusiasm has made the writing act less lonely: Alan Bewell, Don H. Bialostosky, Liz Bohls, Jerome Christensen, Michael Cooke, Geoffrey Hartman, John Hodgson, Mary Jacobus, Theresa Kelley, Herbert Lindenberger, Jerome McGann, Peter Manning, Anne Mellor, W. J. T. Mitchell, Reeve Parker, Ronald Paulson, Sara Suleri, David Wagenknecht, and Carl Woodring. Thanks also to John Bender for advice on photographic sources. Special thanks to my closest readers, in all senses: Helen Tartar, for her early and lasting faith; Jay Clayton, for good talk on narrative and other issues; and Patricia Fumerton, for help at every level from conceptualization to cut-and-paste. The latter's work on "giving" is not just theory.

The intellectual spirit of this book owes much to Herbert Lindenberger, Geoffrey Hartman, and Ronald Paulson—whose interests and individual manners of quest have influenced me directly. I should like to think as well that if this book has both intensity and diversity, those traits express the ample rigor I learned to value among the members of the Yale English Department. Finally, special mention to two courses that, while removed from the subject of this book, have been its invisible partners through the years: thanks to my students at Yale in the Introduction to British Studies seminar and the Age of Johnson lecture for being open to adventure but insisting on truth.

Chapter 1 appeared in earlier form in *ELH* 51 (1984); a section of Chapter 8 appeared in earlier form in *Modern Language Quarterly* 43 (1982). Parts of Chapters 1 and 2 were presented at the Modern Language Association convention, New York, 1983. A section of Chapter 9 was read in the Colloquium series of the Yale Center for British Art, 1981. My thanks to everyone at the Center, past and present, for hosting me through the years and making it easy to love pictures. Thanks also to Yale University for a Morse Fellowship, 1982–83.

PART I

Introduction

CHAPTER ONE

⎯⎰⎯

The History in "Imagination"

At the point of discovery in James Bruce's *Travels to Discover the Source of the Nile*, which Wordsworth knew about by 1803 but may not have read until 1807,[1] there is an agony that must fill any reader of Wordsworth with déjà vu. Bruce believes that he has found the fountains of the Nile, but, strangely, feels disappointment:

I was, at that very moment, in possession of what had, for many years, been the principal object of my ambition and wishes: indifference, which from the usual infirmity of human nature follows, at least for a time, complete enjoyment, had taken place of it. The marsh, and the fountains, upon comparison with the rise of many of our rivers, became now a trifling object in my sight. I remembered that magnificent scene in my own native country, where the Tweed, Clyde, and Annan rise in one hill; three rivers, as I now thought, not inferior to the Nile in beauty. . . . I had seen the rise of the Rhine and Rhone, and the more magnificent sources of the Soane [*sic*]; I began, in my sorrow, to treat the inquiry about the source of the Nile as a violent effort of a distempered fancy:—

> What's Hecuba to him, or he to Hecuba,
> That he should weep for her?—

Grief or despondency now rolling upon me like a torrent; relaxed, not refreshed, by unquiet and imperfect sleep, I started from my bed in the utmost agony; I went to the door of my tent; every thing was still; the Nile, at whose head I stood, was not capable either to promote or to interrupt my slumbers, but the coolness and serenity of the night braced my nerves, and chased away those phantoms that, while in bed, had oppressed and tormented me.

It was true, that numerous dangers, hardships, and sorrows had beset me . . . but it was still as true, that another Guide, more powerful than my own courage, health, or understanding, if any of these can be called man's own, had uniformly protected me. (3:640–41)

Like Wordsworth at the peak of experience in Simplon Pass, Bruce at the source of experience discovers deep emptiness. His true discovery is that he has been led all the while by distempered fancy and a Guide, a pair whose conflation might yield Wordsworth's own spirit of worldly denial at Simplon: "Imagination! . . . Strong in itself, and in the access of joy / Which hides it like the overflowing Nile" (*Prel.* 6.525–48).

The readings we now have of the Simplon Pass episode, among which Geoffrey Hartman's is in the vanguard, are so powerful that the episode has become one of a handful of paradigms capable by itself of representing the poet's work.[2] I seek in this chapter to reimagine Wordsworth's 1790 trip and *The Prelude*'s insertion of Imagination into that trip. To do so, I take as my thought-vehicle the framework of the contemporary touring experience itself. One implication of the comparison to Bruce is that the disappointment at the origin of Imagination in the Alps inheres in any tour aimed toward a goal. Bruce's reflections at the point of discovery show that there are really two models underlying his travels: the voyage of exploration, which points toward an exotic goal, and the tour, which allows only passage through the already known (the Tweed, Clyde, Annan, Rhine, Rhone, and Saône). At the moment of discovery, suddenly, it is tour that dominates and exploration that seems out of place. A tour is designed only to make sense of passage, not of a goal. If an exploration were a sentence, its goal would be the last word. But in a tour, the real goal is the sense of the sentence's overall completion, a sense that cannot appear within the sentence but only on the plane of the grammar framing sentences. From a viewpoint within a tour, therefore, any sense of completion posited at the terminus can only appear a gap, an absence.

In Hartman's reading, Wordsworth's "self" forms in this gap as a self-knowing displacement of nature's sourcehood balanced dialectically against restitution to nature. Holding fast to the tour model with its worldly concerns, as opposed to Hartman's model of the mystic pilgrimage,[3] I offer a reformulation, which, if formally only an addition, ultimately declares something quite different about what we believe the self to be. It seems to me that the self arises in a three-body problem: history, nature, self. In *The Prelude*—as in the nineteenth century with its historicist and evolutionist concerns generally—history is the base upon which the issue of nature's sourcehood is worked out. *The Prelude* organizes the 1790 tour so that "nature" is precipitated in Book 6 only as a denial of the history behind any tour, and the goal of the denial—not fully effective until the purge of

Books 9 and 10—is to carve the "self" out of history. The theory of denial is Imagination.

What is history, whose early detail for Wordsworth is the French Revolution? Let me simply gesture for the moment. Something must rush into the gap discovered on a tour with a determined goal, something whose essence will be a sourcehood *elsewhere*. Such is a preliminary, ad hoc definition of history at its contact point with experience: a sense, not yet formulated into idea, that the completion of the present depends perpetually upon something beyond—whether that force of beyond will ultimately be thought as Hegelian *Geist* (anchored in a future sense) or the later Wordsworthian "realities" of people, nation, and church (rooted in the past). We might think here of the anthem of historical sourcehood in Book 8 of *The Prelude*:

> Great God!
> That aught *external* to the living mind
> Should have such mighty sway! yet so it was
> A weight of Ages did at once descend
> Upon my heart; no thought embodied, no
> Distinct remembrances; but weight and power,
> Power growing with the weight.   (8.700–706)

The Motive of Description: The 1790 Letter

It will be useful first to view Wordsworth's 1790 trip as much as possible from the perspective of 1790 itself. After shipping to Calais on July 13, Wordsworth and Robert Jones spent the summer walking through France, the Savoy, Switzerland, and upper Italy along a route with three segments: *1790a*, a beeline south through France to St. Vallier, highlighted by a boat trip on the Saône (July 13 to August 1); *1790b*, a winding, looping, and at times backtracking passage from St. Vallier through the Savoy, Switzerland, and Italy back up to Basel (August 1 to September 21); and *1790c*, a beeline by boat up the Rhine to Cologne and then home (September 22 to sometime in October).[4] The vertical legs of the tour—each straightforward, each undertaken partly by boat, and each immersed in the sights of Liberty (the celebrations of the French *fédérés* and preparations of the Belgian Republican armies, respectively)—flank the divagations of 1790b as if between facing mirrors.

As will be reported by Book 6 of *The Prelude*, the "variegated journey step by step" of 1790a has the contour of seriality:[5]

> Day after day, up early and down late,
> From vale to vale, from hill to hill we went
> From Province on to Province did we pass.
>   (6.431–33)

So, too, "The Author's Voyage Down the Rhine (Thirty Years Ago)"
(probably composed 1820 or 1821) will describe 1790c as a propagation of scenery by repetition:

> We saw the living Landscapes of the Rhine,
> Reach after reach, salute us and depart;
> Slow sink the Spires,—and up again they start!
> (*PW*, 3: 409)

Between the mirrors of 1790a and 1790c stands the less clearly defined
progress of 1790b. Yet our best direct record of the 1790 tour, Wordsworth's long letter to Dorothy written during 1790b from September
6 to 16, also casts this leg of the tour as simple seriality:

My Spirits have been kept in a perpetual hurry of delight by the almost uninterrupted succession of sublime and beautiful objects which have passed
before my eyes. . . . It was with regret that we passed every turn of this
charming path, where every new picture was purchased by the loss of
another which we would never have been tired of gazing at. (*Letters*, 1: 32,
34)

Seriality reduces at base to duplication, the substitution of one
point-scene for another. By point-scenes I mean precisely the pictures Wordsworth sketches: landscape paintings of the mind, each
composed as if the perceiver were at total rest and as if human vision
permitted only a single-recession system with one vanishing point.
Observe, for example, the absolute point of view and bilateral symmetry in this sketch: "The lake is narrow and the shadows of the
mountains were early thrown across it. It was beautiful to watch
them travelling up the sides of the hills for several hours, to remark
one half of a village covered with shade, and the other bright with the
strongest sunshine" (*Letters*, 1: 33). But how does the traveler move
from one such point to the next? The point-scene pictured in this
passage assumes the petrification of the perceiver: motion has to be
projected outward into landscape itself as the "travelling" of shadows. Here we arrive at the paradigm structure, and dilemma, behind
a tour's seriality: a tour reduces to two points between which a break
poses the problem of continuity.

Of course, a traveler overcomes the break by physically moving.
But physical motion, analyzable variously as muscle contractions,
steps, whole days' journeys, and so forth, has no innate continuity
unless *thought* as continuity. Faced with the gap between points of
scenery, a tourist may exert certain muscles in a certain sequence,
but he cannot "move" from one point to the next unless the logical
relationship between those points is formed in his mind as an accompanying aura of ideas called "description." As emblematized by
the fact that Wordsworth probably read, and was guided by, William

Coxe's *Travels in Switzerland* before his 1790 trip (Coe, pp. 47–48; Wildi, p. 225; D. Hayden, pp. 107–10),[6] no tour can exist as a connected movement unless that movement occurs in a space already described.

It is difficult, however, to discover the real logic of connection in description. The elusiveness of such logic is illustrated in the sketch of the "variegated journey" quoted from *The Prelude* earlier. Wordsworth glosses over vague predication—the connective motion sketched by "went" and "pass"—with a cloud of adverbial prepositional phrases that are themselves vague ("From vale to vale . . .") but so conventional that the reader merely assumes the kind of motion meant. The underlying logic of a tour is always unrecoverable behind the conventional, behind modifiers that narrate the relationship between any two point-scenes according to a plot ready-made. With astonishing frequency in the letter, as in the sentence "My Spirits have been kept in a perpetual hurry of delight by the almost uninterrupted succession of sublime and beautiful objects," Wordsworth adopts the most conventional modifier of all locodescriptive tourist experience: a logic of aesthetic movement (as in "I am moved") expressible in the formula, "sublimity" ←("delight")→ "beauty." As in Denham's "Cooper's Hill," movement between scenes of the sublime and the beautiful transforms into a convention of affective movement, delight.[7] One moves from the mountain to the river in a trajectory that is pleasure.

The root modifier of experience to which aesthetics points may be generalized as motivation, or the psychology of movement. Faced with the gap between point-scenes, a tourist cloaks his physical motion and its logic of relationship behind a calculus of affect, a neverending effort to convince himself, or someone, that even though, as Wordsworth says, "every new picture was purchased by the loss of another which we would never have been tired of gazing at," there is indeed a conventionally understood motive for forward momentum. But such motivation for tours is never fully convincing. Tours, as opposed to journeys or explorations, always seem undermotivated; they always seem to be impelled by someone else's motive. A tour's conventional motivation, perhaps, always represses something indescribable at home—whether ennui or something stronger. This is especially clear in such works as William Lisle Bowles's tour sonnets (or, as we will see, Wordsworth's own *Descriptive Sketches*, composed 1791–92), where motivation for touring is conventionalized as a romantic problem at home—as a heartbreak whose veiled eroticism cannot be addressed except in the tour's vocabulary of aesthetic pleasure.[8]

We might sum up by saying that a tour is motivated by desire for some special *significance* (whether conceived as meaning or feeling) missing at home: a sense of eventfulness whose site is inherently "out there," other, or elsewhere and so from the first adapted to the form of convention. Convention is the sense of a meaningfulness described by someone prior and other, a significance whose mere redescription in any itinerary will result in a feeling of complete eventfulness.

When Wordsworth models 1790b as if it simply mirrors 1790a or 1790c, then, he follows convention, the form of a tour's meaning. Like Bruce, however, he also wants 1790b to localize a goal in a particular segment of the tour rather than on the plane of the tour's overall completion. But since a tour's real goal of convention can never be focused adequately on a segment (conventional expressions of ecstasy at any Alp or Niagara thus show the thinness of conventionality), the stopgap of convention begins to hollow out in Switzerland. In Wordsworth's 1790 letter, the gap between Alpine point-scenes becomes increasingly difficult to fill with modifiers premising behind aesthetic cliché a meaningfulness, a sense of motivated connection, to be acquired merely by redescribing the scene. And as the gaps become ever more insistent, ever more empty of motivated connection, there begins to come to view the fundamental undermotivation of the 1790 tour. Wordsworth, after all, had no good reason to leave England and the chance of a fellowship behind*—an embarrassing circumstance that his letter deals with by emphasizing how frugal he has been (how much money he has *not* spent) and by apologizing to his Uncle William ("I should be sorry if I have offended him"; *Letters*, 1: 32, 37). What can fill the gap in motivation in lieu of the conventional?

Observe the gap in pleasure between lower and upper Lake Geneva in the following passage, a space of desire that conventional aesthetics will not explain and that demands "amends," a sort of scenic version of apology to Uncle William:

The lower part of the lake did not afford us a pleasure equal to what might have been expected from its celebrity. This was owing partly to its width, and partly to the weather, which was one of those hot glaring days in which all distant objects are veiled in a species of bright obscurity. But the higher part of the lake made us ample amends, 'tis true we had the same disagreeable weather but the banks of the water are infinitely more picturesque, and as it is much narrower, the landscape suffered proportionally less from that pale steam which before almost entirely hid the opposite shore. (*Letters*, 1: 33)

We recognize here the two-point model of touring in which description, after a strenuous effort, finally orders the point-scenes as a hierarchy of "low" to "high," as a structure with an innate motive for

* The 1790 letter mentions that he had acquainted his uncle, William Cookson, "with my having given up all thoughts of a fellowship" (*Letters*, 1: 37).

forward momentum. First there is a lower view felt as insignificant: the goal does not match its celebrated description. Then, after a gap, a higher view repeats the former in a key of greater significance. In the interstice is an ill-defined, ambivalent medium of signification apparent only as a confusion of sensation: a hot glare, veil, or bright obscurity. Considered one way, this obscurity projects Wordsworth's difficulty in description, his lack of aesthetic cliché with which to explain the difference/sameness between lower and upper lakes. We almost hear a sigh of relief when, in the last sentence, he resumes the conventional with the word "picturesque."[9] Considered another way, "bright obscurity" attests to dependence on an *alternate* resource of convention even more banal: talking about the weather. "Bright obscurity" is an atmospherics or ambience, something in the air "out there" in which connection can still be posited as commonly understood.

Following the description of Lake Geneva is a more immense bright obscurity. Wordsworth cloaks the sights later to be monumentalized in Book 6 of *The Prelude* within inexpressibility *topoi* and other clichés of circumvention:

We left our bundles and struck over the mountains to Chamouny to visit the glaciers of Savoy. You have undoubtedly heard of these celebrated s[c]enes, but if you have not read of them any description which I have here room to give you must be altogether inadequate. . . . At Brig we quitted the Valais and passed the Alps at the Semplon in order to visit part of Italy. The impressions of three hours of our walk among the Alps will never be effaced. (*Letters*, 1: 33)

Wordsworth says to Dorothy: only *if* you know the description of the Chamonix could I describe it to you. Description only gestures toward a pleasure of description "out there," hanging in air between brother and sister. Just so, when he says that the impressions of the Simplon Pass will never be effaced, it is unclear what impressions were etched in the first place. Impressiveness also hangs in air, in a pleasure of convention.

Let me borrow a reading from Erich Auerbach's *Mimesis* to frame "bright obscurity," the veil under which Wordsworth shifts conventions at his goal. Examining Hebraic narrative as epitomized in the story of Abraham and Isaac, Auerbach probes at the lack of connection between any two points of narrative, at the "paratactic" magic by which characters simply appear on a new scene or enact new deeds without any movement being described. In the gap between points is Auerbach's "background" (pp. 3–23). Traversing the Alps, Wordsworth is Abraham-his-own-Isaac; motion, or motive, between any two points hides in background ambience.

Talking about the weather is always a way to talk about something else. What alternative to the eroticism of aesthetics hangs suspended in the background? What is in the air?

Federation and Convention

Auerbach's "background" houses the Protean spirit of his work, "history." Here the bonus of entering our problem through the worldly tour shows itself. An entire volume of Bruce's five-volume work is devoted to the "Annals of Abyssinia." So, too, Coxe's splendid reportage of his travels is backed up by an enormous amount of Swiss history—synopses whose focus on tyranny overthrown or liberty defended will be footnoted in later editions with ironic reference to the French occupation of Switzerland.[10] Tours always describe motion through a land written over by history, even though they also carefully keep history—however many pages are devoted to it—in the background as if it were supplemental to the delights of the present tour, as if, in other words, it were merely a flourish complementing foreground appreciation. As a convention of tours, history is ornamental.

The notion of the supplement or ornament is very difficult. We say that an ornament beautifies its object; but the object of ornamentation —as is clear in the tradition of courtly love sonnets—is always presumed to be the *ne plus ultra* of beauty: therefore, why does Beauty need the eroticism of ornamentation? In the face of this paradox, theories of ornamentation must enroll it in a structure of signification —whether Platonic (the ornament represents imperfectly the inaccessible beauty of the true), Aristotelian (the ornament expresses an inner beauty), or Chain-of-Being (everything in the universe is part of a necklace allegorizing the prime mover of beauty). Ornament is a mark, a writing. The shyness of its signified, Beauty, can be accounted for by thinking along the lines Angus Fletcher develops in his study of ornament and its Greek form, *kosmos* (pp. 108–46): ornaments mark on the foreground plane (through tokens of place such as dress or the proper accent) a cosmic order of fitness, a total rule of Beauty, otherwise invisible in the background.

Application: tours *require* the ornament of historical synopses in order to provide visible marks for an immense historical, rather than cosmic, order in the background. Background history composes the overall orbit of signification in which tours participate, an orbit that is no other than the social equivalent of cosmos: "conventionality" itself —the very form of shared meaningfulness out of whose mechanism for positing total fitness the individual tourist draws aesthetics or other specialties of appreciation with confidence that they will fit his experience to the understandings of others. Imagine this composite painting of a tour: nature dominates the foreground; toward the back of the foreground, there is a mark composed of historical synopses, a mark like Brueghel's Icarus that seems ornamental because it points to no signified in the foreground; but the mark is crucial because its conventionality establishes the very perspective system, the social history or overall conventionality of vision within which foreground nature can be seen as a "delightful" beauty in the first place. No jewel without its setting: without history in the background, after all, a landscape is not a landscape; it is wilderness.

The conclusion to be reached so far, then, is that history in a tour ornaments nature in order to limn nature's participation in the true background signified: conventionality or civilization. But something is missing in the picture. If we compare a locodescriptive or prospect *paysage moralisé* such as Denham's "Cooper's Hill" or Pope's "Windsor-Forest" with Wordsworth's tour, we notice a striking contrast. History in "Cooper's Hill" and "Windsor-Forest" decorates nature, but points toward the background signified of civilization so unambiguously that it is as if natural landscape itself were the ornament. In a Wordsworthian tour, the arrow of signification from historical ornament toward the background is curiously blunted: historical markers point nowhere and decorate nature to no purpose.

In order to explain the deflection, Wordsworth's tour should be unfolded into three planes instead of two: history marks the background, nature stands in the *middle* ground, and the real foreground stages the tourist himself, or "I" of description. Lawrence Manley's study of convention in the history of criticism suggests a way to approach the tension in this structure causing historical signification to bend. Manley argues that the ancients saw convention as an order of change or of epiphenomena poised against the universal truth of nature. But by the time of the Romantics, convention had enthroned itself so massively as humanistic science and "history" that the relativistic understanding of reality it sponsored made unconvincing the ancient truth of universal nature. Consequently, the Romantics reasserted nature's universal truth against that of history in the new form of individuality: the "original" or transcendentally non-conventional self. If Nature now meant the outdoors specifically, the outdoors was only a setting in which the ancient, universal nature could reappear as the individual. Extending such an analysis, I suggest that in the threefold "painting" of a tour, the middle ground of nature is merely a mediation within the real antithesis of the time between background historical convention and foreground self. Nature, the boundary, is the real mark in the painting. The historical signifier seems to point to no background signified because an interposed veil of nature—really only an idea or mark of naturalness—deflects the arrow of signification so that it points invisibly to the foreground self, which thus originates as if from nowhere, or from nature itself. A tourist in Wordsworth's mold is a historical man who, as soon as he spots scenery, thinks himself primitive and original.

We notice that whether or not guided by Coxe or other tour works specifically, Wordsworth takes care to round out his 1790 letter with homage to social and historical action in France during *l'année heureuse*. Landscape is supposed to be the foreground ("Among the more awful scenes of the Alps, I had not a thought of man"; *Letters*, 1: 34). Historical background is the supplemental delight or ornamental interest: "But I must remind you that we crossed it at the time when the whole nation was mad with joy, in consequence of the revolution. It was a most interesting period to be in France, and we had many delightful scenes where the interest of the picture was owing solely to this cause" (*Letters*, 1: 36).

But I suggest that the letter's perspective should be read in reverse: it is history in 1790 that is the sufficient motive and nature the real supplement or mark. The slightly "mad" truancy of 1790 (the letter mentions those who thought the trip "mad and impracticable," *Letters*, 1: 37) is sanctioned not so much by nature as by the fact that now a "whole nation was mad with joy." History, whose very icon is the Federation, or convention, of a nation, is the common convention of meaningfulness from which the individual with shortcomings in specific motive, in "selfhood," can differentiate himself only by using a province of history—the history of aesthetic taste—to mark a boundary in the middle ground. Only through a flourish of nature can Wordsworth's tourist "I" then appear in the foreground as an "original" denying history and conventionality. An aesthetic tour through France in 1790, after all, is not the same as a tour at other times. Wordsworth's core statement might be phrased as follows: "In 1790, Federation and political spirit are 'in the air' as everyone else's motivation, but I am individual enough to view it all as a matter of aesthetics." Thus the complacent egotism at his letter's end when he spotlights himself in the foreground as the final object of aesthetics. While everyone else may be a sansculotte, he and Jones have the originality to be gypsies at the center of a genre- or subject-painting:

Our appearance is singular, and we have often observed that, in passing thro' a village, we have excited a general smile. Our coats which we had made light on purpose for our journey are of the same piece; and our manner of bearing our bundles, which is upon our heads, with each an oak stick in our hands, contributes not a little to that general curiosity which we seem to excite. But I find I have again relapsed into Egotism. (*Letters*, 1: 37)

The Ego dresses as a "natural" to mark itself off from the historical.

In order to study self-demarcation further, we need to shift at this point from 1790 to the later perspective of Book 6 of *The Prelude*. (I suspend study of *Descriptive Sketches*, which also renders the 1790 trip, until Chapter 5.) The description of the 1790 tour in Book 6, read in its own context, is a sustained effort to deny history by asserting nature as the separating mark constitutive of the egotistical self. It may be helpful to think of nature in its deflective capacity here as a mirror. The aim of Book 6 is to prevent the self from looking through nature to underlying history. Nature must instead reflect the self.[11]

Book 6 creates a mirror denying history in two phases. Instigating the first is a moment of insecurity in the balance between nature and history. Wordsworth begins describing his 1790 trip by confessing his younger self's undermotivation, and then immediately compensates with the main motive, Nature:

> An open slight
> Of College cares and study was the scheme,
> Nor entertain'd without concern for those
> To whom my worldly interests were dear:
> But Nature then was sovereign in my heart,
> And mighty forms seizing a youthful Fancy
> Had given a charter to irregular hopes.
> (6.342–48)

But there is a curious flicker in his main motive, a doubling of viewpoint akin to that in a Renaissance "perspective picture" where, as in Holbein's *The Ambassadors*, we see an attenuated construction to be deciphered only by looking at the picture from the side.* By a conceit carried in diction—sovereign, seizing, charter—Wordsworth already allows history to infiltrate the very core of nature. Nature is the ground, but the figure—the Revolution—tends to usurp the status of the ground with the same hidden *virtù* (in Machiavelli's sense) by which the trick-image of death in *The Ambassadors* seizes every viewer.[12] Book 6 then compounds the danger by declaring the supplemental motive, history, with such enthusiasm that the Revolution's ornamental gilding threatens to distract the eye entirely:

> In any age, without an impulse sent
> From work of Nations, and their goings-on,
> I should have been possessed by like desire:
> But 'twas a time when Europe was rejoiced,
> France standing on the top of golden hours,
> And human nature seeming born again.
> Bound, as I said, to the Alps, it was our lot
> To land at Calais on the very eve
> Of that great federal Day.   (6.349–57)

---

* "Perspective picture" here should not be associated with perspective in pictures generally, which I discuss in Chapter 3.

The implication is that idleness, a perennial concern in Wordsworth's poetry,[13] has the best excuse it will ever have at this time when history supplements scenic holiday with the "work" of nations. History's background helps nature license personal holiday so nicely, indeed, that Wordsworth's oddly passive phrasing of desire ("I should have been possessed by like desire") culminates in the thesis of agency by lottery: "it was our lot / To land" at a particular time in history. The undermotivation with which the 1790 tour begins in Book 6 thus incites overmotivation, a double sufficiency of natural and historical motive only precariously organized so that history is subordinate. If history is work, after all, desire for nature must be indolence.

It is now that Book 6 launches its first defense against history, its initial use of nature as a screen by which overmotivation can seem to mirror the self rather than transmit the historical whole: the great set piece describing the ambience of the Fete of Federation. To appreciate the vanity of this piece, we need to recover with some precision the ambience of 1790. Wordsworth and Jones spent the actual day of Federation, July 14, first at Calais and then on the road to Ardres, and so did not reach the site of the nearest large fete in Arras until late on July 16 (D. Hayden, pp. 9–12). They then passed belatedly through the sites of other major fetes in the department capitals of Troyes, Dijon, and Lyons. In one sense, it did not matter that they missed the celebration of significant fetes. Secondary celebrations in thousands of smaller towns and villages promulgated the spirit of the larger ones in Paris and the local capitals, and preliminary celebrations such as the Federation of the Pas de Calais, Nord, and Somme at Lille in June, as well as subsequent holidays such as the July 18 *Fête Exécutée en Mémoire de la Fédération Générale* at Champs Elysées, further dispersed Federation Day in time. Altogether, the Federation was a month-long background of celebration to be encountered anywhere. "Southward thence / We took our way direct through Hamlets, Towns, / Gaudy with reliques of that Festival" (6.360–62), Wordsworth says, and adds that on the boat trip to Lyons, he met

> a host
> Of Travellers, chiefly Delegates, returning
> From the great Spousals newly solemniz'd
> At their chief City in the sight of Heaven.
> (6.394–97)

But in another sense the poet must have been at a crucial distance from the spirit of the fetes. It is significant that his French at the time was far from fluent.* We have to be aware of two different views

---

* During his second trip to France in 1791–92, he wrote his brother Richard, "I am not yet able to speak french with decent accuracy but must of course improve very rapidly" (*Letters*, 1: 70).

of Federation Day: that of the French themselves, whose architectural, sculptural, visual, pantomimic, and ritual representations of confederation were conventionalized by verbal meaning—by words inscribing ritual in time—and that of Wordsworth, whose access primarily, or only, to the panorama of ritual, "reliques," and the physical behavior of *fédérés* resulted in the need for surrogate verbalization.[14]

We can begin to approximate the French view by noting that the Fete of Federation occurred at a time when the new machinery of state, though already largely operative, hung in suspension between the verbal principles stated by the 1789 Declaration of Rights and the verbal codification still to be completed in the 1791 Constitution. The hollow between declaration and enactment, the gap in the Revolution's own "description," was the space of oath—the Oath of Federation—and the pithiness of the Oath (epitomized in Louis XVI's one sentence)* was such that it had to be supplemented immediately by nonverbal representations—by forms of ritual that were actually all the oath had of substance. An oath is a promise of being, a nation's description to itself of desire fulfilled. Like an *assignat*, the promise had to be seen to be secured upon something tangible, and that security—the visible picture of being—took the form of architecture, sculpture, painting, and performing arts both genteel and vulgar. Most immediately, the oath found visual expression in the relief sculpture on the altar at the Paris Fete imitating David's *Oath of the Horatii*.[15] More generally, it metamorphosed into an astonishingly fertile array of "revolutionary" forms, all cross-referring to each other in unfathomably complex ways. As contemporary engravings show, for example, there was a flow of allusion between the circular towers of the fallen Bastille, the dances in the round or *Carmagnol* performed upon them (the Bastille became a *salle de bal en plein air* for the July 14 and 18 fetes), the spontaneous Liberty Dances in the round at the Paris Fete on July 14, and the evolutions of the military columns at the same Fete. All these demonstrations of revolution were in turn encapsulated within the French version of Shakespeare's Globe, the Paris Champ-de-Mars amphitheater (or such similar concourses as the Grand'Place in Arras).[16]

If this labyrinth of visual and ritual representations provided the Oath with substance, it in return received from verbalization the convention of directed form, of a single, motivated flow of prophecy renouncing the past and pointing toward the future. The Declaration, Oath, and Constitution were the official seals of a massive undernarrative of popular verbalization whose epic was the encyclopedic

---

* After Lafayette's oath binding the *fédérés* to the nation, law, and King, Louis rose and answered: "*Moi, roi des Français, je jure d'employer tout le pouvoir qui m'est délégué par la loi constitutionnelle de l'état à maintenir la constitution décrétée par l'assemblée nationale et acceptée par moi, et à faire exécuter les loix*" (*Collection Complete*, 1: 159).

lists of grievances collected for the Estates General in 1789 and whose episodes were such actions as the Fall of the Bastille collectively described in newspapers, pamphlets, memoirs, and gossip. It was the task of the under-narrative to make sure that the meaning carried in ritual or pantomime would read, destruction → construction, rather than the reverse.

The Fete on the Paris Champ-de-Mars is a telling example of such historicization of visual representation. In her fine study, Mona Ozouf suggests that Revolutionary fetes situated themselves on open amphitheaters and other panoramic spaces designed to project openness to nature, to a new social decorum of fraternity, and—most generally, perhaps—to new meaning.[17] The key point is that open space for meaning, especially in an urban center such as Paris, could only be created by destruction of the old. Nature could not be introduced into a metropolis without displacing something artificial; a fraternal social decorum could not be achieved without tearing down the divisive etiquette of aristocratic fetes; and old symbols could not be written over until erased. Generally, the symbolic actions of the Revolution thus took place either in angry dislocation from traditional sites of meaning (to such peripheral spaces as a Tennis Court, for example) or in violent erasures of meaning on such old sites as the Bastille.

The Champ-de-Mars site incorporated both dislocation and erasure. First, the center of the nation shifted across the river from the Tuileries and Palais Royal to a relatively blank slate. Then the slate was made even cleaner by modeling it upon the violent erasure at the Bastille a year ago. The correspondence between the Paris Fete and the Fall of the Bastille was clinched by a relief of the Bastille at the center of the Champ-de-Mars amphitheater,[18] but such correspondence had already been enacted in the very construction of the amphitheater. The preparation of the site required the labor of thousands of men soon joined, in a famous action, by some two hundred thousand Paris citizens of all descriptions, and involved excavating the flat parade ground in order to build a high ramp all around (as was seen in the splendid watercolor of *La Journée des Brouettes* by Etienne-Charles Le Guay in the Musée Carnavalet). The mood during excavation was festive, but the meaning was violent. As the crowds dug, they sang: "He that is raised up will be humbled, and he that is humble will be raised up."[19] The digging on the Champ-de-Mars reenacted the violent undermining signalized by the destruction of the Bastille. Or, in a secondary allusion, it reenacted the forced removal of the King from Versailles during the October Days—the key act making possible the King's symbolic union with the nation on Federation Day. On October 5–6, 1789, the March of Women broke in upon the royal family at Versailles and brought them to Paris virtually as prisoners (Soboul, p. 156). As Ronald Paulson points out, this action—especially as seen by Burke—had the symbolic form of a rape or penetration (*Representations*, pp. 60–62). The rape finishes on Burke's pages in a splash of "piercing," "scattered limbs," and "mutilated carcasses," as a dismemberment and puncturing—a sort of excavation—of the body politic (*Reflections*, p. 164).

How to make something constructive out of violent excavation? Just as contemporary paintings of patriots planting Liberty Trees depended upon a left-to-right convention of "reading" to specify that the Tree, held at a diagonal, is being planted and not uprooted,[20] so the digging at the Champ-de-Mars required convention-making verbalization, epitomized by the popular song, to show that destructive excavation (humbling) merely prophesies construction (raising up). So, too, the "excavation" of the body politic at Versailles on October 5 required its own verbalizations showing that violent evacuation was really a filling, a reunion in which the King filled the emptiness in Paris. Marat spoke of the event in these terms: "It is a source of great rejoicing for the good people of Paris to have their King in their midst once again. His presence will very quickly do much to change the outward appearance of things, and the poor will no longer die of starvation" (quoted in Soboul, p. 157). It was as if the nation experienced a hunger, an evacuation at its center, that the kidnapping of the King magically filled (the filling was then to be emptied again, of course, in the 1791 flight to Varennes completing this diptych of representation).

As Burke knew, no enactment is complete without such propaganda, or historicizing description, accompanying the very spadework of action. Once excavation had created the amphitheater at the Champ-de-Mars, there arose at the center a large, pyramidal altar—the podium for the nation's ultimate piece of propaganda or descriptive convention enlisting the Fete in a historical process of construction. On this altar, on July 14, the Bishop of Autun (Talleyrand), surrounded by hundreds of white-robed priests, said mass preparatory to the King's Oath. Thus despite the fact that the Fete built itself on undermining the Bastille, on emptying Versailles, and on evacuating religion itself, and despite even the ill omen of unrelenting rain that day, the verbalization peaking in the Bishop's blessing made a totally conventional, but profoundly historical, promise that the explosion of energy seen everywhere in visual form and symbolic action pointed forward to the millennium rather than backward to hell. The blessing transformed the famous rain from ill omen to covenant, a sign of fertility prophesying something like that ultimate celebration of fraternity and nature-become-religion in the Champ-de-Mars: the 1794 Fete devoted to the "Supreme Being and Nature."

We can sum up for our purposes by calling the Fete of Federation the French imagination of history operating under the badge of Reason. The French reimagined the conventions of the past into a convention for the future, and the intersection of past and future was the millennial "now," when the Revolution's transcendental signifieds—Fraternity and Nature—seemed immanent within artistic clichés.[21]

Now we can turn to the alternative verbalization of Book 6 by which Wordsworth takes to an extreme his younger self's aestheticization of Revolution: georgic—the genre closely associated in the eighteenth century with locodescription and the tour but not yet realized in the 1790 letter (even though Wordsworth studied Virgil's *Georgics* closely—especially the third and fourth—at Cambridge soon before the 1790 trip).[22] In 6.355–425, he describes the Revolution as merely a season in vegetable landscape, a "benevolence and blessedness . . . like Spring" that flowers as a rustic May Day or perhaps a harvest festival among "the vine-clad Hills of Burgundy." In this world, the "reliques" of the Fete—"Flowers left to wither on triumphal Arcs, / And window-Garlands"—are not so much garnishes as integral parts of the landscape of growth and decay. Here the very roads along which the young traveler walks appear only as files of "Elms . . . With their thin umbrage." "Enchanting" were "those woods, and farms, and orchards" exclaims the poet-as-*agricola*. In the spirit of the fourth *Georgic*, Wordsworth then inserts within agrarian landscape a simile comparing the *fédérés* to bees that "swarm'd, gaudy and gay." Finally, the set piece of Book 6 reaches its climax in descriptions of *Carmagnol* dances that now, however, appear merely a country dance. "We rose at signal given, and form'd a ring / And, hand in hand, danced round and round," Wordsworth says, and seems so taken with this image of rustic revolution that he repeats it: "round, and round the board they danced again."

Two "snapshots" from the *Georgics*: (1) a plowman working in the field at the end of the first *Georgic* suddenly turns up rusting armor and heroic bones in his fields;[23] (2) Virgil himself, digging for the story behind the spontaneous generation of bees in the fourth, suddenly turns up an entire epyllion, or contained epic, buried in his narrative. Keeping in mind the historical milieu so profoundly in the background of Virgil's work, I offer this preliminary understanding of georgic based on these snapshots: georgic is the supreme mediational form by which to bury history in nature, epic in pastoral. Like the tour mode, it is the form in which history turns into the background, the manure, for landscape. Through georgic, Wordsworth is able, at least at first glance, to make the entire under-narrative of the Revolution sink into unbroken invisibility. In a sense, the young traveler he depicts walks through a landscape that is natural only because it is prehistorical; the possibility of history has not yet evolved. Contemporary engravings depict Liberty pointedly as a woman carrying a broken yoke (Henderson, p. 314); if France was "georgic" in 1790, after all, such fertility harvested the mass destruction of the agrarian

Great Fear of 1789 (on *la Grande Peur*, see Lefebvre, *Great Fear*). But in his georgic, Wordsworth appreciates joy without the haunt of historical fear, the yoke of rustic labor without the jagged edge of break with past oppression.

The purpose of the mirror of georgic nature is to hide history in order, finally, to reflect the self. At the beginning of his "vanity," Wordsworth recounts "How bright a face is worn when joy of one / Is joy of tens of millions" (6.359–60). In the mirror of nature, this proportion is reversed: history's tens of millions focus to foreground the poet's joy of one. Halfway through the set piece, external observation of vegetable process thus deflects momentarily into self-absorption:

> 'Twas sweet at such a time, with such delights
> On every side, in prime of youthful strength,
> To feed a Poet's tender melancholy
> And fond conceit of sadness.   (6.375–78)

The tour's original undermotivation becomes melancholy, the convention in locodescription framing the subjective self. Subjectivity then steps even more vainly into the foreground when Wordsworth elevates his younger self above the celebrating *fédérés*:

> In this blithe Company
> We landed, took with them our evening Meal,
> Guests welcome almost as the Angels were
> To Abraham of old.   (6.401–4)

As in Genesis 18: 1–15, where angels prophesy the birth of Isaac to Abraham, the blessed tourist steps momentarily out of history altogether in prophetic anticipation of his own self, of an "Isaac" that then appears as the deus ex machina of the whole set piece. What is the specific point of rustic festivity and dancing? Says Wordsworth,

> All hearts were open, every tongue was loud
> With amity and glee; we bore a name
> Honour'd in France, the name of Englishmen,
> And hospitably did they give us Hail
> As their forerunners in a glorious course,
> And round, and round the board they danced again.
>> (6.408–13)

Suddenly, the Revolution hails the English poet at the focus of its circle.

Such is the first mirror in Book 6, screening background history from view. Yet, despite its gorgeous polish, the mirror is inadequate because of a basic undecidability in georgic making it at all times, and especially in Wordsworth's time, just as likely to exhume history as bury it. The genres of tour work and georgic, which the Preface of 1815 will call "Idyllic" and "Didactic," respectively, are alike problematic because they tend to fall between the three master genres of Narrative, Drama, and Lyric composing Wordsworth's and literary history's trinity, on the one hand, and true servant genres with clearly defined formal traits (such as Ode as opposed to Elegy), on the other. The generic field in any age, I suggest, distributes itself between master and servant genres with some unstable mediator always filling the role played by tour and georgic in Wordsworth's time. Tour and georgic are preeminently mixed genres in which the stability of genre as a convention is threatening to come apart under the pressure of the times. Tour and georgic in the late eighteenth and early nineteenth centuries are the pressure points where the entire generic field is beginning to rearrange around the massive intrusion of specifically historical reality and the form jury-rigged to imitate it: the novel.

In the era soon to produce a novelist like Scott, history became *the* subject of mimesis, and the georgic mediation of nature projected in Book 6 of *The Prelude* can only bury history out of sight provisionally before turning it up once more. There are, after all, those protruding "bones" in the soil, which, because gothic romance is denied to georgic as an escape valve, cannot be easily covered. Too much energy of repression must be expended to keep the georgic mirror from turning transparent to history. If Wordsworth's simile likening the *fédérés* to bees alludes to the *Georgics*, after all, it certainly also points to the epic use of bees in Homer and in Virgil himself, as well as to the brilliant problem georgic at the close of Book I of *Paradise Lost* where Satanic history threatens to swarm into the pastoral tranquillity of the "belated peasant."

The climactic second phase of the defense against history in Book 6 then begins at Mont Blanc precisely upon the discovery that georgic is transparent. The demands Wordsworth makes at this point upon georgic to bury history create such tension in the convention that the epic pole first seems to disappear entirely, leaving an exaggerated insistence upon pastoral. The Mont Blanc episode begins as a fond, georgic look homeward to pastoral: "Sweet coverts did we cross of pastoral life, / Enticing Vallies" (6.437–38). But like Milton's belated peasant, the young traveler suddenly experiences a near eruption of the demonic in the harvest world: the peak of Mont Blanc discovers itself as a gap in georgic fertility, as a "soulless image . . . Which had usurp'd upon a living thought" (6.454–55). There is some strange devil of history, I suggest, behind usurpation that the poet-as-*agricola* would rather not see. The whiteness at Mont Blanc—like that in *The White Doe of Rylstone*—is the space in which history can ghost into the present; it is not no meaning but a panic of too much possible meaning. Whiteness is the page for a possible epic whose stern mood must either be recognized or thwarted. For the time being, the whiteness at Mont Blanc—protruding like a heroic bone—is simply ploughed under again. In an effort to make "amends" (6.460) akin to that at Lake Geneva in the 1790 letter, Wordsworth returns from intimations of usurpation to fertility in the Vale of Chamonix by means of a suspiciously hyperbolical pastoral:

> There small birds warble from the leafy trees,
> The Eagle soareth in the element;
> There doth the Reaper bind the yellow sheaf,
> The Maiden spread the haycock in the sun,
> While Winter like a tamed Lion walks
> Descending from the mountain to make sport
> Among the cottages by beds of flowers.
>
> (6.462–68)

Not a trace of grimness does the Reaper seem to betray. But notice the suppression of narrative necessary to screen grimness. Arranged around the hinge of the Reaper are two diptychs: the small birds with the Eagle, and the Maiden with the Lion of winter. There is a muted story of predation here, of some spoliation or usurpation in the area of Chamonix that the 1805 Book 6 (still without the Convent of Chartreuse excursus) must prettify.[24]

It is the near eruption of history at Mont Blanc that provokes the climactic veiling at Simplon Pass. It will be useful to retain Hartman's labeling of the sequence: 6a, the ascent ("Yet still in me, mingling with these delights / Was something of stern mood . . ." 6.488–524); 6b, the halt ("Imagination! lifting up itself . . ." 6.525–48); and 6c, the descent through Gondo Gorge ("The dull and heavy slackening that ensued . . ." 6.549–72). Ascent and descent form the paradigmatic two points of the tour, and the halt is the gap. So much work has been done on the sequence that I will offer at present only a schematic of 6a and 6c in order to move quickly to 6b. In 6a we find a trajectory of serial repetition guided at the end by the Peasant, or holdover *agricola* from the georgic universe. More specifically, 6a pictures an implicit struggle between the vectors of the horizontal and vertical. The horizontal, intoned in the tedious diction of "A length of hours," "Ere long we follow'd," and "at length," is the progress of pure repetition, of one foot after another without describable motive. The vertical, heard in the verbs of "we had clomb," "the Travellers rose," and "climb'd with eagerness," is the vector of significance and motivation. Disappointment, first sounded in Wordsworth's and Jones's request that the Peasant *repeat* his message, but fully realized only in the descent pictured by 6c, arrives upon the discovery that verticality is itself simply a disguised form of flat repetition: "downwards

we hurried fast," 6c begins in its record of descent chiastically opposed to ascent. "Downwards" merely repeats without meaningful
connection the previously upward climb. Indeed, 6c is a microcosm
of the disconnected repetition disappointing Wordsworth so gravely.
Gondo Gorge appears as a landscape of binary points separated by
oxymoronic divide: "The immeasurable height / Of woods decaying, never to be decay'd . . . Winds thwarting winds . . . Tumult and
peace, the darkness and the light."

What radical of motivation can connect the "two points" whose
disconnection images the undermotivation of the whole tour? Here
we reach the goal of this chapter, Wordsworth's addition of 6b and
the "bright obscurity" of Imagination:

> Imagination! lifting up itself
> Before the eye and progress of my Song
> Like an unfather'd vapour; here that Power,
> In all the might of its endowments, came
> Athwart me; I was lost as in a cloud,
> Halted, without a struggle to break through.
> And now recovering, to my Soul I say
> I recognise thy glory; in such strength
> Of usurpation, in such visitings
> Of awful promise, when the light of sense
> Goes out in flashes that have shewn to us
> The invisible world, doth Greatness make abode,
> There harbours whether we be young or old.
> Our destiny, our nature, and our home
> Is with infinitude, and only there;
> With hope it is, hope that can never die,
> Effort, and expectation, and desire,
> And something evermore about to be.
> The mind beneath such banners militant
> Thinks not of spoils or trophies, nor of aught
> That may attest its prowess, blest in thoughts
> That are their own perfection and reward,
> Strong in itself, and in the access of joy
> Which hides it like the overflowing Nile.
>
>   (6.525–48)

Here is the great mirror into which Wordsworth looks to reflect upon
his "self." The process of this reflection is complex and sums up the
entire pathway of deflection I have sketched so far.

Crucial is the passage's initial flicker from first person singular ("I
was lost," "I say," "I recognise") to first person plural ("shewn to
us," "whether we be young or old," "Our destiny, our nature, and
our home") and then to the impersonal ("its prowess," "Strong in
itself," "hides it"). Looking outwards, the "I" perceives "we's" and
"our's" that are the pronouns of convention and collectivity. "We"

and "our" are signifiers of background that, given a chance, would point directly into the history heard with such frightening force and precision in the vocabulary of 6b as a whole: "Power . . . all the might of its endowments . . . struggle to break through . . . glory . . . strength / Of usurpation . . . Greatness . . . banners militant . . . spoils or trophies . . . prowess . . . Strong in itself." But there is a deflection here, and the arrow of signification bends, in an extraordinary sentence, to point perpetually "there" into a historically ungrounded "being" we might call objectified subjectivity:

> Our destiny, our nature, and our home
> Is with infinitude, and only there;
> With hope it is, hope that can never die,
> Effort, and expectation, and desire,
> And something evermore about to be.

The perpetual "out there" of such desired "being" is propped up, we notice, upon reference to external nature as pure figure. The "I" comes to see nature as if in quotes: "*like* the overflowing Nile." Anointing itself with a figure of externality as groundless in origin as the Nile itself, which in the 1850 poem pours from a "fount of Abyssinian clouds," the "I" thus comes into the majesty of objectivity seemingly without any further need for the mediation of the most human approach to objectivity: collectivity. History is denied, and the "I" engenders itself autogenetically as the very crown of what I have called objectified subjectivity: a mind knowing itself only in the impersonal—"strong in *itself*."

The "I," in sum, looks into the background of collective history, deflects upon nature's polish of objectivity, and at last sees itself reflected as the awesome, historically free personality of "*The* mind."

Imagination and Napoleon

But Book 6 cannot be read wholly on its own. Let me now open the aperture completely to view Simplon Pass in the overall context of *The Prelude* and 1804, when Book 6 and much of the rest of the poem were composed.[25] In this context, it becomes important to stare fixedly into, and *through*, the mirror of the Imagination. In the construction of the total *Prelude* in 1804, I believe, Wordsworth inserted background reminders of historicity in the Imagination passage as avenues toward a realization that "the mind" must finally enroll (literally enlist, as Wordsworth did in the Grasmere Volunteers in 1803; see MM, 1: 602–3) in a collective system authorized from some source "elsewhere" than the self: in the grounded or demystified Nile that is history.[26] Specifically, Book 6 and the Imagination passage look forward to the direct concern of the Revolution books (Books 9 and

10) with a deluge of history. Wordsworth probably began composing much of Books 9 and 10 soon after finishing 6 in late April 1804 (with additional work in October to December of that year; see WAG, pp. 518–19; *CMY*, pp. 650–53); and there is the possibility that all three books dealing with France were composed in a single manuscript (WAG, p. 519). In the movement of the total poem, the denial (and de-Nile) of history in 6b really warns that the nature and self thus far imagined are antediluvian. Wordsworth is about to go on to open the floodgates in order to let in a ferocious tributary of his Nile: the river of "shapeless eagerness," as we will later see, that rushes us into explicit history at the opening of Book 9.

What preoccupies Imagination in 1804 such that it at once prevents and presages history? MS. WW of *The Prelude*, we know, shows that Wordsworth originally inserted what is now 8.711–27—the first part of the simile of the cave—between 6a and 6b (WAG, p. 216n). Imagination, I suggest, is as hollow as this cave. The more we look into it, the more we submit to an interior, self-motivated reality bodying forth (in the language of the simile) "Shapes and Forms and Tendencies to Shape." Specifically, Imagination cavitates nature to show the protruding bones of the historical world of 1804. In 6b, Imagination sees in nature not just its own reflection but that of a firmly *historical* genius of imagination—of the Imaginer who, in a manner of speaking, wrote the book on crossing the Alps. I believe that if we look into 6b, we will see through the self and mind in the foreground, through even the nature in the middle ground, to a frightening skeleton in the background. Whatever else it is, Imagination is the haunt of Napoleon, the great Bone of the time (a standard play on words in the early 1800's; see below). More precisely, if Imagination reflects upon nature as a mirror, the mirror is of magistrates and shows Imagination to itself as a canny double for uncanny Napoleon. Imagination at once mimics and effaces Napoleon in an effort, anticipatory of Books 9–10 and after, to purge tyranny by *containing* tyranny within itself as what I will study in Chapter 8 as the empire of Imagination.[27]

We need to be careful here with degrees of certainty. An adequate reading of Wordsworth's texts in their historical context, I will suggest, requires not so much positivistic method as a deflected or denied positivism able to discriminate absence. For the moment, however, we can reach our goal simply by positing a ladder of increasing certainty. No single piece of evidence in the following presentation leads absolutely to the conclusion that Napoleon stands in the background of 6b, but the sum, I believe, has plausibility; and such plausibility in the specific thesis will be sufficient to carry the general argument that 6b is decisively engaged with history. I highlight the most telling specifics in italics, but I also include supplementary suggestions based on circumstances and sometimes wordplay that might appear farfetched in normal times. After reading in the literature and art of British reactions to Napoleon in the years of war fever—including the standard plays on the skeletal nature of "Bone-apart" and the fabulous apocalyptic interpretations of Bonaparte's name as the Number of the Beast[28]—I believe that no accident possible to be interpreted should be omitted in detailing an imagination of Napoleon. In any case, the plausibility I aim for does not rest finally on one-to-one correspondence between history and the Imagination passage, but on the alliance between text and context considered as wholes.

18 Brumaire. In 1799 Napoleon returned unexpectedly to France from his Egyptian campaign, reached Paris on October 16 with massive popular support, and took control of the Directory in the coup d'état of 18 Brumaire (actually 18–19 Brumaire; November 9–10).[29] *The Annual Register* (years 1758–92, 1794–96, 1800, 1802–11, and 1814–20 were in Wordsworth's Rydal Mount library; Shaver and Shaver, p. 9) banners the world's astonishment at this advent as if from nowhere, choosing a style of language—"in defiance of reason . . . not any one . . . could have imagined"—that we will need to consider later:

Whether we contemplate the great affairs of nations in a political or military point of view, the return of Buonaparte to France . . . is the grand and leading event in the history of 1800. . . . Who could have believed that a simple sub-lieutenant of artillery, a stranger to France, by name and by birth, was destined to govern this great empire, and to give the law, in a manner, to all the continent, in defiance of reason? . . . There is not any one in the world who could have imagined the possibility of an event so extraordinary. (1800: 66)

"Brumaire" is the month of mists in the vividly imagined Revolutionary calendar, and Napoleon's takeover climaxed in his famously violent personal appearance before the hostile Council of Five Hundred at Saint-Cloud (spoken of simply as "Cloud" in the early Revolution because of antisacral doctrine; see Robiquet, p. 62). In the world's eye, we might say, Napoleon burst upon the scene as a kind of "vapour," or cloud, an upstart and illegitimate spirit.

In 6b Wordsworth begins with a coup d'état of Imagination retracing something like the spirit of 18 Brumaire: an "unfather'd vapour" starts up in defiance of all expectation, comes with "Power" upon a poet who, like France in 1799, was "Halted, without a struggle to break through," and changes the regime with such "strength / Of usurpation" that the astonished poet, like France before Napoleon's renewed spectacles of state,* must say, "I recognise thy glory." Such recognition of glory—the great instance of bright obscurity—

---

* Beginning with the pageantry of Napoleon's symbolic move to the Tuileries on February 19, 1800 (Sydenham, p. 235).

merely makes official what the poet had unconsciously, in an analogy to French popular support for Napoleon, depended upon all along.

Anchoring the reading of Imagination as coup d'état is Wordsworth's strong use of the figure "usurpation," a use prepared for in the chronicle of Mont Blanc. Usurpation in Book 6 is a figure backed up by allusion to *Macbeth*, the poem's preferred exemplar of the usurper.[30] Just after describing the descent through Gondo Gorge, Wordsworth describes "innocent Sleep" lying "melancholy among weary bones" (6.579–80; *Macbeth* II.ii.33). In one sense, the allusion points ahead in the poem, and backward in time, to Book 10 and the night in 1792 when the poet heard a voice in the Paris hotel quoting the regicide Macbeth: "Sleep no more" (10.77; *Macbeth* II.ii.32). Since Book 10 moves on immediately to the confrontation between Robespierre and Louvet, we can guess that Wordsworth's Macbeth, in the context of 1792, figures Robespierre (who in 10.461–62 is also represented as an offspring of Lear). But in another sense, the allusion to *Macbeth* in Book 6 with its addition of the image of bones points to Old Boney: *in the context of the years immediately preceding 1804, "usurper" cannot refer to anyone other than Napoleon.*

After 18 Brumaire, "usurper" was applied to Bonaparte in English parliamentary speeches, pamphlets, and newspapers with the consistency of a technical term and irrespective of party affiliation or sympathy with French republicanism. Whether he was thought merely to epitomize republicanism or to break with it, the premise was that Napoleon was a usurper.[31] Use of the epithet peaked first in 1799–1800 after 18 Brumaire and Napoleon's subsequent offer of peace to George III, which the Government chose to perceive as an insult because Napoleon took the stance of equal. The *Times* of London, for example, named Bonaparte "usurper" immediately after his coup (*T*, November 18, 20, 22, 1799). In his forceful speech of February 3, 1800, Pitt then referred repeatedly to Napoleon as "usurper" and his government as a "usurpation" (pp. 273, 276, 278). Similarly, Sheridan spoke of Bonaparte in 1800 as "this ferocious usurper" (quoted in Maccunn, p. 21). Use of the epithet then peaked a second time in 1803–4 upon the resumption of hostilities after the Peace of Amiens, when *The Annual Register*, for example, labeled Bonaparte "the Corsican usurper" (1802: 224) and the *Times* similarly issued a virtual litany of "usurpers," "audacious usurpers," and "Corsican Usurpers."[32] Perhaps the best way to suggest the possible impact upon Wordsworth of the usurpation epithet in these years is to read Coleridge in the *Morning Post*. In 1800, Coleridge characterized Bonaparte, his regime, or various French decrees in such barbed phrases as "this insolence in the usurper" and a "low Harlequinade of Usurpation." On March 11, 1800, Coleridge's rhetoric drives the point home: Napoleon's rise is a usurpation, he says repeatedly, and "In his usurpation, Bonaparte stabbed his honesty in the vitals" (*STCE*, pp. 63, 91, 207–11).*

Marengo and Aboukir. Completing the coup is the "battle" of Imagination. *A Swiss mountain pass in 1804 was first and foremost a military site*: the avenue of the "modern Hannibal," as Coleridge later described Napoleon's forces (*STCE*, 2: 138). It is even more suggestive that 6b inscribes within the literal setting of the Swiss Alps the figure of the Nile, and so folds into Simplon Pass the two most crucial scenes of battle in the Napoleonic wars prior to Trafalgar in 1805: Switzerland (together with northern Italy) and Egypt. The Alpine region, Wordsworth's model of political independence, was the ground of Napoleon's most brilliant successes, and the mouth of the Nile that of his only major defeat to date. The lamination of the two is interpretive: if 6b begins with coup d'état, such illegality becomes progressively transformed until, by the end, Wordsworth has purged tyranny from Imagination in the flow of the Nile.

To begin with, 6b may be read as the conflation of the several Alpine campaigns: "Halted, without a struggle to break through," the poet is in the position of French troops awaiting the imagination of Napoleon to lead them through the pass. To some extent, Imagination's progress of blockage followed by rapid breakthrough may reflect the 1796 Italian campaign that first made Napoleon famous. Blocked by the numerically superior Austrians and Piedmontese at the Maritime Alps just to the south of Switzerland, Napoleon gestured toward Genoa, stabbed past the Alps to divide and defeat the enemy armies, and created out of Italy the Cisalpine, Cispadane, and Transpadane republics—a creation accompanied by the first of his wholesale "spoliations," as *The Annual Register* terms them, of treasuries and art (1796: 96). To a larger extent, Imagination's progress may reflect France's repeated occupation of Switzerland. Wordsworth later said that this conquest was the culminating factor in his turn of sympathy against France, but linking his various statements on the matter to a specific historical action has proved problematic. J. C. Maxwell argues persuasively that the interventions of 1798 and 1802—the former not directly led by Napoleon—are equally likely (or unlikely) to have provoked Wordsworth's turn. It seems that Wordsworth conflated the two invasions in hindsight and attached them both to Bonaparte. The 1798 occupation of Switzerland by French armies (while Napoleon prepared for Egypt) and the consequent declaration of the Helvetic Republic were also accompanied by vast "spoliations" of treasuries (*AR*, 1798: 36). The 1802 action

---

* Further discussion of Coleridge's complex stance toward Napoleon follows in Chapter 8. In fact, Coleridge's fulminations against Bonaparte as "usurper" in early 1800 coincided with one of his peaks of admiration for him.

occurred during an insurrection against the French-instituted Helvetic Republic when Napoleon, despite promises to the contrary, intervened both by sending troops under General Ney and by transmitting a manifesto that *The Annual Register* says "will ever be memorable for its despotic arrogance" (1802: 233). One of Napoleon's special interests in both the 1798 and 1802 occupations, we may note, was to secure the Valais canton and so the link between Paris and Italy through the Simplon Pass (R. R. Palmer, *World*, p. 171; A. Palmer, p. 148).

To the largest extent, however, Imagination's progress in 6b reflects Napoleon's most astonishing stroke to date: his 1800 passage through the Swiss Alps leading to the Battle of Marengo. Newly become First Consul, Napoleon set off in May as de facto head of the Italian campaign to take the Austrian army from the rear. *Like Wordsworth, Napoleon arrived at Geneva, followed the northern shore of the lake eastward to the Rhone River, and then turned southward toward Chamonix.* Here he diverged, but only slightly, from Wordsworth's 1790 route. While part of his army crossed at Mount Cenis, Little St. Bernard, and Mount St. Gotthard, and a demibrigade of approximately 1000 men was sent to demonstrate as loudly as possible that the crossing would be at Simplon, Napoleon himself accompanied the main army through Great St. Bernard Pass (about 50 miles southwest of Simplon).[33] In an action comparable to Hannibal's crossing by elephant, he broke down his artillery and sledded it through the snow-blocked defile. *This was the first blockage to be overcome in a march widely reported as a series of halts followed by breakthroughs.* The next blockage occurred at Fort Bard, which seemed to impede a narrow defile just past Great St. Bernard. "There was no alternative," *The Annual Register* admires; "the fort must either be taken or another passage sought. Each had its difficulties, but Buonaparte's genius surmounted them" (1800: 191). After some skirmishing, Napoleon raised a cannon on top of a nearby church and battered the fort into surrender.[34] The final, decisive instance of halt followed by breakthrough was the Battle of Marengo itself, which Napoleon turned from defeat into victory. Posted in the rear of the Austrians, Napoleon's inferior forces began retreating under heavy Austrian artillery fire at the village of Marengo. Only with the arrival of Corps Commander Desaix's division from the south could Napoleon mount a charge, supported by all his artillery and cavalry, that broke the Austrian forces.

In the context of 1804, then, any imagination of an Alpine pass would remember the military "genius" of Bonaparte. It seems natural that Wordsworth's halt "without a struggle to break through" at the beginning of 6b should lead to the "banners militant" toward the close. The martial air of 6b, indeed, fairly trumpets itself. If we read in the spirit of the banners, Wordsworth's "visitings / Of Awful promise, when the light of sense / Goes out in flashes that have shewn to us / The invisible world" hint the violence of artillery. Even Wordsworth's great rallying speech has a military ring:

> Our destiny, our nature, and our home
> Is with infinitude, and only there;
> With hope it is, hope that can never die,
> Effort, and expectation, and desire,
> And something evermore about to be.

Whatever else it is, this speech—in its very cadence—is a double of Napoleon's widely publicized rallying speeches to his armies. After the 1796 breakthrough in the Maritime Alps, for example, *The Annual Register* quotes Bonaparte addressing his troops:

You have precipitated yourselves, like a torrent, from the heights of the Appennines. You have routed and dispersed all who have opposed your progress. . . . Yes, soldiers, you have done much; but does there remain nothing more to be done? Though we have known how to vanquish, we have not known how to profit of our victories. . . . Let us depart! we have yet forced marches to make, enemies to subdue, laurels to gather, injuries to revenge. (1796: 91)*

But the parade of banners militant, of course, does not conclude the martial review of 6b. Wordsworth continues:

> The mind beneath such banners militant
> Thinks not of spoils or trophies, nor of aught
> That may attest its prowess, blest in thoughts
> That are their own perfection and reward.

Here, even amid the military anthem, his act of purging Napoleon begins. *Wordsworth's stress in 1804 that the Imagination is its own reward, and so eschews spoils and trophies, should be seen to reject precisely Napoleon's famed spoliations.* His homage to the overflowing Nile—which enriches, rather than, like the "torrent" of Napoleon's armies, robs— then speaks the final "no" to tyranny. Even as French forces occupied Switzerland in 1798, Bonaparte was preparing to sail for Egypt in an effort to disrupt British commerce with the Far East. Despite great successes on land, victory was robbed from him by Nelson, who destroyed the French fleet at Aboukir on the mouth of the Nile and so left Bonaparte's forces suddenly stranded in Egypt. More important than the actual British victory was the fact that Napoleon's myth of invincibility was for the first time broken. Aboukir was a moral

---

* Coleridge's comments in the *Morning Post* for January 1, 1800, on a similar speech of Napoleon's could almost be taken to describe Wordsworth's "egotistical sublime" as well: "Through all these proclamations the fierce confidence, and proud self-involution of a military despot, intoxicated with vanity, start out most obtrusively" (STCE, p. 63).

victory, the prophecy of British triumph even in the years of great-est French conquest. Layering the Nile into the Alps, Wordsworth predicts the "Character of the Happy Warrior."*

The Spirit of Imagination. In sum, Wordsworth in 6b makes a pre-liminary trial of the method by which history can be cleansed of tyranny so that only the shining "genius" figured by Napoleon—and shared by the poet—will reign. Here we reach the most telling point of correspondence between Wordsworth's Imagination and Napo-leon—that of pure spirit. While general British reaction to Bonaparte fluctuated from uncertainty before his usurpation in 1800 to enthu-siasm during the Peace of Amiens in 1802 and finally to renewed hostility, *one species of reaction was constant, if officially inadmissible: admira-tion of the "genius," "sublimity," and "imagination" represented by Napoleon.* Bonaparte, as Scott would later call him in his biography, was the "master-spirit" of the age (p. 216). *The Annual Register*, for example, consistently admired Napoleon's gifts of mind until its first notes of distrust in the 1802 volume (published in 1803). In its character sketch of 1800, for instance, it discovers Napoleon's youthful "spark of genius," and then marvels at his mature genius: Bonaparte possesses "a firm and undaunted spirit, and a genius penetrating, sublime, and inventive," and "his letters, his speeches, his actions, all proclaimed a sublimity of courage, imagination, and design, beyond the limits of vulgar conception" (1800: 11). Hazlitt would later take the same ap-proach in his biography, apostrophizing the Battle of Marengo as "the most poetical of his battles," a battle as "romantic and incredible" as if "Ariosto, if a magician had planned a campaign" (p. 177). And Scott's biography will announce Napoleon's imagination in these terms:

No man ever possessed in a greater degree than Buonaparte, the power of calculation and combination necessary for directing such decisive manoeu-vres. It constituted indeed his secret—as it was for some time called—and that secret consisted in an imagination fertile in expedients which would never have occurred to others. (p. 216)

In his superb rendering of the Battle of Marengo, Scott then makes it sound as if Bonaparte in Great St. Bernard Pass were indeed Words-worth confronting nature in Simplon Pass:

[He proceeded] to the little village called St. Pierre, at which point there ended every thing resembling a practicable road. An immense and appar-ently inaccessible mountain, reared its head among general desolation and eternal frost; while precipices, glaciers, ravines, and a boundless extent of

* Writing in the *Morning Post* for March 11, 1800, Coleridge similarly "grounded" the Nile by reference to Napoleon: "the Chief Consulate . . . pretends to no sacred-ness; it is no Nile, made mysterious by the undiscoverableness of its fountainhead; it exists, because it is suitable to existing circumstances; and when circumstances render it unnecessary, it is destructible without a convulsion" (STCE, p. 209).

faithless snows, which the slightest concussion of the air converts into ava-
lanches capable of burying armies in their descent, appeared to forbid access
to all living things but the chamois, and his scarce less wild pursuer. Yet
foot by foot, and man by man, did the French soldiers proceed to ascend
this formidable barrier, which Nature had erected in vain to limit human
ambition . . . in places of unusual difficulty, the drums beat a charge, as if to
encourage the soldiers to encounter the opposition of Nature herself. (pp.
336–37)[35]

Recall the diversionary force that Napoleon sent to demonstrate in
Simplon Pass. If my presentation has even the barest plausibility, it
will appear that Wordsworthian nature is precisely such an imaginary
antagonist against which the self battles in feint, in a ploy to divert
attention from the real battle to be joined between *history* and self.
Whatever the outcome of the skirmish (called dialectic) between nature and self, history, the real antagonist, is thus momentarily denied
so that when it debouches at last, it will be recognized with shock
by the feinting mind as the greatest power of the Wordsworthian defile. As envisioned in the framework of the total *Prelude*—where the
books of unnatural history then come at the point of climax rather
than, as in *Paradise Lost*, of denouement—denial is the threshold of
Wordsworth's most truly shocking act of Imagination: the sense of
history. The true apocalypse will come when history crosses the zone
of nature to occupy the self directly, when the sense of history and
Imagination thus become one, and nature, the mediating figure, is no
more.

~~⌾~~

CHAPTER TWO

History, Literature, Form

LET ME DRAW BACK AT THIS POINT to locate where I have come and where the tour still leads. In his 1978 essay on the "temporal sublime," Karl Kroeber began with a call to arms: "Despite critical clichés of the 1960's and 1970's, the primary thrust of Romantic art was toward neither apocalypse nor transcendence but toward the representation of reality as historical process" ("Romantic Historicism," p. 149). More recently, David Simpson has sounded the same charge in the field of Wordsworth studies: "My emphasis on the political is a deliberate response to the emphasis marking the most recent and influential reconstructions of Wordsworth, which I see as an emphasis on the visionary and aesthetic self-interrogations in the poetry" ("Criticism," p. 52).[1] Much as I agree with these approaches, it seems to me that the parting of the sea they call for between the representation of history and the apocalyptic or visionary imagination championed by Hartman is too severe.[2] The intent of my own reading in the last chapter has been that strong denials of history are also the deepest realizations of history: apocalyptic Imagination is the very threshold, the "sublime," of the "representation of reality as historical process."[3]

Picture a person—say in a Paris hotel room in late 1792—who pauses and asks, "What is history?" The answer might be something like this dark revelation at the opening of Book 10 of *The Prelude*—a "Paris Passage," as it may be called, precisely pendant to the Simplon Passage:

> This was the time in which enflam'd with hope,
> To Paris I returned. Again I rang'd

More eagerly than I had done before
Through the wide City, and in progress pass'd
The Prison where the unhappy Monarch lay,
Associate with his Children and his Wife
In bondage; and the Palace lately storm'd
With roar of cannon, and a numerous Host.
I cross'd (a blank and empty area then)
The Square of the Carousel, few weeks back
I leap'd up with dead and dying, upon these
And other sights looking as doth a man
Upon a volume whose contents he knows
Are memorable, but from him lock'd up,
Being written in a tongue he cannot read,
So that he questions the mute leaves with pain
And half upbraids their silence. But that night
When on my bed I lay, I was most mov'd
And felt most deeply in what world I was;
My room was high and lonely, near the roof
Of a large Mansion or Hotel, a spot
That would have pleas'd me in more quiet times,
Nor was it wholly without pleasure then.
With unextinguish'd taper I kept watch,
Reading at intervals; the fear gone by
Press'd on me almost like a fear to come;
I thought of those September Massacres,
Divided from me by a little month,
And felt and touch'd them, a substantial dread;
The rest was conjured up from tragic fictions,
And mournful Calendars of true history,
Remembrances and dim admonishments.
"The horse is taught his manage, and the wind
Of heaven wheels round and treads in his own steps,
Year follows year, the tide returns again,
Day follows day, all things have second birth;
The earthquake is not satisfied at once."
And in such way I wrought upon myself,
Until I seem'd to hear a voice that cried,
To the whole City, "Sleep no more." (10.38–77)

In order to map this passage over Simplon, it will be useful to add an exegetical dimension to the bare schematic of 6a and 6c I offered earlier. At some deep level, Simplon evokes the Christological story or, more broadly, the conversion experience.[4] Anticipating the explicit Revelation toward which Wordsworth moves, we might say that the "verticality" of 6a is an ascent of the cross crowned by a type of Christ's forsakenness. The poet "climb'd with eagerness" until, with deep disappointment, he learned he had "cross'd the Alps" (6.508, 524). The downward verticality in 6c is then a harrowing of hell preparatory for last judgment and redemption. Descending from his crossing point, the poet negotiates self-canceling nature in Gondo Gorge ("winds thwarting winds . . .") to open the book of nature to the alpha and omega of his Revelation: "Characters of the great Apocalypse, . . . Of first and last, and midst, and without end" (6.560, 570–72).

Composing the Paris Passage shortly afterwards (WAG, p. 519), Wordsworth simply copied the pattern of his Passion. Just as he climbed with "eagerness" to make the God-forsaken discovery that he had crossed the Alps, so now he "rang'd . . . eagerly" until he "cross'd" the Carrousel, a "blank and empty" zone of missed experience equally forsaken. And just as he harrowed hell in Gondo Gorge in anticipation of apocalypse, so now he spends a harrowing, supernatural night in another self-canceling landscape ("the wind / Of heaven wheels round and treads in his own steps . . .") leading to apocalypse. "Sleep no more," a gigantic voice utters. In part, we know, this voice is last judgment without redemption. "Sleep no more," as we earlier noticed, is the voice of the regicide Macbeth, and so refers Book 10 directly to Simplon and the allusion to "innocent sleep" just past Gondo Gorge:

> That night our lodging was an Alpine House,
> An Inn, or Hospital, as they are named,
> Standing in that same valley by itself,
> And close upon the confluence of two Streams;
> A dreary Mansion, large beyond all need,
> With high and spacious rooms, deafen'd and stunn'd
> By noise of waters, making innocent Sleep
> Lie melancholy among weary bones.   (6.573–80)

The Paris hotel is the Alpine House become a more ample theater for tragedy. But in part also, Wordsworth's Parisian revival of the Globe is truly open to the sky—to an apocalypse not just of doom but of redemption. "Sleep no more" is the clarion of Revelation. It must be taken to be direct rebuttal to the famous antisacral inscription placed over French cemeteries during the de-Christianizing movement in 1793: "Death is an eternal sleep" (EM, Nov. 1793, p. 401; Hampson, Social History, p. 201).[5]

What has become of 6b in Wordsworth's transposition of Simplon? Imagination, I suggest, is now simply this stark, matter-of-fact statement just before the poet surrenders to reading fantasies: "But that night / When on my bed I lay, I was most mov'd / And felt most deeply in what world I was." All that would be needed to read 6b into this profound assertion of place would be to make a few alterations:

> Imagination! lifting up itself
> Before the eye and progress of my Song

Like a *father'd* vapour; here that Power,
In all the might of its endowments, came
Athwart me; I was lost as in a cloud,
Halted, without a struggle to break through.
And now recovering, to *the World* I say
I recognise thy glory; in such strength
Of usurpation, in such visitings
Of awful promise, when the light of *Mind*
Goes out in flashes that have shewn to us
The *visible* world, doth Greatness make abode,
There harbours whether we be young or old.
Our destiny, our nature, and our home
Is with *finitude*.

Except in the matter of meter, no apology is necessary for rewriting the poetry here. Either way, the power of this passage is intact. Historical reality and the visionary are one; and the sense of history that utters in the realization, "I was most mov'd / And felt most deeply in what world I was," is all the force of apocalyptic imagination. We should remember, after all, the origins of apocalyptic literature. Whether in the case of a Book of Daniel or a Revelation, apocalyptic imagination was that which suffered firsthand the most brutal facts of history and then dipped itself in the blood of those facts to etch the handwriting on the wall—the writing that says, "No, this should not be," by means of fantastic figurations saying, in essence, "No, this *is* not." That such figuration denies history is indisputable. But surely such denial is also the strongest kind of engagement with history.

Where we have come in our tour, then, is to the annunciation of the argument of this book. The true apocalypse for Wordsworth is reference. What now shocks us most about Wordsworth's poetry, after all, is its indelible stain of referentiality, its insistent mundanity. We flinch before the topical—the apparition of Napoleon in Imagination, for example—as before a devil; we seek ways to textualize it, to exorcise the mundane daemon through phenomenal, psychic, or metaphoric displacement. We make reference, in short, a figure of speech without remembering that figuration *is* a manner of reference.[6] But reference to history, I assert, is the only "power" of Wordsworth's Imagination (as I will at last call it with examined significance); this power is as unstable, surprising, and full of hidden lights as any figure Mind can conceive; and its hold over Mind is not less but *more* persistent when, as in *The Prelude*, it is manifest only in a poetics of denial, of reference lost.

Where we now have to go in our tour, as is characteristic of Wordsworth's own tours, is *back* from *The Prelude* to retrace the entire itinerary by which the poet learned to create his crowning denial of history: autobiography. Only after such a tour of beginnings can we

conclude by looking with Keatsian wild surmise past the period of
The Prelude into the far pacific reaches of reference regained: the poet's
*un*imaginative restitution to history. This is the critical challenge that
will attend our whole route: can we accept the shock of historical
reference—the hurt and pleasure that "fact" so often generates in excess of any figure of speech—when all the old apparatus of contextual
understanding (influence study or history of ideas, for example) has
fallen away? Can we read in Imagination a Napoleon or, in a humbler strain, a Lakeland yeoman or laborer (not Wordsworth's fictive
"Statesmen," as we will see, but the men and women unearthed by
recent historians and demographers) without seeing our apocalyptic
book of life turn as gray as the newspaper Mallarmé excoriated (in
his "The Book: A Spiritual Instrument")? How can we know without loss of value that any book of life must inscribe the names not
just of imagination, memory, time, affection, and other such Wordsworthian pieties but also the names of nations, peoples, churches,
and other *conventional* pieties enrolled in the newspapers of the day?

An adequate response to this challenge will require rethinking how
we go about establishing historical ground in a critical universe per-
suaded by textual abyssings. It will be useful at the start to lay out
the assumptions I bring to bear. These comprise a critical stance, a
philosophical approach, and a practical analytic.

(1) What I aspire to here is a new derivation of Wordsworth's
poetry. By "new," I denote not originality—for, in a deep sense, my
project is convention—but a particular kind of critical stance or self-
placement. Revisiting the sources of Wordsworth's power, I would
stress the historical *difference* of my own point of view. Whether such
historicist differential or distantiation, as Jerome McGann (*Romantic
Ideology*, pp. 1–2, 30, 34, and *passim*) and Terry Eagleton (*Criticism*,
esp. p. 43; see also p. 18) have addressed it, can by itself complete the
act of criticism is unclear (an issue I will return to in Chapter 9). For
now, all I assume is the functional and, indeed, indispensable value
of historicist difference as a starting point. Difference is especially
desirable in the field of Wordsworth studies, which has tended to
be extremely familiar with its object of study. Criticism, perhaps,
should be an act of boat stealing, in which truly to give restitution
to the other we must first commandeer the artifact of the other and
row away toward as sharply defined a spur of difference as possible.
Criticism of Wordsworth should prepare us to admit that we are
at home in his world only after we have come to a land's end of
familiarity not unlike the universe he himself discovers in the boat-
stealing episode:

> after I had seen
> That spectacle, for many days, my brain
> Work'd with a dim and undetermin'd sense

Of unknown modes of being; in my thoughts
There was a darkness, call it solitude,
Or blank desertion, no familiar shapes
Of hourly objects, images of trees,
Of sea or sky, no colours of green fields;
But huge and mighty Forms that do not live
Like living men mov'd slowly through my mind
By day and were the trouble of my dreams.

(*Prel.* 1.417–27)

Such difference is what I mean by "new." Difference, indeed, is the only substantive meaning that can be conceived in the given names of the two theoretical novelties that are my dialogic partners—agonists and antagonists both—in this book: New Criticism (more generally: formalism together with its deconstructive revaluations) and New Historicism. As I will suggest in Chapter 9 (and have written more fully elsewhere),[7] these seemingly divorced partners are finally both profound formalisms wed to the goal of differentiating themselves from the original work in its world in order to criticize the work from a new world—from a realm of modernism and postmodernism distanced from the original precisely by "huge and mighty Forms." Where the New Criticism propagated the forms of ambiguity, paradox, irony, texture, unity, and imagery, the New Historicism, in rough parallel, studies subversion, transgression, oppositionality, textuality, power, and ideology. Though conceived as situated *in* past literatures and cultures, these critical forms—none of which "live / Like living men"—function as semi-technical abstractions cutting the modern interpreter off from the less clearly or differently shaped forms of experience in the past. The motive is to define the modern/postmodern intellect itself in self-conscious difference. It is the ambiguous or subversive status of modernity/postmodernity, in other words, that the New Criticism and the New Historicism glimpse (often explicitly) when they survey the past.

Thus the New Critical view of the Metaphysicals helped institute Modernism by giving the ambiguous stance toward pluralism of the Fugitive generation a "historical" authority; and the New Historical view of the Renaissance similarly helps institute postmodernism by granting the oppositionality of the post–May 1968 intellect (post-1970 in the United States) a lineage old as Shakespeare. Like over-fastidious quotation marks around a controversial term, in short, "ambiguity," "subversion," and so forth are forms severing past from present while allowing the latter nevertheless to cite the authority of the former.[8] Such is the limitation of formalism; yet such, it must be said, is also its virtue. There is a vital need for the perennially new criticism that worships forms: formalization of past or otherwise alien experience shapes the interval of similarity/dissimilarity without which neither critical reflection on the past (imbued by present concerns) nor critical self-reflection on the present (informed by past perspectives) would be possible.

Formalism in the old sense, then, I would annihilate—implicitly and explicitly—in my project. Yet my own act of enabling denial must in the end acknowledge and make restitution to formalism. Any truly historical criticism must interest itself in the old *and* the new, and so must know the difference relating the two. The moment such differentiating newness is formulated (even if it must be coerced through powerful forgettings of interpretive continuities of the sort studied in the next chapter), *there* is the origin of form.

To make my own opening difference from "Wordsworthianism" as wide as possible, therefore, I nail on the church door a litany of broken faiths.

There is no nature. Since I have already begun upon this refutation, I tender here a brief, Berkeleian argument—in Berkeleian personal voice—merely as a transition to an ongoing critique. Having lived for some years in a part of Connecticut not unlike the Lake District in its reservoirs, brooks, grasslands, and deep forest dells, I would go so far as to acknowledge the existence of a reservoir, brook, field, and possibly even forest (more certainly, trees). But "nature" I have never set axe to. To believe that nature "is" in the way a tree "is" is to abstract the notion of essence while concealing the abstraction. Nature is an idea validating as *rightful* existence the reservoir, brook, field, forest, and—what has remained unspoken here—my own haven in Bethany-away-from-New-Haven. More broadly, nature is the name under which we use the nonhuman to validate the human, to interpose a mediation able to make humanity more easy with itself. To invoke *The Prelude*:

> Ye Brooks
> Muttering along the stones, a busy noise
> By day, a quiet one in silent night,
> And you, ye Groves, whose ministry it is
> To interpose the covert of your shades,
> Even as a sleep, betwixt the heart of man
> And the uneasy world, 'twixt man himself,
> Not seldom, and his own unquiet heart,
> Oh! that I had a music and a voice,
> Harmonious as your own, that I might tell
> What ye have done for me.   (II.12–22)

A full list of corollaries to the above tenet can be unfolded as follows, where the sequence traces the turns we have yet to take in tracking Wordsworth's development, but counteracts any lingering idealism, Berkeleian or otherwise:

There is no time.
There is no affection.
There is no self or mind.
Therefore, there is no Imagination.

(2) What there "is" is history. But to shape critical difference into a flexible approach, of course, we need to make this potentially reductive statement intelligent. The approach of this book rests upon a working philosophy of history skeptical in its ontology but positive in its epistemology.

Both these propositions are true: first that Wordsworth's largest, most sustained theme is the realization of history; and, second, that his largest theme is the denial of history. Both can be true, I suggest, because of the strange status of history as a category of being. Intuitively, history both *is,* because it is the very source of reality, and *is not,* because, no matter whether it is conceived to extend backward in time or outward in social space, the stuff of history is manifestly not "here," available for such ordinary means of verification as sight or touch.[9] Even if a person were present at an event known to be "historical"—the Storming of the Tuileries in August 1792, for example —"history" would not be discernible in the heft of a pike, the shrill of shot, the burning of bodies on the Carrousel, or any of the other sparks in the Carlylean "flame picture."[10] The person may see the phenomena, but the reality of history is the unrevealed essence or "absent cause," to use Louis Althusser's phrase, *elsewhere* than in the phenomena (*Reading Capital*, p. 188).[11] History is the absence that is the very possibility of the "here and now." The reason poetic denial is ipso facto a realization of history, in other words, is that history is the very category of denial. It is history that says, "This 'is' but neither was nor will be." Or in terms of social space: "This is your place but was/is/shall be another's."

Of course, such evacuated ontology would seem to move us very far toward Continental philosophy and its evolutions of negation and absence. These evolutions I do not mean to hide or hide from. Mine is also a variety of "deconstructive materialism," as Marjorie Levinson has insightfully called it (*Wordsworth's Great Period Poems*, pp. 9–13). But just as it was disturbance in ontology that made possible post-Hegelian idealism (the neo–idealism of Dilthey and Collingwood is especially pertinent to the Romantics and history) as well as later hermeneutic and deconstructive transformations,[12] so it was disturbed ontology that sponsored the original instinct of British empiricism: epistemology. If there "is" no history, then the relevant problem becomes the knowledge or *sense* of history in the full sense. This sense may be rendered skeptical in the old empiricist manner and so assimilated to poststructuralist thought,[13] but it may also be rendered affirmative. We might exhume here for fresh application the problem of uncertainty in the collision of two billiard balls. When a text is seen from a distance to collide with, glance off, or receive English from its context, interpretive uncertainty is always an issue. But the uncertainty can be cushioned by probability: by as rigorous as possible a measurement of the particular collision under examination against those we have witnessed occurring within other relevant contexts.

More precisely (since I do not myself find probability a satisfying explanation), I posit a historical epistemology grounded on what may be called denied positivism.[14] I mean by this a negative, but nevertheless determinate, explanation of how we know the relation between text and context. At stake here is the very notion of context. Considered positively, a context is a set of observable phenomena, general laws, and linguistic formulations containing the subset of the text. But I would look aside from logical positivism to rival concepts in the modern genealogy of context. The most useful genealogy for my purposes is that which has developed through and beyond structural definition. I cite selectively Dilthey's world-view penetrated with connectivity (*Zusammenhang*); the Russian Formalist notion of interconnected "motive" (or motif); Lévi-Strauss's and Althusser's cultural structurations; Braudel's pseudo-structural *longue durée*; and Foucault's discursive formation.[15] In varying degrees, each of these formulations of context regrounds positivism upon the special premises of structural thought: first, that the basic stuff of structure is marked difference or negativity; and second, that the organization of such differentiation is *knowable* because it is not just free play (as in the emphasis deconstruction gives the theme), but also a determination of order.

As William Keach has helped me see, the key concept here is the notion of arbitrariness that Saussure applied to language. In a contradiction of long standing, the arbitrary was simultaneously that which is free (whimsical, unconstrained, voluntary) and that which is determined or overseen (as in the legal tradition of the "arbiter").[16] In political usage from Locke through Shelley, Keach thus shows, "arbitrary" implied somewhat oxymoronically an unconstrained despotism or tyrannical freedom; and the desire by the same writers to apply the word neutrally to the workings of language was from the first compromised.[17] Just so, for Saussure it was precisely the arbitrariness of language that led him to formulate the seemingly contradictory thesis that language is subject to cultural forces. Language is arbitrary, but as determined as history: "Since the linguistic sign is arbitrary, a language as so far defined would appear to be an adaptable system, which can be organised in any way one likes," but "we must consider what is brought about by the passage of time, as well as what is brought about by the forces of social integration. . . . When this is taken into account, the language is no longer free from constraints, because the passage of time allows social forces to be brought to bear upon it" (Saussure, p. 78).

For us, contradictoriness suits the arbitrary to cultural study in a way that bears exactly on the problem of historical knowledge. In the modern genealogy of context, as I have called it, structure is arbitrary: always free and unpredictable, yet always also determinate and knowable. It is knowable, indeed, because it is defined from the first as precisely *cognate* with the possibility of "knowledge"—with the epistemological constructs (*epistemes,* in Foucault's term) that cultures create in order to perceive, interpret, and *know* the phenomena referred to as reality. The process by which cultures collectively come to know referential reality might be generalized as follows:[18]

"Reality"
(historical context)

$\downarrow$

Free/determined differentiation
(arbitrary structure)

$\downarrow$

"Truth"
(ordered knowledge)

By itself, the context of "real" history is unknowable. It becomes knowable only insofar as it is acted upon by the collective process of arbitrary structuration—of arbitration, we might call it—by which cultures interpret reality. Collective arbitration superimposes over reality a grid of marked differences (experienced in everyday life as conflicts, breakages, tensions, and other incommensurabilities). Or perhaps "grid" is too Cartesian; a better paradigm for the functional, yet also ornamental or unpredictable, structure of collective arbitration might be "arabesque." As in an arabesque plant motif, whose split leaves are predicated upon a continuous stem, the collective differentiation of reality—of rich versus poor, male versus female, adult versus child, and so forth across the whole spectrum of social interpretation—always at once improvises freely and clings to an axial line or rule of determination. It is the premise of this latter rule (the deepest instinct, perhaps, of Burkean prejudice) that guarantees that the final result of the arbitration process is belief in a determinate and knowable order. Arbitrated by a whole age's prejudicial or creedal differences, reality becomes what "we" (rulers, parents, educators, and so forth) know. What we know are the "positivities," as Foucault calls them, of any age's psychological, grammatical, medical, economic, and other truths.

Later interpreters foreign to the "we" can then share in such knowledge insofar as they extend to a further level the process of arbitration: they must themselves be incorporated with the past by being differentiated *from* the past in the creation of a further structure or arabesque of knowledge. Thus in academic research, for example, the original cultural structures become the historical context, and a new arbitration of structure (the assumptions of scholarship and criticism in their relation to larger society) interprets this context so as to yield a fresh positivity of vested knowledge: a "truth" that, however anti-positivistic its theme in some current fields, is nevertheless still positive in the broader sense I sketch here of a self-evident belief-structure. We "know" the knowledge of the past even if part of what we know is that interpretation, representation, and illusion necessarily separate us from the past. The structure of our knowledge is different, and—precisely in its difference—conjoined with the principle of determined differentiation underlying the very possibility of positivity.

In short, referential knowledge may be an insoluble problem at the level of the individual and his language. But I believe it to be soluble at the level of culture and the *langue* of collective interpretation. Culture *is* the process of interpreting, knowing, and believing in referential truth; and such is true even if the arabesque of structure thus created seems from the standpoint of our later antipositivistic positivity to be wholly arbitrary, ungrounded, decentered, undecidable, labyrinthine, or otherwise *post*structuralist. The requirement for an exact fit between signifier and signified, after all, is premised upon a geometry of one-to-one correspondence suited to the point-consciousness or *cogito* of Cartesian individuality. But collective thought and language are by definition imprecise because transindividual: the signifier of a social structure can mean many things in unpredictable ways and still "refer" to the signified of customary reality. Indeed, it is of the essence that such contextual structures disperse reference laterally by means of contradiction, undecidability, catachresis, deferral, trace-structure, and so forth. Such is the process of shared meaning. Deconstruction, we may say, is really an insight into the dialogism of meaning that is social truth.

I cannot here study in depth, of course, the genealogy of context that leads from Saussurean structuralism and its predecessors to the formulation of shareable historical knowledge I offer above—a formulation designed to elide positivism (in a manner incorporating elements of deconstruction) but *without* rejecting the faith in determinate knowledge that is the core of positivity. An overview of this genealogy, however, may be useful. As early as Dilthey, we notice, structural differentiation emerged with an accent on determinate arbitrariness. To begin with, Dilthey's *Weltanschauung*, or world-view, is by definition *not* the world; it is a partial hollowing out of materiality by the *geistige Welt* (mind- and experience-saturated world). The effect of this basic negativity (the ideal component in Dilthey's thought) is that world-view shares the empty stuff of later structural thought. Dilthey's notion that world-views are articulated through an "inner dialectic" of dynamic differentiation then confirms the structural impulse. In temporal terms, "the inner dialectic . . . drives from one standpoint [in a world-view] to another" such that the "difficulties which are contained in a standpoint drive beyond it." Such inner differentiation is arbitrary, yet also determined and knowable. While "it is erroneous to posit with the school of Hegel that [the difficulties in any one standpoint] lead neatly and directly to the following standpoint," Dilthey argues, nevertheless the inner dialectic that articulates world-views is not relativistic because it is historically determined: it "lets thought progress through historically conditioned orientations . . . to a universality which is everywhere and always tied to historical thought" (quoted in Ermarth, pp. 333, 338).[19] *Weltanschauung* on this model directly anticipates Saussure. The doctrine of world-views, Dilthey comments, "stands to the history of philosophy as comparative philology stands to the history of language" (quoted in Ermarth, p. 328).[20]

So, too, the later contributors in my genealogy of context conceive structure to be a determinate arbitrariness. The Russian Formalists, for example, studied texts and folkloristic contexts as in essence transformable networks of empty slots. Logically prior to the thematic motifs that are their "realistic" content, such networks demonstrate "the dominance of structure, of plot over material" (Eichenbaum, p. 121). Dominance in this fashion is artistic defamiliarization: the recognition that arbitrary structure determines even mismatched, bizarrely whimsical, or otherwise unrealistic content.[21] For Lévi-Strauss, more recently, determinate arbitrariness is the defamiliarization of nature: culture. Social groups cohere on the basis of such supremely arbitrary, but also determinate and determinative, differences as the incest prohibition, which turns the natural family into a cultural unit by forcing it to marry into other families (*Elementary Structures*, esp. pp. 29–68, 478–97). Kinship, we might say, demonstrates the dominance of structure, of plot over biology. For Althusser, analogously, determinate arbitrariness governs a version of Lévi-Strauss's culture: ideology, or the defamiliarization of the economic base. Social groups cohere as structures of contentless differentiation: "the structure of the relations of production," for example, "determines the *places* and *functions* occupied and adopted by the agents of production, who are never anything more than the occupants of these places" (*Reading Capital*, p. 180). The organization of the overall structure is such that a principle of "structural" causality (*Reading Capital*, esp. pp. 184–93) allows the economic base simultaneously to determine the subordinate "ideological state apparatuses" responsible for attitudes *and* to permit the latter a certain "relative autonomy" (just as the latter in turn then allow individual citizens a seeming independence from ideology or "freedom" of thought; *Lenin*, pp. 121–73).

Finally, I invoke Braudel and the *Annales*-style history that has inspired history of mentalities.[22] "Structure," Braudel writes, "dominates the problems of the *longue durée*" (p. 31). But rather than study excessively long durations akin to static positivities, the historian must discriminate "the movement, the different time spans, the rifts and variations" that segment history into incommensurable, but also ultimately unified, levels of structure (p. 47). History, that is, consists of different levels of phenomena interrelated in a manner that may appear arbitrary to the sociologist but that must at last seem to the historian (as Braudel conceives him) as also determined.[23] The prophet of such arbitrarily determined cultural knowledge is then Foucault, whose version of history of mentalities has most affected Anglo-American literary study. For Foucault, the discursive formations that create the positivities of any epoch are buoyed up by a swell of collective *langue* that embraces formations as a shifting sea the continents. In one of the most theoretically problematic and charged passages in his corpus, he names this swell the archive and, while confirming the current of determination that runs through its arbitrary structure, also grows Dionysian or Nietzschean in celebrating its countercurrent of free play. Here, the knowability of cultural structure reaches its limit:

Far from being that which unifies everything that has been said in the great confused murmur of a discourse, far from being only that which ensures that we exist in the midst of preserved discourse, [the archive] is that which differentiates discourses in their multiple existence and specifies them in their own duration. . . . It is not possible for us to describe our own archive, since it is from within these rules that we speak, since it is that which gives to what we can say—and to itself, the object of our discourse—its modes of appearance, its forms of existence and coexistence, its system of accumulation, historicity, and disappearance. The archive cannot be described in its totality; and in its presence it is unavoidable. It emerges in fragments, regions, and levels, more fully, no doubt, and with greater sharpness, the greater the time that separates us from it. . . . The analysis of the archive, then, involves a privileged region: at once close to us, and different from our present existence, it is the border of time that surrounds our presence, which overhangs it, and which indicates it in its otherness; it is that which, outside ourselves, delimits us. The description of the archive deploys its possibilities (and the mastery of its possibilities) on the basis of the very discourses that have just ceased to be ours; its threshold of existence is established by the discontinuity that separates us from what we can no longer say. (*Archaeology*, pp. 129–30)[24]

In its very phrasing as well as theme (backed up by a four-point synopsis of what his method is *not*, in his next chapter), this passage is a sustained meditation on negation or differentiation that brings us to the furthest verge of the Saussurean determination of arbitrariness. We can know after a fashion, Foucault implies, the arbitrarily determinate structurations that create the knowledge of cultures past or present; but such knowledge involves us in a Walk to Emmaus in which the Truth is always in part misrecognized. Beyond this verge, we surmise, would be only the labyrinthine "mycelium" of Freud's meditation on the navel of the dream (p. 564) or the *mise en abyme* of deconstruction.

Such is the background of the understanding of context I propose. Historical context is not a massively stable totality but a domain of collective knowledge (world-view, folklore, kinship system, ideology, *longue durée*, discursive formation). Knowledge or reference of this sort is organized on the basis of arbitrary rifts of internal differentiation, of clashes, divisions, prejudices, and other lived negativities of social experience; and as such is always both capricious and determinate, free as *jouissance* and bound as history. Though never fully ordered or inspectable by the standards of individual consciousness, there is enough determination in such structure shareable with the explanatory structures of the later critical interpreter, I believe, to credit explanation as positive. After all, in everyday existence it is especially those organizing divisions in culture we know from a critical distance to be arbitrary and illusional that we also feel to be the hardest, most recalcitrant facts of life: prejudice, privilege, distinction, antagonism, and all the other elements of social representation. These arbitrary and yet fully determinative facts of life are not "things" to be studied according to the unit-idea principles of positivistic history of ideas; but neither are they precisely nothing. They are, and are not, with all the force of history itself.

One further trait may be noticed about the Foucault passage above: it is also literary. The special virtue of quoting this evocative passage, indeed, is that it allows us to see that Foucault's characteristic exertions of literariness—of the post-symbolist qualities of self-involution, allusiveness, and defamiliarization we now epitomize as literary—hinge precisely on his theme: the negativity at the heart of the differential structures of knowledge. In his very style, Foucault declares that "it is not possible for us to describe our own archive" (or, we may add, any archive) except in a literariness whose estranged "fragments, regions, and levels" of discourse intimate precisely in their disruptions and torsions that positive knowledge speaks itself negatively: by differentiation from "the very discourses that have just ceased to be ours." I finish my genealogy of context, in sum, already predisposed to look to the special problem of literary study: the emergence of literary texts from context. How does historical context as I have defined it give English to literary texts if it is not a simple positivity like a cue stick or billiard ball?

Literary texts emerge, I posit, precisely through a critical or second-order negation: the arbitrary but nevertheless determined differentiation by which they do *not* articulate historical contexts (the latter, of course, themselves constructed as arbitrary differentiation). Or put more empirically: it is not the case that contexts cue texts in the way the stick imparts spin and direction to the billiard ball. Rather, contexts are themselves constituted as masses of difference —as collisions or discontinuities with other contexts or with aspects of themselves. And it is this dynamic mass of marked breaks and shaped absences that determines the text by spelling out in advance the shaped *absence* of context—negative yet determinate—that is the defamiliarized text. I draw here in particular from Pierre Macherey, who defines the literary text as a sheaf of absences and dissonances stitched together by that which is never on the page: the history *not* there. Macherey writes:

When we explain the work, instead of ascending to a hidden centre which is the source of life, . . . we perceive its actual decentred-ness. We refuse the principle of an intrinsic analysis (or an immanent criticism) which would artificially circumscribe the work, and deduce the image of a 'totality' . . . from the fact that it is *entire*. The structure of the work, which makes it available to knowledge, is this internal displacement, this caesura, by which it corresponds to a reality that is also incomplete, which it shows without reflecting. The literary work gives the measure of a difference, reveals a determinate absence, resorts to an eloquent silence. . . . What begs to be explained in the work is not that false simplicity which derives from the apparent unity of its meaning, but the presence of a relation, or an opposition, between elements of the exposition or levels of the composition, those disparities which point to a conflict of meaning. This conflict is not the sign of an imperfection; it reveals the inscription of an *otherness* in the work, through which it maintains a relationship with that which it is not, that which happens at its margins. To explain the work is to show that, contrary to appearances, it is not independent, but bears in its material substance the imprint of a determinate absence. (pp. 79–80)

We may add here Althusser's cryptic definition of art as that which gives us a "view" of its ideology by presupposing "a *retreat*, an *internal distantiation*" from ideology (*Lenin*, p. 204). Or again, there is Ricoeur's notion of "metaphorical reference": "Metaphorical reference

. . . consists in the fact that the effacement of descriptive reference —an effacement that, as a first approximation, makes language refer to itself—is revealed to be, in a second approximation, the negative condition for freeing a more radical power of reference to those aspects of our being-in-the-world that cannot be talked about directly" (p. 80). There is an arbitrary difference between the literary text and its historical context, in sum, but it is precisely this difference, constituted by what we will see to be highly exact swerves of negation and indirection, that refers to the difference—between rich and poor, urban and rustic, English and French, past and present, and so forth —that history itself makes. Or put most broadly: the very scheme of differences that allows certain ages to define a "literary text" separate from historical event (for example, as representation rather than action, aesthetic object rather than utilitarian artifact, medium of the cultured rather than of popular culture) is a reference to, or mimesis of, the scheme of differences that divides and organizes the historical context of that culture.

Such is the regrounding of reference that Jerome McGann, David Simpson, and Marjorie Levinson have also applied to Romantic poetry in their discussions of literary displacement and that I would pursue, if possible, with even more force: the literary text is not just the displacement but the overdetermined and agonic *denial* of historical reference.[25] Like the negations that fracture and so impose interpretive structure over historical context, the differentiating denials that compose literature are arbitrary; but they are also positively determined—indeed, overdetermined—in all substantive senses of the term:[26] they are material because they participate in the principle of structure creating the positivity of all context; they subsume the traditional notions of causation and reference; and they are limited by their historical context to place, time, and manifestation.

All that is necessary now to complete my historical epistemology is to hypothesize a theory of manifestation or expression. What is the efficient cause by which historical context and the collective structure arbitrating it make themselves known to an author such that the author's text can then make it known to the reader? How precisely does literature "sense" the sense of history? The solution to this inquiry, I suggest, requires that we unthink the "idea," which from Locke through modern history of ideas has as much blocked as facilitated the passage between historical context and historical knowledge. In the view of manifestation I argue in this book, ideas and their influence are always after the fact. Historical context first makes itself known to an author in concrete, highly charged phenomena that are accepted as material because they are prior or unacceptable to idea. These phenomenal spots of history (examples I will address: a ruined cottage or Wordsworth's personal debt) are charged because even in their seeming substantiality they intimate immateriality. They mark the aperture of negation or differentiation where at least two facets of cultural context collide in the background so as to define the essential divisions constitutive of that context. (An example from an economic context: the competing notions of industriousness we will see Wordsworth meditating during his crisis of personal solvency.) It is the excess of negativity in such markers of difference that manifests itself in the author's pre-ideational consciousness as an elementary feel for representation—as his sense for the basic material of differentiation, that is, from which collective culture carves its interpretations of reality and from which the individual author can then sculpt further interpretations. Over the deep romantic chasms of differential representation, finally, there arises the pleasure dome or rare device of authorial "ideas" explicable according to history of ideas with its fiction of a continuous historical ground.

Nature, time, affection, self, mind, imagination, and other such Wordsworthian ideas, in sum, are ideological stopgaps: the final, hardened denials of the "literariness" by which rifted and broken texts—themselves a less cogent attempt at denial—communicate the underlying chasms of history. To read Wordsworth's poetry and know the history behind it will mean to descry in the compound shapes of his denial the deep absences that are his sense of history.

Such is the holdfast of qualified positivism that characterizes my approach. A stance of historicist difference or distance on our part does not mean that the relation between text and context can be studied with objective certainty. But neither does distance, with all its hazy hermeneutics on the horizon, entail on my subject unrelieved uncertainty. In the contextual gaps where it has its only being, history "is not" in extremely precise, knowable ways—in calibrated steps and vectors of negation that can be studied with all the certainty or, at least, carefully contained uncertainty, of positivism at its most full-throated. And because history is knowable in this fashion, so, too, is the poetry that would articulate it by denying it. Wordsworth's poetry is a mimetic denial of history so vigorous, full, and detailed that denial, the shaped negation, becomes itself the positive fact.

These, then, are my critical stance and my philosophical approach: the former would differentiate my text from Wordsworth's; the latter addresses the differentiation of Wordsworth's own text from his context. But stance and approach, of course, are nothing without an actual laying on of hands, a practical analytic.

(3) How can we know the manifestation of history and its mimetic denial in poetry practically? Here ontology and epistemology must return to "-logy" itself. To think about the genesis of my chosen texts from their contexts, I choose a logic, or analytic, of form— the necessary recourse, as I suggested earlier, of any criticism that

sets out to differentiate itself from its object of study. In particular, I take genre as the most telling logic of form.[27] By "logic" here I imply that it is useful to conceive of genre as a pre-ideational method of thought akin to classical logic but fundamentally different in its assumptions. Adena Rosmarin in *The Power of Genre* has studied the relation between syllogistic and generic thinking (pp. 39–48). Along similar lines, I suggest that syllogistic logic and genre theory border along an interface of uncanny resemblance.

In Aristotelian logic, we know, there are twelve moods of valid syllogism resulting in 24 valid, particular syllogisms (with mnemonic names such as "Celarent," "Cesare," or "Darapti," indicating by vowel relations their possible transformations). The axiom of the whole system is the "existential quantifier" or, put simply, the proposition of existence coupled with category from which all other propositions are built: $a = a$.[28] (Thus only the fact that "$a = a$" makes possible such propositions as, "All *a* are *b*.") To move from such logic to genre is then only a difference of "modes" and "moods." In the history of genre theory, as Alistair Fowler documents, there are several basic modes (e.g., "lyric") resulting in a varying number of genres and sub-genres (with names such as "ode," "elegy," "sonnet"). The axiom that drives the system is then the exact opposite of the existential quantifier: the proposition of nonidentity or de-categorization ($a = $ not-a) that Anne Mellor has studied as the formula of becoming, change, or (subtracting temporality) differentiation in Continental philosophy (p. 27). I would add that the proposition of nonidentity grounds not just Continental philosophy considered in itself but the literariness that is its distinguishing style. Nonidentity is the basic thought of literature; in Aristotle's own terms of literary logic, it is reversal and discovery. Just as "$a = $ not-a" underlies antithetical philosophy, that is, so the core thought of Shakespeare's play is that Lear is not-Lear. Applied generically: the reversal and discovery by which King Lear becomes not-King provokes a mode (or mood) of tragedy generating—through a process of episode-making akin to syllogistic sorites—a particular form of tragedy.

Genre, in sum, is akin to what Lévi-Strauss calls the thinking of the savage mind. Like the arrangement of cultures into clans, each with its own totem, the distribution of literature in a generic field is a way of thinking, a logic designed to cope with the basic issue of differentiation or internal transformation. Genre is thus a proper logic in which to think about literature and history, differential text and context, together. Genre tells the story of a poet's relation to history even when the story, as we will see, is no longer a story. After all, it is in an author's arbitrary conformity or nonconformity to the historically determined kinds that he most truly knows history even before setting to work. To take the case most ready to hand: the fact that this book is shaped according to accepted modes of academic discourse—and even that it is written in a language that was not mine to begin with—is from the first an act of unfathomably deep conformity to an elsewhereness beyond individual ken or control.

With the notable exception of Hayden White, [29] it is the Marxist critics who have been most preoccupied with the relation of literary form and genre to history. There is the strong precedent of Lukács on the novel, for example. There is Althusser's emphasis on Marx's *Darstellung* and the model of theatrical representation (*Reading Capital*, pp. 188, 193). There is Tony Bennett on the sympathy between Althusser's structural Marxism and Russian Formalism as well as Eagleton on form and ideology (*Marxism*, pp. 20–36; *Criticism*, pp. 100–161). And there is Macherey on the "history of forms" (pp. 91–92). But the post-Althusserian formulation I have learned the most from practically—in its special focus on genres and narrative—is Fredric Jameson's *The Political Unconscious* (supported by his general exposition of form in *Marxism and Form*, pp. 306–416). As I have come to agree, and as the recent recovery of narrative assumptions in historiography proper helps confirm (Stone, *Past and Present*, pp. 74–96), the sense of history is originally and deeply narrative. When a ruined cottage or other spot of history marks a collision of cultural context in the background, such collision is agon; and the first representational form of agon is narrative.

My next chapters will demonstrate that history is quintessentially narrative, not only because the lay forms of historical action and reportage—*journée*, march, massacre, anecdote, grievance, or even joke —are "emplotted," but because the governing institutions of history, such as Church or State, are themselves fully plotted in every sense of the word and can be subverted or revolutionized only by counterplot. The only way to "know" history is through a category of narrative underlying social institutions and literary forms alike. Prior to all other modes or genres, such a category is the very shape of what we mean by historical knowledge. As Arthur C. Danto has put it at the close of his *Narration and Knowledge* (in a statement Collingwood anticipated):[30]

To recognize the present as historical is to perceive both it and one's consciousness of it as something the meaning of which will only be given in the future, and in historical retrospection. For it is recognized as having the structure of what will be a past historical moment. . . . There is an entire vocabulary, the language of narrative as we might call it, the rules of whose meaning presuppose internalization of this structure. . . . To exist historically is to perceive the events one lives through as part of a story later to be told. (pp. 342–43)

Contention or agon, I conclude, is the content of the space of disturbance where facets of cultural context collide, and the form that thinks that differential content is narrative. But the literary text that then takes up this form is determined by content only in a way that frees it from that content. Through the arbitrary process of historical determination, texts refer to their underlying narrative content only by at last differentiating themselves from that content's own scheme of differentiations or agons. Put simply: Wordsworth's poetry is a denial. But history itself is the very form of breakage, difference, and denial. If historical form is fundamentally narrative, then it follows that history can enter the poetry only in denied form as *transformation* of narrative. Wordsworth's work is all a transformation. It is all a poetry of forms of denial.

I have organized my inquiry as a twofold study of poetic emergence and individuation. I use these terms to historicize, respectively, the problems of literary authority and of originality—the composite problem, that is, of where a poet's power comes from. "Emergence" refers to Wordsworth's conversion of political emergency and its improvised authority (the ideological supervision of the People) into the first of the antinarrativistic forms he appended to natural description: time. As we will see, it was the irruption of political narrative within the poet's early descriptive forms that made time—reified finally as an "idea" and ideology—necessary as the obscure allegorization of narrative. "Individuation" refers to the subsequent impressing of nature and time with the forms of denial constitutive of Wordsworth's mature authorities of ego: the lyricism of affection, self, and finally, Imagination. Instead of holding poetry open to the narrative of history, the ideology or supervision of Imagination increasingly fomented antinarrativistic and antimimetic forms culminating in what may be called Wordsworth's great "transform": a lyric mode that was not so much any particular kind of lyric as an *émigré* flight from narrative.

Yet if Wordsworth's corpus escapes narrative to launch itself upon an odyssey of lyrics, its overall momentum will at last bring it round again to something like narrative closure, to an epic return home. In our own argument, we will round back once more to *The Prelude* in order to reprise the poet's lyric transform of history. But such reprise will be truly a prelude. It will put us in position to foresee what *The Prelude* is prelude to: the endless Memorial Tour that is Wordsworth's final restitution to history.

This is the question whose radical simplicity should haunt us throughout: "What *is* the relation of literature to other things, the other things that men make and the other things that men do and think?"[31]

PART II

Violence and Time:
A Study in Poetic Emergence

Before Time

PERHAPS THE SINGLE MOST pervasive preoccupation of Wordsworth criticism in the last twenty years has been "time." Mapped
onto time, the tour with two points that I began with in my first
chapter translates into the modern agony of succession striving to
imagine its own duration. The vigorous, modern critique of Wordsworthian time has phrased the problem variously (as a divorce between outer and inner time, for example), yet has also been remarkably unanimous in its philosophical grounding. As taught in most
cases by Georges Poulet's *Studies in Human Time*, the critique reads
the problem of succession versus duration, or rupture versus continuity, in a modern tradition of thought spanning from Descartes to
Bergson.[1] Put simply, Wordsworth touring from point to point is the
Cartesian *cogito* turned peripatetic. Because *cogito* recognized its own
existence only as a point-instant of consciousness ("I think, therefore I am"), it did not know how to extend through time. If it were
to extend only as a succession of point-instants, it would simply be
another form of corporeal matter, which Descartes conceived to be
infinitely divisible extension (pp. 139–40). To endure, *cogito* required
some means of durational extension or, in Bergson's phrase, "succession without mutual externality" (*Time*, p. 227).

It required God. As Poulet's study makes clear, the divide between
succession and duration modernized the split between the time of
the body and the time of the spirit in Christian thought (pp. 3–7).[2]
Descartes, therefore, could identify the genius necessary to conserve
cogito as God. Thus, in the *Meditations*: "it does not follow from the
fact that I have existed a short while before that I should exist now,

unless at this very moment some cause produces and creates me, as it were, anew or, more properly, conserves me" (p. 105). Wordsworth's secular god is Memory, a divinity arising unbidden and uncontrolled from within *cogito* itself to conserve identity: "I would enshrine the spirit of the past / For future restoration," he worships after the gibbet-mast "spot of time" (*Prel.* 11.342–43).

I will want to emerge upon the spots of time. But the heart of my concern is the *genesis* of philosophical temporality. Imagine, to begin with, the experience of time prior to thought. Several signposts toward such a latent temporality can be suggested. There is Heidegger's massive inquiry into an everyday temporality constituted by consciousness's very stance in its world, its positioning as a "being-in," "being-toward," "being-alongside," and so forth down a series of verbal knots each questioning the intense isolation of the Cartesian *cogito*. There is Braudel's stratification of time into several kinds of spans founded at bottom upon geological or environmental duration. Piaget has studied the way children, and to a lesser degree adults, understand duration only in terms of such primitive phenomena as the relative speeds of objects (the object moving fastest or farthest travels "longest"). Joost A. M. Meerloo has speculated upon the underlying psychology of time: for a child, time may exist only as something to be "killed" in response to parental schedules. And Lévi-Strauss has argued that time exists for tribal societies only in a radically taxonomic form free of the Western preoccupation with passage (*Savage Mind*, pp. 228–69). All these approaches share an appreciation for the time of a subject—everyday, collective, childish, tribal—innocent of the divorce between Christian body and soul or Cartesian succession and duration. All, in other words, are at core reexaminations of modern identity. It may help to Anglicize the problem by applying Dr. Johnson's distinction between conversation, in which there is no "system," and writing (Boswell, p. 624). The conversational use of time—epitomized in commonsense maxims ("A stitch in time") or topical generalizations ("The times are hard")—is a way of everyday being, of adjusting the relations or "timing" between tools and materials, self and others, and society and physical reality.[3] On this level of identity, consciousness is unreflective: it does not remark its own division between subjectivity and objectivity—duration and succession—in such a way as to project that division as a universal crux requiring thought.

To become an Ecclesiastes or Augustine of religious time, or a Descartes, Wordsworth, Bergson, or Poulet of modern time—that is, to write any philosophy, art, or history of time with the explicitness and systematization of thought—requires overwhelming provocation. Some force larger than the self and generated from beyond everyday being must drive into consciousness the idea that life torn between succession and duration is typical (in the religious scheme, typological). It is this larger force motivating the transition from everyday time to philosophy of time that is my concern. To use Ricoeur's phrase (p. 6 and *passim*), thought cannot comprehend such force except by methods of indirection—of connotation, nuance, metaphor—composing the "aporetical style" of temporality. Here is Wordsworth's annunciation of successive consciousness in *The Prelude*:

> A tranquillizing spirit presses now
> On my corporeal frame: so wide appears
> The vacancy between me and those days,
> Which yet have such self-presence in my mind
> That, sometimes, when I think of it, I seem
> Two consciousnesses, conscious of myself
> And of some other Being.   (2.27–33)

And here is Poulet's corresponding discovery of the cleavage in Romantic time:

And so there opens, at the center of man's being, in the actual feeling of his existence, an insupportable void. . . . It is as if duration had been *broken* in the middle and man felt his life *torn* from him, ahead and behind. The romantic effort to form itself a being out of presentiment and memory ends in the experience of a double *tearing* of the self. (p. 29; italics mine)

Poulet's passage accurately divines the force hidden in any "tranquillizing spirit" able to "press" consciousness into time. But thought cannot conceive the danger here. What force *tears* and *breaks* everyday being so that it must suddenly be "thought" in the first place (Wordsworth: "sometimes, when I *think* of it, I seem / Two consciousnesses")?

The force behind philosophy of time, I believe, is the sense of history. It is history that creates the cleavage where succession makes known its difference from duration, interregnum from tradition. Like "Midwinter spring" in the most deliberately historical of Eliot's *Four Quartets*, such history does not occur in time. The unthought continuum of everyday being is "broken in the middle" and *then* time is thought as the explanation, mitigation, and denial of the difference history makes. A more concrete form of this postulate may be ventured: as whispered in Poulet's insistence upon tearing and breaking, or in Eliot's remembrance of the "king at nightfall" (Charles I), any history capable of carving difference in a continuum previously undifferentiated between succession and duration ("The king is dead; long live the king") is a *violent* history. It is always some form of personal or public violence, I believe, that makes necessary the thinking of time as a denial of violence. In the case of Wordsworth, the primary evidence of such violence is public as opposed to private: the evidence of the early poetry is that the poet first "thought" time under the severe ministry of a precise structure of contemporary violence. Specifically, the early tours—*An Evening Walk, Descriptive Sketches,* and (with some latitude in the concept of "tour"), *Salisbury Plain*—trace the development of a terrorized consciousness of time at once miming and denying the violence of the Revolution.

To study such mimetic denial in the period of Wordsworth's poetic emergence, we will need to pay special attention to the earliest apparition of the poet's "nature." Nature is the representational tablet upon which the poet's first poems write history and time together —history as what I will call the poetics of violence, and time as the reinscription of history. I have already argued that by the time of Book 6 of *The Prelude* nature will function as a middle ground or screen deflecting history so that, upon reflection, it will appear as the Romantic self. The mediational structure, History → Nature → Self, may now be seen to derive from a mediation in the early tour works prior to the poet's distinctive self: History → Nature → Time. How did the first use of nature as mediation or blind, and so Wordsworth's first time, come about?

Let me assume for a moment—as an advertisement of future argument—the strikingly imperative voice of such guidebooks familiar to Wordsworth as Thomas West's *A Guide to the Lakes* (1778). *Station 1.* View Wordsworthian nature in its descriptive phase. You will see in *An Evening Walk,* written mostly from summer 1788 to summer 1789, that such nature is "picturesque."[4] *Station 2.* Then turn east and take a view of the unpicturesque landscape of Mountain, Plain, and Gironde in France during the beginning of the Terror in 1792–93.* *Station 3.* Follow Wordsworth as he travels a second time to France during this period of early terror (from November 1791 through November or December 1792) and then as he tours England and Wales in 1793. You will see that the picturesque crosses over to begin resembling and expressing historical violence. Description deforms, first as a sort of evening walk with a revolutionary sunset—*Descriptive Sketches,* written mostly in France in 1792—and then, after the poet's return to

---

* "First terror" usually designates the period of unofficial violence from the overthrow of the monarchy on August 10, 1792, to the fall of the Girondins on June 2, 1793. The high or officialized Terror is then dated from June 1793 to the fall of Robespierre in July 1794. Mountain, Plain, and Gironde were the semi-topographical names used at the time to designate, respectively, the Left, middle, and Right in the National Convention. The Jacobins were known as the Mountain or Montagnards because they sat high in the hall. Opposing them were the Girondins, and in between sat the majority of moderates, variously called the Plain or Marsh (*le Marais*). See *DSFR,* pp. 377–88; Soboul, pp. 281–82. These names were also used in the English press at the time—for example, *T* for July 3, 1793: "The benches of the *Mountain* . . . are constantly well filled; but the *plain* is deserted."

England, as the benighted continuance of that walk, *Salisbury Plain*, composed mostly in summer 1793. As you tour the deform of description that is the latter poem, observe the many antiquities left behind by the ancient Britons. The violent history once performed on these sites may now only be speculated upon. They have been lost in time.

—⊙—

CHAPTER THREE

The Politics of the Picturesque:
An Evening Walk

As signaled by Wordsworth's own footnotes, quotations, and allusions, *An Evening Walk* is a poem whose substance is convention—so many conventions, indeed, that it is difficult to judge whether its tradition is best read as single or multiple. Much of the poem's interest, I will suggest, lies in its own encounter with a slight rift between the assumptions of locodescriptive poetry proper and those of the picturesque tour and guidebooks of the previous two decades known to Wordsworth (especially those by J. Brown, Gray, Hutchinson, West, Gilpin, and Clarke describing the Lake District).[1] To start with, however, I propose to simplify: published in 1793 during the climax of picturesque theory in the years after 1792,[2] *An Evening Walk* may be read for the most part as if it subsumed locodescription wholly within the picturesque.[3]

The perennially difficult question arises: what is the picturesque? What are the possibilities—and also the impossibilities—of the convention from which Wordsworth takes his start?[4]

Motive and Motif

The Arrest of Motive

I will take the radical step in this chapter of hinging all analysis of the picturesque upon a single passage of *An Evening Walk*—the noon-piece opening the scene of description proper:

> When, in the south, the wan noon brooding still,
> Breath'd a pale steam around the glaring hill,
> And shades of deep embattl'd clouds were seen
> Spotting the northern cliffs with lights between;
> Gazing the tempting shades to them deny'd,
> When stood the shorten'd herds amid' the tide,
> Where, from the barren wall's unshelter'd end,
> Long rails into the shallow lake extend;
> When school-boys stretch'd their length upon the green,
> And round the humming elm, a glimmering scene!
> In the brown park, in flocks, the troubl'd deer
> Shook the still twinkling tail and glancing ear;
> When horses in the wall-girt intake stood,
> Unshaded, eying far below, the flood,
> Crouded behind the swain, in mute distress,
> With forward neck the closing gate to press;
> And long, with wistful gaze, his walk survey'd,
> 'Till dipp'd his pathway in the river shade. . . .
>
> (ll. 53–70) *

It will be useful to pause for the moment amid the suspense of these "When" clauses. A first step in our inquiry will be to frame the picturesque as what Jay Appleton calls an "experience" of landscape, or, in the terms I developed in Chapter 1, a "motivated" description.[5] How does the experience of the picturesque begin in Wordsworth's poem?

We notice that noon is populous with figures of arrested desire: cattle gaze at "tempting shades to them deny'd" and horses turn a "wistful gaze" upon the swain while pressing against the closing gate. Such barred desire—often communicated in wistful gazes toward untouchable objects—recurs throughout the poem. There is the way the hens "gaz'd" at the monarch cock (l. 130), for example, or the envy with which the Female Beggar "ey'd" the joy of the swans (l. 242) and then thinks of her dead husband as if turning a "wistful look" upon "hope's deserted well" (l. 255). Perception in the poem is an act of immaculate desire: "I love to mark" the scene (l. 141), declares a poet who "woos"—but never consummates—his affair with landscape (l. 86). If consummated, desire would become an affair of the beautiful, which Burke defined as "that quality . . . in bodies by which they cause love, or some passion similar to it" (*Sublime*,

---

* Citation of *An Evening Walk* in this chapter is as follows: verses from my primary text, the Reading Text of the 1793 version in *EW*, are cited by line number; apparatus and other material in *EW*, including transcriptions of manuscripts associated with the poem, are cited by page number. For a guide to the composition and manuscripts of *An Evening Walk*, see Averill's Introduction in *EW* as well as *CEY*, pp. 21–22, 307–12.

p. 91). The picturesque bars desire from its beautiful object even as it carefully maintains the object in sight. As an experience, it is both motivated and immobilized.

Read conventionally, such arrested desire is the origin of the great fetishistic zone of the picturesque: "intricacy." Intricacy is the *déshabillé* in which fair, smooth, and rococo lines of beauty lie both bared to and barred from the eye of desire, both "free"—to use a particularly telling modifier of the picturesque—and bound. (Gilpin: "A stroke may be called *free*, when there is no appearance of constraint"; *Three Essays*, p. 17n.) In innocent form, it is the winding pathway that teases the wistful gaze in Wordsworth's noon. Less demurely, as we will see, it is a serpentine tree limb that seduces the eye in a picturesque painting only to hide under skirts of foliage. And most brazenly, it is beauty become *erotic*. "According to the idea I have formed of it," Uvedale Price writes in his *Essays on the Picturesque* (first volume published in 1794), "intricacy in landscape might be defined, *that disposition of objects, which, by a partial and uncertain conceal-ment, excites and nourishes curiosity.*"[6] A footnote then glosses the kind of excitement aroused: "Many persons, who take little concern in the intricacy of oaks, beeches, and thorns, may feel the effects of partial concealment in more interesting objects, and may have experienced how differently the passions are moved by an open licentious display of beauties, and by the unguarded disorder which sometimes escapes the care of modesty, and which coquetry so successfully imitates" (1: 22). Or again, we might witness the intricate sexuality of Richard Payne Knight's aesthetics in *An Analytical Inquiry into the Principles of Taste* (first published 1805). Beauty, he says in one of many such descriptions, may be seen in "the fairest nymph of St. James's, who, while she treads the mazes of the dance, displays her light and slender form through transparent folds of muslim [*sic*]" (p. 14; see pp. 13–15 on beauty and sexuality in general).[7]

Secondly, Wordsworth's noon-piece displays arrested violence. On the very front of noon, we notice, "deep embattl'd clouds" shadow the scene with frozen violence,[8] and in the midst of the park, "troubl'd deer" keep watch for predatory danger. The edge of menace at noon is slight, but predicts the Salvatorean effects recurring during the rest of evening. A peasant's sledge comes into view "shot" from the "fearful edge" of a cliff (ll. 111–12); a "blasted quarry" thunders "remote" (l. 124); a "warrior" cock is "sweetly ferocious" when "threaten'd" by challenges from remote farms (ll. 129–38); and a "desperate form" leads a twilight cavalcade of ghostriders "with violent speed" (ll. 179–80). Banditti forces perpetually fret the poem but —except in one anomalous passage we will come to—refrain from becoming Burke's full-length study in violence: the sublime. Wordsworth's picturesque is an experience that bars violence as well from accomplishing its "object" in the landscape—the sublime destruction ("obscurity") of the object—even as it also maintains that object in view in such places of quarantined obscurity as the quarry or spots of shadow under clouds.

Seen conventionally, arrested violence begets the "bold" brother of free intricacy: "roughness" (or, with reference to outline, "irregularity"). Gilpin considered roughness the very signature of the picturesque (*Lakes*, 1: xv and *passim*; *Three Essays*, p. 6) and recommended that the artist render it on canvas in a bold handling complementary to freedom (*Three Essays*, p. 17n).[9] Where intricacy was erotic, however, roughness was *sadistic*. On the one hand, it was certainly violent. Gilpin regularly praised the "violence" of rough lakes, cascades, winds, and so forth in the Lake District (*Lakes*, 1: 110, 128, 129, 129–30) and, by the time of his *Three Essays* (first published 1792), could resemble de Sade at his most murderous: "Should we wish to give [Palladian architecture] picturesque beauty, we must use the mallet, instead of the chissel: we must beat down one half of it, deface the other, and throw the mutilated members around in heaps" (p. 7).[10] On the other hand, violence had to be fettered so that, as in the essential Sadean experience, it could be enjoyed interminably. As Gilpin put it in a formula in his Lakes tour, roughness should dominate the foreground of a view, where the eye enjoys "force" and "richness" (the former a "violent opposition of colour, light, and shade"). But to be truly delicious, it had to be "ruled" by a Claudian background of "tenderness" and an overall "breadth" and "repose" (*Lakes*, 1: 103–4).

The full experience of the picturesque, we can now deduce, must arise from the lamination of eroticism and sadism, intricacy and roughness. It must, that is, be "delight in variety." In conventional usage, "variety" was the global description of intricacy and roughness; and "delight"—a term so common as to be the very oxygen of eighteenth-century description—the universal motive of the picturesque. ("Return Delights!" Wordsworth says as he begins his walk amid the "ever-varying charm" of the Lakes, ll. 27, 18.) Delight in variety implied not only the generic experience of being "moved" toward passional extremes but, as in the case of its component experiences, also a crucial arrest. Here we discover the prime mover —itself unmoved—of the picturesque. As we have already heard mentioned in Gilpin's formula, the state of general arrest inhibiting picturesque motivation was "repose" (the most often named member of a brood that also included "tranquillity," "stillness," "calm," and "composure"). As Gilpin says about the repose of a lake:

If an artificial mirror, a few inches long, placed opposite to a door, or a window, occasions often very pleasing reflections; how noble must be the appearance, when an area of many leagues in circumference, is formed into one vast mirror? . . . The majestic repose of so grand, so solemn, and splendid a scene raises in the mind a sort of enthusiastic calm, which spreads a mild complacence over the breast—a tranquil pause of mental operation, which may be felt, but not described;

> "Soothing each gust of passion into peace;
> All but the swellings of the soften'd heart;
> That waken, not disturb, the tranquil mind."
>
> (*Lakes*, 1: 124–25)

Repose is a terrifically impassive "passion" or "enthusiastic calm."

Price reflects on repose in the same manner:

> when the mind of man is in the delightful state of repose . . . when he feels that mild and equal sunshine of the soul which warms and cheers, but neither inflames nor irritates, his heart seems to dilate with happiness. . . . A mind in such a state may be compared to the surface of a pure and tranquil lake, into which if the smallest pebble be cast, the waters, like the affections, seem gently to expand themselves on every side. (*Essays*, 1: 125–26)[11]

Embodying such moveless reflection would be a picturesque tourist such as Gray or West with his Claude glass: suddenly "moved" by a view, he stops completely, turns his back on the landscape, and stares into a small, oval mirror suspended in perfect stasis by the upper part of its case.[12]

As we will see, the suspense of the "When" clauses in Wordsworth's noon-piece closes precisely in such repose.

Detour 1: "Classic" Repose

But we are not yet ready to finish reading Wordsworth's noon. The picturesque was not simply an experience to be studied in motivational terms, but also a highly specialized experience of *form*. I mean by this not only that picturesque experience required expression—as in the case of any aesthetic—in one form or another, but that it made the very idea of form, or "picturicity," cognate with experience.[13] (Contrast the Burkean sublime, in which such modifiers as "obscure" or "powerful" denoted experience ipso facto in excess of form.) Awareness of form, indeed, *was* repose, the sense of arrest in experience.

To understand how the picturesque acquired its heightened sense of form, we will need to detour into the history of art. The place to start is with Claude, the Old Master of seventeenth-century "Classic" repose.[14] Price's reflection on repose, in fact, looks back for inspiration precisely to *il riposo di Claudio*, that "delightful state of repose, of which Claude's pictures are the image" (*Essays*, 1: 125).[15] As the central exhibit of such *riposo*, I hang here an oil painting with special importance in an English context: *Landscape with Hagar and the Angel* (Pl. 1). With its associated drawing in the *Liber Veritatis* (No. 106), the

PLATE I. Claude Lorrain, *Landscape with Hagar and the Angel*, 1646/47. Reproduced by courtesy of the Trustees, The National Gallery, London. Photo: National Gallery.

painting was the first of five works by Claude on the flight and expulsion of Hagar, her meeting with the angel in the wilderness, and the angel's prophecy concerning her son by Abraham, Ishmael.[16] The painting was such a favorite of Sir George Beaumont, who bought it sometime between 1792 and 1795, that he was reputed never to have traveled without it (Röthlisberger, 1: 269; Greaves, p. 56).[17] Both Constable, who copied it and based *Dedham Vale* on its composition, and Wordsworth himself, who became familiar with Beaumont's collection about 1806, would thus soon be introduced to the painting as the type of Claudian vision.[18]

Hagar and the Angel may be divided into a narrative and an interpretation. Repose is first of all Claude's narrative *subject*,[19] and arises in the foreground in the tradition of *istoria*, the reverence for the sacred (and, secondarily, profane) narrative that had dominated the art of the late Middle Ages and Renaissance.[20] Specifically, repose evolves within the basic Claudian narrative I will call the "journey of creation." The story opens upon an imagination of divine origin. *Hagar and the Angel*, as Martha Shackford has noted (p. 13), was sometimes called the "Annunciation." Both in theme and iconography, Claude's foreground tableau is indeed an Annunciation in the pattern the Quattrocento called *Humiliatio*, the "submission" of the Virgin. Well-suited to Claude's general expressive bias of calm, *Humiliatio* was the quietest of four Annunciation types headed by Mary's initial *Conturbatio* or "disquiet."[21] We might look for comparison to a fifteenth-century altarpiece *Humiliatio* by Fra Angelico (Pl. 2). Claude places his angel on the right instead of the left (the "Annunciation from the right" came into its own at the end of the fifteenth century primarily as a Northern, antipapal reaction; Denny, pp. 146–47). But otherwise the resemblance is close. Hagar wears the blue of the Virgin and sits with hands folded to her breast in a manner resembling most closely the *Humiliatio*—the only type in which the hands join or cross. And not only does the angel's general stance mirror Gabriel's in the Fra Angelico,[22] but his hands point in the double manner that was the characteristic Quattrocento addition to the single hand of the Byzantine Annunciation (cf. Pl. 6).

Claude then gives divinity the narrative plot that H. Diane Russell has called his "single great subject," journeying (p. 83); and so propagates origin as a *translatio* of divinity: *cultural* origin.[23] Characteristically, we notice, Claudian journeys are specially creative. As in the case of the travels of Aeneas, Jacob, or Paul, they mark the creation of some house, race, nation, or religion—of "cultural forms," we may call them, tasked with the custodianship of original divinity in society.[24] In one sense, the journey of creation in *Hagar and the Angel* conceives the nation foretold in Genesis (God will make Ishmael "a great nation"). More generally, however, it should be seen to conceive the universal cultural form that in one way or another is the terminus of all Claude's journeys of creation: a modern, transnational "state" that we can for now simply call "recreation."

To imagine recreation, Claude draws upon journey patterns designed to image a traditionally "universal" cultural form: the Catholic Church. We notice that the Annunciation—like such other images of Incarnational or Trinitarian dogma as the Nativity, Baptism, Trans-

PLATE 2. Fra Angelico, *Annunciation*, c. 1438. Diocesan Museum, Cortona. Photo: Alinari/Art Resource, New York.

figuration, or Virgin and Child[25]—often appeared in compositional stasis (central balance and axial rigidity of the figure group as well as alignment of major figures on a plane parallel to the picture plane). To be propagated, the authority of stasis required a supplementary symbolism of cultural movement. In Orthodox practice, images of stasis hanging on the iconostasis (tiered screen of icons in the church) had to be complemented by literally mobile icons capable of being displayed in processions and of transmitting the authorized image from the cultural centers to provincial regions.[26] A similar, though purely representational, device applied in Catholic tradition. In the Italianate canon, the Annunciation hung thematically pendant to the Visitation, the Nativity to Christ Taking Leave of His Mother, or the Crucifixion to the Walk to Emmaus—all implied or actual journeys peripheral to the great stases of dogma, yet necessary to image the cultural circulation of dogma.[27] The Annunciation in *Hagar and the Angel* hangs thematically beside the favorite such image of circulation in Claude's own canon: the Flight into Egypt. As Röthlisberger

PLATE 3. Claude Lorrain, *Landscape with the Rest on the Flight into Egypt*, 1645. The Cleveland Museum of Art, Leonard C. Hanna Jr. Fund, 62.151. Photo: Museum.

points out, the design of *Hagar and the Angel* derives directly from a vertical-format landscape on the Flight into Egypt theme executed possibly a year earlier (Pl. 3).[28]

Then Claude extends the journey beyond the Church. Traditionally, we observe, such pictorial journeys as the Visitation often required no more room than stasis: throne scene became progress piece without leaving the closed symmetry of an essentially "indoor" house or church.[29] But in *Hagar and the Angel*, the diminishment of the figures and their boldly asymmetrical placement to one side declares open-ended length (an effect even more striking in the two later horizontal landscapes, *Abraham Expelling Hagar and Ishmael* and *Angel Appearing to Hagar*; see Röthlisberger, 2: his pls. 282, 283). Claude's "church," in sum, expands to the scale of an increasingly secular, quotidian, and "realistic" world.

It is in this world that the originating pose of *Humiliatio* is recreated, necessarily, as repose. Seated along physically realized journeys, instants of holy calm such as the *Humiliatio* appear by definition as *rest*. Fully secularized as one of the eighteenth-century French genre-subjects Michael Fried has studied, rest will be "absorption," a recreation of everyday life glimpsed in figures wholly absorbed in everyday life—reading, for example, or sleeping. To apply with special resonance a phrase Fried cites from Diderot, it will be *repos délicieux*, illustrated in such works as Jean-Baptiste Greuze's *Le Repos* (Fried, pp. 130–31, 227–28 n. 51, and his pl. 15).[30] In Claude's work, *repos délicieux* appears in the Italian as *riposo*, the designation for a whole class of "rest" pictures grounded residually upon religious subject. The vertical-format landscape behind the design of *Hagar and the Angel*, we can now notice, was precisely a *Rest on the Flight into Egypt*, the canonical *riposo* dominating the Flight theme in sixteenth- and seventeenth-century art (Osborne, p. 422) and Claude's work in particular. Such "rest" is identical in appearance with the other, wholly secular category of Claude's "rests": the many *Pastoral Landscapes* in which shepherds literally rest (e.g., Pl. 4).

Thus does repose enter Claude's picture as the story of rest. Beyond is all interpretation, the deepening of the story into the landscape proper according to a method so pervasive in Claude's time that it construed even profane narratives: the fourfold "allegorical" scheme of Biblical exegesis.[31] The index of exegesis in *Hagar and the Angel* is the angel, whose left hand points the literal tale.[32] Where in Annunciations, as Mary Ann Caws observes, the corresponding hand of Gabriel (or some mediatory instrument) tells of Christ's conception by "penetrating" through a column or other architectural hymen toward Mary's womb (pp. 109–16), the hand of Claude's angel announces its subject directly. The right hand then appropriates the characteristic second gesture of the Quattrocento Gabriel (often a hand pointing upwards or to the dove of the Holy Ghost) to tell the allegory of the story. It confirms the literal by pointing out Abraham's villa (Röthlisberger, 1: 268). But it also points typologically through the Old Testament to the New: the tableau with the tiny shepherd above the figures in a boat (the latter floats through-

PLATE 4. Claude Lorrain, *Pastoral Landscape*, 1644/45. The Barnes Foundation, Merion Station, Pa. Photo © Copyright 1989 by The Barnes Foundation.

out Claude's work) will later be painted as *Seacoast with Christ Calling Andrew and Peter* (now known only in *Liber Veritatis*, No. 165; Pl. 5).[33] And morally, it points through the Son to Everyman: whatever else it is, the tableau with boat and shepherd is a little vignette showing everyday vocation (the calling of the disciples, in more than one sense) continuing imperturbably even in time of trouble.[34]

The crowning allegory indicated by the right hand of the angel is then the anagogy of the picture: the assumption of all human stories in a single Story (of Creation, Fall, and Redemption) so vast that it cannot be read as *verba* at all but only as the synoptic intuition— and, ultimately, mood—that Origen and Philo called *logos*.[35] Here I suggest a flashback bringing us to the furthest and deepest recess of our detour through art history.

In the beginning, there was the Byzantine imagination of anagogy, which we may describe simply by looking to Annunciation icons and their ancestral gesture of allegory. As demonstrated in an icon such as the one in the National Museum of Ohrid (Pl. 6), this ancestor is a staff—the epitome of Byzantine linear style. The interpretive task of the staff is to teach our eye to jump from the foreground narrative

PLATE 5. Claude Lorrain, *Seacoast with Christ Calling Andrew and Peter*, 1665. Reproduced by courtesy of the Trustees of the British Museum, London. Photo: Museum.

directly to the traditional expansive background of gold, the great instance of what Constantine Cavarnos has called the "non-natural, mystical colors" crowning the "anagogy" of iconic style (p. 37). Gold tells an over-story of *light*—of *lux*, the pictorial Word—transferable from icon to icon without regard for the particular story in the foreground. Unfolded synoptically as space, such light is infinity. Finite space in the foreground of our icon, we notice, is an aggregate of dissociated wedges drawn in "inverted perspective" such that receding parallels diverge rather than converge.[36] Multiple and inside out, such space is "true" only if we imagine ourselves viewing the foreground from the infinity of a God's-eye station deep in the background. The mood of such space—an *ekstasis* or "standing outside"—is the serene ecstasy that was the single allowed expression of Byzantine art: "meekness," "humility," or *apatheia*.[37]

The Italian Renaissance saw anagogy in a different light, space, and mood. If we look once more at the Fra Angelico panel (Pl. 2), for example, we see that the index of allegory in the Quattrocento is not so much iconographic gesture (the hand of figuration points to diminished gold around the Dove) as a vast extension of the iconic staff. The largest "pointing" is the loggia at the left, which notices a strongly marked central-perspective recession akin to those in vir-

PLATE 6. *Annunciation*, anonymous, fourteenth century. The other side of this bilateral icon shows the Virgin and Child. National Museum, Ohrid. Photo: Hirmer Verlag, München.

PLATE 7. Domenico Veneziano, *Annunciation*, c. 1445. Fitzwilliam Museum, Cambridge, England. Photo: Museum.

tually all pictures after the 1430's. Most immediately, the recession populates the area once devoted to gold with the fuller narrative of *istoria*: first the typology of the low fence around the closed garden, or *hortus conclusus* (a symbol of Virginity recalling the "closed garden, my sister, my spouse" of the Song of Songs), and then, beyond the Garden, of the Expulsion of Adam and Eve (Hartt, p. 218). Or again, we might look to the Annunciation by Domenico Veneziano (Pl. 7) in which the recession leads to an arch and then, framed within a secondary arch at the end of the garden, to a type conflating the meanings of Expulsion and Virginity: the *porta clausa*, or shut door, deriving from Ezekiel's vision of a Temple closed to all except the "prince" (Hartt, pp. 261, 69–70).[38] But recession also pointed merely *by means* of narrative to the new anagogy of the time. Whatever their typological meaning, low fences and arches now served to mark with absolute clarity the plane in the middle distance; and Expulsions and shut doors etched with matching precision the plane of the far distance. Organizing the world into fixed "walls" of fore-, middle-, and background, each logically prior to its narrative fresco, Renaissance imagination saw the light not of infinity but of "reality." In the "worldly" Renaissance after the triumph of Albertian perspective, that is, anagogy was finite existence itself—a newly unified, planimetrically defined, and closed space so rationalized by geometry and the laws of the rectilinear propagation of light that an otherworldly *logos* or fiat of light seemed to declare itself *in* the structure of the world. Expressed as mood, such anagogy was a new *ekstasis* or *apatheia*: a spirit of lucid rationality.

Now we can recognize Claude's anagogy. On the one hand, Claude clearly sees "reality," even improving the Renaissance view by allowing his allegorical gesture to join hands with a massive, planimetrically defined recession. But on the other hand, "reality" resumes the older anagogy. Claude posts on the middle plane his version of the Renaissance low fence or arched wall: the "Bridge in the Middle Distance," as Turner will later title a work in imitation (*Liber Studiorum*, No. 13; see Holcomb, p. 50). (Together with such look-alikes as triumphal arches, rock arches, and ruined arches, the bridge in the middle distance is virtually Claude's signature; review, for instance, Pls. 1, 3, 4.)[39] But where Fra Angelico and Domenico then shut the door of the universe by erecting an Expulsion or *porta clausa* in the far distance, Claude leaves the door open. The angel's finger aims for Abraham's villa—the grand Expulsion or *porta clausa* in the work—only at last to bypass it. Pointing into ever more transparent planes in the distance, the finger touches finally upon a deferred version of the old, Byzantine infinity: the vanishing point.[40] Through the vanishing point, which Renaissance pictures worked so hard to screen, Claude pours back into "reality" all the old, Byzantine light of infinity. Reality and infinity, worldly vision and otherworldly translucence wed; and the result is the gold-bled-through-space that is Claude's famously "sinking," "vanishing," or "melting" radiance.

In aureole form, such radiance is Claude's great "arch" without its bridge: the sun, which he was celebrated for first depicting frontally. Suspended more diffusely in *Hagar and the Angel* in air, water, and foliage, it is Claude's immanent sun: "atmosphere."[41] Atmosphere is the technique of sustaining infinite light in finite space—of organizing color progression, contrast reduction, and variation in local color[42] into a single scale of translucent haziness extending in Claude's case from foregrounds of brown-green and chiaroscuro to backgrounds of spirit-hues and virtually no tonal contrast. Expressed as "mood," such atmosphere is repose direct. Studying the early, anti-Quattrocento atmospherics of Giorgione's *The Tempest* (c. 1505), Creighton Gilbert has remarked the inescapable figuration by which technical "tone" became perceived as an emotional "tone" of "gentle quietude" (p. 214).[43] Repose touched with such atmosphere—the final varnish of all stories of rest—is Claude's gentle quietude, his ecstatic recreation of *apatheia*.[44]

Arresting Motifs

Now we can return to our inquiry into the genesis of picturesque form. The picturesque, we can say, forgot half the Classic picture—the narrative—to focus exclusively on the landscape mapping interpretation. (Literally, indeed, some of Claude's works came to be labeled *Pastoral Landscape* precisely because their stories had been forgotten.)[45] Without narrative reference, of course, the very fact of interpretation became unapparent. Thus, I suggest, arose picturesque form: unapparent interpretation *is* form. In specifically pictorial terms, it is the sense that all "motive" must now be fossilized in what Panofsky and Wölfflin called "motifs" (or in the German, *Motive*) prior to or devoid of narrative reference.* We can trace the generation of the most arresting picturesque motifs according to a schedule of forgetting with three logical—and to some extent chronological— steps:

(1) The picturesque reclaimed the Classic universe for the North by skewing its recession along the Netherlandish diagonal more or less toward the distance points (either or both of the vanishing points at 45 degrees to the central vanishing point).[46] An influential intermediary was Gainsborough, whose own rest or repose pictures set the Claudian universe on an angle, as in *Rest by the Way*, Pl. 8.[47] In effect, such composition rotated the old universe on a pivot in the middle distance such that the narrative foreground swung out of view to leave behind the pivot point itself as the subject. In *Rest by the Way* the peasant is thus partly marginalized both by being made anonymous and by being levered to one side by the diagonal.[48] He becomes part of a general dispersion of subject away from the human figure toward animate and inanimate objects in the distance. Most pointedly, we notice Gainsborough's odd emphasis upon a peculiarly English version of the *hortus conclusus* or *porta clausa*: the end of a cow occupying the visual center of the picture and closing off the peasant's line of sight. Like the dog and matted stump stationed at less pivotal sites along the diagonal, the cow is a Not-subject, to use Gilbert's phrase, whose visual blockage mimes the stasis of resting persons so strongly and centrally that Not-subject threatens to become the dominant subject of pictures of rest.[49] In Gainsborough's oeuvre and the picturesque generally, cattle thus serve not only to regulate the distance planes in lieu of a bridge in the middle distance (even to the extent of appearing in silhouetted rows much like Claude's bridge arches) but frequently to provide the bulk of the subject.[50]

* Panofsky defines motifs as the basic "configurations of line and color" elemental to recognizable form, which may then "carry" additional layers of narrative and symbolic meaning (pp. 28–31), while Wölfflin's definition includes such large compositional forms as the principal "motives" (*die typischen Motive, Hauptmotive*) of the linear versus painterly, planar versus recessional, symmetric versus asymmetric, and so forth (*Principles*). My discussion below addresses both elemental and compositional motifs of the picturesque. As I clarify in n. 62 to this chapter, I use Panofsky and Wölfflin to outline two major ideological poles of modern art historiography: the iconological and the stylistic, respectively. "Motif" is the phenomenon axiomatic to both (see Podro, pp. 44–58, on the genesis of motif theory). On the influence of Wölfflin upon the Russian Formalists, whose usage of "motif" I cite in Chapter 2, see Chapter 2, n. 15.

PLATE 8. Thomas Gainsborough, *Rest by the Way*, 1747. Philadelphia Museum of Art. Purchased: W. P. Wilstach Collection. Photo: Museum.

More characteristically, the pivot point was occupied by a topographical motif—often precisely a bridge or similar device—strongly reminiscent of Claude. A prime example is Gainsborough's *Landscape with Cottage and Stream* (Pl. 9), in which the culminating subject —toward which even the massive tree leans—is a footbridge that subsumes the small human figure. As John Murdoch suggests (*Forty-Two*, cat. no. 3), this drawing from the 1750's may have been the original for the actual footbridge Knight later built on his estate and that—with a note acknowledging Claude—he made a central feature of *The Landscape* (p. 51; see also Pl. 10). During the high picturesque, bridges in the middle distance—with single or multiple arches—became a staple in the work of such artists as Gilpin, Richard Wilson, Joseph Farington, Paul Sandby, Thomas Hearne, John Sell Cotman, Francis Towne, John White Abbott, John Varley, and Beaumont.[51] In the picturesque, we might say, *Hagar and the Angel* was repainted without either Hagar or the Angel: the subject vanished into the middle distance and then into air.

(2) Once the picturesque had misplaced any narrative able to diversify its subject, it then had to take the second step of "varying" the remaining view. "Atmosphere" thus multiplied in both kind and expressive range.[52] Where once there was Claude's cerulean air touched

PLATE 9. Thomas Gainsborough, *Landscape with Cottage and Stream*, mid-1750's. By courtesy of the Board of Trustees of the Victoria and Albert Museum, London. Photo: Museum.

with gold, his standard tree, and his ground plane of land descending easily into water, there now appeared a whole range of cloudscapes predictive of Constable's cloud studies; an entire *Gainsborough's Forest* with ancillary groves of oak, elm, willow, and other specialized tree studies; and a wide variety of rock and water studies. Ultimately, it did not matter what objects dominated. Clouds, trees, rocks, and waters were equivalent tonal surfaces, all capable of modeling the glides, twists, whorls, and other motifs of landscape form so minutely that any surface—singly or in combination—afforded sufficient "variety."[53] In expressive range, too, the atmosphere branched out. "Intricacy" entered as a motif by way of the rococo line. A particularly salacious example is Francis Wheatley's *Salmon Leap at Leixlip with Nymphs Bathing*, where a bridge-like arch looks in like a gigantic eye on naked nymphs while overhead trees stretch their serpentine limbs amid foliage (Webster, her pl. 50). "Roughness" entered by way of Salvator. A convenient manual of motifs is Salvator's *The Bridge* (Salerno, his pl. 5), where a bridge poises amid a world increasingly wild at the edges: the ruin of the bridge itself at the left,

PLATE 10. Etching by Benjamin Thomas Pouncy after Thomas Hearne, illustrating the principles of the picturesque in Richard Payne Knight's *The Landscape*, 1794. Yale Center for British Art, Paul Mellon Collection, New Haven. Photo: Yale Center for British Art.

the craggy rock "bridge" above, and the Salvatorean trees at the right with their distinctively broken limbs.

The epitome of counterbalanced tonalities in the picturesque was its view of water. As Stephen J. Spector has observed, "mirror imagery" was the central motif of picturesque water. But calm waters, which we have already seen in Gilpin's and Price's reflections on repose, tended to variety at the extremes. As in Gilpin's *Landscape with River and a Bridge* or Sandby's *Pont-y-Pair over the River Conway*, for example, waters reposed under a bridge in the middle distance drew upon serpentine streams or issued in rough cascades.[54]

(3) Finally, the picturesque normalized the diagonal axis to fit the "various" universe back into the right-angled frame of the Classic. Or more accurately, since diagonal and straight recession became equally acceptable patterns, the picturesque acquired the option of making the diagonal itself a classic form. Any number of illustrations could close our gallery at this point. But I will hang here only a self-proclaimed paradigm: the print by Benjamin Thomas Pouncy (after Thomas Hearne) demonstrating the picturesque in Knight's *The Landscape* (Pl. 10). Here, foreground and background communi-

cate along a recessional avenue regulated in the middle distance by the footbridge. Or, rather, there are *two* avenues of recession. What was once the Claudian, straight recession to the vanishing point has become the picture's minor recession, the diagonal. Whatever the miniature beholder on the bridge sees as he looks off diagonally between trees (perhaps, we can guess, radiance in the background) cannot now be seen from our station. Instead, we look down the recession that in Gainsborough would have been diagonal but that now appears in straight view. In the middle of this latter recession appears our version of the bridge, the arch of the fallen tree at the exact visual center of the picture (the "prostrate tree" that Knight's poem lists in its catalog of bridges; p. 51). Bracketing the center in foreground and background is then a variety virtually sharawaggian in luxury: the intricately rough terrain close up and the intentionally wild irregularities of the Elizabethan house in the distance.[55]

Such is the picturesque perversion—a twist and a recovery—of the Classic. No narrative figures can now be introduced into landscape without provoking the kind of censure Sir Joshua Reynolds directed against the mythological beings in Wilson's *Destruction of Niobe's Children* (pp. 255–56). Wordsworth, who read a set of Reynolds's works given him by Beaumont in 1804 (*Letters*, 1: 490–91, 517), would later criticize Wilson's *Rome from the Villa Madama* by closely following Reynolds's point. As Joseph Farington records in his diary entry for April 28, 1807, "Wordsworth said, He thought Historical subjects shd. never be introduced into Landscape but when the Landscape was to be subservient to them.—When the Landscape was intended principally to impress the mind, figures, other than such as are general, such as may a thousand times appear, and seem accidental, . . . are injurious to the effect" (4: 129; see also Shackford, p. 26). Where small figures remain in view at all—as in the case of Gainsborough's *Rest by the Way* or Knight's illustration (Pls. 8, 10)—they must now be entirely anonymous. They must be what Gilpin called "negative": "neither adding to the grandeur of the idea, nor taking from it" (*Lakes*, 2: 45). Or if allowed to pose in larger scale in the foreground, they must be what Wordsworth calls "general" (a genre-subject) or "accidental" (akin to the "associational" in Knight's parlance).[56]

We can now finish reading Wordsworth's sentence of "noon," which we left suspended earlier, with recognition:

> —Then Quiet led me up the huddling rill,
> Bright'ning with water-breaks the sombrous gill;
> To where, while thick above the branches close,
> In dark-brown bason its wild waves repose,
> Inverted shrubs, and moss of darkest green,
> Cling from the rocks, with pale wood-weeds between;
> Save that, atop, the subtle sunbeams shine,
> On wither'd briars that o'er the craggs recline;

Sole light admitted here, a small cascade,
Illumes with sparkling foam the twilight shade.
Beyond, along the visto of the brook,
Where antique roots its bustling path o'erlook,
The eye reposes on a secret bridge
Half grey, half shagg'd with ivy to its ridge.

(ll. 71–84)

The scene, as Wordsworth footnotes, is the celebrated Lower Falls in the park of Rydal Hall (to be distinguished from a larger falls about a half-mile higher on the same rivulet). It will be useful to hang here four other contemporary views of the Falls. The first, which may have influenced *An Evening Walk*, appears in a note by William Mason on Gray's tour of the Lakes:[57]

Here nature has performed every thing in little that she usually executes in her larger scale; and on that account, like the miniature painter, seems to have finished every part of it in a studied manner. Not a little fragment of a rock thrown into the bason, not a single stem of brush-wood that starts from its craggy sides, but has a picturesque meaning; and the little central current dashing down a cleft of the darkest coloured stone, produces an effect of light and shadow beautiful beyond description. This little theatrical scene might be painted as large as the original, on a canvas not bigger than those usually dropped in the opera-house. (Quoted in West, pp. 80–81)

The second occurs in Gilpin's tour, and possibly contributed even more directly to Wordsworth's poem.[58] Observes Gilpin, the rock faces on either side of the Falls

form a little area; appearing through the window like a picture in a frame. The water falls within a few yards of the eye, which being rather above its level, has a long perspective view of the stream, as it hurries from the higher grounds; tumbling, in various, little breaks, through its rocky channel, darkened with thicket, till it arrive at the edge of the precipice, before the window; from whence it rushes into the bason, which is formed by nature in the native rock. The dark colour of the stone, taking still a deeper tinge from the wood, which hangs over it, sets off to wonderful advantage the sparkling lustre of the stream; and produces an uncommon effect of light. It is this effect indeed, from which the chief beauty of the scene arises. . . . In this little exhibition we had an admirable idea of the magical effect of light picturesquely distributed. (*Lakes*, 1: 162–63)

The final two illustrations are pictorial: Joseph Farington's print of Rydal Lower Falls in his well-known *Views of the Lakes* and Joseph Wright of Derby's *Rydal Waterfall* (Pls. 11, 12).

Viewing Wordsworth's sketch in this company, we see repose so conventional that it is virtually a compendium of picturesque motifs. In the beginning, there is a *Humiliatio*-like subject whose narrative hides in personification: "Quiet led me," Wordsworth says. Quiet leads directly to "repose," which in the foreground consists in an

PLATE 11. Joseph Farington, *The Waterfall at Rydal, Ambleside*, from his *Views of the Lakes*, 1789. Reprinted by courtesy of the Trustees of the British Museum, London. Photo: Museum.

energetic variety of shaggy branches, inverted shrubs, moss, wood-weeds, and rocks all at last collected (as the confusing syntax seems to indicate) in the "wild waves reposed" of reflective waters.[59] Foreground then recedes along the "visto" to the middle ground, where repose reemerges upon a bridge in the middle distance: the "eye reposes on a secret bridge." Middle ground in its turn trails into an endless variety of background foliage that Wordsworth leaves unspecified but that our other views of the Falls help fill in (on Wordsworth's later discovery of the background of the Falls, see note 15 to Chapter 8). Finally, along the whole recession from the stream in the background, through the bridge in the middle ground, down the bright cascade, and at last into the pool in the foreground pours the fount of picturesque atmosphere: *light*—Wordsworth's "sole light," Mason's "beautiful" "effect of light," Gilpin's "sparkling lustre" and "magical effect of light," and Wright of Derby's brilliant "broken reflections" (part of the pebbled effect, he said in a letter, he most wished to reproduce; B. Nicolson, 1: 94).

Noon is the traditional time of rest. Pictured as "repose" in *An Evening Walk*, we now see, rest is the total arrest of experience in form, of passion in *topoi*. Metamorphic passions lurk just under the surface of Quiet: a rill "huddles," moss "clings," a path "bustles," and antique roots—cueing the "eye" in the next line—"o'erlook."

PLATE 12. Joseph Wright of Derby, *Rydal Waterfall*, 1795. Derby Art Gallery. Photo: Art Gallery.

But because narrative has been forgotten, passion has no outlet more exciting than the seductive curve of a branch or rough upthrust of rock. Passion ends arrested in perfect picturicity. For Mason, we notice, Rydal Lower Falls is no more "moving" than the very emblem of picturicity, an opera-house backdrop. For Gilpin, the scene appears similarly motionless "through the window like a picture in a frame." Wordsworth comments no further once his "eye" in the passage reaches its arch point of repose, but we might intimate the frozen picturicity he scans by looking to the gloss on bridges in his most picturesque of later works, the *Guide Through the District of the Lakes.*[60] Remarking upon the compactness of estates in the Lakes, he speculates:

Likewise to the smallness of the several properties is owing the great number of bridges over the brooks and torrents, and the daring and graceful neglect of danger or accommodation with which so many of them are constructed, the rudeness of the *forms* of some, and their endless variety. But, when I speak of this rudeness, I must at the same time add, that many of these structures are in themselves models of elegance, as if they had been *formed* upon principles of the most thoughtful architecture. . . . Travellers who may not have been accustomed to pay attention to things so inobtrusive, will excuse me if I point out the proportion between the span and elevation of the arch, the lightness of the parapet, and the graceful manner in which its curve follows faithfully that of the arch. (*Prose*, 2: 204; italics mine)

When Wordsworth views even the rudest bridge in the Lakes, he becomes a connoisseur of "structure," "proportion," "elegance," visual "*form*."

From Form to Institution

The Baron's Window

Our inquiry into the picturesque can at this point advance to its final stage. *Why* was narrative forgotten so that experience came to be arrested wholly in form? Why form?

To answer this question, I will put to one side formalistic tradition. A working definition of formalism as it developed in an Anglo-American context might be as follows: it is the approach that situates the literary work in an "ambiguous" or "paradoxical" zone of figuration precisely midway between the traditions of *Geistesgeschichte* and philology, of philosophical "meaning" and verbal "being."[61] Between meaning and being, all narrative capable of miming positive reality disappears in "imagery." (Or where narrative is still important, as in Cleanth Brooks's work on Faulkner, it must be treated as a separate domain.) Worshipped as "iconic" by New Criticism, imagery is analogous not so much to Panofsky's "iconology" in art history as to Wölfflin's "stylistics."[62] It is the refusal to look into or behind the icon for the story. Imagery and its associated figurations, we might say, are the empty *istoria* illustrated by that great "sylvan historian" of well-wrought form, the Grecian Urn.

We will need to examine iconic imagery more closely in Chapter 7, but for now this definition of its premises will be sufficient to chart modern appraisals of the picturesque specifically as applied to Wordsworth. Whatever their view of the later works, readers of Wordsworth's early poetry have tended to define its experience precisely in philosophy-of-mind terms as a distance (variously calibrated by Hartman, Sheats, and Ramsey, for example) between subject and object.[63] The subject's experience of its object is then mapped over

Wordsworth's poetic form: that gorgeously contorted canvas of style that has fascinated virtually every reader of the early verse since Coleridge (*Biographia*, 1: 77–79). The fullest example is Emile Legouis's catalog of Wordsworth's stylistic aberrations (*Early Life*, pp. 133–35). Finally, the result of mapping subjective experience over form—philosophy of mind over style parsed with philological rigor—has been preoccupation with figuration and imagery. The finest readings of *An Evening Walk* are thus "complete" when they discover—with differing degrees of emphasis—that Wordsworth's picturesque is a habit of imagery not yet fully capable of imagination. The picturesque in *An Evening Walk* is a forced effort of "personification," "transference of epithets," and "image" (Leguois, *Early Life*, p. 138); an "anthology of images" (*WP*, pp. 92–93); a "rigorous discipline on all figures that distort or obscure the relation between mind and landscape: analogy, personification, and metaphor" (Sheats, p. 53); and a "compressed and difficult texture of images" anticipating the poet's mature "grammar of interfusions" (Ramsey, pp. 378, 389).[64]

But such a formalistic approach—though perceptive in practice and useful as a first platform for any study that then wishes to track Wordsworth "beyond formalism"—cannot answer the question, "why form?" I therefore propose an alternative that holds the potential for explaining, not just the picturesque, but how formalisms in general come to be.

I began this chapter by defining the experience of the picturesque not in terms of the subject-object dialectic but of desire and violence. When applied without the cultural concerns of either *Weltanschauung* or Marxism, dialectical philosophy of mind is enormously resistant to social context: to see Wordsworth's early description in terms of subject and object is to view one man alone in landscape. But a dialectic of desire and violence is always larger than, if rooted in, the relation between an individual subject and its object. It is always also a matter of cultural norms and their transgression. If form arrests motive within the frame of a literary or pictorial text, there must be a larger, cultural context motivating and supervising the arrest. To seek this supervisory over-motive requires that we probe precisely the *cultural* forms, as I previously called them, that the picturesque could not forget, however much it repressed the older narrative medium of those forms. Why the arrest of form? The answer, I believe, is not literary or pictorial formalism, but a historically knowable cultural formalism: institution.

Implicit in my previous sketch of the evolution of the picturesque is the fact that narrative (whose beginning was divine origin, whose middle was cultural propagation, and whose end was the Church) was once the major institutional form—the form through which the Church told the story of human history in such a way as to authorize itself as the culminating temporal mold of that history. With respect to the visual arts, the Church told human history in narrative scenes that were literally part of its institution—of its walls and altars. Given the aniconic and even iconoclastic bias of early Christianity,[65] of course, such assimilation of *istoria* to the institution had to be ideologically disciplined. *Istoria* could flourish only under institutional supervision creedal in authority. As Michael Baxandall observes, pictures in Italy in the late Middle Ages and Renaissance thus fell within "the jurisdiction of a mature body of ecclesiastical theory about images" (p. 40). Fra Michele da Carcano's sermon of 1492, for example, sets forth a standard, three-point agenda:

Images of the Virgin and the Saints were introduced for three reasons. *First,* on account of the ignorance of simple people, so that those who are not able to read the scriptures can yet learn by seeing the sacraments of our salvation and faith in pictures. . . . *Second,* . . . on account of our emotional sluggishness; so that men who are not aroused to devotion when they hear about the histories of the Saints may at least be moved when they see them, as if actually present, in pictures. . . . *Third,* . . . on account of our unreliable memories . . . because many people cannot retain in their memories what they hear, but they do remember if they see images. (Quoted in Baxandall, pp. 40–41)

These precepts adapted pictorial imagination to the processes of Church administration. Very broadly, top levels of administration defined doctrine through the canonization and interpretation of pivotal scriptural stories. They then discharged doctrine to middle and lower levels of administration tasked with its dissemination—with the instruction of the laity in the authorized meaning of Scripture and with the excitement of the proper emotional reactions. And propagation finished in rehearsal, the confirmation of instruction and excitement in memory.[66]

Claude and seventeenth-century Classicism reinstituted imagination by projecting repose—or, to use the concept associated with Gaspard Dughet Poussin, unity—at a time when art in Rome tended by contrast toward the grandiloquent expressiveness of the Italian Baroque (extreme physiognomies and gestures, sudden variances in line and recession, Caravaggio-like dramatics of light and shade). The ideological determinant of such repose—whose institution I earlier called "recreation"—was a deep-seated need not so much to displace as to *restore* the universality of the Church.[67] Recreation in Claude's art, that is, was a sacral nostalgia. As René Huyghe has argued, the turbulence of Baroque style in the late sixteenth through the seventeenth century imitated the troubles of the Counter-Reformation. Specifically, it followed the prescription of the Council of Trent (1545–63) that art become an apologetics propagandizing the aggressive vitality of a new anti-Protestant Catholicism. Explicitly premised upon the goals and methods of rhetoric, art became an instrument of persuasion more creedal than ever: it was no longer responsible for defining truth but only for disseminating the *Church*'s truth with all the resources of imagery that the Reformation had rejected (Huyghe, pp. 329–30, 332–34; see also Bazin, pp. 11–12).

Classicism in the manner of Claude and Poussin originated in the same impulse of Catholic revival, but argued a quietist apologetics.[68] Its rhetorical colors were landscapes of *apatheia* rather than physiognomies of passion, and its underlying *topos* was not Counter-Reformation sectarianism but the nostalgically peaceful universality of the Church *before* the Reformation. Byzantine style had been the official expression of the Universal Church up to the late Middle Ages. And Renaissance style during the Quattrocento and early Cinquecento had then coincided with the last great flourish of true universality: the epoch between the resolution of the Great Schism in 1417 and the beginning of the Reformation in 1517. By marrying the spirit of Byzantine *apatheia* with Renaissance style, Classicism in such pictures as *Hagar and the Angel* concluded its own subdued version of the Council of Trent: it decreed a worldly space unified by light, a whole harmonium of atmosphere older than the stresses of the age. Good form in landscape, in short, apologized for religious contest. It was what made religious subject once more conform to the lay of any land.

The conclusion we now come to, I believe, is inescapable. Arising through the forgetting of both narrative and the major institution served by narrative, the picturesque was a counter-institution. A first formulation: by forgetting narrative, the picturesque instituted the basic *Protestant* method of rehearsing culture. If the picturesque made all experience bow to form, such form was a new reform—specifically, a syncretistic or "Anglican" reform tolerating many of the old forms but unmindful of their past significance.[69] Picturesque arrest was evacuated liturgy. Fixed in a ritual posture of religiosity named repose, back turned to the world, and eyes adoring a mirror with hinged case not unlike a reliquary, the picturesque tourist stood in worship. But what he worshipped was one of the two Protestant arts substituting for the image of the Virgin or of the saints: landscape, which Gilpin compared to the other Northern form by calling it the "portraiture" of scenery (*Lakes*, 1: xxiii–xxx). Where once there rested the image of the Mother of God, now there reposed Mother Nature. It is thus perhaps not accidental that such early leaders of picturesque taste as West and Gilpin were clergymen. West, whom Wordsworth later described in his *Guide* as a "Roman Catholic Clergyman" (*Prose*, 2: 239), opened his Lakes tour by worshipping,

"Whoever takes a walk into these scenes, will return penetrated with a sense of the creator's power and unsearchable wisdom, in heaping mountains upon mountains, and enthroning rocks upon rocks. Such exhibitions of sublime and beautiful objects surprise and please, exciting at once rapture and reverence" (pp. 4–5). Gilpin, the conscientious vicar of Boldre in the New Forest, adapted such reverence to the Anglican institution, even going out of his way to declare that the arts associated with touring were "all very consistent with the strictest rules of the clerical profession" (*Lakes*, 1: xxii).

Following such ordination, the picturesque became in its prime implicitly religious. Witness, for example, the worship of a topographical motif akin to the arched bridge: the ruined abbey (which Gilpin declares is particularly English because "where popery prevails, the abbey is still intire and inhabited"; *Lakes*, 1: 13). Knight writes in *The Landscape*:

> Bless'd is the man in whose sequester'd glade,
> Some ancient abbey's walls diffuse their shade;
> With mouldering windows pierced, and turrets crown'd,
> And pinnacles with clinging ivy bound.   (p. 53)

"Bless'd land!" and again, "Bless'd land!" Knight emphasizes as his poem then moves to its close (pp. 84, 86). Or as Wordsworth puts it in his sunset vespers in *An Evening Walk*: "Now with religious awe the farewel light / Blends with the solemn colouring of the night" (ll. 329–30).

But an understanding of the picturesque as a religious institution can only be provisional because the meaning of Reformation in England was also, more basically, nationalism. It was *state*. Such a formulation at last ushers in the main goal of my inquiry.

Observe once more the bridge in the middle distance at Rydal Lower Falls. How was it that the scene was formed so exactly, we might ask, that contemporary descriptions all composed it in frontal perspective with the bridge arrested exactly in the middle distance? Why did not tourists, for example, station themselves on one of the flanking rock faces to view the scene along the diagonal?[70] The answer is at once practical and suggestive of broader issues. Situated on the estate of Sir Michael Le Fleming, Upper and Lower Falls could be reached only along access routes supervised by the owner or his agents. To view the Upper Falls, the tourist proceeded along a path of about six minutes' walk created by Sir Michael. And to view the Lower Falls, he had to be led by a guide past Rydal Hall down a short path to a small summer house of rubble stone dating from 1668 (which still stands; Pl. 13).[71] Here in an interior kept darkened for effect, the tourist at last removed a shutter in the window to see the falls appearing exactly, as we remember Gilpin saying, "like a picture

PLATE 13. Lower Rydal Falls with Summer House in foreground. A shuttered window in the Summer House looks out upon the Falls. Photo: Frederick Badger.

in a frame."[72] Indeed, the effect was so convincingly pictorial that it made the entire scene of the falls seem what later tourists called dioramic. A nineteenth-century guidebook, for example, marvels:

You enter an old summer-house, purposely darkened for the sake of contrast, and the removal of a shutter reveals the glittering waterfall in all its artistic prettiness, as it glides down a rather precipitous cleft in a black rock, and foams up again in a thousand prismatic ripples beneath an old gray bridge, which, with its covering of ivy, seems to have spanned the waterfall with the sole purpose of increasing its landscape beauty. A peasant seen above the arch, or a wagon crossing with its load of hay or corn, gives that animation to the scene which is really required, not only to add to its dioramic effect, but to convince us, by the introduction of animated objects, that the scene is not a mere cleverly devised illusion of the painter. (Blanchard, p. 32)

To see Rydal Lower Falls was to step into a diorama, camera obscura, or gigantic Claude glass able to change the bridge and even crossing peasants into purely aesthetic effects, into an illusion of workaday life as "animation."[73]

To attempt to see the falls outside this picture frame would have been to trespass against a family proud of its supervision of scenic property. Sir Daniel Fleming, who originally built the summer house, brought the family to Rydal Hall in 1656. Impoverished by

Parliamentary fines because of his Royalist background and by the legal expenses needed to claim his estate, he kept himself busy until the Restoration by becoming a noted antiquarian of the region (*DNB*, 7: 275; Hampshire). Carrying on the high cultural tone of Sir Daniel as well as of George Fleming, Bishop of Carlisle (an intervening heir to Rydal Hall), Michael Le Fleming in Wordsworth's time had sufficient social and literary interests to earn the sobriquet the "brilliant baronet" from Sir Walter Scott (*DNB*, 7: 276). Le Fleming exercised his tastes in great part by managing his estate both as property and as scenery. Wordsworth and Coleridge learned to their misfortune of his proprietorial acumen when they trespassed on his grounds in 1799. Coleridge records in his journal that a "servant, red-eyed &c, came to us, to the Road before the Waterfall to reprove us for having passed before the front of the House" (quoted in *Prose*, 2: 432). And Wordsworth later cautions in the 1810 edition of his *Guide* (in its early version as *Select Views*): "I wish it were in my power to recommend it to the Traveller to proceed northwards, along the slope of the hill-side, till he reaches the Park of Rydale; but this would be a trespass; for there is no path, and high and envious stone walls interpose" (*Prose*, 2: 269). So envious were these walls, indeed, that Dorothy in 1805 observes that they were the final demonstration of Sir Michael's domination over landscape:

Sir Michael Fleming has been getting his woods appraised, and after Christmas the Ax is to be lifted against them, and not one tree left, so the whole eastern side of the Lake will be entirely naked, even to the very edge of the water!—but what could we expect better from Sir Michael? who has been building a long high wall under the grand woods behind his house which cuts the hill in two by a straight line; and to make his doings visible to all men, he has whitewashed it, as white as snow. One who could do this wants a sense which others have. To him there is no "*Spirit in the Wood.*" (*Letters*, 1: 638)

What the baron's (more exactly, baronet's) window at Rydal Lower Falls exemplifies is that the picturesque was in every sense a form of social control. As such, the frames of vision it created should be seen to participate in the basic institutions of control—of "arrest" in another sense—that supervised the British state. Or rather, the picturesque did more than participate; it had the capacity actively to mime the existing, and to imagine the ideal, institutions of state. Such mimetic imagination, of course, was figurative, yet, as we will see, the evidence is that by the 1790's figuration was so polemically charged that the politics of the picturesque became an open topic for debate. The picturesque was a ministry out of office, a shadow government.

The Supervision of the Picturesque

I will compass the picturesque imagination of social institution in three portfolios: property, local government, and national politics. The first and third project an ideology of freedom. The second projects discipline. Seen in overview, the picturesque was the supervision of a precisely disciplined liberty—free, yet never *too* free—identical with being an Englishman, and particularly a liberal, at an epochal moment in history.

(1) *The picturesque was the imaginary ground on which the rights of old property could be adjusted to the demands of new money.*[74]

At issue was the ownership of "property." Michael Le Fleming, as we have noted, saw scenery as identical with property. The importance for the picturesque of such actual as well as symbolic equivalence between scenery and property cannot be underestimated. A parallel case would be that of Beaumont, whose delight in picturesque gardening depended on ownership of his Coleorton property, where Wordsworth helped landscape his "winter garden" in 1806–7 (see Noyes, pp. 93–95, 111–26). But it will be best to focus on the two tutelary geniuses of the picturesque in the 1790's and early 1800's: Price and Knight, the Herefordshire squires whose neighboring properties were the textbook of the picturesque *estate*. Knight's ten thousand acres made him one of the largest landowners in Herefordshire (Messmann, p. 15), a fact that subtly underlies *The Landscape*. Near the beginning of the poem, Knight chastises the owner who would use his property to declare "His vast possessions, and his wide domains" (pp. 12–13). By contrast, the whole of *The Landscape* is an effort not so much to avoid property as to conceal it in "Nature."[75] *The Landscape* is really pendant to the long poem that Knight wrote soon after, *The Progress of Civil Society* (1796), which opens with the imagination of the natural discovery of property (pp. 19–21). For Price also, propriety of form in landscape was first of all a matter of proprietorship. The evidence in this latter case is conclusive. With the example of the French revolution in property in mind, Price during the early fears of invasion organized the gentleman farmers and yeomanry of six Herefordshire parishes into a *posse comitatus* and published his plan in *Thoughts on the Defence of Property* (1797).[76] With the slightest pressure, picturesque landscape reverted to the status of property to be defended against misappropriation.

But the picturesque, of course, was not restricted only to the scenery of old property. The possibility of an imagination of state rather than simply of estate lay in the fact that such special zones as the Lake District offered the opportunity symbolically to broaden and modernize ownership—to "free" property for exchange. The deep interest of the picturesque, we may say, was thus that it imagined a new property whose exchange depended not on hereditary succession but on industrial success, not on "place" but on the displacement and reinvestment of capital. To start with, we notice that the distribution of property in the picturesque zones of Britain was peculiar. Until the decline of its yeomanry in the very late eighteenth and early nineteenth centuries, cultivated land in the Lakes was distributed between a disproportionately high number of small freeholder, tenant-right occupier, and leaseholder estates of £10 to £100 per year and a handful of giant estates owned by the leading families—the Lowthers, for example, owned some forty to fifty thousand acres (*LC1*, p. 229; *LC2*, pp. 7, 61). What was elided from the normal mix in other parts of Britain, as F. M. L. Thompson has pointed out, was the middle ground of the landed gentry (cited in *LC2*, p. 7). Add to this social gap two other elisions in the character of picturesque property. Around 1800, the Lakes had the highest proportion of "wastes" in England, more than 50 percent (Darby, pp. 105, 49–50); and until the Napoleonic Wars, the areas not waste were affected by relatively few enclosures (Darby, p. 23; *LC1*, pp. 233–34; *LC2*, p. 4).[77] The resulting picture is of a property structure with a great white canvas in the middle, a social-geographical free zone that in other parts of the country was the heartland—owned, cultivated, and increasingly enclosed—of the Tory squire.

Onto this white canvas, tourists were free to paint their imagination of "property." They *appropriated* the landscape. Even for the early tourists of the intelligentsia, symbolic appropriation was a deep habit of thought. Gilpin writes in his *Remarks on Forest Scenery* (1791), for example, "Forms, and colours . . . fleet before us; and if the transient glance of a good composition happen to unite with them, we should give any price to fix, and appropriate the scene" (2: 225). Gray had earlier appropriated scenery in the Lakes: "From hence I got to the parsonage . . . and, saw in my glass a picture, that if I could transmit to you and fix it in all the softness of its living colours, would fairly sell for a thousand pounds" (quoted in West, p. 113). And Clarke topped Gray: "Mr. Gray valued one [landscape] at Vicarage near *Keswick* at £1000, I should value this at £1500" (p. 125). With the arrival of increasingly middle-class tourists from nineteenth-century industrial centers (*LC2*, pp. 177–203), such imaginary appropriation of landscape then articulated the actual methods of modern appropriation, capitalization, and industrial development. Essentially, the new monied classes invested unowned property in the Lakes with imaginative capital earned in the urban areas. As Raymond Williams has put it, "The picturesque journeys—and the topographical poems, journals, paintings and engravings which promoted and commemorated them—came from the profits of an improving agriculture and from trade" (p. 128). Tourists saw a potential, that is, for symbolic "production" in the rural wastes that more than justified spending the profits of actual production on a recreational vacation North.

We should not be fooled by the fact that the literature of the picturesque—even as it so busily cataloged mills, forges, tanneries, quarries, mines, canals, fields, and timber—declared that it would rather dispense with such signs of rural productivity.[78] Tourists of the nineteenth century, for example, would have happily endorsed the strictures of West, who finds a forge near a picturesque bridge to be an impairment (p. 192); Clarke, who rejects the introduction of wagons, scenes of cultivation, and other works of men into landscape (p. xxxv); or Gilpin, who thinks that hedges, furrows, fields, and the general "vulgarity" of employment should be expunged from the prospect (*Lakes*, 2: 44–45; see also *Three Essays*, p. iii). In fact, the picturesque tourist was in love with productivity. As John Barrell has suggested, the repose of landscape art was really a recognition of labor finished or performed by others—by the little working figures in pictures of the time, for example (on repose, see esp. p. 162).[79] Just so, rural productivity should be seen to underlie virtually all the leisurely sights that went to make up a picturesque holiday. A whimsical example will set the scene. Visiting the plumbago (graphite) mines in Borrowdale, Gilpin is moved to say: "I could not help feeling a friendly attachment to this place, which every lover of the pencil must feel, as deriving from this mineral one of the best instruments of his art; the freest and readiest expositor of his ideas" (*Lakes*, 1: 205).[80] Artistic production was in love with pencil lead production.

Less whimsically, there was the fascination of picturesque vision for the basic contemporary method of reappropriating land, investing it with vast amounts of new capital, and converting it to more productive use: enclosure.[81] The Lakes, as we have already observed, were relatively little affected by enclosure acts until the war years beginning in the last decade of the eighteenth century. The picturesque was what the region had instead of enclosure. We notice that while picturesque writers and artists generally tried to avoid images of cultivation and rural production in their views, they were oddly willing to accommodate the signature of enclosure—hedges—even when such accommodation required much "hedging," as it were, on artistic principles. Dividing the view into units bounded by straight hedges or roads, enclosure was no friend to "variety." *The Quarterly Review* in 1820 would thus call Commissioners of Enclosure "merciless annihilators of rural scenery" (quoted in Darby, p. 202). But enclosure could nevertheless be adapted to "variety." Gilpin reflects:

On the spot, no doubt, and even in the first distances, the marks of the spade, and the plough; the hedge, and the ditch; together with all the formalities of hedge-row trees, and square divisions of property, are disgusting in a high degree. But when all these regular forms are softened by distance —when hedge-row trees begin to unite, and lengthen into streaks along the horizon . . .—it is inconceivable what richness, and beauty, this mass of deformity . . . adds to landscape. (*Lakes*, 1: 7–8)

Or as he immediately emphasizes again, "Thus English landscape affords a species of *rich distance*." In a long footnote in the 1795 edition of *The Landscape*, Knight speaks in much the same language of enrichment: when seen "horizontally in a flat country" such that their lines blend, hedged enclosures "enrich and embellish" and "are never completely ugly" (pp. 41n, 45n). And Wordsworth in his *Guide* later virtually repeats the point with reference to the property divisions that did affect the Lakes. Hedges, he says, "have frequently enriched the vallies with a sylvan appearance; while the intricate intermixture of property has given to the fences a graceful irregularity" (*Prose*, 2: 199; see also 2: 201 and *Letters*, 2: 506).

Essentially, the picturesque could recognize the artistic richness of enclosure because it was itself *visual* enclosure. Where enclosure acts hedged the land, acts of picturesque vision framed it in an endlessly repeatable enclosure of pure picturicity. But where actual enclosure made the land rich by converting it usually into monotonous pasture (Darby, p. 25), "enclosure" by Claude glass or sketchpad made it rich by converting it into the various and accidental.[82] Answering Humphry Repton's charge that he would change all the nation into a homogenous and unproductive picturesque forest, Knight thus answered in an extensive footnote to the 1795 *Landscape* that he instead wished to foster accidental variety, whether in unenclosed nature, agricultural enclosures, or their intermixture. Such, his vocabulary repeatedly implies, would be picturesque profit: "picturesque effects can only be obtained by watching accidents, and profiting by circumstances. . . . The line of a walk, the position of a seat, or limits of an inclosure, must often depend upon the accidental growth of a tree, and we must always make things, which we can command, conform to those which we cannot" (*Landscape*, pp. 45–46n; see also p. 48n). Properly managed, visual enclosure was a diversified portfolio able to subsume within "variety" not just nature but actual enclosures together with their productivity.

Seen in overview, the picturesque was a deep imagination of the economic institutions then transforming feudal notions of property into the new sense of exchangeable proprietorship that Williams has called the "rentier's vision" (p. 46). Seeking such vision in *An Evening Walk*, Wordsworth in his penultimate verse paragraph utters the strongest possible wish for imaginary property: he pictures to himself the future cottage that is the "sole bourn, sole wish, sole object of my way" (ll. 413–22). With its streamlet murmuring near, this cottage is an imaginary appropriation of something like Rydal Hall with its cascade. Some twenty years later, soon to be secure in Rydal Mount not very far from the Hall, Wordsworth would conclude a section of his 1810 *Guide* by wishing the entire Lake District transformed into purely imaginary property. Though the Lakes, he predicts, will fall increasingly into the ownership of the monied gentry, nevertheless the guidance of "skill and knowledge" may yet preserve the spirit of the place. "In this wish," he ends, "the author will be joined by persons of pure taste throughout the whole island, who, by their visits (often repeated) to the Lakes in the North of England, testify that they deem the district a sort of national property, in which every man has a right and interest who has an eye to perceive and a heart to enjoy" (*Prose*, 2: 224–25).[83] Such is a prophecy of the ultimate appropriation or visual enclosure to free so much of the Lakes for imagination: the National Park.

(2) *The picturesque was the imaginary ground on which an originally feudal, agrarian machinery of rural administration could be policed by a developing urban bureaucracy.*

We can notice first that picturesque guidebooks and theory project an arrest, as I have called it, disciplinary in force. Formulating its principles in reaction against formal gardening and even Capability Brown's looser rules of clumps and belts, of course, the picturesque may initially strike us as emancipation from discipline. But even a quick perusal of its writings will show that such emancipation was secretly obsessed with rules, protocol, and discipline in such a full sense that a chapter on the picturesque would not be out of place in Foucault's *Discipline and Punish*. The object of the picturesque was "command," which, first of all, required the regimentation of the viewer. West, for example, not only practiced the standard descriptive method of locking his viewer on "stations" facing a particular direction,[84] but took to an extreme the tendency of picturesque writers to advise in the imperative: "Return to the gate, and enter the inclosure; turn as soon as you can to the right, having the wall at some distance, till you arrive at the brink of a green precipice" (p. 110). Wordsworth's *Guide* frequently adopts the same voice. Soon after warning the reader not to trespass against the Flemings, for example, the 1810 *Guide* demands what is virtually a tightrope-walk past Rydal:

When you have crossed the Bridge, turn to a Gate on the right hand, and proceed with the road up the Valley of Ambleside, till you come opposite to the Village of Rydale; do not cross over to Rydale, but keep close to the Mountain on your left hand. . . . Advance with the Lake on your right . . . and come in view of Grasmere. Follow the road . . . till you reach the Church; thence into the main road back to Ambleside, looking behind you frequently. (*Prose*, 2: 271)

Command over the viewer was then interchangeable with the viewer's own command over landscape. West can thus command his reader to command: "Return to Bowness, and conclude by taking Mr. Young's general view of the lake, where, at one glance, you command all its striking beauties" (p. 68). Arthur Young himself, in a passage excerpted by West, similarly commands: "Strain your imagination to command the idea of so noble an expanse of water" (West, p. 72). Perhaps the most authoritarian commandant of the picturesque was Gilpin, whose *Lakes* contains a whole sublanguage of "correction." (During his long stint as a schoolmaster at Cheam, indeed, Gilpin devoted much thought to modernizing corrective methods, replacing corporal punishment, for example, with a regimen of fines and imprisonment; *DNB*, 7: 1262.) "It cannot be supposed, that every scene, which these countries present, is *correctly picturesque*," he says in his instructions to the viewer on how to command the landscape; and again, more sternly: "Where little improprieties offend, they are readily passed over," but "where the offence against nature becomes capital, it is not easy to repress indignation" (*Lakes*, 1: 119, xvii).

For Gilpin, the picturesque artist finally exercises a command virtually squirearchical: "Trees he may generally plant, or remove, at pleasure . . . he may certainly break an ill-formed hillock; and shovel the earth about him, as he pleases, without offence. He may pull up a piece of awkward paling—he may throw down a cottage—he may even turn the course of a road, or a river, a few yards on this side, or that" (*Lakes*, 1: xxviii–xxix). Indeed, the picturesque should be seen to substitute precisely for the country squires in their traditionally commanding role as Justices of the Peace. The best way to understand the disciplinary undercurrent of the picturesque, in other words, is to map it over the all-pervasive system of English rural administration —as documented, for example, in Sidney and Beatrice Webb's epic *English Local Government* (supplemented, for our purposes, by *LC1*).[85] It is telling that the Flemings of Rydal had a tradition of being Sheriffs of Cumberland; that Price in 1793 was Sheriff of Herefordshire; that Gilpin actively promoted and wrote an account of a new poor house; and that Richard Burn, a Lakes native, not only coauthored with Joseph Nicolson the *History and Antiquities of the Counties of Westmorland and Cumberland* (1777)—which includes descriptions of the area—but also authored the *History of the Poor Laws* (1764) and the great standard reference work for contemporary magistrates and administrators throughout England, *The Justice of the Peace, and Parish Officer* (1755).[86] Landscape description was an imagination of management. Even if the majority of viewers did not, like Price, Gilpin, or Burn, contribute to the actual management of natural or social resources, the picturesque nevertheless could not but participate in the forces affecting the enormously complex, hodgepodge, undercontrolled, and *changing* system of English local government then responsible for adapting agrarian landscape to an industrial economy.

The old pattern of rural local administration centered upon the Justice of the Peace. Above the Justices sat the Lord Lieutenant and Sheriff of the county. Below stood the officers of the parishes in the county: the churchwarden, constable, overseer of the poor, and surveyor of highways.[87] Two key features of this overall government differentiated it from modern local administration. First, government was a "unit of obligation" rather than of political or vocational opportunity (Webb, 1: 40 and *passim*). Office at both the county and the parish level (with the exception of the respected and relatively easy-to-perform office of churchwarden) was unremunerative and required commitment to unpleasant tasks, often at personal expense. Until the beginning of the nineteenth century, therefore, higher gentry often avoided taking on the responsibilities of Justice of Peace (Webb, 1: 320–21, 382–86). And at the parish level, the much maligned constable, overseer (who was criminally responsible for the death by negligence of a poor person), and surveyor (who had to undertake the unpleasant task of requisitioning road-work teams from neighbors) had to be appointed by annual rotation (Webb, 1: 15–32). Secondly, local government addressed civil and judicial business indiscriminately. As the Webbs observe,

inextricably intermingled with . . . criminal jurisdiction there had, by 1689, come to be carried on at Quarter Sessions the bulk of the civil administration of the county. The repairing of bridges, the maintenance of the King's gaols, the building and management of the newer Houses of Correction, the fixing of wages, prices and rates of land carriage, the licensing of various kinds of traders, the suppression of disorderly houses, the sanctioning of special levies for various parish needs, the confirmation or disallowance of the orders of individual Justices or pairs of Justices on every conceivable subject, were among the multifarious civil functions of Quarter Sessions. (1: 296–97)

Civil business and criminal justice could be addressed together because the two were conceptually identical. Because the individual parish was a structure of obligation, failure to keep highways and bridges in repair or to relieve the poor was treated as dereliction of duty by the parish as a whole to be charged according to the form of indictment, trial, and sentence (Webb, 1: 307–9).

In theory, then, local government was a broadly based, consistent pyramid of authority extending from the yeomanry at the parish level through the squirearchy at the county level ultimately to the King (who appointed the Lord Lieutenant and the Sheriff). Drawing by rota upon all substantial property owners, it brought more or less collective expertise (even given the fact that it excluded from its ranks the laboring poor) to bear on the entirety of social, economic, and judicial business.

In practice, however, local government in the late eighteenth and early nineteenth centuries was inchoate because of a basic contest between old and new notions of government. On the one hand, the squirearchy defended its rule over traditional government ever more stubbornly, establishing what the Webbs call "class exclusiveness" (1: 382–86). Not only did better families enter the ranks of Justice of Peace at the end of the eighteenth century, but the concern of these families—overwhelmingly Tory in politics and conformist in religion—increasingly centered on such actions as the enforcement of game laws and the stopping up of customary footpaths through their property (Webb, 1: 597–602). Protective of ancient feudal prerogatives, these actions were deeply anti-Whig and anti-commercial. By the turn of the century, some counties went so far as to proscribe anyone engaged in trade, manufacture, or commerce from becoming a Justice (Webb, 1: 383n). But on the other hand, the very intransigence of the squires represented a surrender of government at subordinate levels precisely to the forces of commercialization. In essence, the squirearchy retreated into such a tight confine of traditional prerogative that the sheer amount of new civil and judicial business fostered by industrialization at the turn of the century had to be governed untraditionally—and often extra-legally—by professionals substituting for the customary parish officers. The model for such untraditional administration was set first in the industrial parishes of the North and Midlands, as well as near London, where a vast growth in population had made the obligations of parish office so overwhelming that few "substantial" residents would accept appointment as constable, overseer, or surveyor even by rota. Residents instead routinely paid fines. The result was that the offices of constable, overseer, and surveyor became filled either by the most incompetent and venal (leading to notorious cases of "bossism") or by perennial "deputy" officers foreshadowing the salaried overseers and surveyors to come in the nineteenth century (Webb, 1: 18–19, 61–90, 163–66, 512–21). A bureaucracy was coming to be.

Only one further addition was necessary to transform the burgeoning network of professional government at the parish level into a fully functional bureaucracy able to administer both urban centers and rural reaches: statutory legalization. As the Webbs document in their volume on "Statutory Authorities for Special Purposes," one especially salient feature of English local government from the eighteenth to the nineteenth century was a massive improvisation of statutory bodies—most signally the Incorporated Guardians of the Poor and the Turnpike Trusts (4: 107–234). In a movement analogous to the farming out of the King's gaols to private contractors

(Webb, 1: 486), the Incorporations of Guardians of the Poor submitted the poor to organizers who expected the poor in workhouses to earn their own support. Turnpike Trusts similarly ventured to improve the highways for profit.[88] Such bodies drew for membership upon both local yeomanry and squirearchy, but had no logical relation to the chain of county and parish command. Indeed, they often tended simply to bypass public authority and assimilate the duties of the old parish offices. Thus the special surveyor of highways appointed by a turnpike trust, for example, could take upon himself all the traditional right of the public surveyor to demand monies and road labor from the parish (Webb, 4: 166–69). Local government, in sum, changed under the feet of the squirearchy to foreshadow a detached, professional, salaried administration suited to the management of an increasingly industrialized land. Even in the rural North, the local surveyors and attendant bridgemasters who once maintained the many packhorse roads and bridges of the region were no longer competent to deal with the new highways built for carriage transport. In Northumberland, for example, the two stonemasons who served as bridgemasters until 1825 had to be supplemented after 1820 by an "experienced civil engineer" (Webb, 1: 516, 520n).

Now we can return to the command with which Gilpin and other picturesque writers delegated the imaginary power of breaking up hillocks, shoveling earth about, pulling up palings, throwing down cottages, and even turning the course of roads. Visiting Price's estate at Foxley in 1810, Wordsworth would later report with displeasure that the picturesque can appear too much a regimen of "law": "A man by little and little becomes so delicate and fastidious with respect to forms in scenery, where he has a power to exercise a controul over them, that if they do not exactly please him in all moods, and every point of view, his power becomes his law; he banishes one, and then rids himself of another, impoverishing and *monotonizing* Landscapes" (*Letters*, 2: 506). As Martin Price has observed, Price's eye in fact delighted in "the design and improvement of villages," much as if the principles of artistic management in a Gainsborough picture of cottagers could simply be extended into real society (p. 284). The picturesque *was* law and order. It was the imagination of a whole method of managing and ultimately policing the rural landscape cognate with new methods of administration learned in the industrial centers.

Supplementing and replacing squirearchical rule (which the supervision of Price still most closely resembles), the picturesque of the tourists became a rule precisely analogous to the developing bureaucracy of professional surveyors and overseers. Dedicated to opening rather than stopping up parks and footpaths, such tourists were an idealization of the corrupt predecessors of bureaucracy Burn had termed "those spiritless, ignorant, lazy, sauntering people called Sur-veyors of the Highways" (quoted in Webb, 1: 67). They were spirited, enlightened, industrious, sauntering people capable of surveying the landscape so well that picturesque guidebooks were often what rural parishes had instead of an official survey. (The *Gentleman's Magazine* observes in 1787 about actual surveys: "In some parishes, thirty or even fifty years elapse without the bounds and limits of the parish be-ing ascertained, and it frequently happens, in case of lawsuits, that the jury are obliged to depend on the memory of some old man"; quoted in Webb, 1: 12.) And just as the picturesque surveyed the highways, so it oversaw the poor. As Barrell's study of working figures in landscape art attests, it delighted in supervising laborers, cottagers, and their children dressed in their ragged and "shabbily picturesque" attire (esp. pp. 107–9). Even more pointedly, as we might see in Dorothy Wordsworth's journals, the picturesque delighted in super-vising actual beggars in a sort of open-air workhouse of the eye (see, for example, *DWJ*, pp. 71–72).

The picturesque, in sum, was the late-eighteenth- and early-nine-teenth-century idea of bureaucracy as "natural." This idea may at first seem too Kafkaesque for the times, but only so, I believe, can we account for the fact that guidebooks, topographies, and gazet-teers in the late eighteenth and nineteenth century increasingly listed details of local administration alongside scenic descriptions (Clarke, for example, discusses poor relief at Ambleside, p. 132; and a later topography notes that £20 per year from tolls collected on the turn-pike road past Rydal Hall was lent out to raise poor money, Whel-lan, p. 828). Similarly, only so can we account for the fact that the strength of Wordsworth's own *Guide* lies precisely in its supervision of landscape and population together (Sections I and II respectively of the 1835 edition). Perhaps there is no better way to document such supervisory scope in the *Guide* and its satellite treatises than to read two telling passages together. The first is the well-known opening of Section I in which Wordsworth becomes a transcendental Surveyor. In a passage he was especially proud of (*Letters*, 2: 404), he conveys his reader in mind to a station on "a cloud hanging midway" between the peaks of Great Gable and Scafell, then lays out the Lake District as a huge wheel with spokes (*Prose*, 2: 171–73). Similarly, we notice, Clarke had stationed himself at Penrith Beacon to survey the pros-pect as a half-wheel of vision centered around a solitary eye (Pl. 14) —an emblem, as Theresa M. Kelley puts it with allusion to Words-worth's own description of the picturesque in *The Prelude* (11.180), of "the tyranny of eyesight . . . in late eighteenth-century discussions of landscape and prospect" ("Economics," p. 24).[89]

Indeed, "tyranny" is apt: Wordsworth's panoramic wheel is the paradigm for the social vision of the *Guide*. The second passage

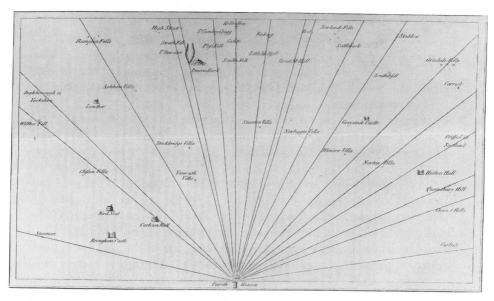

PLATE 14. James Clarke, chart of view from Penrith Beacon, in his *A Survey of the Lakes*, 1789. Note the eye at the viewing station. The Beinecke Rare Book and Manuscript Library, Yale University, New Haven. Photo: Library.

we can consider derives from "An Unpublished Tour," one of the manuscripts intended for an expansion and revision of the 1810 *Guide*. Here Wordsworth becomes a transcendental Overseer. After conveying his reader to the top of Lancaster Castle, he lays out the following "panorama view from the principal Tower of the Castle":

From this lofty station . . . the Spectator looks upon the inferior towers, courts, roofs, walls, battlements, & whole circumference of this vast edifice, & upon the town, shipping, aqueduct, & Bridge—works of art sufficiently splendid for the situation which they occupy in the centre of a magnificent prospect of sea & land. After a hasty survey of the whole Scene, the Castle will naturally become the object of distinct attention. . . .

In the several Courts immediately under the eye, the Debtors and various orders of Prisoners are seen pacing to & fro, amusing themselves or pursuing their occupations in the open air. The construction of their Prison-house makes it evident that it is impossible for them to escape, & at the same time shews that no comfort or accommodation is wanting which their pitiable condition will allow. While the Spectator stands upon this eminence —the breezes passing by in freedom, & the clouds sailing at liberty over his head—the wide circumjacent region exhibits in the fields the cheerfulness & fertility, & in the Waters & Mountains the uncontroulable motions & the inexhaustible powers of Nature. The contrast is striking, & it is impossible not to be touched by a depressing sympathy with the unfortunate or guilty Captives under his eye. There is a counterpoise, however, in the majesty of the building, by its appearance & construction admirably fitted to announce

& give effect to those coercive duties of civil polity which the infirmities of Men have rendered necessary. (*Prose*, 2: 290–91)

In every way, I suggest, this panorama from atop Lancaster Castle corresponds to Wordsworth's wheel vision from between Great Gable and Scafell. We might think here by analogy of the structure of a conversation poem such as Coleridge's "This Lime-Tree Bower My Prison." What is remarkable about the Lancaster Castle panorama is the tidal rhythm by which it alternates between inner and outer directions of vision to create at last a single view of naturalized society—a single landscape able to confine the social irregularities of the foreground within the circumambient freedom of breezes and liberty of clouds in the background.[90] To the picturesque eye, the "uncontroulable motions & the inexhaustible powers of Nature" are finally integral with the "coercive duties of civil polity." Together, nature and polity shape a disciplinary *atmosphere* of freedom, a general breeze or air of regulated release so persuasive that immediately after the passage above Wordsworth is inspired to an extended appreciation of political, corporeal, and mental liberty (*Prose*, 2: 291).[91] Such is Wordsworth's ultimate development of the disciplinary matrix, natural and social at once, implicit at noon in *An Evening Walk*, where, we remember, scenery pens cattle, horses, deer, and schoolboys each in their place amid illusory freedom.[92]

Perhaps a final comparison more arresting than "This Lime-Tree Bower My Prison" can be offered for the disciplinary matrix at the heart of the picturesque. We know that *The Prelude* ultimately amplifies its critique of picturesque tyranny to the scale of epic simile. The picturesque is a despotism in which only a civil war of senses can bring freedom:

> The state to which I now allude was one
> In which the eye was master of the heart,
> When that which is in every stage of life
> The most despotic of our senses gain'd
> Such strength in me as often held my mind
> In absolute dominion. Gladly here,
> Entering upon abstruser argument,
> Would I endeavour to unfold the means
> Which Nature studiously employs to thwart
> This tyranny, summons all the senses each
> To counteract the other and themselves,
> And makes them all, and the objects with which all
> Are conversant, subservient in their turn
> To the great ends of Liberty and Power.
>
> (11.171–84)

We can make Wordsworth's conceit of tyranny concrete by drawing upon the simile spoken by an actual architect of despotism. Imagine that the picturesque is Jeremy Bentham's Panopticon prison, which Foucault and Gertrude Himmelfarb have explored.[93] Proposed in letters almost exactly contemporaneous with *An Evening Walk*, the Panopticon was to have been an inverse Colosseum designed with the same radial geometry as Wordsworth's or Clarke's visionary wheels. A circular perimeter would hold prisoners in solitary cells barring lateral communication but open to sight from the structure's interior, and the central observation tower would allow the "invisible eye" of the Inspector to spy into any cell at any time. Such was Bentham's totalitarian vision. But the vision had a loophole, and it was through this loophole—like the ones the Indian herdsman, we might say, cuts through figs at Milton's moment of original crime (*Paradise Lost*, 9.1108–10)—that a cliché entered to thrust the whole penitentiary scheme onto the plane of simile. Bentham discovered after drawing up his plans that a blank space had inadvertently been left in the central tower in the area of the chapel. This he proposed to turn into a visitor gallery, reasoning that the public would prefer his view of discipline to Bedlam because "the scene would be more picturesque" (Bentham, p. 78; see Himmelfarb, p. 212). The architecture of confinement, in short, was like the landscape of freedom—even to the extent that tourists imposed additional, purely aesthetic requirements. "Building, furniture, apparel, persons, every thing," Bentham says, "must be kept as nice as a Dutch house. The smallest degree of ill scent would be fatal" (p. 78).

We will soon need to address the epic similes that occur throughout picturesque guidebooks and treatises themselves. As in the case of Gilpin's and Price's passages on repose, where the mind is a lake with spreading ripples and a lake is a vast mirror, the extended conceits of picturesque literature seem to emulate the repose of some of Milton's most celebrated similes. At the moment of the picturesque, perhaps, the hearts of all tourists rebound at once with joy and fear, desire and violence; all become belated peasants, careful plowmen, or Indian herdsmen halted in a landscape of hidden animation. But for now we can simply exploit the convention of picturesque simile to close the comparison of Wordsworth and Bentham with a proportion: Milton's Indian herdsman watching his cattle through loopholes, we can say, is to the Shepherd who next descends to judge humanity as Wordsworth's eye reposed on its secret bridge is to the invisible eye of Bentham's Inspector. What the simile of aesthetics-"like"-government tells us—in a style of resemblance integral to our context itself—is that picturesque Britannia rules, if not the waves, then the woods and fields and all who live enclosed therein.

(3) *Finally, the picturesque was the imaginary ground on which Tory and Pittite could be mastered by Whig and Foxite, and thus a "free" Britain established corresponding to the France of the very early Revolution.*

As is clearest in such cases as forests, parks, or dales (a term Words-worth knew stemmed from the way land was "dealt" out; *Prose*, 2: 198), there is no nature except as it is constituted by acts of political definition made possible by particular forms of government. When the governmental understructure changes, nature changes. Each time a nation suffers an invasion, civil war, major change of ministry, or some other crisis, national or international, it must revise its land-scape, the image of its own nature.

In Britain, nature was the Constitution. In the period from the seventeenth century to the high picturesque, British landscape evolved through three identifiably separate revisions, each charting a particular controversy over the proper relation of monarchy to Par-liament and the true nature of constitutional freedom. The first two epochs of controversy may be charted quickly because the trails have been blazed. As James Turner has detailed, the period from roughly 1640 to 1660—the Civil War to the Restoration (and, we may add, ultimately to the Exclusion Crisis of 1679)—was one in which land-scape and statecraft were fully one because both were "partisan, and conceal[ed] their partisanship under a universal doctrine of Nature" (p. 114). Poems such as Denham's "Cooper's Hill" (1642) imagined the contest between Royalists and Puritans so deeply and often ex-plicitly that the "variety" they at last produced must be seen to de-lineate a political solution. Able to balance forms of landscape and, implicitly, of society, variety was a vision of "moderation"—in Den-ham's case, a vision of constitutionalist Royalism (see James Turner, pp. 55, 58–60).[94] It was the imagination of a particular kind of checks-and-balances liberty.

From roughly 1679 to 1730, the landscape of freedom then imag-ined the internalization of civil war that followed the Restoration: party contest. As Nikolaus Pevsner and I. de Wolfe have argued, it is significant that the picturesque arose in its earliest form in these years in the writings of such Whigs as the Earl of Shaftesbury and Joseph Addison. The picturesque was the "garden of liberalism," Pevsner has said, and "Whig is the first source of the landscape garden" ("Gene-sis," p. 146).[95] "Free" landscape, in other words, became the program of the party that first arose after the Exclusion Crisis to defend Prot-estant succession and Parliamentary independence against Catholic and absolutist James—to renovate the checks-and-balances system of the Restoration, that is, in the form of the Glorious Revolution of 1688. In international terms, the Whig landscape of freedom excluded not just James but monarchist and Catholic absolutism as represented by French formal gardening. The garden of liberalism was Richmond or Stowe versus Versailles.[96]

By the time of the high picturesque, therefore, successive sedi-ments of constitutional theory had already been deposited under the

British landscape. Once more the political understructure shifted. The landscape shaped by the Restoration and then the Glorious Revolution changed under the urgency of a growing crisis in government necessitating a new conception of party contest and a new definition of nature. Internally, the crisis began with George III's effort, contrary to the style of the first Hanovers, to rule outside the purview of party politics in Parliament—specifically, to exercise the royal prerogative of appointing ministers independent of Parliamentary and Whig approval.[97] Externally, it was exacerbated in the 1770's and 1780's by dissension over the American War, India policy, and Parliamentary reform. The result was an extended contest between King and Parliament marked by such high points of instability as the emergence of the Whig opposition under Rockingham, the formation of the fantastically unstable Fox-North coalition just prior to Pitt's triumph, and the Regency Crisis. With the addition in the 1790's of controversy over the French Revolution and the Pittite repression, the old structure of party rule that had served the Whigs so well under the first two Hanovers—a loose structure defined more by men and family than by issues—underwent a realignment. While the parties had not yet absorbed the independents and placemen who leavened the characteristic eighteenth-century Parliament (J. Owen, pp. 293–94),[98] party politics in a modern sense—as we will see more fully in Chapter 8—was nevertheless on the rise both in its often confusing practice and in its new theory of *ideological* opposition. By century's end, Whigs such as Burke had joined forces with Government to form a majority of Pittite conservatives, while another nucleus of Whigs created an opposition of Foxite liberals (reinforced by the extra-Parliamentary voice of radical associations). Seen in overview, the outcome was the recognition of a semi-permanent division between Government and Opposition, conservatives and liberals, that transcended the more ephemeral opportunism of earlier party politics and anticipated the modern two-party system (see A. Beattie, pp. 38–46). Pittite and Foxite: each used the French Revolution and its domestic repercussions to hone its own partial view of freedom.

Subjected to such renewed divisiveness in the bedrock of freedom, British landscape once more had to take sides: slowly at first, and then with sudden movement, it followed its original Whig impulse and voted squarely for Foxite liberalism. From the late 1760's through the 1780's, the picturesque must be said to have been politically preconscious—not because it had no politics, but because its understanding of freedom still reflected unthinkingly the principles fixed in the earlier landscapes of the Restoration and Glorious Revolution. It was thus simply conventional to boast the traditional freedom or variety of English landscape. George Mason suggests in his *Essay on Design in Gardening* in 1768, for example, that landscape gardening arose in

England because of native "independence . . . in matters of taste and in religion and government" (quoted in Pevsner, *Englishness*, p. 178). And Gilpin in his *Lakes* repeatedly declares "the freedom of the natural scene" and "the freedom of nature" in England (1: xiv–xv). Even French travel guides and gardening tracts, we might note, habitually confirmed that English landscaping was so various and free that even the cattle were at liberty.[99]

From the late 1780's to about 1810, however, the picturesque awoke abruptly into political consciousness. Discussing fore-, middle-, and backgrounds in his poem "On Landscape Painting" (1792), Gilpin thus suddenly endorses war against France in a simile:

> But tho full oft these parts with blending tints
> Are softened so, as wakes a frequent doubt
> Where each begins, where ends; yet still preserve
> A *general balance*. So when Europe's sons
> Sound the alarm of war; some potent hand
> (Now thine again my Albion) poises true
> The scale of empire; curbs each rival power;
> And checks each lawless tyrant's wild career.
> (*Three Essays*, pp. 104–5)

Again we come upon epic similes in the picturesque—similes, we can now note, that throughout picturesque writings at this time evidenced a preoccupation with political (and, increasingly, Revolutionary) events too deep and persistent to be dismissed as merely ornamental. The case will appear conclusive, I believe, if we turn from Gilpin's endorsement of the war to the climactic battleground of picturesque theory after the mid 1790's: the Price-Knight-Repton controversy. The heated polemics of this contest turned in large part precisely upon an exchange of epic similes associating the picturesque incontrovertibly with Foxite liberalism.

We can begin with an anecdote. Farington records about the Royal Academy banquet on April 23, 1796:

Owing to lack of arrangement most of the guests . . . were obliged to take such seats as were left. . . . C. Fox [sat] between Zoffany & Rooker. After dinner G. Dance came to me to mention his concern that Mr. Fox was so improperly situated; on which I went to Downman & requested He wd. come and sit by me which wd. leave an opening for Mr. Fox between Mr. Price and Mr. Knight. . . . I then went to Mr. Fox and requested He would remove to a seat prepared for him. He very good humouredly said He was very well situated but on my repeating my wish went with me and took his seat between Mr. Price & Mr. Knight. I observed this attention to Mr. Fox was much approved of. (1: 146)

As illustrated by this vignette, the two champions of the picturesque from the 1790's on were perceived publicly to be the flank guard of

Foxite liberalism. Price was a staunch friend not only of the leading Whigs but of Fox in particular. The two were friends at Eton
and Oxford, acted in the same play in 1761, studied Italian under
a common master in Florence in 1767, and undertook the Grand
Tour together in 1768 (*DNB*, 16: 341–42).[100] Knight's association with
Fox's politics may be documented even more strongly. Sitting as a
Whig M.P. for Leominster from 1780 to 1784 and for Ludlow from
1784 to 1806, Knight was a backbencher who appears never to have
made a speech. Yet as shown by his voting record on major issues,
his place on contemporary lists of allegiances, and his participation in
the unsuccessful attempt at the St. Alban's Tavern meeting in 1784 to
set up a coalition government of Fox and Pitt, he must nevertheless
be counted one of the most committed of Fox's legion (Valentine,
p. 514; Messmann, pp. 37–40, 120). Such commitment would at last
issue in his *Monody on the Death of . . . Charles James Fox* (1806–7).

Prima facie evidence alone, then, explains why it was natural for
Humphry Repton in his *Letter to Uvedale Price* in 1794 to attack Price's
Essays on the Picturesque and Knight's *Landscape* (both of which appeared that year) in a sustained political simile. Defending the system of Capability Brown, which Price and Knight derided, Repton
argues in an anti-theoretic manner evidencing the clear influence of
Burke's *Reflections*. He addresses Price:

> Your new theory of deducing *landscape gardening* from *painting* is so plausible,
> that, like many other philosophic theories, it may captivate and mislead,
> unless duly examined by the test of experience and practice. I cannot help
> seeing great affinity betwixt deducing gardening from the painter's studies
> of wild nature, and deducing government from the uncontrouled opinions
> of man in a savage state. The neatness, simplicity, and elegance of English
> gardening, have acquired the approbation of the present century, as the
> happy medium betwixt the wildness of nature and the stiffness of art; in
> the same manner as the English constitution is the happy medium betwixt
> the liberty of savages, and the restraint of despotic government; and so long
> as we enjoy the benefit of these middle degrees betwixt extremes of each,
> let experiments of untried theoretical improvement be made in some other
> country. (pp. 9–10)

Brown's infamous clumps and belts are here the happy medium of
constitutional liberty.[101] By contrast, landscapes of "untried theoretical improvement" à la Price and Knight are too free and, reading
Burke between the lines, *revolutionary*. As Knight reads the simile in
the Postscript to the 1795 edition of *The Landscape*, Repton's implication is no less than that he and Price approve "the Democratic tyranny
of France" (*Landscape*, p. 101).

Once Repton had introduced the simile, neither Price nor Knight
would let it die. In the course of their elaborate rebuttals in the succeeding years, indeed, they allow us to see that Repton served merely

as the catalyst precipitating the political thought suspended in similes throughout their work from early to late. In his *Essays*, for example, Price had taken easy advantage of an anecdote about Capability Brown to initiate an attack with underlying political significance. "I remember hearing, that when Mr. Brown was High-Sheriff [of London]," Price says in a note, "some facetious person observing his attendants straggling, called out to him, 'Clump your javeline men'" (*Essays*, 1: 245–46n). The note grounds the following military assault on both clumps and belts in landscape:

Natural groups are full of openings and hollows; of trees advancing before, or retiring behind each other; all productive of intricacy, of variety, of deep shadows, and brilliant lights. . . . But clumps, like compact bodies of soldiers, resist attacks from all quarters: examine them in every point of view; walk round and round them; no opening, no vacancy, no stragglers! but in the true military character, *ils font face partout.* . . . Clumps, placed like beacons on the summits of hills, alarm the picturesque traveller many miles off, and warn him of his approach to the enemy: the belt lies more in ambuscade. (*Essays*, 1: 245–46)

After being provoked by Repton, Price in his *Letter to H. Repton* (first published 1795) then testified to the political consciousness underlying such rejection of military regularity and other signs of oppression in landscape. Price recognized that Repton's happy medium of liberty in landscape was fully conservative. Fixated on the principles of the Glorious Revolution that Burke in his *Reflections* had used to prosecute untried theoretical improvements of every kind in France, it was precisely the war-mongering platform that Fox was contesting in 1794. Arguing in support of a motion to end the war, for example, Fox declared on May 30:

The House had never sanctioned the dangerous speculation that to secure England we must destroy Jacobinism in France. The experience of ages had proved it to be the will of Providence that monarchies, oligarchies, aristocracies, republics might exist in all their several *varieties* in different parts of the world without imposing the necessity of endless wars on the rest. (*Speeches*, pp. 209–10; italics mine)

To refute Repton, Price's *Letter* simply applies Fox's creed of international political "variety" back to Britain and its landscape. Pride in the British constitution, Price says,

would sink into shame and despondency, should the parallel you have made [between the constitution and Brown's system of gardening], ever become just: should the freedom, energy, and variety of our minds, give place to tameness and monotony; should our opinions be prescribed to us, and like our places, be moulded into one form. (*Essays*, 3: 104)

The clumps and belts that Repton defends and that Price had likened to military formations are leagued with the Pittite warmongers in the background: they would destroy the true Whiggish liberty of "freedom, energy, and variety."

The evidence in the case of Knight is even stronger despite the fact that Knight tried to answer Repton by denying that his *Landscape* had any political content. The Postscript to the 1795 edition of the poem declares:

To say that his [Repton's] own system of rural embellishment resembles the British constitution, and that Mr. Price's and mine resemble the Democratic tyranny of France, is a species of argument which any person may employ, on any occasion, without being at any expence either of sense or science. . . . All that I entreat is, that they [modern improvers] will not at this time, when men's minds are so full of plots and conspiracies, endeavour to find analogies between picturesque composition and political confusion; or suppose that the preservation of trees and terraces has any connection with the destruction of states and kingdoms. (pp. 101, 104)

This statement is remarkable for the sheer magnitude of its untruth: without a doubt, *The Landscape* from its first edition on had itself made political analogies inescapable.

Crucial in this light is the climactic third book of the poem, which, as Frank J. Messmann has put it, enabled "Knight to reveal his broad knowledge of English trees" but is "tangential to landscape gardening and has little relevance to picturesque beauty" (p. 81). The non sequitur of the third book is politically motivated. It is precisely what Knight's Postscript would deny: a sustained comparison between "the preservation of trees" and "the destruction of states and kingdoms." In part, of course, such comparisons were merely convention.[102] But Knight's use of the convention is so full that it should really be seen to outline a sort of Aristotelian *Politics* or Machiavellian *Prince*. For Knight a forest of trees is a nation governed by two alternative types of kings. First, there is the enlightened monarch friendly to variety, the British oak. In a passage included in both the first and second editions of the poem, Knight expatiates:

> Then Britain's genius to thy aid invoke,
> And spread around the rich, high-clustering oak:
> King of the woods! whose towering branches trace
> Each form of majesty, and line of grace;
> Whose giant arms, and high-imbower'd head,
> Deep masses round of clustering foliage spread,
> In various shapes projecting to the view.   (p. 72)

Then, planted in an epic simile, grows a darker majesty tolerating no variety at all:

> lord supreme o'er all this formal race,
> The cedar claims pre-eminence of place;
> Like some great eastern king, it stands alone,

> Nor lets the ignoble crowd approach its throne,
> Spreads out its haughty boughs that scorn to bend,
> And bids its shade o'er spacious fields extend;
> While, in the compass of its wide domain,
> Heaven sheds its soft prolific showers in vain:
> Secure and shelter'd, every subject lies;
> But, robb'd of moisture, sickens, droops, and dies.
>   O image apt of man's despotic power!   (p. 75)

Despite its Eastern referent, Knight's contrast in majesties, I suggest, was really an imagination of the difference between British liberty and the French *ancien régime*. The specificity of this reading is warranted because Knight goes on to close his poem with an explicit declaration of Revolutionary freedom in landscape—a suggestion, indeed, that French tyranny must be destroyed by mass rebellion before a true liberty tree, as it were, can grow. I refer to the fertilizing Deluge of Terror in Knight's final epic simile:

> As the dull, stagnant pool, that's mantled o'er
> With the green weeds of its own muddy shore,
> No bright reflections on its surface shows,
> Nor murmuring surge, nor foaming ripple knows;
> But ever peaceful, motionless, and dead,
> In one smooth sheet its torpid waters spread:
> So by oppression's iron hand confined,
> In calm and peaceful torpor sleep mankind;
> Unfelt the rays of genius, that inflame
> The free-born soul, and bid it pant for fame.
>   But break the mound, and let the waters flow;
> Headlong and fierce their turbid currents go;
> Sweep down the fences, and tear up the soil;
> And roar along, 'midst havock, waste, and spoil;
> Till spent their fury.
>   .   .   .
> So when rebellion breaks the despot's chain,
> First wasteful ruin marks the rabble's reign;
> Till tired their fury, and their vengeance spent,
> One common interest bids their hearts relent;
> Then temperate order from confusion springs,
> And, fann'd by freedom, genius spreads its wings.
>   What heart so savage, but must now deplore
> The tides of blood that flow on Gallia's shore!
>   .   .   .
>   Yet, from these horrors, future times may see
> Just order spring, and genuine liberty.
>   (pp. 91–92)

It is perhaps significant that Knight's own personal experience with the Revolution occurred early in the course of things in 1790, when

he cut short a trip to Paris because of the press of events (Messmann, p. 54). The view of Revolution that closes Knight's *Landscape*
matches precisely the early Foxite view: while deploring violence,
Knight understands its necessity and prophesies that it will usher in a
"genuine liberty."

In sum, Repton was indeed justified in comparing Price's and especially Knight's picturesque to their politics. Knight's true last word
on the subject, we may say, was not the 1795 Postscript to *The Landscape* denying political content, but the fantastic five-page footnote
to the deluge simile in the 1794 edition and after. Forced by the succeeding bloodshed of the Reign of Terror to be less sanguine about
the Revolution, Knight espouses in his footnote—really a political
treatise—the later Foxite position: though the current state of the
Revolution is regrettable, he says, the present war against France is
equally so because it may make the French turn even more militantly
away from true liberty (pp. 93–97n).[103] This last word on the subject, which never rejects the early ideal of revolutionary liberty even
as it deplores the reality, is symmetrical with what may be taken
to be the first word of the 1795 edition: a congratulatory poem by
Edward Winnington inserted at the close of Knight's Advertisement.
The congratulation begins:

> Whoe'er thy classic poem, Knight, hath read
>
> . . .
>
> Must hail, with patriot joy, the approaching hour,
> When trammell'd nature shall again be free;
> Shall spurn the dull improver's pedant power,
> And burst luxuriant into liberty.
>
> . . .
>
> O liberty and nature, kindred powers,
> Shed on this favour'd isle your genial beams!
>
> (p. xiv)

After the Price-Knight-Repton debate, the controversy widened
even further. As Messmann has observed, readers saw Knight's
theory in particular as avowedly Jacobinistic. Anna Seward, for
example, wrote in a letter of 1794: "Knight's system appears to me
the Jacobinism of taste" (quoted in Messmann, p. 83). And Horace
Walpole wrote to William Mason in 1796: "I could make fifty other
objections to this pretended and ill-warranted dictator to all taste,
who Jacobinically would level the purity of gardens, would as ma-
lignantly as Tom Paine or Priestley guillotine Mr. Brown" (quoted
in Messmann, p. 83). When Knight then published *The Progress of
Civil Society* in 1796, the seeds of "liberty" planted in his picturesque
theory became even more visible, and the controversy it generated
—attached willy-nilly to Knight's whole corpus of works as well as
his personal principles—even more turbulent. As if it were merely

exfoliating the politics implicit in the final book of *The Landscape*, the final book of *Civil Society* ("Of Government and Conquest") argues the ideal of Whiggish revolution while carefully distinguishing it from the later stages of the French Revolution—from the ascendancy of Robespierre and the depredations at Lyons, for example (pp. 135, 136–38). The ideal revolution, Knight concludes in a note, would follow the course of liberalism in America rather than Jacobin France:

America having no great manufactories, had none of these mobs, and was therefore able to go through her revolution in peace. . . . I do not mean to undervalue the wisdom, virtue, and temperance of those who conducted the American revolution, or to apologize for the rashness, violence, and ambition of the leaders of the French; on the contrary, I think it probable, that, had the Duke of Orleans, La Fayette, and Mirabeau, been such men as Washington, Franklin, and Adams, France might have been now happy in a free constitution. (pp. 141–42n)

And in the poem itself, Knight concludes that parliamentary reform is necessary in Britain to avoid a native revolution:

> Yet happy Britain! ere it is too late,
> Shun the dire horrors, that thy rashness wait:
>
> . . .
>
> Dismiss the venal and the useless train,
> That waste thy vigour, and thy vitals drain;
> Shake off the leeches, that, at every pore,
> Empty thy veins, and fatten on thy gore.
>
> . . .
>
> For, come it will—the inevitable day,
> When Britain must corruption's forfeit pay,
> Beneath a despot's, or a rabble's sway.
>
> (pp. 143, 152)

The reaction to *Civil Society* was a condemnation of Knight's "Jacobinism" and general principles so strong that it became semi-official. Privately, for example, William Mason wrote to Walpole on March 15, 1796:

Your Lordship may perhaps recollect, that some years ago we differed in opinion about a Parliamentary reform, but I am convinced, that if an *Association* was now formed (much different from that of the present Whig Club) to petition the House of Commons to exclude, instead of rotten boroughs, men of such rotten principles as this writer's, we should both of us very cordially give it our signature. Whether the present author represents such a borough, or holds it in fee, I know not; but this I know, that his principles ought to be exposed before the next general election, that such honest freeholders, who detest the French Jacobins, may be led to make it a point of conscience not to vote for him. (Quoted in Messmann, p. 94)

Publicly, Knight's work suffered a semiofficial drubbing in the *Anti-Jacobin*, the government-backed journal started in 1797 to combat "JA-

COBINISM in all its shapes, and in all its degrees, political and moral, public and private" (quoted in Emsley, p. 65).[104] As Messmann notes, the *Anti-Jacobin* published a parody of *Civil Society* in 1798 with commentary and notes linking Knight to Paine, Priestley, and the French Encyclopedists as well as charging him with writing "against Order and Government" (quoted in Messmann, pp. 88–89).

The picturesque, in sum, was a political platform whose declaration of British constitutional freedom gravitated increasingly leftward in the period that most concerns us toward an idea of revolution cognate with the American or very early French Revolution. The lasting effect of such politicization, no matter a writer's final stance after the French Revolution, was that picturesque landscape became an almost automatic second language of politics. Indeed, efforts to rehabilitate the post-Waterloo landscape simply turned the vocabulary of Whiggish landscape to new purposes.[105] Reviewing the picturesque in his memoirs in 1824–25, for example, a Frenchman, L. P. Ségur, writes:

It has always . . . been a subject of surprize to me, that our government and statesmen, instead of reproaching as frivolous and foreign to the national spirit, that rage for English fashions, which suddenly sprung up throughout France, did not perceive in it the desire of another species of imitation, and the germs of a mighty revolution in the public mind. They were not in the least aware that, while we were destroying in our pleasure grounds, the straight walks and alleys, the symmetrical squares, the trees cut in circles and the uniform hedges, in order to transform them into English gardens, we were indicating our wishes to resemble that nation, in other and more essential points of nature and of reason. (Quoted in Wiebenson, p. 31n)

Or again, witness the passage from Wordsworth's second *Address to the Freeholders of Westmorland* (1818) that James K. Chandler has appropriately made an epigraph to his *Wordsworth's Second Nature*. Here, a conservative Wordsworth reclaims the land from liberalism:

You have heard of a Profession to which the luxury of modern times has given birth, that of Landscape-Gardeners, or Improvers of Pleasure-grounds. A competent Practitioner in this elegant art, begins by considering every object, that he finds in the place where he is called to exercise his skill, as having a right to remain, till the contrary be proved. . . . Modern Reformers reverse this judicious maxim. If a thing is before them, so far from deeming that it has on that account a claim to continue and be deliberately dealt with, its existence with them is a sufficient warrant for its destruction. Institutions are to be subverted, Practices radically altered, and Measures to be reversed. All men are to change their places, not because the men are objectionable, or the place is injurious, but because certain Pretenders are eager to be at work, being tired of both. (*Prose*, 3: 183–84)

For a moment, landscape becomes for Wordsworth no more than an elaborate figure—a sort of epic simile—for the too liberal reform of political institutions. If the simile seems particularly Burkean, and so suited to Chandler's main argument, this is because it resembles the simile in the *Reflections* that may well have originally influenced Repton to compare Price's and Knight's aesthetics to theoretical government. Just after a passage on "theoretic system" serving to preface his sustained excoriation of administrative innovations in France, Burke had imagined a counter-picturesque garden: "The French builders, clearing away as mere rubbish whatever they found, and, like their ornamental gardeners, forming every thing into an exact level, propose to rest the whole local and general legislature on three bases of three different kinds; one geometrical, one arithmetical, and the third financial" (p. 285).

Remember the congruence between the picturesque as landscape panorama and as social panopticon—between Wordsworth's "wheel" and his vision from the tower of Lancaster Castle. We might draw upon West here for a further, specifically political congruency. Stationing his reader atop Penrith Beacon much as Clarke would later, West in 1778 had pointed to a grand panorama of freedom:

The eye is in the center of a plane inclosed with a circle of stupendous mountains of various forms, and awful heights. The plane itself is adorned with many ancient towns, and more ancient castles, stations, and castellums, where the Roman eagle long displayed her wings; but in these more happy days is possessed by a happier people, who enjoy, with freedom, their pleasant seats, and charming mansions, that meet the eye which ever way the head is turned, marked with all the refinements of liberal taste, and flourishing industry. (p. 180)

The great "wheel" of picturesque landscape turns out to be a fully economic, social, and political arena. As we might see in West's remembrance of Roman times, "freedom" was a regime liberated from, but also precisely mappable over, ancient discipline. It was a disciplined freedom or freed discipline—a state of repose one with the ideological norm Repton called the happy medium and that at the time of *An Evening Walk* was left, but not *too* left, of center.

As our valediction to the picturesque, one final epic simile or comparison of our own would not be out of place. It is not stretching the imagination, I believe, to look through West's panorama, through Clarke's or Wordsworth's wheels, through even Bentham's Panopticon to see the picturesque planted at last in an updated version of the arena of freedom and ancient discipline we have visited before: the Champ-de-Mars amphitheater. At the center of this great commonplace of the early Revolution, we saw in Chapter 1, stood an ark of institutional change: the altar where on July 14, 1790, old ceremonies of communion became new ceremonies of fraternity. In the 1794 Fete of the Supreme Being and Nature, this altar would be reshaped into the "natural." It became the very type of the picturesque: a mountain

PLATE 15. *View of the Mountain Erected in the Champ de la Réunion* (previously the Champ-de-Mars), anonymous engraving. Musée Carnavalet, Paris. Photo: Bulloz.

(Pl. 15), as Ozouf has noticed, modeled after Claude's *Sermon on the Mount* (Pl. 16).[106]

Thus is our journey of institutions from religion to the politics of landscape, from Claude to the picturesque, complete.

Toward the Indescribable

Detour 2: The Locodescriptive Moment

It is still only noon in our reading of *An Evening Walk*, of course. Yet it is not necessary to look farther than noon to locate Wordsworth's evening. The cascade at Rydal Lower Falls, we remember, "illumes with sparkling foam the twilight shade." Similarly, Gilpin ends his view of the Falls by adding a touch of dusk: "In every representation, truly picturesque, the shade should greatly overbalance the light. The face of nature, under the glow of noon, has rarely this beautiful appearance. The artist therefore generally courts her charms in a morning, or an evening hour, when the shadows are deep, and

PLATE 16. Claude Lorrain, *Sermon on the Mount*, 1656. Copyright the Frick Collection, New York. Photo: Frick Collection.

extended; and when the sloping sun-beam affords rather a catching, than a glaring light" (*Lakes*, 1: 162–63). The picturesque is shaded so variously that chiaroscuro is the anticipation of evening no matter the time of day. Subsequent description in *An Evening Walk* can thus generate evening simply by repeating noon with greater variety. Characteristically, each framed vignette in the poem thus moves through "various" description to a repose much like that at Rydal Lower Falls. Witness, for example, the atmospheric serenity of smoke that finishes this scene of twilight variety:

> How pleasant, as the yellowing sun declines,
> And with long rays and shades the landscape shines;
> To mark the birches' stems all golden light,
> That lit the dark slant woods with silvery white!
> The willows, weeping trees, that twinkling hoar,
> Glanc'd oft upturn'd along the breezy shore,
> Low bending o'er the colour'd water, fold
> Their moveless boughs and leaves like threads of gold;
> The skiffs with naked masts at anchor laid,
> Before the boat-house peeping thro' the shade;
> Th' unwearied glance of woodman's echo'd stroke;
> And curling from the trees the cottage smoke.
>
> (ll. 97–108)

How can noon then continue into full darkness? The answer sounds already in the "woodman's echo'd stroke." As Hartman has noticed (*WP*, p. 97), night in *An Evening Walk* is the noon of ear, an organ traditionally attuned in picturesque literature to atmospheric echoes and other varieties of sound.[107] Wordsworth can thus later recapitulate Rydal Lower Falls in another cascade view ending in pure sound—a song, a chime, and then a deep repose measured in felt percussions:

> Their pannier'd train a groupe of potters goad,
> Winding from side to side up the steep road;
> The peasant from yon cliff of fearful edge
> Shot, down the headlong pathway darts his sledge;
> Bright beams the lonely mountain horse illume,
> Feeding 'mid purple heath, "green rings," and broom;
> While the sharp slope the slacken'd team confounds,
> Downward the pond'rous timber-wain resounds;
> Beside their sheltering cross of wall, the flock
> Feeds on in light, nor thinks of winter's shock;
> In foamy breaks the rill, with merry song,
> Dash'd down the rough rock, lightly leaps along,
> From lonesome chapel at the mountain's feet,
> Three humble bells their rustic chime repeat;
> Sounds from the water-side the hammer'd boat:
> And blasted quarry thunders heard remote.
>
> (ll. 109–24)

Thus, while I have focused on the opening description in *An Evening Walk*, in fact this description sketches the whole picture gallery of the poem. Or rather, it sketches all except certain crucial anomalies. I have explored so far the possibilities of the picturesque—what it can imagine. It can imagine a state of property, social administration, and politics designed to forget older religious institutions and so project a new, carefully reposed discipline of freedom cognate with the early Revolution. Now I make a final detour to explore the impossibilities of the picturesque—what it *cannot* imagine.

A hypothesis: commitment to a particular kind of freedom as the fact of British identity—its very nature—requires that other kinds of freedom become unimaginable except as unnatural fiction. And a deduction: the sign of such a blind spot in the picturesque must be its inability to assimilate certain anomalous forms into the formal integrity of the whole except across a rift of increasingly strained figuration—of ever more extravagant versions of the epic similes of picturesque tradition that at times simply mask the alternative reality but that at other times, when the alternative is too insistent, overcompensate, call attention to themselves, and otherwise disrupt the norm of descriptive fact. Thus, to invoke the visual analogue of a well-

PLATE 17. Richard Wilson, *The Destruction of Niobe's Children*, 1760. Yale Center for British Art, Paul Mellon Collection, New Haven. Photo: Yale Center for British Art.

known painting of the period in which the picturesque submits to the sublime: Apollo appears in Wilson's *The Destruction of Niobe's Children* perched atop a cloud, a use of "atmosphere" for the purpose of propping up a secondary mythological narrative amid Wilson's primary description of landscape (Pl. 17). As we previously saw, Reynolds viewed the figures in this painting as out of place. In our present context, it is noteworthy that he also saw them as wildly unbelievable. They were figurations:

In the picture alluded to, the first idea that presents itself, is that of wonder, at seeing a figure in so uncommon a situation as that in which the Apollo is placed; for the clouds on which he kneels, have not the appearance of being able to support him; they have neither the substance nor the form, fit for the receptacle of a human figure. . . . It appears to me, that such conduct is no less absurd than if a plain man, giving a relation of a real distress, occasioned by an inundation accompanied with thunder and lightning, should, instead of simply relating the event, take it into his head, in order to give a grace to his narration, to talk of Jupiter Pluvius, or Jupiter and his thunder-bolts, or any other figurative idea. (p. 256)

What refuses to fit formally into *An Evening Walk* except through such disruptive figuration? What, in other words, is indescribable?

To begin with, there is the outsize anomaly at the center of the poem: Wordsworth's abrupt swerve back to the *narrativity* underlying picturesque description. Suddenly, *An Evening Walk* wishes to tell incipient stories of desire and violence excessive of picturesque arrest—stories that threaten to reveal beneath the surface of repose an older reality of narrative catastrophe. I refer to the epyllia of the swans (ll. 191–240) and the Female Beggar (ll. 241–300), characters whose full-scale treatment stands out strikingly in a poem where other entities are fortunate to deserve a single verse.[108]

To understand the effect of this anomaly on the descriptive norm, it will be useful to bring into play the crucial rift between picturesque tradition and locodescriptive poetry proper (together with the close affiliate of eighteenth-century georgic). In locodescription and georgic, of course, a sudden recitation of narrative catastrophe amid descriptive perfection was not anomalous. In such striking, Ovidean stories as the Lodona epyllion in Pope's "Windsor-Forest" (ll. 171–218) or the Celadon and Amelia epyllion in Thomson's *Seasons* ("Summer," ll. 1169–1222), locodescription had always exploited the descent of description from metamorphic narration, from the full Ovidean panic of desire and violence, only the tranquil close of which Claude communicated to the picturesque as repose.

Or more precisely, if the interpolation of self-contained narratives within description necessarily prompted some sense of anomaly, locodescription exploited this sense by building it into its fabric as what I will call the locodescriptive "moment." By this I mean that it demarcated and organized the describable universe around certain specially charged moments functioning in a terminal or liminal manner (something like the Terms of Hymen, we might imagine, once used to mark boundaries). Posted at the transitions between passages of description and of narrative (including the many stray meditations, panegyrics, and historical synopses that locodescription rendered in condensed story form), such moments embodied in their strangely resonant, "trembling," or otherwise supremely sensitized stasis the uncanny interface between the general orders of narrative and description: between motion and stasis, action and variation, reversal and chiaroscuro, development and recession, character and species (as in Narcisuss become narcissus), and so forth. Each expressed subliminally, that is, the incommensurability at once dividing and relating the protocols of good story and of good descriptive form.

With Lévi-Strauss's discussion of Aranda churingas in mind (*Savage Mind*, pp. 237–44), we might say that these transitional moments registered the narrative genealogy of descriptive space creative of the existing organization of that space. In every liminal moment we come upon a totem that has been secreted in a power spot to remind us that ordered landscape—when approached, descried, and interpreted in a certain way—is in itself a testament to the story of how things fell out in the beginning. And the result of being so reminded is salutary to description itself, lending the whole scene a nervous energy—as if the creation story had not quite done, and the earth could still move.

By locodescriptive moment, in short, I mean those antithetical moments marking the bounds of descriptive scenes when a residual feeling for narration daemonizes description even as description contains the chthonic spirit and smooths over the metamorphic ground once more. Thus in "Windsor-Forest," for example, the episode of Lodona chased by Pan and changed into a stream closes in a passage of renewed description at once imperturbably removed from, and tremblingly alive to, the story of watery metamorphosis:

> Oft in her Glass the musing Shepherd spies
> The headlong Mountains and the downward Skies,
> The watry Landskip of the pendant Woods,
> And absent Trees that tremble in the Floods;
> In the clear azure Gleam the Flocks are seen,
> And floating Forests paint the Waves with Green.
> Thro' the fair Scene rowl slow the lingring Streams,
> Then foaming pour along, and rush into the *Thames*.
>
> (ll. 211–18)

This is a clear antecedent of the mirror-like repose figured in the similes of picturesque literature, but with the difference that the story of Panic in the background is still visible. The trembling imagery of the waters recalls Lodona like a "trembling" dove pursued by the eagle (l. 188); and the very pace of the scene, finishing upon the stream's sudden rush to the Thames, recapitulates the movement of the previous story to its breathless climax (see esp. ll. 185–96).

Similarly, Thomson's Celadon and Amelia episode—which Averill has discussed in relation to Wordsworth's Female Beggar (pp. 63–65) —leads to a powerful locodescriptive moment. Narrative closure in the episode arrives just after Amelia has been struck dead by lightning, when Thomson likens the speechless Celadon to statuary on a tomb ("Summer," ll. 1220–22). A transitional passage much like Pope's then follows: Thomson reemerges into a new, washed world of description in which repose subsumes Celadon's frozen pose. First, as Averill observes, thunderstorm changes into heightened atmospheric calm ("Summer," ll. 1223–43).[109] Then, in one of the most strangely effective passages in the poem, atmospheric calm precipitates a pool of repose:

> Cheered by the milder beam, the sprightly youth
> Speeds to the well-known pool, whose crystal depth

> A sandy bottom shows. Awhile he stands
> Gazing the inverted landscape, half afraid
> To meditate the blue profound below;
> Then plunges headlong down the circling flood.
>   (Thomson, "Summer," ll. 1244–49)

Here is the locodescriptive moment. What is remarkable about this pool is its edginess, as we can call it:[110] the liminal fear and trembling (akin to Pope's literal trembling) that attends what the Argument to "Summer" simply names "bathing." Viewed one way, the pool is a mirror with the best picturesque polish; yet seen at a different angle of incidence—of refraction *through* the descriptive medium rather than reflection upon it—the pool shows landscape poised on the edge of submerged narrative. When Thomson's youth pauses "half afraid / To meditate the blue profound below," we seem to see in the profundity not only the "Mysterious Heaven" ("Summer," l. 1215) that has just blasted Amelia but also perhaps a whole hall of mirrors in the narrative background: the "downward Skies" upon which Pope's shepherd muses, the pooled heaven into which Milton's Eve looks upon waking, and, of course, the pool of Narcissus that Milton himself echoes. We sense, that is, a subliminal element in the discourse excessive of description: as when lightning flashes, a retinal image overlays the scene even as we look away.

In *An Evening Walk*, the epyllia of the swans and Beggar lead precisely to such a locodescriptive moment or, rather, series of such moments. Indeed, since we can guess with some security from Wordsworth's reading at Cambridge and his note to "Summer" in *An Evening Walk*, l. 173, that he knew the Celadon and Amelia episode well (he also later remarked upon the popularity of Thomson's stories generally), Thomson's pool may be considered a direct precedent.[111] Borne upon a wave of the poet's love ("I love beside the glowing lake to stray," l. 195) and set within an eroticized, rococo topography ("rills that . . . run in transport to the dimpling deeps," ll. 197–98), the swans perform Wordsworth's great story of desire. They are his version of Celadon and Amelia before the lightning strike or of Thomson's Damon and Musidora (the lovers in the eroticized epyllion in "Summer" immediately after the bathing scene). First there is the Jovian splendor of the male swan, who like some epic or operatic hero "swells his lifted chest, and backward flings / His bridling neck between his tow'ring wings" (ll. 201–2). Then there is the Ledaean beauty of the female surrounded by "tender Cares," "mild domestic Loves," and putti-like cygnets "playing wanton with the floating grass" (ll. 207–12). All the elements for a love story ending in domestic bliss are in place—the same elements, we will see in Chapter 5, that come of age in more developed form in the story of the Female Vagrant in *Salisbury Plain* (where in one of the most elaborate and *outré* epic similes Wordsworth ever conceived the Vagrant's breasts rise like "twin swans").

Of course, when seen through the fabular and mythological haze that surrounds the swans, the story of desire in *An Evening Walk* is still circumscribed. It is held in check by an ornamental air making the swans akin to porcelain figurines: too pretty, too brittle to bear the stress of full narrative development. Even so, the epyllion drifts toward such development in a manner that begins to create a reality entirely separate from the descriptive universe. First, the very preciosity of the episode opens up its own space of reality. Wordsworth witnesses the "affection sweet" of the mother swan as she lets her young climb her back and nestle under her wings; then he feels compelled to add a footnote documenting the truth of what would otherwise be too contrived or precious an observation: "This is a fact of which I have been an eye-witness" (l. 217n). Since the poem as a whole rests on the premise of eyewitness veracity, this declaration has a strange truth-status threatening all the poem's figure-ground relations: the ground that has been the poem's descriptive norm becomes for a moment insubstantial ornament, while the ornament or digression of the epyllion, which now defines a hyperrealistic norm of veracity, becomes ground.

A preliminary version of the locodescriptive moment then arrives, indicating that the extra-descriptive ground thus limned is fully narrative. Painting a scene much like Thomson's pool, Wordsworth addresses a coda to the swans:

> Yon tuft conceals your home, your cottage bow'r,
> Fresh water rushes strew the verdant floor;
> Long grass and willows form the woven wall,
> And swings above the roof the poplar tall.
> Thence issuing oft, unwieldy as ye stalk,
> Ye crush with broad black feet your flow'ry walk;
> Safe from your door ye hear at breezy morn,
> The hound, the horse's tread, and mellow horn;
> At peace inverted, your lithe necks ye lave,
> With the green bottom strewing o'er the wave;
> No ruder sound your desart haunts invades,
> Than waters dashing wild, or rocking shades.
> Ye ne'er, like hapless human wanderers, throw
> Your young on winter's winding sheet of snow.
>
> (ll. 227–40)

Like Thomson's youth bathing himself in the "inverted landscape" of a pool, the swans laving their inverted necks poise in perfect repose. Yet even more so than in Thomson, the scene of watery repose suddenly and unmistakably reveals the refracted shape of narrative— glimpsed in this case in a complex perspective allowing the present scene to be haunted by future story. An edginess, as I earlier termed it, enters the scene via negation: "No ruder sound your desart haunts invades," the poet says, leaving us wondering what sound he expects. Next, the negative expectation strengthens: "Ye ne'er, like hapless human wanderers, throw / Your young on winter's winding sheet of snow." These lines have no place in the description of the swans' place. They cue us instead to the fact that we now reach the ground the epyllion has been struggling to reach all along: not hyperrealism so much as the narrative—and, specifically, tragic—realism of the Female Beggar story waiting in the wings. In a manner foreign to description—no one scene of which really bears any responsibility for developing the next or, again, no part of which acts the chorus for another—the swans are a subplot counterpointing the Beggar's main action. Conflating the two sets of characters in an Ovidian manner, indeed, we can say that the swans essentially *metamorphose* into the Beggar.

A clear predecessor of the Female Vagrant in *Salisbury Plain*, the Female Beggar performs the poem's great story of desire metamorphosed into violence. Not only does she wistfully desire "her soldier . . . her woes to share" (l. 253), but she radiates desire and fulfilled love all around her in the form of affection for her children. Bringing smiles to her crying infants by pointing out a shooting star or glowworm (ll. 257–60, 274–78), she seems the perfect successor to the mother swan with her little loves. Yet from the start, of course, desire is starcrossed. For just a moment, an uncharacteristically topical reference enters the scene with the same effect as the footnote to the swans: the Beggar's desire encounters violence at "Bunker's charnel hill," where her soldier died (l. 254). *Here*, we are suddenly told, is the real truth of her plight. (In the 1794 revision of the poem, indeed, the urge toward extra-descriptive truth at this point generates a whole second family of vagrants anchored, in a footnote, upon "the catastrophe of a poor woman . . . found dead on Stanemoor"; *PW*, 1: 28–29n; see Averill, pp. 65–66.)[112]

This touch of extra-descriptive realism lays the ground for the full story of the Beggar, whose destitution requires that desire submit inexorably to violence. Beaten "by summer's breathless ray" and "shot stinging through her . . . bones" by the sun's "arrowy fire" (ll. 243–46), the Beggar wanders a landscape of violence recapitulating Thomson's "Summer." Indeed, she comes at last to a climactic tempest (though a colder one) akin to that of the Celadon and Amelia episode. Melodrama now creates such an air of unreality (by descriptive standards) that unreality asserts itself as something like a new self-consistent reality: the universe is all a story. I refer to the macabre death scene that readers have perennially derided as grotesque, lurid, and morbid (see, for example, Jacobus, *Tradition*, p. 136; Averill, p. 63). Where the Beggar once desired her soldier on his charnel hill, now—in one of Wordsworth's most Sadean moments—she lusts for the kiss of Death:

> Death, as she turns her neck the kiss to seek,
> Breaks off the dreadful kiss with angry shriek.
> Snatch'd from her shoulder with despairing moan,
> She clasps them [her children] at that dim-seen roofless stone.—
> "Now ruthless Tempest launch thy deadliest dart!
> Fall fires—but let us perish heart to heart."   (ll. 287–92)

Death is so vividly personified that it becomes a fully allegorical personification in the eighteenth-century manner Chester F. Chapin has studied—a quasi-narrative character poised to usher in a morality play or some other narrative of violence. "Deadliest dart," after all, invokes the "dreadful Dart" of Milton's Death; and the Beggar's command to the tempest, "Fall fires," similarly recalls Lear on the heath shouting, "Blow, winds . . . Spit, fire! Spout, Rain!" (III.ii.1–14). The paradise lost of the landscape poises on the brink of revealing whole epics and tragedies. Reality is now the universe of story.

It is at this point that the quintessential locodescriptive moment arrives. At the fatal close of the Beggar's story, we reemerge into description in a sustained passage at once supremely reposed and full of hidden disturbance:

> Sweet are the sounds that mingle from afar,
> Heard by calm lakes, as peeps the folding star,
> Where the duck dabbles mid the rustling sedge,
> And feeding pike starts from the water's edge,
> Or the swan stirs the reeds, his neck and bill
> Wetting, that drip upon the water still;
> And heron, as resounds the trodden shore,
> Shoots upward, darting his long neck before.
> While, by the scene compos'd, the breast subsides,
> Nought wakens or disturbs it's tranquil tides;
> Nought but the char that for the may-fly leaps,
> And breaks the mirror of the circling deeps;
> Or clock, that blind against the wanderer born
> Drops at his feet, and stills his droning horn.
> —The whistling swain that plods his ringing way
> Where the slow waggon winds along the bay;
> The sugh of swallow flocks that twittering sweep,
> The solemn curfew swinging long and deep;
> The talking boat that moves with pensive sound,
> Or drops his anchor down with plunge profound;
> Of boys that bathe remote the faint uproar,
> And restless piper wearying out the shore;
> These all to swell the village murmurs blend,

That soften'd from the water-head descend.
While in sweet cadence rising small and still
The far-off minstrels of the haunted hill,
As the last bleating of the fold expires,
Tune in the mountain dells their water lyres.

(ll. 301–28)

Placed anywhere else in the poem, this passage would simply be another pastiche of calm. But at its present location, it is also supremely edgy with remembered terror. We can read the passage in three movements—the first two touching the surface of repose with tremblings, and the last restoring the full descriptive norm.

To begin with, we notice that the initial sentence of the passage is at once unremarkable in its evocation of peace—of sweet sounds, calm lakes, peeping stars, and feeding fish and waterfowl—and shocking. Such impact derives not from what the sentence includes but from what it leaves out: *any* softening or even notice of the contrast—like a jagged edge—between present tranquillity and the catastrophe of the Beggar that has just concluded in the previous lines. Averill's reading of this sentence is perceptive: "Without editorial upon the tale, or transition to the narrative present, the description of the frozen family ends, and the poet returns to an evening lakeside whose natural tranquillity is made more pronounced, eerie, and moving by the frantic human struggle that has preceded it" (pp. 62–63). Thus, what are we to make of sweet sounds and calm lakes juxtaposed with the death cries and "flooded cheek" (l. 296) of the crying Beggar? Moreover, how can we peep at the "folding star" without remembering the shooting star the Beggar has just pointed out to her children (l. 260)? And most of all, what is the effect of the swan redux here? There is now no such thing, after all, as an innocent swan. As in the case of any Ovidian laurel or nightingale, there are only swans implicated in the story of desire become violence. What fills the whole scene with tension, in sum, is a contrast between epyllion and resurgent description that far exceeds the convention of picturesque chiaroscuro or variety: black and white do not so much distribute the canvas as struggle for dominance. Like the pike starting from the water's edge (or, in *The Prelude*, a drowned man shooting bolt upright from the depths), the catastrophe of the Beggar is always threatening to emerge through the surface of repose.[113]

The second sentence of the passage then repeats in fainter echoes the tense repose of the first. We remember the negations that in the coda to the swans foreshadowed tragedy. Just so, an overpressure of negation now simultaneously confirms the mirror-like repose of the scene and engages in something like a descriptive *occupatio* listing all that breaks the mirror: "Nought wakens or disturbs" the breast's "tranquil tides," Wordsworth says, "Nought but the char that for the may-fly leaps, / And breaks the mirror of the circling deeps" and, again, nought but the "clock" that suddenly strikes the wanderer. It is instructive to set these verses beside the clear antecedent of Gray's "Elegy Written in a Country Churchyard":

> Now fades the glimmering landscape on the sight,
> And all the air a solemn stillness holds,
> Save where the beetle wheels his droning flight,
> And drowsy tinklings lull the distant folds;
>
> Save that from yonder ivy-mantled tower
> The moping owl does to the moon complain
> Of such as, wandering near her secret bower,
> Molest her ancient solitary reign.   (ll. 5–12)

As Roger Lonsdale notes about this passage, the "silence . . . save where" formula had become a convention in descriptions of evening by the 1740's, with such parallels as Warton, Akenside, and Collins (Lonsdale, pp. 118–19n). As such, the formula is perhaps the quintessential rhetoric of what I have called the locodescriptive moment: it is the overfull negation that marks the descriptive surface with intimations of what is not on the surface. Buried beneath repose, Wordsworth's tragedy of the Beggar is much like the "short and simple annals of the poor" underlying graveyard poetry (Gray, "Elegy," l. 32). It is muteness that makes the abundance of present description so expressive.

Only in the third movement of Wordsworth's passage—cued by the "whistling swain"—does the descriptive surface recover fully enough to bury narrative wholly out of sight. A new vista of description opens in which locodescription once more coincides with the picturesque: it forgets narrative in pure atmosphere. Thus while we might be tempted to see in the anchor that drops with "plunge profound" and the "boys that bathe" some half-memory of Thomson's bathing youth about to plunge into the profound, or, again, while we might almost hear in the continued echo of Gray (tolling in the curfew) some half-memory of elegiac death, we know realistically—that is, in the newly restored climate of descriptive rather than narrative realism—that even latent reminders of tragedy have faded entirely to leave only an elegiac atmosphere: a long perspective of slow, solemn, long, deep, pensive, profound, remote, small, still, and far-off repose.

An Evening Walk, in sum, is interrupted by a narrative that leaves the descriptive universe trembling momentarily in the manner of locodescription; and only at the furthest bounds of this instability does the poem recover a composure making locodescription indistinguishable from the picturesque. The indescribable, it thus seems, becomes describable once more.

One further maneuver in the poem then seems to seal the case: the invention of a gigantic epic simile that recapitulates the liminality of the poem's previous locodescriptive moment only to contain or make safe that liminality. Again, the descriptive universe trembles with the hidden urgency of story—with stories, indeed, invoked by clear allusion. But now all the stories are absolute pieces of fiction, mere figures of speech:

> Now with religious awe the farewel light
> Blends with the solemn colouring of the night;
> Mid groves of clouds that crest the mountain's brow,
> And round the West's proud lodge their shadows throw,
> Like Una shining on her gloomy way,
> The half seen form of Twilight roams astray;
> Thence, from three paly loopholes mild and small,
> Slow lights upon the lake's still bosom fall,
> Beyond the mountain's giant reach that hides
> In deep determin'd gloom his subject tides.
> —Mid the dark steeps repose the shadowy streams,
> As touch'd with dawning moonlight's hoary gleams,
> Long streaks of fairy light the wave illume
> With bordering lines of intervening gloom,
> Soft o'er the surface creep the lustres pale
> Tracking with silvering path the changeful gale.
> —'Tis restless magic all; at once the bright
> Breaks on the shade, the shade upon the light,
> Fair Spirits are abroad; in sportive chase
> Brushing with lucid wands the water's face,
> While music stealing round the glimmering deeps
> Charms the tall circle of th' enchanted steeps.
>
> (ll. 329–50)

This is a fairy tale, a romance of description that sublimes all the earlier stories of desire and violence into quaintness. If narrativity still haunts the scene, it does so only in the form of obvious allegory: in Wordsworth's version of Apollo propped up on a cloud, an antique and stylized personification of Twilight moves as in a Spenserian dream.

Now we know how to make sense of the epic similes we have encountered throughout the literature of the picturesque. Such similes are isolated versions of Wordsworth's Spenserian passage so protective of descriptive reality that they forget all reference to an "epic" in the background—to any story drawn from the past or present that could seriously threaten description with an alternative reality. Or again, when the similes do have a specific catastrophe in mind (often, as we saw, a historical one), they keep it so cloudily enwrapped in an atmosphere of pure figure—to use the language of the prefatory

Letter to *The Faerie Queene*—that the "realism" of the action is finally as incredible and adventitious as any of the ostentatious footnotes in Knight's *Landscape*. As our discussion of the political controversy surrounding Price and Knight showed, such similes must be read outside the frame of the work itself to become significant. Epic similes are thus a preemptive strategy: within the frame of the work itself is only a faeryland hollowing out the locodescriptive moment—with its equipollent realities of narrative and description—by occupying the trembling space of that moment with insubstantiality. Instead of a metamorphosis layering story into landscape, there is only empty metaphor.

Such, perhaps, is the ultimate sublimation of the essential negativity we saw in the locodescriptive moment—of the "nought but" or "save where" that utters the appearance/disappearance of story in landscape. "Charming" figuration is a kind of nix, a too-compulsive effort to charm away the daemonization of description by old narratives in the background. The picturesque returns to the oldest of pictorial instincts associated with cave-wall pictographs: the prophylactic impulse to ward off evil or gain good. Nix to tragedy, it says, looking away from the evil eye into its Claude glass of repose.[114]

But for Wordsworth the nix does not work. If earlier I said that the indescribable in *An Evening Walk*, it seems, becomes describable once more, the operative word—I now add with Spenserian intonation—is "seems." As in the case of Wilson's Apollo (as viewed by Reynolds), Wordsworth's epic simile is in the end self-canceling. What is called up so elaborately by the wave of an enchanter's wand can just as easily be waved away. After all, in Spenser's work itself stories never really die; they only pass *through* charmed fictions into uncanny repetitions.

The End of Repose

There are thus two further anomalies or instances of the indescribable in the poem. First, in a passage Hartman has also underscored (*WP*, pp. 97–98), the edge of true night comes upon the poet with all its edginess restored. Indeed, it does so immediately after the Spenserian moment at twilight (and its brief recapitulation in the passage on the halted milkmaid and "Genii" of the scene, ll. 351–58) as if the fiction had never been. Vanishing in an explosive release of negation fulfilling the dark promise of the "nought but" formulations we heard earlier, the Spenserian figuration ushers in a darkness visible of the indescribable. I abbreviate the long sequence:

> —The pomp is fled, and mute the wondrous strains,
> No wrack of all the pageant scene remains,
> So vanish those fair Shadows, human Joys,

But Death alone their vain regret destroys.
Unheeded Night has overcome the vales,
On the dark earth the baffl'd vision fails,
If peep between the clouds a star on high,
There turns for glad repose the weary eye;

　　　.　.　.

Last evening sight, the cottage smoke no more,
Lost in the deepen'd darkness, glimmers hoar;

　　　.　.　.

Nought else of man or life remains behind
To call from other worlds the wilder'd mind,

　　　.　.　.

—No purple prospects now the mind employ
Glowing in golden sunset tints of joy,

　　　.　.　.

Stay! pensive, sadly-pleasing visions, stay!
Ah no! as fades the vale, they fade away.
Yet still the tender, vacant gloom remains,
Still the cold cheek its shuddering tear retains.

　　　.　.　.

　　Now o'er the eastern hill, where Darkness broods
O'er all its vanish'd dells, and lawns, and woods;
Where but a mass of shade the sight can trace,
[The moon] lifts in silence up her lovely face;
Above the gloomy valley flings her light,
Far to the western slopes with hamlets white;
And gives, where woods the checquer'd upland strew,
To the green corn of summer autumn's hue.
　　Thus Hope, first pouring from her blessed horn
Her dawn, far lovelier than the Moon's own morn;
'Till higher mounted, strives in vain to chear
The weary hills, impervious, black'ning near;
—Yet does she still, undaunted, throw the while
On darling spots remote her tempting smile.
　　—Ev'n now she decks for me a distant scene. . . .

　　　　　　　　(ll. 359–413)

Here at the antipodes of noon just after full dark (and before the rising moon and sounds of night can restore the descriptive ground), there emerges an "other world" phrased as pure antithesis: "No wrack of all the pageant scene," "no more" cottage smoke, "Nought else of man or life," "No purple prospects," "Ah no!" Motifs cease. And without descriptive motifs providing "glad repose" for the "weary eye," the narrative motives that lurk within the picturesque begin to escape arrest once more. "No" negates desire ("human Joys") so strongly that it hints the resumption of terminal violence: "Death alone . . . vain regret destroys." Here, we might expect, is where the story of the Female Beggar belongs.

Indeed, something very like a beggar's story begins. We notice that an obvious figuration or epic simile intervenes at the end of the process of negation to compare the moon to Hope: "Thus Hope, first pouring from her blessed horn," the poet begins. But now figuration is transitive rather than intransitive. Instead of halting the development of fatal story, as in the case of the Spenserian passage, it transmits such development to the implied opening of a new story—the life story of the poet himself, or what Hartman calls the "drama" of the poet's "mind" facing the coming of night and the erasure of landscape (*WP*, p. 94). "Ev'n now [Moon/Hope] decks for me a distant scene," the poet says, opening the pseudo-autobiographical passage that then follows:

> (For dark and broad the gulph of time between)
> Gilding that cottage with her fondest ray,
> (Sole bourn, sole wish, sole object of my way;
> How fair it's lawns and silvery woods appear!
> How sweet it's streamlet murmurs in mine ear!)
> Where we, my friend, to golden days shall rise,
> 'Till our small share of hardly-paining sighs
> (For sighs will ever trouble human breath)
> Creep hush'd into the tranquil breast of Death.
>   (ll. 414–22)

Seeking shelter and finding death, this is the poet turned Beggar. The "I" who utters in Wordsworth's early verse, of course, is not yet distinguished from the musing or melancholy personae of loco-descriptive convention; it is certainly not the theorized self and mind of the later poetry. Yet Hartman is right to stress the as yet undeveloped encounter of consciousness with "other worlds" (*WP*, p. 98) that brings *An Evening Walk* to the point of incipient autobiography. If the picturesque successfully arrests the stories of the swans and Beggar, it nevertheless ends by calling beyond description for *some* story—even if it must be the poet's own—able to carry the drama of desire and death to its conclusion. It is the poet who desires (for a cottage of paradise); and it is the poet who foresees "the tranquil breast of Death." Eros coupled with Thanatos, we are now told, has been the "sole bourn, sole wish, sole object" of his descriptive way.

Like Stevens's "death . . . the mother of beauty" in "Sunday Morning," the "tranquil breast of Death" here is a kind of repose. But it is also the end of repose. We have only to dream a little, to paraphrase Stevens, to feel the dark encroachment of some old catastrophe. The tranquillity of death Wordsworth envisions seems to call for a new scene able to supply the particular referent for the "sole bourn, sole wish, sole object" that is his motive. What are the circumstances of this poet, after all, and why does he seek the distant cottage? Is the cottage literal or figurative? These questions cannot be answered in description; they look through the darkened aperture of the "no's" in landscape to indescribable other worlds.

The famous vignette that then ends the poem captures precisely the reposed, but also indescribably disturbed, air I signal:

> The song of mountain streams unheard by day,
> Now hardly heard, beguiles my homeward way.
> All air is, as the sleeping water, still,
> List'ning th' aërial music of the hill,
> Broke only by the slow clock tolling deep,
> Or shout that wakes the ferry-man from sleep,
> Soon follow'd by his hollow-parting oar,
> And echo'd hoof approaching the far shore;
> Sound of clos'd gate, across the water born,
> Hurrying the feeding hare thro' rustling corn;
> The tremulous sob of the complaining owl;
> And at long intervals the mill-dog's howl;
> The distant forge's swinging thump profound;
> Or yell in the deep woods of lonely hound.
>
> (ll. 433–46)

Here is repose as peaceful as any Rest on the Flight into Egypt. Yet we must remember the old catastrophe that motivated Flight in the first place. What gives this passage its strange fascination is its two-edged power: either this is refuge found, or it is a kind of panic. We might remember the "atmosphere" of Panic that touches the back of Lodona's neck in Pope's tale:

> Now fainting, sinking, pale, the Nymph appears;
> Now close behind [Pan's] sounding Steps she hears;
> And now his Shadow reach'd her as she run,
> (His Shadow lengthen'd by the setting Sun)
> And now his shorter Breath with sultry Air
> Pants on her Neck, and fans her parting Hair.
>
> (ll. 191–96)

Just such a bump in the night touches us at Wordsworth's conclusion. In the atmosphere evoked by a sudden shout, echoing of hooves, closing gate, rustling hare, sobbing owl, thumping forge, and howling or yelling dog, there is more than just repose. *Something* is happening in the night even if we cannot quite remember what it is. Something raises the hair on the back of our necks.

In *An Evening Walk*, in sum, nascent stories exert such a torsion upon the picturesque canvas that the craquelure—the cracks in the paint[115]—widens to show traces of the *istoria* underlying all description. Or rather, what shows through the cracks is at last not so much any particular narrative as the generative basis of narrative. Considered together, we recognize, the episodes of the swans and the Beggar compose a fragmented and contradictory story that is really an abstract of all possible stories: the first episode is an idyll of desire commencing, in essence, "once upon a time," and the second is a catastrophe finishing the idyll upon the antithesis of "happily ever after." Beginning and end, white and black, life and death: these are antagonistic binaries sketching the basic structure or synchronic design of narrative. The structure (as we will see in more detail later) is *agony*, or agonic conflict. And if such agony in *An Evening Walk* cannot wholly break through the air of fictionality subordinating it to description—and if, furthermore, the successor agony that is the poet's own life story cannot yet be developed—this is because agon is still void of the complementary structures necessary to express it as the credible movement of arrested motif: plot.

Finally, therefore, we should notice one other indescribability in *An Evening Walk* associated with plot and implicit in what I have called the locodescriptive "moment" with its memory of past stories: the intimation of time. Time, as we will go on to see, is a modernization of "fate" or the "gods" that names—and justifies—all the plot structures enabling entelechial process. In general, as Robert Con Davis points out, the picturesque allowed for a kind of time by posing busy foregrounds against eternal backgrounds (p. 47); and Price and Knight accommodated a version of time as well in their love of accidental decay and old objects (see, for example, Price, *Essays*, 1: 51; see M. Price, p. 285). But on the whole, Wordsworth's description in *An Evening Walk* elides time by locking all parts of landscape into a single schedule. Objects move "in time" only in the sense of marching in step. Almost unbearably stative, syntax in the poem thus bunches phenomena into a massive rather than a linear reading experience. Suspended in the "when's" of noon, for example, hill and cloud, lake and park, deer and horses, boys and swain all appear in a simultaneous tapestry view.[116] Similarly, the present tense in the poem bunches all phenomena into a primitive "now" incapable of poising itself against either past or future to organize the progress of the day. In order to move beyond noon, Wordsworth simply announces the new scene:

> —Sweet rill, farewell! To-morrow's noon again,
> Shall hide me wooing long thy wildwood strain;
> But now the sun has gain'd his western road,
> And eve's mild hour invites my steps abroad.
>
> (ll. 85–88)

Twilight arrives "now" as if description need only turn its eyes from noon to an adjacent part of the prospect. The true tense of the poem, perhaps, is not the seeming present at all but an abnormally frequent participial construction petrifying the "now" in rapt attention: "the still *twinkling* tail and *glancing* ear" at noon, for example. At this pointillistic instant when the present touches upon past and future immediately, indistinguishably, time is not.

Time only encroaches upon description peripherally: in extravagant, and seemingly quite useless, epic similes or conceits crowded into the poem's beginning and conclusion. Just before noon initiates the scene of present description, for example, Wordsworth indulges in a moment of retrospection modeled on Gray's Eton College ode:

> Fair scenes! with other eyes, than once, I gaze,
> The ever-varying charm your round displays,
>
> . . .
>
> Return Delights! with whom my road begun,
> When Life rear'd laughing up her morning sun;
> When Transport kiss'd away my april tear,
> "Rocking as in a dream the tedious year;"
> When link'd with thoughtless Mirth I cours'd the plain,
> And hope itself was all I knew of pain.   (ll. 17–32)

In this opening gesture toward the life story of the poet—as full of figuration as the autobiographical gesture we noticed at the poem's end—a universe of successive consciousness appears in which hope changes into nostalgia aware at every instant of painful distance. The grand epic simile or metaphysical conceit of such time is a sundial, in which the present is overshadowed by the dark gnomon of Memory:

> Alas! the idle tale of man is found
> Depicted in the dial's moral round;
> With Hope Reflexion blends her social rays
> To gild the total tablet of his days;
> Yet still, the sport of some malignant Pow'r,
> He knows but from its shade the present hour.
> While, Memory at my side, I wander here,
> Starts at the simplest sight th' unbidden tear.
>
> (ll. 37–44)

And just before closing, in the simile comparing Hope to the moon we have already considered, *An Evening Walk* revives the fiction of temporality in a prospective rather than retrospective form: "Ev'n now [Moon/Hope] decks for me a distant scene, / (For dark and broad the gulph of time between)." Once more the landscape rifts apart in time to reveal a distant scene—bathed this time not by the hopeful sunshine of the past but the moony hope of the future. And once more the scene is cut off from the present by a gnomic shadow: the dark and broad gulf of time. Such is the intimation of time in *An Evening Walk*: in each duration, we see a rift of succession, and in each succession a hidden agony.

A narrative of desire and violence and a conceit of time, then: these are the indescribables that *An Evening Walk* cannot say except badly, hastily, and figuratively. Yet it strives to say them nevertheless. Considered one way, the poem is thus regressive. A look at its canvas with something like the art historian's X-rays will be illuminating here. Peering into *An Evening Walk* through the apparatus of the Cornell Wordsworth edition and Reed's chronology (together with supporting materials), we discover that the anomalies of description we have been itemizing are part of the deepest and compositionally *earliest* foundation of the poem. *An Evening Walk* first evolved in Wordsworth's notebooks of 1788 in association with materials that included "The Vale of Esthwaite" and a translation ("Orpheus and Eurydice") of the climax of Virgil's epyllion in the fourth *Georgic* (see *EW*, pp. 3–6, and transcriptions of DC MSS. 2, 5, and 7 on pp. 85–125; see also *CEY*, pp. 307–12). All the instances of the indescribable we have noticed belong to these early drafts, which, following Averill in his Introduction to *EW* (p. 5), we can collectively title the proto–*Evening Walk*.[117] The passage of "No's" that follows the Spenserian simile, for example, culminates with lines based on reworkings of "The Vale of Esthwaite" in DC MS. 2 (*EW*, pp. 87–91; see also *CEY*, p. 310), while the Spenserian simile itself descends from the slightly later DC MS. 7, where Wordsworth gathered together the early drafts that became the latter half of the finished poem (*EW*, pp. 111–13). The Female Beggar episode similarly descends from draftwork entered in DC MS. 7 (*EW*, pp. 99–103; *CEY*, p. 310), and the indirect evidence of nearby verses from an early translation of the *Georgics* suggests that missing pages in the same notebook could have held the episode of the swans as well (*EW*, pp. 5–6). Finally, the conceit of the sundial draws upon an early prose fragment (MM, 1: 115n; *CEY*, p. 310), while that of moony hope at the end of the poem derives from revisions of "The Vale of Esthwaite" in DC MS. 7 (*EW*, pp. 115–21).

Viewing the evidence as a whole, we come to the following conclusion: the chief inspiration of *An Evening Walk* lay in a milieu of georgic and gothic juvenilia notably deficient in distinguishing description from narration—that simply made description, indeed, coextensive with narration. Figuration served in these early works in a purely transitive fashion, facilitating metamorphosis between the two orders. Thus while description in the fourth *Georgic* erupts directly into story, in "The Vale of Esthwaite" it opens up through the channel of a "seem," "like," "so," or full-blown epic simile into epyllion-like episodes evocative of gothic romance (see, for example, lines 218, 311, 328, 335, 389; in *PW*, 1: 275–79).[118] No sooner does something go bump in the night in these source-works, in other words, than a whole story appears to identify the demon or spectre responsible. To read *An Evening Walk* amid Wordsworth's juvenilia is to realize that picturesque description—often taken to represent the poet's primitive

beginnings—was in fact already a highly finished device in his repertory, able to assert control over the previous narrative-descriptive
continuum by cleaving that continuum in two.

The indescribable, in short, was the *origin* of *An Evening Walk*.
Wordsworth wishes to describe a landscape in repose; but in the
slips, swerves, and stutterings of his poem, he regresses to landscape haunted by story. Yet considered differently, regress was also
the possibility of the poet's progress to his next works. It is at this
point that we come to a parting of the ways in Wordsworth's early
career. Progress was possible because by the time of publication the
incipient autobiography of the poet we have noticed suddenly *could*
be developed further on the basis of a highly particular and "realistic" narrative referent. Or rather, "autobiography" is getting ahead
of our story. The particular narrative that suddenly revived and re-
furbished the ground of the poem had nothing to do with individual
consciousness or the growth of the poet's mind. Rather, it was a story
of everyman that applied old narrative forms to an avant-garde, collective catastrophe antecedent to the invention of the autobiographical self.

A small detail will point our way. We might wonder why it was
that Wordsworth grounded the episode of the Female Beggar upon
the particular topical reference of "Bunker's charnel hill" (l. 254). The
reference entered the poem very late in composition: in the Errata,
where it substituted for "Minden's charnel plain" (a battleground in
the Seven Years War). Of course, there is convincing evidence that
Wordsworth needed to make *some* change to avoid too near a borrowing from a similar passage in John Langhorne's *The Country Justice* (Jacobus, *Tradition*, p. 144n). Yet such evidence does not explain
the particular change decided upon. Why did it make sense in early
1793 to delete the rout of the French armies in 1759 and introduce
the famous resistance and eventual victory of the American rebels in
1775–76 (in the Revolution, we remember, that Knight also invoked
with reference to the early French Revolution)?

These questions could easily have been moot. We could imagine, for example, Wordsworth putting aside all thought of sustained
narrative and maturing into the descriptive didacticism of an early
Crabbe. Or again, we could picture the poet's narrative urge expressing itself without undermining description by seizing upon some old
mythology or past history as statuesquely removed from present circumstance as the histories he considers at the opening of *The Prelude*
(1.177–219). But as events turned out, our questions are the central
ones. We know that the poet probably finished most of *An Evening
Walk* by late 1789 but continued composition sporadically through
the time of publication in 1793 and of revision in 1794 (*EW*, pp.

7–8). In these years, a master plot of the times, indisputably "fact" rather than fiction or figure, *did* arise to compel the rethinking of description. Not only in *An Evening Walk* itself, as we will see when we peruse Wordsworth's 1794 revisions, but more significantly in its successors, description became merely the thick mediation through which plot structures emerged into an ideologically necessary and just time—a time of agony as fatal as fate. The master plot that prompted this change was the French Revolution; and its politics of agon—which reformed the principles of property exchange, bureaucratic discipline, and liberal freedom in a manner beyond the comprehension of picturesque form—fashioned what I will study as a poetics of desire turned violence.

View once more the picturesque mountain at the center of the Champ-de-Mars amphitheater in 1794 (Pl. 15). By this time, the mountain was also the Jacobin Mountain, the great charnel hill seen in such allegorical representations as those on prints of the Republican calendar (shown in Furet and Richet, p. 331). If the panorama of nature in the amphitheater was picturesque in the manner of Clarke's eye stationed at Penrith Beacon (Pl. 14), that is, it was certainly also supervised by the monstrous fulfillment of the picturesque eye: the Jacobin Eye of Surveillance. We know that the fiery Eye of Reason (itself a displacement of the traditional Eye of God) opened at the top of reproductions of the Declaration of the Rights of Man in 1789 (see Melchior-Bonnet, p. 20; Sieburg, pp. 6, 47) and later, in its character as the Jacobin *oeil de la surveillance* or Vigilant Eye, also opened over the world of the Mountain in 1792–93 (as in the Eye capped by "*Surveillance*" in the depiction of the Mountain in Furet and Richet, p. 331).[119] The embodiment of that Eye was Robespierre, who in contemporary depictions rose like the sun over mountains (see Henderson, p. 417). What the symbolism of the *oeil de la surveillance* supervised was the increasing institutionalization of vigilance in the Revolution—most signally in the Vigilance Committee of the Paris Commune (*Comité de surveillance*) that oversaw the September Massacres in 1792 (Mathiez, pp. 177, 181), the Revolutionary Watch Committees that "redoubled surveillance" to watch all foreigners in 1793 (*DSFR*, pp. 412–14), and the Law of Suspects that allowed Watch Committees that same year to round up an encyclopedic list of "suspected persons" (*DSFR*, pp. 477–79). Such was the modernization of the Inquisition—complete with the auto-da-fé or burning of the bodies on the Carrousel in 1792—that came to watch over the landscape Wordsworth visited on his second trip to France just before publishing *An Evening Walk* with *Descriptive Sketches* on January 29, 1793. Only eight days before the poem appeared, Louis was executed.

Wordsworth's description, quite simply, was surmounted by the

Revolution, the eye of the picturesque by the vigilant eye. The super-vision of this new eye, we must now see, was at once too free and bold, too desiring and violent. It oversaw the discipline-in-freedom —at once similar and monstrously dissimilar to the picturesque—that submitted Wordsworth's repose to Terror.

~~⟳~~

CHAPTER FOUR

The Poetics of Violence

I PROPOSE TO SKETCH the basic action of the Revolution during 1792 and 1793, the period culminating in Terror. The sketch is
of violence, or, as we will need to see, of desire become violence. And
it is double in the sense of being adapted to the perspective of a poet
who was close to events in France after his arrival in late November
1791 but also crucially removed from the most infamous actions:
outside Paris from December 1791 through the fall of 1792 and back
in England by 1793 before the execution of Louis and the onset of the
high Terror.[1] I will thus present events as viewed both "close up" in
Paris (where Wordsworth visited the National Assembly, probably
sat in on the Jacobin club, and "read . . . the master Pamphlets of
the day"; *Prel.* 9.96–97) and as reviewed at a distance in the London
periodicals that would have been the poet's primary access to French
news when he returned to live in London from about December 1792
to early July 1793.[2]

In approach, I draw seminally upon recent studies of the French
Revolution by François Furet, Marie-Hélène Huet, George Armstrong Kelly, Richard Cobb, and others—studies whose common
trait (applied most recently by Lynn Hunt)[3] has been a rejection of
the divide between historical action and representation. "Discourse"
is taken to be an indispensable agency in both actions and their representations. Moreover, discourse in the studies I single out is also
taken to be the sole expressive means by which past action and representation (or, rather, action *as* "representation," in its political sense)
records itself.[4] For our purposes, however, an extra specification
is called for. "Discourse" and such cognate phrases as "language,"

"signs," and "the word" in recent histories of the Revolution are semiotic in orientation, based paradigmatically on analysis of the individual word or sentence, and so relatively insensitive in themselves to generic analysis. A better avenue of approach for us is provided by the occasional emphasis of Furet, and the much more massive accent of Huet, on "theatricality."[5] As we will see, the discourse of Revolution was itself "descriptive" in its propagandistic use of "nature." But more basically, as witnessed by the plethora of plays that sprang up to stage Marat's death (and, indeed, by the self-dramatizing genius that was Marat himself in life), description was a secondary transformation of the true discursive form of Revolution: narrative or, in Aristotle's broad sense, *tragedy*.

We can take as our working model of Revolutionary action and representation the following triadic structure, which I will call "emergency": Narrative → Description → Ideology. The Revolution was a story that sought to describe itself as fact and then to justify the fact after the fact.

London: The Silence

Whether Government or Opposition in viewpoint (my samples: the Treasury-controlled *Times* and *Public Advertiser* and the Foxite *Morning Chronicle*), the London daily press was remarkably consistent in describing the "nature" of French violence.[6] Early in the period, editorials differed depending on their political stance in tolerance for such nature. "Verax" in the *Morning Chronicle*, for example, argued the standard British radical defense, soon to be adopted by Wordsworth in his *Letter to the Bishop of Llandaff*, that violence was the "natural effervescence" of desired change (*MC*, Aug. 31, 1792).[7] (Wordsworth: "The animal just released from its stall will exhaust the overflow of its spirits in a round of wanton vagaries . . ."; *Prose*, 1: 38.) Yet whatever the degree of editorial tolerance, the underlying "nature" described was the same. In both the *Chronicle* and the Government dailies, the nature of violence was constituted in actual reportage by a surprisingly small number of key metaphorical constructs—"radicals" of violence, let us call them—each capable of being compressed into a figure of speech or expanded into an entire conceit as need arose. Echoed and re-echoed (sometimes verbatim) in the weekly, monthly, and annual press (my samples: the *Observer, European Maga-*

zine, *Gentleman's Magazine*, and *The Annual Register*),[8] these constructs composed virtually the whole English description of violence. Their outstanding feature, for our purposes, is the fact that they only partially coincided with the description given by the French themselves: violence in the English and French tongues could not describe the same nature.

We can begin by studying the following major radicals: "savagery," "barbarism," "bestiality," "cannibalism," and "parricide." As we will see, the English press actually shared these epithets with the French— but spoke them with an entirely different intonation. An Eisenstein-like montage of reports on the September Massacres will render the combined effect of English description:[9]

The sanguinary Proclamations of the invaders [the Brunswick Manifesto] have rendered the people desperate and savage. . . . They are attacked and hunted like beasts of prey, and in the toils they act like beasts of prey. (*MC*, Sept. 8, 1792)

The GOTHS and VANDALS, when they levelled the gates of Rome . . . still retained those feelings which distinguished the mind of man from the ungovernable appetite of the brute creation. . . . Far otherwise has been the conduct of the French barbarians. (*T*, Sept. 10, 1792)

Thrice he ran from the flames . . . at last, with their pikes, the sanguinary monsters pinned him there, and, insultingly demanding him to sing *ça ira*, danced around the fire, singing themselves, in the true spirit of North-American Savages. (*GM*, Sept. 1792, p. 855)

France . . . exhibits a frightful spectacle of rapine and barbarity, which is not to be paralleled among the savages of New Zealand. (*GM*, Oct. 1792, p. 880)

The cannibals tore the bodies . . . into innumerable pieces, and shared their mangled limbs among them. (*EM*, Sept. 1792, p. 244)

The streets have this morning exhibited a spectacle of the mangled bodies and heads of the Priests . . . and the multitude who follow this cannibal-feast are singing choruses. (*GM*, Sept. 1792, p. 855)

That the French Maniacs should pay such adoration to Roman murderers as to adore the statue of *Brutus*, who stabbed his father (as Caesar certainly was) is not to be wondered at, when we read of a Frenchman bringing his father and mother's heads to the Jacobin club. . . . The statue of Nero is the next they will bring into their hall . . . for he butchered his mother, his wife, and his brethren. (*T*, Sept. 15, 1792)

Extending and animating the Revolutionary "sunbursts," "tides," "hurricanes," "tempests," and so forth that English writers applied figuratively to earlier *journées* such as the storming of the Bastille (Paulson, *Representations*, pp. 43–47, 52), such language from 1792 on described a realm of "natural" event whose sole significance was that it was *not* "civilized." The nature of French violence, that is, was by definition all that lay on the red-toothed side of the Culture/Nature divide.[10] The firmness of the divide was necessary to maintain the English identity. Paulson has focused on "cannibalism" and "parricide" in particular to sketch an English aesthetics of response opening into psychological compulsion (*Representations*, esp. pp. 8–9, 24, 71; Paulson assimilates the image of sons killing the father to the Oedipal paradigm). We might add Gombrich's thesis of the "exclusionary" in aesthetic response to generalize that the English flinched away from French nature as part of a reflex of self-identification. Epithets such as "savage," "barbaric," and "bestial" are akin, in Gombrich's thesis, to the "Gothic" or "Baroque" as seen from the viewpoint of Classic form (pp. 81–98). Their sole task was to define a zone of cultural exclusion with which to contrast—through a "normative" instinct concealed within "formal" analysis—the English subject as psychologically, socially, politically, and even epochally *different*.[11] As demonstrated by Burke's sustained attempt in the *Reflections* (1790) to distinguish the French Revolution from the English Civil War and Glorious Revolution, the early peril of French violence for the English was not so much physical threat as the threat of resemblance (pp. 99–110). Only by marking a firm divide between accepted culture and excluded nature could the French be seen without too near "reflection." "Savages" with all their "bestial" habits, after all, did not even belong in the same hemisphere, millennium, or species as the civilized.

The English description of violence, in sum, was essentially classificatory.[12] Its function was to fix the difference between species-forms of society on a static table divided vertically between high culture and low nature. But such description had a profound limitation: it could not represent elemental change.[13] Whether evolutionary or revolutionary, change is the traversal of categories. The English language of violence masked the possibility of a developmental universe and thus—with particular relevance for us—also the discourse suited to expressing it. The dominant discourse thus rejected was explicitly narrative.[14] Burke had repeatedly predicted a "great drama" "exhibited on the stage" of Revolutionary "terror and pity" (*Reflections*, p. 175).[15] The press from 1792 on continued to announce a "bloody tragedy . . . exhibiting on the theatre of a once great . . . monarchy" (*T*, Sept. 12, 1792) and invoked comparisons from Shakespeare and other literary sources. After Philippe Egalité voted the execution of Louis, for example, the *Times* stated: "the *ci-devant* Duke of ORLEANS, Mr. *Equality*, in dooming his nephew to death, reminds us of *Richard the Third*, giving orders for the murder of his brother's children" (Jan. 25, 1793). And Wordsworth himself later recalls entering France in late 1791 as if walking "Into a theatre, of which the stage / Was busy with an action far advanced" (*Prel.* 9.94–95). As such testament shows, the English experience of spectating the Revolution was burdened precisely with narrative—and specifically tragic—expectations of change between "high" and "low."[16]

But the Tahitian infatuation of a few years back, when the London theater could actually stage tribal cultures as a sort of Neoclassical Noble Savagery, had passed.[17] Savages, barbarians, beasts, cannibals, and parricides were now the cast of an alien nature whose story was inadmissible in polite society. However much prepared for story, the English thus at last used their descriptive epithets to ban the French story. In reviewing the "great drama" of the overthrow of kings, for example, Burke is shocked to find that some of the world audience respond, not with classical "terror and pity," but with exultation. Like Wordsworth passing into a theater already "busy with an action far advanced," Burke then finds himself suspended—over the course of a page and a half—in the rift between sensible story and no-story. He finally passes judgment and ejects French action from the stage of true story: "No theatric audience in Athens," he says, "would bear" the staging of tragedy as triumph (*Reflections*, pp. 175–76). The French story is un-classic, barbaric.

To grasp the full implications of the English flinch away from Revolutionary story, we need to think in terms of the deep premises of narrative. Imagine the minimum organization required for nature to be viewed as housing an Aristotelian theater and violence as staging a tragic story. To begin with, nature would have to be structured according to an elementary, timeless logic underlying narrative: antagonism, or the dialectical wrestle of agonist and antagonist that Kenneth Burke has studied under the title of the "combat myth" (pp. 380–409). Antagonism *de*classifies as much as it classifies. Othello and Iago, Oedipus and the antagonist of himself: it is of the essence in antagonism, as in antithesis, that the Champion and his Enemy be profoundly complicitous. At the moment when swords meet, the Champion must cleave to as much as from his Enemy.[18]

The linear deployment of such declassification then constitutes change: as in the case of tragedy, the fate of the Champion is to generate an Enemy (sometimes himself) capable of winning and changing places with him. As a second requirement, therefore, narrativized nature must unfold as the entelechial form of change: plot, the deployment of antagonism as "reversal" and "discovery." An implicit condition of such plot is that the stronger its underlying antagonism, the greater its need to represent itself as single or "unified." For our purposes, a negative definition of unity, which in practice tolerates multiple plot lines and episodic structures, will serve: unity is *not* repetition. A unified plot, that is, effectively conceals, or otherwise misrepresents as terminal action, what seems to be the innate repetitional compulsion in strong antagonisms (classic examples: the Trojan wars and the last half of *The Aeneid*).

Finally, a third requirement of narrativized nature is that it must compel the spectator to identify with it. Just as the Champion cleaves from/to his Enemy, in other words, so the spectator offstage must find himself both repelled by and drawn into the violence he sees enacted. Unlike classification, narrative thus ultimately requires what may be pictured as a horizontal rather than vertical plane of difference between observers and observed—a plane on which any perception of difference is also a recognition of underlying parity.

The English description of violence obscured each of these conditions of narrative. First, it could not discriminate even the basic antagonisms in a nature acted by "savages" and "beasts." The London press in the years 1792–93 and after consistently tried to reduce the French agon to a clear opposition of hierarchically differentiated parties: just as English "culture" opposed French "nature" and high opposed low, so, at various times, Lafayette was seen to oppose the Jacobins, the Girondins the Mountain, or the Thermidoreans Robespierre. The consequence was remarkable insensitivity to the transformations, reversals, and affiliations *between* combatants. Such "tragic" episodes as the Fall of the Aristocracy or of Robespierre, after all, depended for *peripeteia* or reversal upon antagonisms in which key Champions of the party previously in power went over to the side of the Enemy. Unable to read such de- or reclassification as development, the English press could only conclude that hostility in France was without structure. The correspondent for the *Morning Chronicle* thus described the increasing hostility between the Girondins and the Mountain after the September Massacres as a kind of non-Euclidean geometry:

It is not in France as with you, parties have not taken consistency. Men are not arranged under distinct standards upon specific principles. There is no steady phalanx acting upon fundamental doctrines. . . . On the contrary, all is fortuitous—their arguments and disunions are both transitory—they rally upon measures, and not upon maxims; and therefore, though there may be lines, they are by no means parallels; for they frequently intersect each other, are one day wide asunder, the next in contact. (Oct. 20, 1792)

The press, that is, saw only a "mob." By definition, we may say, the mob "mobilized" the simple grid of binary opposition into eddying disturbances of three-cornered or, even more uncanny, one-sided agons. After the Storming of the Tuileries, for example, the massacred Swiss Guards seemed a third element foreign to the whole logic of conflict: they could only be explained as victims of all-devouring "savages." And in the aftermath of both the Storming of the Tuileries and the September Massacres, conflict could also seem so unanimous that it appeared to involve all Enemies (from the English viewpoint) and no Champions whatsoever: "heroes" of the People—complete with bloody weapons and other relics—surfaced far in excess of the actual numbers that could have been involved (Cobb, *Police*, pp. 58–61). Knowing no Other, such violence could only be explained as a "cannibalism" or "parricide" violating the most basic of all binary classifications, the distinction between *je* and *vous*—a transgression that uttered itself to the French, we might note, as a solidarity unheard in English, the Revolutionary *tu* (on the egalitarian *tutoiement*, see Robiquet, pp. 56–58).

Second, the English description of violence could not then unfold French nature as a plot or unified development. Or rather, it attempted to fit all French violence into the procrustean mold of two plots so ill-designed and "open-ended," as Paulson has termed Revolutionary plots (*Representations*, p. 55), that they could not properly explain change. One plot simply made classification simulate process such that the only development was ascent or descent on a hierarchical scale. The paradigmatic story of violence in 1792–93 might thus be paraphrased: "things get worse." The *Morning Chronicle* complained, for example, "The contention between the party of BRISSOT and that of ROBERSPIERRE [*sic*] becomes every day more violent, and according to the constant course of the parties in the Revolution, the most inflammatory is gaining ground" (Oct. 20, 1792). The other available plot was a reversion to repetition. An example is an article in the *Times* that, after describing French politics as a process of repetitive violence, extrapolated repetition into the future in an infinite series:

Then shall we behold the factions striving to throw the blame the one on the other;—each will endeavour to find some more culpable than himself. They will recollect, that *Dumourier* was saved by accusing *Marat*: *La Fayette* will prove *Condorcet* to be infinitely more guilty than he is: *Condorcet* may say, he is much less criminal than *Danton* and *Roberspierre* [*sic*]: all of them will be Saints by their own accounts; and perhaps the infamous *Egalité* will discover some one more infamous than himself, in every species of crime. (June 1, 1793)

We might apply to such accounts René Girard's premise in *Violence and the Sacred* that existentially repetitive violence is "vengeance" (pp. 14–15). The *Times* article concluded its report of mutual accusations among the factions by invoking the *lex talionis*: "The day of vengeance approaches:—the villains of every faction must destroy each other, and the death of the virtuous King of France must be avenged, by the very hands of those who imbrued themselves in his blood." Or again, to take just two earlier examples from the prolific vengeance theme in the press, the *Morning Chronicle* reported in the wake of the

September Massacres, "The Commissioners once more attempted to bring back the ungovernable and infatuated multitude to a sense of justice and humanity; but they could not make the least impression on their minds, or check their ferocity and vengeance" (Sept. 10, 1792); and the *Gentleman's Magazine* echoed about September in Orléans, "the mob were delivered from all the restraints of fear, and gave the most savage license to their thirst of revenge" (Sept. 1792, p. 856).[19] Cobb has pointed out that Revolutionary violence in some areas of France—particularly the south—accented a long tradition of family vendettas (*Police*, p. 205). But from the perspective of the English papers, *all* violence in France was a vendetta plot.

The final result of the English inability to understand Revolutionary antagonism and then to follow its plot line was failure to identify with French nature. The best way to demonstrate this lack of sympathy is on the scene of Realpolitik. In order to facilitate the narrative analysis of this scene, I will extend the correlation between literary and political "plot" suggested by Herbert Lindenberger (*Historical Drama*, pp. 30–38) and Peter Brooks (*Reading*, p. 12). Contemporary political discourse on both sides of the Channel in the early 1790's referred to large-scale antagonism within a nation either as overt "civil war" or, with paranoiac frequency, as covert "plot." Such "plot" embodied in *praxis* the antagonism that is the elementary structure of narrative. Political plot was a conspiracy—in French, a *complot* —of Enemies antagonistic to, but nested "secretly" or unclassifiably within, the Champion's state.[20] Moreover, political plot tended to express itself as truly narrative plot. Whatever else it was, political plot was a compellingly told story. To suspect a plot was to "discover" a scenario or story form working behind the scenes toward a climactic "reversal" of power. From the inverse viewpoint, it is thus perhaps not accidental that narratives proper often take their own start from political plots. As Peter Brooks observes, "the organizing line of plot is more often than not some scheme or machination, a concerted plan for the accomplishment of some purpose which goes against the ostensible and dominant legalities of the fictional world" (*Reading*, p. 12; see also Lindenberger, *Historical Drama*, pp. 31–32). In *Lear*, for example, the plot governing the development of the story may thus be seen as precisely a political plot—an action planned by conspiracy under the aegis of the great plotters in drama: "fate" or the "gods."

The English description of violence could not follow the French plot either as narrative or as political agenda, and so could not rationalize identification with Revolutionary conflict through the normal conduct of participatory antagonism at the national level: "war" (with its obverse of "alliance"). If political discourse at the time conceived intranational strife as a theater of plot, it conceived international antagonism symmetrically as a theater of war. The structure of antagonism governing the two theaters was identical to the extent that discovery of plot in a nation's own domain could impute involvement by foreign enemies and thus provide a standard rationale for going to war.[21] Because its description obscured the plot in France, the English press could not easily map the plots and counterplots discovered in England's own politics over those of the Revolution by any identificatory rationale either of "pity" (alliance with foreign factions) or of "terror" (fear of such factions). Therefore, it could not follow the Parliamentary tactic in late 1792 and early 1793 of making Jacobinistic "seditious plots" at home argue the need for alliance with Counter-Revolutionary forces and actual war against France. Put simply, war upon "nature" was inconceivable.[22] Modern war had to be generated on the basis not of a vertical difference between high and low civilizations but of a horizontal parity, called "balance of powers." Only in a world in which difference between nations was also resemblance, after all, could military violence conclude in such methods of restored "identification" as the forging of treaties through diplomacy. Otherwise—as when France in September 1793 promulgated the revolutionary concept of *guerre à outrance*, explicitly rejecting negotiated settlement (R.R. Palmer, *Twelve*, p. 58; Mathiez, p. 370)—war was not, as Joseph Fawcett would soon say with cutting irony in his *The Art of War* (1795), "civilized."[23]

When the theater of war opened in Parliament at the end of 1792, then, the English press experienced a contradictory impulse to follow Parliament in speaking a new practical discourse of "plot" and "war" on the one hand and to continue describing "savagery" and "bestiality" on the other. We notice that Parliament itself simply dropped the language of savagery in order to speak plot and war in tandem. Debate in the House of Commons on December 13–15, 1792, for example, centered on the Government's contention that prosecution of seditious plots at home together with war abroad was necessary to counter a common French menace. The only controversy took the form of the Foxite Opposition's doubt that London corresponding societies in fact hosted a French plot ("a well-arranged methodized plan, for gradually undermining the principles of the British constitution . . . supported by a purse . . . made up in France"; *AR*, 1793: 10). In such a debate, pitting those who decried French calculation and cabal against those who urged approaching France as a nation capable of rational negotiation (and who, indeed, thought the real plot was the "artful designs and practices" of Government ministers; *AR*, 1793: 7), there was no place for a language of savagery quarantining the French as irrational. "Savages" and "beasts," after all, may show native "cunning," but cannot be said to "plot." With the notable exception of Burke's speeches (which had the effect of a sideshow), the descriptive appellations of "savage," "beast," and so forth were thus wholly absent from the debate even during the most violent bouts of invective against "murder," "ruffians," "slaughter," "horrid spectacles," and so forth (see, for example, *AR*, 1793: 25).[24]

Unable to drop its description of savagery, the English press was forced to adopt the alternate formula of simply dividing it from the discourse of plot and war. The former language continued to dominate reports of French domestic affairs. The latter, according to a journalistic tradition at odds with Revolutionary reality, fell into separate columns devoted to Parliamentary reporting and war dispatches. In between, there was no communication at all. Literally, there was "silence." We notice that the English press habitually inserted—by fictional means if necessary—actual silences in French violence. With a heavy varnish of art, for example, this pièce de résistance in the *Gentleman's Magazine* renders the "Murder of Louis" as an episode of silences centered on the deliberate silencing of the King on the scaffold. Never mind that the French themselves heard the "silence" as loud fanfare:

During the night of Jan. 20, Paris was illuminated, and no person whatever was permitted to go abroad in the streets. Large bodies of armed men patroled every part of that immense metropolis, the rattling of coaches ceased, the streets were deserted, and the city was buried in profound silence, more horrid than expression can equal. About two o'clock in the morning of the fatal Monday the 21st, voices were heard, at intervals, through the gloom, of lamentation and distress; but whence they proceeded, or what they were, no person has been able to discover. This circumstance, among many others, has greatly terrified the people. . . .

The Place de Louis Quinze, now called the Place of the Revolution, was the spot appointed for the MURDER. The place was filled with prodigious multitudes of people, and large bodies of horse and foot were drawn up to protect the execution. The most awful silence prevailed, while the coach was advancing slowly towards the scaffold. The dying Monarch ascended it with heroic fortitude, with a firm step, and undismayed countenance. . . . In the middle stood the block, and near it two large ill-looking brutes, one of whom held the axe in his hand. The King for a moment looked around upon the people, with eyes which beamed forgiveness and love; and he was preparing himself to address the spectators, when, horrid to relate! one of the officers cried out, "No Speeches;—come, no Speeches;" and suddenly the drums beat, and the trumpets sounded. He spoke, but all the expressions that could be distinctly heard were these: "I forgive my enemies: may God forgive them; and not lay my innocent blood to the charge of the Nation: God bless my People!!!!"

The Confessor fell upon his knees, and implored the King's blessing, who gave it him with an affectionate embrace. The religious and good Monarch then laid his head upon the block with admirable serenity; and he ceased to live in this world.

The Murder was performed between eleven and twelve o'clock on Monday morning. . . . The Convention, with cruel apathy, passed to the order of the day. (Jan. 1793, pp. 85–86)

Other instances of such deliberately marked "silence" unremarked in Paris abound.[25] In essence, I suggest, the English amplification of silence signaled an aphasia in reportage where the description of savagery had lost its credibility in the face of the terrific design and administration of the Revolution ("voices" of conspiracy in the night, the marshaling of the crowd and control of the execution itself, the Kafkaesque efficiency with which the Convention "passed to the order of the day") but where a narrativistic discourse integral with that of "plot" and "war" had yet to fill the void. Peter Brooks's study of melodrama and the theatrical use of silent gestures speaks loudly here. Where metaphors of savagery drop out to leave a void of speech, melodramatic "silence" amplifies to become what Brooks calls the "trope" of speech (*Melodramatic*, pp. 71–72). For the English, finally, violence was unspeakable.

Paris: The Story

To cross the Channel is to come to grips with a full story that description elaborates rather than censors. The story is of violence evolved from desire—a documentable form of the "desire" that such recent theorists of historical narrative as Paul Hernadi and David Punter and of literary narrative as Jameson and Peter Brooks have located at the origin of the narrative urge.[26] Substituting for the traditional analytic of literary "pleasure" (as in the Horatian dictum that poetry should at once *delight* and instruct), the analytic of desire would account for both a narrative's thematics and the self-indulgent complicity of its spectator.

In Paris, Revolution was first of all the Revolution of desire—of the early, millennial hope whose most urgent form was the libertine Revolution of the notorious Philippe Egalité, Georges Couthon before his paralysis "caused" by indulgence, or Sade, who some days before July 14, 1789, shouted through his Bastille window for the people to liberate him.[27] Revolution, that is, was cognate with "liberty" exercised in brothels in the Palais Royal and with a climate of moral license generally (Robiquet, pp. 65–71). Primarily masculine in expression, such liberty tolerated what Cobb has documented to be an old tradition of seducing and raping women refreshed by the "Rights of Man" (*Reactions*, pp. 142–48). (Preparations for the 1790 Fete of Federation in Paris thus included the publication of a detailed catalog of prostitutes by an author eager to perform the "patriotic service" of counseling "large numbers of strangers attracted to Paris by their love of liberty"; quoted in Robiquet, p. 68.)[28] Significantly, such a Revolution of desire was deeply narrative in imagination. Or, at least, it was narrative in an uncoordinated, polymorphous, and perverse manner. As evidenced by the fact that Saint-Just's first publication was a long, semi-pornographic narrative poem, *Organt* (1789) (R. R. Palmer, *Twelve*, p. 10) and that Restif de la Bretonne would later recognize the continuity of the Revolution with "*Justine, Aline, le Boudoir, La Théorie du Libertinage*" (quoted in Cobb, *Reactions*, p. 148), the early Revolution was strange bedfellows with pornography. Enlightenment pornography was romance for the materialist, rationalist, and atheist: it was the episodic romance of the literal philosophe or "lover of truth." What the evidence of the pornography indicates, we can suggest, is that the early Revolution formed itself as an enactment of the most primitive kind of serial romance—as an endlessly gratifying story as marvelous in its inverse chivalry as "Philippe Egalité's" name. Or to clean up my argument: the early Revolution sought its secular grails as dreamily as any Childe. It conducted itself much like Wordsworth's personal hero of the early Revolution, Michel Beaupuy, who seemed to wander "through a Book, an old Romance or Tale / Of Fairy" (*Prel.* 9.307–8).

Why is desire, whose urge the libertine romance of the early Revolution points so nicely, the opening of narrative? Here I vary the application Peter Brooks makes of Lacan's definition of desire. Desire, in Brooks's paraphrase, is

born of the difference or split between need and demand: for instance, the infant's need for the breast (for nourishment) and his demand, which is in essence a demand for love from the other (for instance, from the mother). To cite Jean Laplanche and J.-B. Pontalis: "Desire is born from the gap [*l'écart*] between need and demand; it is irreducible to need, for it is not in its principle relation to a real object, independent of the subject, but rather to a phantasy; it is irreducible to demand, in that it seeks to impose itself without taking account of language and the unconscious of the other and insists upon being absolutely recognized by the other." In this gap, desire comes into being as a perpetual want for (of) a satisfaction that cannot be offered in reality. (*Reading*, p. 55)

Desire, I suggest, is the necessary precondition of narrative because it defines the primitive locus of the "literary": the split between the urge toward referential fact ("need") and the urge toward shared conventions of non- or cross-referential fiction ("demand"). Desire, that is, marks the central atrium of literariness within which empirical fact is domesticated to the embrace of consensual fiction—the universe of discrete, terminal satisfactions (the knowledge or consumption of "reality") with a universe in which author and "other" (readers and other authors) pursue each other from page to page in an unreal fiction of interminably suspended gratification.[29]

But desire by itself cannot create a fully formed narrative. Desire must become violence. Such, certainly, was the fate of the Revolutionary romance of desire. While in the first years after 1789 brothels and other flagrant "liberties" flourished, by 1793 there arose the Jacobin Republic of Virtue in which, according to the order of the day, "lubricity and immodesty . . . of the female sex" were punishable and "ministers of morals" were appointed to enforce purity (Robiquet, pp. 74–75; see also R. R. Palmer, *Twelve*, p. 324). As shown in pictures of Cupid as a sansculotte and volunteer, or of the feminine, personified French Republic fending off the attentions of male Powers of Europe (Henderson, pp. 231, 245, 327), the spirit of the French rococo enlisted. The High Censor of the new, increasingly violent order was Robespierre, who projected an image so Incorruptible as to be neuter: while contemporary accounts observed the extraordinary number of women flocking to hear him, for example, they also carefully de-eroticized the phenomenon by explaining Robespierre's magnetism as that of a "priest" or "sect" leader (*MC*, Nov. 17, 1792).

The transformation of desire into violence marked the entry of polymorphous romance into the Revolution's organized, Aristotelian narrative: tragedy. The Sadean entelechy according to which desire fulfills itself as violence can be speculated upon as follows. Girard has suggested that "violence" marks the spot where two desires converge —and so clash—upon a single object of desire. Violence, in other words, originates as the sign of *shared* (or, with a sense of rivalry, fraternal) desire (pp. 145–48). We can add that the sign necessarily emerges in negative form. To commit violence is to negate the desire of the other brutally, and so to be forced to negate or rename one's own desire (since it is identical with the other's). While every blow against another thus expresses at some level the fact that one shares the victim's desire (for "happiness" or its tokens), the sharing of desire can only emerge under the name of all that is "*un*desirable" —shocks, cruelty, horror, and so forth. Violence erupts as the "unspeakable" sign of desire. To move beyond the "silence" heard by the English to become a positive utterance in its own right, violence must then take as its great task the authoritative narrativization of undesirability: the rendering of unspeakable horror as a tragic story sanctioned from the start as "classic." At its most inarticulate, that is, violence is a vulgar, "low-class" curse of negation flung at the privi-

leged who possess the signs of one's own desire; but at its most sophisticated, it is a reorganization of desire into a primordially classic
story seeding, as we will see, the ideologizations of violence constitutive of Terror.

We can begin reading the French classicism of violence by noting
that the English press borrowed one other metaphorical "radical"
from across the Channel without recognizing that it was the key
to the whole story of Revolution. This radical was "sacrifice." Of
course, I do not mean to undervalue the fact, as I earlier noticed, that
the Revolution itself indulged in the senseless rhetoric of "savagery,"
"cannibalism," and so forth quite as much as the English. The difference was a matter of intonation not readily communicable across the
Channel. I refer to a subprovince of our topic that cannot be fully investigated here: the "humor" of popular violence. Reported the *Times*
about the September Massacres:

> The Countess PERIGNAN with her two daughters . . . were stripped of their
> cloaths, washed with oil, and roasted alive, while the mob were singing
> and dancing round the fire, and amusing themselves with their cries and
> sufferings. . . . When the mother was roasted, the mob brought six priests
> to the same fire, and then cutting some flesh from the body, ordered the
> Priests to eat it. They all of them approached the horrid scene with their
> eyes shut, and did not speak a word in answer. The mob directly undressed
> the eldest of them . . . and roasted him; saying, they perhaps might like the
> flesh of their friends better than that of the Countess.

> Several pastry cooks, particularly one by the *Palais Royal*, have Pies *de la
> viande des Suisses—des Emigrants—des Pretres*—made of the flesh of the Swiss
> —the Emigrants and the Priests.—I was present when four Marseillois at
> the *Restaurateur Bouvilliers*, in the Palais Royal, sent for two of these pies, and
> eat them, crying out—*Vive la Nation*. (Sept. 12, 1792)

These are jokes, a grand physical humor or sublime slapstick. We
notice that they follow like a main act immediately upon this vaude-
ville of violence in the *Times* report:

> The mob ordered one of the Swiss soldiers to dress the hair of a young
> Swiss officer, a very handsome young man; and when it was done, they
> ordered him with a hand-saw to take off his head, and to be cautious not to
> spoil his headdress, saying it was too fine a head to put upon a pike, but to
> the best advantage.

Like the infamous outrages of the *Bande d'Orgères*, which began operations in the Orléans area precisely during Wordsworth's residency,[30]
humor in this taste belonged to a convention of popular and brigand
violence whose closest approximation in the higher arts was caricature (e.g., cartoons of the priests at the September Massacres having
their "noses" pulled; Henderson, p. 291).

The jokework of violence, of course, is not without its own deep logic. In what Cobb calls the "anti-state" (complete with *départements*) ruled by the gang near Orléans, for example, the arrangement of tableaus of dead farmers and their wives in copulation—possibly as the centerpiece of the gang's own orgies (Cobb, *Reactions*, pp. 190–91, 198–99)—may be seen to stand in the same relation to "fertility" as the tableau David arranged at the Fete of Unity and Indivisibility on August 10, 1793, in which, in a scene that would be humorous on any occasion other than the anniversary of the Storming of the Tuileries, the gigantic statue of Regeneration generated streams of water from her naked breasts by pressing them with her hands (shown in Henderson, p. 356). The point we may take from the comic antimasque of Revolution is that however much the logic of physical humor was cognate with that of classic or tragic violence—or, put another way, however much laughter (especially in the Bergsonian analysis) is a special deflection of violence[31]—it was deliberately marked as the minor or introductory chord. Unperceived by the tone-deaf British, in other words, was the fact that "savagery" and "cannibalism" were a *commedia dell'arte* prologuing a main Racinesque tragedy of "sacrifice" blazoning violence on a more forbidding stage—a stage on which not even the French dared joke. As David reported to the Convention in advance of the Fete of August 10, 1793, the smiling fertility of the statue of Regeneration would only be prologue to the statue of Liberty, "which shall be inaugurated with due solemnity." "At her feet will be an enormous pyre," David says, upon which "shall be offered in expiatory sacrifice the impostured attributes of royalty" (*Chronique de Paris*, July 18, 1793; quoted in Henderson, p. 361).

As proclaimed by the French and echoed woodenly by the English, "sacrifice" appears to have been statistically the most important radical of violence. Again, a montage of revolution (arranged chronologically) will render the spirit of the times:[32]

You should stab them without mercy. Let [twenty deputies at the National Assembly, most later to become Feuillants] be your first victims! Perhaps these bloody sacrifices will ensure you your salvation. (Marat, *L'Ami du peuple*, July 18, 1791; quoted in Gilchrist and Murray, pp. 268–69)

LA FAYETTE . . . is to be hunted down like a wild beast; but he will not resist the torrent—he will rather yield himself up as a sacrifice than be the means of erecting a standard of rebellion even to anarchy. (*MC*, Aug. 24, 1792)

I, unable to do other than speak frankly, will tell you: "This people, whose first need was to love and cherish its kings, today feels only hatred for monarchs and for monarchy; it has changed the objects of its worship; the incense of its sacrifices no longer rises upon the altars of its false gods. . . . Regicide is the gospel of its bloody religion, and everything that will not bend its knee before Baal will be slaughtered on the pavement of its temples." (*Le Journal de M. Suleau*, quoted in Gilchrist and Murray, p. 143)

The mob next proceeded to the *Chatelet*, where they likewise sacrificed all the prisoners. (Report on the September Massacres by a member of the Legislative Assembly; *T*, Sept. 10, 1792; reprinted in *EM*, Sept. 1792, p. 243)

He spoke much of his great patriotism, and made a motion that every Patriot who preferred the ties of blood or nature to those of patriotism, should be looked upon as an *Aristocrat*, and consequently every Jacobin should denounce or sacrifice his parents or friends whose sentiments were not patriotic. (Speech of a man presenting his parents' heads to the Jacobin Club; *T*, Sept. 12, 1792)

If I have a great number of enemies in this Assembly, I recall them to a sense of decency and appeal to them not to greet with vain clamour, hooting, and threats a man who has sacrificed himself for the country. (Marat, defending himself from the Girondins in the Convention on Sept. 25, 1792; quoted in Mathiez, p. 239)

It is for you, for your sacred liberty that your representatives have sacrificed peace, and are braving death every day. (Proclamation of the Convention to the French People, Jan. 23, 1793, two days after Louis's execution and three days after the assassination of Lepelletier; *DSFR*, p. 394)

Posterity, in condemning those infamous Judges who have sacrificed LOUIS to the fury and ambition of the vilest of men, will extend their censures yet further. (*T*, Jan. 25, 1793)

New victims are daily and hourly sacrificed on the *guillotine*. (*T*, Apr. 30, 1793)

'Let us,' says *Roberspierre* [*sic*], 'make a *hecatomb* (a sacrifice) of all the enemies of the Republic. (*T*, July 23, 1793)

[Chabot:] Yesterday evening she again went to his house: and Marat, whose heart has ever made so many sacrifices to humanity, ordered his doors to be opened to her. [Drouet:] He lamented the deplorable death that had terminated the sacrifices which Marat had made to liberty and humanity. (Reports to the Convention; *MC*, July 24, 1793)

[Marat] loved carnage like a vulture, and delighted in human sacrifices. (*T*, July 26, 1793)

They are hardly contented that they have but an insignificant woman to sacrifice to the MANES of the GREAT MAN. . . . I intended, when I left Caen, to have sacrificed him on the SUMMIT of the Mountain of the Convention. . . . At Paris, they do not conceive how one useless woman, whose longest life would be of no avail, could sacrifice it in cold blood, to save her whole country. . . . I have displayed my character; those who regret me, will rejoice at finding me enjoy repose in the Elysian Fields with Brutus and some Ancients. (Letter from Charlotte Corday after Marat's death; *EM*, Aug. 1793, p. 154)

None but spectators of this afflicting scene can conceive the majestic picture of the immortal CORDAY, who, from a perfect sense of rectitude and independent spirit, deliberately sacrificed her life. (*T*, Aug. 10, 1793)

As demonstrated by the London reports of Lafayette "hunted down like a wild beast" preparatory to sacrifice or of Marat delighting in human sacrifices like a vulture, the English simply equated sacrifice with bestiality and the other members of what might be called the "Committee of Nature." But for the French and the Committee of Public Safety, sacrifice was the centerpiece of an entire tragedy of violence untranslatable across the Channel.

I propose the following structural sketch of this tragedy modeled in part upon Kelly's analyses of the Terror (pp. 18–22). Revolutionary violence from the Storming of the Tuileries (Aug. 10, 1792) through the official Terror (Sept. 1793 to July 1794) occurred in two key native phrasings: "sacrifice" and, as a special inflection of sacrifice, "war." The organized speaking of these violences was constitutive of a deeply narrative imagination of the state as antagonism. We know that the Constitution of 1793—the republican replacement for the Constitution of 1791—was finally ratified in summer 1793 but could not be put into effect because of the emergency triggered externally by the First Coalition and internally by dissension (most notably, the Vendéan Counter-Revolution). In the space between external and internal dangers, the Republic emerged as a sort of epic simile or figure for constituted government (as declared officially on October 10, 1793: a "provisional government . . . revolutionary until the peace"; *DSFR*, p. 480).[33] It emerged as a "way of speaking" government that converted what had all along been a French "standard vocabulary of massacre" or "*ABC de l'idiome jacobite*," as Cobb has documented it (*Police*, pp. 87–88), into a discursive form designed to constitute government solely as collective tragedy.

Inflected to address internal danger, the state was a perpetual readiness for domestic sacrifice—whether of its own heroes or of specially designated victims symbolizing "Aristocracy" (the priests at the September Massacres, for example, or the vast number of future victims named in the Law of Suspects of September 17, 1793). Inflected to address external danger, the state was a universal readiness for war climaxing in the *levée en masse* of August 23, 1793. Such "war" was barely comprehensible across the Channel because it was directed as much against purely metaphorical, phenomenologically outward enemies as actual ones. Saint-Just said as early as November 13, 1792, for example, "Louis has combated the people and has been defeated. He is a . . . foreign prisoner of war" (Mathiez, p. 256). Jean Bon St. André similarly declared in the transcript of the sentencing of Louis translated in the *Times*, "This is a combat of liberty against tyranny, and this combat is death" (Jan. 23, 1793). And the placards of the demonstrators marching to the Convention on September 5, 1793, announced, "War on tyrants! War on aristocrats! War on food-speculators!" (Mathiez, p. 368).

The tragedy that was the true Constitution of Terror became possible when inner and outer inflections of violence predicated each other as if grammatically so that no "sentence" moving an action of state (officially, a decree; unofficially, a rumor) could be complete except in the form "war demands sacrifice" or—with subject and object reversed—"sacrifice demands war." These statements may be taken to gloss the simple, frighteningly comprehensive, and all-sufficient plot of Revolution in the years 1792–93: an entelechial development of violence activated as if according to some purely inner necessity. The greater the threat of war, according to the story of decree and rumor, the more necessary the sacrifice at home: sacrifice was the narrative climax of war. Alternatively—and just as satisfying in the chilling narrative of Terror—the greater the sacrifice at home, the more necessary the war against foreign "tyrants" responsible for it all: war was the climax of sacrifice.

Marat may be credited with plotting the necessary relation between external and domestic violences as early as December 18, 1790: "No, it is not on the frontiers, but in the capital that we must rain down our blows. Stop wasting time thinking up means of defence; there is only one means of defence for you. That which I have recommended so many times: *a general insurrection and popular executions*" (*L'Ami du Peuple*; quoted in Gilchrist and Murray, p. 268). Speaking the same voodoo symmetry of inward and outward violence, Danton declared in the Assembly on August 28, 1792: "We must wage a more terrible war," conducted by "purging" the government and throwing "overboard everything which might endanger the safety of the Revolution" (quoted in Mathiez, p. 175). It was such discourse moving "war" on the basis of internal "purge" that was the immediate cause of the "sacrificial" frenzy of the September Massacres. As Gorsas reported: "While a hundred thousand citizens flew to their arms in order to go to the frontiers, a hundred thousand others, or rather all Paris, betook themselves to the prisons, packed with brigands, with the intention of sacrificing everything to the public safety" (*Le Courrier des départements*; quoted in Gilchrist and Murray, p. 270). Or again, as Robespierre tells the story of the Massacres: "Immediately the tocsin was sounded, and 40,000 men were raised in a few hours. These new defenders of their country were ready to hasten to the frontiers, but before they departed, they remembered that the conspirators were still alive—vengeance and fear inflamed their minds—they ran to the prisons, and a general massacre took place" (*MC*, Nov. 12, 1792).

By the time the official Terror came into being, the plotting of external and internal violences had become mandatory in political discourse: it was the single authorized story of France. In one of many such statements from the Mountain setting the basic plot of the Terror, for example, Robespierre sought to remedy the treason

FIG. 1. The Revolutionary ideology of combat.

of General Dumouriez and the defeat of the armies in March 1793 by raising a new "revolutionary army" directed internally against "all those who have been distinguished by their moderation . . . all doubtful citizens, all the intriguers, all those who have proved to lack public spirit" (*Le Journal du Club des Jacobins*; quoted in Gilchrist and Murray, p. 224).[34] We spy here a story with the intense reflexiveness of Sophoclean plot: the state is an Oedipus searching for enemies who lurk deep within.

Altogether, then, the state of Terror may be parsed as an existential *agon* in which two forces clash along a front of antagonistic violence. This front constitutes a single, but bivalent, plot line readable either as "sacrifice" → "war" or vice versa; see Fig. 1. In somewhat different form, Kelly has called such a structure the "ideology of combat."[35] The identity of the state was neither the Terror of Liberty, on the one hand, nor the counterterror of aristocratic Tyranny, on the other. Liberty and Tyranny, indeed, continually changed constituencies. Identity resided instead in the action of combat itself—in a plotted violence, inflected as sacrifice and war, that consolidated the Republic as the form of its own splitting. The Republic, we may say, was the state agonistes. As Furet has put it, "the nation was constituted by the patriots only in reaction to its adversaries, who were secretly manipulated by the aristocrats. . . . [The enemies of equality] were not real, identifiable, and circumscribed forces, but constantly renewed incarnations of its anti-values" (p. 55). Or again, as Kelly has phrased it, the Revolution "demanded the presence of an enemy in its own midst" in order to create a "binary rhetoric" of combat able to "pass from voice to voice as the orators of the Revolution succeeded one another" (p. 20).

To sketch the full emergency of Revolutionary violence, we need now only to explode the plane of narrative into a three-dimensional theater. I imagine this theater or "scene" of violence so as to take advantage of the paradigm of threefold picture-space (in Renaissance *istoria* as well as picturesque form) we conceived in Chapter 3. Revolutionary agon emerged into ideology, we may say, in an imaginal space akin to that in which history-painting evolved into picturesque "atmosphere." But the overall result was a climate of disciplined free-

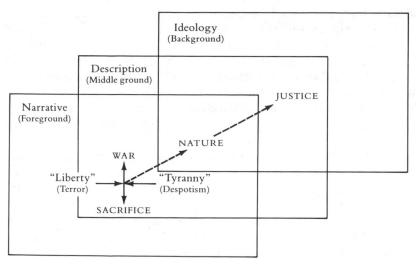

FIG. 2. The scene of emergency, 1792–93.

dom very different from repose: "emergency" (as literalized in the Emergency Decrees of spring 1793 that first created the Committee of Public Safety, Revolutionary Tribunal, Watch Committees, and other instruments necessary to the Revolutionary "provisional government" in the fall; *DSFR*, pp. 408–9); see Fig. 2. In the foreground plays the combat myth or classic narrative of Revolution. From this point on, the action of agony reappears in the light of the Revolution's choric or interpretive functions. First there plays in the middle ground what might be called the "verification" of classic story as constative fact or reality (rather than, for example, epic simile): the Revolution's own grand description of its plot as "natural." As spoken in so many different phrasings and celebrated in so many fetes, we know, Nature was what the Revolution called the entelechial necessity by which sacrifice demanded war (and vice versa).[36] Nature, that is, was the assurance that the Racinesque Revolution was firmly referenced upon what Godwin might call "Things as They Are" (the original title of *Caleb Williams*; p. xv). But verification by itself was inadequate to the optative task of staging the classic story of combat in a manner able to win over all spectators of the Revolution. Things-as-They-Are had to appear Things-as-They-Should-Be: the "natural" classic of the Revolution had to seem a case of classic "justice." Thus arose the background plane of the Revolutionary theater: the explicit ideology according to which combat emerged at last as Revolutionary Justice. The provisional government of emergency declared itself legitimate; agony was *right*.[37]

To spectate the total performance of this theater—to "watch" the action, that is, with the vigilance of a Watch Committee or *oeil de la surveillance* (discussed in Chapter 3)—was to superimpose ideology over tragedy by looking through the drop scenes as if sighting down a line: first from the narrative of "war demands sacrifice" to "nature"; then, by means of the precedent of "natural law," from "nature" to a "justice" seeming both imperturbably removed from immediate action and resident at the self-righteous core of action. In fact, we know that justice appeared at the time to sit officiously in the very thick of bloodletting even while it also claimed to be officially detached from the present scene. Revolutionary justice was first improvised on the pavement in mock street-trials during the Storming of the Tuileries and September Massacres,[38] legitimized in the extralegal trial of Louis, and finally systematized in late 1793 in a legal code (the so-called "Constitution of the Terror"; *DSFR*, pp. 481–90) together with strengthened versions of the Committee of Public Safety, Revolutionary Tribunal, Watch Committees, and other apparatuses (*DSFR*, pp. 476–77). Under the supervision of these latter agencies, war and sacrifice, external and internal violences, were at last legitimized together in the same venue. The paradigm of such a unitary venue was the Revolutionary Tribunal, which had originated on March 9, 1793, with central jurisdiction over "all attacks upon liberty, equality, unity, the indivisibility of the Republic, the internal and external security of the State" (*DSFR*, pp. 409–10). "Terror is nothing other than justice, prompt, stern and inflexible," Robespierre could at last say about the state of Terror in his speech to the Convention of February 5, 1794 (quoted in Gilchrist and Murray, p. 298).

Rooted in underlying narrative, such a state of justice operated throughout its tenure on the basis of the kind of extralegal, *performative* law Furet has called "legitimacy" (p. 74) and Huet, in her study of the trial of Louis, sheer "theatricality" (pp. 1–25, 47–69).[39] Institutionally, the show of law blurred legislative, judicial, and executive functions (Robespierre declared to the Convention, "Because you have established yourselves the judges of Louis, without the usual forms, are you less his judges? You cannot separate your quality of Judge from that of Legislator"; *T*, Jan. 23, 1793). And ethically, it mixed the rationales of punishment, exemplification, and reform (ignoring any distinction between the exemplary and punitive, Danton declared on the same occasion about "Louis the last": "You ought to strike a terror into tyrants—I vote for the punishment of death"; *T*, Jan. 23, 1793). Revolutionary law, indeed, even assimilated wholesale the "vengeance" so deplored by the British. The Report of the Commune on the September Massacres, for example, quoted one of the commissioners on the scene in order to confirm that "The people, in wreaking vengeance, rendered justice also" (*DSFR*, p. 319).

Law during the Revolution, then, was a medium, idiolect, or performative *interpretation* both grounded in the background story and ultimately detachable from the story. The ideology of Justice was something like an Olivier performance of *Hamlet*: a definitive rendition that could not exist without the story but that nevertheless confers some extra essence or dignity upon the story. Thus though the ostensible script of the performance was the Law of the People, we know, the People had no precedent, no clear institutional or ethical identity, except as communicated through the interpretation of the self-delegated street-juries or their representatives in the Assembly—the latter, as Burke noticed, predominantly lawyers by training (*Reflections*, pp. 129–30).[40] A dramaturgy of pure litigiousness, "justice" was the kind of grounded and yet detached interpretation that I previously called the "air" of narrative: *atmosphere*. It was the crowning atmosphere that interpreted Revolutionary violence anagogically so as to declare that it was supervised, if not by God, then by a People otherwise mute and invisible.

Thus where the plot of the Revolutionary tragedy might have remained the angry sentence, "war demands sacrifice," Justice at last legitimized demand to make the sentence read, with an assurance and dignity so supernal that we might well think of the angel-interpreter comforting Hagar: "war *justifies* sacrifice." Sacrifice was just when performed with "the guillotine consecrated by heavenly justice"; and War was just when conducted with the "avenging sword of the laws" (*Le Révolutionnaire*, Nov. 8, 1793; quoted in Gilchrist and Murray, p. 287).

The Revolution, we can sum up, was a poetics of violence that interpreted itself so as to declare that there was neither reality nor right outside its poetics. It was a totalitarian poetics. Seen in overview and with sad hindsight, as John P. Farrell has shown in his fine book on revolution and tragedy, the story of violence could encourage the "moderate" view of a total agony committed neither to left nor right but precisely to left *versus* right. But viewed from within the historical scene itself, which—as we heard Robespierre say, threatened to imprison "all those who have been distinguished by their moderation"—the tragedy of the Revolution was inescapably agonizing for the spectator himself.[41] There could be no middle position, no privileged spectator's vantage, in a totalitarian poetics of terror and pity. It was not possible, quite simply, to be moderate about such as Marat. It was only possible to be to some degree a Corday, who, steeped in Corneille in her youth, would write the tragedy more correctly— would ascend with purer dignity and firmer justice the last stage of the Revolution: the guillotine.[42] On this stage was repose unlike any the picturesque could comprehend:

It was with much difficulty she arrived at the scaffold. The fish women and others, belonging to the markets, were near tearing her to pieces, with oaths and imprecations the most horrid. The *Gens d'Armes* and horse of the Republic prevented this horrid act, by galloping up with lifted sabres.

Mad. *Corday* ascended the scaffold with intrepidity. She appeared serene and reconciled to death. She pulled off her bonnet and handkerchief herself, but recoiled when the executioner went to bind her legs, and said, "Are you so bad as to expose me here?" He answered, "No, it is to bind you." "Do it then," she replied with firmness. (*T*, Aug. 10, 1793)

From out of the savage, barbaric, bestial (and so forth) crush of humanity, Corday emerges as "serene and reconciled" as if she were reposed. Yet in the last episode of her drama—in the "binding" that clinches within a single arresting image the intimation of eros (Corday's illusion of exposure) and violence (the reality of her legs spasming in death)—we know we have emerged into worlds beyond repose. In the universe of tragedy, immobility at the crossing point of motives is in itself *action*: "'Do it then,' she replied with firmness." It is narrative closure. The curtain, or blade, rings down with a sense of fulfilled representation so totalitarian that no further agony can be imagined. Or if imagined, it could not be tolerated. "The inhuman monster" who pulled the *déclic* on the guillotine, we are told, "when shewing her head to the people after her execution, slapped her twice on the cheek!! This was considered as such an atrocious act, that the very Tribunal who had condemned her to death, sentenced her executioner to twelve years imprisonment in irons" (*T*, Aug. 10, 1793). At once wholly improvised and completely scripted, the narrative of the Revolution could not stage further acts of atrocity after the main act. Unable to imagine a more-than-tragic world, the Revolution could only watch tragedy *again*—in further raisings of the blade, in further displays of justified agony. With allusion to Jeffrey Mehlman's thesis, we can thus say that repetition was the essential demonstration of Revolutionary unity—of a unity of action so total that nothing could exist beyond its singularity except further reflections of singularity.[43]

One other feature of totalitarianism will prove relevant: it was in Terror that the Revolution thought time. Repetition became time. Of course, in one sense violence in the Revolution had always been a timed event. As Cobb shows (*Police*, p. 20)—and as Mark Harrison's work on the timing of English crowds helps confirm—*journées*, food riots, protests, killings, celebrations at executions, and so forth occurred in an everyday temporality paced by a practical schedule of holidays, feast days, summer months, and specially turbulent times of day. The People, after all, had to have the leisure to kill; and such leisure was organized according to a calendar in which immediate incitements to riot were fitted into available interstices in the overall pattern of overlapping seasonal, work-week, and religious cycles. The crucial distinction, however, was that such time was rarely thought. Whatever its overall design and philosophy (premised upon its own narratives of agony: of Adam, Christ, or the saints), practical time was customary time. Customary time, we might say, is the recognition that "it is a good day to die" (or to kill) void of any thought about the meaning of "good." Action moves in time; but action *knows* no time.

While violence timed according to the customary calendar raised crowds, therefore, it could not fully articulate temporality as itself a deliberate action—as an *act* of timing able in advance of other actions or representations to register old agonies and communicate new ideology. Summer Sundays during the Revolution might be traditionally good times to raise hell,[44] that is, but not necessarily because of any systematically antireligious polemic conveyed by the choice of time itself. Evolving within such a ragtag or odds-and-ends customary temporality, even the Revolution's more deliberately conceived times could seem lost in miscellany. *Journée* commemorated prior *journée*, but the overall result was somehow not so much a matrix of temporal reference as a labyrinth of cross-reference. Certainly the French police (whose specialized perspective Cobb studies with intriguing results) saw the popular calendar of riot in this fashion. As Cobb puts it in an enactively accumulative passage:

> To the general eighteenth-century pattern of May to September, Sundays and Mondays, feast days, hot days, the Revolution adds the anniversaries of revolutionary *journées*, or of counter-revolutionary atrocities. The recent dead, or the not so recent (so long as there are sons and daughters, nephews and nieces alive, since revenge will hardly extend to the third generation), call out for vengeance, and a revolutionary period multiplies, in each town, the occasions for a collective incitement to murder, and thus gives force to dates, both national and, more often, local: 9 Thermidor, Christmas (in the south only), 21 January (again in the south), 31 May, 15 August, and so on. The police had to be as historically orientated as vindictive crowds; and, in the south-east, the old killing days were still being celebrated in 1798 and even in 1815. They were there so numerous as to be of little use as pointers to massacre, killing in this part of the world going on pretty well throughout the year. (*Police*, p. 20)

Such time, we may say, was *succession* in which each instant generated the next only in a repetitive, associative, and metonymical way.

But in October to November 1793, the Revolution suddenly enrolled succession in an overarching structure of *duration*, and so awoke to the thought of time—to a version of modern philosophic temporality "torn" between the thought of succession and of duration, interregnum and tradition. Specifically, the Revolution thought time as its culminating ideology or over-justification: time was the law of continuous development or entelechial necessity allowing the Revolution to span interregnum with the enduring story, nature, and justice of the People. We might listen once more to Poulet on Romantic time: "And so there opens, at the center of man's being, in the actual feeling of his existence, an insupportable void. . . . It is as if duration had been broken in the middle and man felt his life torn from him, ahead and behind" (p. 29). Now we can fill in the void. If "man" in this era was broken apart to reveal a central absence, that absence had a personality. It was the sans-man whose identity as the state agonistes formed itself within the void as a temporality complicit with the narrative, description, and ideology of new man. Man became the People.

I refer, of course, to the decrees that in fall 1793 instituted the Revolutionary calendar and literally began time anew (with the instant of origin dated retroactively to the beginning of the Republic in 1792). The most telling document is that of November 24, which, after completing the structure of the calendar, continued:

Of the Motives Determining the Decree

The French nation, oppressed, degraded during many centuries by the most insolent despotism, has finally awakened to a consciousness of its rights and of the power to which its destinies summon it. Every day, for five years, of a revolution, of which the annals of the world afford no parallel, it has purged itself of all that sullied it or obstructed its progress. . . . It wishes its regeneration to be complete, in order that its years of liberty and glory may betoken still more by their duration in the history of peoples than its years of slavery and humiliation in the history of kings.

Soon the arts will be summoned to new progress through uniformity of weights and measures. . . . The arts and history, for which time is a necessary element, also required a new measurement of time, freed from all the errors which credulity and superstitious routine have handed down to us from centuries of ignorance.

It is this new standard which the National Convention today presents to the French people; at the same time, by its exactness, its simplicity, and its detachment from every opinion not sanctioned by reason and philosophy, it is to show both the impress of the enlightened members of the nation and the character of our revolution. (*DSFR*, p. 513)

Here in condensed form, we recognize, is a narrative of "purgation" expressing the "character" of the nation; here a verification of natural "regeneration"; and here also the ideology of justice restored after "oppression" and "humiliation." Such is the ultimate ancestor, perhaps, not only of Bergson's temporality but of Braudel's *longue durée*: a philosophy of "*duration* in the history of peoples," according to which repetitive violence coheres in a collective action of awakening character, destiny, and progress. Time was the supra-ideological "thought" that made agony seem as necessary and right as the classical gods or fate: "the French nation, oppressed, degraded during many centuries by the most insolent despotism, has finally awakened to a *consciousness* of its rights and of the power to which its *destinies* summon it."[45]

Remember the "locodescriptive moment" I studied at the unstable interface between narration and description in Chapter 3. To insert the abstract thought of the Revolutionary calendar back into the realm of everyday time, we need at last only look to any of the great fetes marking time from fall 1793 on. What these fetes show in their spectacular imagery is that Revolutionary time—whose total organization Ozouf has perceptively charted (pp. 188–234)—structured the political landscape of the Mountain, Marsh, and Gironde as a firmament composed of nothing but locodescriptive moments.[46] The landscape was a carefully structured itinerary of past and present killing grounds, each one of which, at its proper moment, could come alive with Laocoön-narratives of agon—with fully dramatized stories of hurt forcing their way through the surface of descriptive nature into an atmosphere of ideology at once calm and trembling with agon. The story of the People's "purge" in the decree above, for example, merely generalized such dramatized stories as the allegory staged at the fourth station in the processional Fete of Unity and Indivisibility on August 10, 1793. After moving past the earlier stations (including those we have already viewed at the statues of Regeneration and of Liberty), the procession came to a specially resonant power spot displaying the Mountain's dominance over the Marsh (and the Girondins). As David scripted it in his program: "The fourth halt shall be made in the *Place des Invalides*. In the middle of the *Place*, on the summit of a mountain, shall be represented a colossal figure, the French people, gathering in its vigorous arms the departmental bundle of staves. Ambitious federalism, coming forth from its slimy marsh, with one hand brushing aside the reeds, tries with the other to detach some of the staves; the French people catches sight of it, takes its club, strikes it, and makes it return to its pullulating waters never to quit them again" (*Chronique de Paris*, July 18, 1793; quoted in Henderson, pp. 362–64).[47] Such is the story of the violent, yet eternally natural and just, People.

By 1793, in sum, time was the culminating expression of the story of agony. To quote Ricouer's general thesis about temporality and narrative: "time becomes human to the extent that it is articulated through a narrative mode, and narrative attains its full meaning when it becomes a condition of temporal existence" (p. 52).

———⟲———

CHAPTER FIVE

A First Time:
Descriptive Sketches, Salisbury Plain

WE ARE NOW READY TO OPEN the scene of Wordsworth's time. All that is needed is to pass the picturesque through the Revolution, the picture of repose through the poetics of violence. How could Wordsworth, after touring the Revolution in 1791–92 and returning to England soon before the onset of war with France in 1793, describe nature?

The picturesque, we saw, described nature as the form of liberal freedom—a rest or arrest of motive forgetful of institutionally accepted narratives and carefully balanced between discipline and freedom. Only epic similes and other such telltales marked the survival of narrative as "fiction" within a universe of descriptive fact that was also social and political fact: the majestic repose of the English Constitution. By contrast, the Revolution described nature as a means of verifying narrative fact: an underlying tragedy of the People so radically agonized—so much more riotous in both its freedom and its discipline—as to be hostile to any form duly constituted to arrest motive. Desire was free to become violence according to a "natural" entelechy ideologized as "just."

How could Wordsworth describe nature after the Revolution? The answer, of course, is that he could not. Instead, descriptive form had to deform to apprehend the *tragedy* of nature. As a first approximation, we can call such deform a mimesis of emergency. The mimesis can be derived by aligning in series the three major structures of imagination we have been following. The given of the derivation is the traditional structure of institutional imagination: *Istoria* → Interpretation → Anagogy. Under Church supervision, artists interpreted canonical stories through visual deployments constitutive of the perceptible universe. The crown of interpretation was anagogy: the light or atmosphere of eternal truth.

On the foundation of such imagination, together with its literary and other analogues, arose the basic structure of Revolutionary emergency I have suggested: Narrative → Description → Ideology. Imagination now began upon narratives paradigmatically classical rather than sacred, and acknowledged the supervision of the People rather than the Church. But it also respected the old design in its very expression. Imagination emerged through a descriptive propaganda of nature big with the universe of exegesis—a wholesale typology of natural martyrs, for example, or the implicitly Mosaic landscape of the Jacobin Mountain. And it peaked in an ideology of Terror showing anagogy in a different light: Justice, an atmosphere of inquisitional Vigilance emblematized by the Jacobin Eye of Surveillance in its fiery aureole. Such anagogy implied not eternity but the over-justification, as I called it, of new historical time: duration, an uncanny approximation of Burke's "primaeval contract of eternal society" between "those who are living, those who are dead, and those who are to be born" (*Reflections*, pp. 194–95).[1] Anagogy, that is, was perpetual revolution.

From Revolutionary imagination we can now derive the poetic emergency that is our main concern: History → Nature → Time. Wordsworth mimed the Revolutionary story of man by deforming his early, picturesque description of nature, "agonizing" the landscape so that it told not of repose but of a tragic struggle informed by the contemporary poetics of violence. And the outcome of the mimesis was his first ideology of nature: time. Serene as the *aion* of anagogy, but also urgent as ideology, time justified the tragedy of nature. Time, that is, subsumed all the justifications of the Revolution and legitimized the natural course of things that interposed—from epoch to epoch, or from infancy to adulthood—so painful a break between past and present. The agony of succession, time declares, is for all time: it is what gives you—a People and its poet—the discipline to endure. This is the argument initiated in *Descriptive Sketches*, whose close upon an atmosphere of fiery futurity predicts the time of a brave new world. As the Revolution books of *The Prelude* later recall about 1793, it seemed assured "that time would soon set all things right, / Prove that the multitude had been oppress'd, / And would be so no more" (10.777–79).

Yet mimesis of emergency is finally only half the story. If mimesis were all Wordsworth's concern, time would end only a creature of convention—only a French ideology. Time, that is, would be a calendar of fetes. The other half of our project will be to observe the deflection in mimesis necessary before the poet can write his mature poetry. Time, we know, will indeed become a calendar of fetes: the spots of time.[2] But whereas Revolutionary fetes declared an ideology premised upon nature's transparency to underlying history (the days of Rampion, Field Turnip, Chicory, Medlar, Hog, Lamb's Lettuce, Cauliflower, and so forth thus culminated every year in the days of the *sans-culottides*; *DSFR*, pp. 510–12), Wordsworth's fetes will argue an ideology requiring nature to be opaque to history.[3] After the shock of the high Terror and of the declaration of war between England and France, nature—the verification of imagination intervening between history and ideology—became a blind or screen: a fact for its own sake. Nature obscured history within landscape once more, returned the facts of historical violence to the status of ghostly, unnatural fictions, and so hid any need—or at least conscious need—to justify the brutality of Things as They Are. Left behind at the end of this process, time—the justification of the tragedy underlying nature—became at last Wordsworth's *moot* ideology of justice: a residual law justifying hidden tragedies, obscure sources of agony. We must thus finally apply Ricoeur's thesis, quoted at the end of the last chapter, with severe qualification. For Wordsworth, time becomes human to the extent that it is articulated through a *denied* "narrative mode." Such is the argument begun in *Salisbury Plain*, the first poem to intimate the power of Wordsworth's mature evasions of mimesis or forms of denial. Here, the poet's true time begins.

All that will be necessary to institute the poetry of spots of time, as we will see, will be to invent his version of a Church or People able to supervise imagination: the Romantic self.

The Tragedy of Nature

Agonizing the Landscape

Composed mostly in France between December 1791 and November or December 1792, *Descriptive Sketches* (published with *An Evening Walk* in 1793) begins by refusing to describe. Wordsworth traces his first trip through France in 1790. But while he takes care for most of the poem to respect his actual itinerary of 1790, he opens by refusing to describe either Revolutionary France, which he crossed en route to the Alps, or the Savoy, which he visited just prior to entering Switzerland.[4]

The boundary between France and the Savoy—the free and the still "enslaved"*—marks the proscenium of tragedy. It situates the avant-garde of a Revolutionary agony not yet describable in the picturesque form that *Descriptive Sketches* inherits from *An Evening Walk*. Before the agony can be told, description must know the poetics of violence. Wordsworth must describe nature so as to suppress desire and create a landscape of violence grounded upon Revolutionary action. Nature, that is, must narrate the plot of sacrifice and war and then justify it.[5]

Wordsworth begins submitting desire to violence in two sequences of description, each severely end-stopped and characterized by what may be called "resacralization," a revisionary technique invoking all the old institutional powers of the picturesque. The poem opens upon a sacralized or ritual picturesque seeming virtually to recite dogma:

> Were there, below, a spot of holy ground,
> By Pain and her sad family unfound,
> Sure, Nature's GOD that spot to man had giv'n,
> Where murmuring rivers join the song of ev'n;
> Where falls the purple morning far and wide
> In flakes of light upon the mountain-side;
> Where summer Suns in ocean sink to rest,
> Or moonlight Upland lifts her hoary breast;
> Where Silence, on her night of wing, o'er-broods
> Unfathom'd dells and undiscover'd woods;
> Where rocks and groves the power of water shakes
> In cataracts, or sleeps in quiet lakes.   (ll. 1–12)†

Nature's "GOD" endows man with a spot from which, with a turn of the head, all features of the landscape open to eye and ear in perfectly reposed "rest." So, too, every hour of this long summer's day—evening, morning, sunset, and night—opens to perception in a timeless "now" coordinated by "where's" as simultaneous as the "when's" of *An Evening Walk*.

But Wordsworth then desacralizes the picturesque by propelling beatified "man" forth as *desirer*. In the second verse paragraph of the poem, the wounded heart of the Traveller (so named in the poem's Argument) replaces the eye as the organ of perception:

---

* The Savoy was annexed by France in late 1792 while the poem was being finished. Wordsworth calls Savoy the "slave of slaves" in l. 706 and adds a footnote on the subsequent "emancipation" of the region (*DS*, p. 108n).

† Citation of *Descriptive Sketches* and *Salisbury Plain* in this chapter is as follows: my primary texts are the Reading Texts of the 1793 *Descriptive Sketches* in *DS* (cited by line number) and of *Salisbury Plain* (1793–94) in *SP* (cited by stanza number); later versions of the poems (including the revisions of *Salisbury Plain* titled *Adventures on Salisbury Plain* and *Guilt and Sorrow*), apparatus, and transcriptions of manuscripts in *DS* and *SP* are referred to by page number. For a guide to the composition of the poems, see the Introductions to *DS* and *SP* as well as *CEY*, pp. 24–25, 333–36.

> But doubly pitying Nature loves to show'r
> Soft on his wounded heart her healing pow'r,
> Who plods o'er hills and vales his road forlorn,
> Wooing her varying charms from eve to morn.
> No sad vacuities his heart annoy,
> Blows not a Zephyr but it whispers joy;
> For him lost flowers their idle sweets exhale;
> He tastes the meanest note that swells the gale;
>
> . . .
>
> Moves there a cloud o'er mid-day's flaming eye?
> Upward he looks—and calls it luxury;
>
> . . .
>
> He views the Sun uprear his golden fire,
> Or sink, with heart alive like Memnon's lyre;
> Blesses the Moon that comes with kindest ray
> To light him shaken by his viewless way.
>
> (ll. 13–36)

The fane of landscape becomes the profane of desire—of desire so existential that it sustains the very ground of reality against a negation akin to that we saw in *An Evening Walk*. "No sad vacuities," no veiling of the world by clouds, no scatter of reality into disconnected winds, flowers, and notes can hollow out the wish-substance of this "viewless" world.

And perhaps because the Traveller is older than the Walker in Wordsworth's earlier poem, his "wooing" of shy landscape becomes specifically erotic. The wounded heart at the opening of the paragraph looks through landscape to a virgin heart at the end. The Traveller is

> a brother at the cottage meal,
> His humble looks no shy restraint impart,
> Around him plays at will the virgin heart.
> While unsuspended wheels the village dance,
> The maidens eye him with inquiring glance,
> Much wondering what sad stroke of crazing Care
> Or desperate Love could lead a wanderer there.
>
> (ll. 38–44)

The wounded heart directs humble looks toward its imago, the virgin heart, and receives in answer the flirtation of an inquiring glance. But taboo intervenes: intercourse between hearts must be "brotherly," and humble looks and inquiring glances can mingle only in the buffer zone of vision that is the landscape. Description of nature, so sacred to start with, now "contains" desire: it chaperones it, but is saturated by it.

Having analyzed the picturesque as wanderlust, Wordsworth then personalizes such lust as first-person motive in a strangely listless sentence:

Me, lur'd by hope her sorrows to remove,
A heart, that could not much itself approve,
O'er Gallia's wastes of corn dejected led,
Her road elms rustling thin above my head,
Or through her truant pathway's native charms,
By secret villages and lonely farms,
To where the Alps, ascending white in air,
Toy with the sun, and glitter from afar.

(ll. 45–52)

Just as the Traveller's wounded heart gazed toward a virgin heart, so the poet's heart now gazes toward the Alps. Between heart and Alps extends a landscape of subdued loveliness: a minimally described temptation unnameable except as "Gallia" with all her "native charms."

It is at this point—when the tourist has narrowed from Man to Traveller to Poet, and the landscape to a femininity consonant with the poet's sharpest desire of summer 1792, Annette Vallon—that *Descriptive Sketches* cuts off desire at a monastery. Though the monastery of the Grande Chartreuse belongs here in the 1790 tour, Wordsworth's description of it as already devoid of monks is significantly anachronistic. As Moorman has noted, troops did not arrive to expel the monks until between May and October 1792 (MM, 1: 135–37). In essence, the Grande Chartreuse enters from a different plane of reality. It is a leading from above, a resacralization serving to prophesy that the landscape of desire must reform violently:

Ev'n now I sigh at hoary Chartreuse' doom
Weeping beneath his chill of mountain gloom.
Where now is fled that Power whose frown severe
Tam'd "sober Reason" till she crouch'd in fear?
That breath'd a death-like peace these woods around
Broke only by th' unvaried torrent's sound,
Or prayer-bell by the dull cicada drown'd.
The cloister startles at the gleam of arms,
And Blasphemy the shuddering fane alarms;
Nod the cloud-piercing pines their troubl'd heads,
Spires, rocks, and lawns, a browner night o'erspreads.
Strong terror checks the female peasant's sighs,
And start th' astonish'd shades at female eyes.
The thundering tube the aged angler hears,
And swells the groaning torrent with his tears.

.   .   .

The "parting Genius" sighs with hollow breath
Along the mystic streams of Life and Death.

(ll. 53–73)

Landscape here situates a transition not so much from peace to war as between two faces of totalitarian violence. The peace previously enforced by the Carthusian monks was death-like, the result of a "Power whose frown severe / Tam'd 'sober Reason' till she crouch'd in fear." Such was certainly violence—an inwardly directed or domestic violence that is the poet's first intimation of the Revolutionary spirit of sacrifice. The Carthusian monks, whose place is to be given over unsparingly to the Revolution, are themselves the original spirit of sacrifice. Wordsworth then opens inner violence outward into war by imagining the usurpation of the monks by Revolutionary troops. Yet the transition creates less a difference than a resemblance. The self-inflicted rigor of the monks, we know, had itself been near-military. Travelers to the monastery thus commonly mentioned an atmosphere of extraordinary "severity" supervised by the General of the Order. (Since the Seven Years War, indeed, the monastery had sometimes been fortified by a small body of actual soldiers.)[6] Even in decrying the usurpation of monastic rigor by military rule, in sum, Wordsworth begins to trace over landscape an emergent Revolutionary plot: sacrifice is war. Whatever other hold the anachronism of the Grande Chartreuse has on the poet's imagination, it intrudes so strongly here because it is the perfect vehicle by which to begin ghosting into the landscape of 1790 the narrative shape of events glimpsed at the time of composition in 1792.

A further extrapolation may be risked: violence at the Grande Chartreuse initiates a subtle imagination of ideology. Nature not only verifies the developing world of violence but tentatively justifies it. Certainly the common denominator of the monastic and the military at the Grande Chartreuse is disciplinary rigor. Where the celibate monks once suppressed the desires represented by femininity, now the new monasticism of the military assumes the corrective task: "Strong terror checks the female peasant's sighs." Or again, we might remark the strong allusion to the "parting genius" in Milton's "On the Morning of Christ's Nativity." The *genius loci* or local god (to which Wordsworth compares the monks) departs in the punitive portion of Milton's work. Anticipating the doom that will come when the "dreadful Judge" summons the world to its "last session," all the genii and gods of the old order "troop to th' infernal jail." Updated, such a juridical allusion whispers the "unjust Tribunals" Wordsworth remembers haunted his actual dreams from 1793 on (*Prel.* 10.377).

The overarching result of the Grande Chartreuse passage is the emergence of time. "Ev'n *now* I sigh at hoary Chartreuse' doom," the poet choruses, and again: "Where *now* is fled that Power. . . ?" When, we might ask, is now? Preceded by a brief descent of description into past tense ("Me . . . A heart, that could not much itself approve, / O'er Gallia's wastes of corn dejected led"), now is surely not the descriptive present characterizing the bulk of the poem. Instead, it is the very mark of the anachronism by which the poet has already ascended from the present of 1790—which thus becomes past—to a mountain vision of 1792.[7] It is a first indication that what is important to the poem is a time that has split off from descriptive reality and become a "succession" requiring thought.

But the pattern set in the initial movement of *Descriptive Sketches* is still very tentative. The rhythm of the poem is that of a tide coming in on a series of waves. Wordsworth next repeats the movement from desire to violence with stronger emphasis.

Skirting Chamonix, Mont Blanc, and other parts of the Savoy, the poet suddenly plants himself farther along the tour at Lake Como, where his route had dipped just south of Switzerland into Italy. Here he recovers a deep pleasure: "More pleas'd, my foot the hidden margin roves / Of Como bosom'd deep in chestnut groves" (ll. 80–81). If the synecdoche of desire earlier in the poem was the wounded heart and its imago the virgin heart, the member of desire here is the foot, and its imago—a fetish throughout Wordsworth's early works—the bosom. From line 92 on, the poem lapses into the erotic reverie of a "lingerer" who surveys,

> With hollow ringing ears and darkening gaze,
> Binding the charmed soul in powerless trance,
> Lip-dewing Song and ringlet-tossing Dance,
> Where sparkling eyes and breaking smiles illume
> The bosom'd cabin's lyre-enliven'd gloom.
>
> (ll. 97–101)

A few lines on, "Soft bosoms breathe around contagious sighs, / And amourous music on the water dies" while "Pale Passion, overpower'd, retires and woos / The thicket, where th' unlisten'd stockdove coos" (ll. 114–15, 118–19). When Wordsworth then continues his encomium on Como by exclaiming, "How bless'd, delicious Scene! the eye that greets / Thy open beauties" (ll. 120–21), we wonder what normally kerchiefed beauties lie "open" in landscape. The poem itself refuses to leave the kerchief in place. It suddenly experiences a paroxysm of desire (much self-bowdlerized by the time of the 1836 version) approaching, at times, the intensity of the Sadean vision:

> Farewel! those forms that, in thy noon-tide shade,
> Rest, near their little plots of wheaten glade;
> Those stedfast eyes, that beating breasts inspire
> To throw the "sultry ray" of young Desire;
> Those lips, whose tides of fragrance come, and go,
> Accordant to the cheek's unquiet glow;
> Those shadowy breasts in love's soft light array'd,
> And rising, by the moon of passion sway'd.
> —Thy fragrant gales and lute-resounding streams,
> Breathe o'er the failing soul voluptuous dreams;

> While Slavery, forcing the sunk mind to dwell
> On joys that might disgrace the captive's cell,
> Her shameless timbrel shakes along thy marge,
> And winds between thine isles the vocal barge.
>
> (ll. 148–61)

This second prominence of desire in the poem serves to prepare once more for the translation of desire into violence. First Wordsworth resacralizes the Como environs by glancing at a genius as rigorous as that of the "hoary Chartreuse": a "hoary-headed sire . . . A hermit" (ll. 170–75). Then he shifts the scene slightly to the pleasures of Locarno and the river Tusa, but immediately juxtaposes the violent landscape "where Viamala's chasms confine / Th' indignant waters of the infant Rhine" (ll. 184–85). Finally, and most strongly, he end-stops the second movement of the poem by appending another mountain episode: the story of the Grison Gypsy (ll. 188–242).

Like the Female Beggar in *An Evening Walk*, the Grison Gypsy is a figure of desire whose sole purpose is to become the victim of violence. The poet first paints the Gypsy as a Dark Lady: "Her tawny skin, dark eyes, and glossy locks, / Bend o'er the smoke that curls beneath the rocks" (ll. 190–91). But if this miniature portrait promises a woman as desirable, perhaps, as Wordsworth's own dark-haired and dark-eyed lady of 1792, Annette,[8] desire must be immediately rebuffed. First the poem introduces pain:

> —The mind condemn'd, without reprieve, to go
> O'er life's long deserts with it's charge of woe,
> With sad congratulation joins the train,
> Where beasts and men together o'er the plain
> Move on,—a mighty caravan of pain.
>
> (ll. 192–96)

Akin to the epic similes of picturesque tradition—but with opposite function—this conceit of the mind's exodus marks the re-entry of narrative into the descriptive universe. With a modulation so subtle that the pronoun, "She," could refer to either "mind" or "Gypsy," Wordsworth proceeds to the tragic *story* of the Grison Gypsy:

> —She solitary through the desert drear
> Spontaneous wanders, hand in hand with Fear.
>   A giant moan along the forest swells
> Protracted, and the twilight storm foretells,
> And, ruining from the cliffs their deafening load
> Tumbles, the wildering Thunder slips abroad;
> On the high summits Darkness comes and goes,
> Hiding their fiery clouds, their rocks, and snows;
> The torrent, travers'd by the lustre broad,
> Starts like a horse beside the flashing road;

> In the roof'd bridge, at that despairing hour,
> She seeks a shelter from the battering show'r.
> —Fierce comes the river down; the crashing wood
> Gives way, and half it's pines torment the flood;
> Fearful, beneath, the Water-spirits call,
> And the bridge vibrates, tottering to its fall.
>
> (ll. 199–214)

The roofed bridge, we should recognize, is the very antipodes of the "secret bridge" at the start of *An Evening Walk*; and its stormy atmosphere the death of repose. If the earlier bridge may be called an angel's bridge, in the sense that it descends from pictures such as *Hagar and the Angel*, this later bridge—as Hartman has suggested—may certainly be named a Devil's Bridge akin to another terrorized bridge of this name in Wordsworth's later work.[9] Even if the weather were calm, we notice, the roofed bridge would still commit a violence, an "injury," upon the picturesque. Wordsworth mentions in a note, "Most of the bridges among the Alps are of wood and covered: these bridges have a heavy appearance, and rather injure the effect of the scenery in some places." The actual fall of the bridge in the poem then simply transcribes descriptive injury as the narrative of injury. Opened by allusion to the end of *Paradise Lost* and closed at line 213 by an echo of John Home's tragedy, *Douglas* (as Wordsworth notes), the whole course of the passage records the transformation of description into a story of terror. From this point on, picturesque repose explodes: "Bursts from the troubl'd Larch's giant boughs / The pie, and chattering breaks the night's repose" (ll. 229–30). And in its place enter antagonists threatening to fulfill the promise of "Death" we saw in *An Evening Walk*: not only actual death-dogs, foxes, bears, banditti, and wolves but also metamorphic personifications on the verge of becoming romance characters: "Havoc" rouses the bear, the Moon rides behind her hill, water "slinks" with "red eyes," and so forth (ll. 226–42).

Unlike the episode of the Grande Chartreuse, however, that of the Grison Gypsy does not structure agony precisely. This is the task of the middle movements of *Descriptive Sketches*, which articulate the emergent agony of landscape in ways predictive of Revolutionary imagination. While we cannot read the whole of the poem's middle closely, a glance at the most telling episodes will prepare for the peak agony of landscape yet to be imagined.

Describing the chapel of William Tell with the aid of Coxe's *Travels* (in Ramond's amplification),[10] Wordsworth stages landscape as a theater of war. Specifically, he unfolds a highly selective tale of war contoured along the lines of Revolutionary tragedy:

> But lo! the boatman, over-aw'd, before
> The pictur'd fane of Tell suspends his oar;

Confused the Marathonian tale appears,
While burn in his full eyes the glorious tears.
And who but feels a power of strong controul,
Felt only there, oppress his labouring soul,
Who walks, where honour'd men of ancient days
Have wrought with god-like arm the deeds of praise?
Say, who, by thinking on Canadian hills,
Or wild Aosta lull'd by Alpine rills,
On Zutphen's plain; or where with soften'd gaze
The old grey stones the plaided chief surveys,
Can guess the high resolve, the cherish'd pain
Of him whom passion rivets to the plain,
Where breath'd the gale that caught Wolfe's happiest sigh,
And the last sun-beam fell on Bayard's eye,
Where bleeding Sydney from the cup retir'd,
And glad Dundee in "faint huzzas" expir'd.

(ll. 348–65)

Istoria revives within the picturesque. At the sight of the pictures in Tell's chapel, landscape fills with icons of battle each suggesting that violence against external enemies opens inwardly into martyrdom or self-sacrifice. As in Benjamin West's *Death of General Wolfe* (1771), in which Wolfe's posture quotes a Lamentation or Pietà (C. Mitchell, p. 31 and n.), Wordsworth's heroes simulate Christ's agony: "passion rivets" them with "cherish'd pain." Perhaps the most telling figure of sacrifice here is the bleeding Sidney, who, in the action to which Wordsworth refers, died in an apotheosis of self-sacrifice: "Thy need is greater than mine," he is reputed to have said in giving water to a soldier (Beatty, *Wordsworth*, p. 48n).

Where the Tell fane tells the story of war opening inwardly into martyrdom, the episode of the Chamois Chaser soon follows by telling of sacrifice opening outward into war. The Chamois Chaser is the plebeian version of bleeding Sidney. To reach his icy transcendence, he must ritually let his own blood. The literal anecdote in Ramond, which Wordsworth summarizes in a note, is already striking: "The rays of the sun drying the rocks frequently produce on their surface a dust so subtile and slippery, that the wretched chamois-chasers are obliged to bleed themselves in the legs and feet in order to secure a footing" (*DS*, p. 76n; see Beatty, *Wordsworth*, p. 50n). In Wordsworth's rendition, the anecdote becomes the gospel, if not of the stigmatized Christ, then of a punctured Prometheus offered up to vulture-skies:

Ye dewy mists the arid rocks o'er-spread
Whose slippery face derides his deathful tread!
—To wet the peak's impracticable sides
He opens of his feet the sanguine tides,

> Weak and more weak the issuing current eyes
> Lapp'd by the panting tongue of thirsty skies.
>
> (ll. 392–97)

The Promethean sacrifice reaches its climax when the Chamois Chaser dies after an avalanche under the eyes of the "raven of the skies" and "eagle of the Alps" (ll. 398–407). In a final touch, Wordsworth leaves the bones behind like "reliques" (ll. 408–13).

But domestic sacrifice is also at heart militant. The episode of the Chamois Chaser, we note, recalls an earlier allegory of the chamois in the poem. The allegory had ended upon a conceit:

> Ev'n here Content has fix'd her smiling reign
> With Independance child of high Disdain.
> Exulting mid the winter of the skies,
> Shy as the jealous chamois, Freedom flies,
> And often grasps her sword, and often eyes,
> Her crest a bough of Winter's bleakest pine,
> Strange "weeds" and alpine plants her helm entwine,
> And wildly-pausing oft she hangs aghast,
> While thrills the "Spartan fife" between the blast.
>
> (ll. 323–31)

Following upon armed Freedom as well as upon the warriors in Tell's fane, the description of the Chamois Chaser's life harbors a reserve militancy.

Such vignettes of war and sacrifice in the middle movements of *Descriptive Sketches* together imagine an agony whose ideology is a growing sense of natural law. Visiting the Tell chapel, the poet "feels a power of strong controul . . . oppress his labouring soul" (ll. 352–53), and imagining the Chamois Chaser, he revises power as precisely juridical—as a "Demon" avalanche shutting "for aye his prison door" (ll. 400–401). Some daemonic oppression in the landscape, we may say, begins to make the Swiss Alps a penitentiary of pain, a natural Bastille amplifying the dungeon-like rocks the poet earlier encountered in the Reuss defile: "Black drizzling craggs, that beaten by the din, / Vibrate, as if a voice complain'd within" (ll. 249–50).

Mountain Story

It is at this point that *Descriptive Sketches* brings landscape to its peak agony. In a sweeping conclusion, Wordsworth reveals a myth of Swiss independence and then, as the referent of myth, the Revolution. The myth functions as a gigantic epic simile with a polarity opposite from that of the similes we saw in the picturesque: myth injects within description a narrative of mountains or, more accurately, of the Jacobin Mountain.

The Swiss myth is a proto-narrative of violence founded upon what Sheats has insightfully suggested is the eschatological story of Creation, Deluge, and Millennium (pp. 65–69) and, in closer perspective, upon the tragedy of the Revolution. Switzerland is a state of liberty *not* Edenic, as is often presumed about the poet's early idolization of the Swiss, but tragic. Once, Wordsworth imagines, Switzerland might have been a golden age: "Summer lengthen'd out his season bland, / And with rock-honey flow'd the happy land" (ll. 476–77).[11] And once it might have been a political idyll: "Man entirely free, alone and wild . . . Walk'd none restraining, and by none restrain'd, / Confess'd no law . . ." (ll. 520–24).

But paradise is gone. In its place is a state of supremely harsh liberty. "I see him," Wordsworth says in a vision of the present-day Swiss:

> up the midway cliff he creeps
> To where a scanty knot of verdure peeps,
> Thence down the steep a pile of grass he throws
> The fodder of his herds in winter snows.
> Far different life to what tradition hoar
> Transmits of days more bless'd in times of yore.[12]
>
> (ll. 470–75)

Nature has become a labored paradise. It has become a regime so severe, indeed, that labor is assimilated to violence. Defined on one front, nature in Switzerland verifies a native militancy little short of self-sacrifice. The martial aspect of the Swiss, whose troops died in the Tuileries during the poem's composition, flourishes in the poem's glorification of the battle of Naeffels in 1388, in which "three hundred" Swiss troops defeated "twice ten thousand" Austrians (ll. 536–41). Afterwards, Wordsworth continues, the "sainted Rocks" of the battlefield projected a "holy" air (ll. 542–45), and "savage Nature" herself seemed to join the "rite" (l. 554). Defined inversely, nature in Switzerland verifies a spirit of domestic sacrifice leading to involvement in foreign war. The Swiss are a Spartan race inured by nature to the most rigorous severities at home. The scarcity of arable land, for example, demands a practice that Wordsworth renders as something like an offering up of Isaac: primogeniture. The poem observes:

> The father, forc'd by Powers that only deign
> That solitary Man disturb their reign,
> From his bare nest amid the storms of heaven
> Drives, eagle-like, his sons as he was driven,
> His last dread pleasure! watches to the plain—
> And never, eagle-like, beholds again.
>
> (ll. 616–21)

Where do the exiled sons go? "Lo! by the lazy Seine the exile roves," Wordsworth imagines, "Or where thick sails illume Batavia's groves" (ll. 624–25). They become mercenaries, and so complete the equation between inner sacrifice and outer militancy.[13]

In such a tragically violent land, there can be no true liberty. The Swiss may still be free in the sense of being the slave of none (l. 532), but they are no longer free from what the poem had earlier stayed: law (l. 524). Rather, freedom now demands unswerving obedience to a terrifying natural law felt everywhere in existence—to a justice cognate with life itself. The Swiss, Wordsworth says, must explain the rigor of their present lives by telling their sons that "human vices have provok'd the rod / Of angry Nature to avenge her God" (ll. 486–87). Thus does the poem cap its ideological justification of violence. The climate of nature is justice. Or as Wordsworth immediately says, nature is "ever just" (l. 490).

Having introduced a tragedy of mountains anticipating the Revolution, Wordsworth can then move quickly to the story of the Mountain itself. At line 632, he arrives upon what may be taken to be his denouement: a flashforward of history akin to that at the end of *Paradise Lost*. First there is a flash*back* we will need to consider later:

> Gay lark of hope thy silent song resume!
> Fair smiling lights the purpled hills illume!
> Soft gales and dews of life's delicious morn,
> And thou! lost fragrance of the heart return!
> Soon flies the little joy to man allow'd,
> And tears before him travel like a cloud.
> (ll. 632–37)

Then the poet resacralizes the landscape once more by invoking the monastery at Einsiedeln. Here, "Pain's wild rebellious burst proclaims her rights aloud" (l. 653). We remember that the poem had begun by refusing pain ("Were there, below, a spot of holy ground, / By Pain and her sad family unfound") and that it could think pain only after a strenuous effort of mind in the episode of the Grison Gypsy ("The mind condemn'd . . . joins the train . . .—a mighty caravan of pain"). Only now, after setting the hurtful scene in Switzerland, can pain declaim on nature's center stage. What is pain, the opposite of picturesque delight? When "Pain's wild rebellious burst proclaims her rights aloud," it would not be extravagant to hear an allusion to Paine's *Rights of Man* (1791). Pain is the birth of the Revolutionary story of man from religious institution. While Wordsworth "half wishes" that religious agony at Einsiedeln would be enough to purge human pain, in other words, he knows that such ancient "delusion" will not by itself suffice (l. 679). Only the new institutions of pain developed by the Revolution can purge pain with pain.

After Einsiedeln, we thus discover that the curtain rises on the Revolution as the lone actor. Wordsworth begins by unveiling half of what had been indescribable earlier in the poem: the Savoy and Mont Blanc. The latter is the mountain of old Horror:

> Six thousand years amid his lonely bounds
> The voice of Ruin, day and night, resounds.
> Where Horror-led his sea of ice assails,
> Havoc and Chaos blast a thousand vales.
>
> (ll. 692–95)

It provides the point of supervision from which to spy the Mountain of Terror. As if merely pivoting atop his mountain, Wordsworth thus at last surveys the other half of the poem's initial indescribability: Revolutionary France. Specifically, he moves on from the still "enslaved" region of Mont Blanc to salute a region of liberty not even on the itinerary of 1790, the Loire valley hosting his poetic labors in the summer and early fall of 1792:

> —And thou! fair favoured region! which my soul
> Shall love, 'till Life has broke her golden bowl,
> Till Death's cold touch her cistern-wheel assail,
> And vain regret and vain desire shall fail;
> Tho' now, where erst the grey-clad peasant stray'd,
> To break the quiet of the village shade
> Gleam war's discordant habits thro' the trees,
> And the red banner mock the sullen breeze;
> 'Tho' now no more thy maids their voices suit
> To the low-warbled breath of twilight lute,
> And heard, the pausing village hum between,
> No solemn songstress lull the fading green,
> Scared by the fife, and rumbling drum's alarms,
> And the short thunder, and the flash of arms.
>
> (ll. 740–53)

No more do Gallia's maids sing the siren-note of love in a pastoral world. "Desire" terminates in violence phrased as war and subsequently as the transformation of war into something like a gigantic sacrifice, a Phoenix-rite of regenerative immolation:

> Yet, yet rejoice, tho' Pride's perverted ire
> Rouze Hell's own aid, and wrap thy hills in fire.
> Lo! from th' innocuous flames, a lovely birth!
> With its own Virtues springs another earth:
> Nature, as in her prime.   (ll. 780–84)

From such violent nature at last issues a grand ideologization, a vision of Justice ascendant over the landscape: "With pulseless hand, and fix'd unwearied gaze, / Unbreathing Justice her still beam surveys" (ll. 786–87).[14]

What was indescribable at the start of *Descriptive Sketches*, then, emerges at last as the full story of Revolution. We can note one other salient of the story: fire is the poem's great atmosphere of ideology (cf. Wüscher, p. 33). Leading into the innocuous flames passage, Wordsworth fans the flames:

> —Tho' Liberty shall soon, indignant, raise
> Red on his hills his beacon's comet blaze;
> Bid from on high his lonely cannon sound,
> And on ten thousand hearths his shout rebound;
> His larum-bell from village-tow'r to tow'r
> Swing on th' astounded ear it's dull undying roar:
> Yet, yet rejoice, tho' Pride's perverted ire
> Rouze Hell's own aid, and wrap thy hills in fire.
>
> (ll. 774–81) [15]

We might return to an earlier passage in the poem, the sunset sparking the well-known note in which the poet declares his break with the picturesque:

> the Sun walking on his western field
> Shakes from behind the clouds his flashing shield.
>
> . . .
>
> Wide o'er the Alps a hundred streams unfold,
> At once to pillars turn'd that flame with gold;
> Behind his sail the peasant strives to shun
> The west that burns like one dilated sun,
> Where in a mighty crucible expire
> The mountains, glowing hot, like coals of fire.
>
> (ll. 336–47)

Wordsworth notes: "I had once given to these sketches the title of Picturesque; but the Alps are insulted in applying to them that term. Whoever, in attempting to describe their sublime features, should confine himself to the cold rules of painting would give his reader but a very imperfect idea of those emotions which they have the irresistible power of communicating to the most impassive imaginations" (*DS*, p. 72). Where description began in a noon of repose, it closes upon a sunset of sublime emotion destructive of all repose.

Rather than follow the trail thus blazed toward Wordsworth's later aesthetics and politics of the sublime (which Theresa Kelley has considered), we can here notice only that fire also beacons a crowning ideology of *time*. [16] As in the Grande Chartreuse passage, Wordsworth departs radically from the descriptive present at the end of his poem. Opened by flashback to a personal past ("Gay lark of hope thy silent song resume . . ."), the denouement of the poem suddenly penetrates through the plane of 1790 to 1792 (the "now" of the Loire valley) and at last to a millennial future imagined to be one with the very ancient, Edenic past. "Liberty shall soon, indignant, raise / Red on his hills his beacon's comet blaze," Wordsworth says, annunciating a fiery revelation of time, an epoch in which—precisely in the spirit of the Revolutionary calendar—history's tragic story will purge nature to allow it to recover its primal vigor: "Nature, as in her prime, her virgin reign / Begins" (ll. 774–75, 784–85).

The final justification of the Revolutionary story imagined in *Descriptive Sketches*, in sum, is a primitive thought of time. We might think of the sudden necessity for such thought as follows. The gap between the "two points" of a tour, we saw earlier, originally situated a stopgap of conventional aesthetics. It was bridged by a picturesque aesthetics content to explain movement as moveless repose. All motive for progress merely settled into an assumed "constitution" for traveling (in more than one sense) such that rupture between points, the descriptive version of succession, seemed continuity. But by the time of *Descriptive Sketches*, historical narrative informed landscape with *violent* motive. Necessarily, the closed system of descriptive motivation deformed. If the two points of a tour still seemed continuous in picturesque space, the poet now suddenly generated a more essential two points along an axis of temporal rupture. His perspective split off entirely from the plane of description as if at right angles such that descriptive consciousness became past and narrativized consciousness present. (Just so, *The Prelude* writes time by projecting descriptive vignettes of past youth into the poet's older, epic consciousness.) Of course, since Wordsworth has not yet fully thought out or "constituted"—either aesthetically or politically—the violent motive thus impelling temporal rupture, movement across the tour's revised two points cannot yet be true continuity. While attempting to imagine a new time, *Descriptive Sketches* thus poises merely on the threshold of the Revolution's own "duration in the history of peoples." In practical terms, therefore, the poem remains highly discontinuous in its effort to justify succession as a new discipline of duration. Though it closes by looking forward to the joining of the millennial future with the far Edenic past, it itself only jumps from description to emergent narrative, and from past to present or future.

A flashforward of our own may not be inopportune here. In the Grande Chartreuse passage of the 1850 *Prelude*, Wordsworth will once more endorse Revolutionary violence and the fiery atmosphere of Justice. Then he invokes a philosophy of time able to transform ruptured history into a supernal vision of duration:

> Discerning sword that Justice wields, do thou
> Go forth and prosper; and, ye purging fires,
> Up to the loftiest towers of Pride ascend,
> Fanned by the breath of angry Providence.
> But oh! if Past and Future be the wings
> On whose support harmoniously conjoined

> Moves the great spirit of human knowledge, spare
> These courts of mystery.   (1850 *Prel.* 6.444–51)

How can the primitive revelation of time upon which *Descriptive Sketches* closes mature into such an angel of duration, a spirit of justice dedicated to transcending violent succession upon its harmonious conjunction of wings?

Unexplained Violence

Three Voices of Agony

"All . . . was progress on the self-same path / On which with a diversity of pace / I had been travelling," the Revolution books of *The Prelude* later record, "this a stride at once / Into another region" (10.238–41). Progress through history was mapped in *Descriptive Sketches*. But when war broke out between England and France, the tour abruptly turned into "another region." The progress-piece of this turn is *Salisbury Plain*, which Wordsworth wrote largely between late July and September 1793,[17] just before making his possible third trip to France to witness the execution of Gorsas (*CEY*, p. 147). *Salisbury Plain* maps the crux of the poet's emergence: the evasion of mimesis that allowed him, even while witnessing the brutal facts, to acknowledge historical emergency only in the form of its denial: poetic time. Only in time's denial could history be endured.

Unlike *Descriptive Sketches*, *Salisbury Plain* does not develop its argument sequentially. It may best be studied by adapting for our purposes Sheats's analytic of "three voices" (pp. 85–94) or, more generally, of a polyphony led by the voices of the Traveller, the Narrator, and the Vagrant.

(1) *Traveller*. The most useful voice to begin upon is that of the Traveller, which is essentially not a "voice" at all, as Sheats has recognized (p. 88), but a window of third-person, limited omniscience through which the poet describes landscape. To say that the resulting description is plain would be an understatement. The Traveller appears like Spenser's knight "pricking on the plaine" with "too solemne sad" visage:

> The troubled west was red with stormy fire,
> O'er Sarum's plain the traveller with a sigh
> Measured each painful step, the distant spire

That fixed at every turn his backward eye
Was lost, tho' still he turned, in the blank sky.
By thirst and hunger pressed he gazed around
And scarce could any trace of man descry,
Save wastes of corn that stretched without a bound,
But where the sower dwelt was nowhere to be found.

No shade was there, no meads of pleasant green,
No brook to wet his lips or soothe his ear,
Huge piles of corn-stack here and there were seen
But thence no smoke upwreathed his sight to cheer;
And see the homeward shepherd dim appear
Far off—He stops his feeble voice to strain;
No sound replies but winds that whistling near
Sweep the thin grass and passing, wildly plain;
Or desert lark that pours on high a wasted strain.

(st. 5–6)

It would be possible to map where the Traveller loses sight of the "distant spire" of Salisbury Cathedral as he paces north; and a report dated July 29 in the August 2 issue of the *Times* (roughly when Wordsworth himself crossed Salisbury Plain) confirms that wheat, hay, and corn crops in the area were extraordinary. Nevertheless, description is really no more accurate than the Woods of Error. *Salisbury Plain* is beyond description. Specifically, it is beyond *Descriptive Sketches*. Where the earlier poem had finished at sunset on a trail without delight (a "various journey, sad and slow," Wordsworth ends), the later introduces the Traveller in another fiery sunset after a near, verbal echo ("turns of chance . . . Various and sad"; st. 4). *Salisbury Plain* begins upon what *Descriptive Sketches* had worked so hard to achieve: the end of picturesque description. The stanzas quoted above thus survey *in*visibilities (a lost spire, blank sky, absent traces of man) harvesting the negativity we saw first seeded in the vale of "No's" in *An Evening Walk*. "No shade . . . no meads . . . No brook . . . no smoke . . . no sound" appear here.[18] A repetition of "No's" several stanzas later underscores the vacancy of the universe:

No moon to open the black clouds and stream
From narrow gulph profound one friendly beam;
No watch-dog howled from shepherd's homely shed.

.   .   .

No transient meteor burst upon his sight
Nor taper glimmered dim from sick man's room.
Along the moor no line of mournful light
From lamp of lonely toll-gate streamed athwart the night.

(st. 12–13)

Salisbury Plain, we may say, is description become plain as a *tabula rasa*.

The Plain is the blank slate on which the poem can write the *narrative* of the Traveller and so complete the tragedy *Descriptive Sketches* had launched. Or so it first appears. Where the earlier poem told of collective "pain," the later expects an individual dramatization of pain. The Traveller's tour, we note, begins upon a calculus of pain: he "measured each painful step" (st. 5). And it ends in stanza 45 upon a remembered pain, a blight (the exact poison of delight), demanding narrative background:

> He half forgot the terrors of the night,
> Striving with counsel sweet [the Vagrant's] soul to chear,
> Her soul for ever widowed of delight.
> He too had withered young in sorrow's deadly blight.
>   (st. 45)

The alexandrine here, to which Enid Welsford has drawn special attention, functions as a narrative lure (p. 17). Like Redcrosse's dented armor, the Traveller's "deadly blight" provokes a sense of narrative mystery. What catastrophe exiles him on the plain of pain (a rhyme Wordsworth himself makes in stanza 1)? What tragic tale explains pain?

(2) *Narrator.* We may reinforce our questions by adding the voice of the Narrator, the early spokesman of what Stephen Gill has called Wordsworth's "poetry of protest" (esp. p. 50). The Narrator exists to give narrative expectation historical context. At first, however, he prefaces the Traveller's pain with a four-stanza protest wholly insensitive to historical difference. The protest compares savage and modern pains. Beset by boars and other beasts, by war, and by the "fruitless pains" of the hunt, the life of the "savage" is nasty, brutish, and short (st. 1–2). And "beset with foes more fierce" because more refined, the life of civilized man is by even crueller "pain depressed" (st. 3–4). But rather than truly distinguish pre- and post-historical agencies of pain—Hobbesian nature and Rousseauian civilization[19]— the Narrator submits both to an ahistorical default agent: "hard lot," "sad reverse of fate," "Fortune," and "turns of chance" (st. 2–4). Pain is a grand accident. *Salisbury Plain* itself, we know, drew seminally upon accident. Enroute to Wales in late July or early August, just before the composition of the poem, Wordsworth and his traveling companion, William Calvert, suffered an "accident" with a horse-drawn "whiskey," which Dorothy recorded "might have had fatal consequences." Calvert took the horse, and Wordsworth wandered by foot for some days through Salisbury Plain (*Letters*, 1: 109).

But accident, of course, is not a very enlightened explanation of pain. In Wordsworth's later poetry, where chance meetings with a pedlar, a leechgatherer, or a discharged soldier seem "leadings from above," accident is simply not a viable concept. As early as the spring of 1793 preceding *Salisbury Plain*, it was inadequate. The evidence lies in the unpublished prose treatise Wordsworth wrote in London (either in February and March or in June and shortly after): *A Letter to the Bishop of Llandaff.*[20] The single most violent work he ever attempted, the *Letter* consistently glosses pain—most signally Louis's execution in January—as a kind of leading from below: necessity. Wordsworth exclaims in the strongest of many such usages: "Alas! the obstinacy & perversion of men is such that [Liberty] is too often obliged to borrow the very arms of despotism to overthrow him, and in order to reign in peace must establish herself by violence. She deplores such stern necessity" (*Prose*, 1 : 33).[21]

Godwin's influence on Wordsworth prior to the meetings of the two in 1795 has been a matter of dispute, but certainly the parallel is instructive.[22] Appearing in mid-February 1793, *Political Justice* had opened its critique of political institutions upon a first axiom of human character: character is shaped not by innate principles but by "various external accidents" determined by prenatal circumstance and education within a historical milieu (pp. 108–15). Fixed throughout life by such historical circumstance, the "accident" underlying human behavior is finally "necessity" analogous to strict, mechanical causality (pp. 335–60); it appears arbitrary simply because reason cannot discover the true causes of things. Only gradual improvement or "perfectibility" of reason, it follows, will then allow humanity to ameliorate by discriminating life's true necessities and adapting accordingly (that is, "voluntarily," or with full recognition of necessity; pp. 118–19). Thus does *Political Justice* prepare the ground for its anarchistic program, which in part decrees that the problematic ideal of free will (pp. 354–55) and its political institution as freedom—indeed, all political institution—will at last be superfluous in the project of human improvement. Free will, after all, is only a strange double of accident, and its instituted "freedoms" have proved either arbitrary tyranny in established states or, as Godwin deplores in his chapters on revolution, bloody accident in new ones (see esp. p. 271).[23] Only when violent accident becomes subsumed in historical necessity will freedom mature into perfectibility.

Wordsworth reputedly advised a student in 1795, "Throw away [your] books of chemistry and read Godwin on necessity" (*CEY*, p. 163). The earlier *Letter* distinguishes itself from any such straightforward endorsement, of course, because it still tolerates violence in the service of freedom. But already it anticipates the main Godwinian charge: accidental freedom must be supervised by historical necessity. Specifically, freedom must be supervised by a concept of necessity supplementing the Revolutionary poetics of violence. Wordsworth's rhetoric in the *Letter*, we observe, is instinct with "sacrifice" and "war." Immediately before declaring the "stern necessity" of Revolutionary violence, for example, the poet underscores his repeated use of sacrifice by alluding strongly to a tragedy about sacrifice: Racine's *Athalie* (*Prose*, 1: 33 and Wordsworth's note).[24] And immediately after the "stern necessity" dictum, he uses war figuratively to declare that Revolutionary violence is "indispensable from a state of war between the oppressors and oppressed" (*Prose*, 1: 34).[25] Violence is precisely the French agony of sacrifice and war. Verifying the agony in the *Letter* is the figure of nature. Wordsworth says, for example: "having dried up the source from which flows the corruption of the public opinion, . . . the stream will go on gradually refining itself," or again, in a figure we have already cited, "The animal just released from its stall will exhaust the overflow of its spirits in a round of wanton vagaries" (*Prose*, 1: 38). And justifying the total project of violence, finally, is law—the republican law that Wordsworth confidently predicts will evolve under the supervision of the People into an "expression of the general will . . . enacted only from an almost universal conviction of their utility" (*Prose*, 1: 39). Such justification completes his rehearsal of the Revolutionary poetics of violence.

But with the onset of the Terror, we notice, natural violence seemed to be terrorized by accidents or "wanton vagaries" mimicking what the *Letter* had earlier called monarchy's "arbitrary power" (*Prose*, 1: 35). (Making their last stand against the Jacobins at the time, the Girondins also blamed chance. Guadet declaimed in his speech of May 18, 1793: "How long will you [citizens] leave the fate of liberty to chance? . . . Up to the present, fortune has done everything for you"; *DSFR*, p. 435.) How to ensure that the story of violence could still produce systematic justice? The answer lay in reinforcing the supervision of the People, or convention, with an impersonal agency: Necessity. Necessity was Wordsworth's first displacement, abstraction, or "representation" (in the *Letter's* political sense) of collective imagination.

Given the contemporaneous evidence of the *Letter*, in sum, we can predict that if the Narrator in *Salisbury Plain* first views pain as accident, he must at last review it as historical necessity—and specifically, as the necessity of Revolution. Thus the epilogue the Narrator appends to the poem in stanzas 47 and following, which embeds the concept of pain in a violent flux and reflux of current historical necessity. First, the Narrator deplores the pain ("murder, pain, and tears") necessitated by the status quo of Oppression, Injury, Strife, Avarice, Superstition, Tyrants, Misery, Exile, Terror, Bonds, and Force (st. 49–58). "Say, rulers of the nations," he asks in a characteristic, necessitarian phrasing, "from the sword / Can ought but murder, pain, and tears proceed?" (st. 57). But stanzas 57 and 58, we notice, grow ambiguous in reference: the war and terror they cite could stem from the regimes of either Oppression or Revolution. Such ambiguity preparcs for a crucial transition in the epilogue's last surviving stanza (st. 54–56 and 59–60 are missing). Here, the Narrator concludes his observation of pain by exhorting a program of necessitarian perfectibility far more violent than Godwin's. The combat against pain, he argues, requires the necessity of a new, corrective pain of Revolution. The last stanza stages Wordsworth's exact reenactment of the Herculean colossus clubbing the Marsh monster at the Fete of Unity and Indivisibility in Paris on August 10, 1793 (the proposal for which had appeared in French newspapers in July; see Chapter 4 and n. 47 to that chapter).[26] For Wordsworth, Reason—identified somewhat against legend with Hercules—must resistlessly bludgeon humanity into improvement:

> Heroes of Truth pursue your march, uptear
> Th' Oppressor's dungeon from its deepest base;
> High o'er the towers of Pride undaunted rear
> Resistless in your might the herculean mace
> Of Reason; let foul Error's monster race
> Dragged from their dens start at the light with pain
> And die; pursue your toils, till not a trace
> Be left on earth of Superstition's reign,
> Save that eternal pile which frowns on Sarum's plain.
>
> (st. 61)

Thus does the Narrator at last develop a political vision that, for all its resemblance to the sacking of Rome, is "enlightened." Looking back on the first four stanzas of the poem, we can now see that by themselves they could only envision a politics confirming reports in the English press of the mob action, or *randomness*, of French savagery: since the bestial life of the savage is actually better than that of civilized man, the solution to modern pain would seem to require the savaging of civilization. Savagery may still be required in the violence the Narrator finishes upon (which depends figuratively on such antique weaponry as maces, for example), but now savagery must seem Reason.[27]

We can now perceive the overall historical frame prepared for the poem's argument of pain. Between the opening universe of savage accident and the terminal one of historical necessity lies the blank page of pain, the Plain. The Plain is where the poem must write the full process of the Narrator's Reason, the logic that explains why accidental pain is indeed historical necessity. But the poem, of course, cannot practice discursive reason in the manner of *Political Justice* or the *Letter to the Bishop of Llandaff*. How to explain the necessity of pain? The answer amplifies the sense of narrative expectation we have already discovered: *Salisbury Plain* must write a *tragedy* more fully developed than the one begun in *Descriptive Sketches*. Tragedy, after all, is the poetic logic designed precisely to stage accidental pain, or "sad reverse of fate" (st. 3), as a necessity of character and of the fateful history bringing character to catastrophe. Jay Clayton's chapter on Wordsworth and George Eliot's narrative in his *Romantic Vision and the Novel* is particularly apt here. Tragedy in our sense of an entelechially developing agony epitomizes the "stubborn, autonomous power" or "hardness" of causal necessity, as Clayton has put it using Eliot's term, that is the implicit condition of narrative progress itself (p. 146).

We may now repeat our earlier questions with amplification: what catastrophe of *history* exiles the Traveller on the Plain? What tragedy explains pain as historical necessity?

(3) *Vagrant.* I propose an allegory. "I will unfold a tale—!" Caleb Williams exclaims near the end of the novel of pain Godwin wrote in 1793–94 (p. 314). But the possibility of ever truly unfolding any tale is suspect in a novel that is in part a sustained critique of narrativity itself. Caleb realizes that his "half-told and mangled tale" (p. 326) will no more unfold the true cause, the necessity, behind all his pain than Falkland's trunk would open to reveal the origin of pain in this universe: Falkland's own written narrative, Caleb at last believes, of murder and pain (p. 315). Unable to explain pain and the necessity of such contributing causes as the burning curiosity of its hero or the obsessive chivalry of Falkland, *Caleb Williams* will not unfold; it will not explicate (from *explicare*, "to unfold"). Indeed, as its method of successively telling the tales of Tyrrel, Falkland, Caleb, and so forth illustrates (and as Caleb's brief career in London of writing criminal tales confirms), the best it can do is *replicate* pain.

And the application: *Salisbury Plain* also cannot—or, perhaps, will not—explain pain. Everything we have read points toward the writing of some tragic tale able to explicate the historical necessity of pain. But the "herculean" struggle of the poem is not therefore to unfold that tale. Rather, the poem denies explication by suspending narrative in ever more obscure replications.

The most obvious replication of the pain initiated by the Traveller occurs in the third leading voice of the poem: the Female Vagrant's. Like some articulate Dido of the underworld, the Vagrant takes center stage once the Traveller enters "the dead house of the plain" (st. 14). The Vagrant, we are told, has breasts—a baroque cathedral of the breast worship we remarked earlier—making clear her descent from both the swans and Female Beggar of *An Evening Walk* (cf. "Beauty and Moonlight," 1786; *PW*, 1: 264). She is a "Delight" of pure desire:

> Like swans, twin swans, that when on the sweet brink
> Of Derwent's stream the south winds hardly blow,
> 'Mid Derwent's water-lillies swell and sink

> In union, rose her sister breasts of snow,
> (Fair emblem of two lovers' hearts that know
> No separate impulse) or like infants played,
> Like infants strangers yet to pain and woe.
> Unwearied Hope to tend their motions made
> Long Vigils, and Delight her cheek between them laid.
>
> (st. 24)

The figure of Derwent's stream opens into the Vagrant's tale proper, which recapitulates the entire trajectory we have traced from pictur-esque delight to tragic pain. The Vagrant was raised in gardens of delight:

> By Derwent's side my father's cottage stood,
>
> . . .
>
> Can I forget my seat beneath the thorn,
> My garden stored with peas and mint and thyme,
> And rose and lilly for the sabbath morn;
> The church-inviting bell's delightful chime . . . [?]
>
> (st. 26–27)

But delight suddenly knew pain. As the Vagrant reports, her father's property was seized (st. 29–30), her husband enlisted during wartime depression (st. 31–34), "pains and plagues" killed him and their chil-dren (st. 35–36), and she returned to England with "pain" (st. 42–44). Such is certainly a "tale of woe" and "human sufferings," as the poem puts it, able to relieve the Traveller of the need to tell his own tale of deadly blight (st. 45). But the relief, I suggest, can only be provisional because the Vagrant allows no real progress in narrative understanding. A *Lear* in which the "why" of Cordelia's death is not even wrestled with,[28] the Vagrant's tale is deeply unsatisfying as a tragedy because it refuses even to attempt explaining the necessity of pain. "How changed at once!" (st. 34), the Vagrant characteristically marvels. She is a passive register of hurt, a witness perpetually sur-prised by painful, incomprehensible events. The critical stanza is that in which the Vagrant tells of her first pain:

> The suns of eighteen summers danced along
> Joyous as in the pleasant morn of May.
> At last by cruel chance and wilful wrong
> My father's substance fell into decay.
> Oppression trampled on his tresses grey:
> His little range of water was denied;
> Even to the bed where his old body lay
> His all was seized.   (st. 29)

Why pain? Says the Vagrant with no attempt at logical connection: chance "and" oppression. All she can do is redefine the rift between accident and historical necessity demanding the explanation of the

Traveller's tragedy in the first place. Her tale, we might say, is a compulsive tic, a repetition that does not so much discharge the need for the Traveller's tragedy as block its full utterance.[29] It is a regression in tragedy (literally, it may have been the earliest portion of the poem drafted; *CEY*, p. 333).

As we must now see, *Salisbury Plain* continually impedes its essential narrative in this manner, propagating a series of replicate narratives that confirm the inexplicability of pain. Before proceeding, however, it will be useful to identify the tradition of such replication. First, a Romantic cross section of the tradition I seek. As appears even more clearly in its subsequent versions (*Adventures on Salisbury Plain* and *Guilt and Sorrow*), *Salisbury Plain* is akin to *Caleb Williams* and such later novels of pain as *Frankenstein* in following a principle of "shell" narration. Story glides into interior or parallel stories not by causal process but by a strange magic of figurative resemblance or sympathetic identification—a voodoo doubling that exceeds pure accident or coincidence yet refuses the full onus of narrative necessity. As Wordsworth himself observed in his Fenwick note on *Guilt and Sorrow* (his 1842 revision of *Salisbury Plain*):

It may be worth while to remark, that, though the incidents of this attempt do only in a small degree produce each other, and it deviates accordingly from the general rule by which narrative pieces ought to be governed, it is not therefore wanting in continuous hold upon the mind, or in unity, which is effected by the identity of moral interest that places the two personages upon the same footing in the reader's sympathies. (*PW*, 1: 330).

Unity is to be found in plurality, the end of one story in another; and the overall result is a narrative line that "deviates" from the level "rule" into what we might image as a shell-form—a spiraling, centrifugal series of narrative revolutions whose whole, while more than episodic, is certainly less than classically tragic or unified. Though there may really be a single core story, the very fact of its ceaseless volution suggests incomplete or repressed explanation: there is always some remainder of tragic truth, some excess of pain, that the shell with all its redundancy—like the shell in *The Prelude* "that was a God, yea many Gods, / Had voices more than all the winds" (5.107–8)—resists articulating. Such narrative is the emphatic form of what J. Hillis Miller, extending his work on Wordsworth's shell, has imaged as the labyrinth of narrative repetition.[30]

We can now extend our cross section back into literary and exegetical history. In traditional terms, shell narrative is a strangely disoriented version of the narrative method that I enacted some pages ago and that Wordsworth himself introduces with similar surreptitiousness in his Spenserian form: allegory.[31] Having forgotten the universe of *istoria* in Chapter 3, we thus at last come full circle to resume that universe in altered form. Replication in *Salisbury Plain* expands narrative once more precisely to the dimensions of *istoria*. As in a Renaissance painting, story duplicates itself on successive displaced planes of story charged with exegetical function: the Vagrant's tale, we can thus say, is a new testament of pain *interpreting* the Traveller's old testament of "deadly blight." But expansion into the old, manifold space of interpretation in *Salisbury Plain* also entails an uncanny subversion of *istoria*. It makes possible not so much totality of narrative truth as *distance* upon some Minotaur's center of that truth —some core tragedy whose burden of historical pain has become unbearable. Where *istoria* unfolded according to an ordered scale of exegesis closing upon overall anagogical vision, then, *Salisbury Plain* generates a thick tangle of allegories designed to deny the monstrous truth that would complete the overall vision. The poem, we may say, finally cultivates only a vast, negative anagogy or sense of narrative bewilderment. It wanders on a Plain that is the deforested version of the archetypal labyrinth Spenser planted in his work: the Wood of Error.

The Other Voice

To finish reading *Salisbury Plain*, we need now only complete our analytic of voices by discovering that the poem has one further voice, ipso facto allegorical. Literally, we know, "allegory" is an "other voice" or "other speaking" (from *allos* + *agorein*, "other" than "speaking publicly"). *Salisbury Plain*, I suggest, at last has no voice to tell its tragedy because it has only *other voices*: the quintessential Other Voice of allegory. Speaking throughout in secret syncopation with Narrator, Traveller, and Vagrant, the Other Voice *denies* the tragedy of historical necessity.

I will collect the allegory of the Other Voice into a sort of censored or blackout tragedy—an impeded, fragmentary replica of Wordsworth's true story akin to the subversive pantomimes censored by French law prior to the Revolution (F. Brown, p. 52). With the exception of one scene set in the Dead House, the allegory revolves around Wordsworth's primal scene of violence: a single spot on the Plain. Guarding the spot from too close approach is Wordsworth's Den of Error, Stonehenge.

i. [*Near Stonehenge.*]
Enter the Traveller near what "seems an antique castle."
A disembodied "voice as from a tomb" warns:
Oh from that mountain-pile avert thy face

.   .   .

For oft at dead of night, when dreadful fire
Reveals that powerful circle's reddening stones,

'Mid priests and spectres grim and idols dire,
Far heard the great flame utters human moans,
Then all is hushed: again the desert groans,
A dismal light its farthest bounds illumes,
While warrior spectres of gigantic bones,
Forth-issuing from a thousand rifted tombs,
Wheel on their fiery steeds amid the infernal glooms.

(st. 10–11)

ii. [*Dead House of the Plain*]

The Vagrant wakes at the entrance of the Traveller.
She remembers a warning tale:

For of that ruin she had heard a tale
That might with a child's fears the stoutest heart assail.

Had heard of one who forced from storms to shroud
Felt the loose walls of this decayed retreat
Rock to his horse's neighings shrill and loud,
While the ground rang by ceaseless pawing beat,
Till on a stone that sparkled to his feet
Struck and still struck again the troubled horse.
The man half raised that stone by pain and sweat,
Half raised; for well his arm might lose its force
Disclosing the grim head of a new murdered corse.

(st. 16–17)

iii. [*Stonehenge and a nearby "mystic plain."*]

"Voices" speak as if from "other worlds" (st. 18). On cue,
the Vagrant remembers another monitory tale of "an old man
beckoning from the naked steep":

Much of the wonders of that boundless heath
He spoke, and of a swain who far astray
Reached unawares a height and saw beneath
Gigantic beings ranged in dread array.
Such beings thwarting oft the traveller's way
With shield and stone-ax stride across the wold,
Or, throned on that dread circle's summit gray
Of mountains hung in air, their state unfold,
And like a thousand Gods mysterious council hold.

And oft a night-fire mounting to the clouds
Reveals the desert and with dismal red
Clothes the black bodies of encircling crowds.
It is the sacrificial altar fed
With living men. How deep it groans—the dead
Thrilled in their yawning tombs their helms uprear;
The sword that slept beneath the warriour's head
Thunders in fiery air: red arms appear
Uplifted thro' the gloom and shake the rattling spear.

Not thus where clear moons spread their pleasing light.

—Long bearded forms with wands uplifted shew
To vast assemblies, while each breath of night
Is hushed, the living fires that bright and slow
Rounding th' aetherial field in order go.
Then as they trace with awe their various files
All figured on the mystic plain below,
Still prelude of sweet sounds the moon beguiles
And charmed for many a league the hoary desart smiles.

(st. 20–22)

iv. [*Epilogue.*]

Enter the Narrator with a warning for modern times.
He begins by recalling old voices of terror:

Though from huge wickers paled with circling fire
No longer horrid shrieks and dying cries
To ears of Daemon-Gods in peals aspire,
To Daemon-Gods a human sacrifice;
Though Treachery her sword no longer dyes
In the cold blood of Truce, still, reason's ray,
What does it more than while the tempests rise,
With starless glooms and sounds of loud dismay,
Reveal with still-born glimpse the terrors of our way?

(st. 48)

Thus ends the allegory of the Other Voice. Repeatedly, Wordsworth's scene of violence opens; yet always before we approach near enough to recognize its full story and historical meaning, the scene closes. "Beware!" the Other Voice simply says, confirming Stonehenge's monumental warning that *this* spot, this amphitheater on a new, bloodier Champ-de-Mars is totem and taboo.

We might imitate here the rhythms of Blake's questions in "The Tyger" ("What dread hand? & What dread feet?"). What tragedy, urgent with what historical pain, hides on Wordsworth's primal scene of violence? What the terror? What the mountain-pile?

To ex-plain the allegory with some assurance, it will be useful to consult the Rosetta Stone of Wordsworth's Druidism. I refer to DC MS. 12, the notebook he appears to have used as a commonplace book before setting down early versions of *The Borderers* in 1796 and 1797 (see *B*, p. 7). As Gill notes (*SP*, p. 35n), a page of the notebook includes the following bibliography labelled "Druids":*

---

* To make Wordsworth's shorthand citations more accessible, I have standardized, expanded, Anglicized, and, where I am able, added missing information in brackets. The dashes are Wordsworth's, and appear to indicate the equivalent of "ff." or "*passim.*" A facsimile reproduction of this notebook page, together with a full transcription (the essentials of which are reproduced in *SP*, p. 35n), may be found in *B*, pp. 420–21.

Caesar. *Commentaries on the Gallic Wars.* Bk. 6.
Pliny. *Natural History.* 16.44—29.3.
Drayton, Michael. *Polyolbion.* Ninth Song—
[Rowlands, Henry]. *Mona Antiqua Restaurata.* Pg. 338.
Dion Chrysostom.— — —[*Orations*].
Tacitus. *Annals.* 14.29— —
Lucan. *Pharsalia.* Bk. 3— — — —
Ammianus Marcellinus. [*Rerum gestarum*; "Chronicles of Events"].
   Bk. 15.
B. Procopius. *Goth.* Bk. 4—

Wordsworth may not have read all the modern authors on this list by the time of *Salisbury Plain* in 1793, but many of the classical sources would have been familiar from his readings at Hawkshead and Cambridge (see Schneider on Wordsworth's reading of Caesar and Tacitus, p. 68). Applying these selections (especially the classics) to the allegory of the Other Voice, I pose five sequential hypotheses.

(1) *Wordsworth's allegory mimes the Revolution.*

Standard in the literature on the Druids, we note, was the belief that the Celts of Britain and Gaul were culturally identical. The original notes to the Ninth Song of Drayton's *Polyolbion* thus speculate that the "community of name, customes, and originall" between Britons and Gauls were so alike that the two nations communicated etymologically in the term "Gualsh," which became "Welsh" (p. 145). And the most authoritative text on Wordsworth's list, Caesar's *Gallic Wars*, notes that Druidism in particular assured the identity of the Celts. Druidical worship in Gaul not only originated in Britain, Caesar says, but had to be renewed by study at its source (quoted with translation in Kendrick, p. 78).[32]

Coincidence between the Britons and Gauls may be taken to be the *raison d'être* of Wordsworth's Celtic allegory. Why did the ostensibly Celtic monuments the poet saw on Salisbury Plain seem so ready for allegorical deployment? In part, perhaps, because Celtism was the ground of the poet's own closest recorded brush with violence. While touring Wales in either 1791 or 1793, Wordsworth was threatened at the point of a knife by a Welsh parson who believed himself "an ancient Briton" insulted by a "vile Saxon!"[33] But the deepest reason, I believe, must have been the confusion of geography —or in Coleridge's words, the Spenserian "true imaginative absence of all particular space or time"—that Celtism made possible.[34] On the Faeryland of ancient Salisbury Plain, Britain *was* France. Without the least nationalistic resistance, in other words, British violence (especially the war preparations Wordsworth saw from the Isle of Wight just before setting off for Salisbury Plain and Wales)[35] could mime violence across the Channel.

Wordsworth was not alone, we might add, in inventing a Celtic Britain imitative of the Revolution. Other radicals of the time inhabited the same Faeryland. (For a fuller study of the "Welsh Wordsworth" in the context of contemporary radical Celtism, see my "Wordsworth and Subversion.") As reported in the *Gentleman's Magazine* for October 1792, for example, Welsh nationalists led by "Iolo Morganwg" (Edward Williams) joined to revive a Bardic and Druidic ceremony in which a sword was placed upon an altar in a circle of stones (Piggott, pp. 164–65). Such nationalism also feted radical internationalism. Iolo and his clan were infamous for their sympathies with Thomas Paine and the French Revolution (Piggott, p. 166). Similarly, the contemporary revival of "Bardic" and "Druidic" poetry feted primitivism and radical reform in the same breath. "EB" in the *Gentleman's Magazine* for December 1792, for example, strikes a "Druid harp" to declaim upon British "Corruption" and the need for true Liberty:

> Curs'd be the man, whoe'er he be,
> That will not struggle to be free,
> Nor give his life for Liberty!
>
> (p. 1134)[36]

We might bring our initial hypothesis to a head, as it were, by looking to Scene ii in our staging of Wordsworth's allegory above. The scene tells of violence on British soil. But as in Book 10 of *The Prelude*, which records England's aggression against France but neglects to mention that France first declared war, British violence masks Revolutionary precedent. Book 10 will excuse French Terror by making it seem to originate on native shores. England's decision to go to war, the poet says, is the true Terror or violence:

> Oh! much have they to account for, who could tear
> By violence at one decisive rent
> From the best Youth in England, their dear pride.
>
> (10.275–77)

In precisely the same manner, Scene ii of the allegory in *Salisbury Plain* masks murder across the Channel by making it seem to come to a head at home. Foregrounded with exaggerated prominence in the alexandrine of stanza 17 is "the grim head of a new murdered corse." In the historical frame of the poem, such obsession with a "grim head" surely points not only to domestic violences such as those committed by Jarvis Matchem or John Walford (which Wordsworth will soon try to incorporate in *Adventures on Salisbury Plain*) but also to the guillotine.[37] ("Head after head, and never heads enough," Book 10 of *The Prelude* recalls about the Terror in France; 10.335.)

(2) *Specifically, Wordsworth's allegory mimes the Revolutionary tragedy of war and sacrifice.*

The *Gallic Wars* is most authoritative in Wordsworth's bibliography because it predates a key divergence in the classical experience of the Druids. How were the Druids related to the barbaric warriors and knights, the other noble caste in Celtic society? One tradition of thought developed from Caesar's analysis of Druidic sacrifice. According to Caesar, warriors "who are engaged in the perils of battle either sacrifice human victims or vow so to do, employing the Druids as ministers for such sacrifices" (quoted in Kendrick, p. 78). The Druids, in other words, participate in the practical workings of the barbaric war-state, conducting sacrifices in the spirit of efficient magic. From this observation (as well as Caesar's description of the Wicker Man) evolved what may be named the "barbaric," "savage," or, at best, what A. L. Owen calls "militant patriot" theory of Druidism (p. 138). According to this view, Druidical sacrifice was an act of savagery in complete alliance with barbaric warfare. Tacitus, for example, thus confounds the savagery of British warriors and Druids in a single view of violence: after describing a battle between the British and Romans, he concludes, "[The British] deemed it, indeed, a duty to cover their altars with the blood of captives and to consult their deities through human entrails" (quoted in Kendrick, p. 93).

The savage theory of Druidism provided Wordsworth with the materials to stage a crypto-Revolutionary tragedy of war and sacrifice in Scenes i and iii of his allegory. In Scene i, sacrifice sparks a visionary war: illuminated by the sacrificial flames of Druid priests, warrior spectres spring "from a thousand rifted tombs." And war in turn fuels sacrifice in Scene iii. Giant warriors hold mysterious council. But in the next stanza, we see a "sacrificial altar fed / With living men" and a revisionary hallucination of war painted the color of sacrifice: red arms of warriors lift up like so many flames.

What the "terror"? What the "mountain-pile"? The answers, of course, are the Terror and the Mountain. The hegemony of Stonehenge over the Plain* is tantamount to the final victory in 1793 of the Jacobins over the Girondins. It mimes a Revolution that conducted war and internal sacrifice simultaneously.

(3) *Nature verifies the tragedy, but now nature is "Other Nature."*

A second tradition of thought on the Druids also descended from Caesar. "The Druids," Caesar says, "usually hold aloof from war, and do not pay war-taxes with the rest; they are excused from military service and exempt from all liabilities. . . . The cardinal doctrine which they seek to teach is that souls do not die. . . . Besides this, they have many discussions as touching the stars and their movement" (quoted in Kendrick, p. 78). From such a passage springs what may be called the "mandarin" tradition, which held that Druids were

---

* As noted earlier, the Plain or Marsh was also a name for the moderates who sat between the Girondins and the Mountain in the French National Convention.

priestly scholars living a purely meditative life removed from the practical concerns of the war-state.[38] They were the administrators of nature. Pliny, for example, catalogs their intimate knowledge of nature (Kendrick, pp. 88–90); and Drayton, as Geoffrey G. Hiller observes, stresses that they understood "great Natures depths" (p. 7). But the scholar-Druids were more than the shamans of oaken groves. In a manner beyond the ken of what I earlier called picturesque "bureaucracy," their administration of nature penetrated to a celestial nature above nature. According to Caesar, they searched the stars and taught immortality. Ammianus Marcellinus echoes: "they were uplifted by searchings into secret and sublime things, and with grand contempt for mortal lot they professed the immortality of the soul" (quoted in Kendrick, p. 84).

We can now remark the critical divergence of Wordsworth's allegory from Revolutionary tragedy. By drawing upon the "mandarin" tradition, Wordsworth *doubles* the role of the Druids in his plot of war and sacrifice—and so doubles the nature verifying that story. One nature in the poem conforms to the "savage" theory of Druidism. This is the red-toothed, primal nature of mountain and tempest. But in the central third scene of his allegory, Wordsworth suddenly stages a disconnected, alternative view of the Druids and the nature they ritualize. Where stanzas 20 and 21 stage "fiery" war and sacrifice, as we have observed, stanza 22—after a negation opening up an ambiguous distance—embarks upon a strong revision. Druids, it says, minister to a different kind of "living fire" in a nature ascendant above savagery:

> Not thus where clear moons spread their pleasing light.
> —Long bearded forms with wands uplifted shew
> To vast assemblies, while each breath of night
> Is hushed, the living fires that bright and slow
> Rounding th' aetherial field in order go.

After this sea change, the stanza then returns us to a transformed world staging what almost seems a delightful tour:

> Then as they trace with awe their various files
> All figured on the mystic plain below,
> Still prelude of sweet sounds the moon beguiles
> And charmed for many a league the hoary desart smiles.

On this still spot at the center of Wordsworth's allegory of violence, nature deflects us momentarily out of the world to the final intent of the Other Voice: what we might call Other Nature. Other Nature no longer functions to verify the story of violence. Instead, it simply looks away from violence to affirm itself as an independent fact. It becomes a newly various description of form ("various files / All figured on the mystic plain") signifying no more than the magisterial sense of formality itself.

(4) *Verified by Other Nature, the tragedy of sacrifice and war is no longer just.*

It will be useful to juxtapose two further strands of Druid lore. The first, which writers such as William Hutchinson in Wordsworth's time thought essential, is that the Druids administered the law.[39] Caesar records: "In fact, it is they who decide in almost all disputes, public and private; and if any crime has been committed, or murder done, or there is any dispute about succession or boundaries, they also decide it, determining rewards and penalties: if any person or people does not abide by their decision, they ban such from [participating in] sacrifice" (quoted in Kendrick, p. 77). The second strand of belief is that the Druids had nothing to do with Stonehenge and that Stonehenge, indeed, was so far from being a site of justice as to be the very monument of injustice. Here I append a source not on Wordsworth's bibliography. Francis Celoria has shown convincingly that the poet borrowed for his setting and vocabulary from Chatterton's verses on Stonehenge in "The Battle of Hastings II." Based in its turn upon Geoffrey of Monmouth's legend that Merlin erected Stonehenge to commemorate the Saxon massacre of 460 Celtic chiefs met in truce (the so-called "treason of the long knives"), Chatterton's poem records an act of total injustice removed from the jurisdiction of Druids: "Hengyst did the Brytons slee," he says, "As they were mette in council" (*Poems*, p. 265).[40]

To grasp the relevance of these beliefs, we need only look to Scene iv of Wordsworth's allegory—the epilogue in which the Narrator summons up huge wickers of human sacrifice and envisions "Treachery" dyeing "her sword . . . In the cold blood of Truce." Clearly, Wordsworth has superimposed over the Stonehenge of Druid sacrifice the treacherous, non-Druid Stonehenge of the Geoffrey of Monmouth legend. (We now recognize, indeed, that earlier scenes in which "warrior spectres" issue from "a thousand rifted tombs" must also draw upon the legend as well.) Stonehenge may stage a tragedy of war and sacrifice, we can thus deduce, but it at last voids the tragedy of any legitimizing ideology. *Salisbury Plain* mimes a Revolutionary story *no longer just*.

During the high Terror, in sum, the state of historical emergency supervised by the People suddenly seemed to Wordsworth a blocked tragedy incapable of completing the process of verification and justification. The blockage lay in nature itself. Nature *sous la Terreur* now appeared a perpetual savagery of war and sacrifice fulfilling the direst expectations of the English press (and anticipating the "savage" analysis of all warfare that Joseph Fawcett would publish in his *Art of War* in 1795).[41] By speaking in his Other Voice, however, Wordsworth avoided the tendency in the British press to treat savagery with silence. The poetry of denial, of impeded allegory, was what took the place of silence. Such poetry marked the return on a grand scale of Spenserian allegory or epic simile in the manner of the twilight fairy tale we saw in *An Evening Walk*. On Wordsworth's scene of revised emergency in 1793, Other Nature is the new fairy tale. Other Nature intervenes in the vector of historical emergency to deflect agon away from its proper ideological conclusion of justice (as shown in Fig. 3). History thus at last reemerges upon the new ideological site I have marked as mystery.

Thus in the middle of the Vagrant's tale, we notice, the Traveller calls for an intermission. For a moment, we exit the theater of savagery to spy a new world of nature somehow serenely *right*:

> "Oh come," he said, "come after weary night
> So ruinous far other scene to view."
> So forth she came and eastward look'd. The sight
> O'er her moist eyes meek dawn of gladness threw
> That tinged with faint red smile her faded hue.
> Not lovelier did the morning star appear
> Parting the lucid mist and bathed in dew,
> The whilst her comrade to her pensive chear
> Tempered sweet words of hope and the lark warbled near.
>
> They looked and saw a lengthening road and wain
> Descending a bare slope not far remote.
> The downs all glistered dropt with freshening rain;
> The carman whistled loud with chearful note;
> The cock scarce heard at distance sounds his throat.
>
> (st. 38–39)

Such, I suggest, is a vision of Other Nature at once immanent in the world and—as heard in the strong figurations in stanza 38 ("Not lovelier did the morning star appear . . .")—designed to transpose that world to the heavens. At the end of the poem, the Narrator then makes the intermission permanent by breaking off the stories of the Traveller and Vagrant and looking to an Other Nature of fresh woods and pastures new:

> Along the fiery east the Sun, a show
> More gorgeous still! pursued his proud career.
>   .   .   .
>   now from a hill summit down they look
> Where through a narrow valley's pleasant scene
> A wreath of vapour tracked a winding brook
> Babbling through groves and lawns and meads of green.
> A smoking cottage peeped the trees between,
> The woods resound the linnet's amorous lays,
> And melancholy lowings intervene

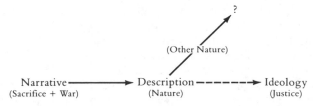

FIG. 3. The scene of revised emergency, 1793.

> Of scattered herds that in the meadows graze,
> While through the furrowed grass the merry milkmaid strays.
>
> Adieu ye friendless hope-forsaken pair!   (st. 45–47)

The "?" marked in Fig. 3 is Other Nature transformed into a substitute for justice. All is right in the world, we know, as *Salisbury Plain* closes. But such rightness no longer has to do with the historical ideology of justice. Rather, the rightness of lyrical Other Nature justifies human pain *despite* the fact that it assumes the presence of some unspoken injustice, some invisible history of pain, in the background. "Adieu ye friendless hope-forsaken pair," the Narrator laments, thus acknowledging—and screening—a whole world of pain. What can the substitute justice promised by Other Nature be?

(5) *The total meaning of Wordsworth's allegory is Time.*

Here I reach the close of my argument. The justice that will deliver us from evil in *Salisbury Plain* is Wordsworth's first true thought of time. As the poet says in his Advertisement to the later version of the poem, *Guilt and Sorrow*, "The monuments and traces of antiquity, scattered in abundance over [Salisbury Plain], led me unavoidably to compare what we know or guess of those remote times with certain aspects of modern society" (*SP*, p. 217). Not in an incidental or peripheral way but in a manner that makes it the overwhelming anagogy of the poem, time triumphs over history. Nature buries all history within a remote prehistory of ruins on the Plain, deflects the poet into a purified reality, and so at last allows him to emerge upon a scene of time become a self-sufficient ideology of justice.[42] An analogue is the unfinished poem in elegiac quatrains that Wordsworth probably drafted in 1793 during the trip to Wales that occasioned *Salisbury Plain* (*CEY*, p. 146). The quatrains begin:

> The western clouds a deepening gloom display
> Where light obscurely sleeps in purple streaks,
> And see the slowly sinking orb of day
> Dilating through the Darkness dimly breaks:
> So traveller full before this central bridge
> Whose lofty arch o'erlooks the winding dale
> Yon towers with [chasing?] walls and broken ridge
> More solemn gleam through Nature's [   ] veil:

So through the dim eclipse of antique days
Each moral image to that pile assigned
But half distinguished from [?] [cottage?]
More awful features to the darkened mind.
What though yon [trees?] perchance their voice have lent
To fill the shriek that pierced the murderer's ear
Or deeper groans by captive anguish sent
Till Nature stilled the cry that none could hear.
'Tis past and in this wreck of barbarous pride
Now mortal weakness only views the tomb
[?] though savage still to man allied
And o'er their terror breathes a softening gloom.
(J. O. Hayden, p. 117)

Here also, Nature is a mediation or "veil" that, while it invokes with accentuated solemnity some hidden terror in the background, buries the history of that terror in the ruins of prehistory, deflects the poet from violence into an atmosphere of softening gloom, and so allows him at last to leave behind the disturbance of tragedy for the time-heavy serenity of elegy. " 'Tis past," the poet says. "Now" terror has its Thermidor.

In *Salisbury Plain* and these quatrains above, time surely contains within itself—within the rupture opened between past and present—a thought of historical violence. But the rupture is a wound become its own scar. If time is a succession from past to present felt to be latently violent (in Poulet's terms: a tearing and breaking), so, too, it becomes a way to *dis*imagine the rupture of violence. Time is an "other" history, or other-than-history, that purges the story of agony and leaves the stage—to use the phrase Wordsworth first invented in another violent poem of this period—bare except for "the unimaginable touch of time" (fragment of the "Gothic Tale," 1796; B, p. 752). To vary Hartman's thesis on the subject, we might say that Wordsworth's later "touching compulsion" only comes about because of a fastidiousness in his historical touch: in a tic of time the poet withdraws by reflex from the "substantial dread" of such scenes of history as the September Massacres, which can be almost "felt and touch'd" (*Prel.* 10.62–66; see n. 9 to Chapter 2).

On Salisbury Plain, in sum, Wordsworth turns into his Mosaic wilderness—his zone of temporal rupture lasting, as it were, forty years. Here he receives his poetic commandment. The commandment is a "No" to history whose ultimate decree is time. In Blake's terms (p. 494), such negation sets a "limit" to the rupture of historical violence. The limit of negation is the start for the positive philosophy of time that Wordsworth then develops—a "thought of time" able to transform rupture into a sense of continuity restored.

What could such continuity be? We can look once more to the

1850 *Prelude* and the winged angel of time that bears "the great spirit of human knowledge." In *The Prelude*, of course, the true angel is the poet's personal Mnemosyne: memory. And the knowledge to which memory conducts is a special, profound amnesia of historical knowledge: Mind or Self. Where the continuity of the human spirit had been ruptured by the Revolution, now the rupture will be closed by a supervision of self able to redeem rupture as itself a kind of continuity. Historical rupture must be rethought as a *personal* version of a "duration in the history of peoples." The perpetual Revolution we glimpsed at the end of the last chapter must become the Growth of the Poet's Mind.

The Terror of Time

A Map of Coming Times

Thus does Wordsworth's first time begin. Since we have yet to trace the rise of the Romantic self, it will be convenient to break off pursuing the full evolution of time into spots of time. But it may be useful simply to map the symbolic topography that grounds the route of this later evolution.

We can begin our tour of time with a detail from a broader picture. In his next major work, *The Borderers* (1796–97), Wordsworth regrounds the allegorical landscape of *Salisbury Plain*. For the moment, a political interpretation of the play complementary to David Erdman's will serve ("Wordsworth as Heartsworth"). Briefly, the Plain becomes the Solway Plain, and the tragedy another crypto-Revolutionary "plot" (Early Version, V.iii.27–28) of warriors familiar with sacrifice (Rivers: "We recognize in this old man [Herbert] a victim / Prepared already for the sacrifice"; II.iii.400–401, see also II.iii.377–78, 428). Just as the Revolutionary poetics of war and sacrifice had required verification and justification, so Rivers now offers Mortimer "proofs" and leads him in invocations of "justice" so repetitive as to be formulaic (see n. 1 to Chapter 6). And just as the Revolution had been ostensibly supervised by necessitarian benevolence, so now Mortimer is supervised by what we will see in the next chapter to be Rivers's "friendship." Yet ultimately, of course, Rivers is malevolent, and all his plot lies and injustice. What neutralizes the shocking discovery of such *unnecessary* malevolence in the play is an evasion or "othering" wholly congruent with that in *Salisbury Plain*. Rather than communicate its true historical referent, the allegory of *The Borderers* obscures the referent in a thick opacity of time. We can take our cue from Mortimer, who ends by turning *émigré*: he flees the scene of injustice to wander in "intensity of thought" toward "blank forgetfulness" (V.iii.271–75). Just so, the play as a whole retreats from disclosure of contemporary injustice into a forgetful sense of time. It invents its version of a Druid past: the semilegendary world of the thirteenth-century Border. Like *Salisbury Plain*, that is, it mimes Revolutionary tragedy only to screen it at last behind a veil of otherness, of "then" as opposed to "now."

Such is the raw stuff of temporality, which *The Borderers* then begins to shape into a spot of time. The central totem spot in the play is a sort of Gothic Stonehenge: the ruined castle where Mortimer had first planned to kill Herbert (II.iii). Through a symbolic shift, however, the murderous spot opens out into another spot: the bare heath upon which he abandons Herbert. Suggestively, this latter killing ground stages a precursor of the gibbet mast and blasted hawthorn in Book II of *The Prelude*: "a tree, ragged and bent and bare" (III.iii.37). (As Marijane Osborn suggests, this description refers to an actual tree the poet knew near Penrith; pp. 153–54.) More tellingly, the tree is then immediately overshadowed in the following scene by what Robert Osborn suggests may be a facsimile of Penrith Beacon: "an eminence—a Beacon on it" (III.iv; see *B*, p. 202n).[43] The scenes of the Border begin to resemble the mature spots of time to come.

What our "detail" map shows, in fact, is the pattern of the poetry as a whole in this period: the topographical displacement I mark in *The Borderers* characterizes a number of works, each of which carries on the task of transforming the early allegory of the Druids into spots of time. As Hartman has put it, Stonehenge is one of the earliest power spots in Wordsworth's work (*WP*, pp. 120–23). After *Salisbury Plain*, this spot descends into the poet's symbolic landscape along an overall route that may be mapped by means of certain specially potent landmarks (as in Fig. 4)—with the overall result that the Spenserian allegory or epic simile of Other Nature is naturalized.[44]

On the one hand lies a path of fixation (scored with a broken line). Wordsworth simply shuttles the spot of Stonehenge from one work to another—from the 1793 *Salisbury Plain* to the 1795 *Adventures on Salisbury Plain*[45] and finally to the Sarum Plain vision of the 1805 *Prelude*. Yet the sameness of the spot makes a subtle difference. We notice that at each stage of repetition, the spot of Druid power diminishes in importance. In *Adventures* the three scenes set at Stonehenge in *Salisbury Plain* clarify into a single scene of just over three stanzas (*SP*, pp. 127–28). And in the 1805 *Prelude*, the Sarum Plain vision is a subordinate spot of time. Occurring at the close of the two-book unit

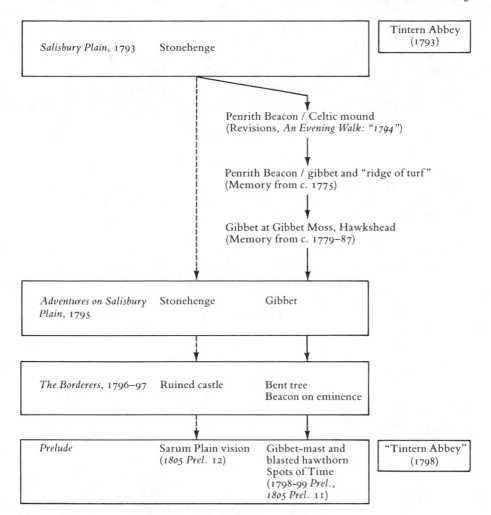

FIG. 4. The scene of time, 1793–1805.

titled "Imagination, How Impaired and Restored," it does little actual work in the poet's project of reimagining the world after the Revolution. Relieved of the main task by the spots of time that open the task of Restoration, it is free to apply itself to a further investiture of Imagination. After recapitulating Scene iii of the allegory in *Salisbury Plain* (again the Britons with "shield and stone-axe," again the "sacrificial Altar, fed / With living men," and again a final glimpse of Druids pointing to the skies; 12.312–53), the Sarum Plain vision adds a personal ambition. The vision was early proof, Wordsworth says, that he could be a "Prophet," a "power like one of Nature's" (12.298–312). Stonehenge predicts the ultimate Druid of his poetic self.

The fixated descent of Stonehenge into the later works, in short, is only at first glance stasis. What was originally allegory at Stonehenge is so far from unchanging, indeed, that by the time of the 1805 *Prelude* it barely seems allegorical at all. It is attracted into a more complex symbolic landscape of nature capable of figuring a self at last more than natural, more than can be contained in descriptive poetry.

What intervening force has pulled the allegory of Stonehenge into a new orbit of meaning? The force is memory, the supervision of time by selfhood. I look aside at this point from the path of descent to that of denial (scored in Fig. 4 with a solid line). The true fate of allegory is to follow a trajectory of symbolism into what Christopher Salvesen calls Wordsworth's "landscape of memory."

After finishing *Salisbury Plain*, we know, the poet returned in body and spirit to the Lake District. Living at Windy Brow in Keswick during spring and summer 1794 (and briefly at Rampside during late summer), he set his hand to revising *An Evening Walk*—first on pages facing *Salisbury Plain* in DC MS. 10 and then in fuller form in DC MS. 9 (*EW*, pp. 12–13). These revisions, which nearly double the bulk of *An Evening Walk*, create a version of the poem that Averill, following Selincourt, titles *1794*. To start with, *1794* dismantles the allegory of *Salisbury Plain* and relocates it in symbolic form in the Lakes. The spot marked by Stonehenge becomes by dreamwork another spot presided over by a dual marker: Penrith Beacon and a Celtic mound.

Here we need to follow the complex transference made possible by fire (the culmination of the fiery atmospherics we saw earlier). The original *Evening Walk* had briefly mentioned Druid stones at Broughton (the Sunkenkirk or Swinside Stone Circle), and then, a few lines later, Penrith Beacon:[46]

> The Druid stones their lighted fane unfold,
> And all the babbling brooks are liquid gold;
>
>   . . .
>
>   silent stands th'admiring vale below;
> Till, but the lonely beacon all is fled,
> That tips with eve's gleam his spiry head.
> (ll. 171–72, 188–90)

1794 embellishes both the Druid stones and the Beacon. It lights the stone circle at Broughton with a fiery sun, then an actual fire, and finally a comparison to past sacrificial fires. "Refulgent" in the sun's "parting blaze," Wordsworth says, "naked druid stones" appear attended by "piles of burning fern . . . Where once the savage viewed mysterious fires" (*EW*, p. 142). Then *1794* fires Penrith Beacon to summon up another, specifically Druidical scene—a scene that intimates sacrifice and war in a manner reminiscent of the allegory in *Salisbury Plain*. The Beacon, we know, had once housed a pitch-fire pot or grate (Jefferson, 1:78). In a long interpolation, Wordsworth draws figuratively upon the original apparatus of the Beacon to spark thoughts of the "torch of War." Then he allows the fire of war to prism wildly through fiery sunlight to end in a Druid-like vision of war restaging the sacrifices we saw at Stonehenge:

> Why, shepherds, tremble thus with new alarms
> As if ye heard the din of civil arms?
> Peace now is yours; the brother swains that view
> Romantic Tiviot's rocks are still as you.
> Lighted by flames flushed from the torch of War,
> No more that beacon sends his dismay afar;
> But now, while dances his exulting spire,
> Red with the thunder-tempest's splendid fire,
> There, from the bursting of the summer clouds,
> All unconcerned the mountain shepherd shrouds.
>
> · · ·
>
> And when the sun declining pours the tide
> Of heat redundant from the mountain-side,
> Behind a mound, which rose in ruder days
> For other use, that shepherd shuns the blaze;
> His flocks across the beacon's shadow bound
> In antick race beneath that mossy mound,
> Nor with their noiseless feet the earth molest,
> Where side by side the slain and slayer rest.
> Not thus where Labour bids yon marsh recede.
>
> · · ·
>
> There rent the fen before him and—behold,
> A horseman skeleton of giant mould!
> Half-shown, erect, his mighty bones he rears,
> An unknown being of forgotten years.
>
> (*EW*, pp. 143–44)

Where Stonehenge in *Salisbury Plain* had once staged war and sacrificial flames, in sum, Penrith Beacon and the Celtic mound now restage the scene.[47]

Thus does *1794* layer the allegory of Revolutionary war and sacrifice into the Lake District. The other key revisions in *1794* then direct us away from the historical referent for such allegory to a myth of nature and time.[48] By way of allusion to the rite of sacrifice in Horace's ode on Blandusia, we notice, *1794* appends to its version of the Rydal Falls passage a long meditation upon sacrificial violence. Horace, whose passage Wordsworth includes in a footnote in his own translation, had colored the scene of repose with wanton desire and bloody violence:

> Blandusian Spring, than glass more brightly clear,
> Worthy of flowers and dulcet wine,
> To-morrow shall a kid be thine,
> Whose brow, where the first budding horns appear,

> Battles and love portends—portends in vain,
> For he shall pour his crimson blood
> To stain, bright Spring, thy gelid flood,
> Nor e'er shall seek the wanton herd again.
> Thee Sirius smites not from his raging star;
> Thy tempting gloom a cool repose
> To many a vagrant herd bestows.   (*EW*, p. 135n)

The interpolation in *1794* applies Horace to the repose at Rydal Falls
by way of negation. Wordsworth summons up Horace's scene only
to flinch sharply away:

> Did Sabine grace adorn my living line,
> Blandusia's praise, wild stream, should yield to thine!
> Never shall ruthless minister of Death
> In thy brown glooms the glittering steel unsheathe;
> No goblets shall for thee be crowned with flowers,
> No kid with piteous outcry thrill thy bowers;
> Stabbed when Desire first wantons in his blood,
> No dying kid shall stain thy [   ] flood.
> (*EW*, pp. 134–35)

The reflexive flinch away is *so* sharp, indeed, that we might suspect it
to respond to more than the threat of a prior poet in the background.
With just the slightest nudge of topicality, for example, the "ruthless minister of Death" might seem to intimate some member of the
Committee of Public Safety (or, with English reference, Pitt during
the period of the treason trials of 1793 and 1794).

   Yet any opportunity to deploy the swerve from Horace in a historical manner quickly passes. The instability in the text marked by
negation—a locodescriptive moment implicit with suppressed agony
—is elided. Wordsworth converts negation into the great naturalized
epic similes or fictions that from this period on give his work its
characteristic air: nature and time as supervised by selfhood. The poet
finishes his allusion to Horace by invoking "a more benignant sacrifice" to be conducted by the ruth*ful*—rather than ruthless—ministers
of Mind and Heart. He addresses the waters at Rydal Falls:

> The mystic Shapes that by thy margin rove
> A more benignant sacrifice approve;
> A Mind, that in a calm angelic mood
> Of happy wisdom, meditating good,
> Beholds, of all from her high powers required,
> Much done, and much designed, and more desired;
> Harmonious thoughts, a soul by Truth refined,
> Entire affection for all human kind;
> A heart that vibrates evermore, awake
> To feeling for all forms that Life can take,

That wider still its sympathy extends,
And sees not any line where being ends;
Sees sense, through Nature's rudest forms betrayed,
Tremble obscure in fountain, rock, and shade;
And while a secret power those forms endears
Their social accents never vainly hears.

                    (*EW*, p. 135)

Sympathizing with all life in a manner circumventing the full tragic response to agony, Mind and Heart are "mystic Shapes" akin to the Druids looking heavenward in *Salisbury Plain*: they transform the scene of sacrificial violence into an Other Nature of purified existence. The "trembling" of the incipient locodescriptive moment is harnessed to a new meditative repose.

   Such Mind and Heart are the developing anatomy of Wordsworth's self. They are the organs of Imagination and Affection that from this point on subordinate any engagement with the social scene to love of Nature—a mediating realm now serving to verify, as in a mirror, only the subdued agon or gentle ache that is the Romantic self itself. Nature is what tells the self that its feelings and imaginings are natural. The ideology of such nature is Wordsworth's time in its mature personality—temporality supervised by the faculty of self that conjoins Imagination and Affection: Memory. In what is probably its most significant revision, *1794* opens a meditation upon "favoured souls" (*EW*, p. 138) who know how to feel and imagine in Memory:

   Blest are those spirits tremblingly awake
To Nature's impulse like this living lake,
Whose mirrour makes the landscape's charms its own
With touches soft as those to Memory known;
While, exquisite of sense, the mighty mass
All vibrates to the lightest gales that pass.

                    (*EW*, p. 137)

   In the next stage of Wordsworth's developing scene of time, the allegory of Stonehenge is then assimilated even more thoroughly to the Lakes landscape and the memorial self. Here a conjectural reconstruction of the poet's memory is required to explain a metamorphosis in the symbolic markers of Penrith Beacon and the Celtic mound. Sometime soon after *1794*, we speculate, he must have returned in mind to his Penrith boyhood to recall—and indirectly apply—his celebrated gibbet mast experience of about 1775 (later detailed most fully in Book 11 of the 1805 *Prelude*). As recorded directly for the first time in the "Two-Part *Prelude*" of 1798–99, we know, this episode focused upon a power spot dominated by Penrith Beacon and—in place of the Celtic mound and giant warrior of *1794*—"a long green ridge of turf . . . like a grave" marking a vanished gibbet mast (WAG,

p. 9). The Celtic tumulus of *1794* was changing form. A supplementary act of memory then probably furthered the metamorphosis by invoking yet another gibbet mast from slightly later in the poet's boyhood. I refer to the less well known scene of Gibbet Moss near Hawkshead (see *Prose* 2: 445–46, and T. Kelley, "Economics," pp. 22–23) where, as Wordsworth later vividly describes in "An Unpublished Tour,"

> the body of some atrocious Criminal had been hung in Chains near the spot where his crime had been committed. Part of the Irons & some of the wood work remained in my memory. Think of a human figure tossing about in the air in one of these sweet Valleys. 'Tis an object sufficiently fearful & repulsive upon Hounslow heath or in the solitudes of Salisbury Plain, but in a populous enclosure like this where no one could look round without being crossed by the sight—what a dismal annoyance! (*Prose*, 2: 333)

The comparison to Salisbury Plain here is telling. Altogether, the poet's invocation of native killing grounds allowed him to establish an equivalence between his entire landscape of allegorical Druidism and that of the memorial self rooted to the Lakes. Penrith Beacon and a gibbet mast—the former a remembrance of war, the latter a monument to what the old allegory ritualized as sacrifice—were the means by which markers of Celtic violence could be transformed into tokens of the native and *personal* allegory of violence commemorated in the spots of time in Book 11 of the 1805 *Prelude*: the death of the poet's father.[49]

Such, in any case, is one explanation for what is perhaps the single most striking innovation in *Adventures on Salisbury Plain* in late 1795: the introduction of a gibbet mast. Through some process of recall akin to that reconstructed above, Wordsworth deployed his newfound equivalence between the landscapes of Druid allegory and of the memorial self to renovate even the barren expanse of Salisbury Plain into a partial look-alike of the Lakes. Though he had now actually moved from the Lakes to Racedown near Bristol, that is, he regrounded the earlier *Salisbury Plain* upon the terrain of boyhood memory and so began detaching his allegory of time from too strict a Druidism. Of course, the Plain could not be entirely refitted to reproduce the significant features of his new symbolic landscape of memory. Penrith Beacon, for example, could not easily be added. But the other symbolic marker of boyhood memory proved eminently adaptable to "the solitudes of Salisbury Plain," as the account of Gibbet Moss in "An Unpublished Tour" describes it. The Traveller in *Adventures* is now a criminal Sailor who, near the poem's opening, falls senseless before a gibbet foreshadowing the poem's ideology of justice:

> For as he plodded on, with sudden clang
> A sound of chains along the desart rang:

He look'd, and saw on a bare gibbet nigh
A human body that in irons swang,
Uplifted by the tempest sweeping by,
And hovering round it often did a raven fly.

It was a spectacle which none might view
In spot so savage but with shuddering pain
Nor only did for him at once renew
All he had feared from man, but rouzed a train
Of the mind's phantoms, horrible as vain.
The stones, as if to sweep him from the day,
Roll'd at his back along the living plain;
He fell and without sense or motion lay,
And when the trance was gone, feebly pursued his way.

(*SP*, p. 126)

What kind of justice is administered by phantoms of mind? The answer is justice cognate with the experience of memorial time. At the conclusion of the poem, the Sailor confronts a living memory of the past he gave up by committing murder: he meets his old wife, who is now dying. Torn by remorse at her fate, he at last surrenders to "Justice" and is himself actually gibbeted. The poem ends:

Blest be for once the stroke which ends, tho' late,
The pangs which from thy halls of terror came,
Thou who of Justice bear'st the violated name!

They left him hung on high in iron case,
And dissolute men, unthinking and untaught,
Planted their festive booths beneath his face;
And to that spot, which idle thousands sought,
Women and children were by fathers brought;
And now some kindred sufferer driven, perchance,
That way when into storm the sky is wrought,
Upon his swinging corpse his eye may glance
And drop, as he once dropp'd, in miserable trance.

(*SP*, p. 154)

This fete is Wordsworth's first recognizable spot of time. Through a process of memory that fulfills the amnesiac allegory of Druidical time, Terror becomes personal terror, and justice a gibbet. Time ends by making all things—legitimately, if harshly—*right* once more.

Thus it is that when Wordsworth turned in 1796–97 to *The Borderers*, as I have already detailed, Stonehenge was ready to be transformed first into a ruined castle and then into the spot on the heath marked by the equivalent of Penrith Beacon and the gibbet mast: a beacon on its eminence and a bent tree. And thus it is that when in 1798–99 he began *The Prelude*, the paradigmatic markers of the spots of time were already in place. Stonehenge (which, as we saw, will be restored in a minor position in the 1805 *Prelude*) is suppressed en-

tirely in the 1798–99 "Two-Part" poem. In its place is a spot marked
by Penrith Beacon and the gibbet mast that synthesizes the boyhood memories of gibbeting at Penrith and Hawkshead (WAG, p. 9).
Finally, of course, the Beacon/gibbet is then recapitulated in a further spot of "chastisement": an eminence surmounted by the blasted
hawthorn (WAG, pp. 9–10). On these spots of time, the landscape
of memory becomes one with justice. All is wrong in the agonized
world; yet all is somehow supremely right as well. Here is where a
Poet, whose loyalty to the People has shrunk to friendship for Coleridge, declares his own history of agony to be legitimate.

Revolutionary Vision: A Panoramic View

Along this overall path of symbolic markers, then, tours the poet's
self—the subject whose full Imagination, as we will later see, at last
crowns itself in the 1805 *Prelude* atop Snowdon as a self-sufficient
power little short of imperial. Indeed, we might look once more
to the residual allegory of Druidism in the 1805 *Prelude*—the Sarum
Plain vision in Book 12—to review the whole itinerary of poetic
emergence we have toured and to predict the itinerary of poetic individuation yet to come. The Sarum Plain vision, we recall, showed
the poet he could be a "power like one of Nature's" (12.298–312). The
passage that follows the vision to close Book 12 then points directly
toward Snowdon in the next book:

> This for the past, and things that may be view'd
> Or fancied, in the obscurities of time.
> Nor is it, Friend, unknown to thee, at least
> Thyself delighted, who for my delight
> Hast said, perusing some imperfect verse
> Which in that lonesome journey was composed,
> That also then I must have exercised
> Upon the vulgar forms of present things
> And actual world of our familiar days,
> A higher power, have caught from them a tone,
> An image, and a character, by books
> Not hitherto reflected. Call we this
> But a persuasion taken up by thee
> In friendship; yet the mind is to herself
> Witness and judge, and I remember well
> That in life's every-day appearances
> I seem'd about this period to have sight
> Of a new world, a world, too, that was fit
> To be transmitted and made visible
> To other eyes, as having for its base
> That whence our dignity originates,
> That which both gives it being and maintains

A balance, an ennobling interchange
Of action from within and from without,
The excellence, pure spirit, and best power
Both of the object seen, and eye that sees.

(12.354–79)

Here, Wordsworth summons Coleridge to witness the first fount of all his later ideology: the atmosphere he absorbed on Salisbury Plain. The "imperfect verse" is *Adventures on Salisbury Plain*, which he recited to his new friend in 1795 or 1796 (*CEY*, pp. 167, 185); and the "tone" he so effectively communicated—as Coleridge's reminiscences in *Biographia Literaria* inform us—was precisely atmosphere: "It was not however the freedom from false taste," Coleridge says, "which made so unusual an impression on my feelings immediately, and subsequently on my judgement. It was the union of deep feeling with profound thought; the fine balance of truth in observing with the imaginative faculty in modifying the objects observed; and above all the original gift of spreading the tone, the *atmosphere*, and with it the depth and height of the ideal world" (1: 80).

It is such ideal atmosphere that Wordsworth shapes into the tenets of his personal ideology. First there is nature. Atmosphere forgets everyday reality—and, we can add, historical agon—not in the manner of the picturesque but through the discovery of Other Nature: "I remember well," the poet says, that "I seem'd about this period to have sight / Of a new world, a world . . . To be transmitted . . . To other eyes." Then there is time. The newness of the world projects the overall atmosphere of the passage: a thick opacity of memorial *time*. The new is the obscurity of the old; "I remember well," that is, invokes a temporality serving to *dis*remember remarkably well: "This for the past, and things that may be view'd / Or fancied, in the obscurities of time," the passage as a whole begins. Thus is dismissed —as if out of court—all the agon the poet originally allegorized on Sarum Plain. The history of agony is thrown out of court so that the most atmospheric of all ideologies—a poetry whose recourse for wrongs is only the natural course of time—can at last sit in a mood of self-sufficient righteousness: "the mind is to herself / Witness and judge," Wordsworth says.

Taken as a whole, we can conclude, the Sarum Plain unit functions to mediate between the earlier spots of time and the poet's crowning statement of ideology in Book 13. Sarum Plain sounds a march from the spots of time toward the aggressive and expansionist self-righteousness we will witness on Snowdon: the imperialism of Mind. Already, we notice, the poet marches across the Plain to the beat of ever more insistent *power*. He will be "a power like one of Nature's," "a higher power," and the "best power / Both of the object seen, and eye that sees." In short, the poet promotes himself. He prepares to *crown* himself with a glory succeeding both the picturesque vision of repose and the Terrorized *oeil de la surveillance*: a vision of the Mind's empire. As we will hear him say in Book 13:

> Such minds are truly from the Deity,
> For they are Powers; and hence the highest bliss
> That can be known is theirs, the consciousness
> Of whom they are habitually infused
> Through every image, and through every thought,
> And all impressions.   (13.106–11)

Such minds are supremely reposed; but they are also implicitly tyrannical.

It will not be out of place to close by summing up in one view the visions and revisions that have taken us to the threshold of incipient imperial vision. Revolving through all the arena-structures we have witnessed—the dioramic summer house, the "wheel" vision of the Lakes, Clarke's or West's views from Penrith Beacon, the prospect from Lancaster Castle, the Panopticon, the Champ-de-Mars, Stonehenge, and, at last, the spots of time—is the grand panorama that is the age's vision of itself. In one sense, this panorama is all the same. All its versions predict David's painting of Napoleon ringed by coronation spectators or Debret's painting of Napoleon adored by recipients of the Légion d'Honneur.[50] All, that is, prepared not only the imaginal form of revolution but also that of the fulfillment of revolution in empire—in the ultimate panopticism that saw Napoleon as the new Sun King (and Britain as the realm on which the sun never set).

Yet if the revolution of vision was essentially unchanging and so incapable of progress—except in the sense of expressing its innate form in ever more totalitarian fashion—it could still digress. As in the digression of an epic simile, it could look away from the agon, the gladiatorial combat, staged in the center of history's arenas to some other scene allowing at least the relief of suspended disbelief—of naturalized fiction. We might look for our model to the actual panorama, exactly contemporary with Wordsworth's poems of the 1790's, that initiated the panoramic craze of the period: Robert Barker's gigantic 360° rotunda (later called Burford's Panorama) in Leicester Square (Pl. 18). Opened in 1794, Barker's structure housed not one but *two* panoramas (for details, see Altick, pp. 128–34; also R. Hyde, pp. 130–32). The celebrated first exhibit, for example, featured Barker's view of the Grand Fleet lying off Spithead (with the Isle of Wight in the background and a capsized boat in the foreground) and, in a smaller upper gallery, his view of London from the top of Albion Mills (before its destruction by fire the highest point between St. Paul's and Westminster Abbey).

PLATE 18. Cross-section of Robert Barker's panorama rotunda in Leicester Square, from Robert Mitchell's *Plans and Views in Perspective of Buildings Erected in England and Scotland*, 1801. Yale Center for British Art, Paul Mellon Collection, New Haven. Photo: Yale Center for British Art.

Wordsworth's revolutionary vision, we may say, became exactly such a rotunda. If the capsize of his political beliefs in the main chamber of history-seen-in-nature was too painful—emblematized precisely in the fleet at Spithead the poet saw off the Isle of Wight in 1793—then the solution was denial. The self had only to withdraw to a different chamber entirely: transcendence was a climb of three flights of stairs. When we come to "Composed Upon Westminster Bridge" in Chapter 9, we will see that the poet's higher chamber of vision could indeed seem to transcend history by projecting a strangely veiled analogue of Barker's London view. (Meanwhile, we may note, the actual panoramas of London and Paris took the opposite tack by increasingly concentrating on the logical outgrowth of Barker's Grand Fleet picture: spectacular scenes of battle exploiting what Altick calls "newsreel" interest in the history of the Napoleonic wars; pp. 134–36; see also n. 12 to my Chapter 9.) But it was primarily a *rustic* transcendence of history that Wordsworth embraced in his Great Decade of poetry after the mid 1790's. Enacting a revolution of mind, he pictured himself in the surround of Other Nature and all that such circumambience allowed him to digress toward: first his dark allegory of time and then—at the close of the series of symbolic displacements on the scene of time we sketched above—his smallest, and yet most ambitious, of all viewing chambers, the self.[51] Here was room for the Mind to expand into *its* empire.

Digression from history through corridors of time, in sum, was the special denial that became the mind's expansive "growth." It was prelude to a legitimized and authoritative self that, however much it experienced the gaps, breaks, and agonies of historical succession, nevertheless locked itself away in the small closet of Mind to declaim an ideology—and poetry—of ever-widening duration. Life viewed from the closet became the panoramic round of One Life without end.

Here, once more, is the confession of successive temporality in *The Prelude*:

> A tranquillizing spirit presses now
> On my corporeal frame: so wide appears
> The vacancy between me and those days,
> Which yet have such self-presence in my mind
> That, sometimes, when I think of it, I seem
> Two consciousnesses, conscious of myself
> And of some other Being.   (2.27–33)

And here, just after the Revolution books, is the historical authority for such temporality:

> Shall I avow that I had hope to see,
> I mean that future times would surely see
> The man to come parted as by a gulph,
> From him who had been, that I could no more
> Trust the elevation which had made me one
> With the great Family that here and there
> Is scatter'd through the abyss of ages past,
> Sage, Patriot, Lover, Hero; for it seem'd
> That their best virtues were not free from taint
> Of something false and weak, which could not stand
> The open eye of Reason.   (11.57–67)

Whether inspecting the personal or collective past through the "open eye of Reason," Wordsworth in his Great Decade was threatened by a tearing and breaking in time creative of deadly *ricorso*. Where there was one consciousness or Man, now there was another, diminished one.

But finally, here is the culmination of the argument of time on the last page of *The Prelude*:

> Oh! yet a few short years of useful life,
> And all will be complete, thy race be run,
> Thy monument of glory will be raised.
> Then, though, too weak to tread the ways of truth,
> This Age fall back to old idolatry,

Though men return to servitude as fast
As the tide ebbs, to ignominy and shame
By Nations sink together, we shall still
Find solace in the knowledge which we have.

　　　　　　.　.　.

Prophets of Nature, we to them will speak
A lasting inspiration, sanctified
By reason and by truth; what we have loved,
Others will love; and we may teach them how;
Instruct them how the mind of man becomes
A thousand times more beautiful than the earth
On which he dwells, above this Frame of things
(Which, 'mid all revolutions in the hopes
And fears of men, doth still remain unchanged)
In beauty exalted, as it is itself
Of substance and of fabric more divine.

(13.421–45)

In the eye of Imagination rather than of Revolutionary Reason, *ricorso* (the return of the age to idolatry; "revolutions in the hopes / And fears of men") will be redeemed. Personal or collective succession in time rounds back upon itself as *duration*. It becomes a new *ricorso* ("what we have loved, / Others will love") signing "lasting inspiration." And the ultimate identity of such duration is poetic Mind: a "mind of man" transcendent above the world.

Or put another way, succession becomes the new authority that increasingly ideologizes the poet's work: originality (in Leslie Brisman's thesis, the redeemed *ricorso* of Romantic reorigination). Originality is the enduring one life of a Mind for which there can exist nothing, past or future, but intimations of itself. It is to Wordsworth's post-Revolutionary argument of originality—or, more broadly, of the full individuation of the poetic self and its triumvirate Directory of memory, affection, and imagination—that I now turn. From this Directory, the First Consul of the Mind, Imagination, at last usurps power.

Simply to provide a shared resting place in advance of new argument, I enter into evidence here a poem that in the past few years has suddenly become a commonplace, and battleground, of historicist and antihistoricist readings of Romanticism—a work seeming at once far removed from imperialism and, as it were, already a young lieutenant of artillery. I refer to "Tintern Abbey," the quintessential poem of Wordsworthian time. Inspired by a visit to the Wye valley immediately after the poet's wanderings on Salisbury Plain in 1793, and composed in 1798 a few months before the first sustained work on the "Two-Part *Prelude*," "Tintern Abbey" precisely brackets the whole scene of temporality we have surveyed in the 1790's. But as others have ably suggested, it may do so by recording a revolution in Wordsworth's development that was fundamentally historical rather than psychobiographical or spiritual. Specifically, the poem may be "about" the displaced stance he took toward political and social history when, in the aftermath of the French Revolution, he learned to digress into his own mind.[52] A choice of three questions confronts us with regard to this poem: can we ground "Tintern Abbey" in historical and political reference? Is it *im*possible to ground it in such reference (with the corollary that the effort to do so betrays the over-historicizing impulse of historicist readers themselves)? Or does the real issue transpose these two questions to a different level entirely, where it appears that it is the very *undecidability* of the poem with regard to historical reference that is historically and politically grounded (in a way that opens an interpretive link between the undecidability of the poet's engagement with history and our own postmodern anxiety of engagement)?

Without rehearsing the studies of Robert Brinkley, Kenneth Johnston ("Politics"), Marjorie Levinson (*Wordsworth's Great Period Poems*, pp. 14–57), and Jerome McGann (*Romantic Ideology*, pp. 85–88), I should here declare that I concur with these and other readers of the poem who argue the relevance of historical concerns—especially insofar as such argument addresses permutations of the last question above.[53] The most celebrated—and criticized—portion of "Tintern Abbey" is the passage in which reference seems to disappear entirely to leave only *something* "rolling" through something else:

> For I have learned
> To look on nature, not as in the hour
> Of thoughtless youth; but hearing oftentimes
> The still, sad music of humanity,
> Nor harsh nor grating, though of ample power
> To chasten and subdue. And I have felt
> A presence that disturbs me with the joy
> Of elevated thoughts; a sense sublime
> Of something far more deeply interfused,
> Whose dwelling is the light of setting suns,
> And the round ocean and the living air,
> And the blue sky, and in the mind of man:
> A motion and a spirit, that impels
> All thinking things, all objects of all thought,
> And rolls through all things.   (*PW*, 2: 261–62)

Empson, in his well-known discussion, criticizes: "Whether man or some form of God is subject here, [Wordsworth] distinguishes between *things* which are objects or subjects of *thought*, these he *impels*; and *things* which are neither objects nor subjects of *thought*, through these he merely *rolls*. . . . The only advantage I can see in this distinction is that it makes the *spirit* at once intelligent and without intelligence; at once God and nature. . . . There is something rather shuffling about this attempt to be uplifting yet non-denominational" (pp. 153–54).

Empson's criticism, I believe, is essentially right—though God is in the end a wrong identification of what is at stake. The ambiguity of the poem is not between "man or some form of God," or even nature and God, but between Man—that is, the People—and self. "*Spirit* at once intelligent and without intelligence," as I have written elsewhere, is the very definition of the entity that historicism after the French Revolution as well as formalism and New Historicism in our own century have tried to think in a safe manner: the People or pluralistic mob ("Power of Formalism"). Wordsworth revolves in his mind a counter-Spirit whose anonymity at once mimes and denies the shuffling mob that first authorized his emergence as poet. The signature of this latter Spirit is "I" ("For *I* have learned," "And *I* have felt"). It is the "I"—the great impersonator of history able to be anyone at any time—that makes reference inconsequential. Just as "I, Bonaparte," can divide and rename the Italian peoples at will, so "I, Wordsworth" can make a leechgatherer a stone, a sea beast, and so on in an ambiguous process of referral, deferral, and *re*-referral. It is neither reference nor its lack, in short, that is the issue in reading the poem, but the sheer will and ambition of a poet who makes reference or lack of reference precisely a non-issue.

This ambition resident in the historical undecidability of the poem is what our own ambition to rehistoricize poetry engages. As I have argued in Chapter 2 and will return to in Chapter 9, the historicity of past texts and the historicity of present interpretation must of necessity differ; but precisely in their difference they will agree— thus making critical interpretation and understanding possible. Our own postmodern sense of history chooses controversies such as that over the history/not-history in "Tintern Abbey" because they offer a different way (for example) to ask whether the academy itself, after May 1968 or 1970, is in or out of history. Our chosen controversies, in other words, reproduce with a critical difference the controversy *in* a work like "Tintern Abbey" itself, which may be said to be "about" the very split between existence in and out of history.

"I" am everywhere in history, Wordsworth's Spirit declares, and yet nowhere in particular in history. "I" am the empire of the light of setting suns, of the round ocean and the living air, of the blue sky, and of the mind of man. "I" am the commander of motion and spirit that impels—indeed, *coerces*—all thinking things, all objects of all thoughts, and rolls through all things. And though my very being is denial, "I" will not be denied.

Such is the transcendence of reference that we must now go on to study in its evolving ideological phrasings from the mid 1790's through the 1805 *Prelude*. In this period, re-ideologization generates the affective and imaginal forms that make it possible to change allegories of time into the "symbolic" landscape of self we have already previewed—the Druids working magic at Stonehenge, in other words, into a poet writing "imagery" about spots of time. And throughout this whole process of transformation, I will argue, transcendence of reference is at every point itself referable to historical context. Or more properly, the effort of individuation that conducts Wordsworth to the full imagining of his spots of time is referable to plural *contexts*. As small as a family or a cottage, as large as Parliament or a battlefield: the contexts that determine the Romantic self to overcome its limiting referentiality are so ample and varied that any handful we now choose to study will necessarily be in part arbitrary. Yet arbitrariness, as I have said, does not exclude determination. To borrow from *The Prelude*:

> The road lies plain before me; 'tis a theme
> Single and of determined bounds; and hence
> I chuse it rather at this time, than work
> Of ampler or more varied argument.
>
> (1.668–71)

PART III

The Flight of Forms:
A Study of Poetic Individuation

Lyric and Empire

PERHAPS I MAY BE PERMITTED at this midpoint to invoke the poet's own rebeginning at the midpoint of *The Prelude*:

> Five years are vanish'd since I first pour'd out
> Saluted by that animating breeze
> Which met me issuing from the City's Walls,
> A glad preamble to this Verse.
>
>   .   .   .
>
>   my favourite Grove,
> Now tossing its dark boughs in sun and wind
> Spreads through me a commotion like its own,
> Something that fits me for the Poet's task,
> Which we will now resume with chearful hope,
> Nor check'd by aught of tamer argument
> That lies before us, needful to be told.
>
>   (7.1–56)

It is indeed time for a rebeginning. To trace the full genesis of Wordsworth's poetry, we need now to turn from its emergence under collective authority to what I will call its individuation under the new authority of the Romantic self. Where we have traced the origin of time, in other words, we must now watch the ascendancy of Imagination proper, Wordsworth's culminating ideology.

Time in its raw state, we saw, followed upon a bewildered allegorization, an amnesiac "othering" of history. What we will now be in a position to see is that in the period after his emergence, Wordsworth became preoccupied with a particular inflection of bewildered otherness: irony. Irony is the deep structure of the works of the mid-

1790's. But irony is also the foundation of a new superstructure. In the mid to late 1790's, the irony of time became "affection"; and affection begat the latest Druid of time, self. This is the argument initiated in *The Borderers*, whose stumblings toward selfhood I turn to in the next chapter.

But a distinction needs to be made. We are not concerned here with the unfolding of the poet's "real" self. Whatever the priority of such self, it is clear that no systematic thought of self—that is, no philosophy organizing and justifying everyday experience—is recoverable from textual evidence before about 1796. The poetry prior to Wordsworth's twenty-sixth year is essentially anonymous in its concern with the politics of collective consciousness. Where "I" or "mind" occurs, it is as stiffly conventional as any personification from a descriptive or Sensibility poem.[1] The ideology of self in the poet's work, it follows, is knowable only as an invention. As such, it must be explained on grounds other than incipient "self-consciousness," the teleological opening of so much modern analysis of the philosophy and psychology of Wordsworth's subjectivity. Self-invention must be explained on the basis of historical conventions generating not only the Romantic self but modern notions of subjectivity themselves.

What is the history of Wordsworth's self? Because this is the period of the poet's turn away from politics, it will be most useful to recover the history we need from "tamer arguments" of cultural experience exclusive, for the time being, of politics. In *The Borderers* (and, to some extent, *Adventures on Salisbury Plain* just before it), social history domesticates political agon, creating a new mimesis of the agony the poet thought he had buried on Salisbury Plain and forcing him to bring home his strategies of denial for fresh application. The social history most instrumental in domesticating denial in *The Borderers* is the history of the family. The adolescence of Wordsworth's poetic self lies in an ironized "family tragedy" both mimetic of family agony and selfishly unfaithful to it.

But this is only half the argument and half the social history I wish to explore. To follow the process of individuation in Wordsworth's poetry beyond *The Borderers* requires that we continue to track form. The entelechy of Wordsworth's ideology of self, we might say, is to create itself a form serenely detached from its origin in tragic form. To borrow from Hartman's essay on Milton, the Romantic self must assume the form of a "counterplot," of a remove from narrative reality able to redeem for self all the old imperturbability of anagogy.[2] Tragedy, of course, had always included forms that appear removed when taken separately: soliloquy, chorus, descent of the god, and address to the audience. But tragedy also provided for resistance to remove by engaging each of these forms in the others by identification: the chorus dances the plight of the soliloquizing hero, the god in the machine comes down to earth, and the audience finds itself touched by the entirety of the action. Wordsworth's ideology of self is driven to be as much as possible a self-enclosed soliloquy, chorus, god, or spectator of history.[3] In the mid to late 1790's, Wordsworth's poetry thus creates the self-expressive form that is his censored or elided tragedy: lyric.

This I take to be the central enterprise of *The Ruined Cottage*, which inaugurates lyric as the counterplotted form, or rather the "trans-form," of self. Whatever the poet's ostensible form from this point on, lyric will flower with sudden, inexplicable "imagery" to project an eye, and an "I," blind to narrative agony. Where family history had shaped the denied agony of *The Borderers*, now economic history performs the same function in *The Ruined Cottage*. As we will see in Chapter 7, the imagery of the hungry eye is "rich" no matter the evidence of poverty strewn all around. It is full of itself.

Wordsworth's Imagination, in sum, denied political history to emerge from collective imagination as a first time; and now it denies social and economic history to give time a local habitation and a name, a self and authentic form. When we at last return to *The Prelude* in Chapter 8 to watch the transformation of the French Revolution—and, at last, empire—into lyrical autobiography, it will thus be with full awareness of the extent of social and economic denial needed to fortify Imagination for politics once more. At its climax of "shapeless eagerness," as we will see, Wordsworth's epic of self has no form other than the transform of history. It becomes what I will at last call a refugee flight of forms, a rush to escape history in which each transitional genre (ending in lyrics of pure refuge like the epitaph we will come to on Leven Sands) harbors denied knowledge of the nation, family, and riches that must be left behind for the self to be free.

CHAPTER SIX

~⊙~

The Tragedy of the Family:
The Borderers

WORDSWORTH FIRST COMPOSED *A Tragedy*, as *The Borderers* was originally titled (see *B*, p. 444), mostly between fall 1796 and spring 1797, in a series of states culminating in what Robert Osborn has labeled the Early Version of 1799 (the first surviving manuscript of the complete play).* Read one way, the social agony preoccupying the play is a domestication of the problem of political justice: crime and punishment. A police sheet would include at least these counts: conspiracy to commit fraud (convictions: Rivers, Female Beggar), manslaughter (convictions: Rivers, Mortimer), pimping (charges dropped: Herbert), robbery and murder (charges dropped: Robert), and possibly even pickpocketing (charges pending: Mortimer, who takes Herbert's scrip of food). But of course, the whole premise of the play is that there is *no* police apparatus able to distinguish crimes objectively from what Mortimer actually believes he is upholding: a self-promulgated, ritualistically announced "justice."[1]

Set in a land that owns, as Rivers says, "no law but what each man makes for himself" (II.i.53), and that acknowledges only the "immediate law / Flashed from the light of circumstances / Upon an independent intellect" (III.v.31–33), *The Borderers* is an extreme case

* Citation of *The Borderers* in this chapter is as follows: verses from my primary text, the Reading Text of the Early Version in *B* (based on MS. 2 in DC MS. 23), are cited by act, scene, and line number; other material in *B*—including the fragmentary Rough Notebook drafts of late 1796 and early 1797 (MS. 1 in DC MS. 12), the Late Version of 1842, facsimile reproductions of the MSS., transcriptions, and textual apparatus—is cited by page number. For a guide to the composition and manuscripts of *The Borderers*, see *B*, pp. 3–17, 299–301, 445–49; and *CEY*, pp. 329–30.

of the purely ideological law Douglas Hay studies in "Property, Authority and the Criminal Law." In the absence of a true police force, Hay argues, the propertied interests in eighteenth-century England could govern only by virtue of an ideology of law enforced largely by elaborations of pomp and circumstance—by judicial "majesty." Just so, what allows Mortimer to govern in the absence of workable, official enforcement in *The Borderers* is an existential, perpetually advertised *style* of justice—an inflated pomp and circumstance of righteousness that, until the end of the play, covers for the crimes of self-interested appropriation (of Matilda and the scrip symbolic of her) he himself unwittingly commits.[2] Rivers's law of the "independent intellect" is merely the extreme jurisdiction of such righteous majesty.

But crime, I believe, is not the heart of the issue. Circumstantial evidence will prepare for my working thesis. Records of indictments in eighteenth- and early nineteenth-century England show that crime stood in precise inverse relation to the occurrence of war. As the age itself recognized, crime went down in war years and rose drastically in peace when the soldiers returned (J. M. Beattie, p. 103; Hay, "War," pp. 124–46). Indictments for theft and other crimes against property, for example, (1) remained low in England during the American War, (2) rose substantially in the peace years, 1783–93, (3) dropped radically as the Revolutionary wars began (reaching a nadir in 1795), and (4) shot up again to unprecedented peaks with the first returning veterans (and the crisis in food prices) from 1798 or 1799 through the Peace of Amiens in 1802 (Hay, "War," pp. 124–27; J. M. Beattie, pp. 104–5).

Evidence this broad, of course, cannot dictate interpretation of the poetry. Nevertheless, plotting Wordsworth's work against the national crime statistics gives us at least a prima facie case for suspecting that poetic criminality was in excess of criminal history. On the one hand, some direct relation between the poetry and social history is suggested by the fact that poems associated with crisis periods (2) and (4) show a deep-seated and sometimes spectacular emphasis upon crime. One instance is *Adventures on Salisbury Plain* (1795), whose addition of a criminal Sailor may testify to the just-concluded era of high crime, (2).[3] The other striking instance is *The Prelude* in its earliest phases—the episodes of the stolen woodcocks (1.316–32), stolen boat, gibbet mast, or Discharged Soldier, for example. Upon seeing a returned soldier in the latter episode (drafted early 1798) Wordsworth experiences a "specious cowardise" (4.434) that may well compound the high awareness of crime in the years after 1798, our period (4), with that of the previous crisis era, (2), when he actually saw the Discharged Soldier (probably in 1789; *CEY*, pp. 95, 88n). But on the other hand, works massively preoccupied with crime also flourished throughout the low-crime period, (3), between about 1795 and 1798. These works include "The Convict" (probably mid-1796), *The Borderers*, and *A Somersetshire Tragedy* (mid-1797; surviving only in brief fragments).

What the general evidence suggests, then, is that our best tactic lies not in seeking direct correspondence between the poetry and criminal history but in isolating some determinant behind Wordsworth's criminal interest semi-independent of the overall facts of crime. Several such determinants may be hypothesized, each entailing its own agenda of research. It would be useful, for example, to seek a hidden local factor by sifting Wordsworth's biography in conjunction with the regional criminal history of the Lakes and Dorset (where, at Racedown, the poet wrote the Early Version of *The Borderers*). The evidence in these fields, however, appears to be crucially inadequate.[4] Alternatively, we could probe for the basis of the poet's criminal interest in phenomenological or psychological consciousness, and so premise a general determination eliding the need for detailed external evidence. But for our purposes, this approach is disallowed because our final goal is to account for the very notion of the ideal psyche as an explanation of history. More fruitful, perhaps, would be investigation into the influence of intellectual or literary histories that at once realize such contemporary issues as penal reform and idealize them. We could thus look, for example, to the controversy surrounding the political "criminals" tried for treason and sedition in the mid-1790's or to the literature of crime written by Godwin, Schiller, and others.[5] Yet in our study, such factors can at best be only supplementary. Given the extreme choices of a local history void of adequate evidence and an ideal history void of the need for such evidence, the middle range of collectively formulated ideas, ideologies, and literature is not necessarily the best compromise. Ideas at a high level of formulation, as I earlier argued, are for our purposes already too far removed from basic historical context to be granted the status of premise. Unless we redefine "idea" to admit the looser structures and contradictions of "mentalities," history of ideas and its affiliates must stand at the close rather than beginning of study.

The approach I elect is to look slightly askance from criminality to a *contiguous* social context—a realm where the evidence is amply recoverable and spans the whole domain from the general to the local. As in the case of an erasure in a document, that is, the print around the blank can be revealing. Or rather, the thesis I propose is stronger than mere contiguity suggests: *The Borderers* and Wordsworth's other early works stage crime as the epiphenomenon of a *deeper*, more central social agony. We might witness here, for example, the spectacularly excessive criminality of *A Somersetshire Tragedy*.[6] In the real-life incident inspiring the play (as related to Wordsworth by Thomas Poole), a charcoal burner who loves one woman marries instead a "near-idiot" who had borne him bastard children. Two weeks later, he murders his wife by striking her with a hedge stake and savagely cutting her throat. After a wrenching valediction scene with his lover, he ends his life on the gibbet (J. Wordsworth, "A Wordsworth Tragedy").

In theatrical form, this would surely have been melodrama. Some deeper drama, we feel, invests the melodrama, inciting the poet in the period of *The Borderers* to portray sensational crime as implicitly typical of modern times regardless of the norm of actual crime at the time. The essential drama underlying Wordsworth's criminal melodrama, I suggest, is the social agony that in the later eighteenth century laid so much of the groundwork for the reception of the phenomenological and psychological explanations we now favor for understanding the self: the family.[7]

A pastiche from the poet's surviving works of the period will extend the scene rehearsed in *A Somersetshire Tragedy*. From *Adventures on Salisbury Plain*: a returned veteran murders a stranger while journeying home and thereafter abandons his family to become a fugitive. Many years later, he witnesses a strange repetition of his crime: a father brutally beating his child. Only after seeing such an in-family reenactment of the violence he had himself committed upon a stranger can he then encounter his family again in the person of his dying wife. From "The Convict": a criminal lies fettered in a cell for unknown crimes. The poet wishes to be his "brother." A chorus from Coleridge's "This Lime-Tree Bower My Prison" (1797): the poet languishes in "prison" after a household calamity in which his wife poured scalding milk on his foot. He thinks of the "strange calamity" of his friend, Charles Lamb, whose sister had killed their mother the previous year. Only then—as if through an exchange of prisoners, of the strange for the familiar—does he feel himself emancipated.[8] Finally, strange calamities from *The Borderers*: Rivers promises a woman he will never forsake her father, but leaves him to die on an island. Mortimer loves Matilda but, led by his "friend," Rivers, emulates the latter's crime as if somehow deeply familiar with it: he abandons Matilda's father on the heath. Meanwhile, in the subplot, a cottager who had once been falsely imprisoned must be reminded by his wife, "Robert, you are a father" (IV.iii.63).

No single generalization will account for all these tragic evolutions. But the following is a start: what we perceive in *The Borderers* and its satellite works is a complex scale of emulations or "affiliations" —ranging from the brotherly to the friendly to the purely symbolic —all serving to "familiarize" crime, to bring criminality by representation into the household. Only there, in the nuclear family updating the aristocratic "houses" of tragic tradition, can criminality be understood. For Wordsworth, as we will see, the family is the crime. Or phrased so as to ground the "excess" of poetic criminality we began upon: crime is a projection of the excess that *is* the family. As we will see, the family was a structure innately excessive of its own structure. Its identity was transgression. To keep the mentality of the family together—if not the actual family—required casting such transgression out of the house as an illegitimacy that could be safely pointed to in the stocks. The family, that is (as Mary Jacobus and Michael Ragussis help me conceive), pointed the finger at an illegitimacy and criminality staged across a spectatorial or theatrical remove.[9]

In pointing his own finger at criminals on the Border, in a stolen boat, on a gibbet mast, and so forth, Wordsworth then replayed at a still further remove the family dramatization of illegitimacy. He named the criminal in the stocks the Self, a proto-phenomenological and proto-psychological self that transumed both the family's agony and its means for casting—and casting out—agony. Denying the family by absorbing the agon of the family, the self became at once the actor and the spectator of its own illegitimacy. Such was the de-familiarization, in every sense, that ushered Wordsworth into originality. In the defamiliarized universe of the Border where domesticity and the family are always over the horizon, the self has no choice but to watch itself originating in splendid isolation like a god in descent —or, with bend sinister here, a bastard without descent.

A Question of Legitimacy

The Text of Illegitimacy

It will be best to open *The Borderers* first neither to the retrospective plot in which Rivers abandons the sea captain nor the ongoing reenactment in which Mortimer abandons Herbert. Rather, the key to the play is what I will call the "pre-plot" (on the model of Freud's threshold "preconscious") that allows the former action to impress itself on the latter and so makes possible the conceptual unity of the total plot. In I.iii, Rivers commissions the Female Beggar to perform a lie, a play-within-a-play.

Why does the lie act so powerfully on Mortimer?

We can play I.iii in four movements. The first opens with a prologue in which Rivers tells Mortimer the Beggar's history and so establishes her basic character as illegitimacy. Goes the tale: the Beggar is a fallen woman who went crazy after being abandoned by the orgiast, Lord Clifford (I.iii.4–15). In her madness (and presumably before her marriage to the recently deceased "poor Gilfrid" of Kirkoswald; I.iii.140–43), illegitimacy may have gone further: perhaps to bastardy and infanticide. A forerunner of Martha Ray in "The Thorn" (1798), the Beggar returns every midnight to a graveyard and paces "round and round" the "self same spot" (I.iii.16–22)—an obsession Rivers recounts again in II.i.20–31.[10] When the Beggar then comes onstage to bear out Rivers's story, she intensifies the pathos of illegitimacy by communicating it in "mad" terms. She rises from sleep with a prop, a "child in her arms." But rather than lull suspicions of illicit doings, the baby maintains them in surreal form: the Beggar announces dreams of violent infant death. She dreamed a bee stung her infant to death and, again, that a strange dog bit off her baby's head (I.iii.23–33, 36–41).

But Mortimer does not care. He says to Rivers after the Beggar's first dream, "We have no time for this," and casually dismisses her with tuppence: "My babbling gossip, / Here's what will comfort you" (I.iii.34–35).

The second movement of I.iii succeeds only marginally better in engaging Mortimer. Talking disconnectedly of her hard life and the illusion she sometimes has that she will somehow find money in the road (a coinage of mind we will need to come back to), the Beggar at first persuades Mortimer to see her only as a nuisance—"This woman is a prater"—and an object of fun: "Pray, good Lady, / Do you tell fortunes?" (I.iii.61–62). Only when she likens him to those who view her illegitimacy in an especially cynical way does his interest stir. The Beggar says:

> Oh! Sir! you are like the rest.
> This little one—it cuts me to the heart—
> Well! they might turn a beggar from their door,
> But there are mothers who can see the babe
> Here at my breast and ask me where I bought it:
> This they can do and look upon my face.
> —But you, Sir, should be kinder.   (I.iii.62–68)

Essentially, illegitimacy is rethought here according to the folkloric convention of the changeling, updated from the feudal imagination of agency by magic to the bourgeois imagination of agency by money. The perception of a basic mismatch between hag-mother and fairy-child is explained not on the basis of the little people but, as it were, of small change. We might paraphrase the Beggar as follows: "You, Mortimer, are like those who can look at my child and see only a product of illegitimate 'exchange.'"

"Come here ye fathers, / And learn of this poor wretch," Mortimer responds, sympathizing for the first time (I.iii.68–69).

It is only in the climactic third movement of I.iii that the Beggar fully draws Mortimer into her plight—so fully, indeed, that he discovers with total self-absorption that the plight is his own. First she reveals that she had met Herbert the previous day (I.iii.70–85). Then she hints that she has unfinished "business" with him, that "he owes / The best of all he has to me and mine," and finally that "If there's a lawyer in the land, the rogue / Shall give me half" (I.iii.109, 113–18). "What's your business / With Herbert or his daughter?" Mortimer asks (I.iii.121–22). The "business" is not long in coming. The Beggar gives Mortimer the "business," the bottom line of which, of course, is that Herbert's daughter, Matilda, is not really Herbert's daughter at all but her own, sold to him in infancy (I.iii.135–37). Thus is all the mysterious illegitimacy in the Beggar's history first rethought as "exchange" and then brought home to Mortimer as illicit "business" touching him nearly: the family he himself had thought to marry into is illegitimate to the core.

Now Mortimer cares. He cares, indeed, to a distraction already suggesting his own later madness. "Enough!" he shouts. Rivers elaborates, "We've solved the riddle" (I.iii.143–44). What follows is not "get thee to a nunnery"—not yet that madness. But already Mortimer is Hamlet shuffling off his mortal coil (and perhaps also Lear falling off the cliff and Richard II coming "down, down").[11] After sending the Beggar away with a curt promise of "justice," he acts his depression broadly:

> Sinking, sinking,
> And feel that I am sinking—would this body
> Were quietly given back unto the earth
> From whence the burthen came.
> (I.iii.157–60)

Mortimer has little sympathy left to spare the Beggar. He really feels pity and fear only for himself—for a tragedy of illegitimacy in which he must now act.

The fourth and final movement of I.iii then comes as a surprise. "Enough! or Too much," Blake might say. Despite the fact that "Enough!" has occurred and that the Beggar has left the stage, the scene continues into a supernumerary deception—a final, outrageous refinement of illegitimacy prompting further solipsism. Earlier, the Beggar had hinted, "There's a Lord— / I spied him sculking in his peasant's dress" (I.iii.119–120). But Mortimer had not been ready to listen. Now Mortimer calls her back on stage and learns at Rivers's instigation the identity of the "peasant" lurking at Herbert's door (I.iii.165–76): Lord Clifford, the orgiast and—considering the chronology of the Beggar's tale—possibly the natural father of Matilda.

We can guess with some assurance, after all, that Wordsworth conceived Matilda to be about twenty years old. (As indicated in V.iii.238, Mortimer is twenty-three, and men in the lower and yeoman classes normally matched with women two to three years younger; Stone, *Family*, p. 50 and notes 12–13 on pp. 692–93.)[12] Because it would be highly improbable for Gilfrid to have sired Matilda and then, some two decades later, the Beggar's current infant—and because, in any case, the Beggar presumably did not marry Gilfrid until after the period of her dalliance with Lord Clifford and of Matilda's birth—the distinct possibility arises that Matilda is a bastard. By implication, therefore (unless the Beggar's infanticidal dreams mean that she killed her earlier bastards), Matilda may well be the illicit offspring specifically of Clifford, who took the Beggar as mistress sometime prior to "ten years" ago (I.iii.14–15). Realistically, of course, we can imagine Wordsworth inventing such complex family history in piecemeal fashion without realizing its overall, baroque implications. What is of interest, however, is the general tendency of his logic of illegitimacy to spill beyond bounds: each premise of wrong spawns additional premises in a bottomless regress until, if we are willing to follow the logic to its conclusion, there is no escape from the unthinkable. Either the Beggar is infanticidal, for example, *or* Matilda may be the bastard of Clifford, whose lust for her thus becomes incestuous.

The ultimate result at this point in the play, whatever the exact details being whispered in the background, is that Rivers can use the Clifford subplot to persuade Mortimer of a monstrous sequel to child-selling big with hushed pornographic and incestuous intimations. Herbert bought Matilda as an infant, Mortimer comes to believe, only at last to sell her once more to Clifford for unspeakable purposes. Child-selling matures into a practice of daughter-prostituting that is at least pseudo-incestuous (if not actually so).[13] "Enough!" Rivers concludes, echoing Mortimer's earlier expression of surfeit (I.iii.176). And once more Mortimer sinks into himself—almost as if he had seen the ghost of Hamlet's father:

> Father! To God himself we cannot give
> An holier name, and under such a mask
> To lead a spirit spotless as the blessed
> To that abhorred den of brutal vice!
> The firm foundation of my life appears
> To sink from under me.   (I.iii.177–82)

Here both the scene and the first act close.

Why, then, does the Beggar's lie act so powerfully on Mortimer? It becomes clear that we do not know. We know only where to look: at a mysteriously narrow portion of the pre-plot staged by the Beggar. So long as the Beggar points a tale suggestive only of premarital sex, bastardy, infanticide, or violent infant death unconnected with himself, Mortimer remains unmoved. Similarly, the outrageous allegation of prostitution in the scene's last movement—while certainly inflammatory—is beside the point. Outrage is not the rage itself. For Mortimer it is more than "Enough!"—a flourish, a curtain call. The *only* phrasing of illegitimacy that makes a critical difference is that which builds in the scene's second movement to dominate its third: the charge of child selling, or what I have called "exchange."

Such narrow intensity of concern, we should realize, is exceedingly odd. The play itself later foregrounds the anomaly. When Mortimer's gang interrupts him during his indecisiveness in act II, he undertakes to prosecute Herbert's guilt publicly. With "an appearance of relaxed gaiety," he first rehearses the evidence he himself had found enough:

> Hark'ee, my Friends—
> Were there a man who, being weak and helpless
> And most forlorn, should bribe a mother pressed
> By penury to yield him up her daughter,
> A little infant, and instruct the babe
> Prattling upon his knee to call him Father—
> (II.iii.345–50)

But such evidence is not enough for others. Lacy interrupts, "Why, if his heart be tender, that offence / I could forgive him" (II.iii.351–52). This assessment puts things in perspective. After all, the fact that a blind old man wishes to buy a child may also be evidence of merciful or, at the least, pitiable intent. Mortimer continues,

> And should he make the child
> An instrument of falshood; should he teach it
> To stretch its little arms, and dim the light
> Of infant innocence with piteous looks
> Of misery that was not—   (II.iii.352–56)

And again the evidence is not enough. Lacy interrupts mildly, "Faith, 'tis hard, / But in a world . . ." (II.iii.356–57). It is only at this point that Mortimer broaches in a "serious tone" the evidence he himself had never needed:

> This self same man,
> Even while he printed kisses on the cheek
> Of this poor babe, and taught its innocent mouth
> To lisp the name of father, could he look
> To the unnatural harvest of that time
> When he should give her up, a woman grown,

> To him who bid the highest in the market
> Of foul pollution—   (II.iii.357–64)

"Hell itself / Contains not such a monster," Lacy finally agrees. " 'Tis too horrible," Wallace concurs (II.iii.364–65, 373–74).

What was enough for Mortimer, in sum, is not enough to convince others of Herbert's guilt—a fact Mortimer himself seems to sense when he introduces child buying merely as a casual preliminary. The only evidence that will do is that of intended prostitution.

Mortimer's decisive response to the illegitimacy of "exchange," we conclude, is severely undermotivated in the play. The strength of his response is so overdetermined relative to any apparent motive, indeed, that it must be presumed to rest upon some undisclosed, *selective* standard of significant illegitimacy—upon some prejudice, in Burke's term, making certain kinds of crime especially heinous. Unexplained prejudice, we can deduce, is the motive of the "justice" Mortimer upholds generally and promises to the Beggar in particular.

In his own catastrophe, we know, Rivers had judged the sea captain on the basis of a prejudice named "honour" and "pride." "I was convinced a foul conspiracy / Was laid against my honour," he remembers (IV.ii.9–10), adding that "Pride" itself had tamed his "pride" until a blow from the captain compelled him to act (IV.ii.14–36).[14] We might look for precedent here to the crucial blow Falkland receives from Tyrrel in *Caleb Williams* (B, p. 228n). As in the case of Falkland's fetish of honor, Rivers's similar prejudice is essentially chivalric or feudal in context. The reason he is such an inscrutable Iago in the play is that he is the *only* character truly a creature of the time of the Crusades. Perhaps, indeed, Rivers descends from an ethos even earlier than that of the Crusades. Honor and pride remember the code of the comitatus, of the earliest form of commitment to liege lord and lineage. Compare, for example, another seafarer, the speaker of the Old English poem, *The Wanderer*:

Thus I, wretched with care, removed from my homeland, far from dear kinsmen, have had to fasten with fetters the thoughts of my heart—ever since the time, many years ago, that I covered my gold-friend in the darkness of the earth; and from there I crossed the woven waves, winter-sad, downcast for want of a hall, sought a giver of treasure—a place, far or near, where I might find one in a mead-hall who should know of my people, or would comfort me friendless, receive me with gladness. (pp. 79–80)

Rivers is a wanderer whose honor and pride drive him to kill his own ring-giver, the sea captain, and so to end even more solitary, brooding, and desperate for a boon-friend than his Old English forerunner.[15]

What prejudice moves Mortimer to react so strongly to the Beggar's tale of debased ring-giving—of the exchange of coin for child—that he ends himself "a wanderer on the earth . . . Living by mere intensity of thought" (V.iii.265–72)? Moreover, what context of mores camouflages his prejudice (in the way feudalism had normalized honor and pride) so that overreaction appears unremarkable?

The answer to these questions cannot be discovered onstage. The evidence of the manuscript is telling in this regard. Though Wordsworth later reviewed I.iii with pleasure, remarking on the occasion of the play's publication in 1842 that the scene was "thoroughly natural and yet not commonplace nature" (*LY*, p. 1122), it appears at the time to have been the most difficult part of the work to write. Until fairly late in the early stages of composition, the scene and the deception sequence it caps were essentially unimaginable. As Robert Osborn shows in studying the two initial stages of draftwork for the play in the Rough Notebook (DC MS. 12), Wordsworth must have from the first conceived some such pretext for Mortimer's rage as Herbert's "murder of his wife," "exploitation of Matilda's filial piety," or other perversion of the family (*B*, p. 9). But the poet just could not get the pretext, or pre-plot, right.

To begin with, Wordsworth drafted what Osborn calls the *Ur-Borderers*—a disconnected series of scenes and prose synopses all centered on the results of Rivers's deception of Mortimer (*B*, pp. 48–60; see Osborn's discussion, pp. 13, 15).* Then he went back and, in a second stage of drafts, began by interpolating in the blanks between entries for the *Ur-Borderers* a number of attempts at fleshing out the exact nature of the earlier deception—portions of which still survive at the end of I.i in the Early Version (*B*, pp. 355, 359–71; see Osborn's commentary, pp. 13–14).[16] Still without the Beggar as his accomplice at this stage, however, Rivers cannot quite get the lie out. At no point in the "Drafts for the Deception," as Osborn calls them, does his tale about Herbert's illegitimate connection with Matilda become fully speakable, let alone comprehensible. Instead, what we read at crucial moments is a more than normally impenetrable texture of dashes, elisions, circumventions, and thematized "suppressions" obscuring the nature of Herbert's crime. For example (in Osborn's transcription):

RIVERS:

~~I am ashamed to see you thi~~s̶ ̶disturbed — ̶u̶[
~~How now~~   ~~thing~~
You force me to give utterance to a ~~thought~~

---

* For clarity in this chapter, I use the names Mortimer and Rivers in referring to all versions of the play even though these names appear only with the second stage of draftwork in the Rough Notebook. The *Ur-Borderers* uses Ferdinand and Danby, and the Late Version of 1842 then uses Marmaduke and Oswald. See *B*, p. 8, for a table of the name changes.

> Which now I would suppress as dangerous
> But at another time 'twould move your Laughter
>   In
> ~~For~~ truth there's not a shadow to support it
> But at the time it crost meᴧand those
>   kisses
> I did not like them —
>   that this girl
> We know not whence she comes her history
> Is what he makes it — and in truth those
>   kisses
>
> MORTIMER:
>
>   ~~kisses~~ — sayst thou — ha
> ⎧T
> ⎨   (a pause
> ⎩tis even so — plain as the day ——— the thought
> — It is not to be born — things terrible
> Do hang upon it — if this same suspicion
> Be slightly taken up — better thou wert
>   ~~idly [?bred]~~
>   the
>
>   (B, p. 363)

This is a closed hermeneutic circuit. We witness not Sherlock forced by the slower Watson to divulge his reasoning but two Sherlocks communing intuitively over their detection. "Her history" is indeed "what he makes it," we may say, but "he" really implicates Rivers and Mortimer, for whom Herbert's illegitimate relationship with Matilda alters without need for either corpus delicti or explicit charge from "there's not a shadow to support it" to "plain as the day." Only later in the second stage of draftwork did Wordsworth then begin drafting what is now I.iii with its addition of the Beggar and her slightly clearer lie (B, pp. 325–33).[17]

To recover more fully the pretext or "history" of illegitimacy Wordsworth conceives in I.iii and its predecessor drafts, we need at this point to walk offstage to probe context. The context is not the feudalism of Rivers but the thoroughly contemporary middle-class mores of Mortimer. Why does the Beggar's lie act so powerfully on Mortimer? The answer cannot be discovered until we proceed to a related question about the honor and pride of the middle class: the nuclear family.

The Context of Legitimacy

We will soon need to think more carefully in this chapter about the relation between social context and the text it engenders. But for now it will serve to divide offstage from onstage entirely—to define our context, that is, as if it were independent of any textual complications more involved than the availability and representativeness of historical records.

The context consists of the "middle class" in the latter half of the eighteenth century. Configured as a mix of rural and urban occupations not yet mediated by "suburbia," this class may be taken to range from the average farmer and artisan, on the one hand, to the upper-yeoman farmer, entrepreneur, professional, and lower gentry, on the other. Altogether, it accounted for a thick plane in the English population pyramid (roughly half of a total 17 million circa 1800) distinguished in practical terms from both higher and lower planes by what might be called its proprietorial acuity: an intensive, rather than broad-based or flexible, attachment to the small landholding or clearly defined occupation. (For a convenient visualization and breakdown of the population pyramid of England as a whole around 1800, see Cook and Stevenson, p. 145.)

Within this context, our area of inquiry is the nuclear family during the period of its consolidation—a crucially rifted organization distributed between two levels of existence: actual family experience and an ethos of legitimacy that historians of the family have come to call family "idea," "ideology," or "state of mind" (Ariès, *Centuries*, p. 9; Laslett, *Household*, pp. 63–67; Shorter, p. 205). Of course, our context is still overbroad. But it is possible to make useful generalizations if we open our aperture in a series of calibrated stops—the early ones specific in focus but uncertain as to the wider picture, and the later ones, by way of compensation, low on detail but more indicative of the whole. I start with Wordsworth's own family portrait and work outwards.

If Wordsworth were to imitate the gentry of the time and sit for a "conversation piece," a group portrait showing family members, house, and possessions, who would be included? Clearly, the poet at no time lived in what we now think of as the nuclear family: (1) father, mother, and unmarried children sharing the same household and (2) linked more closely to each other than to other kin or occupational associates by strong emotional bonds (the kind of family Lawrence Stone has called the "closed domesticated" family of "affective individualism"; *Family*, pp. 221–480). Leaving the secondary definition aside for the moment, we need only gauge the primary definition of family constituency against the available evidence to remark the magnitude of the misfit. If Wordsworth's conversation piece were to be true to life, it would have to be capacious indeed. As a matter of course, the poet grew up in, and then habitually duplicated, varieties of the extended family.*

* For reasons that will be apparent, I use "family" in this chapter somewhat elastically to mean primarily, but not exclusively, kin living in the same household. It will sometimes make sense to apply the term to the household generally (including

To start with, Wordsworth's childhood home at Cockermouth was other than strictly nuclear because of the long absences of his father on business and the attendance of live-in servants—a female staff and liveried manservant (MM, 1:9). More importantly, his true early "home" extended beyond Cockermouth. Along with his siblings, he probably spent almost half his time at Penrith in the household of his maternal grandparents, the Cooksons, and maternal uncle, Christopher Crackanthorpe Cookson, called "Uncle Kit" (MM, 1: 11; CEY, pp. 41–45 and notes). In addition, he and his brothers and sister often visited the large Whitehaven household of their paternal uncle, Richard Wordsworth (MM, 1:13–14). In later childhood, the scope of the poet's effective family then broadened further. After their mother's death in 1778, Wordsworth and his siblings were essentially "fostered out" to widening circles of kin and strangers. Dorothy went to live with maternal kin in Halifax (their mother's cousin, Elizabeth Threlkeld), and the older boys boarded in Hawkshead with Ann Tyson while splitting their vacations between their father at Cockermouth and the Cooksons at Penrith (CEY, pp. 46–58).[18] When Wordsworth's father then died in 1783, the family at last came to exist entirely in its extensions. While Dorothy remained at Halifax, the poet and his brothers lived a life fractured between the Tysons, the Cooksons, and the Wordsworths of Whitehaven (CEY, p. 61n).

In his manhood, the poet then deliberately continued the pattern of complex family ensembles. Simplifying somewhat: after Cambridge, he established his household with Dorothy at Windy Brow, Racedown, Alfoxden, and Grasmere so that it embraced other kin and friends (in long visits from his brother John, Coleridge, and Mary Hutchinson, for example) and even, at one point, formally fostered Basil Montagu's son. Then he set up his mature household from Grasmere onwards to include not only his wife, Mary Hutchinson, and their children but also Dorothy and at times his sister-in-law, Sara Hutchinson.[19] Throughout the period of these evolutions, of course, there was also the bend sinister represented by Annette Vallon (or Veuve Williams, as she came to call herself; MM, 1: 554); her bastard daughter by Wordsworth, Caroline; and the entire troubling Vallon clan—virtually a whole phantom family.[20]

Stem, laterally branched, and finally even alternate kin relations: Wordsworth's family experience was always excessive of the nuclear form. Once the conjugal nucleus had accomplished its task of generation, it passed into other family forms with continuing responsi-

---

servants, lodgers, and live-in friends) or a cluster of geographically separate households. "Extended" is generic for a number of family forms: stem families organized along the line of descent (e.g., parents and a married son or daughter living in the same house), laterally extended families (e.g., married brother and sister), and combinations or partial versions of the two (see Shorter, p. 29).

bilities: guardianship, education, financial support, occupational and marital advice, and so on.

Expanding our frame outward, we can see that such elasticity of form must have been a general fact of middle-class life. The first step is to look more fully at the circle of families around Wordsworth.[21] There were the Crackanthorpes on his mother's side of the family, for example. Of gentry background, the Crackanthorpes could afford families approaching the upper-gentry, large-household structures Stone has studied (*Family*, pp. 24–25). At times, indeed, their arrangements were unclassifiably mixed. In her widowhood, Wordsworth's maternal great-aunt Anne Crackanthorpe thus joined in a post-nuclear or quasi-stem household with her widowed mother and unmarried sister. Meanwhile, her mother-in-law lived at Newbiggin Hall (the Crackanthorpe estate that Wordsworth's Uncle Kit would inherit in 1792) in a similarly mixed family with the aunt of Anne's late husband (Hudleston, p. 139). In a humbler, entrepreneurial background, the Hutchinsons on Wordsworth's wife's side of the family traced similar complexities. One parallel to Wordsworth's own experience is striking: after losing both parents, Mary Hutchinson and her siblings also had to be taken in by kin, in this case, their maternal aunt (MM, 1: 77).

The next step in broadening our picture is to consider Lake District society as a whole. Here it will be helpful to shift our focus from the primarily professional and town milieu of the Wordsworth circle to the region's single largest occupational group: the agricultural population. A preliminary survey of this group will be useful. Statistical information from the early nineteenth century shows that it accounted for between two-thirds and three-quarters of the rural population in the Lake District and between one-third (in Cumberland) and one-half (in Westmorland) of all families (*LCI*, pp. 326–27, 339). Altogether, the group took the form of a pyramid, as shown in Fig. 5.

The highest tier was occupied by a very small elite of large and *very* large property owners. Numbering about 30 families in late eighteenth-century Cumberland, for example (*LC1*, p. 229), these included the great landed families of the Lakes—the Lowthers, Grahams, Hothfields, Howards, Leconfields, Lords Muncaster, Tuftons, and others (*LC2*, pp. 7, 55). Together with lesser landowners, these families not only held vast acreages but in some instances aggressively built up their estates by amalgamating smaller holdings (*LC2*, p. 60; G. P. Jones, "Decline," p. 211; *LC1*, pp. 328–29, 238).

The next highest tier was occupied not by the usual squirearchy and lower gentry, who were notably few in the region (*LC2*, pp. 7, 55; see my discussion on p. 92 in Chapter 3), but by the small-farm occupiers. Including not only the yeomen (freeholders together

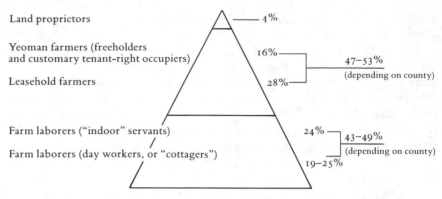

FIG. 5. Agricultural population structure: Cumberland and Westmorland, 1829–51. All figures except those distinguishing yeomen from leaseholders are based on 1851 census data for persons ten years old and over in *LC2*, p. 249. The separate figures for yeomen and leaseholders (16% and 28%) are based on 1829 census data as adjusted in *LC1*, p. 335, and are slightly incongruous relative to the total pyramid because they count families rather than individuals, assume a smaller population base, and discount the small group of landed proprietors at the top.

with the more numerous customary tenant-right occupiers) but also the leaseholders, this group constituted what G. P. Jones ("Decline," p. 198) and Millward and Robinson (pp. 180–82) have called a true "rural middle class."[22] Holding land usually under 100 acres, the class accounted for between 60 and 93 percent of the total number of farms in the Lakes—a vastly greater percentage than in other parts of England.[23] Altogether, the small-farm occupiers had much prospered by the late eighteenth century: not only had most become self-sufficient, but some were now sufficiently rich and "market-orientated," as C. E. Searle has termed it (p. 117), to accrue savings and household goods, buy extra land, lend out money, and pass for (or marry into) lower gentry.[24]

The bottom tier in Lakeland agricultural society, finally, was occupied by the immense group of agricultural workers who held no property at all: proportionally one of the largest populations of farm laborers in England (*LC2*, p. 56).

Working from documents antedating the nineteenth-century census data (anecdotes, surveys, directories, probate inventories, hearth-rate taxes, churchwarden and household accounts), historians of the Lakes have made guesses that allow us to adjust this pyramid more nearly to the later eighteenth century as follows. First, it appears that the proportion of yeomen to leaseholders in the middle class was still relatively high—with some two-thirds of land, for example, held by customary tenant-right alone between 1777 and 1805 (Searle, pp. 109–10). The famous "decline of the yeomanry" in the region, in other words, probably did not reverse the ratios until after the 1820's or 1830's (G. P. Jones, "Decline," pp. 211–13; *LC1*, pp. 237, 334–35).[25] Secondly, the farm-laborer population was not as large as in the early nineteenth century, but must already have been substantial. Because cultivation methods in the Lakes—especially in some terrains—were extremely labor-intensive (*LC2*, pp. 5–6), the average farmer usually needed more workers than resident kin could provide. One sample of eighteen farms in about 1771, for example, showed that the number of laborers ("indoor" servants and day workers) employed per farm averaged 3.4 and ranged from just one on the smallest farm to six on the largest (*LC1*, p. 240).[26] Since the average number of family members in the Lakeland rural household was probably between five and six, this indicates that the proportion of laborers to farmer-occupiers even in the days of yeoman ascendancy could approach parity.[27] (In the Solway Plain, the ostensible setting of *The Borderers*, there was an even heavier dependence on day laborers; *LC2*, p. 56.) The advent after the end of the eighteenth century of increasing numbers of leaseholders (who probably used more hired help), larger amalgamated estates, and even more labor-intensive cultivation and extraction methods (together with the stubborn retention of old ones) then simply intensified the region's traditional dependency on labor (*LC1*, pp. 239, 335; see also *LC2*, pp. 5–6).

Altogether, our adjusted picture of agricultural society in the later eighteenth-century Lakes shows that we will do best to make the yeomanry (together with the overlapping segments of the leaseholder group; see note 22 to this chapter) our norm of middle-class rural life. It also prepares us to understand why complex family forms, though somewhat different from their urban counterparts, must have been basic to this norm. The key is to grasp the special relationship between the yeomanry and the already large farm-laborer population it employed.

This relationship had two faces. One may be termed "inclusion." Among farm laborers, those known as "indoor" or live-in servants —males and females generally 5 to 34 years old (*LC2*, p. 251)—not only resided in the farmer's family but in real terms were *part* of that family. One evidence is the architectural record of their literal place in the family. We will soon need to consider the housing of the actual "cottagers," or day-workers, but for now we can use the ambiguous term "cottages" to refer only to the farmhouses of the yeomanry built during or after the onset of the vernacular housing revolution in the seventeenth century (when Lakeland small-house builders began using permanent construction materials; see *LC1*, pp. 108–9; Brunskill, *Vernacular*, pp. 16–17). These, we know, were more uniform in the Lakes than anywhere else in England (Barley, p. 234 and n.). As R. W. Brunskill shows in his survey of small houses in the Eden Valley, virtually all followed either the so-called "statesman"

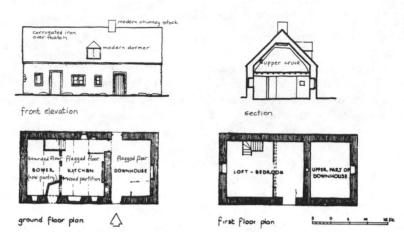

FIG. 6. Midtown Cottage, Brampton, Westmorland. From Brunskill, "Small House," facing p. 165. Reproduction courtesy of R. W. Brunskill.

plan (built from roughly 1670 to 1770) or late eighteenth-century variations.[28] The basic template may be taken from the plans for the Westmorland cottage shown in Fig. 6. From a modern perspective, the outstanding feature here is the lack of differentiation in space. Entrance to the house was by way of a cross-passage conducting on one side to the "downhouse," a service and storage area open to the second story, and on the other to the living unit proper. The ground floor of this unit consisted only of a "kitchen" or "fire-house" (a communal space equivalent to today's living room, dining room, and kitchen all in one) and "bower" (master bedroom or, in later houses, "parlour"). Even less differentiated was the cruck loft on the top floor. If we discount a partition added in modern renovation, the loft in this cottage was simply an open space extending the length of the living unit.

It was in the "kitchen" that servants, with the rest of the family, lived and ate.[29] And it was in the loft that they slept, sharing the space with all family members except the master and mistress. John Gough, a firsthand observer of Lakes social customs, describes the use of the loft in the eighteenth century clearly: "here the children and servants lodged, without the least distinction of rank or attention to decorum, except that the men occupied one end of the place and left the other to the women. A rope was stretched across this nocturnal receptacle of the family, upon which coats, gowns, and other articles of apparel, both male and female, hung promiscuously" (p. 12).[30] Writing for popular consumption early in the next century, Gough already sounds a certain Victorian uneasiness about the "promiscuity" of traditional sleeping arrangements (intimated here in worry about the intercourse of clothes at night but more directly expressed later in his work; p. 38).[31] Clearly, however, it was no more odd in the eighteenth century for servants to sleep "promiscuously" than it would have been for any family member to sleep beside another.

The other evidence helping us place Lake District servants is conclusive. Servants could mix comfortably with the families of their employers because in many cases they were themselves either children of neighboring families in the same class or, at the remove of a generation or two, descendants of such families. They were the younger sons (and presumably also daughters), in other words, of yeoman farmers themselves (*LC1*, pp. 240, 335–36). As one writer in the nineteenth century put it, "Even those who are enumerated as 'labourers' in Westmorland and the other yeomanry counties are probably not in the same social position, generally speaking, as the labourers of the south-east. They are without doubt the sons of yeomen, too numerous to find employment on their father's land, and glad, therefore, to hire themselves out for a time to the neighbouring occupiers" (quoted in *LC1*, p. 240). A more recent historian imagines the typical Northern situation as follows: "Ties of blood must often have linked the yeoman and husbandman with the labourer, and even when the latter was not in fact a younger brother or a cousin he was treated as a member of the family. If he lived in the house he was nursed as affectionately when sick; helped to find or build a cottage when he married, and reckoned as a full member of the community" (Barley, p. 124). Such intimacy in the hiring customs of the Lakes, we can speculate, descended from the older tradition of familiar service: "fosterage," the custom by which English families at every social level from the middle ages through the early seventeenth century had given or hired out their children to live in the service of other families (Fumerton, "Exchanging Gifts").[32]

The other face of the relation between the yeomen and laborers, however, was the very reverse of inclusion. The rural middle class took servants into their families only at last to "exclude" them once more. We know that though some "indoor" servants stayed regularly with a single farmer's family, the hiring customs of the Lakes also allowed many to change farms at the twice-yearly Whitsuntide and Martinmas hiring fairs (*LC2*, pp. 68–69; see also Kussmaul). It was as if, in the final analysis, it was not an individual farm servant so much as a constant "slot" or role that a middle-class farmer included in his family. Such impermanence with regard to the individual servant was preparatory for the great change in life that occurred when the servant married, usually in his or her mid-twenties through early thirties (Stone, *Family*, p. 50; *LC2*, p. 251). At this time, the servant left the employer's household and entered the other bracket of the laborer population: that of the older day-laborer or "cottager" (*LC2*, p. 251).

Communing with the employer's family only in the fields, the laborer now lived nearby in a very different style of "cottage." Though some estimates suggest that these cottages may have accounted for up to 40 percent of houses in the Lakes since the seventeenth century (Marshall, *Old Lakeland*, p. 44; see also Flandrin, p. 96), the transience of building materials, coupled with the rosy myth of the English cottage that has privileged documentation of more substantial homes, has ensured that virtually no tangible evidence survives prior to the late eighteenth through nineteenth centuries (Brunskill, *Vernacular*, p. 66).[33] Except for increasingly "upscale" cottages after the late eighteenth century, Brunskill shows, laborers' cottages permanent enough to leave evidence were primarily only two very small rooms normally one above the other (the equivalent of a "kitchen" and a parlor-bedroom; *Vernacular*, pp. 66–74). The slender evidence about earlier or less permanent cottages suggests they were probably even more cramped—possibly as small as a single-roomed ramshackle hut—and much less wholesome. A visitor to the Lakes in 1698, for example, records: "sad little hutts made up of drye walls, only stones piled together and the roof of same slatts, there seemed to be little or noe tunnels for their chimneys and have no mortar or plaister within or without" (quoted in Marshall, *Old Lakeland*, p. 32). Similarly, William Hutchinson described the typical laborer's cottage in nearby Northumberland in the 1770's as follows:

The cottages of the lower class of people are deplorable, composed of upright timbers fixed in the ground, the interstices wattled and plastered with mud; the roofs, some thatched and others covered with turf; one little piece of glass to admit the beams of day; and a hearthstone on the ground, for the peat and turf fire. Within there was exhibited a scene to touch the feelings of the heart; description sickens on the subject . . . the damp earth, the naked rafters, the breeze disturbed embers, and distracted smoke that issued from the hearth . . . the midday gloom, the wretched couch, the wooden utensils that scarce retain the name of convenience, the domestic beast that stalls with his master, the disconsolate poultry that mourns upon the rafters, form a group of objects suitable for a great man's contemplation. (quoted in Fussell, p. 62)

"Cottages" they may have been called, but clearly such huts were far from the "cottages" of the yeomen (see also Flandrin, p. 96; Burnett, p. 33; Stone, *Family*, pp. 255–56). Some might almost be spoken of in the same breath with the region's traditional shielings, or migrant shepherds' huts (on the latter and other hut-structures in the Lakes, see H. G. Ramm et al.).

Altogether, we perceive, the entire system of inclusion and exclusion was a sophisticated mechanism designed to ensure that the yeoman farmer could benefit from a large, in-"family" labor pool without thereby having to leave his property divided among that pool. What we have been witnessing, in other words, is the institutional possibility of primogeniture in the Lakes: not only a symbolic mechanism by which the discharge of farm servants—like a *memento mori* —prepared a farm family to lose its own younger sons (and daughters) but also a *real* mechanism for expelling those offspring from the class entirely. As Marshall has put it, "the eighteenth and nineteenth centuries scattered the sons and daughters of the dalespeople to the winds" (*Old Lakeland*, p. 49). Because only one son succeeded to the family holding, other siblings had to hire themselves out as farm servants and day-workers, turn ironmongers and (in the case of daughters) mantuamakers, or enter into trade and the professions (Marshall, *Old Lakeland*, pp. 48–49; *LC1*, pp. 335–36). The result was their eventual displacement into a lower agricultural class or into town and urban life.

The practice of the rural middle class in the Lakes, then, argues a variant of the family complexity we saw in Wordsworth's immediate circle. Whether urban and professional or rural and agricultural, the "family" in the poet's environs was an elastic, multilayered structure whose constituency and function extended well beyond the conjugal nucleus.[34]

Having broadened our frame thus far, I open the aperture to its widest at last to suggest that complex family forms were typical— though with uncountable local variations—of the English middle class as a whole. Here the demographic evidence needs to be handled with care. Perhaps the single most controversial discovery of historical demography in recent decades has been the announcement by the Cambridge Group for the History of Population and Social Structure, led by Peter Laslett, of a single number serving as a gravitational constant of family history: "4.75." Arrived at by computer-assisted analysis, "4.75" represents what appears to have been the constant mean household size in England (including many specified locations in the Lake District) since the late sixteenth century (Laslett, *Household*, p. 126 and *passim*). Laslett and his group have used this figure to argue that the old sociology of Frédéric Le Play (extending with variation to Ariès) is wrong: the family did not develop from extended forms to the nuclear model. Rather, it has always been nuclear (Laslett, *Household*, pp. 126, 144).

But subsequent work by historians of the family outside the demographic discipline—including Shorter, Stone, and, most incisively, Flandrin—makes it clear that if the "4.75" figure denotes the constancy of the nuclear family, then "nuclear" is an empty, tautological term.[35] So far I have used the term "elastic" to describe family form.

But such an essentially spatial stretch of the imagination conceals the influence of a different stretch—that of time, of the social basis for the "succession" we previously studied in political terms. What should now become clear is that our portrait of the middle-class family has all along really been a moving picture. Elasticity of family form is a function of the fact that there has never been such a thing as "the family"—fixed, bounded, and mounted as if in a photo album of just one page. There is only the *evolution* that is the family—of the unit that in Wordsworth's period especially, as Stone has put it, "expanded and contracted like a concertina, moving from the extended stem family to the nuclear and back again" (*Family*, p. 24; see also Mitterauer and Sieder, pp. 48–62). As Stone pictures it in composite, a family of the middle or upper class might evolve as follows:

A young couple might begin their married life for a year or two in the house of one of their parents, thus becoming part of an extended stem family. But they would very soon move out on their own and set up a nuclear family, usually first without and then with children. Eventually the children would grow up and leave home for apprenticeship, school, or service in someone else's house. Very soon after, in some cases the father of one of the couple would die and the widowed mother would move in with them, or in other cases both might move in since the old father was no longer able to work. The family thus became extended stem again. Soon afterwards the eldest son would marry, and he and his bride might also move in for a short period, so that it might become a fully extended stem family of three generations. Then the old couple or the widow would die, the married children would move away, and the family would become nuclear once again. (*Family*, p. 24)

The "4.75" figure thus has no referent in felt reality. A more meaningful measure of family form in the past is not the mean number of family members at any single point of time but what might be called the amplitude of variation—the range of possibilities through which the family form could pass without transgressing the sense of the norm. As Stone and others have documented, and as we have confirmed in our more limited area of interest, all indications are that in the later eighteenth century this amplitude was far wider than modern standards of the nuclear family would allow.

Why such amplitude? Besides such economic factors as the need to maximize labor, of course, there was the influence of what Stone has argued was perhaps the single greatest fact of life at the time: death. As Stone's stress on the typical death of a parent suggests, every family was its own mutability canto. Generally speaking, life expectancy in England rose slowly after the 1750's to reverse the disastrous dip of the late seventeenth and early eighteenth centuries (Stone, *Family*, pp. 66–73; Wrigley and Schofield, p. 178). Nevertheless, mortality rates in this period were still remarkably high by modern standards. The effect on the middle-class family can be gauged in two complementary ways. (With the provision that some correction must follow, I approximate the middle-class condition here by drawing primarily on available figures for the English population at large.) One side of the coin was adult mortality as it affected marriages. Even as late as the early nineteenth century, Stone points out, adults 25 to 40 years of age still stood a 1 percent chance of dying each year, meaning that 2 percent of all marriages ended annually in the death of one of the spouses. As a result, roughly 30 percent of all marriages ended within fifteen years; the median duration of first marriages was only 17 to 22 years (except among the upper class, where it was longer in the late eighteenth century); and remarriages were so common as to account for roughly a fourth of all spousals (Stone, *Family*, pp. 54–60).

The other side of this coin of Charon was the high incidence of orphanage. Infant and child mortality rates, of course, were themselves high. Between one-fourth and one-third of all English children still died before age fifteen despite a decline in child death rates after 1750 (Stone, *Family*, pp. 68–69; Wrigley and Schofield, p. 178 and table 13 on p. 177). Nevertheless, children could barely die fast enough to keep up with their elders. Because up to 30 percent of marriages ended with the death of a spouse in the first fifteen years, the proportion of children orphaned was of the same fearsome magnitude. From 1600 on, orphans who had lost at least one parent thus accounted for approximately 21 percent of all English children (defined in the data as unmarried dependants living in their family of origin), with the proportion only falling to between 13 and 17 percent in the 1790's (Laslett, "Parental Deprivation," pp. 13–14). If we include servants and other children not residing with their family of origin, however, these figures would have to be raised (Laslett, "Parental Deprivation," p. 15). Indeed, selective evidence from the late seventeenth century indicates that about half of all brides and bridegrooms at their first marriage had lost their fathers (Laslett, "Parental Deprivation," p. 15; Stone, *Family*, p. 58).

The conclusion to emerge from these figures is that the family form in the later eighteenth century was *compelled* to layer the conjugal nucleus—perennially "truncated" or "fragmented," as some historians of the family have called it (Wheaton, p. 7)—into longer-lived, flexible forms. The conjugal nucleus, of course, was often restored in some manner either through the remarriage of the widowed parent or the transfer of orphans to a different intact family (as when an uncle or aunt took in orphaned nephews and nieces). Up to a fourth of all families, Stone thus points out, were "hybrid" in such ways (*Family*, p. 58).[36] The larger truth, however, is that whether or not the conjugal nucleus was restored, the surviving members of a family had to be fitted into a broad mosaic of kin, village, parish, occupational, and other affiliational networks able collectively to disperse the responsibilities of "family."

The full range of contemporary family experience thus appears only when we add to our picture of elastic family forms such institutional extensions of the family as apprenticeship and schooling. Apprenticeship was a traditional way to take care of orphans and other children (Stone, *Family*, p. 58); but it was the educational system—as Ariès has studied extensively in his *Centuries of Childhood*—that for the middle class increasingly became the predominant surrogate for family life. Whereas apprenticeship supplanted the family (because the child was in essence sent away to a different family), live-away schools and colleges created a suddenly lengthened period of dependency complementing the original family's custodianship. The child was thus never fully out of the home even when boarding away: parents took care to visit, send money, and show other signs of intimate, if distanced, involvement (Ariès, *Centuries*, pp. 137–336, and esp. pp. 369–71). When Wordsworth went away to school at Hawkshead and Cambridge, in other words, he enrolled in an evolving modern institution eminently suited to taking in orphans along with those from intact homes because it was already on the way to subsuming—and redefining—the experience of familiarity.[37]

We might look back at this point, indeed, to the Wordsworth family portrait upon which we began. The status of the poet (and of the Hutchinsons) as an orphan with *both* parents dead in childhood was relatively rare (Laslett, "Parental Deprivation," p. 18). But we now see that his experience of orphanage itself and of the family diaspora it initiated—the exodus of survivors into the kin network together with its institutional complements—surely was not. Though readers of Wordsworth have often premised his uniqueness on his absence of parents, nothing could be further from the truth. It is more accurate to stress the relative normalcy of parental absence —of absence, in fact, that was really social presence. To lose a parent was to enter normatively into the storehouse of complex family forms making up the reality of contemporary family experience.

Such, then, is a picture of middle-class family life in the later eighteenth century centered on the poet and his native region. Yet, of course, such a picture sensitive primarily to matters of family constituency is still deeply untrue in a manner that has nothing to do with possible errors of fact. To be sufficient, a historical picture of the family would need to record not just constituency but also that distinctively fading, tattered, musty patina of ideation and valuation —of wish, pride, and regret—that has always been part of the reason actual family pictures are taken. To be sufficient, that is, our historical picture of the family must also look to the ethos or *mentalité* that is family "legitimacy."

Here I bring into play our secondary definition of the nuclear family as an affective construct. On the basis of massive documentary evidence gathered by family historians (Ariès, Stone, Shorter, and others), we can make the following deduction: the middle-class nuclear family consolidated itself in the eighteenth century through the regulation of actual family form by a much more narrowly defined form resident in the concept of "love."[38] The family created its ethical form by rethinking the conjugal nucleus. Specifically, it intensified the affective tone of three crucial axes of relation—what might be called "affective radicals"—so that they suddenly far exceeded their original function. Affected were the bonds between husband and wife (in the "companionate marriage"), parent and child, and, as a special beatification of the latter, mother and child (as indexed most tellingly in the diminishing use of wetnurses; see esp. Shorter, pp. 120–254; Stone, *Family*, pp. 221–480). Then the family closed the ranks of these radicals to create a novelty in its history: a wholly self-reflexive or inward-looking idea of "normalcy" restricted to love at the conjugal core. The result for the family was an idea of itself that diverged radically from the original idea. Where once the nucleus was subordinate to kin, settlement, and occupational groups that distributed the tasks of support, education, guidance, and so forth, now it imagined it could accumulate within itself all functions.[39] In the middle-class family, that is, love between husband and wife, parent and child, and mother and child colluded to eject from the perceived identity of the family a whole host of competing relationships that were at the time just as necessary and emotionally fraught: most notably, relations between child and stepmother, father and apprentice (or servant), brother and sister, and (of special importance to Wordsworth in his rebellious years at Penrith) child and grandparents or uncle.[40]

We might think here by way of illustration. Just as pictures of the Holy Family from the seventeenth century on reinterpreted tradition by giving Joseph a central place in the composition and a strong family resemblance to the Son (Ariès, *Centuries*, pp. 362–64),[41] so the new ethical form of the family may be said to have revised its self-image. In the light of emotion (the latest anagogy to descend from Orthodox *apatheia*), only one family form could now be seen as *the* family. All other configurations, however "familiar," were reseen as figurations. At best, they became "like"-families. At worst, they became "illegitimate."

The evidence for such revisionism is especially clear in our specific context. Just as it is certain that family form in Wordsworth's experience was actually varied and far-flung, so it is documentable —at least from the days of Windy Brow, Racedown, and *The Borderers*—that the poet worshiped exclusively the ethos of the nuclear family. A few cursory looks ahead will be sufficient to make our case. To start with, there is the evidence of the poetry. Soon after the period of *The Borderers*, such works as "The Brothers" (1799–1800) and "Michael" (1800) demonstrate that while Wordsworth's poetry acknowledges the realities of parental deprivation, orphanage, and the hiring out of children, it preempts them by making its norm a nuclear ideal beatified above mortality. Put simply, it will not be "normal" in Wordsworth's poetry to survive family death—to be deprived of parents, fostered out, or otherwise inserted into the network of complex family forms. Better, as in the Lucy poems, that the child outstrip its parents in the race of mortality and die first. Or, where the child survives the conjugal core, it will be legitimate for him or her only to live a myth: a life devoted entirely to the remembrance of the nuclear crèche.

In "The Brothers," for example, the nuclear ethos is so prescriptive that the death of Leonard's parents leads at first only to the reconstitution of the nuclear family in a "like"-family: the grandfather Walter Ewbank, the Priest remembers, became both "a father to the boys, / Two fathers in one father" and "half a mother to them" (*PW*, 2: 7). The deaths of old Walter and Leonard's brother then lead to a further symbolic reconstitution of the nuclear family—this time revealed in its true otherworldly rapture. On one panel of the poem's diptych, as it were, we see Leonard communing with his family gathered in their graves, while on the other we see the worldly manifestation of such a tableau, the Priest surrounded by his wife and children (*PW*, 2: 1, 3). In "Michael," the same mythic ethos of the nuclear family holds. "Michael" commemorates a nuclear norm so immaculate in conception that not only mortality but the economic realities sending Luke away from home appear abnormal. The family imagined in the poem consists of husband, wife, and a single son. Rendered invisible, therefore, is the fact that nuclear form in the Lakes had always been compromised by the need to hire out or otherwise expel supernumerary sons or to take in servants.

Finally, there is the evidence of the poet's life as discovered in letters and other higher-order documents. Just a few instances will close our family album. Witness, for example, the recent find of letters between the poet and his wife (*Love Letters*). Reading this volume, we realize that however austere our older poet could be, the slightest disruption of his family life—here his journeying from home—could elicit an outrush of sentiment symptomatic of the new-style "companionate" bond between husband and wife. So, too, the poet's later thoughts on his children, as collected by Moorman ("Wordsworth and His Children"), show how far he could bend from the traditional, deferential tone of parent-child relations set in his grandfather's and uncle's household at Penrith. Only with severest "agony of my spirit" (*Letters*, 3: 51) could he acknowledge the death of a child and accept what would have gone without saying just two generations or so earlier in English history: that such death was part of normal life. "I seem to possess all my children in trembling," he said in 1814 (*Letters*, 3: 183). We need then only add the fond attachment of the poet to his mother—at least as evidenced in memory (for example, *Prel.* 5.256–90)—to conclude with a complete portfolio of his participation in the ethos of the nuclear family, in the revisionary ideal of a family founded upon love between husband and wife, parent and child, mother and infant.

I thus arrive upon my essential question of context. Given a strongly divergent reality, how was it possible for the contemporary middle-class family to imagine with any conviction its revisionary form? By what means did it imagine the nuclear ethos to be not only an ideal but an attainable norm?

This, after all, seems to me the deepest truth I know about the nuclear family (whether in the eighteenth century, in what Stephen Kern has called its Victorian era of "Explosive Intimacy," or in our own times): it is not just joyful presence but also the slow ache of absence, not just simple legitimacy but also a complex haunting of broken wishes, promises, and wills reflecting in their collective trespass reality's rupture within the ideal. Our family: it is strong in the bonds of intimacy linking husband to wife, parents to child. But in every moment of intimacy, of affection so strong as to seem to shut out contrary bonds pulling toward the outside world, there is also acknowledgment of the demand of those contrary bonds, of a "trans-parent" reality whose every message is that bonds to others are important because parents and children at last absent themselves.

If the nuclear family arose as an ethical revision of the mortality, economics, and overall social complexity that permeated the conjugal crèche, how did it screen the transparency of that revision?

The Crime of the Family

The Bad Poor

With my two key questions in hand, one textual and the other contextual, I now invert the order of inquiry in order to explain *The Borderers* in its milieu. A solution to the contextual issue will make possible an answer to our earlier textual question: why does the Beggar's lie act so powerfully on Mortimer?

Hypothesis: The middle-class family screened the rift between reality and its nuclear form by throwing up the representation of a virtually tribal rift between itself and a specially designated class of "illegitimates," the poor. Nuclear form could thus stand for Us because non-nuclear illegitimacy stood for the impoverished Other.

Here I leave behind the style of explanation favored by the historians. The shortcoming of a work such as Stone's, despite its avowed intention to address *mentalité* (*Family*, p. 18), is its massive dependence on causal explanation.[42] Characteristically, Stone explains attitudes, beliefs, or customs on the basis of plural "causes" unrelated except by the very primitive heuristic of "convergence." Thus "semi-independent developments" in economic, social, ideological, and political contexts add up to "convergent forces" causing the growth of "affective individualism" (pp. 258–68). The dispersed quality of such explanation is then exaggerated by a consistent strategy of following causes horizontally through a single class or organization at a time. The overall result of such study as an explanation, however invaluable Stone's overall blend of "explanation" and "anecdote" (as he describes it; p. 17), is that the history of cultural consciousness reduces to traditional history of ideas—a positivism that in Lovejoy's application, for instance, managed unit-ideas very much as if they were particles obeying physical forces or ebbs and flows of convergence, divergence, and so forth (see Mink, pp. 9–16). Or rather, the outcome is a very restrained history of ideas. Crucial punches are pulled in an explanation that proposes plural explanations with no attempt at overall coherence or consistency.

What is pulled is what I propose to press here: the explanation by structured representation that in any study of cultural consciousness must complement explanation by cause. Rooted in epistemological rather than physical paradigm, the category of representation refers positivistic explanation to the only universe in which laws of cultural cause have consistent meaning: that of conventional perception and expression. After all, rarely does causality communicate itself in the social cosmos by means as direct as one billiard ball hitting another. Rather, events cause other events through intermediary "arbitrations" (as I called them in Chapter 2) of economic, social, legislative, religious, moral, educational, rhetorical, and other suasive representations of reality whose interconnected and transformable structures are better understood on the basis of the *langue* model than by analogy with Newtonian physical space.

How is it possible for social contexts to engender texts? The answer, as I earlier argued, is that contexts are themselves from the first differential representations structured less by causal than by perceptual, interpretive, and expressive act—that is, by all the words, pictures, gestures, frowns, sleights, beatings, killings, and so forth along the whole scale of social discriminations that create a consensual notion of culture out of the agons and dissensions that are the elemental basis of that culture. With as little as a single gestural or verbal slur, that is, "we" tell bad stories about others that can be given constative as well as optative value—that may be verified by natural truth (as I termed it in Chapter 3) and then ideologized as just. Higher-order "texts" are a representation-with-a-difference of such cultural representation. To descend for a moment to the gut-level crudity of social life from which all strong literary texts may be said to take their start: if culture is that which gives the finger to particular elements of itself, then literary culture is that which reverses, problematizes, covers up, and otherwise changes the direction of the finger so that—like the middle fingers pointing up on some eighteenth-century tombstones (signifying the place of the dead in heaven)—we are pointed out of the original context of agonic difference to a revalued representation of difference. The world becomes another world.

To apply to family history this understanding of social context and the texts that defamiliarize it, we need to consider one further facet of Stone's work. *The Family, Sex and Marriage*, we notice, builds itself around certain structural interstices—fault lines or border zones of salient silence. One such border zone is Stone's silence about any communication, causal or otherwise, *between* social levels—a habit of explanatory segregation whose extreme result is that the poor appear throughout as virtually an untouchable caste.[43] I wish to posit a seminal act of social representation or discrimination situated precisely in the perceived border zone between social groups—most tellingly for our purposes, between the middle class and the poor. The poor were "akin" to the middle class because their families were compelled by the same basic facts of life: death and economic necessity. But the poor were also untouchables because the severity of mortality and necessity in their case led to a critically different style of family management. Thus arose the difference-in-sameness, the agon of contestatory identification, that founded the dominant cultural representation of the family as well as the marginal or Border-zone *literary* representation of the family—a defamiliarization and "defamilying" —that is my final concern.

First, the poor died more quickly and in greater numbers. I now review my earlier general picture of mortality in an attempt to factor out the mortality of the less well documented lower classes. Paradoxically, one of the strongest clues is that the poor respected the numerical ideal of the nuclear family more strictly than their betters. We now know that the lower the class in English history, the smaller the household (despite popular belief to the contrary) and the more likely it was to be restricted to the conjugal unit (Laslett, *Household*, p. 153 and table 4.15 on p. 154; Wall, p. 172; Stone, *Family*, pp. 64–66; see also Shorter, pp. 26–27, 329–31). But the inadequacy of the "4.75" criterion is especially striking here. All that low numbers meant for the poor, it appears, was attrition compounded by poverty (Stone, *Family*, p. 25; Burch, pp. 91–92). Not only were poor adults subject to higher mortality rates, but, as we will soon need to detail more carefully, so were their children (Stone, *Family*, pp. 55, 72, 421–22). Burnett's study of life in the average laborer's cottage is informative:

The whole nature of the labourer's environment—his home, his habits, his diet, and his work—had debilitating effects on his health and physique. Contrary to the romantic belief that rude health engendered by an open-air life would bring him to a ripe old age, the labourer's chances of survival were notably less than those of other classes in the countryside. As Chadwick's Report [*Report . . . on . . . the Sanitary Condition of the Labouring Population*, 1842] showed, the average expectation of life in the rural districts of Wiltshire in 1840 was:

> Gentlemen and persons engaged in professions, and
>   their families   50 years
> Farmers and their families   48 years
> Agricultural labourers and their families   33 years

Much of this mortality was due to the early deaths of children in overcrowded and insanitary cottages where . . . epidemic diseases like typhus and cholera could spread unchecked, but even in adult life confined and unventilated rooms made the labourer a prey to tuberculosis and respiratory complaints which often proved fatal.

  Such facts were known empirically, if unproved statistically, long before the 1840's. (p. 47)

Few parents of laborers thus survived to move in with their married children, despite the fact that sheltering widows and widowers was the norm set by the yeomanry and upper classes (indeed, few old parents of any class survived; Stone, *Family*, pp. 25, 58–60). Lack of adequate room and board, moreover, ensured that few elders *could* have moved in (Stone, *Family*, p. 25). The same applied even to the younger generation: the poor consistently put out their surviving children to service at an early age (Wall, p. 172; Stone, *Family*, p. 393). Low numbers, in sum, were not so much an index of stable family form as of the enormous flux in family life all around—the same flux engendered by fatality and exacerbated by poverty that in a family of more expansive means could have been accommodated in larger complex households (with room for widows, sisters, and others) but that for the poor made the small conjugal unit the only option. The poor nuclear family, we may say, was the exhausted family: it was the family left behind after the evacuation of its old and young.

  But, secondly, the poor were not simply passive victims of circumstance: they also actively *managed* their families to maintain the optimum size. In a style of "birth control" whose apparent profligacy coupled with cruel parsimony had only suppressed parallels in the middle class, the poor—if we may be pardoned the vulgarity—sowed their oats and mowed them too. I refer to what may be the single most striking period-specific fact about the poor in the later eighteenth century: their fantastic rise in bastardy rates coupled with continued insistence upon infanticide. Generally, as we have already noted, the English poor (like the peasantry of northwest Europe generally) delayed marriage until relatively late—the mid-twenties through early thirties in the Lakes, for example (*LC2*, p. 251). Indeed, age at marriage—and so the number of years between puberty and legitimate sexuality—was high in England overall (Stone, *Family*, pp. 46–54). Other classes invested their bottled-up energies differently.[44] But let us think ourselves poor, in service, and young. We have worked since childhood. Our reward—a home and spouse of our own—is far in the future. How to seize the day?

One part of the answer in the later eighteenth century was to enjoy illegitimate sexuality and so, in due course, to generate infants outside the family form. Various explanations have been offered for the urgent rise in extramarital sex among the lower classes at the time.[45] What is clear is only that customary sexual activity among youth—for example, at the semiannual hiring fairs and during "night courting" or "bundling" (the widespread practice of sleeping together semi-chastely with family approval)—indeed burgeoned beyond the power of old controls.[46] Bastardy, especially among the poor and landless, rose at an astonishing rate in the late eighteenth century to reach a first peak in the period between about 1790 and 1810 (Laslett and Oosterveen, pp. 260, 268; Stone, *Family*, p. 614).[47] In the rural Lakes in particular, the rate of illegitimate births was so high that by the middle of the next century Cumberland and Westmorland earned the scandalous reputation of bastardy capital of England, with rates running 80 percent above the national norm (*LC2*, pp. x, 81–82; Laslett and Oosterveen, pp. 276, 282, and statistics on pp. 274, 280).

The other part of the answer, of course, was necessitated by the fact that the excess infants had to be supported in some manner. But mothers had less than adequate help from kin or community. Among the poor, as we have seen, there were few households able to afford taking in the infant of an unwed daughter, as well as few grandparents surviving to help with care or housing. Other routine outlets for excess children—fostering or hiring out offspring aged five and above (Stone, *Family*, p. 393) or letting the parish place illegitimate children in apprenticeship (*LC1*, pp. 296–98)—were often simply not timely enough. Nor could fathers of bastards be depended upon for partial support even when paternity could be proved. As shown in records of legal action against such men in the eighteenth- and nineteenth-century Lakes, fathers often either could not or would not pay (*LC1*, pp. 295–96). And the final safety net—poor relief—

was already overstrained. Parishes in the Lakes, for example, were at times so unwilling to care for additional pauper bastards (who took settlement in the parish of birth) that they moved expectant mothers to other parishes—a problem aggravated in the Border region by the frequency with which unwed women were said to have been carted with an attending surgeon from Scotland into England at the point of delivery (*LC1*, p. 296).

Thus we arrive upon the only method of relief—short of active begging—over which poor mothers exercised some element of control (and through which, of course, they sought relief as well from the strong social stigma attached to illegitimacy in village communities; Stone, *Family*, p. 474). This was their customary insistence upon killing some of their bastards and other excess children through infanticide, exposure, and—what often amounted to the same—abandonment.[48]

The key word here is "customary." Over the course of its long history, we know, English infanticide increasingly became a target for official condemnation. In medieval times, the killing of infants was not consistently illegal (Hanawalt, pp. 9–10). But once a statute defining the crime was passed in 1624,[49] infanticide was charged frequently enough to figure, for example, in some 14 percent of the parishes in Essex from 1601 to 1665 (Wrightson, pp. 11–12). In eighteenth-century Surrey, to take a later example, the number of infanticide prosecutions then rose virtually to equal all other homicide cases brought against women (J. M. Beattie, p. 85). And in the nineteenth century, the numbers throughout England swelled to account for one-fifth of all homicides in the population at large (almost one-half if we include children as well as infants; Hair, p. 18).

Unofficially, however, a habit of popular tolerance—or at least willingness to look aside—continued. To begin with, we need only anatomize contemporary infanticide cases to realize that they in fact comprehended a wide variety of practices some of which were either borderline legitimate or undetectable. In tabulating the causes of death in infanticides, for example, Wrightson lists strangulation and exposure as most frequent, followed by blows, suffocation, drowning, and burning (p. 15). The last three causes here, and to some extent exposure, overlap with the category of neglect, for when a child was suffocated (often when a parent turned over in bed), drowned, or burned, there was room for reasonable doubt. Moreover, official counts against infanticide did not even include some of the most popular strategies of neglect. As DeMause and Stone suggest, a full measurement of infanticide would also have to count instances of premature weaning, deliberate use of wet nurses or certain infanticidal "killing nurses" for the purpose of decreasing a baby's chances of survival, dosing with opiates or alcohol, swaddling to the point of gangrene, bathing in ice water, and abandonment in foundling hospitals and workhouses (DeMause, pp. 29–39; Stone, *Family*, pp. 68–70, 471–78; see also Wrightson, pp. 16–17). The last practice made for some spectacularly visible eruptions of child death in the eighteenth century. Among other cases, Stone recounts that of the London Foundling Hospital, which Thomas Coram established "to prevent the frequent murders of poor miserable children at their birth, and to suppress the inhuman custom of exposing new-born infants to perils in the streets" (quoted in Stone, *Family*, p. 476). As soon as Parliament in 1756 did away with limits on the number of children accepted, the gates opened to an astonishing three or four thousand infants each year from all over England. Many were sent to the Hospital as if they were so much produce to be remaindered. As Wrightson shows, fathers of bastards had in the past often paid vagrant or beggar nurses to take their illegitimate infants (pp. 16–17). Upon the change in the Hospital's acceptance policy, a similar practice reached enormous proportions: itinerant baby transporters earned a guinea or so a head to carry baskets of children—"dead, dying or half alive," as Stone puts it—to the Hospital and there to dump the human surplus at the doors. As a result, of fifteen thousand children sent to the Foundling Hospital during the first four years of its general acceptance policy, some ten thousand died (Stone, *Family*, pp. 475–76; also DeMause, p. 29).[50]

Infanticide cases thus often opened with uncertainty about the degree of culpability. And they then closed—even if the facts were known—with surprising leniency. As in the case of the popular food riot (which I study in Chapter 7), infanticide was often "acceptable" after the fact: it was a practice to be excused on the grounds of hardship or, occasionally, insanity. In medieval England, infanticide was dealt with by Church, as opposed to secular, courts, and merited at most public whipping (Stone, *Family*, p. 474). The legacy of such a court of shame continued in our period. As J. M. Beattie finds in his study of female criminality in eighteenth-century England, "judges and juries went out of their way . . . to find evidence that would justify acquittal" rather than punishment (p. 84).

What we discover among the poor, in short, is an overall system of child procreation/decimation classifiable (in Wrightson's words about infanticide) as partly criminal but also in part "a socially sanctioned form of population control analogous to that found in certain ancient or 'primitive' societies" (p. 10). Procreation at the opening of the system may have been motivated by spontaneous desire and frustration, and infanticide or abandonment at the close by individual emotion and shame: infanticide, that is, was the desperate serving girl hiding her dead baby in a chest.[51] But in its broader extensions, the system was also deliberate and collective: it was the hiring of third-party "killer nurses" with what Wrightson calls the "calculated intention of removing a source of expense, shame or inconvenience" (p. 16). Or again, it was the possibility that whole groups of kin and accomplices would conspire to murder a child. In a case Hanawalt reports: "Alice Grut and Alice Grym were indicted for drowning a three-day-old baby in a river at the request of Isabell of Bradenham, her son, and her daughter" (p. 9).[52] The essential point, in short, is that child procreation/decimation among the poor was not just an effect of the facts of life—of sexuality and mortality—but also a determined effort to take those facts in hand. To have a baby or to kill a baby was more than simply "natural" or "unnatural": it was also a cultural act, a way of *containing* biological imperatives within social structure and purpose. The lone mother, mother with father, family and clan, and, in the end, sympathetic judge and jury took life in their hands. They shaped mortality into a fully social action, a sort of reverse passover, able to make the procreative urge—with all the freedom and hope such urge once stood for as itself a social action— come to terms with economic reality within the fragile equilibrium of the family form.

Now let us think ourselves middle-class once more. How pitiable the poor with their thoroughly "illegitimate" families: illegitimate because pierced through by a whole scale of domestic evil braced on one extreme by bastard births and on the other by infanticide deaths. But also how *instructive* the illegitimacy of the poor. No wonder the poor families we know, even if they have no actual skeletons in the closet, are rife with child-, wife-, and sometimes husband-abuse, bitter jealousy and sullen anger, general callousness and all the unruliness of an uncaring life so different from our own.[53] No wonder the poor families in our village—see, look at them with their dirty feet and pinched faces, so different from the poor that must inhabit other parts of England, the kind that live in the engraving we own of rosy-faced cottagers by Francis Wheatley—no wonder they are their own worst punishment!*

I have slipped into ventriloquism here, of course. But I hasten to add that my tone, while meant to highlight prejudice, is not mocking. To mock the prejudices of the middle class would be to discount the prejudices of other social levels, the contemporary poor not excluded. The point of the ventriloquism, rather, is precisely the necessary fact of Burkean prejudice. Consider the practical problem of

---

*For the purpose of addressing *The Borderers*, I leave aside here the flip side of such prejudice: the poor could also be valorized as the reservoir of all genuine legitimacy. In this case, the social field is reversed. The poor become the true gentry and the gentry—as in Goldsmith's "The Deserted Village"—the source of all corrupt illegitimacy. The necessary constant is that the illegitimacy of *some* other social group demonstrate "our" legitimacy.

teaching "our" children why "we" are a good, a normal, middle-class family. The norm is very hard to point to in a vacuum. In practice, therefore, it is instructive to point instead—in so many implicit, everyday, often unconscious ways—to telling abnormalities teaching that "we" are normal because we are not like "them." As homily, I recite here a poem from Isaac Watts's *Divine Songs* (first published 1715), the most influential of the "good godly" books for children in the eighteenth century.[54] The poem is titled, "Praise for Mercies Spiritual and Temporal":

> Whene'er I take my Walks abroad,
>   How many Poor I see?
> What shall I render to my God
>   For all his Gifts to me?
>
> Not more than others I deserve,
>   Yet God hath giv'n me more;
> For I have Food while others starve,
>   Or beg from Door to Door.
>
> How many Children in the Street
>   Half naked I behold?
> While I am cloth'd from Head to Feet,
>   And cover'd from the Cold.
>
> While some poor Wretches scarce can tell
>   Where they may lay their Head;
> I have a Home wherein to dwell,
>   And rest upon my Bed.
>
> While others learn to Swear,
>   And Curse, and Lye, and Steal:
> Lord, I am taught thy Name to fear,
>   And do thy holy Will.
>
> Are these thy Favours Day by Day
>   To me above the Rest?
> Then let me love Thee more than they
>   And try to serve Thee best.

Such is the core of the representation I hypothesize. The poor, as Watts says, "learn to Swear, / And Curse, and Lye, and Steal." They are the glass of illegitimacy in which the middle class sees reflected its own legitimacy.

What we are dealing with, in sum, is representation indeed premised upon what I termed difference-in-sameness or contestatory identification. It is at this point that the suppressed parallels between the poor and the middle class should be brought to the fore. The middle class, of course, also suffered from mortality. The middle class was itself not innocent of bastardy, though the lapse was perhaps less visible because bastards were not as much a problem above the poverty line (on Lakeland yeomen and bastardy, see *LC2*, p. 82). And the middle class was itself constrained by economics to rid itself of younger children according to a primogenitural hiring-out process that, if not infanticidal, was nevertheless still appreciable by Wordsworth as cruel. Infanticide among the poor, after all, was in actuality continuous with a whole scale of severe treatment of children extending—in the Lakes, for example—right up through the middle class. We might remember here the episode of brutal child abuse in *Adventures on Salisbury Plain*, where a father batters his five-year-old son about the head until he lies outstretched on the ground (*SP*, pp. 148–49). The episode mimes what we saw previously was a leading cause of infant death among the poor: "blows." But the evidence of local dialect suggests that blows were also one of the most common communications between yeomen parents and children in the Lakes. As an example of the vim of "hill-farmer" dialect (descended from that of the yeoman) in his native Lakes, Melvyn Bragg (pp. 64–73) has recently collected a list of traditional verbs meaning "to beat." What is most striking about this glossary of violence is not simply its size (110 entries plus variants) but the fact that so many of the verbs refer specifically to beating children. Besides verbs applying to adults as well as children, the glossary includes:

bensal To thrash severely and repeatedly, say a sturdy lad or truant.

bray To pound; chastise and bruise, mostly in reference to children.

break To beat with a stick (used chiefly as a threat), generally applied to boys.

hidin' A thrashing administered to a boy or girl by the parent.

leas To chastise a boy with a switch.

ledder To thrash a boy severely, similar to "bray."

nointin', ointin' The punishment which the schoolmaster gives to the scholars, evidently with "strap oil."

paik A very severe beating given by the schoolmaster. "Paiks" is also said of a continuance of blows whereby a person becomes exhausted.

pay Any form of punishment administered for the correction of a fault committed by a child. To settle a grievance by beating.

peg A beating less severe than a "paikin," generally with the fist.

skelp A smart blow applied by the mother's open hand on the child's bare buttocks.

smack Same as "skelp" but on any part of the body.

spank Same as "skelp" but on any part of the body, and less severely than "noint."

stirrup oil, strap oil Chastisement given to a child with a leather strap similar to that one used by a shoemaker to hold his work firmly on his knee.

trim To whip a child.

troonce To thrash deliberately as a punishment.

twank To beat with a stick, similar to "welt."

warm To beat, but especially said of children; these last four are very akin to one another in meaning.

Primogeniture, we may say with an American intonation, was simply the ultimate such "what for" used to administer children in the Lakes. Or at least such was the view of Wordsworth, who denounced primogeniture so strongly as to make it sound not only abusive but virtually infanticidal. We might witness once more his protest against Swiss primogeniture in *Descriptive Sketches*:

> The father, forc'd by Powers that only deign
> That solitary Man disturb their reign,
> From his bare nest amid the storms of heaven
> Drives, eagle-like, his sons as he was driven,
> His last dread pleasure! watches to the plain—
> And never, eagle-like, beholds again!
> (ll. 616–21)

The poem then follows by recounting the legendary ability of the sons—now become Swiss mercenaries—to die of literal homesickness (ll. 622–31 and Wordsworth's note). In effect, primogeniture becomes an act of exposure.

In every instance, in short, the relationship between the middle class and the poor was what I earlier called inclusive before it was exclusive. We remember that there was actual blood relation, after all, between middle and lower classes in the Lakes (though not necessarily between any one farmer and the laborers he excluded as "poor"). Or again, we might take as our crowning example of the family resemblance between classes the case of Wordsworth himself, who personally contributed to the bastard boom and—at least symbolically—infanticide. The birth of the poet's natural child in France coincided within a few years with the first great peak of English illegitimacy. How to take care of this child? In imagination at least, the answer was the poor man's: kill it. As Jacobus has asked incisively about the fate of the baby in the Vaudracour and Julia episode in Book 9 of *The Prelude*, "is this a displaced suicide, a mercy-killing, or an infanticide?" ("Law Of/And Gender," p. 55).

If the middle class itself housed the facts of life so disruptive of poor families, then, how was it possible to view the nuclear ethos as normative without seeing through its transparency? Let me ventriloquize once more a voice not mine: Children, death has come to our family. Your brother has died. Three years ago—John, you are old enough to remember—your grandfather and grandmother died. Last year, your little sister died. But be good. Remember we are still a family. We shall go to the churchyard tomorrow dressed in our best. We shall cry quietly because others would stare. You know those poor children from down the road who sometimes come to beg at our door. Their father died many years ago. Some say he was murdered. Their mother drinks, and worse. Every year one more of their number is buried. Sometimes they run away, and the villagers find them crying and cold at their door. Be glad you are not like them. We are still a family.

I write this short fiction to gather together as many of the relevant strands of contemporary middle-class family ideology as possible—strands, for example, that may be located in closely analogous form (with the exception, perhaps, of the more objectionable or "adult" aspects of the poor) in late eighteenth-century children's literature. Ideological by design and addressed even more clearly than Watts's work to the middle class, such literature provides particularly fertile documentation of the family ethos. We could look at Mrs. Barbauld's *Hymns in Prose for Children* (1781), for example.[55] But it will be most instructive to read the children's literature translated or written by Mary Wollstonecraft at the end of the century. In both Christian G. Salzmann's *Elements of Morality*, which she essentially rewrote to Anglicize its setting and characters for her translation of 1790, and her own *Original Stories from Real Life* of 1788, Wollstonecraft trains children not only in middle-class mores but in the "affectionate" sensibility she believes must underlie spontaneous adherence to mores (see, for example, the Introductory Address to Parents in *Elements*). Most compellingly, she does so by exposing the middle-class children who are her protagonists to wrenching scenes of family death. Death breaks up the bourgeois nuclear family, which then recreates itself as pure ethos by viewing the even deadlier circumstances of the poor and their families.[56]

Elements of Morality, for example, arrives upon its great object lesson when it thrusts its definitively bourgeois family (a rich Bristol merchant named Jones, his wife, and their two children) out of their round of civility into apocalypse. In a symbolic reenactment of Genesis at the work's conclusion, a flood suddenly devastates the much-loved garden of the Joneses as well as the surrounding landscape. Afterwards, the father must rewrite the covenant in a modern idiom by justifying God's destruction as benevolence. "But, dear father," Mary complains, "I am not a wicked child; why has the good God destroyed my auriculas?" "My dear children," Mr. Jones insists, "the God who can do all these things is your father and friend" (3: 182). In essence, the destruction of the world is made safe by assimilating it to the ideal of the nuclear family. Jones's argument is that God "does many things which you do not like" just as he himself, as a loving father, has sometimes "taken from you playthings, which gave you pleasure" (3: 182–83).

But the deluge is not over. In the succeeding final chapter of the work, it is internalized in the flood of tears attending the abrupt sickness and death of the children's mother. It is now that the modern covenant—God as he signs himself in the nuclear ethos—must be finally confirmed. In a sudden gestalt change, all the elements of morality that the work has taught—good behavior founded upon sympathetic affections—at last cohere to form the mature personality of the children. Crucially, however, such maturation can occur only after the poor display themselves so as to allow the children to reflect upon the essential goodness of their own family and so to devote themselves from this point on to maintaining the *ideal* of the family. After Mrs. Jones dies, the poor "collected themselves from every corner" to see the body and lament the "best of women!" (3: 197–98). One poor woman in particular rushes from the crowd and exclaims: "God bless you! dear woman. . . . You brought me up, a poor orphan" (3: 198). Only after thus chorusing all that Mrs. Jones had done to redeem the poor can the narrative then deliver a version of my ventriloquized speech above. In a highly affecting, and also subtly coercive, disquisition, Mr. Jones tells his children:

Your dear mother [God] has called to Himself, to reward her for all the love she has shewn us, and such a number of poor people. Now, there is nothing so dear in the world to me as you. If you should become wicked, I shall not long remain in this world—grief would soon bring me also to the grave. But if you continue to be good, obedient, industrious children, and attend to truth, I shall still find some comfort even after the loss of your mother. (3: 199)

If the children wish to keep their father alive, Mr. Jones says, they must never sink into the wickedness, disobedience, lack of industry, and dishonesty from which their mother had tried to save them—just as she had ever tried to rescue the poor. Poverty and such sins as lack of industry come to occupy the same symbolic position in the father's discourse (even though the *Elements* as a whole has served up examples of virtuous as well as intemperate, envious, gluttonous, ungrateful, dishonest, or otherwise sinful poor folk). Indeed, there is an insidious way in which poverty then becomes even more strongly identified with lack of industry and its attendant sins. In the final two paragraphs of the work, we watch the children grow up into a virtue synonymous in their father's eyes with being not-poor, or prosperous. In its very phrasing, goodness becomes all that the poor cannot *afford*: "For a long time Mr. Jones saw in the conduct of his children the fruits of the good lessons which he and his wife had given them: and though in the following years he considerably increased his fortune, yet he was still more and more convinced, that among all his treasures, he found nothing that afforded him so much pleasure as the gratitude of his children. *And their good behaviour in his old age rewarded*

him for the pains which their education had cost him" (3: 200). Only by becoming "worthy" enough financially to continue the family tradition
of relieving the poor (3: 200) can the children keep the spirit of their
mother alive and so the integrity of their family intact (so much so,
indeed, that the daughter is soon praised as "another Mrs. Jones";
3: 200).

Similarly, Wollstonecraft's own *Original Stories* teach goodness by
exploiting family death together with the exemplum of the poor. The
premise of this work is that the middle-class nuclear family is already
broken: Mary and Caroline's mother had "died suddenly," leaving
them "shamefully ignorant" and susceptible to "every prejudice that
the vulgar casually instil" (p. xx). It is the task of Mrs. Mason, the
children's governess, to drive out the vulgar habits "of servants, or
people equally ignorant" (p. xx) by repeatedly subjecting Mary and
Caroline to object lessons about poverty and about death—lessons
that, to cite the work's subtitle, will teach them to "Regulate the
Affections" and so "Form the Mind to Truth and Goodness." These
lessons include such spectacular episodes as that of Crazy Robin, a
"poor man" who had been driven to madness by poverty, debtor's
prison, and what seems almost a census of contemporary mortality:
the cruel deaths of his wife and many children one after the other (pp.
10–13). What this episode argues, in essence, is that the distress of
Mary and Caroline's own family and the danger posed by their vulgar prejudices are as nothing compared with the suffering of Crazy
Robin's brood and the ultimate prejudice or bad habit: madness. The
children of the well-to-do may be purged by spectating, and relieving, the poor.

The most poignant of such lessons then comes in the idiom of Mrs.
Mason's own experience. In what amounts to a lyric autobiography
of sentiment, Mrs. Mason tells the children about death in her own
family: "I lost a darling child . . . in the depth of winter—death had
before deprived me of her father, and when I lost my child—he died
again. . . . I was unhappy, and the sight of dead nature accorded with
my feelings—for all was dead to me" (p. 72). Here Wollstonecraft
touches upon not just actual death but the fatal antithesis of her entire
system of morality: the extinction of family *feeling* and so of general
sympathy. Recovery, however, is possible. Family feeling and sympathy at last revived, Mrs. Mason recalls, after a series of encounters
with poor persons whose own families had been broken apart by
death and were in even greater need of redemption (pp. 72–74). Only
in offering poor relief could she resurrect her sensibility and thus the
foundation of good conduct: "I cheered the widow's heart, and my
own was not quite solitary" (p. 74). The family ethos thus survives
by spectating the death of the family across a social remove; once
more able to care for others—for the orphaned Mary and Caroline in
particular—Mrs. Mason is still essentially a mother.

In these and other children's books, in short, the presence of the poor—with all their heightened vulnerability to mortality, to family fragmentation, and to degraded ethics and sensibility—was crucial to the process of contestatory identification by which the middle class sustained the nuclear ethos in the face of contradictory reality. In this regard, children's literature was merely one index of a general need for social differentiation communicated at every level of contemporary family discourse from the table talk of parents through higher-order moral disquisition. To guard against the transparency of the middle-class nuclear ethos, it was necessary to increase social distance as prejudicially as possible in order to demonstrate that whatever the complications in the class's own normalcy, the poor were *surely* abnormal and, in the end, illegitimate (somehow at once innately piteous *and* incorrigibly wicked, disobedient, indolent, dishonest, and so forth). Social separation, in sum, had to be exaggerated to such an extent that it could become the medium for distinguishing— within what was really the same family of man—the outcast others, the exempla of all that in reality crossed the dignity and stability of the nuclear form and so had to be crossed out of the symbolic identity of that form.

Indeed, it is instructive to note that the effort to represent the poor as abnormal and illegitimate could be so extreme that the poor were often in popular lore akin to "gypsies." Their families and ethics were not just shiftless but existentially "criminal." As in medieval England, when one-third of all recorded group crimes were committed by family units (Stone, *Family*, p. 95), crime in eighteenth-century England was a labor of the family—and particularly of poor families. I do not mean to suggest that the English poor all inclined toward gangsterism, of course, but a few spectacular instances from Lakes criminal history will serve to show how powerfully the correlation between poverty and criminality could influence representation. There were the infamous Castlehows of Hawkshead, for example: wallers, husbandmen, entrants in the Poor Accounts, and petty *thieves* precisely in the period of Wordsworth's school years at Hawkshead. T. W. Thompson in *Wordsworth's Hawkshead* recounts the colorful activities of this small-time gang, the raid on one of their houses in 1784, the daring escape that followed, and the subsequent exaggeration of the Castlehows' exploits in local lore (pp. 223–33).[57] And there was also Thomas Lancaster, an earlier Hawkshead native infamous for a different kind of family crime. Lancaster, who ended in 1672 on the Hawkshead gibbet that accompanies the Penrith gibbet into *The Prelude*, used poison to kill his wife and several members of her family (*Prose*, 2: 445–46).

Thus was the revisionary ethos of the middle-class nuclear family normalized on the basis of a representation, and misrepresentation, of the tribe of social others. Or, in any case, such is the hypothesis I offer, which I now punctuate by acknowledging that a full proof must remain largely absent. What opens to view here is a research field not as fully investigated as others and too vast to fit within my present project: the tone of past family life as revealed in documents witnessing how families viewed *other* families. What needs to be written, in other words, is the history of prejudice. Possible materials to be consolidated in such a history would include not only children's and instructional literature but letters, journals, memoirs, novels, genre paintings (what do we make of Gainsborough's moving, crowning passion for his *The Woodman*, for example?),[58] the literature and legislation of poor relief, and court proceedings and reporting.

Perhaps there is no better way to instance the abundance of such material—and its importance in Wordsworth's milieu—than to quote a passage from Dorothy Wordsworth's Grasmere journals. Preoccupied on December 22, 1801, with what I have elsewhere called "purity" ("Autobiographical Present," pp. 130–31) but will here name "legitimacy," Dorothy speculates about the past of a vagrant beggar and then closes her entry with gossip about yet another of the local poor, the impure "Queen of Patterdale":

—When we were at Thomas Ashburner's on Sunday Peggy talked about the Queen of Patterdale. She had been brought to drinking by her husband's unkindness and avarice. She was formerly a very nice tidy woman. She had taken to drinking but that was better than if she had taken to something worse (by this I suppose she meant killing herself). She said that her husband used to be out all night with other women and she used to *hear* him come in in the morning for they never slept together—"Many a poor Body a wife like me, has had a working heart for her, as much stuff as she had." (*DWJ*, pp. 72–73)

Such, I have said, is the portrait of Dorothy's uncanny opposite ("She was formerly a very nice tidy woman"). For Dorothy, the legitimacy of home life depends on representation not only of pure "nature"— the ultimate verification of legitimacy in the journals—but also of an antonymic *impure* nature whose social avatars must be watched askance with mixed pity and terror. These avatars are the "naturals," in another sense, of the illegitimate poor.

Toward the Unhomely

Now we can return to our initial, textual question. Why does the Beggar's lie act so powerfully upon Mortimer?

Thesis: Mortimer feels such a strong anxiety about "exchange" because this is the one illegitimacy that unravels the essential prejudice of the middle-class family and makes the very concept of such family suspect. Exchange has all the force of incest: it is an illegitimacy whose transgression of the family concept is structural.

We need at this point to begin grasping the overall shape of *The Borderers* as it develops from the Beggar's lie. To do so, I suggest an analytical restaging of the play whose full rationale will come clear later. Imagine on the basis of the play's preoccupation with justice that its phenomenal space is the same as that of *Caleb Williams*: a grand courtroom. The court on our stage is dedicated specifically to the examination of families and is predisposed to judge defendants innocent until proven guilty. But what "innocent" or "legitimate" has meant until now is simply "middle class."

Enter as defendant for the first time, the Middle-Class Family itself.

Identification of such a family in the line-up of the play requires two stages of inspection. First, we need to penetrate the disguise of Wordsworth's costume drama to discern that it is indeed the middle class that is the culprit even though, with the exception of the Host at the inn in I.ii, no such literal class appears. To start with, there is the curious pattern of class designation in the play. We notice that both Mortimer and Herbert are essentially classless—but only because they are double in class. Baron Herbert is both a noble and one of the landless poor. Mortimer is supplied with no social or familial background whatsoever. Yet this remarkable omission—an immense blind spot in the text—does not mitigate our certain impression that he is also one of the play's ignoble nobles. (He is leader of a band devoted to "noblest ends," Rivers lauds; I.i.33. He is a "base freebooter," Herbert charges; I.i.175.) Conflating high and low in a manner reminiscent of Robin Hood (Sharrock, p. 172), such class redundancy is an unstable fiction. Given a backdrop to any degree "realistic," I suggest, what each of these class chimeras would reveal within himself is the rural middle class. As Marijane Osborn's mapping of *The Borderers* over the Penrith landscape helps us further deduce, the relevant middle class is that specifically of the Lakes.

The "white metaphor," or self-masking viewpoint, of *The Borderers*, then, is the yeomanry. The hard evidence for this assertion is architectural. Early in the play, Herbert recounts to Matilda that, "as thou knowest," the abbot of Saint Cuthbert gave him a "little cottage" (I.i.167–70). But scattered clues in the play suggest that the "cottage" is almost certainly larger and more comfortable than any laborer's cottage either of feudal times or of the eighteenth century. Earlier, we notice, Matilda had stumbled upon a small hut without recognizing anything more than a quaint miniature of some larger, actual habitat:

> midway on the heath, ere the night fell,
> I spied a little hut built with green sods—
> A miniature it was: and, as it seemed,
> Some shepherd's boy had raised it, half in sport

> To cheat the lazy time and half to screen him
> From rain and the bleak wind.   (I.i.88–93)

The implication is that Herbert must live in the larger version of such miniatures in the Lakes: a yeoman's "cottage" or small house. As the play proceeds, indeed, it becomes clear that the yeoman's standard of space and comfort sets the norm, no matter the ostensible social level of the occupants. When Matilda later visits the "poor cottage" of Robert and Margaret, for example (the former identified as a "Cottager" in the Dramatis Personae), she has occasion to retreat "into *an* inner room of the cottage" (IV.iii.22; italics mine). Though it was not impossible for the best late-eighteenth-century laborers' cottages to have two rooms on the same floor, the normal pattern was two rooms "one up and one down" (with the bedroom above the living space and reached by a ladder-like staircase; Brunskill, *Vernacular*, pp. 71–72).[59] In any case, only a yeoman's small house with additional "outshut" (as we will see in more detail later) or perhaps a larger laborer's cottage with a fairly capacious scullery off the living space could be both roomy and comfortable enough to offer a guest the choice of more than a single interior retreat. What Wordsworth calls Robert's "poor cottage," in short, is imaginatively larger than realism permits. Robert is as much a "cottager," perhaps, as Wordsworth would become at Dove Cottage (whose rooms numbered more even than the normal yeoman's house): he lives in the fiction of a cottage.[60]

Identification of our culprit is then complete when we recognize that the key imagination of the rural middle class in the play is precisely the nuclear family—and one family in particular serving as the "primal scene" or originating matrix of the narrative. To discover this Family, we need only view synoptically the play's elementary catalog of relations. As in the case of Ike McCaslin reading the family ledger in *Go Down, Moses*, narrative in *The Borderers* is an agony chronicled at heart merely as genealogy. What we discover is that Wordsworth has at base only four true characters, a tetragonal crystal of humanity into whose mold—akin to Blake's Four Zoas—all successive generations of characters must wedge. Indeed, comparison to Blake is helpful. Wordworth's foursome is inscribed on what might be called his mythopoeic plane: the tablet of half-truth/half-lie formed by conjoining the Beggar's Vala-like deception (which Mortimer thinks true) and Herbert's autobiography (which Mortimer thinks false). On this tablet finally appear four names: first "Herbert and Matilda" as half of something like a broken recognition-coin, and then "Beggar and Son" as the missing half Blake would call an "emanation." Together, "Herbert and Matilda" and "Beggar and Son" are the play's primal-scene family. But here lies the charge before the court: the play's Family is also, like a primal word, the Not-Family.[61]

Consider first Herbert's "legitimate" view of things (as shown in

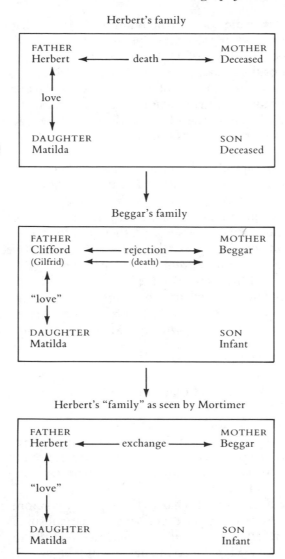

Herbert's family

FIG. 7. The "family" in *The Borderers*.

Fig. 7, top).[62] From his autobiography early in act I, we learn that his family once consisted of himself and his wife, daughter, and son (I.i.144–55). But during the razing of Antioch, Herbert could rescue only Matilda before the flames blinded him. Even as he lost his sight, he remembers, mother and son perished: a single "death-shriek" told the tale. The final result is a fragmented nuclear family in which mortality on one axis is compensated for by increased love on another. Herbert ends blindly loving Matilda.

Now add the Vala story (shown in Fig. 7, middle). Suppose that

Matilda's mother did *not* die (the blind evidence of that single death-shriek, after all, is very slender). Or suppose that she dies but lingers in spirit, like the shade of Dido, with augmented presence. In the underworld of the manuscripts, we know, Matilda's mother literally reappears: the prose synopsis of act III in the *Ur-Borderers* begins with Matilda meeting "a pilgrim whom she discovers to be her mother" (*B*, p. 48). In the Early Version itself, the mother reappears in another kind of underworld—that of the poor. "The girl / Is mine," the Beggar lies, opening Mortimer's eyes to the revived spectres of mother and son. To recapitulate her story: early in her career she was the mistress of Clifford and mother of Matilda (possibly by Clifford himself). Later, after becoming wife to Gilfrid and probably shortly following his death, she bore her present infant son. Her total family form may thus also be parsed as father (Clifford/Gilfrid), mother, daughter, and son.[63] Thus is a homology created between Herbert's and the Beggar's families premised in part on convergence: Gilfrid is a residual type of the legitimate Herbert, and the death that separates him from the Beggar reenacts in reverse the mortality intervening between Herbert and his wife. But convergence serves only to make divergence more uncanny. On one axis of relationship in the Beggar's composite family, death becomes destabilized: it overlaps symbolically with Clifford's rejection of the Beggar. And on the other axis, parental love comes into question: Gilfrid is probably only the stepfather of Matilda, and Clifford would "love" her in unthinkable ways.

What makes the homology between Herbert's and the Beggar's families most uncanny is the allegation substituting Herbert for Clifford/Gilfrid such that he combines in one person both the aristocratic and landless, the natural and adoptive fathers (as shown in Fig. 7, bottom). This allegation, of course, is what I have called exchange. Indexed by child selling, exchange is the purely economic transaction —an alienation of labor, in every sense—that subsumes all the relations between father and mother we have seen in the top and middle of Fig. 7. Exchange is a depersonalization of love that absorbs not just Clifford's exploitative rejection of the Beggar but the most absolute of divorces: death. Whatever our modern view on the matter, that is, in *this* universe a surrogate mother is as good as dead; she is dispensable. On the other axis of the family, the relation between father and daughter similarly embraces the destabilized possibilities we have witnessed: Herbert's love for Matilda seems to grow so unfixed that it can strike Mortimer at one moment as genuine (as in III.iii.62–68) and at the next as rankest obscenity. Even the relation between mother and son (which I have for clarity elided from Fig. 7) grows insecure: as we earlier noticed, the Beggar's love fills with infanticidal dreams.[64]

Now we can understand why the Beggar's lie acts so powerfully on Mortimer. What the play as a whole demonstrates is that social illegitimacy in the way of illicit sexuality, bastardy, prostitution, and so forth are bad things, but not so terribly bad so long as they can be seen from Mortimer's habitual holier-than-thou perspective (inverted at play's end in his more-cursed-than-thou demeanor). Cognate with Mortimer's manner of governing the Border, such a differential perspective quarantines illegitimacy in the province of a reprobate Them across the moral border from an elect Us. "They" are such poor folk as the Beggar, to whom Mortimer condescends, or Robert, whom he treats virtually as a vassal to be manhandled (see, for example, V.ii.51–60). (Less importantly in the play, "They" are also such off-stage aristocrats as Clifford, for whom Mortimer has only contempt.) Mortimer, in short, normally rules the Border with an armory of condescension, ruthlessness, and contempt able to erect within no-man's-land an essential moral and social border. His universe is stable because bad things happen to other people.

But at a single stroke, the border of mores collapses. This stroke is exchange, which horrifies Mortimer more than even such outrages as Herbert's alleged prostitution of Matilda because it is the one illegitimacy that is *structural*. Exchange may not seem especially heinous when considered independently (as the reactions of the gang show), but when placed in context it is the flaw that determines how the whole crystal fractures. Exchange undermines all the normative representations of difference allowing Mortimer to distance, contain, and regulate his universe of pervasive illegitimacy; and it does so by contravening not just a vulnerable section of his moral border but the very premise of such a border. This premise is class difference as defined by economic and social standing. Exchange, we recognize, participates in the system of accumulation, commodification, and transaction by which the middle class (even the rural yeomanry of the Lakes, as we will see in the next chapter) became not-poor in the first place. But it also subsumes within its depersonalized vision of personal relations all the essential illegitimacy and mortality of the poor. The transaction by which a parent buys a child, after all, is symbolically equivalent to the reputedly lower-class practice of infanticide: commodification turns an infant into an object; infanticide leaves it for dead.[65]

Or put another way, exchange breaches an unspoken code integral to the nuclear ethos: the rule that the family deals with others through economic transactions characterized by competitive and exploitative values, but with itself through transactions of love, kindness, fostership, and custodianship. Exchange confounds these two modes of transaction; and once business values thus infiltrate the home ideal (at least in an early industrial milieu before the rise of banking, insurance, and corporate structures created a mediating *mentalité* of "trust" and "security"), insiders must be treated indiscriminately as if they were themselves outsiders. As the case of Herbert seems to show, "love" for one's daughter thus becomes interchangeable with acquisition and profit, custodianship with attention to the bottom line. Love, in short, is cupidity. Perhaps this is why the greed causing Herbert allegedly to pander Matilda takes on the unmistakable taint of incest—of sexual-cum-economic disregard for the distinction between the family member and non–family member. Whether or not we conceive Clifford to be Matilda's actual father, the imputed wish of Herbert (as her stepfather) to sell her services to the voluptuary comes near to being sexual abuse in its own right. In the end, therefore, I suggest that exchange fascinates Mortimer so horribly because it is the economic imagination of a perversion equivalent in structural significance to incest (as Lévi-Strauss conceives it): exchange makes the middle-class nuclear family, in a sinister inversion of *caritas*, love its brothers, sisters, sons, or daughters as it loves others.

Nor does such illegitimacy in *The Borderers*, we can add, trouble only the home. The dirty business of child-selling is merely the leading indicator of Wordsworth's growing preoccupation in this period with generalized economic exchange and capitalization. Reserving detailed study of this preoccupation for the next chapter, we can itemize a single telling motif in *The Borderers*: "coins" as they intersect with the notion of the "coiner" or counterfeiter. Literary works, we know, often represent the onset of modern economy by focusing on such figures bordering between legitimacy and illegitimacy as the Usurer or Shylock. *The Borderers* shifts this entire border zone further into the demimonde by posing as its primitive capitalist the Coiner—an ultimate moneychanger in the temple. Here we come to the basic economic significance of Wordsworth's setting, the ostensible feudalism of which harbors an early modern industrial milieu. Defined with special relevance to the long contest in the Lakes between manorial system and yeoman enfranchisement, feudalism was a system of coercing surplus from the peasantry authorized not by the invisible hand or impersonal handling of capital but by a highly personalized regime of landed property.[66] As its mythic role in such works as *Richard II* or Burke's *Reflections* shows, property was bound up with the notion of "impress" or the sign of landed family identity. Or rather, it was bound up with a regulated system of propagating identity both lineally within the family and laterally to customary and other tenants owing duty to the landed aristocracy.[67] Property, in short, was the marker of genealogy and allegiance.

Money, by contrast, was the token of anonymous, exchangeable, and transportable goods as well as factors of production; and the counterfeit money of the "coiner," a representation of the modern extreme of such anonymity: paper scrip secured initially upon the outright *dispossession* of identifiable property with its lineal and liege affiliations. What Wordsworth imagines in the money created by a coiner, in other words, is something like the *assignat* as Burke assessed it: a medium of exchange grounded on the unrightful seizure of land in the French Revolution. Or phrased to address Lakeland economics, which I will later study, "coinage" in *The Borderers* conceives a system of transportable capital and exchangeable commodities in which credit and debt were finally more important than tangible possession. Such credit was by definition "counterfeit" because it was property disenfranchised of proper name and made "improper." A family may own money, after all, but money owns no family. Modern money as imagined in *The Borderers*, in sum, is in itself already the principle—and principal—of the black marketeering we will examine in Chapter 7: a coercion of surplus value authorized by anonymous, propertyless, and thoroughly illegitimate middlemen in the background.

This is the systemic illegitimacy nested within "coins" that *The Borderers* exploits to make even blacker its black market of child selling. Preparing for the Beggar's lie, we thus notice, the play lays down a trail of dirty money. The economic axiom of the play is that Herbert is an aristocratic property owner without property—a fact that Rivers immediately seizes upon to begin divesting him of his proper identity: "The tale of this his quondam Barony / Is cunningly devised," he says (I.i.52–53). Indeed, Herbert seems to Rivers to have the character not of the propertied at all, but of the entirely venal. As Rivers puts it, Herbert hoards his daughter as he would treasure: he thinks Mortimer a "rapacious" bandit out to steal Matilda's affections "as if 'twere robbery" (I.i.28–39). Answering to such venality, Mortimer himself begins to count small change. If Herbert thinks him a robber, then he will square the account by figuring Herbert as the very antithesis of the true property owner: a coiner. Rivers prompts: "I suspect unworthy tales / Have reached [Herbert's] ears— you have had enemies" (I.i.227–28). Mortimer rises to the occasion: "Away! I tell thee they are his own coinage" (I.i.229). A few lines on, Rivers then underwrites Mortimer's figure: "he coins himself the slander / With which he taints her ear," he says (I.i.236–37).

Thus is the backdrop prepared. When the deception scene then arrives, the play is ready to cue the climactic recognition of exchange in its form of child selling by using the prop of a literal coin. First, as we have seen, the Beggar's lie is greased by coins in the hand—the charity money Mortimer gives the Beggar as unwitting commission for the bad-penny tale to follow. Then the Beggar poses Mortimer a puzzle:

                                    —but oh! Sir!
         How would you like to travel on whole hours
         As I have done, my eyes upon the ground,
         Expecting still, I knew not how, to find
         A piece of money glittering through the dust.
                                        (I.iii. 56–60)

This is the Sphinx's riddle of the play. It is immediately after misin-
terpreting the omen of the glittering money ("Pray, good Lady, / Do
you tell fortunes?") that Mortimer first hears the kind of illegitimacy
he has to deal with. "Oh! Sir! you are like the rest," the Beggar says,
and introduces the slander of "mothers who can see the babe / Here
at my breast and ask me where I bought it." It is not accidental, perhaps, that *A Somersetshire Tragedy* was shortly afterward inspired by a
family crime also turning upon a coin (a shilling found in the murderer's clothes and used to convict him).[68] In both of Wordsworth's
family tragedies, the coin's the thing wherein to catch the conscience
of the king. Exchange buys out the feudal milieu and establishes an
incipient entrepreneurship of very insecure—or as yet only credited
—legitimacy.

   To sum up our total argument: Mortimer is told a lie about the
family that is potent because it draws upon and turns to opposite purpose the innate lie or, more fairly, the representational *mentalité*, not
just of the nuclear ethos, but of its complicit economic and social institutions. Just as monetary exchange in the increasingly transactional
world of the Lakeland yeoman (as we will see in Chapter 7) occupied an uncanny interface between traditional and modern senses of
worth, so child selling in the play occupies a transgressive border.
Child selling is a mean-spirited transaction that brings the uncaring
world of the market so uncannily near to the conjugal and filial relations valued by the legitimate family that it implicates those values.
Legitimacy becomes illegitimacy; the middle-class family becomes
the crime of the family. It becomes not-family. We might think here
of Freud's study of the uncanny, or *unheimlich*. That which is most
uncanny in *The Borderers* is precisely the homely become "unhomely."
Or again we might think back to romance, in which haunt arises
when a changeling is "fairied" out of native lands. The same family
romance haunts Wordsworth's play. What legitimacy of family identity can there be if—as the case of Matilda seems to prove—any
middle-class family member can be shown at any time to have been
changed (like one coin for another) with the uncanny other: the illegitimate poor?

   One more effect of the Beggar's lie may be tallied: the disturbance
it creates in the "family" considered as a purely discursive system. Indicted for exchange, the nuclear ethos becomes for Mortimer only a
transparent figure of speech or way of talking about—and around—

a devastating social reality. As a way of apprehending reality, that is, the whole family discourse of affiliation becomes for him a language void of referential content. We will soon need to probe in more detail the rhetoric of tropes that hollows out the truth of family and interpersonal relationship; but for now it will serve to notice that "family" for Mortimer becomes, broadly speaking, an obviously catachrestic trope for social experience: a fictive *abusio* that refers to harsh experience by abusively misnaming it "the poor." The alternative, however, is not yet the silence that claims him at play's end ("No human ear shall ever hear my voice"; V.iii.267). Rather, Mortimer still requires *some* idiom of abuse by which to castigate illegitimacy. Thus it is that family discourse, in a shift paralleling what we will see to be the play's fundamental descent into irony, becomes itself his language of abuse. "Love," "father," "brother," and so forth turn in his mouth into cynical figures of speech for all that is unspeakable: premarital intercourse, bastardy, infanticide, prostitution, child selling, and callousness in personal relationships generally. All of the social illegitimacies we have seen in the later eighteenth century, indeed, are thus figured in a play that can never refer to them directly. Killer nurses and baby-transporters, for example, are cast in exact inversion as a child-selling Beggar (who gives up, rather than takes, a baby); and the latter in turn as a thoroughly ironized "mother." As we earlier heard Mortimer exclaim in what is virtually a pique of philology:

> Father! To God himself we cannot give
> An holier name, and under such a mask
> To lead a spirit spotless as the blessed
> To that abhorred den of brutal vice!
> The firm foundation of my life appears
> To sink from under me. This business, Rivers,
> Will be my ruin.—   (I.iii.177–83)

The one word that undermines the foundation of "father" and all family discourse, we may say, is "business."

Toward a Discourse of Self

From Irony to Justice

All that happens in *The Borderers* after the Beggar's lie is the emplotment of the configuration of issues established by the pre-plot as an "action": Mortimer's self-revelatory attempt to restore the border of mores once structuring and containing illegitimacy. Conceived generically, such emplotment requires fitting—and, in this play, slightly misfitting—the pre-plotted family history to the contours of tragic development. Specifically, it requires a generic elaboration of the most primitive of all dramatic gambits expressed in the pre-plot's imputation of child selling or exchange: the device of mistaken or substituted identity (which survives nakedly in the recognition of Matilda's mother in the *Ur-Borderers*). Considered purely as a literary convention, that is, the pre-plot performs no more than an exchange in identities (between Herbert's family and the Beggar's and, more generally, between legitimacy and illegitimacy) whose plot outcome must at last be some variation upon the plot of recognition. With all the necessity of entelechy, Mortimer—in failing to restore the moral border—must recognize Herbert to be truly what he claims, and himself to be the genuine illegitimate.[69]

But what is the best plot, or Aristotelian "mythos," by which to articulate the transformation from a family history of exchange to a tragedy of recognition? Here, Frye's *Anatomy* is helpful. We could imagine plotting the transformation of exchange into recognition in several manners each adding to the "high mimesis" of classical tragedy a slightly different modern nuance. For example, a literal family romance might plot the play as something like a *Winter's Tale*, in which the lost wife is recognized in her statuesque substitute, or, with a gothic twist, a *Wuthering Heights*, in which Heathcliff, that changeling and complete bastard, at last lies by the window to grasp the only ghost of a chance he ever had to be recognized for himself. In this case, the movement from exchange to recognition would be spoken within the work itself not as tragic Fate but as its romance equivalent: magic or, in the psychologistic idiom of some Romantic romances, inspired madness. Again, a low mimetic, comic, or "realistic" modality might plot the play as something like *Tom Jones*, in which the bastard is at last recognized as All-worthy. Here, the movement from exchange to recognition would be signed within the work as an everyday form of Fate or magic: good luck or coincidence.[70]

Wordsworth plots his play by degrading high-mimetic tragedy with a conflation of the possibilities above: the vector from romance to realism that Frye has defined as the ironic mythos (*Anatomy*, p. 223).[71] Of course, romance in *The Borderers* is merely vestigial. Magic lurks just outside direct vision in the play's insistence upon subliminal hauntings: its daemonized dreams, fears of a dead dog, visions of dust eddying windlessly or of a phantom staff blocking a path (I.iii.23–42; II.iii.34–40; V.i.14–15; V.iii.197–200). What produces the ironic mythos, therefore (and, as we will see, a complementary rhetoric of irony), is actually a further extension of the vector from romance to realism: an even more cynical descent from realism to a baser realism. Deploying the implications of exchange in the pre-plot, the play's plot degrades the ethos of classical tragedy from the level of the aristocratic "house" not just to that of the middle-class family but ultimately to that of the lower-class household.

This, after all, is the entire purpose of the cottagers Robert and Margaret in acts IV and V, whose otherwise unnecessary subplot ensures that the recognition of Herbert as innocent—revealed to Mortimer in Rivers's autobiographical confession in IV.ii—is *not* finally as tragically grand and romantically mad as Rivers would have it. Flanked in IV.i and IV.iii, respectively, by the first entrances of Robert and Margaret, Rivers's autobiography of heroic illegiti-macy is in essence outflanked by a lower-class milieu in which ille-gitimacy is *not* the heroic embrace of criminality but the fearful, ner-vous, and perpetually harassed effort of the laboring poor to avoid the prejudice of criminality (specifically, the crimes with which Robert was once falsely charged). Indeed, there is a sense in which it is Rivers who is the minor character and the anti-heroic Robert the major one. It is Robert who actually reveals the fate of Herbert to Matilda as well as to Mortimer (IV.iii.93–95; V.ii.69–79). It is Robert, in other words, who is the efficient agent of recognition. *His* actions alone reveal what Rivers's autobiography with its Faustian idealiza-tions of guilt would transcendentalize: the dead body. In V.ii.77–79, Robert indicates Herbert's corpse and so literalizes the fact that at the end of any severe illegitimacy there is always a dead body. It is ex-traordinary, indeed, how long the corpse hovers on the threshold of vision from this point on, refusing either to rot or to sublime within Robert's cottage.

Wordsworth's play, in sum, moves from a pre-plot of exchange governed by the Beggar to a plot of recognition supervised by a cottager. Tragic fate and romance magic thus collapse not just into everyday luck but the especially craven form of luck that the middle class sees exaggerated in the poor: the finding of coins and money. Even his own wife, we notice, first fears that Robert had robbed Herbert: "you are no richer than when you left me?" (IV.iii.35–36). Nor is she herself immune to the money motive: she speculates about Herbert: "this man may be rich.—And could he be saved by our means, his gratitude—" (IV.iii.87–88). The grandly illegitimate ethos of tragedy (concerned with kingly parricides or incests) thus threatens to degenerate wholly into petty illegitimacies of anxiety, recrimi-nation, greed, small-mindedness in general, and a dead body that refuses to be transcendentalized. Robert says superstitiously about Herbert's body at one point:

> He has been dead and silent many hours.
> If you should hear a groan or from his side
> He should uplift his hand—that would be [evidence].
>
> (V.iii.42–44)

"Fie!" Margaret responds, dismissing even this lowest attempt at redemptive transcendence.

Thus the problem that confronts Wordsworth as tragic playwright: how to plot the action of ironic mythos *and* reinflate his ethos so that the play will end with recognizably tragic dignity? How, that is, to respect the essential imperative of his developing corpus of works: to give even the stigmatized poor their own high sphere of action? Dignity, we note, does not really come by way of the Hamlet-like madness giving Mortimer a spurious sense of grandeur at the end. Indeed, Mortimer's disconnected and extravagant phobias actually do more to adapt him to the crudely superstitious sensibility of Robert than to raise him to the threshold of purgative transcendence. It is now that the full rationale for our restaging of the play as a courtroom drama comes clear. The solution to Wordsworth's problem of tragedy, I suggest, is what Hay has studied as the performative aspect of law: spectacle or "majesty" ("Property," pp. 26–31). If the ironic plot of the play is a lèse majesté, then such affront to the dignity of majesty may be compensated for by what I earlier called the "excessive" or epiphenomenal idiom of crime and punishment—an entire ethos of "justice" brought in from outside the domestic center of the play to compensate for debased action with the dignified public ideologies the poet had previously learned on the scene of politics. The class-based differential structures once representing illegitimacy as Them can be reestablished and Our dignity thus restored, in sum, if Mortimer can only insist on Justice so strongly and repeatedly that a new juridical hierarchy of high versus low, the just man versus the criminal, will replace his original economic and social hierarchies.

Trial, in short, is the extra-generic means by which the degradation of tragedy by realism and baser realism can be counteracted, and irony redirected toward transcendence once more. Having charged the culprit of the middle-class family in court, indeed, we can at this point pursue our juridical restaging to its close by witnessing the fact that—though there is no literal trial—the full plot of the play may very usefully be conceived precisely as due process:[72] a defense, prosecution, punishment, and rehabilitation of the family constitutive at last of Wordsworth's developing transcendentalization of irony, the Romantic self. The self is the illegitimacy of the family reconceived. It is the criminal whose autobiography will have all the dignity of self-justification.

Defense

We can first consider Mortimer in defense of the nuclear family. Defense opens with the argument that the alleged illegitimacy of the middle-class nuclear family is merely circumstantial—that Herbert, in other words, is so far from being representative of the class as to be only an accident or *lusus naturae*. Yet such defense is doomed. Every effort by Mortimer to demonstrate Herbert's "monstrous" nature admits of uncanny insights into his essential normalcy. Thus even as he is spurred by Rivers into furious righteousness against Herbert, and even as he himself traces and retraces the proofs justifying zeal, he cannot convince even the jury of his own conscience that Herbert is the devil. "Nay, be gentle with him," he remonstrates early in the play, remembering all that had endeared the old man to him (I.i. 59–71). Such misgivings dog him continually—in the form of Herbert's actual dog, for example, whose death provokes guilt (II.iii. 34–45)—and lead at last to the play's great climaxes of fastidiousness: first the dungeon scene in which, a Hamlet-become-Claudius, Mortimer kneels in fitful prayer (II.iii.287–91) and then the scene of his final interview with Herbert, when he washes his hands of the matter (III.iii).

How to defend the Family from illegitimacy when Mortimer cannot convince even himself that Herbert is a freak of nature? The answer is to brave illegitimacy with illegitimacy itself: to resort to gangsterism and—to adapt a bit of modern slang especially apt here—to "waste" Herbert before the trial can proceed. One way to put the belief driving my whole inquiry into Wordsworth is that there is no such thing as the innocent imagination. In the case of *The Borderers*, the question may be put: where did the imagination of the climactic trial-by-waste to which Mortimer submits Herbert come from?

We can notice first that intimations of infant death and infanticide—first seeded in the Beggar's dreams—propagate elsewhere in the play. In one of Mortimer's periodic fits of zeal, for example, he declaims a "philosophy" alluding to similar thoughts in *Macbeth*:

> Now for the corner stone of my philosophy:
> I would not give a denier for the man
> Who could not chuck his babe beneath the chin
> And send it with a fillip to its grave.
> (III.ii.92–95)[73]

To understand such infanticidal urges in *The Borderers*, we need only notice that it is Herbert who is the great "child" of the play. Herbert is helpless. But, strangely, helplessness fires rather than damps the instinct to kill him. After Rivers worries at one point that some may think it "unseemly" to "take the life of one so helpless" (II.i.46–47), Mortimer answers, *con brio*,

>   Oh,
> Would he were older! would he were more weak,
> A thousand times more helpless; verily,
> I do not think the tale will be believed
> Till I have shed his blood.   (II.i.47–51)

Like so many other utterances by Mortimer, this bit of braggadocio is astonishingly odd. Its deep rationale only comes clear when we realize that it is Herbert's very helplessness that allows Mortimer to savor his death as eye-for-eye justice. What more fitting punishment for a perpetrator of child-exchange, after all, than symbolic infanticide? The full expression of such symbolism belongs to Rivers, who, in the dungeon scene, first speaks of drugging Herbert with "A gentle dose! / That will compose him to a child-like sleep" (II.iii.170–71) and then figures murder as "baptismal" rite:

>   we kill a toad, a newt,
> A rat—I do believe if they who first
> Baptised the deed had called it murder, we
> Had quaked to think of it.   (II.iii.231–34)

The result of such figuration is that Rivers can at last answer all objections to killing Herbert as follows: "His tender cries / And helpless innocence, do they protect / The infant lamb?" (II.iii.391–93). Uttered shortly before "sacrifice" comes to the fore in the play (II.iii.401, 428), this declaration is conclusive. Herbert is the Lamb—a type of the infant Christ to be offered up.

The "wasting" of Herbert, in sum, mimes the exposure of infants. Or perhaps a broader phrasing is more accurate: the only truly shocking action Wordsworth could imagine for Mortimer turns out to be a crime indistinguishable from lower-class infanticide. It was the exposure of children, after all, that was the only contemporary analogue of trial-by-waste.[74]

With such defense, what need for prosecution? The defense itself is deeply implicated in "the crime of the family."

Prosecution

But this is a heavy-handed play. Wordsworth ensures that the agent provocateur who set up the case remains on hand to prosecute the middle-class nuclear family as fully as possible. The prosecutor, of course, is Rivers. And his case is "friendship"—the great subversion

W.W., M.H., D.W., S.T.C., J.W., S.H.

S. T. Coleridge.

Dorothy Wordsworth.   William Wordsworth

Mary Hutchinson.   Sara Hutchinson.

William.   Coleridge.   Mary.

Dorothy.   Sara.

16th May

1802

John Wordsworth.

FIG. 8. "Sara's Rock" (above) and Dorothy Wordsworth's blotting paper (below).

of the family. Friendship adds to the ironic mythos of the play a rhetoric of irony giving the coup de grace to the nuclear ethos.

I refer to a theme of friendship so large and central to the study of Romanticism that no full justice can be rendered to it here.[75] Remember the genealogical register or tablet of the play I postulated with its arrangement of four names: "Herbert and Matilda" and "Beggar and Son." To be actors rather than merely spectators of the family drama, all other characters in the play must link their names to this matrix. Mortimer, for example, had intended to assume the role of the son. But what about Rivers, the remaining lead in the cast?

For cross-reference, I set down in Fig. 8 two actual tablets inscribed with names. First, there is "Sara's Rock" on the road to Keswick, a "visual charm" of "shared faith," as John Beer has called it (*Wordsworth and the Human Heart*, pp. 165–66), which by May 1802 displayed the collectively carved initials shown (MM, 1: 551).[76] Second, there is the blotting paper that Dorothy inserted in her journal in May 1802 (MM, 1: 551). Among these mosaics of identity there is one name that both belongs and does not belong, because it is related to the Wordsworth clan neither by blood nor impending marriage (between William and Mary Hutchinson in October 1802). This name, of course, is "S.T.C." or "Coleridge."

And as the reference for this cross-reference, I set down Wordsworth's clumsy equivalent of Othello's handkerchief, the telltale "letter" he mentions so often that we are misled into thinking it must be a crucial plot-device. When Mortimer finally shows the letter to

Matilda to prove his involvement in Herbert's death, however, it leaves her wholly uninterested. The letter, it turns out, has no functional role in the play. Its only purpose seems to be to set down together the names of the play's Father and would-be Son:

Be not surprized if you hear that some signal judgment has befallen the man who calls himself your father—he is now with me, as his signature will shew—suspend your judgement till you see me—

Herbert
Mortimer
(V.iii. 126–30)

Or rather, the letter's two signatures should really be seen to bracket an invisible third drawn from outside the paradigmatic family ensemble yet somehow indispensable to the internal correspondence of that ensemble: "Herbert [Rivers] Mortimer." It was Rivers who authored the letter and took care to have Herbert and Mortimer affix their signatures (II.i. 124–29). (And it was also Rivers who earlier conveyed the Dear-John letter from Matilda to Mortimer; I.i. 22–26.)

Coleridge is to the Wordsworth clan, I propose, as Rivers is to the "family" of *The Borderers*. Coleridge/Rivers is the type of the Romantic friend. As I will further detail in the next chapter, the period from about 1795 to 1799 saw Wordsworth not only suddenly extending and deepening his "friendships" (e.g., with Coleridge, the Calverts, the Pinneys, Mathews, Wrangham, Montagu, Lamb, and Cottle) but rethinking the meaning of friendship. The match he made with Coleridge was particularly new, experimental, and significant precisely in the period of *The Borderers*. Wordsworth met Coleridge in August or September 1795 and began correspondence with him in the spring of 1796, soon before going to work on his tragedy (*CEY*, pp. 167, 179). It was Coleridge, indeed, who in 1797 also wrote a tragedy, *Osorio*; it was Coleridge who gave Wordsworth's play its first informal audience at Racedown in June 1797; and it was Coleridge who took charge in the long, troubled attempt to produce the play in London (*B*, pp. 3–7).

What is a Romantic friend? Here I improvise upon Ariès, who suggests the great interventionist role in the history of the family played not only by such institutions as school, but also—first as a traditional alternative to, and then as a component of, the socializing experience of school—by friendship (*Centuries*, pp. 369–71, 376–81). School was an extension of traditional fosterage, and schoolfriends were a new kind of foster-family. Extending the thought, we observe that Wordsworth made his friends in school and the early postgraduate years, as they may be called, of his poetic craft. Then he cherished those friends to such an extent both actually and in idea—in his correspondence, talk, and poetry—that they became "like" family.* A first definition of the Romantic friend may thus be offered: as in the case of the earlier periods studied by Ariès, the friend is precisely the "like"-family. William Galperin has recently studied the relationship between Wordsworth and Coleridge in terms of the latter's concept of "desynonymization." We might think in similar rhetorical terms.[77] Put rhetorically, the friend is the stranger whose name attaches itself to the family's, not by blood-affiliation or organic resemblance, which we may conceive as "metaphor," but by a pure "liking" essentially "metonymic."[78]

Highly suggestive in this regard are Coleridge's despairing efforts in the next decade to fit himself securely into the crèche of Wordsworth names. While absent from the Grasmere ensemble (during his Malta exile from 1804 through 1806), he filled his notebooks with his own versions of such name games as Sara's Rock or Dorothy's blotting paper (MM, 2: 85n). As Moorman notes, he thus addresses the Wordsworth household at one point:

> Friend, Lover, Husband, Sister, Brother!
> Dear names close in upon each other!
> Alas! poor Fancy's bitter-sweet—
> Our names, and but our names can meet.
>   (quoted in MM, 2: 84–85)

But even the meeting of names he fancies is finally illusory, purely a matter of metonym. His own name, it appears, communicates with the closed circle of the Wordsworths only by "substitution." Thus under his name and the names of the Wordsworth clan in a book of German philosophy (as Moorman observes) he inscribes the following signature of alienation: "Shall I ever see them again? And will it not be better that I should not? Is my body, and the habits and state of mind induced by it, such as to promise that I shall be other than a new sorrow? O dear John! would I had been thy Substitute!" (quoted in MM, 2: 85). As will become increasingly clear in the years to come (with the writing of "To William Wordsworth," for example), Coleridge's true Imagination or "I AM" is activated only by such Dear-John letters to his self—to a self of promise, hope, and poetic genius forever banished from its home paradise. Within that paradise of "Dear names close[d] in upon each other," "Coleridge" can exist only as metonym: "I AM" as "John [Wordsworth]" is.[79]

---

*It was in the 1795–99 period of intense experimentation with "friendship," indeed, that Wordsworth initiated his lifelong pattern of actually housing friends in his family for extended periods. One case clearly shows the ancestry of such habits in traditional fosterage: out of considerations of friendship, and also of income, Wordsworth in 1795 agreed to foster Basil Montagu's son (*Letters*, 1: 146–47).

But the Romantic friend is more central to the family than metonymy by itself implies. We can fully romanticize friendship by
taking as our emblem the opening of *The Prelude*, which, considered
one way, invokes the muse of "Friendship":

> Oh there is blessing in this gentle breeze
> That blows from the green fields and from the clouds
> And from the sky: it beats against my cheek,
> And seems half-conscious of the joy it gives.
> O welcome Messenger! O welcome Friend!
>
>   .   .   .
>
> For I, methought, while the sweet breath of Heaven
> Was blowing on my body, felt within
> A corresponding mild creative breeze,
> A vital breeze which travell'd gently on
> O'er things which it had made, and is become
> A tempest, a redundant energy
> Vexing its own creation.
>
>   .   .   .
>
>   Thus far, O Friend! did I, not used to make
> A present joy the matter of my Song,
> Pour out, that day, my soul in measur'd strains.
>
>   (1.1–57)

Between the first flush of "Friend"-ship here, referred to the wind,
and the second, referred to Coleridge, flourishes the "corresponding
mild creative breeze," the fluid spirit of such friends as Rivers. A
second definition can be offered: the Romantic friend is indeed a "correspondent" spirit. He is the outer, objective, or exogamous identity whose correspondence (literally, his letters) communicates to a
family its own inner identity. Rhetorically: a friend is the metonymic
medium in which a family writes its intuition that it is itself structured by communications of metaphorical identity closer than mere
metonymy or "liking." Thus, for example, Dorothy draws more near
to William when corresponding with Coleridge: Coleridge is what
allows Dorothy to say "we"—to express her identity with, care for,
worry over William.

But one further complexion of Romantic friendship requires account. Like the "corresponding mild creative breeze," the friend is
also a source of deep "vexation." This is because to allow a friend
to attach his name metonymically to the family's is to allow a virus
within: a particle of otherness with the uncanny ability to render the
inner, affiliative metaphor of the family itself metonymic, other. To
begin with, the friend is truly "redundant," or in excess of the central family germ. In practice, this means that it is the friend who
draws the family member out of the family to partake of such other
social identities as the club, pub, salon, or the friend's own family.

And with the introduction of a larger social surround, there arises the possibility of conflicting obligations and reciprocal recriminations. Somewhere, after all (as we will see Wordsworth learning in his vexed financial relations with Montagu), the line must be drawn between family and friend.[80] Moreover, the friend vexes because he is the rhetorical medium that allows a family to tell itself truths it would rather not know. From William and Dorothy's viewpoint, therefore, the perpetually ailing Coleridge allowed them to tell themselves how close to indolence (William's preoccupation) and sickness (Dorothy's) they themselves lived.[81] And from Coleridge's perspective, Wordsworth's status as a true poet allowed him to tell himself in 1800 that by comparison he was no poet (*Collected Letters*, 1: 656, 658). A third definition thus seems necessary: the Romantic friend is the irony of the family. Rhetorically, he is the metonym that allows a family to see how precarious, "like"-family, or metonymic its own identity appears in the face of greater social or physical realities.

Now we can understand why friendship is the rhetoric that allows Rivers so effectively to prosecute the family in *The Borderers*. "Friendship" is mentioned so frequently in the play that it must be ranked after "justice" as Wordsworth's second most important discourse. "Friendship" and "justice," indeed, begin as synonyms: Mortimer would bring Herbert to justice out of friendship to humanity at large. "I have a friend," Matilda says, who "lives but to protect the injured" (IV.iii.17–18). And again: "Art thou not here the friend of all the helpless?" (V.iii.85). "I am the friend of all men," Mortimer can still declare at the close of the play (V.iii.227).

The real question, however, is not whether Mortimer remains friends with all but what "friendship with all" means. On the one hand, universal benevolence refreshes the old ambiguity in the word "friend" by confounding family and non-family.[82] To be friends with all is to treat all as part of the family of man. Mortimer, in other words, wishes to be "fraternal."[83] More broadly, he wishes to be "familiar." Thus he makes "friend" convertible with "father" in an early speech of self-identification:

> If I ever knew
> My heart, and naked saw the man within me,
> 'Tis at this moment.—Rivers! I have loved
> To be the friend and father of the helpless.
> (II.i.87–90)

But, on the other hand, to be "friends with all" is to be promiscuous with family feeling and so to end by ironizing the very notion of family. Such is the empty friendship that Rivers, the great rhetorician of benevolence in the play, insidiously teaches Mortimer, leading the latter to see that the familiar friendship he practices is finally a very

shallow thing—an admission that family feeling itself has no more integrity than metonym. Rivers is the special "friend" of Mortimer. "I
still will be your friend, will cleave to you / Through good and evil,
through scorn and infamy," he says at one point with such ceremony
that we might think his commitment one of feudal allegiance or even
marriage (III.v.36–38). Rivers is "friends" with everyone else as well
—with the Host at the inn, with Herbert himself, with the Beggar,
and even with two anonymous woodmen (I.ii.69; II.iii.138; II.iii.244;
V.i.25). And Rivers, finally, also holds friendship dear as family. "My
good friend . . . My good old brother," he calls Herbert (II.iii.138–
41). Or again, as the Host reports later, Rivers seems Herbert's
"familiar friend" (III.i.4). But, of course, "friendship" and "familiarity" drop from Rivers's lips only as conscious rhetoric, as a sophistry
of endearment aware in every syllable that it is false "liking." Friendship and family are equivalent, in other words, only because both
are empty terms. "Dead?" Rivers asks about Herbert at the end.
"Quiet," responds Mortimer. "As his best friends could wish," Rivers
concludes, wholly ironizing "friendship" (V.iii.225). Or again, with
universal irony: "I felt that to be truly the world's friend, / We must
become the object of its hate" (IV.ii.156–57).

"Come, my friends, / And let us house together," Herbert says
early in the play (II.iii.174–75). "A stranger has done this to me," he
says later, "And in the arms of a stranger I must die" (IV.i.21–22).
Herbert learns to distinguish between family and friends. Mortimer
never does. Led on by the rhetoric of his "correspondent spirit," he
also comes at last to see friendship and familiarity as equivalent because both are nothing. "I am the friend of all men," we earlier heard
him asseverate. But now we can recognize that this is one of the most
ironic lines Wordsworth ever wrote. It is only after Rivers observes
that Herbert is "quiet" as his "best friends" could wish and then seeks
rapprochement with Mortimer by suggesting, "We are then friends,"
that the latter responds with total emptiness, "I am the friend of all
men" (V.iii.225–27).

Punishment

Aided by the self-incrimination of the defense, the prosecution of
"friends" is conclusive. All that remains is the punishment and rehabilitation of the family. The punishment is one of the great originals
of Wordsworth's poetry: "affection."

Extending K. E. Smith's study of "love" in *The Borderers*, we can
observe that the play contains what is virtually a *Symposium* of men
of feeling, of philosophers of sentiment whose colloquy of family
and friendship ultimately intends a supra-familial and meta-friendly
"love" so powerful, uncontrollable, and shockingly contrary in its

felt effects that we may well be reminded of Girard's definition of the sacred: "The sacred consists of all those forces whose dominance over man increases or seems to increase in proportion to man's effort to master them" (p. 31). In our gradually filling glossary of *The Borderers*, the place of third rank would have to go to the word "love." Love is like Milton's Christ come down to the first family in the Garden: it is there first of all to judge and give pain.

Mortimer loves Matilda. "O could you hear his voice—," Matilda swoons at one point, "All gentleness and love" (I.i.133–36). Mortimer also deeply loves Herbert. As R. F. Storch has insightfully observed, indeed, his love for Matilda is consistently superficial and unconvincing compared to the complicated love he bears for her father ("Wordsworth's *The Borderers*," p. 347)—for example:

> methinks
> There cannot be a time when I shall cease
> To love him.—I remember, when a Boy
> Of six years' growth or younger, by the thorn
> Which starts from the old church-yard wall of Lorton,
> It was my joy to sit and hear Matilda
> Repeat her father's terrible adventures
> Till all the band of play-mates wept together,
> And that was the beginning of my love.
>
> (I.i.60–68)

But, crucially, love is not love. Love is also fear and loathing.[84] Again, the gadfly who leads Mortimer to such a view is Rivers, whom Mortimer also loves. Here it will be useful to go back to page one of the play:

> WILFRED: Be cautious, my dear Master!
> MORTIMER: (*smiling*)   I perceive
>   That fear is like a cloak which old men huddle
>   Around their love, as 'twere to keep it warm.
> WILFRED: Nay, but my heart is sad
>   To part with you.—This Rivers—
> MORTIMER: What of him?
> WILFRED: You know that you have saved his life—
> MORTIMER: I know it.
> WILFRED: And that he hates you! (*seeing* MORTIMER *displeased*)
>   Pardon me, perhaps
>   That word was hasty.
> MORTIMER: Fie! no more of this.
> WILFRED: Dear Master! Gratitude's a heavy burthen
>   To a proud soul.—Nobody loves this Rivers;
>   Yourself you do not love him.
> MORTIMER: I do more,
>   I honor him.
>
> (I.i.1–12)

What is apparent is that Mortimer's more-than-love for Rivers is the envelope for a whole complex of emotions opened by fear, centered upon hate, and sealed with honor. It is precisely this Pandora's box that Rivers teaches Mortimer to open as the play progresses. " 'Tis plain he loves the girl," Rivers can thus say about Herbert's relation to Matilda (I.i.201), and then, contrarily: "But sure, he loves the girl; and never love / Could find delight to nurse itself so strangely, / . . . thus to plague her with *inventions*!" (I.i.206–8). Or again, witness the strange love Rivers speaks upon remembering that Mortimer once saved his life:

> The villains rose in mutiny to destroy me.
> I could have quelled the cowards—but this stripling [Mortimer]
> Must needs step in, and save my life—the look
> With which he gave the boon—I see it now—
> What if he did the deed in love—so be it,
> I hate him not—now I begin to love him.   (II.iii.220–25)

Such love is hateful and fearful in the very contrariness with which it utters itself.

Tutored by such a Socrates of the anti-Eros, Mortimer at last also learns to complicate love with all that is unlovely. By the time he is ready to expose Herbert, indeed, he knows love to be the climactic irony of the play. Looking at Herbert, he declaims:

> And I have *loved* this man? and she hath loved him,
> And I loved her, and she loved the Lord Clifford,
> And there it ends—if this be not enough
> To make mankind merry for evermore.
>
> (III.iii.12–15)

Later in the scene, Mortimer sums up the entire transition he has made from love of mankind to misanthropy:

> Even such a man [Herbert] my fancy bodied forth
> From the first moment that I loved the maid
> And he was still a brother in my love—
> These tears—I did not think that aught was left in me
> Of what I have been.—Yes, I thank thee, heaven:
> *One happy* thought has passed across my mind.—
> It may not be—I am cut off from man,
> No more shall I be man, no more shall I
> Have human feelings!   (III.iii.64–72)

To love in *The Borderers* is to fixate in fear and hate; and to feel is to be forced to cut oneself off—pitifully and terribly—from human feelings. Such monstrous contrariety is indeed sacred: "Yes, I thank thee, heaven," gratulates Mortimer before sacrificing all his feelings.

Love tending toward its pathological border-states is what Wordsworth in the mid to late 1790's eventually categorizes as "emotion" —the poetic principle whose inflection as "recollection" in the 1800 Preface to *Lyrical Ballads* will at last be collected in the 1815 "Poems Founded on the Affections." The need for such a category was urgent. As we have seen, the deep structure of Wordsworth's poetry at the time of *The Borderers* was irony—a mythos and rhetoric whose combined effect was to make his fundamental social ethos, familial love, illegitimate. But to provide the basis for a full poetic program, irony had to convene at least as much authority as the convention in the poet's immediate background: tragedy. In the mid 1790's, we know, Wordsworth had access to some ironic conventions. Shortly before beginning work on *The Borderers*, for example, he collaborated with Francis Wrangham to imitate Juvenal (*CEY*, pp. 163–80). But such old conventions proved inadequate. Classical satire thus survives into the mature poetry primarily in such cul-de-sacs as the Juvenalian set pieces in the London book of *The Prelude*.

Wordsworth had to create a new convention of irony: what the 1798 Advertisement to *Lyrical Ballads* calls an "experimental" poetry. The parallel with other Romantics is instructive here. We might think of Blake's "proverbs of hell" or "contraries," Schlegel's aphorisms, Byron's stanzas, or even Coleridge's Notebook entries—all experiments in which self-canceling, fragmentary form creates the transcendental casualness of Romantic irony.[85] As we will soon see, Wordsworth's experiment consolidates itself as "lyric," the form in which dispersed images, ballads, epitaphs, or sonnets fashion his version of the contrary, the aphorism, and the Byronic stanza. But crucially, Wordsworthian lyric will transcendentalize irony by intending the very opposite of casualness: affection.

I hazard here a pun that is both etymologically and conceptually more than pun. If irony is Wordsworth's *langue*, or deep structure, in the period initiated by *The Borderers*, then poetic affection will be his *parole*. *The Borderers* begins the painful task of respeaking familial affection as a "sentence," in the dual sense of words and punishment, able to parole irony in the form of the rehabilitated irony resident in lyric: the Romantic self.

To explain this parole, I will outline the overall discursive system of Wordsworthian affection in the mid to late 1790's as follows. Imagine that the most straightforward depiction of irony in *The Borderers* and other works of the period is a line, a single descent of discursive conventions, as shown in Fig. 9. The line originates in a social convention, the ethos of family love. It submits social convention to the destabilizing mythos and rhetoric of irony we have witnessed. Then it closes upon a restabilized social convention: a terminal ethos of irony that integrates family love *with* its ironization. But because the institution of the family is no longer sufficient to define this ethos,

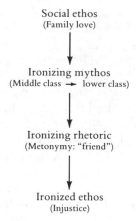

FIG. 9. The structures of irony.

Wordsworth deploys most fully at this point his framing institution of social ideology in the 1790's, "justice." (An analogy would be today's soap operas, which define their essential family drama within such framing institutions as the divorce court, boardroom, or general hospital.) The irony of domestic affection becomes the origin of social "injustice."

To speak irony as the poetry of affection, Wordsworth adds to this evolution what might be called his cathectic apparatus of affection—a sort of afterburner of irony. Rather than being exhausted by irony, the disturbance created by reduction of the poet's original ethos is shunted aside into the parallel evolution of conventions shown in Fig. 10, with the final result that ironic injustice is rejustified and restored to the old high dignity of tragedy. Such, I suggest, is the core romanticization altering irony into Romanticism as we know it. It will be useful to chart here at least the main turns in the new channel of feeling.

(1) *Ethos*. As the feudal never-never-land setting of *The Borderers* highlights, the first step in Wordsworth's discourse of affection is the romanticization, in the full sense, of middle-class mores. Specifically, affection displaces family love into the late-feudal ethos of "courtly love." The gain from such a maneuver of love is enormous. Courtly love was the cathexis of difference between family and non-family, house and non-house. Adulterous difference, indeed, was its crowning passion. In extreme form, courtly love was the Petrarchan lover's devotion to a lady married to another—to a lord more noble, powerful, or, in the case of Sidney's Stella, "Rich." More broadly, courtly love was the passion of such lovers as Chaucer's Palamoun and Arcite for Emelye, a lady inaccessible because of allegiance to a lord outside the lover's circle of allegiance. The gain from aligning family love with courtly love stems from the fact that the latter code had le-

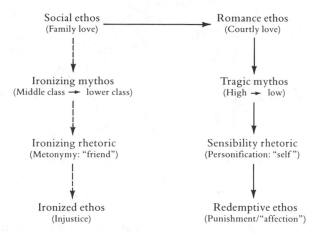

FIG. 10. The structures of affection (solid arrows indicate the new line of descent).

gitimized precisely the condition that the middle-class nuclear family knew as its mortal lot but could not admit without bastardizing itself: its own internal "difference," fragmentariness, or subordination to societal networks outside the conjugal core. It was the romance of the fey, strange princess, we might say, that allowed the middle class to idealize its everyday enactments of a grimmer fairy tale: for example, the tale of the stepmother (or true *belle dame sans merci*) whose societal otherness was too much at home.

Or again, we might look ahead to a fairy tale closer to home: the Vaudracour and Julia episode in Book 9 of *The Prelude*. In this short-form *Borderers* (to which we will need to return in Chapter 8), Wordsworth romanticizes social and, in this case, class difference between his lovers so thoroughly that difference—and the fragmentation of the nuclear family it enforces—becomes canonical. As his allusions spell out, the pattern of "Vaudracour and Julia" is *Romeo and Juliet*.

(2) *Mythos.* Wordsworth then inflects ethos within mythos, romance within the one aspect of Aristotelian tragedy to survive through the mid to late 1790's, "action." But action is no longer necessarily narrative. It need only be the field of residual action, or essentialized tragedy, Wordsworth calls "suffering." One of the poet's own favorite passages in *The Borderers*, we know, is the meditation in which Rivers deepens action into suffering:

> Action is transitory, a step, a blow—
> The motion of a muscle—this way or that—
> 'Tis done—and in the after vacancy
> We wonder at ourselves like men betray'd.
> Suffering is permanent, obscure and dark,
> And has the nature of infinity.
>
> (III. v. 60–65) [86]

Mortimer responds in the Early Version, "I do not understand you," but in the 1842 version, "Truth—and I feel it." The difference, we might say, is that he must have read Aristotle in the meantime. Reversal and recognition in *The Poetics* are well known. Less often cited is the conclusion of the chapter on *peripeteia* and *anagnorisis*: "These things, reversal and recognition, are two parts of the plot. A third is suffering. . . . Suffering (*pathos*) is a fatal or painful action like death on the stage, violent physical pain, wounds, and everything of that kind" (Ch. 11). Suffering, in short, is pity and fear affecting not the spectator but the person on stage. At heart, it is the stigmata of what Aristotle originally meant by "ethos": the heroic *character*.

In the discourse of affection, we can deduce, the burning lover must end a hero agonistes, Vaudracour a Prometheus bound. Only so—to play on Erdman's Anglicization—can Wordsworth's essential Vaudracour become "Heartsworth," his core persona of affection. The genius of this persona is to *interiorize* the intuition of social difference. Character swallows difference (the tragic vector from high to low) within itself to create the rift of soul across which the high hero at last suffers his basest other self: his *hamartia*.

(3) *Rhetoric*. To achieve its full personality, Romantic affect inflects its developing character within a rhetoric descended most immediately from Sensibility poetry. Here I draw upon Frances Ferguson's insight that affection for Wordsworth, which she studies under the 1815 category of "Poems Founded on the Affections," consists in an illusion of "metaphorical" relationship with the object of love (e.g., "you are my world") so deeply unaware of itself as trope that the loss of the original object of love leads inevitably to a revaluation of affection itself (pp. xiii, 42–53). Affection concludes as the highest degree of what I earlier called the rhetoric of metonymy or "liking." It becomes the cathexis—in rhetorical terms, the overdetermined construction—that occupies the evacuated site of the copula ("you *are* my world") where relations of identity suddenly dissociate into empty figures of speech.[87] Affection, that is, consists of the whole catalog of uncopulated syntactical relations—ruptures, elisions, inversions, and repetitions—that Longinus theorized as sublime *pathopoeia* and that Collins (my type of Sensibility here) applied in what Dr. Johnson called his "clogged and impeded" verse: anacoluthon, anantapodoton, asyndeton, catachresis, hyperbaton, polyptoton (in Longinus's sense), and so on.[88]

Above all, affection is the rhetoric of the Archimago of metonymy: personification, in which the human identity is substituted for an attribute (for example, an emotion) or contiguous association (a feature of landscape, for instance). Personification packages what would otherwise be the disturbed syntax of *pathopoeia* in the nominative (e.g., "Pity" or "Fear") so as to restore the capacity of sentences to copulate. If "you" no longer *are* "my world," that is, then the Pity and Fear that arise metonymically in the space of the exploded copula provide a surrogate noun subject by which to copulate the object of passion at one remove: "You ~~are~~ [Fear is] my world." It is precisely in this fashion, for example, that personification unclogs rhetoric in one of the great poems of Romantic passion, the "Dejection" ode. Where Collins characteristically fills the evacuated copula between "you" and "world," or subject and object, with Fear, Coleridge invests it with mythic Joy. Only when he names Joy does his syntax recover the primal copula or "I AM" of his imagination: "Joy, Lady! *is* the spirit and the power . . . / Joy *is* the sweet voice, Joy the luminous cloud" (italics mine).[89]

In Wordsworth's case, whenever we read of love, passion, or feeling in the blocked syntax of the early works or even in the colloquialness of the later "Poems Founded on the Affections," we should be aware how easily the poet lapses into an allegory of personified Passions in the tradition from Collins to Coleridge.[90] I take as illustration here "'Tis Said, That Some Have Died for Love," a Lyrical Ballad of 1800 that Wordsworth later included in the "Poems Founded on the Affections." After listening to the orphic elegy of a lover for his deceased lady, the speaker in this poem of uncopulated love (in every sense) concludes with a strange fit of passion:

> Ah gentle Love! if ever thought was thine
> To store up kindred hours for me, thy face
> Turn from me, gentle Love! nor let me walk
> Within the sound of Emma's voice, nor know
> Such happiness as I have known to-day.
>
> (*PW*, 2: 34)

Or again, we can look to "Nutting" (1798), which Wordsworth later elevated to the status of a "Poem of the Imagination." Here, affection is raised a spiritual body:

>   unless I now
> Confound my present feelings with the past,
> Ere from the mutilated bower I turned
> Exulting, rich beyond the wealth of kings,
> I felt a sense of pain when I beheld
> The silent trees, and saw the intruding sky.—
> Then, dearest Maiden, move along these shades
> In gentleness of heart; with gentle hand
> Touch—for there is a spirit in the woods.
>
> (*PW*, 2: 212)

All that would be needed to inflate "gentle Love," "sense of pain," or "spirit in the woods" in such poems into full-blown personifications would be to address them in the vocative. Personification would then be entirely cognate with what we previously saw to be the genius of metonymy, the friend. "Ah gentle Love," "dearest Maiden," and "O Coleridge!" are like expressions.

The ultimate function of the rhetoric of affection is to accent what I have called the interiorization of difference. At first glance, of course, character that knows itself only as Pity, Fear, Mercy, and so forth seems destined to project itself "outward" into a detached realm of feeling. We might think, for example, of the vulture passions Gray personifies with such cruel detachment in his "Eton College" ode. Or again, we might think of Wordsworth's "Three Years She Grew in Sun and Shower," in which a daemon-queen of personification, Nature, administers Lucy's "glee," "calm," and "feelings of delight" with such detachment as to seem utterly inhuman. But there is also a deep sense in which the seeming detachment of personification is the sign of imminent internalization. For the moment, it will be sufficient to abbreviate with the aid of Owen Schur's thesis on personification and the poetic persona in Victorian poetry. As Schur has helped me see, the logical end of Sensibility personification will be a unique Romantic version of the tragic "character" we witnessed above. We might conceive of the total evolution of character as follows: *hamartia* or tragic flaw → Theophrastan "character" or Jonsonian "humour" → ruling passion (e.g., Pride) → Sensibility personification → Romantic self. An apt emblem is the huge personification Blake names the spectre "Self." The *ne plus ultra* of personification will be the alienated, memorial, or otherwise self-differentiated person-within-a-person that we are rapidly approaching: the Romantic self. Self will be the ultimate "friend" or personification. Self is the tragic character whose ability to externalize itself—as in the "two consciousnesses" meditation in Book 2 of *The Prelude*—will provide Wordsworth with his deepest imagination of social difference.

(4) *Redemptive Ethos*. We thus come to the close of Wordsworth's discourse of affection: the social convention that allows him to collect the romance, tragic, and Sensibility deflections of irony into an over-all inflection or "sentence." To read this final sentencing of the ethos of family love, we can begin by noticing that the poet's exaggerated emphasis on crime and punishment in the mid to late 1790's attends so closely his equally hysterical stress on personal affection that the two become a single phenomenon. Criminal *mentalité* and sentimen-tality draw together into a single figure of emotional torture.[91]

In *The Borderers*, the climax of *pathos* thus arrives when Mortimer experiences pangs of criminal guilt and affection simultaneously. In act 5, he reflects:

> A man may be the father's murderer
> And to the daughter the most precious thing

The world contains.—Matilda, at this moment
I feel a most unusual fondness for thee.
                    (V.iii.54–57)

Criminal guilt and fondness flourish together across a separation no
thicker than a Sternean dash. Criminality and sentimentality then
draw even closer as the scene of pathos continues. "May vengeance
haunt the fiend / For this most cruel murder," Matilda begins in a
curse calling punishment down upon her father's killer (V.iii.64–72).
"Heaven is my witness that my heart has joined thee," Mortimer
immediately rejoins (V.iii.73). Heartfelt sympathy then builds until
Mortimer experiences one of his most truly affectionate moments in
the play. When Matilda imagines her dying father calling for "his
beloved child!" (V.iii.75), Mortimer choruses, "Aye, come to me and
weep," and kisses her (V.iii.76).

Other works in the period of *The Borderers* extend the *pas de deux*
of criminality and sentimentality. Witness, for example, the end of
Adventures on Salisbury Plain (composed 1795; MS. 2 from 1799–1800),
where the criminal Sailor experiences a pang of feeling so sharp that
Wordsworth likens it to an instrument of torture. The Sailor

> stroked the child, outstretch'd
> His face to earth, and as the boy turn'd round
> His batter'd head, a groan the Sailor fetch'd.
> The head with streaming blood had dy'd the ground,
> Flow'd from the spot where he that deadly wound
> Had fix'd on him he murder'd. Through his brain
> At once the griding iron passage found;
> Deluge of tender thoughts then rush'd amain
> Nor could his aged eyes from very tears abstain.
>   (*SP*, p. 149)

Sentiment is the Sailor's presentiment of capital punishment. Or
again, witness "The Convict," a poem Wordsworth first published in
1797 under a pseudonym descended from *The Borderers*: "Mortimer"
(MM, 1: 351; Pollin, pp. 32–33). Here the confine of criminal mentality becomes so saturated with sentimentality—with "deep sad-
ness," "steadfast dejection," "sorrow," "grief," "terror," and "compassion"—that it becomes clear that sentiment is the whole regimen of
torture.[92] Grief and guilt rack the criminal with their "tortures," and
pain and terror submit him to "a thousand sharp punctures" (*PW*,
1: 312–14). Or once more, witness the demented witch-love of the
mother in "The Three Graves." In Wordsworth's contribution to this
strange collaboration with Coleridge (written 1796–97), the mother
at last experiences passions akin to the tortures of a witch-trial:

> And she was pinched and pricked with pins,
>   And twitched with cord and wire;

> And starting from her seat would cry,
> "It is a stool of fire."
>
> *(PW*, 1: 312)[93]

Perhaps the best exhibit upon which to close our survey of emotional torture, however, is *Peter Bell*, Wordsworth's quintessential tale of unfeeling man converted to feeling by the mere idea of punishment. Despite its drollery, *Peter Bell* (first drafted 1798) is remarkable among the early works for the vigor with which it imagines the anti-type to the Matthews and other "feeling" personae of this era. Wordsworth first gives us Peter's character in a memorable sequence of stanzas depicting the world of the utterly unfeeling *(PW*, 2: 339–43). Peter is married to twelve wives, none of whom he loves, and communes like some ignoble savage with nature, no scene in which he loves. He is ancestral to such literary types as Crabbe's Peter Grimes or one of the wildmen in Robert Service's Yukon ballads:

> Within the breast of Peter Bell
> These silent raptures found no place;
> He was a Carl as wild and rude
> As ever hue-and-cry pursued,
> As ever ran a felon's race.
>
> *(PW*, 2: 341)[94]

Redemption comes to Peter only when he encounters the Ass, a Mary's mount of infinite feeling whose identity is no more than the capacity to absorb torture. In an action that is the very rebus of corporal punishment, Peter beats the Ass. But as Blake might put it, "He became what he beheld," and at last suddenly experiences a "conviction strange" that "Vengeance . . . will fall" upon his own head *(PW*, 2: 363). After this point in the poem, Peter becomes a disciple of what Alan Bewell has analyzed as virtually criminal punishment, surrendering himself to a bottomless sense of guilt and retribution seemingly devoid of external cause. Peter comes to believe, Bewell writes, "that the surrounding dark powers, a cosmic tribunal, have condemned him, and that his slow ride on the ass is really that of a convicted criminal on the cart to the place of execution. Metaphors of crime and guilt appear early in the poem, and gain in power and intensity as Peter approaches the Methodist chapel" ("Wordsworth's Primal Scene," p. 339; see also pp. 340–42). The end of such a pure *mentalité* of punishment is that Peter *feels*. He feels the tortured love that Wordsworth, like Coleridge in his play of the title, calls "remorse" (cf. Thorslev, p. 88, on *The Borderers* and remorse). "Smitten to the core / By strong compunction and remorse," Peter is suddenly haunted by the memory of one of the wives he had made so unhappy *(PW*, 2: 374). Uncharacteristically, "His heart is stung" *(PW*, 2: 374). Thus it is, Wordsworth concludes, that Peter is

> taught to feel
> That man's heart is a holy thing;
> And Nature, through a world of death,
> Breathes into him a second breath,
> More searching than the breath of spring.
>
> (*PW*, 2: 380)

A Lazarus of feeling, Peter then ends by rejoining the world of his fellow man. In the poem, this means that for the first time he approximates our own condition as compassionate reader. He watches from the shades as the son of the Ass's dead master enacts a passion play:

> Forth to the gentle Ass he springs,
> And up about his neck he climbs;
> In loving words he talks to him,
> He kisses, kisses face and limb,—
> He kisses him a thousand times!
>
> (*PW*, 2: 382)

Touched to the heart, Peter, "the ruffian wild, / Sobs loud, he sobs even like a child" (*PW*, 2: 382).

How can we understand the deep affection of Romanticism for punishment? Why is love nothing without laceration?

One way to frame an answer is to reflect upon the social history of criminal punishment. Here I condense conclusions drawn by Foucault in his *Discipline and Punish* and emphasized by Marie-Hélène Huet. We can first observe that Continental and English justice began as an *ancien régime* of punishment descended from feudal convention. Finishing in a literal marking or "writing" of the criminal's body, such justice was a *peine forte* signing with state authority the principle of social difference we have been following. As Foucault puts it, capital punishment in eighteenth-century France exhibited

the corpse of the condemned man at the scene of his crime, or at one of the near-by crossroads. The execution was often carried out at the very place where the crime had been committed. . . . There was the use of "symbolic" torture in which the forms of the execution referred to the nature of the crime: the tongues of blasphemers were pierced, the impure were burnt, the right hand of murderers was cut off; sometimes the condemned man was made to carry the instrument of his crime—thus Damiens was made to hold in his guilty right hand the famous dagger with which he had committed the crime, hand and dagger being smeared with sulphur and burnt together. As Vico remarked, this old jurisprudence was "an entire poetics." (*Discipline*, pp. 44–45)

Torture, in sum, was mimetic, a referential writing reproducing in characters of blood the place, kind, severity, and often even the means of the offense. The ultimate purpose of such writing was to make the mutilated body of the criminal stand for, or "refer to," the whole body that was the integrity of the king's justice. Indeed, the writing made the body of the criminal stand symbolically for the king himself. As Huet argues in her application of Foucault, "The ceremony of justice, and its justification, endlessly reproduced the image and the majesty of the king. To judge in the name of the king was to place the condemned in a relationship with the one whom his actions had offended" (pp. 50–51). Social *difference* rather than identity declared itself because the bond thus imaged between criminal and king was finally one of inversion. As displayed on the scaffold with his catalog of wounds, the criminal was the impress or intaglio of the giver of wounds: he was a "symmetrical, inverted figure of the king" (Foucault, *Discipline*, p. 29) serving to witness the higher lawgiver in the same way that man is an "imprint" marking the existence of God in Descartes' *Meditations* (p. 107).

But the *ancien régime* of punishment succeeded to modern justice roughly at the time of the epochal change in the visibility of death studied by Ariès and others (Ariès, *Western Attitudes* and *Hour*; Stone, *Family*, pp. 206–15, 246–53). We can witness such change in the eighteenth and nineteenth centuries in smaller compass here because the end result is familiar to us in our own regimes of punishment, which make punishment—like death itself—mute, secret, *invisible*. As Foucault details, the spectacle of punishment began its retreat from the public stage of the scaffold to behind prison walls (*Discipline*, pp. 7–10, 115–16). Or where the scaffold was still public, punishment became veiled in a different way. Torture was standardized, mechanized, minimalized (the original motive for Dr. Guillotin's device), and so rendered mimetically neuter (*Discipline*, pp. 12–13, 104–31 and *passim*). Masked by the roll of the drums and preempted by the instantaneous action of the *déclic*, or lever actuating the guillotine, the suffering of the victim could no longer be articulated on stage. From the spectator's vantage, it had to be imagined—as in Wordsworth's "The Convict"—within the mind and heart of the victim. The discourse of punishment, in sum, became *privatized*.

Of course, fuller study would be required before we could transcend a cliché application of Foucault. If nothing else, we would need to research the particularly English aspects of the subject— the evolution of common law, the science of hanging as opposed to guillotining, the increase in the number of capital statutes versus the decrease in actual executions in the eighteenth century (Hay, "Property," pp. 17–24), the history of transportation, the literature of criminality, and, most tellingly, the collision of the new, "sentimental" intelligentsia with the practice of public punishment (as registered, for example, in the fascinated revulsion such punishment set off in Boswell and Wordsworth). But our conclusion can already be hazarded: "men of feeling" in our period came to abhor public punishment not because the concept of punishment was in itself objectionable but because it had been fully privatized, locked within, interiorized. Every man alive to "affection" was a Werther-his-own-punishment or Coleridge-his-own-*Remorse*. Every Heartsworth, that is, knew that true punishment was not a mimetic discourse putting social difference on show but an internal discourse—let us call it a "symbolism"—in which the self domesticated the allegory of difference and became its own criminal and king, its own offense and tribunal. We might well apply our modern epithet, "bleeding-heart liberal," to Wordsworth simply as an analysis of his developing symbolism of the invisible gibbet ("The Gibbet-mast was moulder'd down, the bones / And iron case were gone"; *Prel*. 11.291–92). In such symbolism, the heart itself is the only manifest of punishment.[95]

Now we can begin to understand the deep affection of Romanticism for punishment. Indeed, we might notice that an underlying trope of punishment has all along informed the courtly, tragic, and other conventions in Wordsworth's discourse of affection. Consider, for example, a well-known miniature portrait, Nicholas Hilliard's *Young Man Among Roses* (c. 1587–88), in which a courtly lover stands under a golden motto: *Dat poenas laudata fides* ("Praised faith brings sufferings [or penalties]") (Fumerton, "'Secret' Arts," p. 69; shown in her pl. 9). Or again, we might think of tragedy's love of crime and punishment—most suggestively in such tales as *Oedipus Rex* in which the agonized criminal must punish himself. In the poetry of the mid to late 1790's, I suggest, Wordsworth makes explicit such tropes of "feeling punishment" because changes in the increasingly interiorized institution of justice now meant that the trope was the best means to articulate the crucial rite of passage in his work. This passage is the process by which the irony of family love transforms into the self-ironized, self-tortured genius whose articulation is the finale of the discourse of affection: the self. The interiorization by which punishment is mapped over feeling, in sum, caps the interiorization of social difference I have sketched. The irony that is the "crime of the family" finishes in the inner character, personification, and punishment of the self.

Such is the "sentence" that finishes Wordsworth's discourse of affection. The irony that is the nuclear family speaks itself in a discourse of affection, and affection speaks itself at last as the great Romantic punishment: a feeling for self. From such self-feeling arises the possibility of redemption. For the performative function of the sentence of affection is at last to parole or release the ethos of the nuclear family in its new form: the ideology of the Romantic self or mind.

Rehabilitation

I now reach the goal of this chapter, the point at which my argument can be referred back to the mainstream of criticism on *The Borderers*. My goal is the Romantic self and the poetry such self supervises, a poetry in which "familiarity," a generalized family-feeling for the world, becomes defamiliarization. We might apply anew Coleridge's account of the genesis of *Lyrical Ballads*:

Mr. Wordsworth . . . was to propose to himself as his object, to give the charm of novelty to things of every day, and to excite a feeling analogous to the supernatural, by awakening the mind's attention from the lethargy of custom, and directing it to the loveliness and the wonders of the world before us; an inexhaustible treasure, but for which in consequence of the film of familiarity and selfish solicitude we have eyes, yet see not, ears that hear not, and hearts that neither feel nor understand. (*Biographia*, 2: 6–7)

In the poetry of Wordsworth's self, we might say, all the unfamiliar world will now be "felt" to be as fresh and new—and also as frightening—as the world seen through an orphan's eyes. Such is the social basis of defamiliarization, which is so far from abnormal (as we earlier noticed about Wordsworth's actual orphanage) that it is really a deep recognition—affirmation and denial both—of the true social norm.

What is the Romantic self or mind? In terms of *The Borderers*, what is the principle of subjectivity that utters itself in Rivers's declaration of "independent intellect"? Addressing Mortimer, Rivers justifies murdering Herbert as follows:

> You have taught mankind to seek the measure of justice
> By diving for it into their own bosoms.
> To day you have thrown off a tyranny
> That lives but by the torpid acquiescence
> Of our emasculated souls, the tyranny
> Of moralists and saints and lawgivers.
> You have obeyed the only law that wisdom
> Can ever recognize: the immediate law
> Flashed from the light of circumstances
> Upon an independent intellect.
> Henceforth new prospects ought to open on you,
> Your faculties should grow with the occasion.
>
> (III. v. 24–35)

To start with, we can echo the answers given by modern readers of *The Borderers*, who in one way or another chorus Rivers's credo. Put simply, the play appears to us to be about the birth of the philosophy of self. The most telling modern interpretations merely embed the principle of the "independent intellect" in more general contexts drawn from outside the play. There have been two main kinds of readings: those that apply late-eighteenth-century contexts to inflect the philosophy of self as moral philosophy, and those that apply nineteenth- and twentieth-century contexts to inflect it as philosophy of mind or psychology.

In the former group belongs the sustained sequence of readings initiated by George McLean Harper, Legouis, and H. W. Garrod— all concerned with the influence of Godwin's moral philosophy upon Wordsworth.[96] A late instance in this lineage is Donald G. Priestman's essay, "*The Borderers*: Wordsworth's Addenda to Godwin," which focuses on the play's development of Godwinian "conscious egoism." Associated with such readings is Peter L. Thorslev, Jr.'s, essay "Wordsworth's *Borderers* and the Romantic Villain-Hero," which adds to Godwin the context of gothic drama. Wordsworth, Thorslev argues, displays in his gothic villain-hero Oswald (Rivers), "the terrible dangers of [the] self-sufficiency of the individual mind," a danger whose "dreadful freedom implies also a dread responsibility, not to anything outside the self, but to the self itself" (p. 93). Thorslev adds an effective chorus of allusions:

[Oswald's] sense of the powers of nature serves rather to reinforce his sense of the powers of his own mind (not of the poet's mind as representative, or part of, the immanent mind of the universe, as in Wordsworth's case), and the conclusion he comes to is one which he shares with a whole tradition of Romantic hero-villains, from Milton's Satan ("the mind is its own place") to Captain Ahab, and from Manfred and Cain ("The mind will be itself / And centre of surrounding things—'tis made / To sway") to Nietzsche's *Übermensch*. (p. 95)

To the second group of readings belong those that import dialectic and/or psychoanalysis into *The Borderers*. We might instance the studies of Roger Sharrock and Hartman, which on one level privilege the issue of dramatic form. (Sharrock: "the dramatic form . . . is best suited to communicate a form of thinking that is occupied with the tensions and dynamic pressures of the human situation"; p. 171. Hartman: "*The Borderers* as a whole stands irresolutely between ancient tragedy and modern philosophical drama"; *WP*, p. 126.) But "drama," with its antithesis of agonist and antagonist, serves finally to model dialectic and philosophy of mind. As Sharrock puts it, "The drama is a drama of the mind and it only originates when the Wordsworthian man is divided against himself; Marmaduke and Oswald are the two aspects of his divided mind" (p. 175). Such psychodrama is in essence a play of thesis and antithesis dedicated to the production of synthetic idealism, or what Sharrock goes on to specify is the play's failed "moral and philosophic idealism" (p. 176). In Hartman's case, the argument of dialectic and philosophy of mind is clear: "*The Bor-*

derers, though caught between two worlds, or at least two genres, . . . is one of the first plays to focus on the subject of an intellect that has become fully conscious of its powers, including its political powers. It projects, in fact, a myth of the birth of the modern intellectual consciousness" (*WP*, p. 126). For Hartman, the importance of criminality in the play is thus that *"punishment . . . is simply life itself under the condition of consciousness"* (*WP*, p. 132) or, again, under the condition of "genuine consciousness of self" (*WP*, p. 128). The value of *The Borderers*, in sum, lies in the fact that it reveals "the perils of the soul in its passage toward individuation, or from a morality based on 'nature' to one based on the autonomous self"—at which point Hartman appends a note to Hegel's *Phenomenology of Mind* (*WP*, pp. 129, 369n).

We can close our quick survey by adding to this second group of readings R. F. Storch's fine essay "Wordsworth's *The Borderers*: The Poet as Anthropologist." By "anthropologist" Storch means that Wordsworth bridges the realms of "psychology and sociology" (p. 342). More accurately, Storch argues that Wordsworth moves from social concerns *to* psychology—specifically, to the universe of psychoanalysis that Storch elucidates as his counterpart to Hartman's universe of dialectic. The operative context is now Freud rather than Hegel; and the crucial agon is Oedipal struggle rather than the clash of thesis and antithesis:

Wordsworth's concern is not with social factions or the battle of ideas, but with energies of the mind: joy, hope, guilt, and despair. His imagination probes what the psychologist understands to be the drives behind historical movements, and behind the sense of destiny. The dramatic action of *The Borderers* takes its inception from the child's feelings towards its parents, feelings at the root of all human energy, however transformed or disguised. (p. 343)

Modern readers, in sum, have defined the "independent intellect" as "egoism," Geist, or (in a later sense) ego. The answer I add to these possibilities is not different in kind but, I believe, has priority. It has priority not because it draws upon some more absolute or *a priori* context but simply because the context it engages is historically prior and deeper. Consider that a gambit of this chapter has been to attach the analysis of family history to psychoanalysis through the liberal borrowing of certain cachets: "primal scene," "family romance," "pre-plot" (on the model of "preconscious"), "primal word," "fixation," "cathexis," "defense." An observation by Thorslev will help bring this opening gambit to its endgame: "Above all, [the Romantic villain-hero] is a rebel, first against the family and community, then against the state and the church" (pp. 92–93). Indeed, the family belongs at the head of the list of prior social institutions against which the self defines itself. The design of my cachets is to preempt modern subjectivity by subordinating it to social history.

The entire strategy of this chapter, in sum, is predicated upon the kind of inquisition into the privilege of the modern subject that Carl E. Schorske and William J. McGrath have undertaken in relation to Freud. As Schorske concludes in his chapter on "Politics and Patricide in Freud's *Interpretation of Dreams*":

The brilliant, lonely, painful discovery of psychoanalysis, which made it possible for Freud to overcome his Rome neurosis, to kneel at Minerva's ruined temple, and to regularize his academic status was a counterpolitical triumph of the first magnitude. By reducing his own political past and present to an epiphenomenal status in relation to the primal conflict between father and son, Freud gave his fellow liberals an a-historical theory of man and society that could make bearable a political world spun out of orbit and beyond control. (p. 203)

Or to choose the most relevant example, the design of this chapter is congruent with the aggressive move Mark Poster has made in his *Critical Theory of the Family* to situate Freudian (and post-Freudian) notions of self within the dynamics of historical family situations. The common strategy of such critics of psychological subjectivity is their insistence that there is no "self" except as it is shaped by a collective history necessitating the experience and theory of subjectivity in the first place: not a timeless or mythical family romance, then, but culture-specific forms of family staged in equally culture-specific genres (romance or otherwise).

So, too, dialectical philosophy of mind may be submitted to similar criticism. The politics behind Hegelian method will concern us in Chapter 8. For the moment, we can concentrate simply on the section on "The Ethical World" in the *Phenomenology*, where Hegel draws upon social history to imagine self-conscious Spirit. Particularly relevant is Hegel's discussion of the family, whose basic method can be suggested by touching upon just two passages:

Amongst the three relationships . . . of husband and wife, parents and children, brothers and sisters, the relationship of husband and wife is to begin with the primary and immediate form in which one consciousness recognizes itself in another, and in which each knows that reciprocal recognition. Being natural self-knowledge, knowledge of self on the basis of nature and not on that of ethical life, it merely represents and typifies in a figure the life of spirit, and is not spirit itself actually realized. Figurative representation, however, has its reality in an other than it is. This relationship, therefore, finds itself realized not in itself as such, but in the child—an other, in whose coming into being that relationship consists, and with which it passes away. And this change from one generation onwards to another is permanent in and as the life of a nation. (pp. 474–75)

[The relationship between brother and sister] is the limit, at which the circumscribed life of the family is broken up, and passes beyond itself. The brother is the member of the family in whom its spirit becomes individualized, and enabled thereby to turn towards another sphere, towards what is other than and external to itself, and pass over into consciousness of universality. The brother leaves this immediate, rudimentary, and, therefore, strictly speaking, negative ethical life of the family, in order to acquire and produce the concrete ethical order which is conscious of itself. (p. 477)

What is evident here is that the dialectical unfolding of Spirit in social life (of self-consciousness sublating the bond between parents into other bonds and finally the brother-sister relationship) is logically dependent on social history—on the history, specifically, that first ideologized the three nuclear bonds as exclusive. Recalling our survey of family history and demography, indeed, we can recognize that every step in Hegel's movement of Spirit toward a primogenitural individualism of outward-turning "brothers" is premised upon datable innovations in family form (for the heightened importance of the brother-sister bond after the sixteenth century, for example, see note 40 to this chapter). Freud's primal horde and Hegel's "brother," in short, stem from the same family; and it is this historically discrete family—in all its complex friction of experience and ideology —that has fostered readings of Romanticism predisposed to view the outward-turning loneliness of "independent intellect" as the symptom of psychological or phenomenological selfhood.

The Romantic self and its methodological progeny, I thus conclude, are a testament of social denial. "Rebellion," to invoke Thorslev's phrasing once more, is negation: the *adolescent* rejection of family history whose ultimate theory was repression/sublimation or *Aufhebung*. Opening to view in the conceptual middle of such formulations as Wordsworth's "the Child is Father of the Man," adolescence was the enlarged border zone of personal development whose historical discovery and early narrativization, naturalization, and ideologization (in the Prolific Energy of Blake's *Marriage of Heaven and Hell*, for example) prepared precisely for the propagation of psychoanalytic and phenomenological interpretation.

My attachment of repression/sublimation and sublation to "adolescence" is thus not pejorative but historical and analytical. Indeed, it is a precise way to phrase one crucial further aspect of social negation: if the Romantic self and its developing interpretations were denials of family history, they were also *mimetic* denials. Like an adolescent in our modern acceptation, the self attended by its psychologies and philosophies negated the confining family form only by at last incorporating that form in its deep structure. Self and its methods were the negation of family, that is, but family itself (or what I earlier called Family/Not-Family) was the precursor of negation. It was the nuclear family, as we have seen, that originally denied the multifarious and fragmented permutations of social organization to declare itself the only significant tribe. Modern selfhood then merely shrank the already counterfactual tribe into a single mind, within whose compass all the contestatory ideologies of the self's social orbits— not just parental but also kin, class, professional, and so forth—now wrestled.

It will not be excessively anachronous, perhaps, to liken Mortimer and Rivers to the heroes of our own great Romantic drama of adolescence: the cinema, whose theater and associated marginal spaces (e.g., the car, the roadside) situate one modern Border of extrafamilial socialization and individuation. Mortimer, we may say, is rebel without a cause. Or filmed more broadly: the Romantic self is the imagination of adolescent selfishness as tragic heroism; it is the agonic adolescent who acts "selfishly" and unfaithfully toward the family only because, at heart, he or she is faithful to the family's own necessary unfaithfulness to its ideals.

Historical context and literary text, I have said, pursue each other in highly specific arabesques of denial and counter-denial, in precise patterns of overdetermined and agonic no-saying to lived experience; and one of the names identifying the specificity or precision of such denial, we now see, is "I." "I," in my internal rifts and faults, am the exact denial of the rifts and faults composing the nuclear family. "I" am the figure of a family that is not just wholeness but also brokenness, not just presence but also representation or—in the most real, fatal sense possible—absence. And in my criminal fantasy life of Oedipal love and death, "I" closet within myself the lingering drama of originary absence: the history of family rupture which is also the tragedy of my own breaking into self-consciousness.

Thus did the Romantic self arise to succeed the family as the defining frame of social identity. As Poster has put it, "the family is the secret of the individual" (p. 2).[97] The family, whose historical contours Freud displaced into his version of *The Borderers*, the Oedipal drama, is what we *mean* by "self." The self is the rehabilitated family. It is the family "transported" to an inner exile.

And thus the poetry of defamiliarization, whose final intention is the perpetually frustrated effort to *re*familiarize self with the universe. We might apply here the figure of "marriage" that M. H. Abrams has studied in a Biblical context (*Natural Supernaturalism*, pp. 27, 31, 37–46) but whose social context, I suggest, is what Stone calls the "companionate marriage" of the nuclear family. As Wordsworth imagines it in the Prospectus to *The Recluse*, the defamiliarized self or mind wishes to become family once more by being "wedded to this outward frame of things / In love." But "the spousal verse / Of this great consummation" can never be realized (*Home at Grasmere*, pp. 102–4). As the death of John or of his own children told the poet, the familiarity of a universal nuclear family remains always just out of reach, purely in manuscript. In its every effort to be familiar, the Romantic self at last rediscovers its essential loneliness.

As the mate in my endgame, therefore, it is appropriate at this point to move the discovery of solitude. Recall Rivers's declaration of the "independent intellect." Framing this declaration in III.v is the will to be solitary. "I would be left alone," Mortimer responds after Rivers's speech (III.v.38). True to his opportunistic genius, Rivers then seizes the moment by rephrasing the "independent intellect" as what amounts to a whole metaphysical conceit of "solitude":

> It may be
> That some there are, squeamish, half-thinking cowards,
> Who will turn pale upon you, and call you murderer,
> And you will walk in solitude among them—
> A mighty evil! Bodies are like ropes:
> When interwoven, stronger by mutual strength.
> Thanks to our nature! 'tis not so with minds.
> Join twenty tapers of unequal height,
> And light them joined, and you will see the less
> How 'twill burn down the taller, and they all
> Shall prey upon the tallest.—Solitude!
> The eagle lives in solitude.   (III.v.43–54)

Here, we may guess, lies the origin of such passages as that on "potent" Solitude just before the Discharged Soldier episode in the 1850 *Prelude* (4.354–70). In *The Borderers*, the prototype of the Discharged Soldier is the abandoned sea captain in Rivers's autobiography:

> A man by men deserted,
> Not buried in the sand—not dead nor dying,
> But standing, walking—stretching forth his arms:
> In all things like yourselves, but in the agony
> With which he called for mercy—and even so,
> He was forsaken.   (IV.ii.44–49)

What is solitude, the Romantic version of the forsaken Christ? We can look to one of Mortimer's earliest moments of sustained introspection. After deciding to kill Herbert, he declares:

> If I ever knew
> My heart, and naked saw the man within me,
> 'Tis at this moment.—Rivers! I have loved
> To be the friend and father of the helpless,
> A comforter of sorrow—there is something
> Which looks like a *transition* in my soul,
> And yet it is not.   (II.i.87–93)

Solitude is the interiorization of family feeling. It is the moment in which the self cuts itself off from those for whom it had felt familiar love in order to look into its own heart and there, invisibly, reconstitute love (thus Mortimer's emphasis on a change of heart that is not a change). Proof positive of such interiorization is the daughter of the betrayed sea captain. After hearing of her father's death,

> She neither saw nor heard as others do,
> But in a fearful world of her own making
> She lived—cut off from the society
> Of every rational thing—her father's skeleton.
>
> (IV.ii.86–89)

Amputated of family feeling, the sea captain's daughter creates a widow's walk of solitude, an interior world. Or to give this world the title we must finally arrive upon, she displaces family feeling into the world of "imagination." Here is a sketch of Rivers offered by one of Mortimer's gang:

> restless minds,
> Such minds as find amid their fellow men
> No heart that loves them, none that they can love,
> Will turn, perforce, and seek for sympathies
> In dim relations to imagined beings.
>
> (III.iv.33–37)

Solitude is the social history of Imagination.

The king on the chessboard that my mate is at last designed to take, of course, is Mortimer, whose "transportation" from the world of human feeling on the final page leaves him in a lonely "mere intensity of thought." At the very close of the play, Mortimer sentences himself to what we may conceive as the epiphany of solitude:

> No prayers, no tears, but hear my doom in silence!
> I will go forth a wanderer on the earth,
> A shadowy thing, and as I wander on
> No human ear shall ever hear my voice,
> No human dwelling ever give me food
> Or sleep or rest, and all the uncertain way
> Shall be as darkness to me, as a waste
> Unnamed by man! and I will wander on
> Living by mere intensity of thought,
> A thing by pain and thought compelled to live,
> Yet loathing life, till heaven in mercy strike me
> With blank forgetfulness—that I may die.
>
> (V.iii.264–75)

Such is the Epiphany of the Magus we know as the Romantic self. The self is not a Coming of the Magi to that still, rapt scene in the manger where once rested the type of the nuclear-family/not-nuclear-family. It is instead a Going of the Magi, a flight from the manger of contemporary family history.

To point down the road we must now pursue, it will be helpful to view Lucy, the child in the manger of the *Lyrical Ballads*. I reask the old question, "where is the body?"—that is, what is Lucy and is there a referential or interpretable sense to these poems at all?[98] The answer I hazard is partial and meant only to socialize the moment of shock at the heart of all these poems and their affiliates—the moment of sudden, but also strangely foreknown and so gentled, horror. Viewed in the context of rural social history, "Lucy" is the evidence of a particularly fatal fostering of children. I refer to the fosterage of the personification Wordsworth names "Nature." Here, for example, is Nature as the foster mother of Lucy in a poem of 1799:

> Three years she grew in sun and shower,
> Then Nature said, "A lovelier flower
> On earth was never sown;
> This Child I to myself will take;
> She shall be mine, and I will make
> A Lady of my own." (*PW*, 2: 214–15)

There is strange sympathy, I suggest, between the beautifully colored "hill of moss" "like an infant's grave in size" in "The Thorn," the "violet by a mossy stone" prefacing Lucy's grave in "She Dwelt Among the Untrodden Ways," and the lovely "flower" Nature gathers to herself here in "Three Years She Grew in Sun and Shower." Lucy as "natural" child is the body of Lakeland bastardy. The concealment of the body is Nature: the personification of the unspeakable practices that produce natural children and then make them disappear. What does it mean for Nature to foster Lucy? It means to kill her. On one level, "Three Years She Grew in Sun and Shower" is about a natural death miming, and denying, child exposure.[99]

The road we must take is signposted "lyric," the new home of the Wordsworthian self in its fugitive flight from social history. How does the poet move from a work like *The Borderers* to lyric?

The possibility for such movement lies in a fact that readers have agreed upon: *The Borderers* is a bad play (see Hartman, *WP*, p. 125; Sharrock, p. 170; Storch, "Wordsworth's *The Borderers*," p. 340; Thorslev, p. 103; Wüscher, p. 70). The reviews are in part deserved.[100] But I would add this qualification: *The Borderers* intends to be a bad play. It does so in this special sense: it is the very principle of "intent" or subjectivity in the play that drives it from accepted form into a "closet" of drama where all action halts in paralyzed asides of the self (cf. Hartman, *WP*, p. 126, on the irresolute status of the play between tragedy and philosophical drama). *The Borderers* is a bad drama, I suggest, because the self intends lyric. The self, that is, demands expression not as tragic Mortimer but as the lyric persona soon to be epitomized in the speaker of the Lucy poems. In "Strange Fits of Passion Have I Known," for example, a lover's proleptic bereavement exiles him from the haunts of the familiar and leaves him only with the passive core of Mortimer's character, consciousness of self:

> What fond and wayward thoughts will slide
> Into a Lover's head!
> "O mercy!" *to myself* I cried,
> "If Lucy should be dead!"
> (*PW*, 2: 29; italics mine)

If drama is the discourse of interlocutors, we may say, then lyric transforms drama into a discourse in which there are no true interlocutors, only the locution that is the self and certain mute circumlocutions (e.g., Coleridge, Dorothy) standing in place of the chorus. Or again, self at last discourses only with itself via the great circumlocution of self to come: Nature elevated from the metonymy of "friend" into the self's "symbol," from Sensibility personification, that is, into what I will study in Chapter 7 as the Romantic "image."

From the first, in sum, the tug of self unravels tragedy in *The Borderers* and urges it toward some further form, some "transform" that will know how to deploy static soliloquies in rapt devotions of imagery. But closet drama by itself, of course, is not lyric. How to realize the lyric possibility in such drama, and so change theater props into imagery?

It would be possible at this point to socialize the rise of Wordsworthian lyric much as Ian Watt socialized the rise of the novel: by looking at the precondition of closet drama, the "closet" itself or private reading chamber. Actual "closets" akin to those in the Georgian large houses Watt considers (p. 188) do not appear to have been a feature of Lakeland architecture either in the homes of the yeomen or of the lower gentry. But one analogue is suggestive. As Brunskill's study of architecture in the area shows, some yeoman cottages at the close of the eighteenth century added onto the stock plan such features as "outshuts" (a rear extension on the ground floor) and two-room deep construction (on both floors). The final result was that individual bedrooms could be partitioned off on the top level ("Small House," pp. 181–87).[101] Private space was coming to be.

Of course, such space apart reflected not only desire for privacy but also increased prosperity. This is the aspect of the problem of privacy, of selfhood, that must now become our central concern: the economics of the Romantic self and its destined form. What the architectural precondition of closet drama presages is that Wordsworth's "lyric" will arise from a context of economic history complementing the family history that conceives his "self." Consider, for example, the letter the poet wrote to Fox in 1801 recommending *Lyrical Ballads*. Praising the Lakes yeomen under the mythic, neologistic title, "statesmen,"[102] the letter specifies that the leading features of the class were family affection and an "independence" grounded in a certain kind of property holding:

In the two Poems, "The Brothers" and "Michael" I have attempted to draw a picture of the domestic affections as I know they exist amongst a class of men who are now almost confined to the North of England. They are small independent *proprietors* of land here called statesmen, men of respectable education who daily labour on their own little properties. The domestic affections will always be strong amongst men who live in a country not crowded with population, if these men are placed above poverty. But if they are proprietors of small estates, which have descended to them from their ancestors, the power which these affections will acquire amongst such men is inconceivable by those who have only had an opportunity of observing hired labourers, farmers, and the manufacturing Poor. Their little tract of land serves as a kind of permanent rallying point for their domestic feelings. . . . It is a fountain fitted to the nature of social man from which supplies of affection, as pure as his heart was intended for, are daily drawn. (*Letters*, 1: 314–15)

Just as Wordsworth thinks "self" on the basis of family history, so he will express that self in a form conceived on the basis of his growing interest in economic history. In economic terms, selfhood is "independence." And the text of independence is an economy of lyric told in bright, shining coins of imagery.

But to study the economy of lyric, we need to look not to prosperous yeoman cottages with their outshuts and additions so much as to their inverse: a ruined cottage.

CHAPTER SEVEN

The Economy of Lyric:
The Ruined Cottage

THE GREAT DISCOVERY OF *The Ruined Cottage* (begun in 1797; MS. B by early March 1798) was the "image."[1] Attended by a theory of natural vision, the image for the first time became a separate principle of form not only fundamental but exclusive in generating Wordsworth's meaning. Or, at least, such was the belief, whose aggressive teacher in the poem is the Pedlar: "no longer read / The forms of things with an unworthy eye," he says at the end, pointing to the celebrated "spear-grass" and its "image of tranquillity." In such imagery lies meaning beyond expression. "She sleeps in the calm earth," the Pedlar glosses simply (*RC*, p. 277).* "She" is Margaret. Yet like Donne's inexpressible "Shee" in the "Anniversaries," "she" is also the spirit of universal "cohaerence." What the Pedlar would make our eyes worthy of reading is that "she"—expressed at last only in her cottage and garden—is the very principle of enduring coherence that the poem also names the "bond of brotherhood" or "humanity."

At our present critical moment, however, it is hard to distinguish the Pedlar's reading of imagery—and so ultimately of humanity—from that of the New Criticism. As Frank Kermode's *Romantic Image* suggests, New Criticism caps what is essentially a single tradition of

---

* Citation of *The Ruined Cottage* in this chapter is as follows: verses from my primary text, the Reading Text of MS. B in *RC* (based on DC MS. 17), are cited by line number; verses from the draftwork added to MS. B immediately after its Reading Text stage (reproduced in facsimile and transcription in *RC*) as well as other material and apparatus in *RC* are cited by page number. For a guide to the composition and manuscripts of *The Ruined Cottage*, see *RC*, pp. x–xii, 7–35, 130–31; and *CEY*, pp. 337–39.

concern with the image and its apotheosis, the symbol (pp. 155–59).[2] To read Jonathan Wordsworth's *Music of Humanity* with its sensitive observation of "symbolic details" in *The Ruined Cottage*, for example, is thus to know that it is precisely "close reading" that has most loved the humanity of imagery.[3] Put in terms dating to the nativity of New Criticism, imagery rests upon an irreducible poetic quantum, the "icon," which "resembles" its referential object. John Crowe Ransom's analysis in his *The New Criticism* (1941) is especially useful. Normal discourse refers to only one "value-property" of the referent, Ransom argues, but "aesthetic discourse" refers by means of iconic resemblances themselves on the "ontological" order of the object and so themselves as universally full of possible values as real particulars. "The icon is a particular," Ransom stresses, and "a particular has too many properties, and too many values," to be restricted to precise significance (p. 291).[4] Denotation of a single meaning, therefore, cannot be privileged over metaphorical connotation of others, and the icon perpetually opens out into what Wellek and Warren—in their sliding scale of "image, metaphor, symbol, myth"—identify as figuration or "tropology" (p. 186).

The true value or property of an iconic image, we might sum up, is its tendency always to exceed reference through unaccountable acts of appropriation. Compounded as "indeterminacy" and "texture," "paradox" and "irony," "tension" and "ambiguity,"[5] such unaccountability at last projects, in place of the humanity the Pedlar finds in rustic society, the purified pluralism of a new humanism originally rooted in the Southern Fugitive and Agrarian movement.[6]

The result of superimposing New Critical vision over the Romantic image of humanity is mystification. Close readers of *The Ruined Cottage* have thus tended to grow misty-eyed about "humanity" to such an extent that the term has become a purely inflationary valorization communicating much feeling but virtually no (or, what is the same, too much) meaning.[7] The only way to read Wordsworth's image of humanity with precision, I suggest, will be to undermine the illusion that humanity can be a timeless personality spanning without difference from Romanticism to our own century. We need to find a strategy, in other words, by which to read through the unchanging "icon" to humanity as a historical formation.

I propose a tactics of disillusion. Rather than resist conflating the Pedlar's worthy "reading" with close reading, I will commit a deception and begin as if engaged upon a full-scale New Critical analysis. But I will do so with final emphasis on the structure of imagery so as to prepare for a further maneuver, which will not be deconstruction, but the kind of historical reconstruction Levinson has named deconstructive materialism (*Wordsworth's Great Period Poems*, p. 9). The maneuver will become possible when close reading shocks itself out of close reading. Where Ransom has opened our close reading of imagery, Cleanth Brooks will finish it by discovering with shock that such reading fails to account specifically for *The Ruined Cottage* and a humanity that suddenly seems, from a differentiated viewpoint, inhuman. Only at this point will the historical form of Wordsworthian humanity emerge, signaling the need to turn our gaze from the iconic text to the context generating the need for imagery in the first place.

Why imagery? This is an inquiry into poetic kind as well: why lyric? The great ruin recorded by Wordsworth's poem, perhaps, is that of his earliest kinds: description in *An Evening Walk* and *Descriptive Sketches*, narrative in *Salisbury Plain*, then drama in *The Borderers*. As has been remarked by others, *The Ruined Cottage* is at best a sort of fossilized narrative or drama.[8] Eliding action and sinking all dialogic tension into monologue, the poem ruins Aristotelian tragedy and returns us to Wordsworth's earliest land of description. Or, rather, it returns us to description defamiliarized into a collage of disassociated souvenirs and bric-a-brac (epitomized in the broken bowl the Pedlar singles out at one point).

The bricolage that pieces this universe together again is Wordsworthian lyric. Generated along a series of short, haunting still lifes of imagery, *The Ruined Cottage* is a record of the early evolution of Romantic lyric—of the kind of experimental poetry Coleridge was already writing and Wordsworth himself would soon attempt in his first sustained period of short poems immediately after the completion of MS. B. The stem that reaches from the "long lank weeds" of Coleridge's "This Lime-Tree Bower My Prison" (July 1797) to the "spear-grass" in Wordsworth's *Ruined Cottage*, in other words, will at last effloresce in such posies of imagery as follows:

> all at once I saw a crowd,
> A host, of golden daffodils;
> Beside the lake, beneath the trees,
> Fluttering and dancing in the breeze.
>
> . . .
>
> I gazed—and gazed—but little thought
> What wealth the show to me had brought.
>
> (*PW*, 2: 216)

To appreciate lyric imagery, as we will see, is indeed to value strange "gold" and "wealth."

The Value of Imagery

The Tropics of Revision

MS. B begins upon a dream of imagery copied with variation from the noon prospect of *An Evening Walk*:

> Twas Summer; and the sun was mounted high.
> Along the south the uplands feebly glared
> Through a pale steam, and all the northern downs
> In clearer air ascending shewed their brown
> And [   ] surfaces distinct with shades
> Of deep embattled clouds that lay in spots
> Determined and unmoved, with steady beams
> Of clear and pleasant sunshine interposed;
> Pleasant to him who on the soft cool grass
> Extends his careless limbs beside the root
> Of some huge oak whose aged branches make
> A twilight of their own, a dewy shade
> Where the wren warbles, while the dreaming man,
> Half conscious of that soothing melody,
> With sidelong eye looks out upon the scene,
> By those impending branches made [   ]
> More soft and distant.   (ll. 1–17)

Picturesque description seems to revive with all its repose. Yet the resemblance to the earlier poem also harbors difference—most noticeably in the replacement of the scene at Rydal Lower Falls by an arboreal enclosure with roots in Marvell, Thomson, and topographical tradition. In this enclosure traditionally reserved for the "amused" or musing seer, Wordsworth reveals that description turns upon a genius not so much of repose as of re-vision.[9] This genius is the "dreaming man" who looks through foliage with "sidelong eye." By means of revision (whose early type was the eye reposed on its secret bridge in *An Evening Walk*), landscape becomes an *image* of landscape projected upon an "impending" screen of vegetation. It becomes a green thought in a green shade whose softening and distancing effect is dream stuff.

Without revision, the scene would not please. Proof is the Poet,* who enters in stark counterview to introduce a reality of blind spots. One blind spot, which we may call an origin of the need for imagery,

---

* The "Poet," of course, is unnamed in MS. B. However, I follow J. Wordsworth in naming him professionally for convenience in discussing what I will call Wordsworth's "vocational imagination." Dorothy, we may note, referred to this character as the "Poet" (*Letters*, 1: 200).

is the architecture of the ruined cottage itself, which centers the populous order of artifacts, utensils, and tools in the poem (fragment of a
bowl, well, garden wall, footstone, cornerstones, loom, and so on).
Seeking refuge upon a "bare wide Common" as empty as the Ancient Mariner's "wide wide sea," the Poet comes upon an arboreal
enclosure that merely compresses agoraphobia into claustrophobia.
"I rose," he says,

> and turned towards a group of trees
> Which midway in the level stood alone,
> And thither come at length, beneath a shade
> Of clustering elms that sprang from the same root
> I found a ruined Cottage, four clay walls
> That stared upon each other.—'Twas a spot!
> (ll. 26–31)

Ruin is stopped sight: "four clay walls / That stared upon each other."

The other blind spot is Margaret, who centers the order of persons. Margaret is also stopped sight. "Her gentle looks" once refreshed the traveler (l. 153), the Pedlar recalls, but on his first visit
after Robert's disappearance, she "looked" at him "a little while" before turning away speechlessly (ll. 306–7) and, a little later, gave him
a desperate "look" that seemed to "cling" (ll. 314–15). The outlook
is dim. Thereafter, Margaret looks once with "brighter eye" (l. 339)
and then closes her eyes. The Pedlar mourns, "evermore / Her eye-
lids drooped, her eyes were downward cast" and "she did not look
at me" (ll. 415–18). After the Pedlar's four visits in the poem, Margaret ends in a paralyzed stare: "evermore her eye / Was busy in the
distance, shaping things / Which made her heart beat quick" (ll. 491–
93).[10] Searching for a vision never to appear, she is as much an origin
of the need for imagery as the wall-eyed cottage.

Knowing the origin of the need for imagery, as well as the sidelong
glance through vegetation capable of propagating imagery, we have
all that is needed to generate the rest of the poem. Wordsworth must
find a way to plant what I will call the vegetable "tropics" of the
revisionary eye around his blind spots. Only through the trope of
vegetation can he re-see his twin sites of emptiness as sights of being.
And only so, as we will see, can he then communicate the burden
of his poem: humanity. If the two centers of revisionary being can
be made to look toward each other by means of overlapping imagery,
then a sense of human community will revive.

To give the argument of imagery authority, however, Wordsworth
must first transplant the "sidelong eye" from vegetable slumber into
full consciousness. He must first, in other words, make the "dreaming man" wake into the Pedlar in such a way that the latter is *not*
what he himself fears to be thought: merely a "dreamer among men"

(l. 289).[11] Like the dreaming man beside his "root," after all, or Rousseau associated with a similar root in Shelley's *Triumph of Life*, the Pedlar seems merely to vegetate when he first crops up on his bench. He is literally defined by a fret of moss: "Stretched on a bench whose edge with short bright moss / Was green and studded o'er with fungus flowers" (ll. 37–38). Without extra work by the poem at this point, our next view of the Pedlar on the bench (ll. 105–10) would then simply confirm the triumph of dream: where the "dreaming man" had eyed the world through the shade of impending branches, the Pedlar is such a camera obscura that he can lie on the bench with "eyes . . . shut" while the pure revisionism of vegetation impresses itself directly: "The shadows of the breezy elms above / Dappled his face."

To differentiate a principle of conscious revision from vegetable dreamwork, the poem inserts between our two views of the Pedlar on the bench his biography, which, as Diane C. Macdonell puts it, validates the "second-order sign system" of "visual language" to come in the poem ("Place of the Device," p. 432; Macdonell's argument on pp. 433–37 is relevant to my following discussion). The first purpose of the biography is to demonstrate the reality of revisionism. Specifically, it shows the Pedlar to possess "eyes" of such intensity that they emulate the sun,[12] the fount of Platonic reality in a shady universe. Immediately after our first view of the Pedlar on the bench, the poem thus recalls a scene from the day previous when he stood vertically with "eyes . . . turned / Towards the setting sun" (ll. 42–43). Then the biography plunges fully into the past to root his eyes in a phenomenology of brilliance, verticality, and depth standing for essential reality.[13] The Pedlar, we learn, had always had a "luminous eye" (l. 49), an "eye / Flashing poetic fire" (ll. 70–71), and an "eye which evermore / Looked deep into the shades of difference / As they lie hid in all exterior forms" (ll. 94–96).

Much of what may be called the "supertext" of MS. B then accomplishes the second purpose of the biography. The basic text of MS. B consists of 528 lines written by early March 1798. But immediately after completing these lines, Wordsworth added leaf after leaf of revisions consisting mainly of drafts and insertions that expand the Pedlar's biography and a series of concluding drafts attempting the "moral addendum" to the poem.[14] The expanded biography illuminates the true meaning of the link between the Pedlar's eye and the sun: the real sun powering his eye is "mind." In his youth, the Pedlar attained "an *active* power to fasten images / Upon his brain, & on their pictured lines / Intensely brooded"; "from the power of a peculiar eye / Or by creative feeling overborne," he "traced an ebbing and a flowing mind"; "Nature and his spirit was on fire / With restless thoughts—his eye became disturb'd"; and he began to scan "the laws of light" themselves "with a strange pleasure of disquietude" (*RC*, pp. 153, 153–55, 171, 173).

Only after thus rooting the Pedlar's eyes in conscious reality does Wordsworth allow them to open—or rather to flower. The Pedlar rises from his bench and "points" to a vegetable image of the ability to stare at the sun: the sunflower (l. 114). Now, however, we have been reminded of his mind and so can differentiate conscious revision from vegetable dream. Without a mind able to view imagery from across an interval of reflection, after all, it would not be possible to point at all. More than anything else, the Pedlar is he who "points out" images to consciousness. He is the great archivist able to index, cross-index, and interpret the tropics of revision. After pointing out the sunflower, he can thus deliver the poem's great credo of revision: "I see around me [   ] / Things which you cannot see" (ll. 129–30). Imagine that the blank in the MS. here emblematizes the blind spots of the ruined cottage and Margaret. By means of his sunny mind, the Pedlar can fill blankness with a sense of being so convincing that it requires no more evidence than a screenwork, a trope of vegetation heliotroping all around.[15]

The heliotrope marks the spot of access over the garden wall (ll. 113–16) and so—as in *Paradise Lost* when Satan bounds over the wall—the opening of the tale proper. From this point on, the Pedlar throws around the blind spots of the cottage and Margaret one luxuriant still life after another, each superimposing sidelong images of vegetation over our direct vision of artifacts and persons. In some of the most luxuriant still lifes, vegetation tropes persons. Weeds, spear-grass, and nettles "sun" themselves where Margaret once nursed her infant (ll. 162–65). Honeysuckle "crowded" around the door, and bindweed spread "his" bells while border tufts "straggled out into the paths" (ll. 366–77). Most poignantly, an apple tree with an encircling chain of straw (ll. 458–61) predicts Margaret with her "belt of flax" (ll. 496–98). "I fear it will be dead and gone / Ere Robert come again," Margaret says about the tree of her paradise lost, making it impossible for us to see it as anything but her image (ll. 464–65). Other still lifes show vegetation troping artifacts. Hedgerows of willow boughs, for example, create a "damp cold nook" exactly like the well they harbor (ll. 122–24), and spilled books with "straggling leaves" resemble the disorder of the garden (ll. 443–48). Vegetation, in sum, substitutes for the human being and the human place. To use the language of Keats's "To Autumn," the universe of human fall is plumped out with ripeness to the core.

By the time the poem ends, the husks of persons and artifacts then resemble not only vegetation but, through the commutative power of vegetation, each other. Because Robert no longer repaired its thatch with "fresh bands of straw," the cottage fell apart in "frost, and thaw, and rain." Simultaneously, Margaret—whose link with straw had just been cinched by her double, the apple tree—suffered "nightly damps" and winds that ruffled her "tattered clothes" (ll. 512–22). Artifact and person, cottage and Margaret, disintegrate to leave a straw of pure resemblance in the middle. Ripeness is all.

The "moral addendum" in the supertext then harvests the most famous of such scarecrow images allowing persons and artifacts to trope together. The Pedlar instructs his acolyte, the Poet (in a somewhat simplified version of the manuscript transcription):

> no longer read
> The forms of things with an unworthy eye
> She sleeps in the calm earth & peace is here
> I well remember that those very plumes
> Those weeds & the high spear-grass on that wall
> By mist & silent rain-drops silvered o'er
> As once I passed did to my heart convey
> So still an image of tranquillity
> So calm & still and looked so beautiful
> Amid the uneasy thoughts which filled my mind
> That what we feel of sorrow & despair
> From ruin & from change & all the grief
> The passing shews of being leave behind
> Appeared an idle dream that could not live
> Where meditation was.
>
> (*RC*, pp. 277–79)

This passage could virtually replace Coleridge's "To the River Otter" as W. K. Wimsatt's paradigm in his chapter on "Romantic Nature Imagery" in *The Verbal Icon*. Like the "bright transparence" of waters in Coleridge's sonnet, we may say, the silvery sheen on the spear-grass interposes a mirror upon which "forms of things" reflect an increasingly mercurial "image of tranquillity," a film of affiliation akin to what Lindenberger has called Wordsworth's "images of interaction" (*On Wordsworth's "Prelude,"* pp. 69–98). On this film, persons and artifacts condense together in a single dream of vegetation. Strange sympathy thus allies the tranquil spear-grass to the "sleeping" Margaret, while strange convenience (to use Foucault's term for resemblance by proximity; *Order of Things*, pp. 18–19) joins the spear-grass to the ruined wall. Person and ruin commune beneath the weed that is their living monument, icon, or image. Predicted earlier in the poem in the tear the Pedlar notices in his own eye (l. 250), such imagery washed in "silent rain-drops" is nothing less than the ichor of revisionism, the very sap of a vegetable tropics forced by the sun. Immediately after the image of spear-grass in the poem, the sun shoots "a slant & mellow radiance" as if the blinding genius of sidelong revision had revealed itself at last (*RC*, p. 279). "Look" in such a fluid, brilliant way as to "read" the images of things, the Pedlar says, in sum, and dead persons and ruined artifacts will flourish together again.

We are now in a position to read the humanity of the Pedlar's imagery. Persons themselves cannot be humanity in this sense. Only relations, affiliations, or—conceived semiotically—communications of care can be humanity. In the paradise remembered by *The Ruined Cottage*, humanity once communicated itself during most of each day in the cares of labor—in the relation of person to artifact, the hand to the universe of its tools, utensils, products, and domicile.[16] Looking at the garden well at one point, the Pedlar recalls,

> the bond
> Of brotherhood is broken—time has been
> When every day the touch of human hand
> Disturbed their stillness, and they ministered
> To human comfort.   (ll. 136–40)

Such care, or, in the poem's own language, bonding, between persons and artifacts did not so much displace the humanity we might normally expect to reside in familial bonding—between husband and wife, for example—as immerse family in the lover's touch of a weaver on his loom or of a housewife on the waters of a well. If humanity were a Saussurean sign, the care a person takes with a tool would be the signifier, or articulation, and the signified would be the care persons express for each other.

Now, in the ruined present of the poem, the "bond of brotherhood" is no more. Predictive is the fragment on "The Baker's Cart" linked to the origins of *The Ruined Cottage* in MS. A. As a baker's cart passes by her famished children, a woman much like Margaret declares, "That waggon does not care for us" (*RC*, p. 463). Just so, the full meal of care once articulated by the bond with artifacts in *The Ruined Cottage* ends piecemeal in what we can call the layoff of its signifier. No longer able to signify his care through the bond of labor, Robert must desert the social meaning of that bond, marriage, in favor of a new bond with the army. Margaret similarly breaks the bonds of motherhood to bond her eldest child to the parish (ll. 403–5).[17] The bonds of human care scatter like fragments of a broken bowl.

How can the meaning of humanity survive the dismissal of its signifier? The answer, of course, lies in a strangely laborless trope of vegetation. As divined in the leaves, the relation between persons and artifacts must now be seen to be a bond of affiliative vision—of "convenient" and sympathetic imagery—rather than of labor in the first place (as shown in Fig. 11). Imagery as a structure of resemblance, in other words, is powered by an inner structure of displacement

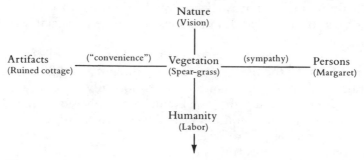

FIG. 11. The structure of Romantic nature imagery in *The Ruined Cottage*.

(represented by the vertical axis in Fig. 11): in place of the labor once bonding persons and artifacts together to articulate humanity, let there now be a splendidly tranquil or effortless vision of humanity as Nature. Let human culture, in other words, be cultivated such that the only work necessary will be a dreamwork/branchwork of visual resemblance, a look-alike of Nature's own effortless work: pure being. The vegetation iconic of such work, we notice, proliferates across all boundaries precisely in the total absence of labor, which, as in Milton's paradise, would trim, lop, define.[18]

Humanity, in sum, revives as spontaneously and effortlessly as a weed. Just before the Pedlar invokes the spear-grass, his auditor, the Poet, identifies the secret race of such humanity:

> Yet still towards the cottage did I turn
> Fondly & trace with nearer interest
> That secret spirit of humanity
> Which 'mid the calm oblivious tendencies
> Of nature, 'mid her plants, her weeds & flowers
> And silent overgrowings still survived.
>
> (*RC*, pp. 275–77)

The Well Wrought Ruin

But now the turn in my argument: *there is also something shockingly dehumanizing about imagery.* The humanity of spear-grass, as it were, sticks in the craw. I turn for guidance here to Cleanth Brooks, whose own lifelong love of imagery reaches a sticking point precisely in the encounter with *The Ruined Cottage*. My reference is to what seems to me still the single most compelling study of the poem to date (in its form as *The Excursion*, Book 1), Brooks's "Wordsworth and Human Suffering: Notes on Two Early Poems," first published in 1965.[19] Brooks shrinks from concluding that Wordsworth compensates for human suffering only with "rich" images composing a "total pattern" of Nature or Art. Reflecting upon the "image of tranquillity" at the end, he asks with relentless inquisition,

Is Wordsworth saying here that, seen in the full perspective of nature, seen as a portion of nature's beautiful and unwearied immortality, Margaret with her sorrows is simply one detail of an all-encompassing and harmonious pattern? One can, for example, look at the rabbit torn by the owl in something like this fashion, and the rabbit's agony, no longer isolated and dwelt upon in itself, may cease to trouble us when understood as a necessary part of a total pattern, *rich* and various and finally harmonious, in which even the rabbit's pain becomes not a meaningless horror since it partakes of the beauty of the whole. ("Wordsworth," pp. 385–86; italics mine)

Brooks rejects this first solution as inhuman and goes on to suggest that Wordsworth might really be demonstrating the "reconciliation of suffering in the aesthetic vision":

I should describe this latter in something like this fashion: man is so various, so wonderful, capable of so much triumph and agony, suffering and joy, malice and goodness, that if one can take his stance far enough away from the individual case to allow him to see life in its wholeness, with all its *rich* variety—if one can do that, he can accept not only suffering but active wickedness as an inevitable and necessary part of the human drama, and can even rejoice in it as a testimony to the depths of man's feeling and his power to experience and endure. ("Wordsworth," p. 386; italics mine)

Yet Brooks at last rejects this "rich" vision of suffering as well with a barely concealed scorn reminiscent of Dr. Johnson's review of Soame Jenyns ("Wordsworth," pp. 386–87).

Brooks's protest, we should realize, is especially powerful because it questions all that his early criticism valued as rich. For "richness" in the above quotes, we can read "paradox," "irony," or what I earlier called "unaccountability" in general; and for "total pattern," the "unity" or whole treasure house of "imagery." What Brooks sees in Wordsworth's ruin is the unmaking of *The Well Wrought Urn*. The early Brooks took his first examples from a pair of Wordsworth sonnets (*Well Wrought Urn*, pp. 3–7) before canonizing Donne's poem as the pattern of poetry ("Countries, Townes, Courts: Beg from above / A patterne of your love!"). In his Wordsworth chapter, Brooks then identified the richness of poetic pattern specifically as imagery:

In reading the poem [the "Intimations" Ode], I shall emphasize the imagery primarily, and the success or relative failure with which Wordsworth meets in trying to make his images carry and develop his thought. (*Well Wrought Urn*, p. 126)

But if the type of analysis to which we have subjected the "Ode" is calculated to indicate . . . deficiencies by demanding a great deal of the imagery, it is only fair to remind the reader that it focuses attention on the brilliance and power of the imagery. (pp. 149–50)

As he then concludes in the chapter on "The Heresy of Paraphrase," the beauty of poems inheres in their "total pattern" (p. 194), and such pattern—visible in the case of Wordsworth primarily as imagery—cannot be accounted for in referential discourse because "immediately the imagery and the rhythm seem to set up tensions with it, warping and twisting it, qualifying and revising it" (p. 197). Such is Brooks's account of the verbal icon.

Two decades later, however, the unaccountable "richness" of imagery is no longer rewarding. When *persons* such as Margaret become patterns in an imagery wholly distanced from normal human concerns, equanimity in the face of suffering seems inhuman. Playing figuratively upon "richness," we might say that the urn of poetry suddenly seems unearned: it is a cheat, a fraudulent account of human poverty able to create a luxury of nature or art with no usable cultural value at all. If poetry is rich, in other words, then its value arises like the Phoenix in Donne's poem. It springs up either in immaculate remove from the realities devaluing culture (from the "owl" subjecting culture to raw nature in Brooks's metaphor) or, even more inhuman, perhaps precisely in concealment of the fact that poetic richness is "urned" by preying upon cultural value.

It is here at last, in the account of poetry's *value* relative to culture, that we reach the heart of Brooks's objection. Significantly, he later reprinted his study in a collection of his works headed by an essay on "The Uses of Literature" (written a year before the Wordsworth essay). The goal of "The Uses of Literature" is to determine the link of usage between poetic and cultural value: "The knowledge that literature gives, we might say, is always knowledge of a value-structured world, not the abstract world of the mathematician or the physicist but a world conceived in human terms" ("Uses of Literature," p. 11). Shock in Brooks's subsequent reading of *The Ruined Cottage* comes from realizing that appreciation of the poem's rich imagery seems to require suppressing all thought of useful value. These questions of use, we can now notice, initiate his analysis: "Why is the younger man [the Poet] calmed and strengthened by the Wanderer's [Pedlar's] recital of Margaret's sufferings? Why does the Wanderer feel that the 'purposes of wisdom' are served by attendance on her story? What consolation was there for Margaret herself?" ("Wordsworth," p. 382). These questions Brooks cannot answer. When he then immediately thinks of De Quincey's objection that the Pedlar "would have done better to give Margaret some cash rather than mere sympathy," he reaches the bottom line: "richness" is useless ("Wordsworth," p. 382).[20]

Remember the Pedlar's instructions for reading imagery: "no longer read / The forms of things with an unworthy eye." Here is the bottom line of our question, "why imagery?": how much is "rich" imagery "worth" in usable cash? What is the cultural use or value to be gained in piling up "total patterns" of images? What is the cash value of spear-grass?

A discrimination, perhaps, is in order here. We should notice that the objection Brooks develops is not finally philistine. Put in a way that extends the conceit of "riches" even further, the point is not that the imagery of spear-grass must actually be reduced to hard cash. The point is that any legitimate commerce between culture and poetry requires *some* medium of exchange, some pricing mechanism based on a demonstrable, earnable, and commonly held "cash" of human value allowing cultural and poetic premiums to be weighed alike. Only so could poetic value be validated. In the absence or deliberate concealment of such a medium of worth—most literally but not exclusively the cash once earned in the world of *The Ruined Cottage* by labor—there can be no accountable method by which to understand the cultural value that poetry speculates upon, the profit to be gained, and so, ultimately, the motive or deep *why* of the imagery Wordsworth discovered to be his talent in early 1798.

Or more exactly, there would be no way to trust in poetry's account of its value unless we already knew from the first, as if on the basis of some blind trust fund, how much poetic talent is worth. Imagery that conceals the source of its riches is at last compelled to draw for speculative trust only from the already converted. Put another way, such icons as spear-grass—whose worth the Pedlar makes no attempt to account for in open terms—are religious in nature. Such imagery has the shibbolethic quality of allegory as Michael Murrin has analyzed it (pp. 18–53). Like the holy of holies behind the veil of the Jerusalem Temple, spear-grass is an icon whose unrevealed worth has the effect of separating believers from nonbelievers, the sheep from the goats (or perhaps the parable should be reversed, since only goats, presumably, would find nourishment in spear-grass).

Brooks at last simply blesses Wordsworth's image of humanity, extending infinite credit in the form of religious tolerance. Inspired by doctrinal refinements in *The Excursion*, Brooks ends, "In any case, the view of human suffering taken by [the Pedlar] is much more than what I have called the aesthetic vision. It is deeply tinged with religion" (though Brooks immediately qualifies that the religion is not specifically Christian; "Wordsworth," p. 387). Where there can be no account of the sources of poetic richness, perhaps we should simply believe. But MS. B of *The Ruined Cottage* is still void of the religiosity added most strikingly to the conclusion of *The Excursion*, Book 1, in 1845. How can *we* brook the humanity of spear-grass? Is there, indeed, any provable cash or demonstration of commonly held value backing up the humanity of imagery other than the stuff of famine?

We spy here seeds of the deconstruction of the icon succeeding New Criticism, of the criticism that has no avowed God-term and whose talent is iconoclasm. De Man writes in an early essay on the Romantic image: "The existence of the poetic image is itself a sign of divine absence" ("Intentional Structure," p. 6).

Yet there are alternatives to thinking about the concealed or absent value of imagery in deconstructive terms. The great forms of absence are historical. If the medium of exchange between cultural and poetic values is absent, I suggest, the best way to define such absence is as itself a medium of exchange, as a "value" formed in a moment of historical transition when old values disappear and new ones have yet to be recognized. In order to assess such value in the imagery of *The Ruined Cottage*, we will need to begin afresh by converting our figure into the ground. The figure is the commercial conceit I have already tendered on the basis of Brooks's "richness." "Rich" is so far from being accidental in Brooks's critical vocabulary that it is virtually a verbal tic; and, generally, the vein of "richness" (and such associated terms as "wealth" and "profit") runs so deeply in New Criticism that it constitutes the method's bedrock paradigm of poetic appreciation.[21] It will be instructive to return to Ransom's theory of imagery. From start to finish, we can now notice, his account of iconic "value-property" is underwritten by the financial imagination. The essence of an iconic image is that it is "property" that cannot be sold so as to divorce the measure of its "value" from the actual object. Ransom confirms his market metaphor in a telling note: an icon, he suggests, must not be merely something like an advertisement, an "image of a body so obviously meant for consumption, so ripe for immediate consumption, that nobody could resist knowing" its denotative "value" independent of the actual object (*New Criticism*, p. 291n).[22]

In a passage from *The Ruined Cottage*, MS. B, later applied to himself in *The Prelude*, 3.141–44, Wordsworth hawks the Pedlar's talents as follows:

> In all shapes
> He found a secret and mysterious soul,
> A fragrance and a spirit of strange meaning.
> Though poor in outward shew, he was most rich;
> He had a world about him—'twas his own,
> He made it—for it only lived to him
> And to the God who looked into his mind.
>   (ll. 83–89)

This, we might say, is the original Romantic patent for the icon antedating even the Keatsian rift of ore. Following the lead of Marc Shell, Kurt Heinzelman, and R. A. Shoaf, who have explored the economics of the imagination,[23] I suggest that the best approach to the absent cash flow between culture and poetry in *The Ruined Cottage* will be to follow a figure of "richness" so central to the understanding of poetic talent from the Romantics to the New Critics that I believe it is actually the ground. If we can track the figure to its contemporary ground—that is, if we can remove "richness" from the sphere of imagery in order to let it tell us from a literal perspective *about* imagery—then we will be able to arrive at a standard by which to relate cultural and poetic value.

Given the fact that the value of "rich" poetry seems absent, what historical value constituted the ground of such absence? What economy underwrote the "iconomy" of lyric?[24]

The Economy of Debt

The history of the value of absence may be blocked out as follows: if rich imagery is not secured upon any cash visible in normal usage, then it must be secured upon *lack* of cash. Such lack, I suggest, marked a value of industrial economy that did not yet have form for Wordsworth except as "debt." Or rather, it had no form except as Wordsworth capitalized upon debt by strange speculations of imagery until the inhumanity of actual capitalization could seem to disappear. *The Ruined Cottage*, I fear, is not a poem of humanity. It is a capitalization upon inhumanity. A specific kind of capitalization, that is, is the historical form of Wordsworthian humanity. Endorsing a transition in the industrial method of the contemporary Lakes and in the poet's own livelihood at the time even as it looks away from such transition, *The Ruined Cottage* is one of the strongest cases of the denial, the overdetermined and precise absence, that is the poet's sense of history.[25]

Careful definition of the economy of debt is necessary before we can detail the Wordsworthian capitalization. The leading indexes of this economy in the poem are Robert, whose vocation defines a crux in contemporary industry, and the Poet, whose entrance in existential "toil" defines a corresponding crux in Wordsworth's own industry of writing. As intimated by the etymological link between "textiles" and "texts," as well as by such stock metaphors as the "warp and woof" of verse, Robert's weaving and Wordsworth's writing are really one labor I will call "textualization."[26] Whereas the Pedlar indexes the sun as the blinding source of reality, Robert and the Poet point to a different kind of sun: a strangely hollow "purse of gold."

Weaving

Wordsworth is careful to detail Robert's status both before and after his ruin. An "industrious," "sober and steady" weaver with the by-occupation of gardening (ll. 172–84), Robert lapses into unemployment for reasons itemized in three steps. The poem depicts a general economic depression "some ten years ago" caused by bad harvests and "the plague of war" (ll. 185–96), adds that a "fever seized" Robert after two years and "consumed" all his savings (ll. 196–205), and finally recapitulates the calamity of general depression with stress on unemployment: "As I have said, 'twas now / A time of trouble; shoals of artisans / Were from their daily labour turned away" (ll. 205–7). The result is that Robert ends in a state of permanent unemployment. Becoming fretful and unbalanced, he increasingly absents himself from home (ll. 234–36) and finally deserts Margaret to enlist in the army for a "purse of gold" (ll. 320–23).

Upon close examination, however, Wordsworth's explanation is puzzling in its overdetermination. Why is "fever" necessary as the centerpiece of the explanation when general depression would seem sufficient? An answer appears if we notice that in reality bad harvests in the English Northwest in 1794–95 (as well as 1799–1800) together with the outbreak of war with France (1793) initiated unstable cycles of falling wages and rising prices (300 percent in the Northwest by 1800).[27] But Wordsworth imagines a *constant* ambience of depression displaced slightly before the 1790's "some ten years ago." While he first mentions unemployment specifically in the third part of his explanation, he does so not to notice a new development but to recapitulate constant conditions ("As I have said, 'twas now / A time of trouble"). The implication is that unemployment was steady throughout. Because we know that Robert subsists for two years of depression possibly underemployed but not unemployed, an additional reason must be offered for his fall into permanent unemployment and, despite his "industrious" character, such idleness that he no longer even gardens. The reason is "fever." But the only practical effect of fever, it seems, would be to idle Robert temporarily. In a constant depression, Robert would regain at least his prior level of employment even if all his savings were consumed. Fever could have such drastic effects only if there were something special about contemporary hard times making temporary disability equivalent to a permanent layoff. Insofar as the poem does not reveal any such special circumstances, however, "fever" appears only another image.

The "plague" of war compounds with Robert's fever to create an increasingly figurative malaise: "Ill fared it now with Robert" (l. 213).

To uncover the crisis screened by "fever," we need to establish as accurately as possible Robert's vocational situation. It is not unlikely, after all, that Wordsworth had technical knowledge of the weaving profession. While a schoolboy in Hawkshead, he often entered spinners' cottages and "admired the cylinders of carded wool which were softly laid upon each other" (quoted in MM, 1: 24). He probably also saw weavers' homes because textiles and clothmaking were Hawkshead's second leading nonagricultural occupation, and he knew at least one weaver, John Martin, well enough to go fishing with him.[28] (It is also possible that he had read John Dyer's *The Fleece* by the time of *The Ruined Cottage*.) But it will be sufficient to assume only what seems certain: whatever his acquaintance with techne, Wordsworth understood profoundly the ethos of weaving as the traditional exemplar of British labor. If we require more detail ourselves, it will be in the service of reproducing the poet's own deeper brand of familiarity.

First, we can be certain that Wordsworth conceived Robert as a traditional wool, as opposed to cotton, weaver. Among other evidence: the cotton industry was so new that it did not arrive in substantial form in the Lakes until the last decades of the eighteenth century ("cottons" still commonly referred to the area's trademark coarse woolens).[29] Woolen manufacture had been divided for centuries between two systems of production: the "household" domestic industry of Yorkshire and the North (including the Lakes) and the "putting-out" domestic industry of the West Country around Bristol and the Racedown-Alfoxden area (where Wordsworth wrote MSS. A and B of *The Ruined Cottage*). In the Northern system, to start with, a weaver controlled all the factors of production. He bought his own wool, carded and spun it at home with the aid of his family (and sometimes apprentices), worked it upon his own loom, and then sold the product to the clothier.[30] After fulling and dyeing, the clothier then distributed the product either through middlemen to stores or—and this will have special bearing for us—through an extensive network of peddlers directly to the rural public. Wordsworth's Pedlar with his "pack of winter raiment" (l. 192) is typical of contemporary peddlers in selling primarily women's clothes and accessories on an economically significant scale (on peddlers and the textile trade in the North, see Lipson, p. 90).

From this system arose the famous character of Northern weaving: "independence."[31] When operating above a certain scale, weavers who held land by freehold or customary tenure, owned both wool and loom, and controlled an in-house pool of labor tended to keep producing even if a depression meant that their products could not be sold for some time. As the Northern weavers represented themselves to Parliament in 1806, "Winter or summer, bad trade or good, we go on straight forwards" (quoted in Lipson, p. 78). By their own account, indeed, Northern weavers were so independent that their universe seemed to know no economic other at all. A petition of the Northern weavers to Parliament in 1794 pictured them as men "who, with a very trifling capital, aided by the unremitting labour of themselves, their wives and children, united under one roof, decently and independently have maintained themselves and families" (quoted in Lipson, p. 70).

Another way to measure "independence" is to observe that Northern laborers traditionally saved up a special kind of free-standing credit. Study of Lake District probate inventories and wills by J. D. Marshall shows that until the middle of the eighteenth century Northern laborers—including weavers—were dedicated savers who preferred to invest profit in credit instruments (bills, bonds, and mortgages) rather than new goods and services transcending traditional standards of comfort (e.g., clocks or expensive funerals).[32] Such credit, however, had a status more like treasure—a pure accumulation symbolizing "independence"—than of exchange value. It did not seem to imply a corresponding amount of debt as well. As Marshall observes, the striking evidence of the inventories is that, except in the case of the hill areas of rapidly industrializing Kendal, there was substantially more credit in the Lakes than debt ("Agrarian Wealth," p. 511 and table 1 on p. 509; see also his "Kendal"). Who, then, owed money to the creditors?

Part of the mystery is explained by assuming that some credit was in the form of bills and bonds taken by agencies outside the Lakes, though contradictory evidence shows an extreme localism of credit (Marshall, "Agrarian Wealth," p. 511). But an additional hypothesis can be suggested: the formal recording process undervalued debt because it was conceptually different from, rather than simply the obverse of, credit. Northern weavers, we know, characteristically bought their wool on loan, but such debts necessary for production were individually very small.[33] Moreover, while profit was invested in credit instruments with long maturities, small debts incurred in production—even if extended over the month or so necessary to loom one batch of wool—existed on a different time scale, a subsistence schedule of week-by-week debit and repayment (Lipson, p. 79). In short, credit piled up visibly, but debt stretched thinly throughout working life in a different kind of space and time. The practical reason for such debt to fall out of the recording process is that the records available to us cover only estates above a certain level of wealth in which the overhead debt required for production was proportionally small.[34] Much of the missing debt in the Lake District must hide in the unrecorded operating costs of the lower yeomanry and the laborers. The conceptual corollary of this circumstance is that however much the small debts extending throughout working life added up to a high overall debt level, Lakes society as a whole—at least in the prosperous mid-century—estimated debt as insignificant except in the case of marginal producers. Such debts were no more than operating expenses, a sort of static noise of economic existence with no impact worth recording. *In the Northern system of labor as epitomized by weaving, debt was invisible.*

In the Bristol-area putting-out system, by contrast, the weaver worked at home usually upon his own loom, but it was the clothier who owned the wool, had it spun and carded, and contracted it to the weaver. The clothier then paid piece-rate for the woven product before selling it through the same network of middlemen and peddlers.[35] The sum effect was that the weaver worked in a nascent wage system not yet fully differentiated from the piece-rate system of payment. Such a system made crucial what Northern industry deemphasized: the essential indebtedness upon which production floated. In contemporary economic thought, indeed, a putting-out economy was analytically identical with debt financing. As Adam Smith argued, "In all arts and manufactures the greater part of the workmen stand in need of a master to advance them the materials of their work, and their wages and maintenance till it be compleated" (1: 73–74). While the weaver controlled other factors of production, in other words, he could acquire materials only as an "advance" from the clothier. Unlike his Northern counterpart, then, who accumulated profit as what I have called free-standing credit, the putting-out weaver earned only unsavable subsistence, a continual refinancing of labor drawn upon capital controlled by the other. Indeed, only in such a system did there appear a true economic other. The social distance between wealthy clothiers and poor weavers was much greater than in the North (Lipson, pp. 13–20) and expressed itself in perennial disputes over weavers' embezzlement of wool (Lipson, pp. 59–61). *In the putting-out economy, indebtedness, or dependence on capital advanced by the other, was central.*

The application we can make of the facts of weaving is as follows. Wordsworth situates Robert in a crux *between* the traditional economies of weaving. We notice to start with that Robert resides both in the Lakes and in the Bristol sphere of influence. The poem's opening prospect with its southern "uplands" and "northern downs" clearly locates Robert in the Lakes of *An Evening Walk,* and the fact that Margaret later need not worry about eviction suggests specifically that he is a Lake District yeoman holding his land by freehold or customary tenure.[36] But Robert also has clear ties with the West Country near Bristol from which, according to the Fenwick note on *The Excursion,* Book 1, Wordsworth collected much of his local color

(*RC*, p. 476). We know that Robert inhabits an unenclosed common covered with "bursting gorse" (ll. 18–25), for example, and that sheep cross his threshold and garden in his absence (ll. 388–94, 461). These details depict the area around Racedown, where the Wordsworths walked up gorse-covered Pilsdon Pen and themselves had trouble keeping livestock out of the garden (MM, 1: 282–84).[37]

Correspondingly, Robert's industrial situation is double. While he lives within the orbit of Northern "independence," he is also victimized by a method of production resembling the Bristol-area putting-out system. Even after being idled, we notice, Robert "tasks" himself in ways confirming his Northern habits:

> The passenger might see him at the door
> With his small hammer on the threshold stone
> Pointing lame buckle-tongues and rusty nails,
> The treasured store of an old houshold box,
> Or braiding cords or weaving bells and caps
> Of rushes, play-things for his babes.
>
> (ll. 224–29)

"Braiding" and "weaving" as if in a dream of occupation, he relives an "independent" career whose whole goal was to save a free-standing credit or "treasured store." His psychological decay begins only after a discovery that would be traumatic to any Northern saver: "the little he had stored . . . Was all consumed."

Yet Robert also certainly works according to something like the putting-out system. A first hint is the fact that he does not buy his own wool. Even in times of distress, we notice, Margaret does not help Robert by spinning or carding; indeed, she later subsists on the much more impoverished by-occupation of spinning flax (ll. 495–502).[38] Robert must be "advanced" wool already spun and carded. Confirmation of Robert's dependence on the capitalist other comes when Wordsworth recounts that it was "A time of trouble; shoals of artisans / Were from their daily labour turned away." The implication is that Robert depends for employment on others with the power to "turn him away." MS. A is even more specific: "Shoals of Artisans / Were from the merchants turn'd away" (with "daily labour" entered interlinearly above "merchants"; *RC*, p. 87). The ultimate marker of such dependence on capitalists, perhaps, is the "purse of gold" Robert at last accepts. In a sense, the purse of gold is the poem's imagination of a wage. In the economy of debt, the self mortgages itself for a wage and then disappears, in total indebtedness, into the armies of the other.

Robert thus exists at a troubled crux in the structure of industry. The historical significance of such crux is that it marks transition: Robert is the poem's paralyzed imagination of the shift by century's end from Northern to Bristol-area systems.[39] In fact, depression caused by bad harvests and war—as well as such regional factors as Yorkshire's increasingly successful competition against the Lakes (Musson, pp. 86–89)—did cause unemployment in Lake District wool weaving as well as a distortion of the whole system in the direction of the putting-out method. Weavers operating above a certain scale remained self-sufficient, but others saw their "independence" disappear as depression raised the static noise of operating debt above the threshold of significance. Poorer weavers subsisted entirely on a week-by-week supply of wool bought on credit and paid for upon delivery of the woven fabric to the clothier. In a depression, clothiers were often slow to pay for finished work or to extend credit (Lipson, pp. 70–71, 78), and weavers therefore had to use savings to buy wool if they wished to work at all.[40] Any interruption in the weaver's ability to work or market his product, and so to refinance himself, would thus indeed have left him unable to start up again except in complete indebtedness to a capitalist.

We might look once more at Robert's illness:

> A fever seized [Margaret's] husband. In disease
> He lingered long, and when his strength returned
> He found the little he had stored to meet
> The hour of accident or crippling age
> Was all consumed.   (ll. 201–5)

As in the actual case histories Marshall records of debt-ridden yeomen in the Lakes afflicted by illness ("Domestic Economy," p. 215), Robert's "seizure" would realistically have put him out of business. But the real seizure consuming his living by sinking him irrecoverably into debt was financial. "The finances of many a family," Marshall observes, "might be miserably disorganised by prolonged illness on the part of its head or its members" (p. 215).

Writing

Preoccupying the poem just as deeply as weaving is the "stitching and unstitching" (as Yeats calls it in "Adam's Curse") of the poem's own writing. Prima facie evidence is the manuscript's physical state. We need only look at MS. B with its supertext or, even more tellingly, MS. D as Wordsworth obsessively revised it in early 1802[41] to realize that the poem—to an extent unusual even for Wordsworth—is virtually obscured under the massed tracks of its own labor. The personification of these tracks in the poem is the Poet, who leaves his footsteps all over the opening. The Poet can find no repose. He is belabored:

> Across a bare wide Common I had toiled
> With languid feet which by the slippery ground
> Were baffled still; and when I sought repose
> On the brown earth my limbs from very heat
> Could find no rest nor my weak arm disperse
> The insect host which gathered round my face.
>
> (ll. 18–23)

The significance of the Poet is that he points us to the deep concern underlying the "toil" of poetic feet: Wordsworth's own preoccupation in the period of the poem's composition with the industry of writing. We can take a page here from Dorothy, who, when she sent Mary Hutchinson a partial transcript of the poem in March 1798, prefaced the Poet's entrance with a sketch of William's labor: "William was very unwell last week, oppressed with languor, and weakness. He is better now. . . . His faculties seem to expand every day, he composes with much more facility than he did, as to the *mechanism* of poetry, and his ideas flow faster than he can express them. After having described a hot summers noon the Poet supposes himself to come in sight of some tall trees upon a flat common" (*Letters*, 1: 200). The transcription then picks up at the equivalent of l. 26 in MS. B. In effect, William's recovery from "languor" and "weakness" in Dorothy's letter exactly substitutes for the Poet's "languid" and "weak" toil in MS. B, ll. 18–23.[42]

What Dorothy recorded was a belabored, Sisyphean state perfectly expressing the tone of Wordsworth's vocational imagination at the time. The vocational imagination, as it may be called, is the concern not just with the work of writing but also with the need to *place* such work in the field of contemporary industry.[43] This was the century, after all, of such great Idlers and self-Taskers as Thomson, Johnson, and Cowper (or, in another medium, Hogarth in his *Industry and Idleness* series). This was the period, in other words, when preoccupation with the labor of writing was so important that it often generated the subject of writing itself. In Wordsworth's case, the central fact of his vocational imagination in the 1790's was that writing suddenly seemed to reach a crux exactly congruent to that of weaving. On the one hand, writing was an independent, Northern industry. On the other, it was a bookseller-dominated industry whose reliance on external capital placed it on the order of the Bristol-area putting-out system. The crux was marked by another "purse of gold," the Calvert legacy, within which, unexpectedly, loomed a frightening debt.

We can pick up the story of Wordsworth's vocational imagination in 1794, when he first thought seriously of writing as a profession.[44] The need to find *some* vocation, certainly, had become urgent by early that year. Writing to William Mathews in February, he fretted: "I have been do[ing] nothing and still continue to be doing nothing.

What is to become of me I know not: I cannot bow down my mind to take orders, and as for the law I have neither strength of mind purse or constitution, to engage in that pursuit" (*Letters*, 1: 112). *An Evening Walk* and *Descriptive Sketches* had appeared the year previous but were not vocational. As Wordsworth wrote in another letter to Mathews in May, the poems had been essentially collegial exercises in lieu of university honors: "I had done nothing by which to distinguish myself at the university, [and] I thought these little things might shew that I could do something" (*Letters*, 1: 120). Only now in May 1794 did he show professional interest: "have the goodness," he requested Mathews, "to call on Johnson my publisher, and ask him if he ever sells any of those poems and what number he thinks are yet on his hands." Almost in the same breath, he also considered publishing *Salisbury Plain* specifically for "pecuniary recompence" (*Letters*, 1: 120).

Wordsworth's imagination then became fully vocational when in spring and early summer he came near to joining Mathews and one of the latter's friends in producing a monthly magazine to be titled, at Wordsworth's suggestion, *The Philanthropist* (a somewhat different version of which, Kenneth R. Johnston suggests, Wordsworth may then actually have helped produce during his 1795 stay in London among the radical set; "Philanthropy or Treason?").[45] Shaped in letters to Mathews from May to June 1794 (*Letters*, 1: 118–20, 123–29), *The Philanthropist* was to have been the express form of what I will call the "endowed" industry of writing. The way Wordsworth intended to put himself in the business of philanthropy is instructive: "at our own risk" and with as little venture capital as possible from booksellers. "You have probably . . . had more experience amongst booksellers than myself," he wrote Mathews, "and may be better able to judge how far our publisher may be induced to circulate the work with additional spirit if he himself participates in the profits. For my part I should wish that if possible it were printed entirely at our own risk and for our own emolument" (*Letters*, 1: 127). But like his partners, Wordsworth was absolutely poor: "I am so poor that I could not advance anything" (*Letters*, 1: 118). How, then, could he raise capital to venture the magazine "at our own risk"?

The answer lay in advance subscription. Under the management of a Pope or a Hogarth, the subscription method had historically mediated between the patronage system and the modern bookseller, or publisher, method of financing authors. But in Wordsworth's imagination, subscription was meant to *resist* modern capitalization. Material for at least two issues, he proposed, should be "circulated in manuscript amongst my friends in this part of the world as specimens of the intended work," and, "after this is done, we should then see how much money each of us can raise" (*Letters*, 1: 127). The naive reliance on "friends" is telling. In his letters, Wordsworth mentioned only two acceptable sources of capital, the "patronage of the public" (*Letters*, 1: 118) and the aid of "several friends who though not rich, I daresay would be willing to lend me assistance" (*Letters*, 1: 127). These sources are identical in abetting a flight from the bookseller system. The very phrase, "patronage of the public," is nostalgic for the old system of financing; and the notion of supportive peers merely gives nostalgia form: the "patrons" Wordsworth would solicit in lieu of booksellers will be "friends." [46] A generalization may be useful here: friends, which we began studying in the last chapter, are what Romantic poets have in place of patrons. A fuller study of Romantic patronage centering on Beaumont, the Wedgwoods, and William Hayley would measure the special tensions created by the displacement of the patron-poet relationship toward middle-class friendship—particularly as idealized from the eighteenth century on in such literary pairs as Pope and Swift, Johnson and Boswell, Wordsworth and Coleridge, or Pound and Eliot.

We can return to the title, *The Philanthropist*, to epitomize the theory of friendly or, put philosophically, benevolent endowment. As Godwin later remembered, he converted Wordsworth to "benevolence" in early 1795 (*CEY*, pp. 164). But Johnston is surely right that the plans for *The Philanthropist* in 1794 were already crypto-Godwinian ("Philanthropy or Treason?" p. 375). *The Philanthropist* was to have embodied benevolence in a perfectly circular conservatorship of endowment: endowment would come philanthropically to the author with no more obligation than that of friendship, and would allow him in turn to endow the world with the very spirit of philanthropy—the political and moral rationale of "welfare" for "mankind" promised in Wordsworth's prospectus of editorial principles (*Letters*, 1: 123–29).

Whether or not the *Philanthropist* that then ran for eleven months in 1795–96 actually involved Wordsworth (as Johnston maintains), the project as the poet conceived it financially folded early. The manner of this dissolution in 1794 is instructive. Coleridge's experience with the chimerical subscription lists for *The Watchman* (1796) and later for *The Friend* (1809–10) suggests how impractical the patronage of friends would have been (*Biographia*, 1: 175–87). And Mathews's employment later in 1794 on *The Telegraph*, which was financed chiefly by the moneylender John King (*Letters*, 1: 139n), attests to the actual extent of capitalization in the contemporary periodical trade. *The Philanthropist* in its first conception, however, never even reached the stage of confronting the difficulties of subscription because of an even more basic impracticality: Wordsworth's refusal in 1794 to come to London. "As to coming to town this step I must at present decline" (*Letters*, 1: 126), he wrote to Mathews, seeming to think he would be able to engage fully in the life of Grub Street by mail.[47] At the root of such impracticality was a new bonus in Wordsworth's vocational imagination. The poet could afford to shelve *The Philanthropist* because it was replaced even during the process of its planning by a more substantial endowment: the Calvert legacy. Indeed, it was precisely the legacy, first offered probably in mid-May 1794 (*CEY*, p. 154), that excused Wordsworth from London. He wrote to Mathews in June: "I have a friend in the country who has offered me a share of his income. It would be using him very ill to run the risque of destroying my usefulness by precipitating myself into distress and poverty at the time when he is so ready to support me in a situation wherein I feel I can be of some little service to my fellowmen" (*Letters*, 1: 126–27). Where *The Philanthropist* required the endowment of multiple friends, a single friend would now do.

From this point on, the Calvert legacy (initially set at £600 but finalized at £900; MM, 1: 252–53) became the holdfast of Wordsworth's early vocational imagination. Even the form in which it was finalized emphasized its status as pure endowment. Calvert wanted the legacy drawn up in late 1794 so as to block Wordsworth's relatives in Whitehaven from ever seizing it in repayment for £460 they had lent primarily for his education (*Letters*, 1: 130–31; MM, 1: 252). William thus asked his brother Richard to bond himself for the £460 in the event it came due. The condition was that "if ever [William was] worth more than . . . six hundred pounds [the original sum of the legacy]," he would repay Richard (*Letters*, 1: 131). In essence, Richard bonded himself in return for a promise of repayment having only an "if" status predicated upon brotherly affection, the extreme of friendship. Buffered entirely from the claims of normal economy, the Calvert legacy became tantamount to an inalienable birthright.

William's management of the legacy after Calvert died in January 1795 then further confirmed its status as a fund seemingly immaculate of market exigencies. Though the legacy arrived in tardy payments amounting to only £525 by the end of 1795 (MM, 1: 269), Wordsworth immediately began to loan it out at high interest—but extremely bad risk—to the habitually indebted Basil Montagu and his friend Charles Douglas. In lieu of more sensible plans to invest the legacy upon good security,[48] he loaned Montagu £300 in October 1795 in the form of what he later sheepishly called an "irregularly" drawn-up annuity at 10 percent interest. The following January, he loaned another £200 to Douglas, also at 10 percent (*Letters*, 1: 183). Montagu paid on time his first year's interest on the £300 (*CEY*, p. 187); and at least part of the interest on Douglas's £200 (for which Montagu had made himself liable; *CEY*, pp. 178, 184) came in by the beginning of 1797 (*CEY*, p. 193). But while Douglas kept up interest payments (*CEY*, pp. 193, 213, 261; *CMY*, p. 66) and paid back

half the principal to Montagu (who did not transmit it to Wordsworth; see W. Douglas, p. 629), Montagu fell behind in 1797 (a
month late on the £300; *CEY*, p. 208) and eventually missed 1798 and
1799 altogether (see *CMY*, p. 58 and n. on Montagu's indebtedness
to Wordsworth).[49] Moreover, for many years none of the principal
for either the £300 or £200 was returned to Wordsworth (MM, 1:
297). The sum effect was that Wordsworth gave his treasure away
to "friends." He could not manage the Calvert legacy sensibly as an
investment because it was not really money: it was benevolence.

Upon the mythic base of the Calvert legacy arose the possibility
of a poetic character cognate with Northern independence: "genius."
The complex vocational structure of Wordsworth's "genius" cannot
be fully rendered at present. For the moment I will only sketch its lar-
val stage in the period from Racedown to Grasmere (1795 to 1799 and
after) by looking ahead to *The Prelude*'s summary of these years. We
remember that *The Prelude* closes by recording the financial endowment of writing: Wordsworth thanks Calvert for the legacy enabling
him to "walk / At large and unrestrain'd" in "pursuits and labours
. . . Apart from all that leads to wealth, or even / Perhaps to necessary maintenance" (13.351–57). Yet the poem also makes it seem
as if Calvert's aid merely reveals some original endowment granted
at birth. The legacy, Wordsworth says, came on trust "That I had
some endowments by which good / Might be promoted" (13.346–
47).[50] The poem's preamble in Book 1, indeed, had already subsumed
the Calvert legacy within an invocation of prior endowment. What
the preamble pre-ambulates is in part precisely the "walk / At large
and unrestrain'd" sponsored after 1794 by the Calvert legacy.[51] But
any thanks for worldly sponsorship disappears in the celebration of a
genius endowed by no patron more substantial than "A corresponding mild creative breeze" (1.43). "Now I am free, enfranchis'd and at
large," the poet says, owning the charter of his independence (1.9).
Such charter sponsors poetry-as-vocation on the basis of a prior invocation of purely poetic talent. "Genius," in sum, is the title under
which the poet appropriates the facts of his industry as original to
himself.

We can capsulize the early character of poetic genius by looking at
just one other passage in *The Prelude*. Wordsworth writes his resumé
as follows:

> When, as becomes a man who would prepare
> For such a glorious work, I through myself
> Make rigorous inquisition, the report
> Is often chearing; for I neither seem
> To lack, that first great gift! the vital soul,
> Nor general truths which are themselves a sort
> Of Elements and Agents, Under-Powers,

> Subordinate helpers of the living mind.
> Nor am I naked in external things,
> Forms, images; nor numerous other aids
> Of less regard, though won perhaps with toil,
> And needful to build up a Poet's praise.
> Time, place, and manners; these I seek, and these
> I find in plenteous store.   (1.157–70)

This is the workshop, complete with apprentices, of a "household" domestic artisan. Poetry is a mythic independence based upon Northern control of all factors of production: poetic soul, general truths and forms (means of labor), toil in the service of "glorious work" (labor itself), and "Time, place, and manners" (materials). *In the industry of "endowed" writing, indebtedness to others is invisible.*

But now the complication: "endowed" poetry in its character as genius was traversed brutally in Wordsworth's vocational imagination by another development after May 1797 precisely when he was at work on *The Ruined Cottage* (in its form as MS. A). Endowment was "put out." Here we reach the outstanding feature in the early biography of Wordsworth's writing: the discovery of personal debt. The groundwork for Wordsworth's education in debt had already been laid in the latter stages of his mismanagement of the Calvert legacy when he suddenly woke from the dream of philanthropy into an accountant's nightmare. Before Montagu's loan of £300 had run its first year, Wordsworth drew up a second annuity bond for the principal and, beginning to fear the worst, took out insurance on Montagu's life (*CEY*, pp. 186, 205; see note 49 to this chapter). Then, after lending Douglas £200, he had the sum and its interest bonded by Montagu and subsequently rewritten as a promissory note signed by both Montagu and Douglas (*CEY*, pp. 178, 184). The lesson of these continual, overlapping assurances of security was that even "friendly" benevolence had to be accountable by strict rules of indebtedness. But even so, the lesson was slow in the learning. Asked by Richard in early 1797 to declare his dealings with Montagu and Douglas, William responded on May 7 with a confused ledger complicated repeatedly by worry that he charged "usurious" interest (*Letters*, 1: 182–85). "In this case," he said at one point, "I trust to the honour of each, (if there can be any honour amongst usurers)" (*Letters*, 1: 184).[52] The poet was still fundamentally uncomfortable not just about specific interest rates, I suggest, but the very morality of holding others in debt.

Only after early May 1797 did Wordsworth truly understand the nature of debt. By the time he responded to Richard's demand for an accounting, he had already received another, more unsettling demand. Part of the £460 he owed their relatives in Whitehaven came due when his cousin, Robinson Wordsworth (who was planning to marry), insisted that £250 be paid back. In his May 7 letter to Richard, William wrote with disturbance:

I do most ardently wish that these matters were settled. Has any thing been done with respect to my Uncle Crackanthorpe? This claim of Robinson certainly must be attended to. Do let me know what is the best that can be done. Do not fail to write to me upon this subject. . . . Did you see my Uncle Crackanthorp? Could 150 £ or 200 £ be paid by way of pacifying them for the present and shewing that we have a disposition to be just? (*Letters*, 1: 184)

We remember that Richard had bonded himself to pay the £460 debt if it came due. But Richard took no action, and the problem seems to have been deferred until 1812 (MM, 1: 338n). The result for William, as witnessed in four subsequent letters to Richard in the following months (*Letters*, 1: 185–86, 187, 188, 193), was escalating anxiety. On June 4, 1797, for example: "I am very anxious to hear from you in order that I may give an answer to those letters . . . from Whitehaven" (*Letters*, 1: 187). And again on June 12, with some desperation: "What *is* to be done in this business? I cannot express my anxiety" (*Letters*, 1: 188). The tone of these letters would only be approached again in 1802 in another troubled exchange between William and Richard concerning the largest default circumscribing the entire period under consideration, the Lonsdale debt to the Wordsworths (esp. *Letters*, 1: 369–73). What Wordsworth suddenly glimpsed, we might say, was an expanding universe of debts—Montagu's, William's, Richard's, and, at the outer periphery, Lonsdale's—each inscribed within the orbit of larger debts. (The largest of all, of course, was the national debt, which sources available to Wordsworth put at some £397 million in 1797; see *Oeconomist* 1: 98–99.) In such a universe, there could be no endowment pure and simple. There could only be something like a sinking fund marking the intersection of monies collectible and payable.

Sensitive to indebtedness, to the everyday demands of poverty, and by mid-1798 to the added financial worries imposed by his planned trip to Germany, Wordsworth at last entered a new phase of the vocational imagination. As late as March 1796 he had still wanted to publish by "friendly" subscription. We know that he transmitted *Salisbury Plain* to Joseph Cottle, whom he had recently met, and that Cottle gave the MS. to Coleridge to offer in published form to subscribers of *The Watchman* (*CEY*, p. 179). When Wordsworth then wrote of the project on March 7 to Francis Wrangham, he was merely taking over for himself an informal plan of friendly subscription: "I mean to publish volume-wise; could you engage to get rid for me of a dozen copies or more among your numerous acquaintance. . . . I do not mean to put forth a[ny] formal subscription; but could wish upon my acquaintances and *their* acquaintances to quarter so many as would ensure me from positive loss; further this adventurer wisheth not" (*Letters*, 1: 168).

But immediately after the onset of the Robinson Wordsworth affair in early May 1797, Wordsworth reappraised his profession and adventured vigorously in search of less friendly capital. One means of "putting out" his work was to have been the production of *The Borderers* on the London stage. He first planned in late May to send the tragedy to Drury Lane (*Letters*, 1: 186); then rewrote the work after September with the stage specifically in mind (*CEY*, p. 205); and by November 20—soon after a resurgence of worry over his debt (see *Letters*, 1: 193)—sent it to Covent Garden (*Letters*, 1: 194). Together with Coleridge's *Osorio*, however, *The Borderers* was at last rejected (*Letters*, 1: 196). On March 6, 1798, Wordsworth could thus write to James Tobin with strange fatalism:

I am perfectly easy about the theatre, if I had no other method of employing myself [Monk] Lewis's success would have thrown me into despair. The Castle Spectre is a Spectre indeed. Clothed with the flesh and blood of £400 received from the treasury of the theatre it may in the eyes of the author and his friend appear very lovely. There is little need to advise me against publishing; it is a thing which I dread as much as death itself. (*Letters*, 1: 210–11)

If publishing was "death," however, then it was also inescapable. Probably by March 13, 1798, Wordsworth thus turned fatalistically to the bookseller system proper, offering Cottle not only *The Borderers* but *Salisbury Plain* and *The Ruined Cottage* (MM, 1: 371; *CEY*, p. 226). The story of his relation with Cottle from this point on, which James Butler has described as the "rise and fall" of "close friendship" (p. 140), provides a crucial record of the poet's new professionalism. One way to understand this rise and fall in amity is to observe that while Wordsworth retained at least a semblance of friendship with Cottle, the concept of friendship itself ultimately became reduced as he sought to supplement it with a relation of mutual *profit* that Cottle, soon to go out of business in 1799, clearly could not supply.

As defined in Wordsworth's letters to Cottle from January 1796 to mid-1798, friendship was constituted as the reciprocal exchange of literature (Cottle lent Wordsworth books such as Erasmus Darwin's *Zoönomia*, for example, while Wordsworth promised his own works) as well as refusal of Cottle's "pecuniary" assistance (*Letters*, 1: 163, 191–92, 196, 198–99, 215, 217–18). Sending literature to Cottle without any declared thought of money, Wordsworth would not acknowledge the fact that his friend was indeed a bookseller. But when the plan to publish *The Borderers*, *Salisbury Plain*, and *The Ruined Cottage* fell through and Cottle agreed instead to pay Wordsworth 30 guineas for *Lyrical Ballads* (*Letters*, 1: 219, 227), friendship suddenly became too limiting. While Wordsworth wanted to stay on the same terms of friendship (as late as July 1799 he resisted accepting any extra interest for money owed on *Lyrical Ballads* because Cottle was "a friend"; *Letters*, 1: 267 and see the full text in Butler, pp. 148–49), he also wanted Cottle—precisely because he was a friend—to transfer the rights for *Lyrical Ballads* to the London bookseller Joseph Johnson, under whose management more copies might be sold (*Letters*, 1: 259). The complex bind Cottle then found himself in and the deceptions he may have practiced to extricate himself after Wordsworth left for Germany have been well recounted by Butler. By the time Wordsworth returned to England in 1799, the harm had been done and the rift between friendship and business was fixed in his mind. He wrote to Richard on May 23, 1799:

I must add that I entirely disapproved of [Cottle's] not surrendering his claim to Johnson because as he repeatedly assured me that he published the work for my benefit (and as I only suffered him to have it on this account) he ought to have resigned his claim when I had a so much better prospect before me than I possibly could have if the work continued in his hands. . . . Now in my Letter I told him plainly that I wished him to give up his claim for *my advantage* and mine alone. (*Letters*, 1: 260)

All Cottle ought to be, Wordsworth is saying, is a friend, and out of friendship he should have transferred *Lyrical Ballads* to a more efficient capitalist.

From the worry of debt, at last, arose a character of labor exactly counter to that of independent "genius": "industriousness." On March 11, 1798, when Wordsworth had just finished work on MS. B of *The Ruined Cottage*, he wrote to James Losh: "I have not yet seen any numbers of the *Economist*, though I requested Cottle to transmit them to me. I have been tolerably industrious within the last few weeks. I have written 1300 lines of a poem which I hope to make of considerable utility; its title will be *The Recluse or views of Nature, Man, and Society*" (*Letters*, 1: 214). I will look more closely at *The Oeconomist* later. Here we can observe only that Wordsworth appropriately invokes *The Oeconomist* to open the scene of *The Recluse*. Measured by length like a piece of cloth, *The Recluse* unfolds as a "utilitarian," "industrious," salable product. Advertisements of industriousness continue in the succeeding months. Wordsworth refers to his work as "my stock of poetry" (*Letters*, 1: 215), for example, and, as Dorothy mentions, justifies the trip to Germany by planning to learn enough of the language to succeed at translation, "the most profitable species of literary labour" (*Letters*, 1: 221). By the time the poet returned from Germany, he could thus speak of himself in such day-laborer terms as follows: "Southey's review [of *Lyrical Ballads*] I have seen. He knew that I published those poems for money and money alone.

He knew that money was of importance to me. If he could not conscientiously have spoken differently of the volume, he ought to have declined the task of reviewing it. . . . I care little for the praise of any other professional critic, but as it may help me to pudding" (*Letters*, 1: 267–68; full text published in Butler, p. 145). *In the bookseller's industry as Wordsworth learned it after 1797, preoccupation with debt was central.*

The Ruined Cottage in its earliest form (MS. A) evolved from March to June 1797 when the debt to Robinson Wordsworth was freshest in Wordsworth's mind. MS. B then developed from January to early March 1798, just in time to be offered to Cottle along with *The Borderers* and *Salisbury Plain* in Wordsworth's first major scheme to publish for money. Of the poems collated together in this package, indeed, *The Ruined Cottage* was the only one substantially written during the encounter with personal debt. We thus arrive precisely at the moment of *The Ruined Cottage* upon a crisis in Wordsworth's industry of writing parallel to that of weaving. Weaving and writing: the partners of textualization together entered the economy of debt.

Now we can account more fully for the "layoff of the signifier" in the poem's structure of humanity. Labor, we remember, was once the signifier of a value immanent in household economy: humanity. As framed between the labors of weaving and writing, such humanity was an "independent" textuality. But in the moment of economic crisis, labor became part of a sign-structure displaced from the independent household—an industrial sign-structure in which, as Saussure has suggested, wages became the signifier and labor itself the signified.[53] Before labor could signify humanity, in other words, it now had to await the outcome of a previous adjustment of meaning, or negotiation of wage-value, occurring wholly outside the household. Labor, we might say, became intertextual, and what was once the value of domestic humanity opened out into the inhuman value or cash of the economic other.

What capitalist, with what funds, can allow the labors of textualization to produce even in debt the text of humanity?

Peddling Poetry

The Pedlar

Peddling has been de-emphasized in readings of *The Ruined Cottage* as an occupation whose only significance is that it is peripatetic. But

I believe the specifically vocational status of peddling is crucial. Not in a superficial or loose sense, but deeply and precisely, peddling is the Wordsworthian capitalization. It is a capitalization of ruin not the less identifiable for being denied.

By way of contrast, we can glance at the "benevolent" but undeniable capitalization of ruin recommended by *The Oeconomist, or, Englishman's Magazine*, which ran for two years beginning January 1798. As mentioned in his letter of March 11, 1798, to James Losh (a frequent contributor to the magazine; *Letters*, 1: 214n), Wordsworth asked Cottle for copies of *The Oeconomist* immediately after finishing MS. B. He then repeated the request on May 9 (*Letters*, 1: 218). Because we do not know if he actually received the magazine, we can only assume that he understood its mission in a general way from Losh. But even cursory knowledge, given the magazine's singlemindedness, would have been instructive. *The Oeconomist* was a *Philanthropist* schooled in business. Taking as its primary task the improvement of agriculture and particularly the lot of the agricultural poor, it argued in such essays as those on "Leasing" practices and, in the premier issue, "On the Importance of the Middle Ranks of Society" that poor relief could only come through participation in the methods of middle-class capitalization. Charity schemes should be managed by benevolent entrepreneurs; or, even more to the point, the poor themselves should be educated in the principles of modern "oeconomy." And if they could not themselves own property, then they could be given long or indefinite leases allowing them to be motivated as if they did own property. The overall vision of *The Oeconomist*, in sum, was that rural "economy," which previously meant only the regulation of the household, had no choice but to enroll fully in the great national phenomenon of middle-class capitalization (*Oeconomist*, esp. 1: 5–8, 9–20, 28–32, 58–65).[54]

Wordsworth's Pedlar is a denied Oeconomist whose talent is to capitalize rural ruin *secretly*. However benevolent he may be—an issue we will need to address—his capitalization is at least in form furtive and illegitimate. The best historical analogue I know is the contemporary black market as protested in the popular antecedent of Wordsworth's "The Baker's Cart": the food riot (see also Wüscher, pp. 77–78, on "The Baker's Cart" and hunger). As Alan Booth documents, from 1793 to 1801 there were 46 riots (often involving weavers) against high grain prices in the English Northwest alone, including a wheat riot in Penrith in July 1795, a flour and oatmeal riot in Ulverston in February 1800, and an oatmeal riot in Whitehaven in January 1801 (p. 90).[55] A parallel to the English food riot was the French Revolution. Just as French laborers in 1792–93 fixed food prices through strong-arm tactics and, with the aid of the *Enragés* left, campaigned for sumptuary regulations (Mathiez, pp. 200–213,

268–74, 304–5, 312; see Tilly on the politics of French food rioting in general), so crowds in the English Northwest hijacked bakers' carts and other grain shipments for auction at "fair" prices fixed at levels prior to the great price increases of 1795 and 1800 (Booth, pp. 93–97). The crucial difference between the food riot in France and in the English Northwest was that the latter did not become manifestly or fully political until about 1800 with the rise of the United Englishmen and their "Big Loaf" watchword (Booth, pp. 101–4; E. P. Thompson, pp. 472–73).[56]

Merely to describe the food riot in its prepolitical phase, I suggest a psychological paradigm: food riots represented a repression of capitalism. Relevant are Cobb's findings that the ideology of "hunger" in popular protest is to some degree independent of actual hunger (*Police*, pp. 246–52). Hunger in culture is at times as much symbolic as real. In the English Northwest, hunger and price-fixing were in part a fetishistic fixation upon grain that repressed the fact that grain had become a modern commodity. Food riots, that is, enacted the desire to regain Mother Nature by repressing the capitalization signaling her removal from rustic control. The "large sticks" in the hands of rioters (Booth, p. 97) were raised to repress the Invisible Hand of the father-economy. Ultimately, such manipulation was so strong that repression became a kind of legitimacy: price-fixing often acquired either the explicit or de facto consent of the local magistracy (Booth, pp. 104–6; see also E. P. Thompson on the legitimating "moral economy" backing the food riots, pp. 66–68).

But capitalism, as our own century teaches us, is never fully repressible. The ad hoc legitimacy constituted in the food riot thus could not defend itself against an irrepressible monster of capitalism erupting from within: the black market. French laborers in 1792, we know, increasingly turned their anger on "speculators" in food and currency—that is, on the profiteers of the black market and "black money" always resident in any economy where, to cite a standard definition of parallel economy, artificial price ceilings create excess demand.[57] The black-hearted profiteers of such excess economic desire extorted higher prices not only by hoarding and cornering supplies but by exploiting regional differences in demand. Food rioters in the English Northwest thus targeted not only manipulative corn dealers in general but especially "itinerant speculators" who came into an area to buy up all the grain (Booth, p. 92).

Peddling is Wordsworth's black-market capitalism, his itinerant speculation mandating a poetry of repressed or denied economy. I enter as evidence the actual status of peddling at the time. By the end of the century, and especially in the English Northwest, peddling had become precisely a parallel economy akin to a black market. Wordsworth, we know, knew the peddling trade remarkably well even before he had heard of James Patrick of Kendal and introduced him into the Pedlar's biography in 1801–2 (*RC*, p. 26). In the Fenwick note on *The Excursion*, he remembers a peddler ancestral to Patrick:

At Hawkshead also, while I was a schoolboy, there occasionally resided a Packman (the name then generally given to this calling) with whom I had frequent conversations upon what had befallen him & what he had observed during his wandering life, &, as was natural, we took much to each other; & upon the subject of *Pedlarism* in general, as *then* followed, & its favorableness to an intimate knowledge of human concerns, not merely among the humbler classes of society, I need say nothing here in addition. (*RC*, p. 478)

There is even the possibility that "Pedlarism" undergirds *The Ruined Cottage* so thoroughly that the tale of Margaret and Robert could have been generated solely from the circumstances of Hawkshead peddlers. One of the six peddlers Wordsworth might have known at Hawkshead, according to T. W. Thompson, was related to a weaver the poet also knew and had once joined the army, and one had a wife named Margaret (pp. 207, 239–45).

Such familiarity with "the subject of *Pedlarism* in general" allows us to deduce that Wordsworth almost certainly knew of the Parliamentary controversy over peddlers in 1785–86, precisely when he was in Hawkshead. Changing regulation of the peddler's trade had stabilized in 1697 with the imposition of a barely enforceable system of licensing and taxation (Lipson, pp. 90–93). In 1785, however, a campaign suddenly began to persuade the House of Commons to ban the living of the nation's 1400 or so peddlers entirely by revoking or withholding their licenses. The motive was to compensate retail-store merchants—the competitors of peddlers—for a new tax. From spring 1785 to the following spring, scores of petitions on both sides of the issue came before the House. Among these, a disproportionately high number originated in the North country of Lancashire and the Lake District (especially Kendal and Westmorland generally, but also Cumberland).[58]

The debate can be summarized as follows, where "no" to the proposal to ban peddling was argued not only by peddlers but sympathetic farmers, weavers, wholesale merchants, and clergy, and "yes" exclusively by town retail-store merchants (cf. Lipson, pp. 91–93). *No*: peddlers (also known as hawkers, chapmen, and scotchmen) were a "useful Class of People" in the North, where distribution of cloth goods to rural customers would otherwise be much hampered. More than useful, peddlers were absolutely necessary. Without them, innumerable existing debts owed by rural customers to peddlers and, through peddlers, to merchants (some of whom circulated many thousands of pounds of goods at a time in this fashion) would become uncollectible and so plunge "Thousands of worthy Families in Distress and Ruin." Finally, peddlers were dealers of "Integrity and Uprightness" who stemmed what would otherwise be a rampant black market of "contraband Goods" detrimental both to merchants' profits and tax revenues.[59]

Yes: peddlers were "unfair" competition for retail outlets because they practiced "fallacious" advertisement and other flimflam, paid no parochial taxes, and could not be held to strict account for the licensing fees they did owe. Moreover, peddlers were not really useful in the Northern distribution system because they merely took trade away from "Retail Shops now established in all Parts of the Country." They were also so far from being necessary because of the credit line they controlled that they actually harmed all merchants because of "the Uncertainty of the Returns of Hawkers" and the fact that many were "profligate Tradesmen [who], in Contemplation of Bankruptcy, become itinerant for the sole Purpose of defrauding their honest Creditors." Finally—and this was a constant refrain—peddlers were *themselves* black marketeers engaged in "Smuggling," distribution of "stolen Goods," and "illicit Traffic" in general.[60]

Because peddlers lived on the outer fringe of documentation, the truth of the matter is hard to determine. But the lack of proper documentation is itself a clue to the deep truth of the controversy: peddlers were holdovers from a system of production and distribution that, in the transition to modern production by wage labor and distribution by retail outlet, became objectionable precisely because it represented the undocumented, unaccountable, and unregulated. Controlling in their informal way an extensive credit line, they stood for a recalcitrant unaccountability of debt, a refusal to make debt financing emerge from traditional Northern invisibility into the institutionalized form of the wage system. In other words, in an economic age of legitimate wage workers and merchant-capitalists, peddlers were unclassifiable except as dangerous "vagrants." They were reminders of an old Northern system now seen as itself an extralegal black market secreted within lawful business.

Wordsworth reverses the locus of legitimacy in *The Ruined Cottage*, but retains peddling in its black-market capacity. Traditional Northern economy is fixed as legitimate; capitalization as illegitimate; and peddling as the occupation that smuggles capitalization irrepressibly within. As the supertext of MS. B tells us, the Pedlar in his youth disregarded his father's advice to become a schoolmaster and took up what may seem the most disinterested of all trades: peddling (*RC*, pp. 175–77). In the 1801–2 revisions in MS. D, where the father (now a stepfather) is himself a schoolmaster (*RC*, p. 331), Wordsworth will emphasize that the son's vocation is so disinterested as to be wholly avocational. Because "he had an open hand / That never could refuse whoever ask'd / Or needed," the Pedlar "was slow / In gathering wealth" (*RC*, p. 359).[61] But such neglect of his father's business in books, as teaching might be called, is really a repression that smuggles the occupation of brokering textuality inside as preoccupation. Dealing in textiles and at one point in the supertext of MS. B in poetic texts as well (he "fitted to the moorland harp / His own sweet verse," "many a ditty"; *RC*, p. 191), the Pedlar is indeed the "itinerant speculator" of textuality. His talent is to capitalize secretly the labors of weaving and writing. He is the middleman, intertextual dealer, or interpreter of the text of "humanity" who allows the debt or absent value of the text to be pocketed as "riches" by that special economic other, the reader.

Now we can account for the poem's riches. In the Pedlar's youth, there was a primal "textuality" to be negotiated. As the supertext tells us, the Pedlar exchanged all his actual earnings for books (*RC*, p. 161) and "greedily . . . read & read again" (*RC*, p. 163). He also conned the book of Nature, a larger ledger of the riches to be gained from a ghostly, absent value of textuality. In a 1798 draft in the Alfoxden Notebook (DC MS. 14) later transferred to *The Prelude*, Wordsworth thus deems "not profitless these fleeting moods / Of shadowy exaltation" when the Pedlar strove for gain from the "ghostly language of the antient earth" (*RC*, p. 119). The net gain from early dealings in textuality, the supertext of MS. B then adds, consisted of "accumulated feelings" that "press'd his heart / With an encreasing weight" (*RC*, p. 169). The Pedlar capitalized upon textuality so successfully, we might translate, that he banked in his heart emotions recollectible, with interest, in tranquillity. With such funds available, "He could afford to suffer / With those whom he saw suffer" and in "best experience he was rich" (*RC*, p. 183). Or to cite again the passage about the Pedlar later applied to Wordsworth himself in *The Prelude*:

> In all shapes
> He found a secret and mysterious soul,
> A fragrance and a spirit of strange meaning.
> Though poor in outward shew, he was most rich
> (ll. 83–86)

The maturity of the Pedlar's riches is then the hidden currency or black money of imagery. Appreciation of spear-grass, in other words, is akin to speculation in wheat futures with the exaggeration, as in the case of hoarders and cornerers generally, that it is the total absence of wheat that the Pedlar most appreciates. The Pedlar had "an eye / So busy," Wordsworth says (ll. 268–69). The eye is precisely the Pedlar's instrument of business, his jeweler's loop or—to invoke Shell's study of the mythic origin of money and its ability to make property visible or invisible at will—his Gyges's Ring (pp. 11–62). Designed as the consummate instrument of exchange, the Pedlar's eye is in the business of seeing traditional cultural values disappear and the intertextual marker, debt-note, or "image" of such values appear instead.[62] The crowning speculation of his eye is the tale of Margaret, which, because it is "hardly clothed / In bodily form" (ll. 292–93) virtually invites the capitalist of textuality to work his deal of imagery.

Here is how the Pedlar deals with the tale of Margaret:

> Within her casement full in view she saw
> A purse of gold. "I trembled at the sight,"
> Said Margaret
>
>   .　.　.
>
> This tale did Margaret tell with many tears:
> And when she ended I had little power
> To give her comfort and was glad to take
> Such words of hope from her own mouth as served
> To chear us both—but long we had not talked
> Ere we built up a pile of better thoughts,
> And with a brighter eye she looked around
> As if she had been shedding tears of joy.
>
>   (ll. 322–40)

First there is the "purse of gold" marking the absence in Margaret's world; then the Pedlar's inability to contribute anything of value and, indeed, his need to "take" textual value—"words of hope"—from Margaret herself; and finally, through strange dealings in absence, a "pile of better thoughts" for the "brighter eye."

S. K. Ray writes in his *Economics of the Black Market*, "The parallel economy . . . thrives under the patronage of the unscrupulous element of our society. . . . It is based not on the official monetary system, but on a secret understanding and involves a complex range of undisclosed deals and transactions pushed through secretly with unaccounted sources of funds, generating in the process income and wealth which escapes enumeration and cannot be easily ascertained" (p. 29). With the elision of the word "unscrupulous," this would be a strangely resonant definition of Wordsworth's denied capitalization in *The Ruined Cottage*—of the "secret understandings . . . deals and transactions" by which the Pedlar turns "unaccounted sources" of imagery into "income and wealth which escapes enumeration."

The Economy of Lyric: Three Laws

Such, I conclude, is the economy of lyric. But at the last I must risk an evaluation without which any purely analytical conclusion would be incomplete. What *about* the possibility of the "unscrupulous" in poetic peddling? Is Wordsworth's capitalization "benevolent"? I invoke for my chorus here the lost play Aristotle mentions in which Sophocles speaks the "voice of the shuttle." [63] To speak the "voice of the shuttle," as tongueless Philomela does to tell of her violation by Tereus, is to weave a tale out of inhumanity and then to present it to the textual other, the reader, for the strange, humanizing gain of tragedy: the purgation that redeems "changes in fortune." As literalized in debased form on the London stage at the time of *The Borderers* (witness the work Wordsworth derided, Monk Lewis's *Castle Spectre*), tragedy had always been a legitimate way to capitalize upon cultural misfortune. Every *Oedipus Rex*—to call upon that other Sophoclean play central to Aristotle's imagination—is also an economic Oedipus in which the representation of "change of fortune" profits from the Theban economic crisis circumscribing the action.

Wordsworth's "voice of the shuttle" weaves the misfortune of Margaret rather than of Philomela. But instead of presenting such misfortune as a narrative or drama able to capitalize upon tragedy with traditional authority, Wordsworth peddles his tale as incipient lyric. The danger is that when we spot the hidden capitalization in lyric we will feel defrauded. Stripped of the full tragic grandeur by which "change in fortune" once opened out from private to public concerns and set within a history of literal economic crisis, poetic peddling seems unscrupulous and exploitative. Peddling ruin brazenly affronts our scrupulous post-Romantic belief that money should be unthinkable in "disinterested" poetry. After all, lyric consciousness gained by converting ruin into "rich" souvenirs (called "images") is by definition selfish: dedicated to the increase of the lyric "I." Having appreciated the poem's "sun," in short, we pall before a line of inquiry making us Blake's Idiot Questioner: " 'What,' it will be Question'd, 'When the Sun rises, do you not see a round disk of fire somewhat like a Guinea?' " (Blake, p. 617). [64]

If there is one evaluation upon which I would be content to rest this chapter, it is that money does indeed matter deeply and *legitimately* to poets, not just because everyday subsistence demands attention by right of reality but because everyday dealings infiltrate purely poetic imagery itself through shuttlings of mimesis working all the more powerfully the stronger the denial. If we cannot appreciate poetic peddling as it mimes the unscrupulous processes of contemporary economic history without stigmatizing such peddling—without compounding the poetry's denial with our own—then "appreciation" is too limited a response. A fuller reading would follow the initial stage of appreciating a poem's own declared values with a twofold process at once depreciative and reappreciative. A perspective that is truly critical, perhaps, requires at last something like a con man's bait-and-switch practiced in reverse: look once at imagery and see the sun depreciate into a mere guinea; look twice and appreciate the deeper fact that the world of spending and getting has always itself been shot through with what Heinzelman calls "mythic force" (*Economics of the Imagination*, p. 13). Such, after all, is the core sense of Heinzelman's expansive book as well as of Shell's work: economy exerts so powerful a hold over everyday imagination because it is a *primary* poetics of the imagination. Economics tosses the coin of golden hope and brass fear, illusion and disillusion; and in the Platonic cave that is the speculative imagination, such is all the sun there is. If the "dreaming man" or Pedlar in Wordsworth's poem plays the con game of the "sidelong" glance, then a fully critical appreciation must not so much avoid the shifty glance of ideology—for that would be to attempt to look outside history—as con the poem's values in reverse. The imagery that the poem appreciates, we should finally depreciate as a precondition of critical reading; and, inversely, the economy that the poem's imagery depreciates, we should learn to re-appreciate—but without any illusion that our own idols of the marketplace (such terms as "capital," "labor," or "value" approaching at times the reified abstractions Bacon attacked) are less ideologically implicated than Wordsworth's idols *denying* the marketplace.[65]

To allow us to read certain values in order to re-appreciate them, I conclude, must be the true use of a poem like *The Ruined Cottage*, for "use" is a concept necessarily suspended between the horizons of the text "in itself" and of the reader. In this sense, the dictum that a poem should not mean but be is exactly wrong (with the caveat that our current sense of decentered "meaning" alters that of the New Critics). Just as the use of a tool lies not in its form but in its function of changing other forms to suit the purpose at hand, so the use of a poem lies not in its iconic "being" but in the open market of multivalent, transformable, and perennially negotiable "meanings" it passes from hand to hand. Economics is merely one of the largest markets capable of situating such negotiation or sharing of meaning. Because the sharing is as much brutally contestatory as consensual, economics is an imagination of the world that allows us not so much to "explain" the meaning of poetry univocally as to reground poetry's own processes of consensualism and contestation (named "unity" and "paradox," respectively) in a larger domain. Only in such a larger offering of shares does the poem truly become of critical use, and criticism itself—if such hope is not merely sunny illusion—also potentially a useful offering.

Of course, there is a limit to how far we can evaluate our own method of evaluation (though we will need to resume the problem in a new way in parting from Wordsworth in Chapter 9). But it is proper to close our reading of *The Ruined Cottage* with some such reflection because evaluative stance is even more crucial in reading the poet's mature economy of lyric after MS. B of early March 1798.

The black-market economy of *The Ruined Cottage* is the groundwork of Wordsworth's fully legitimate economy to come; and with the maturity of this latter white market or mythology, more rests upon our avoiding the false choice between a criticism of appreciation and one of depreciation. It is simply not useful in approaching the work of the middle and later years, I suggest, to view the poet's economy of lyric as *either* a generous vision of humanity *or* a petty capitalization upon inhumanity. It is more useful to "see Wordsworth through" (to vary Levinson's haunting, bivalent dedication to McGann, "who sees me through," in her *Romantic Fragment Poem*)—that is, at once to read the Romantic ideology of the image supportively so as to allow it to express its proper value *and* to see through the illusions of those values to a critical transvaluation (the latter through the two-step method of depreciation and re-appreciation I suggested above).[66] Appreciation and depreciation are two sides of the hermeneutic coin that criticism risks upon its chosen poets. As in the experience of reading Poor Susan in Wordsworth's reverie, we must risk being enchanted before we can be so richly disenchanted.

In a mood both appreciative and depreciative, then, I will close by seeing Wordsworth through to the period of *The Prelude*. To read the lyric imagery of the poetry from early March 1798 on is to discover an economy of lyric regulated by three basic laws.

Less is more. This is the law of lyric investment that allows the poet to speculate upon debt. In the words of the supertext of MS. B, "littleness was not" because to the Pedlar "the least of things / seemed infinite." All who see things aright, the supertext continues, will be able to "multiply / The spiritual presences of absent things" (*RC*, pp. 159, 263).

The law of lyric investment multiplies such least quanta of textual value as white space—whether actual white space on the page (as in the rich pause between the two stanzas of "A Slumber Did My Spirit Seal") or, more generally, loss of the object of reference. We might instance here "Lucy Gray," where the footsteps of the missing girl stop in the middle of the bridge to leave the untracked whiteness of snow beyond. What lies beyond the tracks of reference? Only a ghost-form to be *imaged* in imagination:

> —Yet some maintain that to this day
> She is a living child;
> That you may see sweet Lucy Gray
> Upon the lonesome wild.
>
> O'er rough and smooth she trips along,
> And never looks behind;
> And sings a solitary song
> That whistles in the wind.
>
> (*PW*, 1: 236)

What kind of ghost image flickers—there and not there—in lucid grayness? The answer must lie in something like the Coleridgean "translucence" of symbol, that phenomenon in which More—Coleridge: the "general" and "universal"—embodies itself iconically in Less—the "special" and "individual" (*Lay Sermons*, p. 30).

To share is to own. This is the law of lyric exchange. Even the smallest or most intense of Wordsworth's lyrics, we observe, does not aim to monopolize significance in a single, all-sufficient symbol like the "shell" in Book 5 of *The Prelude*. As the shells of things, images are empty at origin and must re-originate their value repetitively and in the congress of their fellows. This means that imagery must be like a cowrie-shell money constantly validating its meaning in a communal exchange owned by no one individual. Individuals may own particular shells, of course, but not the system of exchanging shells.[67] As if in a purged dream of business, Wordsworth's lyricism thus insistently points us from the pile of the poet's "original" shells to the unowned congeries of shells. To start with, such lyrics as the Lucy poems continually circulate images not only internally but also within the society of their sibling poems. Witness, for example, the sharing of flowers and stars in "She Dwelt Among the Untrodden Ways" and "Three Years She Grew in Sun and Shower." Secondly, Wordsworth's lyrics programmatically eschew competition not only with each other but also with commonwealth. The more "common" a poem's wealth of imagery, that is, the better it introduces us to the vast, circulating fund of "the real language of men" (as appreciated in the Preface to *Lyrical Ballads*).

I hazard the following extension of the law of lyric exchange: if the law of lyric investment suggests the translucence of Coleridgean symbol, then that of lyric sharing suggests another Coleridgean concept to which Wordsworth owed much in his 1798 and 1802 work on the Pedlar's biography: the "One Life."[68] The One Life is a Chain of Being in which what had traditionally been static, hierarchical correspondence (e.g., "lion" for "king") becomes fluxile exchange.[69] The One Life, in other words, is the sharing of images among a universe of equals. Wordsworth writes in the supertext of MS. B:

> All things there
> Looked immortality, revolving life
> And greatness still revolving, infinite;
> There [then] littleness was not, the least of things
> Seemed infinite. (*RC*, p. 159)

In Wordsworth's mature idiom, such an economy of shared imagery is "Imagination" as formulated in the Preface of 1815. Able to confer "additional properties upon an object," abstract "from [the object] some of those [properties] which it actually possesses," and

modify clusters of images such that one is "endowed" with the properties of another (*Prose*, 3: 32–33),[70] Imagination is quintessentially a
sharing of what Ransom would call iconic "value-property." Perhaps
not accidentally, Wordsworth opens his disquisition on Imagination
in the Preface by quoting this simile from Milton:

> As when far off at sea a fleet descried
> *Hangs* in the clouds, by equinoctial winds
> Close sailing from Bengala, or the isles
> Of Ternate or Tidore, whence merchants bring
> Their spicy drugs; they on the trading flood
> Through the wide Ethiopian to the Cape
> Ply, stemming nightly toward the Pole: so seemed
> Far off the flying Fiend.
>
> (*Prose*, 3: 31; Wordsworth's italics)

Imagination is trade in imagery. Milton's business of imagery thus
opens out precisely, even down to the placement of the crucial verb
at the start of the second line, into the climactic example of Imagination as an exchange of images. Wordsworth quotes from his own
"Resolution and Independence":

> As a huge stone is sometimes seen to lie
> Couched on the bald top of an eminence,
> Wonder to all who do the same espy
> By what means it could thither come, and whence,
> So that it seems a thing endued with sense,
> Like a sea-beast crawled forth, which on a shelf
> Of rock or sand reposeth, there to sun himself.
>
> Such seemed this Man; not all alive or dead
> Nor all asleep, in his extreme old age.
>
> (*Prose*, 3: 33)

To imagine is to labor. At this point, my study of the economy of
lyric should be seen to pass the baton to Heinzelman's exploration
of imaginative economics in the works Wordsworth wrote after *The
Ruined Cottage*. The mimesis of physical labor by imagination is the
maturity of Wordsworth's economy of lyric: it is the insistence that
the work of giving birth to works of imagination is indeed "labor"
in both Adam's and Eve's senses. And because it is a sweat-of-the-
brow, it may legitimately take its place in the marketplace in which
contemporary culture valued the worth of one labor relative to another. This market is the labor market where the imaginative effort of
the poet can be equated—in a sublimated version of normal supply-
and-demand—with the labors of the reader. As Heinzelman puts it,
Wordsworth will conceive a direct exchange of writer's and reader's
labors:

In Wordsworth's poetic exchanges, labor bestowed and labor commanded—the relationship between systems of production and consumption, text and implied reader—could still be computed directly. . . . Wordsworth proceeds to create *through his poems* his most inclusive figure of compensation: the literary work as a form of labor to be exchanged for the reader's. In respect to the economics of poetry, the successive labor of the reader is a recompense for the original work bestowed upon the text. (*Economics of the Imagination*, pp. 200–201)

Thus is the original bond of labor in *The Ruined Cottage* at last redeemed: as an act of imagination whose labor is to be valued on a par with any other specie of human work.

This is Wordsworth's economy of lyric. "Riches" arise through sublimated denials of normal economy: though you have less, you shall have more; though you share, you shall own; though you merely imagine, you shall labor.

The Gift of Poetry

The full story of Wordsworth's "genius" can now be told. If a poet is in debt, how can he enfranchise genius? The answer Wordsworth offers is his whitest economy: the "gift of poetry." Here, I take my argument to its furthest extent by spilling out of the confines of economy to study Wordsworth's mature theory of "giftedness" in terms of the anthropology of human value, especially as pioneered by Marcel Mauss in his study of gift societies and as recently applied to literature by Lewis Hyde.[71] Just as primitive gift societies have the potential to open inward into an overlapping transaction economy (Mauss, pp. 70–73), so modern transaction societies have the potential to open reciprocally into the primal spirit of gift (p. 74). As Mauss observes, the "gift" is defined by the intersection of three separate obligations—to give, to receive, and to reciprocate—whose sum effect is to free the receiver from strict obligation to the donor (esp. pp. 10–12, 37–41). The act of reciprocation closing the system is not so much a repayment as a gift in its own right (sometimes to someone other than the original giver).

Mauss's analysis allows us to distinguish Wordsworth's "transactions of genius," as they may be called, into two successive theaters: one staging the act of "presentation" between the gift and its reception, and the other the art of "re-presentation" between reception and reciprocation.

The story begins immediately after the poet's arrival at Racedown, when, from late 1795 to his first work on *The Ruined Cottage* in early 1797, his poetry centered on presentation. Crucial was his fascination with theft. Between September and November 1795, Wordsworth changed *Salisbury Plain* into *Adventures on Salisbury Plain* primarily through the addition of the Sailor and his tale. The Sailor committed murder in the service of robbery. If, as in Stephen Gill's Reading Text, we then include in the poem the revised "Female Vagrant" (despite Wordsworth's temporary excision of the tale in hopes of writing a substitute), we can recognize that the Vagrant's experience confirms the main narrative of theft. A "greedy" lord appropriated her father's pastures, the Vagrant remembers (*SP*, p. 133); and the chain of calamity thus initiated—in a phrase retained from *Salisbury Plain*— "robbed" her of her "perfect mind" (*SP*, p. 141).

Wordsworth then elaborated the phenomenology of theft in *The Borderers*. In the Early Version, the death of Herbert comes as the climax of a series of thefts. From the start, we know, the outlaw Border was the site of theft. Upon returning from Palestine, for example, Herbert had found his lands "usurped" (I.i.159–61). As the Early Version intimates (II.iii.328–37 and *B*, p. 172n), and as the 1842 version then more fully explains (*B*, p. 73), it is precisely such original theft that then justifies Mortimer's Robin-Hood–like countertheft. The living of the Borderers is to "defend" the "genuine owners" of land and to plunder "rich Spoil" from usurpers and Scottish forces. On the basis of such actual theft then arises a dreamwork of alleged or hypothetical theft. Rivers imputes Herbert's "quondam" Barony to some "cunning" fiction or past embezzlement (I.i.49–59) and credits Herbert's fatherhood to a malfeasance committed with the aid of the Female Beggar. Moreover, he hypothesizes that Herbert projects his own illegitimacy upon others—thus coming to the view that Mortimer wishes to "rob" him of Matilda (I.i.29). The culmination of actual and fictional thefts in this universe is then the robbery by which Mortimer finally kills Herbert. In the act of exposing Herbert on the waste, Mortimer unwittingly "forgets" that he bears away the old man's scrip of food (III.v.166–67). Such kleptomania, another version of the Female Vagrant's "robbery" of mind, is a theft committed as if in pure dream. Like a nightmare, the dream then recurs once more in the subplot of Robert and Margaret. After finding and reabandoning Herbert on the heath, as we saw in Chapter 6, Robert comes home to face Margaret's groundless fear that he may have committed a fatal robbery: "You have not *buried* any thing? you are no richer than when you left me?" (IV.iii.35–36).

The significance of theft in the poems preceding *The Ruined Cottage* is that it is the misrecognition of what Wordsworth at last conceives as the gift. Not recognizing their proper gifts, human beings cannot partake of existence except through acts of misappropriation. How to redeem spiritual larceny? The answer Wordsworth gives is "forgiveness," the horizon of the recognition of the gift. We might look once more to *Adventures on Salisbury Plain*, for example, to see that theft ultimately seeks forgiveness as its obeisance to the spirit of the gift. The Female Vagrant had told of the terrifying inability of society to give anything to anyone. In her diaspora of estrangement upon returning to England, she at one point comes upon a "wild brood" of other vagrants who "gave me food, and rest" (*SP*, p. 143). But such exceptional giving merely underscores the uncharitableness of a world in which she must learn a Song of Experience: "homeless near a thousand homes I stood, / And near a thousand tables pined, and wanted food" (*SP*, p. 141). It is after such preface that the Sailor then closes the overall narrative by imploring the redemption of society's misgiving: forgiveness. "Forgive me, now forgive," he asks of his dying wife (*SP*, p. 153).

Considered in the same light, *The Borderers* also enacts misgiving in search of forgiveness. The poem's outlaw universe and its entire dreamwork of theft, we notice, have their ground precisely in an original misrecognition of the gift. The space traversed by Herbert on his journey, after all, is the waste of the gift. Leaving behind the charity of the abbot of Saint Cuthbert's, who "gave me that little cottage" (I.i.169), he tries to cross a strange zone toward the promised "bequest" of Matilda's "kind patroness" (I.i.125–26). But this zone is a Border of wasted gifts where all rightful owners have been stripped of their lands and reduced to the condition of waiting for Henry III to recognize their grants once more (II.iii.330–34). The very daemon of the land of wasted gifts is Rivers, whose own original misgiving may be traced to his abandonment of the sea captain. As rendered in the confession scene, he left the captain "stretching forth his arms" (IV.ii.46) upon a rock where "There was no food, no drink, no grass, no shade / No tree" (IV.ii.24–25). Such is the antipodes of giving. In the present of the play, the crucifixion of the captain parallels Mortimer's forgetful exposure of Herbert, which we can now see is precisely a misgiving. "That belt" was "the first gift of my love," Matilda says when she sees the scrip Mortimer took from Herbert (V.iii.167–68). "Oh! misery!" he cries, "the scrip which held his food! / And I forgot to give it back again" (III.v.166–68). The Early Version then ends upon Mortimer's deepest misgiving: "No human dwelling ever give me food" (V.iii.268). It is in the 1842 version that Wordsworth at last calls for forgiveness. Mortimer will wander, he says, "In search of nothing, that this earth can give, / But expiation" until "Mercy gives me leave to die" (*B*, p. 295).

It is at this point that we reach *The Ruined Cottage*, which evolved in early 1797 and 1798 as the beneficiary of a succession of stolen gifts. The money robbed by the Sailor in *Adventures on Salisbury Plain*, we may say, enters *The Borderers* as the theft Margaret thinks Robert committed; and the latter larceny then devolves upon *The Ruined Cottage* as the purse of gold left another Margaret by another Robert. By laundering this purse in imagery, *The Ruined Cottage* can then at last dedicate itself to the full recognition, and so reception, of the gift. It can dedicate itself, that is, to recognizing the forgiveness of Nature. If only men recognized that Nature in her forgiveness abundantly gives, we might hear the poem say, they need no longer steal. They need only receive.

MS. B invokes from its very beginning the spirit of the gift. "Give me a spark of nature's fire," the poet says in his epigraph from Burns, thus making "give" his first word (*RC*, p. 42). The call for the gift is then thematized in the body of the poem itself by Margaret, who is in need of someone "to give her comfort" (l. 335), hopes "that heaven / Will give me patience" (ll. 412–13), and begs for news of Robert that passers-by "gave" not (ll. 480, 505). To be fulfilled, such receptiveness to the gift must look away from the example of Robert, who is a throwback to the misrecognition of the gift. Robert will accept no gifts, parish charity or otherwise (l. 208). The call for the gift must instead look for its answer to the Pedlar, who embodies the conscious reception of gifts. As his biography tells us, the Pedlar was from the first endowed with the gifts of Nature: "He was a chosen son: / To him was given an ear which deeply felt / The voice of Nature" (ll. 76–78). Crucially, the Pedlar knew how to receive gifts. "He had received / A precious gift"; he "was prepared / . . . to receive / Deeply" and, indeed, "cannot but receive." And "From nature . . . He had received so much, that all his thoughts / Were steeped in feeling" (*RC*, pp. 145, 155, 173). Given such blessings, the Pedlar's "mind" was at last "a thanksgiving to the power / That made him," and all his heart was "meek in gratitude" (*RC*, pp. 157, 159).

Thus is the "gift" received in *The Ruined Cottage*. From this point on, Wordsworth enters the theater of reciprocation, or re-presentation. The great thanksgiving for Nature's gifts must be the reciprocation of his poetry, a representation that to be truly "gifted" must pass on the gift so that all readers will receive it in turn. *The Ruined Cottage* merely opens this scene of representation. After showing the Pedlar to be a "chosen son" to whom much had been given, the poem immediately goes on to sketch the kind of reciprocation he must accomplish: "To every natural form, rock, fruit, and flower, / Even the loose stones that cover the highway, / He gave a moral life" (ll. 80–82). Such outpouring of spirit is what Wordsworth would soon call "silent Poetry" in "When, To the Attractions of the Busy World." In the next several years after *The Ruined Cottage*, the poet then increasingly stressed the need to reciprocate for Nature's gifts with such poetic spirit. Where the original blockage in the theater of presentation had been theft, the outpouring in the theater of re-presentation was identified with *charity*, especially—as demonstrated in "The Old

Cumberland Beggar" and the drafts of the Discharged Soldier episode of *The Prelude*—to beggars and vagrants. By the time of "Tintern Abbey" in 1798 (whose initial commemoration of "five" years passed seems almost to pick up where the "Five tedious years," l. 482, at the close of *The Ruined Cottage* leave off), the legacy of Nature's gift has devolved fully upon the poet. First he recognizes receiving the "gift" of "that blessed mood / In which the burthen of the mystery . . . Is lightened" as well as "gifts" of "Abundant recompense." And then he reciprocates in the form of the sustained thanksgiving of his blessing of Dorothy.

With *The Prelude*, where it will be convenient to close our story of the gift of poetry, the total sequence of reception followed by reciprocation had become so conscious for Wordsworth that he could recapitulate it in its entirety. It would be sufficient to study just the episodes in the "Two-Part *Prelude*" of 1798–99, but I will release myself from chronological discipline here to sketch the vision in full. Remember that the 1805 poem closes by thanking Calvert for his endowment but opens by subordinating such endowment to a prior legacy of genius. The prior genius, we can now see, was a gift. What, after all, is "free" about the genius of the preamble ("Now I am free, enfranchis'd and at large")? Precisely the gift: gifts are free. Freedom of spirit, Wordsworth thus says, comes by "miraculous gift" (1.22) or, again, by a "corresponding mild creative breeze" constituting a "gift that consecrates my joy" (1.40–43). As the poem then repeatedly confirms, such are Nature's "gifts" (e.g., 7.383; 8.145). In early episodes such as those of the woodcocks stolen from others' snares, the plundering of the raven's nest or, most importantly, the boat stealing, Nature's gifts were at first misrecognized as objects to be stolen.[72] Only after such misgivings are put aside can there be true recognition of the gift. As Wordsworth declares after the boat stealing: "Wisdom and Spirit of the universe! . . . That giv'st to forms and images a breath / And everlasting motion" (1.428–31).

Recognition then opens into the poem's subsequent theater of reciprocation or representation. "From nature largely he receives" (2.267), Wordsworth says about the exemplar of reception in the poem, the Infant Babe. But the Babe cannot be satisfied with his gift except as he "largely gives again" (2.268). Transferred to the end of the poem and into Wordsworth's own life, such early instruction in the gift provides the moral of the spots of time:

> I am lost, but see
> In simple childhood something of the base
> On which . . . greatness stands, but this I feel,
> That from thyself it is that thou must give,
> Else never canst receive. (11.330–34)

> and I would give,
> While yet we may, as far as words can give,
> A substance and a life to what I feel.
>
> (11.339–41)

The total lesson to be learned from spots of time, Wordsworth continues, is that Nature "lifts / The Being into magnanimity" and disposes the mind "to seek in Man, and in the frame of life" the fount of "gifts divine" (12.31–42).

Magnanimity, we now see, is mature "philanthropy," and demands as restitution for original endowment the whole lifework of reciprocation that is poetry. It is fitting, then, that *The Prelude* should at last dedicate itself to Coleridge as a "Gift / Which I for Thee design" (13.404–5). *The Prelude* is a reciprocation rendered to the very theorist of the gift—to a poet who in his "Dejection" ode of 1802 had himself declared: "O Lady! we receive but what we give."

CHAPTER EIGHT

A Transformed Revolution:
The Prelude, Books 9-13

PERHAPS I MAY PAUSE at this point to take stock. Wordsworth's genius, we now see, is a given. All our effort has been
to recover the origin of the given. In Part II of my study, I posited
an axis of emergence meant to historicize the problem of literary
authority. For Wordsworth, I argued, the supervision that oversees
poetry derives from a layered emergency converting the authority of
historical narrative into a moot ideology of time:

$$
\begin{array}{lll}
\textit{Istoria} & \longrightarrow \text{Interpretation} & \longrightarrow \text{Anagogy} \\
\text{Narrative} & \longrightarrow \text{Description} & \longrightarrow \text{Ideology} \\
\text{History} & \longrightarrow \text{Nature} & \longrightarrow \text{Time}
\end{array}
$$

Time authorizes (authors, sanctions) all things.

My corresponding concern in Part III has been to construct at right
angles to emergency an axis of individuation able to historicize the
problem of literary originality. Authority becomes originality when
we sight vertically down the series, Anagogy → Ideology → Time,
to extrapolate a further organization of memorial time: self. Indeed,
the "scene of time" I mapped at the close of Chapter 5 foresaw such
supervision. As indicated in Fig. 4 in that chapter, the poetry after
Salisbury Plain grounds two avenues of descent from the poet's early
universe of time—a blind alley of residual allegory and a path of
nascent symbolism leading to the spots of time proper. But how
does the poet create the symbolism necessary for spots of time? The
answer appears if we look from Fig. 4 to the congruent map of affection in Fig. 10, Chapter 6. In the works after *Salisbury Plain*, the path
of residual allegory becomes irony; and the way of symbolism, affec-

tion. Affection is the new symbolic apparatus of memory. Through conventions of affection, Wordsworth reformulates narration and description into inward-turning mythos and rhetoric, respectively. And the outcome of the reformulation is his new authority, self, together with its regime of supervision, Imagination. As we then saw in Chapter 7, the ultimate form of such reformulation is lyric, whose business is the very idiom of symbolic Imagination: imagery.

A comprehensive account of Wordsworth's corpus would go on at this point to study the *Lyrical Ballads* as a unit, as well as other lyrics leading up to the 1805 *Prelude*. But having watched the genesis of Wordsworth's lyricism, I advance apace toward the end of my tour by resuming where I began *in medias res* in Chapter 1—with the debouchment of Imagination in *The Prelude*. Compositional history, we noted in that chapter, suggests that to trace the triumph of Imagination after Simplon is to turn to politics—to the Revolution books written soon after Book 6. But to recur to the scene of politics we last left in Chapter 5 is also to diverge into a strangely post-historical world transformed by all the intervening years of political and social denial. Spotlighted at the place of climax in *The Prelude*, Books 9 and 10—our first topic in this chapter—epitomize Wordsworth's whole process of transform.

I take my cue here from recent work on Wordsworth and genre. Stuart Peterfreund has written of *The Prelude* as a "metamorphic epic" in which a progress of genres serves to internalize the progress of civilization within the individual ("Metamorphic Epic"); Clifford Siskin has studied the general method of interpretive revisionism and "mixing" by which Wordsworth reformulates all genres as essentially lyric ("Romantic Genre," "Un-Kind Imagination"); and Mary Jacobus—in a provocative extension of genre theory—has argued the relation between gender, politics, and the self-legitimation of autobiographical genre in *The Prelude* ("The Law Of/And Gender"; see also note 27 to Chapter 2). The common insight of all these investigations of Romantic genre may be understood by reference to Lacan's essay "Of Structure as an Inmixing of an Otherness Prerequisite to Any Subject Whatever"—which, psychoanalysis aside, is in essence an intense scrutiny of the logic of classification, typification, and the creation of units or "integers."[1] To apply Lacan's basic insight to genre theory, there are ultimately only two literary kinds: genre and *other* genres—the latter experienced within any self-conscious kind as its barely contained "lack" of control over generic boundaries or, what is the same, as its immersion within a literary history of dynamically interrelated kinds (see Fowler on the constitutive role of change in genre history, pp. 18, 23, and *passim*). Organized as a metamorphic, revisionary, or self-legitimating process, *The Prelude* is in its very structure an inmixing of otherness (other genres with their separate histories of reference and authority). Such inmixing is the origin of the poet's declared originality, authority, or lyric self-consciousness. As the sustained lyric of the Wordsworthian Subject, that is, autobiography in *The Prelude* originates through the refashioning of unstable generic differentiation into the very signifier, the unconscious language, of selfhood.

Or to clarify the catalyst of Lacan from my mixture of genre criticism: self in *The Prelude* truly *becomes* self only when it finds a discourse that affirms-in-order-to-deny the absences, differentiations, mutabilities, "elsewhereness," or *otherness* of history. That discourse, at the level of higher-order structure, is generic transformation. *The Prelude* is a poem that says, in effect, "I am most myself, most intensely lyric and Imaginative, in those moments when I reflect how unlike myself and like others—like description, like romance, like tragedy, like epic (and so forth)—I have been."

Recapitulating the entire flight of forms from description to lyric that we have traced in Parts II and III, Books 9 and 10 situate *The Prelude*'s most intense scene of generic transformation. In these books, the poet is most unlike himself. But through the antithetical logic of genre traced above (an elaboration of the "proposition of nonidentity" in my logic of genre in Chapter 2), Books 9 and 10 are therefore also the originary otherness that makes possible the intensity of the poem's lyrical self-consciousness in Books 11–13. The declaration of personal ideology in these latter books—of a poet who remembers what it is to be himself—will be the second topic of this chapter. In the official spots of time and the ascent of Snowdon, as we will see, Wordsworth's ideology of self becomes a seemingly impenetrable defense against history. On guard against the very empire of otherness across the Channel, Books 11–13 announce what I will call the poet's "ideology of logos," whose Revelation—marking the transformation of history into personal history, and French empire into the mind's empire—is simple autobiography. Autobiography is the interior contest, transgression, or cross-channel invasion of genres that provides the discourse for denying the invasiveness of history. And for that very reason, autobiography is history's strongest communication. In 1804, self, genre, and nation were correlative kinds; the self's discourse of genre versus other genre was also its politics of nationalism versus imperialism.

The Contest of Genres

Shapeless Eagerness

Because the Revolution books are among the most difficult sections of the poem to grasp as a whole, it may be useful to begin with an overview of their design. A look at the strangely shapeless river that opens Book 9 will point the way:

> As oftentimes a River, it might seem,
> Yielding in part to old remembrances,
> Part sway'd by fear to tread an onward road
> That leads direct to the devouring sea
> Turns, and will measure back his course, far back,
> Towards the very regions which he cross'd
> In his first outset; so have we long time
> Made motions retrograde, in like pursuit
> Detain'd. But now we start afresh; I feel
> An impulse to precipitate my Verse.
> Fair greetings to this shapeless eagerness,
> Whene'er it comes, needful in work so long,
> Thrice needful to the argument which now
> Awaits us.   (9.1–14)

From the hypothetical river in Book 1 whose floating twig points the poet's way (1.31–32) to the figurative Nile in Book 6, rivers have throughout imaged Wordsworth's act of touring. What makes the river in Book 9 more than ordinarily interesting, however, is that in a historical context the image is not just another insignia of inspiration. Wordsworth's characteristic river of history, as Barbara T. Gates has identified the image ("Wordsworth and the Course of History"), is here an inspiration especially oblique to actual history.

Imagine, for example, what the poet would have seen in the river had his drift been toward realism. He would have had good reason to be "Part sway'd by fear." Like the Street, the River was one of the most celebrated killing grounds of the Revolution. As Cobb and others have noted, it was the bloodbath not only of popular violence but of the organized violences that allowed the Mountain to suppress the Vendéan counterrevolution. Popular riots thus began so frequently on river banks (and seaports) that the French police became "obsessed" with keeping rivers under surveillance (Cobb, *Police*, p. 16). And in the Vendée, late 1793 saw some of the most infamous of all French violences: the *Noyades* on the Loire as well as other deaths-by-water.*

---

* Mathiez describes the *Noyades* organized by Jean-Baptiste Carrier at Nantes as follows: "Lighters or rafts were got ready, in which scuttle-holes had previously

In this direction Wordsworth's shapeless eagerness must not turn. Rather, with a touch of the pen that is his Moses' rod, he stains the water clear. The shapeless eagerness of his Revolution books will indeed carry a full freight of violence—a stream of disassociated names, events, topics that even at the time of writing (and certainly in our time) are finally only as interesting as drowned corpses: distended with irrecoverable meaning. But shapeless eagerness washes away such debris of realism by at last converting history into myth. The myth is a story of deluge followed by lyric peace. As we will see, Wordsworth's shapeless eagerness is the very genius of transform allowing him at last to deny the deluge of revolution—to recover the antediluvian Loire he knew firsthand in 1792 and to prophesy the postdiluvian zone at Leven Sands.

We can chart the precise route of shapeless eagerness in Books 9–10 against the course of waters in two other histories of the poet's revolutionary involvement. On the one hand, there is the devouring sea in *The Borderers*. Rivers is a Robespierre-figure who, in the action antecedent to the play's main action, arrives at a sea figuring mental, moral, and social overthrow, suffers a sea change, and returns to show Mortimer the land's end of all order (IV.ii). The barely stageable plot and style of *The Borderers* are themselves a turbulent river, a type, indeed, of disordered Rivers. When we as readers puzzle over plot, motive, and sometimes even the sense of sentences, we enter into the character of Mortimer asking Rivers repeatedly, "What hast thou seen?" "What do you mean?" (I.i.234, 249). Except in those passages that verge toward lyric (when irony-become-affection, as we have seen, anticipates full subjectivity), the play exhibits a narrative turbulence that refuses to let us stand at a reflective or emotionally "recollective" distance: it is *enactive*.[2]

On the other hand, there are the still waters of Book 3 of the later *Excursion* (*PW*, 5:75–108).[3] Following Shakespearean precedent, *The Borderers* had achieved closure by calling for a future stately recapitulation: Mortimer, we remember, instructs his band to "Raise on this lonely Heath a monument / That may record my story for warning" (V.iii.262–63). In a sense, it is an even more mortified Mortimer that then reappears as the Solitary in Book 3 of *The Excursion*, where he becomes his own historian erecting the final memorial to the revolutionary spirit. In a natural amphitheater with stones like "monumental pillars" (l. 57), the Solitary renders his tale of personal and political disillusion in the aftermath of the French Revolution with

---

been pierced; Carrier's guard crowded them first with priests and afterwards with Vendeans, floated their human cargoes into the middle of the Loire, opened the scuttle-holes, and sank them. . . . At the lowest computation the Noyades accounted for two thousand victims" (pp. 402–3). On violence in Lyons, "with its two rivers, and a dozen or so bridges," see Cobb, *Police*, p. 41.

nearly marmoreal composure. For just a moment, the enclosure converts into a theater proper, and he becomes a Mortimer projecting his agony: he spoke "As skill and graceful nature might suggest / To a proficient of the tragic scene" (ll. 465–66). But the moment of narrative enactment passes, and the Solitary becomes a historian condensing his life's story into schematic chapters pointed with studied or mock exclamations. Past joy surfaces only as "faint echoes from the historian's page" (l. 603), and past grief survives archaeologically: "Only by records in myself not found" (l. 705).

At the last, the narrative urgency of the Solitary's tale fades entirely into the lyric brilliance of the stream at the end of Book 3. His present life, he says in an outpouring of imagery as lyrical as any in Wordsworth's work, is like "a mountain brook / In some still passage of its course." The brook is wholly reflective, recalling only in murmurs the echoes of past precipitations:

> The tenour
> Which my life holds, he readily may conceive
> Whoe'er hath stood to watch a mountain brook
> In some still passage of its course, and seen,
> Within the depths of its capacious breast,
> Inverted trees, rocks, clouds, and azure sky;
> And, on its glassy surface, specks of foam,
> And conglobated bubbles undissolved,
> Numerous as stars; that, by their onward lapse,
> Betray to sight the motion of the stream,
> Else imperceptible. Meanwhile, is heard
> A softened roar, or murmur; and the sound
> Though soothing, and the little floating isles
> Though beautiful, are both by Nature charged
> With the same pensive office; and make known
> Through what perplexing labyrinths, abrupt
> Precipitations, and untoward straits,
> The earth-born wanderer hath passed; and quickly,
> That respite o'er, like traverses and toils
> Must he again encounter.—Such a stream
> Is human Life; and so the Spirit fares
> In the best quiet to her course allowed.
>
> (ll. 967–88)

Fulfilling the call of *The Borderers* for monumental finish, the starstruck, hushed lyricism of the Solitary's narration becomes itself a kind of still passage. The river of stars that is its figure-within-a-figure functions like some actual constellation to awe him into composed acceptance of mortal process—into an idealization by which stories of mortal struggle and pain are transmuted into tracings of eternal peace above.[4] On the strength of a recent paradigm for Wordsworth's poetry, we may call such reflective lyricism "epitaphic."[5] To raise a monument, Wordsworth writes in his first "Essay upon Epitaphs" (composed in 1809–10), "is a sober and a reflective act," and the passions in the inscription "should be subdued, the emotions controlled; strong, indeed, but nothing ungovernable or wholly involuntary" (*Prose*, 2: 59–60). Such could be the very definition of lyrical "emotion recollected in tranquillity." When Revolutionary history vanishes, what remains is a lyric inscription whose zero-degree story —like the bare name, span of dates, or short verses of an epitaph— points away from the buried narrative to an imagined, eternal history.[6] "My particular current," the Solitary thus anticipates at the close of Book 3 of *The Excursion*, will soon "reach / The unfathomable gulf, where all is still!" (ll. 990–91).

The Revolution books of *The Prelude*, I suggest, flow in form from the troubled waters of *The Borderers* to the milky way of *The Excursion* at its best—from enactive narrative to epitaphic lyric. The bulk of Books 9–10 is enactive because Wordsworth engages the reader in his younger self's perpetual confusion about the kind of agon the Revolution is and the kind of narrative appropriate to tell it. He portrays himself wandering at first into an inaugural tour poem of history. But descriptive form is suddenly appalled by irrepressible stories of Revolution. Like a curtain on the proscenium stage, description splits in two to reveal a bewildering succession of story forms—most importantly, romance, drama, and epic. Each generic frame in turn rifts apart in its effort to grasp the two aspects of the Revolution, the bright and the dark; and the overall accumulation of genres merely accentuates a sense of shapeless eagerness. Such shapelessness—really an excess of shapes—reduces the distance between the reader and the "I" on the page. We enact the character of the young Wordsworth whose bewilderment the poem figures as the reading, or misreading, of history. He came to look upon the Revolution, the poet says,

> as doth a man
> Upon a volume whose contents he knows
> Are memorable, but from him lock'd up,
> Being written in a tongue he cannot read,
> So that he questions the mute leaves with pain
> And half upbraids their silence. (10.49–54)[7]

Yet shapeless as much of Books 9–10 may be, a peculiar grace of lyric at last subsumes their enactive agony. As we will see, shapeless narrative first stops at Leven Sands to lyricize the death of Robespierre and that of a beloved teacher, William Taylor. "I" mourn and "I" prophesy, the orphic self sings. The narrative then resumes, but only to lead once more to an orphic moment, an elegy-become-prophecy, devoted to the sick Coleridge. Again the "I" is paramount: "I feel for Thee, must utter what I feel," the poet laments (10.986). Like Edward King in Milton's *Lycidas*, Robespierre, Taylor, and Coleridge are stand-ins. Each moment of lyric recollection really records the poet in the act of celebrating the death of his own revolutionary spirit and the triumph of his true self. Such are Wordsworth's fetes to end all fetes, his post-Revolutionary holidays celebrated in moments of sandy peace when the tide of history has gone out.

Having surveyed the overall terrain, we can now focus on the precise march of genres leading to poetic Thermidor and the regime of terminal fetes that Wordsworth will next institute: the spots of time.

The Beauty of the Revolution

The river inspiring Book 9 is just the first signal that history in the Revolution books begins as a tour poem: cities, people, and events are a landscape to be described. Wordsworth depicts his younger self as a "sauntering traveller," for example, leaving the "field" of London with its bookstalls like "Wild produce, hedge-row fruit" (9.31–34) to enter France in an exclusively tourist frame of mind. "Through Paris lay my readiest path," he says, "and there / I sojourn'd a few days, and visited / In haste each spot of old and recent fame" (9.40–42). Such spots include those that disappoint the naive enthusiast. At the site of the demolished Bastille, for example, the young poet retrieves a souvenir more to follow the etiquette of enthusiasm than because, like Childe Harold in the Colosseum, he feels any grand response to history's ruins:

> Where silent zephyrs sported with the dust
> Of the Bastille, I sate in the open sun,
> And from the rubbish gather'd up a stone
> And pocketed the relick in the guise
> Of an Enthusiast, yet, in honest truth
> Though not without some strong incumbences;
> And glad, (could living man be otherwise)
> I look'd for something that I could not find,
> Affecting more emotion than I felt.   (9.63–71)[8]

Already the tourist of political France senses a disjunction between his expectations and the actual lay of the land. The rubble of the Bastille "Seem'd less to recompense the Traveller's pains" (9.75) than did a single painting: "the Magdalene of le Brun, / A Beauty exquisitely wrought, fair face / And rueful, with its ever-flowing tears" (9.78–80).

The Magdalene is the genius of the landscape Wordsworth tours. He saw Charles Le Brun's *Repentant Magdalene* (Pl. 19) in its original setting at the Carmelite convent in Paris soon after his arrival in 1791 and before the convent's art works were seized the next year.[9] The

PLATE 19. Charles Le Brun, *The Repentant Magdalene*, c. 1656–57. Louvre Museum, Paris. Photo Giraudon/Art Resource, New York.

painting shows three sets of subjects related emblematically: the over-thrown riches and trappings of the Magdalene's life (epitomized by the spilled jewel box at her feet), the Magdalene herself partly reclining upon a seat and facing away from a mirror at the extreme right, and a landscape with tower visible through the window at the left. The congruence of the three subjects brings out their significance. Just as brilliant gems and pearls pour out of the rectilinear confines of the jewel box, so the brilliantly lit Magdalene—herself a kind of jewel or "Beauty exquisitely wrought"—pours across the Cartesian grid of the room's groundplane with a Baroque fluidity repeated in her clothes and hair. The Magdalene, indeed, escapes the figurative jewel box of her past life entirely by turning away from the darkened mirror of *vanitas* that might have boxed her beauty within its frame. And just as both the gems and the Magdalene represent brilliant beauty escaping worldly confines, so the landscape in the background of the recession through the window illustrates the liberation of light. The real reflection of the Magdalene is not in the mirror but in the miraculously released atmosphere of the landscape. Radiance near the horizon refuses to stay boxed in the window, but spills according to the conventions of fresco into the room itself as a suggestion of glory borne upon clouds.

Furthermore, there is a striking way in which Le Brun's painting reached out of its frame to involve the viewer in its subject. *The Repentant Magdalene*, along with six less famous paintings also illustrating the saint's life (designed but not executed by Le Brun), hung in a chapel devoted to the Magdalene. Facing the ensemble and set upon a large, boxlike pedestal was Jacques Sarrazin's kneeling statue of the Cardinal de Bérulle (Eriau, p. 88 and his pl.). Not only did the statue's expression emulate the Magdalene's, but its total form —white marble leaning slightly along diagonals across the pedestal's rectilinear coordinates—imitated the painting's subjects: gems, woman, and radiance escaping worldly confines. The statue provided a model for viewer response to the painting. We can imagine that the viewer—and Wordsworth—would place himself in mind in the emulative posture of the Cardinal and so in alignment with the painting's upward series of subjects culminating in landscape.

Together, then, painting and statue form a tableau allowing us to sketch the traveler's world the young Wordsworth expects and the response he wants this world to unlock in himself. He wants to see a revolutionary country in which liberation arrives, not with the pike thrusts of violence, but with the soft, fluid undulations of a necklace spilling from a box, of clouds rolling through a window, or of the clothes, hair, tears, and body of a woman flowing out of old constraints.[10] In the pictorial terms available to Wordsworth—for whom "Baroque" was not a possibility—Revolutionary France should embody the *beautiful* (the "intricate" side, that is, of the picturesque).[11] Set beside a radiant landscape, the Magdalene's "fair face . . . with its ever-flowing tears" is a paradigm of beauty standing in for such native belles as the Lake District widow "Wetting the turf with never-ending tears" in *Prel.* 8: 533–41. The young Wordsworth, in sum, has not truly left home upon arriving in France in 1791: he seeks to glimpse an idealized land of childhood watched over by a weeping feminine genius. Only there, in a land like Blake's Beulah, could he achieve self-liberation; only there could he assume the posture of the kneeling Cardinal de Bérulle releasing himself from worldly cares. We should remember, after all, the poet's anxieties at this time about worldly maintenance and his thoughts of entering the clergy (MM, 1: 166). The search for a "relick" at the Bastille leads him directly to the Carmelite convent; the tour through France becomes a pilgrimage toward a Madonna's beauty bypassing historical reality.

But the point of *The Prelude*, surely, is that the traveler of 1791 misread *The Repentant Magdalene* and the beauty of the revolution. Of crucial importance in the painting is not beauty without context, but the condition or aspect in which beauty appears. The 1805 *Prelude* records the young traveler's impression of a sentimental beauty in the condition of ruefulness. The 1850 poem, which details "hair / Dishev-elled" and "gleaming eyes," comes closer to the truth by introducing a touch of wildness. In fact, Le Brun's painting depicts beauty, not in the aspect of sentimental sorrow, but in the act of being emotionally ravished or violently transported. The Magdalene's face duplicates most closely the expression of Ravishment or Rapture (similar in many respects to Acute Pain) in Le Brun's widely known illustrations of the passions, and differs markedly from the physiognomies of Sad-ness or Dejection. Approximating Le Brun's paradigmatic Sadness more closely (coupled, perhaps, with Veneration) is his *Le Repas chez Simon*, also known as *La Madeleine aux pieds de Jésus Christ*. This latter painting, apparently unnoticed by Wordsworth, hung in the church nave of the same convent and shows the Magdalene kneeling before Christ with head lowered and eyes closed (Pl. 20).[12] It could have displayed to Wordsworth a truly gentle revolution of spirit before the consoling Son. The contrasting figure in *The Repentant Magdalene*, we might say, expresses in her upward look only a violent revolution of spirit before the fearsome Father. Even the landscape in *The Repentant Magdalene* is at best only darkly beautiful, showing a Claudian radi-ance near the horizon that must be acted upon by storm clouds before it can be sublimed into the nebular glory overhead.

In Burke's terms, what the young Wordsworth has difficulty see-ing is that *The Repentant Magdalene* really illustrates not so much beauty as the rape of beauty by the *sublime*, the other pole of pictur-esque experience.[13] Jewels, Magdalene, and light are being liberated

PLATE 20. Charles Le Brun, *Le Repas chez Simon*, c. 1653. Academy, Venice. Photo: Alinari/Art Resource, New York.

not by gentleness but by a cataclysmic, "masculine" revolution forcing the Magdalene with her ever-flowing tears into the mold of a punished Niobe. Indeed, it is helpful to notice that *The Repentant Magdalene* bears interesting resemblances to a famous "sublime" painting that Wordsworth probably did not see until 1806 but (as we noted in Chapter 3) read about in Reynolds's *Discourses* between July and December 1804, possibly during his autumn work on Books 9 and 10: the Wilton–Beaumont version of Richard Wilson's *Destruction of Niobe's Children* (Pl. 17).[14] The latter is a kind of *Repentant Magdalene* in which landscape is writ large. Where the Le Brun work shows spilled jewels, the upward-looking Magdalene, clouds projecting past a tower into the foreground, and a hint of supernatural glory above, the Wilson shows Niobe's offspring spilled in death, the figure in the center foreground looking upward in an attitude like the Magdalene's, storm clouds jutting over a fearful landscape into the foreground (there is a tower in the distance), and Apollo upon the clouds shooting arrows. In terms Wordsworth would have known after mid-1804, after he read Reynolds and placed himself under the informal guidance of Sir George Beaumont (see note 18 to Chapter 3), *The Repentant Magdalene* is like Wilson's painting in exposing beauty not to a Claudian but to a Salvatorean or Burkean setting—a landscape that suggests violation by rough forces.[15]

The older Wordsworth, we should note, knew that his younger self would soon be implicated in the violation of France's feminine genius. Part of the fame of Le Brun's painting rested upon popular belief that it was a masked portrait of Louise de la Vallière, a maid of honor who became Louis XIV's mistress, suffered from court intrigue, and retired at the age of 30 into the Paris Carmelite convent.[16] Like Julia forced into a convent at the end of Book 9, the Magdalene is a type of Annette Vallon (the fact that both Vallon and La Vallière came from Blois further links the two). Looking at the Le Brun painting in 1791, the young Wordsworth half falls in love with a Madonna, but really spies a violable Mary who will come to represent a violated land.

Now we can better understand his strange mental state at the site of the Bastille, a condition not so much of disaffection as of suppressed, unfamiliar emotion on a taboo spot of violation. Just as the young traveler misreads Le Brun's painting, so *The Prelude* shows him misjudging the overall type of pictorial experience political France offers. The razed Bastille is a signature, not of beauty ("something that I could not find"), but of sublime violence, and it affects him with "strong incumbences"—powers incumbent or pressing down from overhead like Apollo on Niobe. The young Wordsworth would suppress such incumbencies under a shield of "gladness." "Could living man be otherwise," he half states, half asks in a strange parenthesis.

Yet such gladness rings hollow. Everywhere the traveler looks, he sees a landscape contoured like the rubble of the Bastille and mandating that he be indeed otherwise than glad; everywhere the beautiful Revolution is violated by the characteristic earthquakes and storms of the sublime. "I saw the revolutionary Power / Toss like a Ship at anchor, rock'd by storms" (9.48–49), he says. In a seeming lull in the political climate, he observes that "the first storm was overblown, / And the strong hand of outward violence / Lock'd up in quiet" (9.109–11). The lull passes, and the eruptions of history continue: "The soil of common life was at that time / Too hot to tread upon" (9.169–70); "The land all swarm'd with passion, like a Plain / Devour'd by locusts" (9.178–79); and the names of politicians were "Powers, / Like earthquakes, shocks repeated day by day, / And felt through every nook of town and field" (9.181–83). No longer a picture of beauty exquisitely wrought, France comes to resemble a John Martin canvas in which whole populations succumb to devastations of sea, sky, and land.

As a tour poem, in sum, the first portion of Book 9 surveys a land that has undergone a revolution of terrain before the traveler's eyes. The challenge for the tour mode of perception—as for any framework—is to explain a Revolution beginning in golden promise and ending in dark upheaval. But such radical transition between the greatest "two points" yet faced by his tour framework distresses Wordsworth because he now possesses only an outmoded generic frame no longer able to hold rough sublimity and intricate beauty together in the same world of the picturesque.[17] We might think in terms of the complementary model of locodescription. Just as landscape in a poem such as Denham's "Cooper's Hill" touches off miscellaneous historical or political reflections, so historical events in the tour sections of the Revolution books generate scattered images of landscape. The reversal of ground and figure does not so much indicate difference of kind as nostalgia for an established principle of organization. Wordsworth as he portrays himself in 1791 wants to fix history to a linear route able to index otherwise unrelated sights. But in Book 9, the merely associative coordination of the sublime and beautiful no longer suffices. It is now precisely because he cannot find "a regular Chronicle" explaining the origin and development of "the main Organs of the public Power" that events in France appear "loose and disjointed," leaving his affections "without a vital interest" (9.101–8). Challenged by changes in historical topography, Wordsworth's younger persona suddenly comes to the point where it yearns to see history, not as a loose variety of beauty and sublimity, but as an organic whole.

The Prelude, of course, argues that in the realm of actual landscape the poet of 1791 had already formulated a philosophy of nature able to integrate the beautiful and sublime at a deep level. (The critique of the tyranny of the eye in Book 11, indeed, accounts the picturesque to the period *after* France.) The beautiful and sublime in nature became organically linked because they participated in forming, and in being formed by, his self. In the Lakes, "beauteous forms or grand" (1.573) thus cooperated to influence his growth. Reciprocally, his fancy, as in 8.542–86, made landscape even more beautiful while his imagination, as in the Simplon passage, enhanced sublimity. Landscape came to compose a single, coherent picture washed by consciousness in which nurturing and chastising, beautiful and sublime elements complemented each other. Only in such a view of nature where all chastisement is borne with awareness of consolation can the sublime transcend mere horror.

But for the bulk of the Revolution books, the traveler through France not only cannot apply his philosophy of nature to history but seems unaware of any such philosophy separate from what I have called the verificatory nature of the Revolution itself—the time's own idiom of storms, earthquakes, and so forth. One example will demonstrate this point clearly. As remembered in the early books of the poem, beauty and sublimity in the Lakes complemented each other such that a child hanging over a raven's nest could surrender to sublime winds trustingly, mindful of balancing forces (1.341–50). But *history's* sublime winds cause vertigo, a total loss of balance and trust. After England declares war on France,

> I, who with the breeze
> Had play'd, a green leaf on the blessed tree
> Of my beloved Country; nor had wish'd
> For happier fortune than to wither there,
> Now from my pleasant station was cut off,
> And toss'd about in whirlwinds.
>
> (10.253–58)

Wordsworth's conceit merely witnesses the random destruction of beauty by the sublime. Contrary to the hindsight of Book 11, a fully organic philosophy of nature does not arise until after the Revolution makes it necessary.[18]

Bad Stories

With the failure of description, the curtain rises on the underlying narrative scene. The genre of the tour poem extends into the succeeding portions of the Revolution books: "All else was progress on the self-same path / On which . . . I had been travelling," the poet says, "this a stride at once / Into another region" (10.238–41). But increasingly, Wordsworth disrupts the facade of description with

GENRE	PARADIGM SHIFT IN GENRE	
Tour poem	Beautiful——(Picturesque)——► Sublime	
Narrative genres		
Romance	Chivalric————————► Gothic	
Drama	Comic————————► Tragic	
Miltonic epic	Millennial————————► Hellish	
Lyric	Elegiac————————► Prophetic	

FIG. 12. The contest of genres in Books 9 and 10 of *The Prelude*.

narrative genres enacting his younger self's shapeless perception of events. Altogether, the kinds of Books 9–10 form a layered structure conducting us toward lyric, as shown in Fig. 12. Concentrating for the present on the three narrative genres of romance, drama, and epic, we can see that each produces a version of the tour poem's inadequate split-image of the Revolution: each first projects a golden-world France, then limns a terrible iron age. Or rather, each genre follows the pattern of the travel poem in representing the sudden appearance, not of an iron age conceptually related to the golden past, but of a whirlwind energy—call it gothic, tragic, or hellish—canceling the line of history and confronting the perceiver with a merely monstrous experience.

We might think by contrast of the Revolutionary "ideology of combat" (see Fig. 1, Chapter 4), which had organized the forces of liberty and tyranny in a structured agony constitutive of the state. The rift in each of Wordsworth's narrative genres marks something like agon—a combat, for example, between the chivalric and gothic Revolutions. But such agon potentially mimetic of historical combat is never comprehended as such. Rather, the moment an agony occurs sharp enough to focus a coherent narrative of revolution, the frame of generic expectation shifts and the lines of combat must be redrawn. The contest of genres in Books 9–10 is thus a denied mimesis of Revolutionary combat. It flinches back from one genre after another in search of some perfectly purgative narrative form— a tragedy beyond tragedy—able to make acceptable the underlying facts of combat. But a purgation so complete that agony hurts not at all is unimaginable in narrative. Abandoned in mid-performance in all its available narrative forms, history in the Revolution books thus becomes only what we know it intuitively to be: a bad story.

Chivalric romance dominates the middle portion of Book 9 before yielding to its dark gothic brother.[19] In what we can call the "Beaupuy Tale" (9.294–555), Michel Beaupuy appears as a knight wandering "through a Book, an old Romance or Tale / Of Fairy" (9.307–8) and inspires the young Wordsworth to recall "each bright spot" of "truth preserv'd and error pass'd away" (9.373–75). Wordsworth thoroughly romanticizes the history seen under this bright spotlight. First, his younger self "slipp'd in thought" to the marvelous realm of Ariosto's Angelica, Tasso's Erminia, and Spenser's Satyrs where enchanted woods replace the tourist's landscape of history (9.445–64). After imagining Spenser's Satyrs dancing about "A mortal Beauty, their unhappy Thrall" (probably Una),[20] he slips to the cognate actual sight of a "Convent in a meadow green" violated by "violence abrupt" (9.468–81). Finally he is fired with "chivalrous delight" (9.503) after visiting a castle near Chambord where Francis I once wooed a mistress "bound to him / In chains of mutual passion" (9.481–93). Altogether, this rapid montage creates a composite bright spot focused upon helpless ladies or symbols of innocence awaiting champions. Book 9 acquires such an aura of romance, indeed, that it is easy to see the succeeding scene as the epitome of the romantic bright spot: " 'Tis against *that* / Which we are fighting," the outraged Beaupuy declares at the sight of a "hunger-bitten Girl," a damsel-in-distress or secular version of the weeping Magdalene (9.511–20).

Yet the romantic story cannot continue. One of the spots of romance, we notice, is anomalous because it does not contain a simple example of innocence awaiting her champion. At the castle near Chambord, Francis I, a traditional courtly lover, is both villain and champion, both the seducer and defender of his mistress—probably a maid of honor like Louise de la Vallière (*Prel.*, p. 295). Just surfacing in Wordsworth's younger mind on this spot is recognition that the chivalric world is the very emblem of the *ancien régime* that necessitated revolution in the first place. The castle, the poet says, commemorates not only the "better deeds" but the "vices" of kings (9.496). If we may vary Marie Antoinette's dictum, to love romance in this case is to have one's cake and eat it too: to temporize on politics. On spots of royal vice, Wordsworth says, his "Imagination" would thus often need to "mitigate" the "virtuous wrath," "noble scorn," and "civic prejudice" of his "youthful Patriot's mind" (9.494–501). But the compromise between romance and revolution is stillborn, its narrative climax unimaginable. When Wordsworth's hero declares, " 'Tis against *that* / Which we are fighting," he throws down his glove in challenge to invisible antagonists as if *this* were the moment the combat of the Revolution should come to a point. But Wordsworth's romance necessarily misses the point because it cannot grasp the underlying nature of Revolutionary combat. Urging the good fight between a Childe and a clearly identifiable enemy, it cannot comprehend that the purpose of Revolutionary fighting is to *establish* (test, fix, confirm) identity in the first place. Which is the enemy, after all, the aristocrat or his foe? And in insisting upon a fight to the finish, Wordsworth's romance then compounds its error. As we have seen, a revolution in which protagonists in one phase of action turn antagonists in the next necessarily perpetuates the state of war as the very condition of its being. Thus, for example, an event that will completely mystify the young poet: "become oppressors in their turn, / Frenchmen . . . changed a war of self-defence / For one of conquest" (10.791–93).

In the event, then, no enemy appears to pick up Wordsworth's gauntlet; and the Beaupuy tale simply stops. Beaupuy indeed dies fighting; but he dies in an *anti*-climactic battle (as Wordsworth believed) against the "deluded Men" of the Vendéan civil war.[21] This meaningless death is buried early in Wordsworth's tale (9.431) so that, like the Redcross Knight fighting the great dragon, Beaupuy can seem to come vividly to life again. But he lives to no purpose; there is no final canto of triumph.

Wordsworth then appends to the Beaupuy Tale the episode of Vaudracour and Julia, and romance turns gothic. Vaudracour, a romantic hero like Beaupuy, attempts a doomed revolution against social and political institutions represented by his father.[22] "Arabian Fiction," Wordsworth says, "never fill'd the world / With half the wonders that were wrought for him" (9.584–85). But failure plunges Vaudracour into a much darker kind of romance—an increasingly gothic tale much like *Caleb Williams*, where, to use Godwin's words, the plot consists of "a series of adventures of flight and pursuit; the fugitive in perpetual apprehension of being overwhelmed with the worst calamities, and the pursuer, by his ingenuity and resources, keeping his victim in a state of the most fearful alarm" (p. 337). Like the hero of Godwin's quasi-gothic novel, Vaudracour both flees from and is drawn to the father figure, experiences the gothic horrors of prison, and (as in the original conclusion of the novel) ends in madness. We come to recognize in his "dark and shapeless fear of things to come" (9.749) and his "savage" appearance to visitors ("he shrunk, / And like a shadow glided out of view"; 9.925–26) the characteristic demeanor of what Peter Thorslev calls the gothic villain-hero. Godwin's novel makes an especially apt analogue because in its original state it leaves its hero in unmitigated horror, refusing to liberate him from dungeons of the soul. The shift from the Beaupuy to the Vaudracour romance, in sum, duplicates exactly that from the beautiful to the sublime Revolution. Like the sublime, the gothic of history ultimately appears to the young Wordsworth as an isolated, monstrous detour from history breaking with, rather than developing from, the *ancien régime* of the romantic past. Such a freak horror must be kept at a distance, and so becomes for Wordsworth merely a tale "I heard" perhaps "worth memorial" (9.553).[23] The romance framework, whether chivalric or gothic, cannot comprehend the Revolution as historical phenomenon.

Complementing and, indeed, overlapping with the genres I have traced so far is a dramatic frame staging a shift from comic to tragic Revolution. The Vaudracour and Julia romance serves to announce the theater at hand because it is itself simultaneously a special kind of "tragic Tale" (9.551). Wordsworth opens this tale in l. 559 with an allusion to *Romeo and Juliet*, II.ii.15, goes on to give Julia/Juliet her own balcony scene (9.626–34), and even refers explicitly to Shakespeare's play (9.635–42). Like *Romeo and Juliet*, the Vaudracour and Julia episode is a play profoundly transitional between comedy and tragedy. "Oh! happy time of youthful Lovers!" (9.556), Wordsworth says, establishing expectations of a comic universe in which love triumphs over insubstantial woes. But as in Shakespeare's play, such expectations perish as the full tragic implications of the plot unfold. The structure of society victimizes Vaudracour/Romeo and poisons his life. So pronounced is the wrench in expectations from comic to tragic that Vaudracour changes scripts entirely to become villain rather than victim, a malcontent rather than Romeo. "From that time forth he never utter'd word / To any living" (9.912–13), Wordsworth says, echoing—as Selincourt suggests (*Prel.*, p. 297)—Iago's last words in *Othello*: "From this time forth I never will speak word."

An allusion-filled passage near the beginning of Book 10 then restages the shift from comedy to tragedy and initiates the strong emphasis on tragedy in the rest of the Revolution books. This is the passage centered in the Paris hotel room (10.38–77) that we previewed in Chapter 2. The scene is "a spot" in Paris evoking the same blend of strong incumbencies and too-eager gladness evident at the site of the Bastille (or of patriotic wrath and chivalrous delight near Chambord). Keeping watch like Hamlet on his castle or Brutus in his tent, the young Wordsworth allows "true history" to dematerialize (at the touch of "pressing" incumbencies) into a phantasmal, dramatic chorus (cf. Peterfreund, "Metamorphic Epic," p. 462). The chorus begins by quoting the first scene of *As You Like It*, in which Orlando complains that his tyrannical brother treats his horses better than his sibling. Then, turning specifically tragic, it rehearses a topos of such plays as *Julius Caesar* and *Hamlet*: a catalog of unnatural perturbations in earth, sky, and ocean heralding apocalyptic doom. A climactic allusion finishes the scene. As we have already remarked, Wordsworth hears the regicide Macbeth crying, "Sleep no more." Altogether, this passage shows Revolution changing from a comedy such as *As You Like It*, in which an Arden world can reform political tyranny, to a tragedy such as *Macbeth*, in which the very woods must be uprooted in a cataclysmic battle against oppression.

After the Paris-hotel passage, tragedy then seizes center stage in Book 10. Wordsworth, who read *Hamlet* again in March 1804 shortly before beginning the Revolution books (*CMY*, p. 254), crowds the pages with allusions not only to *Hamlet* (10.313–14), but to *Julius Caesar* (10.167), *King Lear* (10.462), and *Samson Agonistes* (10.377). All revolutionary incidents come to seem staged. Appearing so soon after the "Sleep no more" cry, for example, Louvet seems an avenging Macduff confronting Robespierre/Macbeth (10.91–100). "I, Robespierre, accuse thee!" Louvet says in much the same tone as Beaupuy declaring, "'Tis against *that* / Which we are fighting." [24] Yet, of course, Louvet is a failed Macduff. The young Wordsworth continues seeking a Macduff figure—"one paramount mind" that "Would have abash'd those impious crests, have quell'd / Outrage and bloody power" (10.179–81). But Macduff cannot appear in Book 10 because the tragedy so carefully staged refuses to yield cathartic release. Just as the sublime and the gothic of revolution seem merely terrifying when perceived in isolation from their counterparts, so the tragic climax of Book 10 remains perpetually unfinished, thoroughly Jacobean, when viewed as canceling rather than complementing the possibility of comedy. The revolutionary tragedy refuses to purge dark elements from society in order to allow restoration of a bright, comic universe. Book 10 is the bloody fifth act of a Shakespearean play in which the duel or battle never ceases; or again, it is a *Samson Agonistes* in which freedom cannot be achieved through any number of temple destructions. Drama is no more able than romance to comprehend the Revolution.

Superimposed upon the dramatic frame of Book 10 is then the last of the narrative genres of revolution I will consider: a Miltonic epic that shifts disturbingly from what may be called the millennial to the hellish (cf. Peterfreund on the Miltonic allusions of the Revolution books, "Metamorphic Epic," pp. 461–66). Book 10 opens with a millennial story that stresses the insignificance of evil and the importance of a special heroism in achieving immediate human regeneration. In the first lines, Wordsworth perceives the Revolution's foreign enemies through a Miltonic lens:

> say more, the swarm
> That came elate and jocund, like a Band
> Of Eastern Hunters, to enfold in ring
> Narrowing itself by moments and reduce
> To the last punctual spot of their despair
> A race of victims, so they seem'd, *themselves*
> Had shrunk from sight of their own task, and fled
> In terror.   (10.13–20)

The phrase "punctual spot" derives from *Paradise Lost*, 8.23, as Selincourt points out (*Prel.*, p. 297), but the simile as a whole echoes the similes concluding Milton's first book, in which the devils suddenly swarm like bees and play jocund music like fairy elves. As in Milton's similes, in other words, the opening of Book 10 diminishes evil and predicts "confidence / And perfect triumph to the better cause" (10.22–23). Wordsworth's opening simile, however, only introduces the millennial form of revolution. The theory of evil it contains makes no link between evil's fall and good's rise: evil declines by itself because it is a terrorism that can only redound upon the terrorist's head. Wordsworth follows the opening simile by predicting a similar fate for the Revolution's domestic terror: "lamentable crimes" of violence are "Ephemeral monsters . . . / Things that could only shew themselves and die" (10.31–37). But as Book 10 continues, Wordsworth shows himself developing a full theory of good as well. Repeating the essence of Milton's argument, he pictures the triumph of good over evil as the shift from a violent martial ethos —in which the "senseless sword / Was pray'd to as a judge" (10.33–34)—to one of Christian heroism. Wordsworth prepares for someone like Milton's Messiah, a savior confident in himself and God. In Wordsworth's terms, the Revolution requires a "Spirit thoroughly faithful to itself," endowed with "desires heroic" and with invincible "self-restraint, . . . circumspection and simplicity" (10.146–57). The young poet's trust that "the Godhead which is ours" will triumph over "tyrannic Power" is so strong, indeed, that it has "a revelation's liveliness" (10.158–75). Such millennial expectation amounts to a creed that France will be "Redeem'd according to example given / By ancient Lawgivers" (10.187–88).

Yet here the millennial epic ends as Wordsworth encounters betrayal, apostasy, and the declaration of war between England and France. Suddenly, the Revolution is no longer a *Paradise Lost* heralding redemption but instead a *Paradise Lost* in which no hint of salvation mitigates the calamitous history of Michael's vision. Alluding to Book 4, ll. 393–94, of Milton's work, Wordsworth recalls that "Tyrants, strong before / In devilish pleas were ten times stronger now" (10.309–10). The implications of the opening simile of Book 10 are reversed: the devils grow rather than shrink. Now the Christian heroism of the just and faithful becomes indistinguishable from "the blind rage / Of insolent tempers, the light vanity / Of intermeddlers," and the "steady purposes / Of the suspicious" (10.315–26). Now Wordsworth sees everywhere a return to the old violent code of justice: "The Herculean Commonwealth," he says in a recapitulation of the Fete of Unity and Indivisibility of 1793 (see Chapter 4 and note 47 to that Chapter), had "throttled with an infant Godhead's might / The snakes about her cradle" (10.362–64). Instead of heralding a Messiah, the Revolution gives birth to a pagan destroyer, a Hercules or Satanic Robespierre who, as Wordsworth says with an echo of *Paradise Lost*, 6.370, "Wielded the sceptre of the atheist crew" (10.457). (We might remember here with some irony the "herculean mace" the poet picks up at the close of *Salisbury Plain*.) This is a vision of the hellish Revolution.[25] Like the sublime, gothic, and tragic Revolutions, it cancels rather than complements its happier counterpart and provides not so much a form of history as a frightening terminus to history. It is a vision of the origin of Death. "Domestic carnage now fill'd all the year" (10.329), Wordsworth says, beginning his tribute to the guillotine. Epic can no more comprehend the Revolution than Adam and Eve can understand the personified shapeless eagerness that is Milton's Death.

A Dead History

Yet, of course, this is not the end of Wordsworth's account of revolution. Book 10 goes on to envision a new shape of history about to begin—a history signaled by allusion to Milton but not achieved in the framework of Miltonic epic or, indeed, of any of the narrative frameworks I have sketched. A tragedy beyond tragedy or perfect purgation, as I earlier called it, is imaginable only in lyric form. It will be instructive to focus on a preliminary passage in which narrative history reaches its height of generic clash, then watch the formation of an island moment on Leven Sands witnessing the death of history and the birth of lyric.

At 10.439, there is a figurative "deluge" of guilt and ignorance over the land. In the next verse paragraph Wordsworth shows us the remains of old history. There are remnants of a tour-poem landscape:

> And as the desart hath green spots, the sea
> Small islands in the midst of stormy waves,
> So that disastrous period did not want
> Such sprinklings of all human excellence.
> (10.440–43)

There is an echo of the language of romance we heard in Book 9: Wordsworth recalls "those bright spots, those fair examples . . . / Of fortitude, and energy, and love" (10.445–46). There is a stage scene: Arras, the town that fathered Robespierre, seems a Lear reproaching the winds (10.462). And there is Miltonic epic: Robespierre appears the leader of the "atheist crew" (10.457) and, a little later, "chief Regent" of the "foul Tribe of Moloch" (10.468–69). Genre piles upon genre in a storm of narrative contradiction: "human excellence" and "fair examples" clash with types of Lear's madness and Satan's foulness. The whole form of this passage of history is a contradiction and "mocks" the poet under a "strange reverse" (10.465). Narrative history can no more contain the deluge (the "devouring sea" predicted at the opening of Book 9) than the false "rainbow made of garish ornaments" at Arras (10.452) can shape the Covenant.

But the false passage of history acts as prelude to the new. In the three verse paragraphs following his strange reverse, Wordsworth launches a "separate chronicle" (10.471), a fresh kind of history. The deluge-sea recedes, and he shows us his younger self walking home in 1794 over Leven Sands estuary beneath a prospect of Miltonic splendor: "Creatures of one ethereal substance, met / In Consistory, like a diadem / Or crown of burning Seraphs" (10.480–82).[26] But the prospect of Miltonic glory is not the core of the experience. Prospect originates in a retrospective moment that makes "fancy more alive" (10.488): the poet's morning visit to Cartmel Priory and the grave of his Hawkshead teacher, William Taylor. At the center of this retrospection is his reading of a special kind of history on Taylor's tombstone:

> A plain Stone, inscribed
> With name, date, office, pointed out the spot,
> To which a slip of verses was subjoin'd,
> (By his desire, as afterwards I learn'd)
> A fragment from the Elegy of Gray.
> A week, or little less, before his death
> He had said to me, "my head will soon lie low;"
> And when I saw the turf that cover'd him,
> After the lapse of full eight years, those words,
> With sound of voice, and countenance of the Man,
> Came back upon me; so that some few tears
> Fell from me in my own despite.   (10.495–506)

This is epitaphic, or self-epitaphic, history. The passage, we notice, begins by alluding to a pastoral elegy sealing off, rather than releasing, the history of the dead. Taylor's tombstone adds to a plain chronology of events a close variant of the last four lines in the self-epitaph closing Gray's "Elegy Written in a Country Churchyard":

> His Merits, Stranger, seek not to disclose,
> Or draw his Frailties, from their dread Abode.
> There they alike, in trembling Hope, repose,
> The Bosom of his Father, and his God.[27]

Such an epitaph is not far removed from the purely prophylactic variety (e.g., the verses guarding Shakespeare's grave: "Bleste be the man that spares thes stones, / And curst be he that moves my bones"). But precisely because the epitaph is a *self*-epitaph, it allows the reader to pick up the bones of the dead in a different way. The nature of the self-epitaph is to trigger further stages of self-epitaphic consciousness in the reader himself. Viewing the stone in Cartmel Priory with its allusion to Gray, Wordsworth in 1794 thus first recalls Taylor's self-epitaphic words, "my head will soon lie low," and then goes on to write what is really the epitaph for his own passed-away self. Taylor "loved the Poets," he says,

> and if now alive,
> Would have loved me, as one not destitute
> Of promise, nor belying the kind hope
> Which he had form'd, when I at his command,
> Began to spin, at first, my toilsome Songs.
>
> (10.510–14)

Thrice-compounded as if in some magic spell, self-epitaphic consciousness at last wholly seals off the enactive quality of narrative history, causing a shift of perspective by which the self, caught up in the deluge of contemporary events, suddenly elegizes itself in past tense. When the 1794 Wordsworth reads the stone in Cartmel Priory, it is not so much that he brings to mind his 1786 self in the year of Taylor's death (and, indeed, an even younger self spinning its first songs) as that he abruptly gains eight years' distance on himself in 1794. Epitaphic history creates such a sense of elegiac finish, that is, that even the present becomes *as if* past. Only in such a moment of temporal *ekstasis*, a standing outside the present self, can strong incumbencies force the 1794 poet into an attitude of mourning like that of the repentant Magdalene ("some few tears / Fell from me in my own despite"). And only such *ekstasis* can then transform elegiac mourning into the profound, rather than superficial, gladness of Miltonic ecstasy on Leven Sands. Only epitaphic historical consciousness, in sum, can lay the past to rest with acceptance of loss because it lays to rest the present—with all its hopes and fears—as well.

But Wordsworth's wake for history is not simply elegiac. Rather, in both the self-epitaph (by its very nature) and the tradition of pastoral elegy generally, elegy wakes to prophecy. Just as Gray looks forward to a supernatural realm in his last line, so the 1794 Wordsworth, after meditating Taylor's epitaph, reenters immediate reality on the estuary to celebrate Robespierre's death in a hymn of supernatural prophecy. He spies a "rocky Island" grounding a ruined "Romish Chapel, where in ancient times / Masses were said" (10.517–22). This is the new island of history: the point of Ararat in the Revolution books. Here, while the "great Sea" of the deluge "Was at safe distance" (10.528–29), the poet learns of Robespierre's death and launches a "Hymn of triumph" (10.543) celebrating the passing of the revolutionary daemon. "Come now ye golden times," he begins as if the present were part of times so ancient as to be Biblical (10.541). Thus does he fulfill the spirit he had assumed just before the Leven Sands episode: that of one of the "ancient Prophets" (10.401–10).

We now come to the burden of our argument. Modulating in this fashion from pastoral elegy to prophetic hymn, Wordsworth's epitaph contains in seed the whole span of his characteristic lyricism. The oscillation from pastoral elegy to prophetic hymn, after all, mirrors his general oscillation in this period between Classical and Hebraic or near-Hebraic forms (including the psalm-like form of the ballad, whose common measure was identical with that of the hymn).[28] Writ large in early 1804 in the "Immortality" ode, for example, the alternation between pastoral and prophetic, elegiac and hymnal, and Classical and Hebraic assumes the dignity of the very epitome of passionate oscillation: the Pindaric ode (as it was conceived at the time). Indeed, the first three kinds of lyric listed in Wordsworth's later classification of genres in the Preface of 1815 encapsulate the span of lyricism I sketch here: "The Lyrical," he says, contains "the Hymn, the Ode, the Elegy" (together with "the Song, and the Ballad") (*Prose*, 3: 27).[29] Of course, much closer study of the interplay of lyric genres—of the sort I will attempt in Chapter 9—must accompany any description of the matrix of Wordsworth's lyricism in this period. What we should witness at present is that the epitaphic mood, which will at last be reified in such clear-cut genres as the sonnet (my crowning example of the poet's lyricism), is really the potential for a whole symphony of lyric.[30]

We might compare the epitaph buried in the Leven Sands episode, indeed, to the shell's "loud prophetic blast of harmony" or "Ode" in the Arab-Quixote dream (*Prel.* 5.96–97).[31] As in the case of this latter Ur-lyric as well, the function of lyric poetry is to sound the death of history. In particular, the lyricism introduced in epitaph lays history to rest through precise strategies designed to transform the scene of collective authority into that of the poet's original self. Its basic strategy is a strangely selfish manner of allusion. From the perspective of the Revolution itself, we have seen, the story of combat was supervised by the collective People. It was the People who governed the process of splitting constitutive of the state agonistes. In the Revolution books, however, the People are a mob of allusion. Here I venture upon a purely literary-historical aspect of authority and originality that I have so far underemphasized. It is indisputable that in the Revolution books and elsewhere Wordsworth wrestles with such "strong" poetic ancestors as Milton. But in the case of Wordsworth, I believe, anxiety of influence is secondary to fear of a more direct influence. In Harold Bloom's terms, a great, invisible trope underlies the system of swerves by which Wordsworth rereads his predecessors. This is the trope by which the entire system of misreading swerves away from something not even on its map: the influence of the People—of that frightful, pervasive, yet all but anonymous author of events that Furet and Cobb title Rumor or Opinion (see note 4 to Chapter 4). Where the rumored People once governed the splitting of the state, now only a madding crowd of allusions seems to govern the splitting apart of narrative genres that is the misprision of the Revolution books.[32]

How to reauthorize and individuate the collective authority that compels allusion? It is suggestive that the last, redemptive swerve in Bloom's system is *apophrades*, or "the return of the dead" (*Anxiety*, pp. 139–55). Epitaphic lyric, of course, is Wordsworth's version of the return of the dead—of a mode of return that is more than simple recurrence. We can take our paradigm here from the common type of epitaph in which, as Wordsworth knew, the actual voices of the dead seem to utter again from a transformed world. Wordsworth comments in his first "Essay upon Epitaphs":

The departed Mortal is introduced telling you himself that his pains are gone; that a state of rest is come; and he conjures you to weep for him no longer. He admonishes with the voice of one experienced in the vanity of those affections which are confined to earthly objects, and gives a verdict like a superior Being, performing the office of a judge, who has no temptations to mislead him, and whose decision cannot but be dispassionate. Thus is death disarmed of its sting, and affliction unsubstantialised. (*Prose*, 2:60)

In the context of the Revolution books, we may add: thus is *history* "unsubstantialised." The function of Wordsworth's lyric return of the dead is to allow the voice of past history to utter again only in the service of leading us into a purer, eternal history ruled by a transcendent authority. In actual epitaphs, of course, the realm of eternity is heaven and its authority God. But in Wordsworth's epitaph for Revolutionary history, there is a new heaven and God: nature and self. By modulating from pastoral elegy to prophetic hymn, epitaph in the Revolution books introduces a nature compounded from idyllic nature and supernature—the inheritors of picturesque beauty and the sublime, respectively. Such heavenly nature is what I called in Chapter 5 Wordsworth's other, or historically alienating, nature, and its genesis in the Revolution books leads directly to a new, transcendental authority of history: Wordsworth's "I."

Here we may look once more to the detail of the Leven Sands episode. "Other nature" in the episode, of course, is assimilated to the Lakes (the true other nature in the Gallic world of Books 9–10). Such a historically alienated nature makes possible the new, individual authority of the self by "quoting" collective allusion according to a process exactly like Bloom's *apophrades*: as if collective allusion were really *an allusion to the poet himself.*[33] The power of the whole episode thus originates in the fact that Wordsworth never alludes *directly* to Gray or any other precedent of pastoral elegy. Rather, he seizes upon a natural scene in the Lakes that allows Gray to be quoted by Taylor, the spirit-medium who can bring the wayward ghost back to native haunts. When the poet then wakes from his seance, the collective authority that mobs the rest of the Revolution books is thus suddenly recentered within a field of purely personal meaning. Just as Gray becomes Taylor, so Taylor at last becomes no more than an excuse for the poet to cite himself.

The prophetic hymn that closes the Leven Sands episode then completes the process of individuation precisely by allowing Wordsworth to allude to himself. Indeed, we need only listen to the hymn in full to confirm that the entire process of Revolutionary emergency —its Herculean narratives, its bloody scenes of natural verification, and its culminating ideology of justice—is now reincarnated in the poet's "I":

> Great was my glee of spirit, great my joy
> In vengeance, and eternal justice, thus
> Made manifest. "Come now ye golden times,"
> Said I, forth-breathing on those open Sands
> A Hymn of triumph, "as the morning comes
> Out of the bosom of the night, come Ye:
> Thus far our trust is verified; behold!
> They who with clumsy desperation brought
> Rivers of Blood, and preached that nothing else
> Could cleanse the Augean Stable, by the might
> Of their own helper have been swept away;
> Their madness is declared and visible,
> Elsewhere will safety now be sought, and Earth
> March firmly towards righteousness and peace."
> Then schemes I framed more calmly, when and how
> The madding Factions might be tranquillised,
> And, though through hardships manifold and long,
> The mighty renovation would proceed;
> Thus, interrupted by uneasy bursts
> Of exultation, I pursued my way
> Along that very Shore which I had skimm'd
> In former times, when, spurring from the Vale
> Of Nightshade, and St. Mary's mouldering Fane,
> And the Stone Abbot, after circuit made
> In wantonness of heart, a joyous Crew
> Of School-boys, hastening to their distant home,
> Along the margin of the moonlight Sea,
> We beat with thundering hoofs the level Sand.
>
> (10.539–66)

Whose voice, we may ask, sings out, "Come now ye golden times"? Surely not Wordsworth's so much as that of a whole assembly of other speakers, past and present, poetic and prosaic, scriptural and secular. By naturalizing the voice within his childhood landscape, however ("Along that very Shore which I had skimm'd / In former times"), the poet succeeds in capturing it within his own orbit—so fully, indeed, that his refrain is a line from earlier in *The Prelude* itself. "We beat with thundering hoofs the level Sand," he says, reciting from Book 2.144.

Thereafter, the next portion of Book 10 (which becomes a separate book in the 1850 poem) recapitulates the descriptive and narrative genres of revolution, fashioning an enactive history specifically of the poet's intellectual development up to the time of the writing of the poem. The young political thinker, for example, approaches "the Shield / Of human nature from the golden side" (10.662–63) as if he were a knight and enters upon social philosophy as if on a quest through "a Country in Romance" (10.696). Again he becomes a tourist of historical landscape, describing contemporary society in terms of beautiful prospects (10.701–7) and historical winds (10.749–51). He anticipates a time "When some dramatic Story may afford / Shapes livelier" to convey his thoughts (10.879–81). And again he alludes often to Milton and an intellectual, millennial story turning hellish.

But Book 10 then culminates in a coastal region much like Leven Sands—a zone of epitaphic rather than enactive history where lyric resumes its song of pastoral elegy and prophetic hymn. In 10.940–1038, Wordsworth displaces his "grief" for Napoleonic France (10.954) into an elegiac lament for the sick Coleridge at Syracuse—a "pastoral interlude," as Lore Metzger has shown, woven from strands of Theocritean idyll and Miltonic elegy. The overall movement of this pastoral elegy reproduces that of the Leven Sands episode. First there is a vision analogous to the earlier deluge: Wordsworth imagines in Sicily "a Land / Strew'd with the wreck of loftiest years" (10.959–60). "How are the Mighty prostrated!" he exclaims (10.951). Then there is a glorious prospect like that on Leven Sands, where angels met in consistory. "There is / One great Society alone on earth," the poet says, opening to view a new earth of "The noble Living and the noble Dead" (10.967–69).[34] But like the Miltonic prospect earlier, this view also looks back to retrospect. In the next verse paragraph, Wordsworth reads what is essentially an epitaph for Coleridge parallel to that for Taylor:

> Thou art gone
> From this last spot of earth where Freedom now
> Stands single in her only sanctuary,
> A lonely wanderer, art gone, by pain
> Compell'd and sickness, at this latter day,
> This heavy time of change for all mankind.
>   (10.980–85)

As in the Leven Sands episode, the home chord of pastoral elegy sounded in this epitaph (with its allusion to line 37 of *Lycidas*: "But O

the heavy change, now thou art gone") causes Wordsworth suddenly
to memorialize a lost version of self. "Child of the mountains, among
Shepherds rear'd," he remembers, "Even from my earliest school-day
time, I loved / To dream of Sicily" (10.1006–8). Like Taylor's epitaph, in sum, the elegy for Coleridge finally guides the poet back to
Hawkshead school days. But having reached the depths of elegy, self-
epitaphic consciousness then at last ascends once more to a mountain
vision of prophecy at the conclusion of Book 10. "Thou wilt stand /
Not as an Exile but a Visitant / On Etna's top," Wordsworth predicts
to Coleridge, and "Shalt linger as a gladsome Votary, / And not a
Captive, pining for his home" (10.1031–38).

We might perform a simple addition to evaluate the cumulative effect of Books 9–10. There are spots of enactive history—the tourist's
"spot" of the Bastille, the romantic "bright spot," the dramatic "spot"
in the Paris hotel, and the epic "punctual spot"—over which flows a
riverlike shapeless eagerness, a historical version of the breeze's "redundant energy" inaugurating *The Prelude* as a whole (1.46). Such
spots are instinct with the energies that will characterize the gibbet
mast and blasted hawthorn episodes to come in Book 11.[35] Yet they
remain unrealized, merely redundant. Only when they are removed
from the enactive flow of narrative history-made-present can they
be seen to sum up on the essentially single spot of time, of denied
history, repeating itself in Wordsworth's poetry without fear of redundancy.[36] On this "last spot of earth," as the poet names freedom's
sanctuary at the close of Book 10, the shapeless eagerness of the sense
of history gathers into the strength of Wordsworth's poetry at its
most powerful. There is muscular poise in this poetry, a sense that
the whole story of history has been folded into passages of utterly
lyric peace. Repose is come again.

Indeed, it would be possible at this point to refer back to "repose"
in the penultimate line of Gray's self-epitaph. But it will be more
useful to point ahead in our argument by reciting a stanza from the
"Ode to Duty" of early 1804. In DC MS. 44 of the time:

> From no disturbance of my soul,
> Or strong compunction in me wrought,
> I supplicate for thy controul;
> But in the quietness of thought:
> Me this perpetual freedom tires;
> I feel the weight of chance desires:
> My hopes no more must change their name,
> I wish for a repose that ever is the same.
> (*P2V*, p. 106 and *appar. crit.*)

Picturesque repose, we saw, had projected a carefully controlled freedom. Now repose must be reconstituted under a new control of
freedom: duty.

Autobiography and Ideology

The Ideology of Logos

There are other sections of *The Prelude* we could focus on to close our study of Wordsworth's denial of history. But it will serve simply to stop where the Revolution books have deposited us: at Book 11 and the official spots of time. Here, in the hushest, frankest tones of what we have received as Wordsworth's authentic voice of autobiography, we witness the announcement of his final ideology of self—a "correct" ideology that is no less than doctrine in the oldest sense.

Recall the God-Mind apotheosized at the close of the Simplon episode in 6c:

> The unfetter'd clouds, and region of the heavens,
> Tumult and peace, the darkness and the light
> Were all like workings of one mind, the features
> Of the same face, blossoms upon one tree,
> Characters of the great Apocalypse,
> The types and symbols of Eternity,
> Of first and last, and midst, and without end.
>
> (6.566–72)

Or again, recall the hieratic stance Wordsworth assumes at the close of the Revolution books. Framed between the Carmelite convent and the "Romish Chapel," these books of shapeless eagerness are not unlike what C. S. Lewis (p. 125) has called the "untransmuted lump of futurity" of Milton's history books: after history's deluge, the poet-his-own-Michael sings of golden times in full-throated prophecy.

As such mounting religiosity prophesies, Wordsworth's culminating ideology of self—his greatest denial of history—will indeed be apocalyptic in the old, high sense. But what sense in particular? What final doctrine or formalized ideology of transcendence will the Imaginative self choose to invest? This we may take to be the function of Books 11–13 in *The Prelude*: to impose not only a natural limit on Imagination, as Hartman has argued, but also a supernatural limit aligned with the deepest traditions of religious doctrine.[37] The official spots of time in Book 11 address themselves to the task by indoctrinating the Imagination in a regime of nature identical with God. Wordsworth teaches himself about his childhood terror in three clearly doctrinal passages posted at the beginning, middle, and end of the spots of time. Abbreviating slightly:

11a

There are in our existence spots of time,
Which with distinct pre-eminence retain
A vivifying Virtue

. . .

This efficacious spirit chiefly lurks
Among those passages of life in which
We have had deepest feeling that the mind
Is lord and master, and that outward sense
Is but the obedient servant of her will.
Such moments worthy of all gratitude,
Are scatter'd everywhere.   (11.258–75)

11b

        When, in a blessed season
With those two dear Ones, to my heart so dear,
When in the blessed time of early love,
Long afterwards, I roam'd about
In daily presence of this very scene,
Upon the naked pool and dreary crags,
And on the melancholy Beacon, fell
The spirit of pleasure and youth's golden gleam;
And think ye not with radiance more divine
From these remembrances, and from the power
They left behind?

      . . .

         The days gone by
Come back upon me from the dawn almost
Of life: the hiding-places of my power
Seem open; I approach, and then they close;
I see by glimpses now; when age comes on,
May scarcely see at all, and I would give,
While yet we may, as far as words can give,
A substance and a life to what I feel:
I would enshrine the spirit of the past
For future restoration.   (11.316–43)

11c

         The event
With all the sorrow which it brought appear'd
A chastisement; and when I call'd to mind
That day so lately pass'd, when from the crag
I look'd in such anxiety of hope,
With trite reflections of morality,
Yet in the deepest passion, I bow'd low
To God, who thus corrected my desires;
And afterwards, the wind and sleety rain
And all the business of the elements,
The single sheep, and the one blasted tree

. . .

> All these were spectacles and sounds to which
> I often would repair and thence would drink,
> As at a fountain; and I do not doubt
> That in this later time, when storm and rain
> Beat on my roof at midnight, or by day
> When I am in the woods, unknown to me
> The workings of my spirit thence are brought.
>   (11.368–89)

The two end panels of the triptych rehearse the mature self in its correct posture. Passage 11a signs the supervision of a transcendental subject: before the lord and master of the mind, objective reality must stand as properly as an obedient servant. And 11c signs the control of the older transcendence: before God, subjectivity itself ("anxiety of hope," "reflections of morality," "desires") must stand corrected. Taken together, the two passages convert the raw moments of childhood correction experienced at the gibbet mast and the blasted hawthorn into a unitary doctrine. The powerful analogy that appears when we read them together may be parsed, God is to Subject as Subject is to Object. Imagination is correct only when it assumes the position *between* divinity and objectivity, the two limits of autobiographical error.

The epitome of such transcendence-in-between (or of bordering, as it has also been called; see *WP*, pp. 198–202, also J. Wordsworth, *Borders*) is the passage we literally read in between: 11b. Here, just after adoring images akin to relics of the Cross (the missing gibbet with its Mariology of a "Girl who bore a Pitcher on her head"), the mature poet knows himself to be fully correct. He knows that his essential self, his Imagination, is neither God nor a worldly creature chasing early love and pleasure. It is instead the missive angel in between whose charge is to communicate grace, in glimpses of radiance more divine and of enshrined spirit, *to* the creature who must live in the world.

More formally, we can call Wordsworth's doctrine of transcendence-in-between his ideology of logos. Here it is useful to take the poem's religiosity at its word for a moment and think about Romantic autobiography exegetically. To start with, we can concur with James Olney (pp. 239–40) that autobiography is the record not just of personal being, but of ontic Being. Its primary function, that is, is to register within the discrete actions of existence a sense of existence *qua* existence—the fact that "I *am*." But what defines Being as opposed to loving, lusting, fighting, talking, and the other classic actions of autobiography? Conceived one way, an action occurs when a subject takes an object: "Boswell loves Louisa." But listen to the primal Western autobiography: "I AM THAT I AM," God said to Moses.

This construction, in which a subject reproduces itself as its own object (or predicate nominative) may be taken to be the core sentence of being. In the tradition of conversion or confession literature from which modern autobiography descends, the sentence is rewritten to introduce an element of temporary difference: "God is that I am."[38] A sense of true being, that is, originates only when the sign of the supreme Being is read in the personal being. Paul is not Paul until caught up into paradise to hear the "unspeakable words."[39] Nor is Augustine truly Augustine until he hears the voice of the child, and the miraculous page can be opened. Only at this moment can the Pauline or Augustinian self know that it "is" because it is "of God," thus restoring the tautological essence of definitive being in the form, "God is that I am (of God)."

But the Romantics, as Leslie Brisman has argued, would give birth to their own true selves. They would read within their everyday being the sign of a Supreme Being who is really their own deeper, earlier, or purer self. Whether we think of *The Prelude, Milton, Biographia Literaria, Sartor Resartus,* or even *The Phenomenology of Mind,*[40] "God is that I am" thus becomes once more "I AM THAT I AM"— but in such a way that the subject of the construction is now what Coleridge calls the I AM of primary Imagination. Or more accurately (since the first-generation Romantics, at least, cannot be said to be unbelievers): the Romantics embedded their new formula of autobiographical being within the older formula. The full statement of autobiography thus came to read: "God is that Imagination is, and Imagination is that I am." Or as I parsed Wordsworth's essential autobiography above, God : Subject :: Subject : Object. Imagination became the relational *sign*—akin to "unspeakable words" or the miraculous page—between God and the world. Or more accurately, it became the imaging (as in the formula, "man the image of God") that substituted for the originally aniconic doctrine of the Word.

To use the language of the original exegetes (Philo and Clement, as well as Origen), the sign of Imagination or Subjectivity thus intervening between God and the everyday self is precisely a type of the Word, "Logos." It is logos that is the aspect of unknowable divinity revealed to worldly reality. Or put in a manner that bridges the universes of old and modern hermeneutics: it is logos that is the *consciousness* of divinity given to worldly sense (see note 35 to Chapter 3). Wordsworth's religiously phrased doctrine of Imagination, in sum, contains deep inside an entire apparatus of traditional indoctrination predetermining the correct form of Imagination as a type of God's Word. We cannot press such implicit hermeneutics too far into the foreground, of course, but certainly some such primal, rather than merely contemporaneous, doctrine had to be in place for the poet to discover his Imagination haloed from the start in complete and sudden glory. The position of the concept, as it were, was already defined. All that was necessary was for a new kind of consciousness, self-consciousness, to assume the position.

But now the turn in my argument: having tracked Wordsworth's denial of history to its final doctrine and then gloried in a purely doctrinal reading of such doctrine, I wish to close by recapitulating the basic *criticism* of the poet I have pressed throughout. As in the case of any truly critical act, such criticism must at last correct the poet's own correctness—that is, evaluate, justify, and/or repudiate his own assumptions in the light of others.[41] To leave the study of Wordsworth's most glorious moments of autobiography upon a peak vision of logos, after all, would be to risk assuming the position ourselves. We would be in danger of simply confirming that the poet's work recovers the spirit implicit in his deepest influences, and that therefore our critical standards of "correct" or "good" poetry from this point on may be referenced upon the poetry of Spirit. All the work prior to the late 1790's, perhaps, may now be called pre-Imaginative; and all that after about 1807, post-Imaginative. Such would be our complicity in what McGann has called Romantic ideology.

How to resist complicity and correct the poet even in those passages where he declares himself most correct, most fit to be ordained a Poet? Our final *coup de critique*, of course, must not itself become too doctrinaire if it is to be a criticism rather than a counter-poetry. But for the moment, let me pursue assertively, and to the end, the historical criticism that has been my program throughout—a doctrine, let it be called, whose orthodoxy I have in part defined by recourse to the perennial strategy of dogma: rejection of a more heterodox doctrine. Here I bring into full play the phrase I have created as a signpost at a critical fork: ideology of logos. In recent criticism as it has developed from New Criticism, the trajectory from Philo to Clement—and thus from Jewish to Christian meditations upon Logos—has had its counterpart in the movement from Derrida to Anglo-American deconstruction.[42] It would be possible at this point to proceed as others have done and—starting upon the observation that Wordsworth's mature Imagination is avowedly logocentric—go on to read the endless decenterings that signal the necessary reversion of logos to those things that begot it: "absence, darknesse, death; things which are not" (to borrow from Donne's self-epitaphic "Nocturnal"). Such would be one way to correct the poet. Surely, for example, such passages in *The Prelude* as the revelation of language at the close of Book 5 would provide ample authority for readings of both the logos and the shadow it casts:

> Visionary Power
> Attends upon the motions of the winds
> Embodied in the mystery of words.

> There darkness makes abode, and all the host
> Of shadowy things do work their changes there,
> As in a mansion like their proper home;
> Even forms and substances are circumfus'd
> By that transparent veil with light divine;
> And through the turnings intricate of Verse,
> Present themselves as objects recognis'd,
> In flashes, and with a glory scarce their own.
>
> (5.619–29)

But while the particular bent and texture of this book would not have been possible without some devotion to the turnings intricate by which deconstruction itself illuminates its texts, it is also true that my purpose all along has been to put the content back in the method of absence—and so to validate the power of such method upon that of the most basic absence there "is": history.

The limitation of deconstruction as a critical act, I suggest, is that its conscious heterodoxy constrains it from adequately finishing the task of correction or evaluation (cf. Goodheart, pp. 175–76). Let me be clear on this score: deconstruction is not without value, as it is sometimes too easily charged. We have only to open a page of de Man, Miller, or Hartman to appreciate how full the method is of cherish, of nurture, of the sense that literature's word is the trust of value.[43] But like the New Criticism from which it inherits its trust in literature, the *explicit* argument of the method is tremendously resistant to the declaration of any normative frame of reference upon which to secure the determination of value. Such lack of normalcy allows the method to discharge its ontological and epistemological tasks brilliantly: the inquisition of absolute being and truth. But in the process, the problem of literary *value*—of correctness *qua* correctness—becomes invisible. Without its own producible norm of critical evaluation referred to some historical context (past or present), deconstruction cannot criticize the normative essence of "correctness" except by translating the whole problem of value, of ethics in a broad sense, into ontological or epistemological terms.[44] It cannot, that is, knowingly evaluate the transient motives, as opposed to timeless being or truth, of doctrinal position—of having a "*right*" position as opposed simply to plural *Positions* (to play on the title from Derrida's corpus). Motive caught in the differentials of historical value can only appear as the freak whimsicality deconstruction appraises in such terms of disengaged value as "playful," "odd," or "exorbitant."[45] Such are the second-generation "ironies" and "ambiguities" that establish between orthodoxy and heterodoxy a Zen of doctrine very like the older New Critical paradox.[46]

Logos may not *be*, in sum, but certainly the *value* of logos is in the way any cultural value is. It is a position whose external or internal "difference" (epitomized in holy wars and dark nights of the soul, respectively) is not so much absence as a ritual of determination constitutive of being "right." This is why my instinct, when confronted at last with the Gospel of John according to Wordsworth (declaring Poetry the Word of God), is to finish my doctrinal argument, *con brio*, where I began—by correcting the Word not in the light of absence but of the felt plenitude of history, the absence, as I have said, that is constitutive of what we mean by cultural reality.

At this point, I join company with other recent inquirers into Romanticism by taking the second road signed in the phrase, ideology of logos. What we must finally see is that Wordsworth's logos is ideologically determined in the full historical sense—a sense cognate, in fact, with what McGann (*Romantic Ideology*, pp. 7–8, 10), James Chandler (pp. 217–23), and Donald R. Kelley (pp. 14, 17) have pointed out was the origin of the very notion of "ideology" during our period in the friction between the French Ideologues and Napoleon. To criticize Wordsworth's autobiographical correctness historically is to recognize that autobiography is the most powerful ideological form the Romantics ever achieved. In particular, it is to recognize that the spots of time in *The Prelude* project Imagination as a highly specific, if denied, historical ideology. Some rough beast of history, its time come round again, slouched—if not towards Bethlehem—then towards Snowdon to be born again. It was this beast, antithetical to the poet's ideology of self and yet monstrously implicated in it, that forced the issue of correctness in the first place.

Toward a Discipline of Hatred

To make my case, I begin by borrowing seminally—if divergently—from chapters 8 and 9 in Chandler's *Wordsworth's Second Nature*, which has accomplished the most radically new reading of Wordsworth's spots of time in some years.[47] I refer to Chandler's very powerful thesis about the "discipline of mind" evidenced in the spots and their cognates throughout *The Prelude*. "Discipline," which Chandler borrows from *Prel*. 13.263–64 ("the discipline / And consummation of the Poet's mind") is the general pattern of what I have designated, in the idiom of Book 11, correction. Wordsworth was influenced by Burke's respect for prejudice and tradition, Chandler argues, to demonstrate in his spots a mental discipline reverential of the oldest, most emotively inchoate habits of his mind. Mind disciplines itself by rehearsing those past episodes that first taught it discipline: it makes of itself its own tradition (pp. 184–215). In the context of the late 1790's when the spots were originally drafted for the "Two-Part *Prelude*" of 1798–99, Chandler continues, such neo-

Burkean and paradigmatically English ideology may best be understood as a precise reaction against the ideology then being instituted by the French Ideologues (in their *Institut National des Sciences et des Arts*). Implicit rather than explicit in style, and habitual rather than theoretical in substance, Wordsworth's English ideology countered ideology *à la mode*. It became an "ideology against ideology" expressed as pure psyche (pp. 216–34).

The variation I wish to play upon this thesis is motivated by two differences in emphasis. First, where Chandler's work centers on the influence of political philosophy and ideas, my own has been sensitive to a different notion of how history influences poetry. As set forth in the discussion of historical manifestation or expression in Chapter 2, my working premise is that ideas are always after-the-fact in the process by which historical context emerges in literary texts. A poet first "senses" context in the form of highly charged and concrete phenomena that are prior to thinkable "idea" because they mark a constitutive—if morally or otherwise unacceptable—differentiation, contradiction, or contest in the historical context itself (and so also a contradiction in the once commensurable or, at least, sensibly opposed ideas aligning the facets of that context into ideological unity). Historical sense becomes poetic sensibility when, through a second-order differentiation implicating the poet in his context even in his attempt to distance or deny that context, the literary text emerges as a tissue of internal contradictions or ambiguities covered over by its own ideology of unity (characteristically declared through such critical "ideas" as Organic Unity, One Life, or Imagination). Accepting Chandler's basic insight that the creed of Wordsworth's spots of time was indeed an ideology against ideology, then, I would go on to suggest that the influence behind such ideology was not only Burke's philosophy of prejudice applied against a specific French philosophy but also a pre-philosophical exercise of denial—an effort by the Imagination to contain the phenomenal event that most seized imagination at the time of composition.

My second point of variance concerns only what to specify as the relevant time of composition. Studying the 1805 poem, Chandler argues incisively that Wordsworth grounds the discipline of the official spots of time in a textual structure homologous with a similar structure earlier in the poem: just as the powerfully imagined vignettes of childhood in Book 1 correct the lapse of mental discipline in the poem's introduction (where the poet records his writer's block), so the official spots of time correct the lapse of mental discipline registered in the preceding Revolution books and early sections of Book 11 (pp. 187–98). The felicity of Chandler's analytic lies in the efficiency with which it appropriates for the study of Wordsworth's ideology the older study of his revisionism and of its basis in crisis autobiography. The great crisis of the poem is historical; and the great instance of revision or recovery is an ideological correction leaving massive traces in the poem's textual integrity. But the history to which Chandler refers such revisionary structure is focused upon that of the Ideologues of the mid to late 1790's when the official spots of time were drafted. For our purposes, however, there is another relevant time frame: 1804, the year when Wordsworth conceived, primarily wrote, and assembled his full poem. At this time, the Burke/Ideologue conflict may be seen to be subordinate to another conflict so much more phenomenally pressing that it created—at the close of the poem's pattern of lapse and correction—an entirely different revisionary structure.

Our question becomes: what seized imagination *in 1804*?

A first step in historical reconstruction will be simply to recover the major compositional fact of the time: the changeover from the five-book plan of the poem to the thirteen-book scheme and *the relocation of the official spots of time this change entailed*. Drawing upon the complex manuscript evidence presented by Selincourt in his Introduction to *1850 Prel.*, Jonathan Wordsworth in his "Five-Book *Prelude*," WAG (pp. 515–20), and *CMY* (Appendix 5), we can summarize the contents of the five-book poem of January to about March 10, 1804, as follows (I cite books in the five-book version by roman numeral). Books I–III corresponded essentially to Books 1–3 of the 1805 poem; Book IV contained elements of the 1805 Books 4 and 5; and Book V—the crucial piece in our puzzle—contained in *inverse* the core elements of the 1805 Books 11 and 13. As recorded in the extant and implied sections of the so-titled "fifth book" of MS. W,[48] the last book of the five-book poem included (1) the ascent of Snowdon (now 13.1–65), (2) a transition addressed to Coleridge and leading into an early version of the meditation upon Snowdon, (3) a series of Snowdon-corollaries immediately canceled in manuscript (including the portrait of the "statued" horse; WAG, p. 498), (4) a fuller version of the meditation on Snowdon (corresponding to 13.77–165 in the 1805 poem) leading into a transition on the forces that wage "unremitting warfare" on imagination, and finally (5), after some work toward what is now the early part of Book 11, the gibbet mast and blasted hawthorn episodes. For our purposes, the outstanding fact here is that the last book of the five-book poem was to have *begun* with Snowdon and *ended* with the spots of time.

When Wordsworth then changed his mind after about March 10 and began on the thirteen-book poem, his basic method of expansion was to introduce enormous interpolations into a clearly marked zone of elision in the previous plan. Here we may look closely at the two transitional passages that framed Snowdon and its applications—(1) through (4) above—in the "fifth book" of the five-book poem. The first passage prefaces the Snowdon unit with an apology for a jump in time:

> Once (but I must premise that several years
> Are overleaped to reach this incident)
> Travelling along the region of North Wales,
> We left Bethkellert's huts
>   (quoted in J. Wordsworth,
>   "Five-Book *Prelude*," p. 16)

The second follows the Snowdon unit by sketching the world's unremitting warfare against Imagination:

> The unremitting warfare from the first
> Waged with this faculty, its various foes
> Which for the most continue to increase
> With growing life and burthens which it brings
> Of petty duties and degrading cares,
> Labour and penury, disease and grief,
> Which to one object chain the impoverished mind
> Enfeebled and [?], vexing strife
> At home, and want of pleasure and repose,
> And all that eats away the genial spirits,
> May be fit matter for another song;
> Nor less the misery brought into the world
> By degradation of this power misplaced
> And misemployed [?where] [? ?]
> Blind [?], ambition obvious,
> And all the superstitions of this life,
> A mournful catalogue.   (WAG, pp. 499–500)

These passages mark the fault line where history is elided in the five-book poem—specifically the history of Wordsworth's first Continental trip of 1790 and subsequent London stay just before his ascent of Snowdon (in summer 1791) and the history of his second trip to France in 1791–92. (A conjectural interpretation of the "unremitting warfare" passage might thus refer the first half to the poet's experience of London after graduating from college and—more certainly—the second half with its thoughts of the ambitious abuse of imagination to the Revolution. The "mournful catalogue" of degraded imagination at the end thus resonates against the "mournful Calendars of true history" [10.68] Wordsworth records in the Paris hotel room passage just before staging his paragon of ambition, Macbeth.) To expand his poem, as J. Wordsworth has said, Wordsworth had to fill in these elisions with the "poetry of experience" ("Five-Book *Prelude*," p. 24): first, from late March to April 29, Book 6 (accounting for the 1790 trip); then, from late April to early June, probably much of Books 9 and 10 (the Revolution) as well as perhaps Book 7 (London); and finally, from early October to December, Book 8 together with the rest of the Revolution books. With composition from late 1804 onward of the bulk of Book 12, additions to the already written materials for 11 and 13, and assembly of the whole poem, he was then able to complete his task by May 1805.[49]

The overall effect of this expansion, we know, is that the *Bildungsroman* of the five-book poem—tracing the progressive education of the poet up to Snowdon and then recapitulating the essence of the whole in the spots of time—for the first time became crisis autobiography.[50] Once the darkness visible of social and political history entered the five-book poem, that is, the linear progress of the poet's development had to be reseen as fall and recovery. Thus in the latter half of the poem: the fall in London followed by the recovery of Book 8, then the greater fall of the Revolution books followed by Imagination "Restored" in the concluding movement of the poem, Books 11–13.

But at least one highly salient mystery remains: why was it necessary to alter the original conception of the poem's conclusion by reversing the order of the spots of time and Snowdon (the latter, of course, itself the grandest spot of time)? It would seem to make perfect sense, for example, to proceed from the fall of the Revolution books to the recovery *allegro molto* at Snowdon and then to finish— *pace* the poet's original intent—with the quieter coda or recapitulation of the official spots of time. Rounding from childhood experience in Book 1 to childhood experience in Book 13, the poem would thus close upon itself symmetrically (see J. Wordsworth, "Five-Book *Prelude*," p. 20). One further aspect of the problem may be added: why was it also necessary at this time to raise the official spots of time to their highest pitch of doctrinal correctness? In his original drafts in the "Two-Part *Prelude*" of 1798–99, we observe, Wordsworth had minimized doctrine. While the passage I labeled 11c earlier in this chapter was already largely extant, 11a occurred as follows:

> There are in our existence spots of time
> Which with distinct preeminence retain
> A fructifying virtue, whence, depressed
> By trivial occupations and the round
> Of ordinary intercourse, our minds—
> Especially the imaginative power—
> Are nourished and invisibly repaired;
> Such moments chiefly seem to have their date
> In our first childhood.   (WAG, pp. 8–9)

Only in 1804 (whether in the five- or the thirteen-book plan remains unclear) did Wordsworth add the verses pledging fealty to the mind as "lord and master."[51]

The case of 11b is even clearer. Wholly missing in the "Two-Part *Prelude*," the passage appeared only in 1804. First there was a draft for the five-book poem ending:

> the hiding-places of my power
> Seem open, I approach, and then they close;
> Yet have I singled out—not satisfied
> With general feelings, here and there have culled—
> Some incidents that may explain whence come
> My restorations, and with yet one more of these
> Will I conclude.   (WAG, p. 517)

Then there followed the thirteen-book version with its additional verses testifying to complete doctrinal correctness. After recognizing the hiding places of poetic spirit, Wordsworth now deems it his duty to preserve spirit in strictest sanctity: "I would enshrine the spirit of the past / For future restoration," he concludes.

What we encounter here, I suggest, is a difficult problem in Wordsworth's aesthetics of closure. By the beginning of 1805, only one of two available orderings of the spots of time and Snowdon "felt right"—that is, aesthetically correct. And aesthetic propriety somehow corresponded with the effort in the spots of time to foreground Wordsworth's doctrinal correctness as a Poet. What decided Wordsworth's aesthetics of closure on this solution? Much attention, after all, has been given to the poem's opening: the infamous "Was it for this?" question at the head of the "Two-Part *Prelude*" (1.271 in the 1805 poem) that in early 1804 necessitated the writing of an introduction filling in the antecedent. What we can now see is that there is a kind of "Was it for this?" question suspended in the poem's ending as well.

It may be useful for a moment to inquire semiotically how it is possible to answer any question so absolutely as to create the sense of total closure. The only solution, it would seem, is a formal one: a recoding of the initial question in the form of closure. Seen in overview, the task of the thirteen-book *Prelude* is thus to create closure through the simple stratagem of reversing the "Was it for this?" construction to create an answer that might be phrased: "This is what it was for." Witness, for example, the place of honor given the demonstrative pronoun (and modifier), "this," in Book 13: "This proceeds / More from the brooding Soul, and is divine" (13.157–58); "This love more intellectual cannot be / Without Imagination" (13.159–60); "This faculty hath been the moving soul / Of our long labour" (13.164–65); "And now, O Friend! this History is brought / To its appointed close: the discipline / And consummation of the Poet's mind" (13.262–64); and so on. But what generates the meaning of "this" as the poem moves from its beginning question to its ending answer? The "this" that is the alpha and omega of the poem, we know, belongs among the other contentless "shifters" or deictic pronouns ("I," "you," "me," and so forth) that Jakobson has studied in a well-known essay ("Shifters"). This suggests that it would be possible to undertake a wholly contentless reading of *The Prelude* based simply on the relation between Wordsworth's shifters, which he structures in the course of the poem into reversible symmetries creative of his essential meaning or content.[52] A sense of significant being thus arises only when he refers "I" reversibly to "You" (Coleridge) or, in the spirit of what I called in Chapter 1 objectified subjectivity, "I" to "it": "I am it (the Mind)" or, put in reverse, "it is my genius." It is this latter reversible relation between "I" and "it," we may say, that is the primary content of the "this" upon which the poem closes. "Was it for this?" is answered, in effect: "This shifting relationship [I ↔ Mind] is what it was for."

Most disturbing, therefore, is any relation of the shifters "I" and "it" in the poem's concluding movement that cannot be referred to the pre-established network of reversible symmetries—that is, to the essential synchrony of self and genius that is the poem's burden. The strong inversion that occurs between the official spots of time (which spotlight the "I") and the Snowdon episode (which spotlights "it," "the Mind") is such a disturbance. Such a decisive inversion signals that the field of synchrony (the poet's habitual shifting between the sense of personal self and impersonal Mind) is being distorted by diachrony, by some field of meaning that commands: "*this* order of shifting and no other." The entirety of the previous books with their record of self-consciousness growing in rhythmic interchange with the sense of transcendent Mind, in sum, is inadequate to govern the closing aesthetic choice of spots of time → Snowdon, I → Mind. Or more simply: the decisive close of the poem on a crescendo of impersonal Mind is unconvincing based on everything the poet has so far told us about his shifting sense of self.[53] To create decisive closure, something other than the formal or structural means of generating an ending must be at work. In Jakobson's terms in his "Closing Statement," context is needed to supplement the purely poetic, phatic, and metalinguistic dimensions specifying "this" ending. Some *other* "this" must be exerting its force upon the poem's closing torsions—something whose very element is diachrony.

Here I proceed to my second step of historical reconstruction—a step that cues my own act of closure by completing the basic flanking maneuver of criticism I earlier deployed in Chapter 1 to study Book 6. To understand the aesthetics of closure in *The Prelude*, we will need to immerse ourselves in the full sweep of history in 1804. This can be accomplished by reading not only the journalistic and other materials available to the general public of the time but also the sources of public information most accessible to Wordsworth—particularly the *Morning Post*, the only periodical he was then reading.* As even a cursory examination of these sources will show, the overwhelming historical concern of 1804 was Napoleon triumphant. As 1804 continued, English hatred for Napoleon reached a zenith of hysteria whose closest modern analogue was the English view of the "Nazis" (in Churchill's caricaturing pronunciation) during the Battle of Britain. But Wordsworth hated Napoleon in a special way that had everything to do with how he chose to close his poem.

Wordsworth hated, I suggest, dialectically. It is in the years immediately preceding 1804, indeed, that we can for the first time name his methodology of denial "dialectical" without anachronism. Of course, it is important that we do not grow too philosophical here. It will be useful to allude to the true *Recluse* or philosophical statement of his method just around the corner, Hegel's *Phenomenology of Mind* (1807). But the presence of dialectic must not be thought to coincide with the ripening of its ideation. One thing that past seasons of war and invasion-fear teach us, after all, is that "ideas" are radically derivative of history. In times of trouble when "Spinoza" can be interpreted as "Spy Nozy" (at least as Coleridge tells the Alfoxden spying incident of 1797), the rules governing not only the interpretation of specific ideas but also the acceptance of larger systems of philosophy are radically reduced to the kind of *bricolage* Lévi-Strauss has called savage thinking.[54] It is the *bricolage* of dialectic that we must recover to reconstruct the torsions of Wordsworth's hatred in 1804.

Let me begin by hypothesizing, then, that the ground of dialectic, as of any logical method, is to be discovered in the purely practical domains of social problem solving—domains that include but are not restricted to the economics of class struggle treated by dialectical materialism. For our purposes, the two theaters that will be most useful in reconstructing the shape of Wordsworth's hatred in 1804 are the military and the political. Whatever else it is, dialectic is a tactics of contest. The *longue durée* view of the problem is intriguing. It may well be, for example, that just as Classical logic with its axiom of fixed identity ($a = a$) is the logic of the Greek city-state or archipelago, so dialectic with its axiom of negational identity ($a = $ not-a) is the logic of the Central European plains lacking defensible boundaries. But what is practicable here is only a history of shorter view preparing us to grasp the specific tactics of Wordsworth's poetry.

(1) *The Art of War*. At the risk of platitude, we can begin by ratifying the contemporary opinion that Napoleon was the premier military mind of his time. But what kind of mind? How did Napo-

---

* Wordsworth wrote in mid-January 1804 to John Thelwall: "I neither read reviews, magazines, nor any periodical publications whatsoever except the Morning [Post]" (*Letters*, 1: 433).

leon think war? The answer, as David Chandler's massive study of *The Campaigns of Napoleon* makes clear, must be sought primarily in the lower-order records of Bonaparte's battlefield practice and only secondarily in his unsystematic *Correspondance* and other writings (D. Chandler, esp. pp. 133–36). What the record shows is that Napoleon's "genius" lay in a logic of moving armies that was remarkably unified in conception if multifarious in application (see also Connelly on this point). Not only did Napoleon meld strategic and tactical planning ("It is often in the system of campaign that one conceives the system of battle"; quoted in D. Chandler, p. 178), but he practiced on both levels of military thinking a style of warfare so unified that it may be called organic in a Romantic sense.

It will serve to look primarily at Grand Tactics, the art of moving men, horses, and artillery in battle that contemporary military thought set between higher strategy and the lower tactics of hand-to-hand fighting.[55] As David Chandler suggests, Napoleon's Grand Tactics stand out in clearest relief in his "ideal type of action," or normative battle plan (pp. 178–91). What stands out, we might say, is something like Reynolds's Ideal or Central Form. At least at first glance, Napoleon's art of war was a Classical unity. His operative paradigm was Aristotelian tragedy: just as strategy dictated that armies be moved and disposed in three actions (D. Chandler, p. 162), so Grand Tactics dictated that "A battle is a theatrical piece, with a beginning, a middle, and an end."[56] And just as strategy was the unity specifically of space and time ("Strategy is the art of making use of time and space"; quoted in D. Chandler, p. 161), so Grand Tactics was the unity of the Center and the Moment.

Center and Moment are the axioms of Napoleon's distinctive system of concentrated force coupled with fluid maneuver. By the center, or "point," he meant the vulnerable hinge or joint in the enemy formed by turning the flank and folding him up into an L-shape.[57] To the attack upon this center he dedicated his *masse de décision*, or general reserve force. But how to take the center when his army was characteristically outnumbered? The answer lay in the mediation of the whole notion of the Center by that of the Moment: the frontal assault had to be held back until the developing hinge had been brought to just the right instant of crisis. It is clear from Napoleon's constant preoccupation with temporality in his *Correspondance* and his battlefield actions that this moment had near-mythic significance. It registers on the same clock as Goethe's *Augenblick* and other pregnant Romantic Moments.[58] The moment, the minute, the mystical heart of time he sought in battle was eternity in an instant. Or to use the conceit of the *Correspondance*, it was the instant when the universe of fluid maneuver brimmed: "There is a moment in engagements when the least maneuver is decisive and gives the victory; it is the one drop of water which makes the vessel run over" (quoted in D. Chandler, p. 189; see also p. 149).

But the theater pieces of Romantic art, of course, are never just unified in an Aristotelian sense. As Goethe's *Faust* displays so largely, they achieve their unity only through an entelechy that at last redraws the very notion of unity. Thus if Napoleon's system of Center and Moment is a Classical unity in one sense, in another it resolves into what we may aptly call—in the idiom of the latest descendant of dialectic—decentering and deferral. Consider his ideal plan once more.

Center: As we read in accounts from both sides of the line, Bonaparte's secret in taking the center was that he never let the enemy know where the center was. Through his own act of dangerous unbalance, he kept his enemy in a constant state of actual and psychological unbalance. Here we may look in detail at the maneuver of turning the flank by which he created an attackable center. The maneuver was accomplished by means of his very signature: his famously demoralizing enveloping movement. Even as he gathered his *masse de décision* behind his lines, he would form up under the leadership of his ablest commander a strong secondary force consisting of cavalry, horse artillery, and sometimes infantry (D. Chandler, p. 186). Marching behind a concealing cavalry screen, this force would advance to the flank or rear of the enemy, then suddenly discover itself in an *attaque débordante* announced by an explosion of cannon from an unexpected quarter and—to the eyes of the opposing commanders—an ominous, nearing line of dust and smoke (D. Chandler, p. 188). What Napoleon called "the Event" would then occur when the opposing general felt compelled to draw off troops from the previous center of engagement to meet the threat on the flank. The enemy was thus decentered, folded up in its attempt to meet *two* apparent centers of engagement.

Moment: Witness this vignette recounted by David Chandler:

The process of the enemy's weakening his position at the appointed sector [the "hinge"] had to be completed or at least well-advanced before the main French attack could be unleashed; this was a time in the battle when Napoleon always held his watch in hand, closely scrutinizing the passage of every minute. At Austerlitz he asked Soult how long it would take his divisions to storm the Pratzen Heights: "Twenty minutes, Sire!" was the reply. "Then we will wait a further quarter of an hour," replied the Emperor, anxious that the Russian and Austrian columns of the Allied center . . . should have all the time they needed to be drawn into the fierce battle raging at the southern extremity of the line. (p. 189)

Our traditional image of the imperturbable Emperor with hand in waistcoat, perhaps, should be replaced by the picture of a more anxious Napoleon with watch in hand. How did he divine the right moment to attack the center? The answer lay in his carefully conceived, deliberate calculus of deferral designed to decenter the enemy *in time* —to make him misjudge not only the place but the decisive instant of battle. Only after the enveloping movement had been allowed to develop for a perilously long time—a time that weakened the enemy at the critical hinge but also, in the era before rapid battlefield communication, perpetually threatened to unhinge the attacking army as well—would Napoleon at last release his *masse de décision* against the center: first a devastating concentration of artillery to make the rupture, then infantry and cavalry charges to occupy the breach, and finally the commitment of his cavalry "heavies"—cuirassiers, carabiniers, mounted grenadiers—to split the enemy in two and win the battle (D. Chandler, pp. 189–90).

The judgment of modern military history is instructive. What has most impressed the historians about Napoleon's battles is not so much their brutal efficiency as their preeminently indirect or doubling approach. As B. H. Liddell-Hart puts it in his *The Strategy of the Indirect Approach*, Bonaparte's method consisted first in "the principle of calculated dispersion to induce the enemy to disperse their own concentration preparatory to the swift reuniting of his own forces" and secondly in the principle of "a 'plan with several branches,' . . . of operating in a line which threatened alternative objectives" (p. 106). Or as R. Ben Jones sums up: "Normally, Napoleon preferred . . . subtle methods, for example, the so-called 'double battle' as at Austerlitz, where the main forces were engaged on one front and a secondary battle was fought on the wing, three miles away; or a frontal attack combined with a surprise attack on the flank, the psychological effect of which would be tremendous" (p. 61).

In our own context, pure military history must be pressed into new service. What should strike us about Napoleon's quintessentially indirect or doubling logic of war is that it was deeply *dialectical*. Napoleon split his enemies by performing upon them an analysis requiring his own splitting, his own dispersion in space and time. In the terms of the Hegelian triad (as reified by received tradition): he developed a thesis; then a powerful, semi-independent antithesis (the enveloping movement led by his best subaltern); and finally an extension of his original thesis on a higher synthetic level (the final attack on the hinge formed in the fold between thesis and antithesis). Thesis and antithesis doubled each other from opposed directions even to the extent of opening on the same massive discharge of artillery. Explosive main attack and equally explosive feint: these together paralyzed the enemy as if between facing mirrors. Other frames of analysis could also serve to map Napoleon's phenomenology of war. We can prepare for future argument, for example, by noticing that in battle Napoleon doubled action and *representation*. Parallel to his main actions, he propagated deceptive, figurative, yet also wholly convincing side actions whose relation to his true intent was negational. Napoleon's celebrated use of propaganda and of misdirectives designed for enemy interception was thus integral with his logic of war.

Whatever terms we use, however, the essential fact remains: for Napoleon, warfare was a way of *thinking* incommensurable with classical military thinking. Indeed, it is instructive to turn to the war columns of London newspapers in the early Napoleonic years—to coverage, for example, of the Italian campaign prefacing the Battle of Marengo in June 1800. What is striking about this coverage is the disparity between the massive amount of French military thinking available (presented in the form of army bulletins and reports translated from the *Moniteur*) and the virtual incomprehension in editorial commentary until well after the event. In the *Morning Post*, for example, the basic Napoleonic concept of massing on a central point was documented as early as April 28, 1800, when the paper translated a *Moniteur* article on the French strategy for defending Genoa. But there was no recognition that such massing was the central device of Napoleonic strategy and tactics in the campaign until after the climax of events at Marengo, at which point the *Post* broached the tactics of center and moment in consolidated form as follows: "The Austrian force was spread out, while the [French] every where presented themselves in close and consolidated column. The one had therefore all the advantage in direct and immediate effect that impulse possesses over pressure, the very principle on which French military tactics are formed" (June 30, 1800).

Prior to this moment of realization, all was confusion of a sort that confirms the antithetical nature of Napoleon's thinking. Misunderstanding of Napoleon's indirect or doubling manner of bringing force to bear arose because the *Post*—and the style of military thought it represented—was wrong from the start on three assumptions: that Genoa was the center of conflict; that Napoleon's straightforward objective must be to break the Austrian siege of Massena's army in that city; and that the Army of the Reserve still in France was only a marginal, defensive force. In fact, the exact reverse of all three was true: the Army of Reserve was actually the *masse de manoeuvre* (or strategical reserve) that Napoleon staged at Dijon as his main offensive force;* the direct drive to Genoa was only a feint; and the true center of conflict lay in the debouchments of the Alpine passes through which the Army of Reserve soon poured upon the Austrians from the rear. As each of these reversals came to light, the *Post* expressed wonder: its essential statement was amazement that the European community

---

* The *masse de manoeuvre* was the strategic equivalent of Napoleon's tactical enveloping force, with the difference that in this case the antithetical movement of the *masse* to the flank or rear of the enemy usually *was* the main attack.

had been so taken in by the feints, ploys, and gambits—that is, enabling antitheses—facilitating Napoleon's opposite intents. Thus the paper's rapt wonder that the Army of Reserve was actually an offensive force (June 2 and 14, 1800) and that the direct move on Genoa was really an indirect feint (June 25, 1800).

The climax of such amazement occurred in a long article of June 13 in which the total explanation of events is that no explanation is possible: conventional military thought cannot explain Napoleon's mind. The article opens:

No period of the war has been so astonishing as the present; at no time have we felt ourselves so unable to develope [*sic*] the views of the enemy, to reconcile their movements with common prudence and common sense. While we believed Bonaparte was marching to raise the siege of Genoa, he appeared to have a reasonable object. . . . In forming these opinions we were guided by a review of the ordinary operations of the war; but the movements of Moreau [acting under Napoleon] and Bonaparte have overset all our speculations, and effected a greater change in the state of the campaign than could have been produced by any battle; and we are left to decide whether these great Generals are guilty of the greatest misconduct, or attempting enterprises so gigantic, that they appear to be impracticable.

To make the comparison to the Battle of Britain: Bonaparte's strategy and tactics were as fatally incomprehensible to eighteenth-century military thought as the Luftwaffe's *Schwärme*, or "split-finger four" (four planes widely spaced, line abreast), to the thinking that marshalled the English Vic and other tight formations of the early Battle of Britain. Indeed, this last comparison—with its testament to the enduring organic paradigm behind military thinking—may serve to cue our exit from military history.[59] The unity of Napoleon's warfare, as I have suggested, is indeed an instance of Romantic organicism. How did such organism differ from the imaginal body—with head, hand, flank, tail, rear, etc.—that has always haunted the military mind? Imagine for a moment what it was like to join battle with Napoleon. Unlike a traditional army with a clear head, flank, and tail, his forces were strangely formless before battle. More accurately, his *corps d'armée* system with its loosely but carefully arranged matrix of semi-independent units (not unlike the elementary tactical unit of the Luftwaffe) was only potential form—only the base for any number of possible dispositions or avenues of attack. Whichever *corps* first made contact with the enemy became the head, and the other units rearranged themselves accordingly (D. Chandler, p. 185). Or rather, no clear organism resulted at all. In the course of the enveloping movement, the limb of the organism would seem to improvise independent status and become itself a main body.

It will not be too far afield, as we will see, to call such organism Coleridgean. Unity was the effect of a rhizome-like, almost obsessive predilection for antithetical splitting. Napoleon conducting battle bore a strange resemblance to Coleridge talking at table. To transume the military idiom: genius lay in developing "several branches," "alternative objectives," "double" entendres.

(2) *The Art of Politics*. But as Machiavelli teaches, military thinking is finally just one aspect of a larger political logic. What we must now see is that the military tactics we have been studying are a salient of the general formation of late-eighteenth-century politics. The link between the two is especially clear in the context of French Revolutionary politics, where strong-arm maneuvers enforced a vertiginous process of faction formation, transient alliance, and continued division. It is no accident, after all, that the Jacobin, Thermidorian, and Directorial regimes were at last superseded by Napoleon, for whom *coup de force* was only a more muscular *coup d'état*. For our purposes, however, it will be most useful to cross the Channel at this point and concentrate not on the French scene but on its closest home front homologue: the politics of Opposition. I will outline the contemporary theory of opposition by focusing on the Parliamentary scene and on the one out-of-doors extension linking politics directly to Romantic poetics: the politics of journalism.

Parliament. To start with, we require a discrimination of oppositions. As documented by such historians of party politics as Alan Beattie, opposition in the earlier eighteenth century was an unfocused, plural concept caught within the field of a Constitutional ambiguity of long standing. Dating from the start of party labels during the Exclusion Crisis of 1679–80, the ambiguity concerned the proper relation of Parliament to monarchy after the Restoration. Should this relation be one of "institutional opposition" (pitting the whole of Commons against the King) or of "formed" or "faction" opposition (pitting the "outs" among the politicians in Commons against the king's ministers)? In the former case, monarchy and Commons were seen as wholly separate entities; in the latter, Commons was held to be infiltrated by appointees of the king whose influence had to be counteracted by factional antagonism (A. Beattie, pp. 1–12; see also J. Owen, pp. 109–10). If through no more than seating "on the left," it was clear by the 1730's and 1740's that there was indeed a settled opposition of outs in Commons (A. Beattie, pp. 7–9). The concept of *the* Opposition, though not yet legitimized, was beginning to emerge. Yet in its theory, such opposition was still far from differing in any essential way from the Government it sought to replace. The outs wanted above all to get in, with no admission that once they were in they would recognize any further opposition (A. Beattie, p. 7; J. Owen, pp. 106, 108). The two-party system of government and the concept of Opposition *qua* Opposition did not yet exist.

It was the accession of George III in 1760 that initiated the modern era of opposition. At this point, we enter the zone of debate between Whig historiography, initiated by Burke, and modern criticism of the Whig myth (see J. Owen, pp. 277–78). But whatever our view of the contention by Burke and others that George III set out to subordinate Parliament (through corruption) to a small circle of King's Friends headed by Lord Bute, it is clear that the King did indeed exercise his prerogative of appointing ministers independently of Commons more aggressively than his predecessor (under whom the Old Corps of Whig families—the Pelhams, Yorkes, Walpoles, Cavendishes—had held long sway). Beginning with the appointment of the ill-fated Bute ministry of 1760–63, George III touched off a period of political instability that lasted through the end of the century and encompassed the American war, the Reform movement, the Wilkes debacle, the India problem, the Regency crisis, the Irish problem, the French Revolution, and the growth of the out-of-doors radical movements (see also my discussion of the politics informing landscape aesthetics in Chapter 3).

For our purposes, the chronology of the period may be written as a saga of declining Whig power with five moments: (1) the period of purge from 1760 to 1765 when the Government of Bute and then Grenville cut off the old Whigs and their associates; (2) the brief respite of the first Rockingham ministry of 1765–66 when the Old Corps Whigs and such younger Whigs as Burke returned to Government; (3) the first long period "in the wilderness" of 1766–82 when ministries under Chatham (Pitt the Elder), Grafton, and North relegated the Whigs to the margins; (4) the second brief Rockingham ministry of 1782–83 when the Whigs pushed through Burke's economic reform act (followed after Rockingham's death by the passing of the ministry to the Shelburne branch of the Whigs); and finally, (5) the second long period in the wilderness from 1784 through century's end when, after the famously unprincipled Fox-North coalition of 1783, Pitt the Younger brought the Whigs to heel (key dates: the triumph of Pitt and the reduction of the Foxites in the general election of 1784, the Regency crisis of 1788–89 when Fox again deserted principles to bid for power at the coattails of the Prince of Wales, the split between Burke and Fox in 1791, the Addington ministry and the Peace of Amiens of 1802–3, and finally the return of Pitt in May 1804 to lead the war effort).

What may be read in this chronology is the fact that our modern notion of opposition was authored primarily in the two periods of the wilderness—(3) and (5)—by a specific group of Whigs organized by Rockingham, propagandized by Burke, and carried to its *fin de siècle* by Fox. In the wilderness, as it were, Opposition transformed its antipathy to Pharaoh into a self-sufficient sense of itself as an elect tribe:

a group with a full "theory of opposition," to use L. Stuart Sutherland's term (p. 52), that knew itself to be perennially out of power
and so in need of a theory justifying the necessity in any regime,
at any time, of the out-of-power tribe. The immediate prompting
for such opposition occurred in the first period in the wilderness
when Chatham—in an anti-faction and anti-Rockinghamite move—
resolved to stand on "not men but measures" (J. Owen, pp. 185–87;
Winstanley, p. 31). Such goading was reinforced just before the onset
of North's durable ministry by the climax of the Wilkes issue, which
determined the Rockingham Whigs to join with the now out-of-
favor Chathamites to compact a "united Opposition" (see J. Owen's
summary, pp. 194–96).

In actuality the united Opposition of these years soon degenerated
into intramural contest between the Rockinghamites and Chathamites. But the theory that undergirded it survived and indeed flourished the greater the marginalization of actual Opposers. The leading
document here is Burke's *Thoughts on the Cause of the Present Discon-
tents* (1770), which sets forth the manifesto of opposition founded on
modern tribe: party. "Party," Burke defines anew, "is a body of men
united for promoting by their joint endeavours the national interest
upon some particular principle in which they are all agreed" (quoted
in A. Beattie, p. 53). Such is the celebrated formulation by which
the Rockingham Whigs circumvented the credo, "not men but measures," and authorized themselves as a formal unity subsuming *both*
men and measures. By this formulation they legitimized not only
their own Opposition but the notion of a perpetual out-of-power
Opposition. For the uniting of men on principle implied the uniting
of other men on other principles (from the *Declaration of, and Form of
Association Recommended by the Whig Club,* 1796: "When bad men conspire good men must associate"; quoted in A. Beattie, p. 73). The
function of an out-of-power party was to provide a counterbalancing check to the party in power, though with recognition that in the
event of the Government's fall the new out-of-power party would
in turn serve as counterbalancing check. The two-party system of
alternating government was coming to be.

The eventual outcome of the Whig theory of opposition was the
establishment in 1784 of the Whig Club, which Archibald S. Foord
has called the first party of "a more than temporary or local character" (p. 406). More generally, the outcome of the Whig theory was
the consensus by century's end that a formed Opposition conducted
on the basis of party indeed had a proper place in government. To
underscore this consensus, Beattie has collected excerpts from contemporary writings of diverse political persuasions. In his *A Short
History of the Opposition During the Last Session of Parliament* (1779), for
example, James Macpherson comments: "In every popular govern-

ment, opposition is not only natural, but, when conducted on liberal principles, useful, and even necessary." The Earl of Camden adds in 1788 that "he honoured an opposition; and . . . that he thought an opposition of great service to the country" (A. Beattie, pp. 61–62). Two passages representative of opinion early in the next century may serve to sum up the matter in an especially suggestive manner. Writing in 1811, John Ranby observes: "The opposition is an exact counterpart of the ministerial party. . . . The two parties thus composed, are to be considered as the principals in that legitimate warfare of parties in parliament from which much benefit is derived to the public" (quoted in A. Beattie, p. 61). And *The Quarterly Review* declares in an essay on "The Opposition" in 1822:

The inseparable attendants of freedom are party and faction. . . . As the body which is successful must be removed whenever its rival can produce a majority of votes, and as its removal constitutes in effect the election of this rival, the latter, under the name of the Opposition, daily resorts to every imaginable artifice to strengthen its interest, and procure the dismissal of its opponent. The ministry has therefore not only to transact the business of the state, but to carry on an offensive and defensive war on its own private account. (Quoted in Beattie, p. 62)

To exploit the trope of politics as warfare: Opposition became a legitimate *tactics* of political contest.[60] After 1783 when note-taking in Parliament was officially sanctioned, therefore, contemporary newspapers could report actual warfare and Parliamentary debate in perfect tandem.

But we must also observe that if the politics of Opposition was a tactics, it was like Napoleon's Grand Tactics in resembling no combat the Parliamentary system—and public perception of it—could yet fully conceive. If Parliamentary reportage accompanied war news in the newspapers, then, both alike were behind the times. Just as traditional coverage of military actions, as we have seen, could not understand warfare as conducted by Napoleon, so coverage of Parliamentary debate could not grasp the change in Opposition conduct imposed by Whig theory. Editorial commentary during the early Revolution, for example, repeatedly contrasted the shifting formlessness of French faction with an assumed standard of party constancy or unity in England.[61] But the standard no longer accurately represented the true state of politics at home because parties were anything but constant. Here we reach the crux of our issue: as in the case of Napoleon's warfare, the unity of the new Opposition was also a deep predilection for disunity of a special kind. To adopt the terms of Hegelian tradition once more: the Whig justification of Opposition as a partner in a legitimate alternation of power was deeply dialectical. Properly constituted government was an interaction of thesis and antithesis in which the Opposition party was charged with preserving the essential reflex of negation, of political differentiation, making the whole process possible. As a party, we may say, Opposition was negation raised to the level of policy.

With its awakening recognition of the two-party norm, public perception of politics was ready for such negation at the level of interparty contest. The Whigs, it was understood, were anti-Government. What public perception was not prepared for, however, was the thoroughness with which the dialectical or negational essence of Opposition penetrated intraparty relations as well. As became clear in the Whigs' second period in the wilderness, for example, there was no such thing as a party united in Opposition that did not immediately reproduce its dialectical relation with Ministry internally as the kind of divisiveness, rancor, and recantation that culminated in Burke's public break with Fox in 1791 and in the desertion of Burke and other conservative Whigs to Government in the early war years. It is at this point that the vexed issue of apostasy—of shifting loyalties —arises in our period. The leaders of Opposition could seem both wholly principled and *un*principled in their loyalties. From our perspective, this is because apostasy was endemic to the basic negational structure of opposition. Referenced on a pure relation, Opposition was in the final analysis a will to oppose independent of settled object. We might instance Burke's quixotic tilting against corruption in his Reform and India crusades, both of which were perhaps less founded on verifiable corruption than on a sheer will to contest (see J. Owen, p. 237). So, too, there is the oath Fox swore in 1793 that "there was no address at the moment Pitt could form he would not propose an amendment to, and divide the House upon" (quoted in J. Owen, p. 289).

In the eyes of contemporaries, such a stand could seem no true stand at all. To stand for Opposition was to be willing to give up old principles and allies as the relational essence of negation dictated. Thus the apostate views of both Burke and Fox: when Burke found in the French Revolution a more powerful object to oppose than Ministry, he deserted Fox to take his position within the Pittite perimeter and, in an action parallel to his earlier invention of the Whig myth of history, created in his *Reflections* a history spanning from the Glorious to the American Revolutions to explain what would otherwise seem his inconsistent stand on the French Revolution. (The *Morning Chronicle* of May 12, 1791, thus prosecutes Burke for falling off from pure Whig doctrine as follows: "The great and firm body of the Whigs of England, true to their principles, have decided on the dispute between Mr. Fox and Mr. Burke, and the former is declared to have maintained the pure doctrines by which they are bound together, and upon which they have invariably acted"; quoted in Werkmeister, *Lon-*

don, p. 344.) And when Fox found any means to gain the upper hand over Ministry, whether during the Fox-North coalition or the Regency Crisis, he seemed to desert all his previous principles in even more spectacular fashion.[62]

Opposition, in sum, was a habit of splitting with Government that compelled splitting within the self. To oppose—and this is the dark implication of the wilderness conceit—was at last to be a party of one, a cult of personality. Thus the late, doomed persona of Burke in his *Letter to a Noble Lord* (1796) where he figures himself as a modern Job accused of apostasy for taking a pension. And thus the essentially cultic nature of the Fox circle in the years just before his death in 1806.[63]

Again, one more aspect of the topic will be useful. Opposition was also a dialectic between ordinary political discourse and representation. Accepted political discourse, of course, could not proceed without a repertory of conventional figures or topoi designed to assimilate the topical to known history.[64] But it was the fate of Opposition discourse to stage the received topoi *as* figuration. When Burke threw the dagger to the floor in his famous "daggers" speech in Commons, for example, topos did not so much interpret topical reference as create its own theater—and bad theater at that.[65] Burke's taking the podium, it was known, created a showcase—but often also sideshow —of oratory. As Boswell remarked: "It was astonishing how all kinds of figures of speech crowded upon him. . . . It seemed to me however that his Oratory rather tended to distinguish himself than assist his cause. There was amusement instead of persuasion. It was like the exhibition of a favourite Actor" (quoted in Kramnick, p. 102). Or as Fox put it in 1794: "Burke's eloquence . . . rather injures his reputation, it is a veil over his wisdom" (quoted in Kramnick, p. 103; also see the other contemporary reactions to Burke's speeches gathered in Kramnick, pp. 100–103). Of course, Fox was himself not unknown for his illusionist's veil of words. Indeed, he was at last the master theatrician, conjuror, or, perhaps, carnival freak, of rhetoric. In a caricature of 1788 during the Regency Crisis, for example, he was billed as the great Word Eater: consuming words at one end and vaporing them forth at the other in an endless stream of verbiage (see Barnes, his pl. 8). Audiences in Parliament sat in something like suspended disbelief before the force of his rhetoric, distanced from full persuasion by consciousness that they were witnessing not so much truth as Fox speaking in the mode of truth. One instance of such rapt audience will cue our exit from this theater. On Fox's return to Commons in 1800 after his secession (with Grey) in 1797, Coleridge records that the "full & overflowing Eloquence" of the "great orator" met all his "pre-formed" conceptions (*Collected Letters*, 1: 568).

Thus did the master rhetorician of Opposition appear to the master rhetorician of newspaper opposition.

Journalism. To understand the impact of Opposition politics on the press—particularly the daily newspapers—at the end of the century, it is again necessary to start on a discrimination of oppositions. The most direct approach would be to study the Opposition press as a bought medium—as a counterpart, that is, of the Government press controlled by subsidy. But as we must see, this approach is inadequate for the years after 1793, when the majority of Opposition newspapers were forced to rethink their economic base and the political ideology allowed by that base. From this point on, our best measure of newspaper opposition is an indirect one: the reproduction of Whig opposition mentality *at one remove* in an ad hoc, adversarial mentality ancestral to journalistic impartiality. In the years around the turn of the century, the *Morning Post* led the Opposition press in a process of party-hopping that would later be remembered as the origin of the new journalistic norm: a neutral and/or adversarial stance "opposed" equally to Government and Opposition.

To understand the genesis of such independent journalistic opposition, we need to pick up the story in the years 1788–89 when the Regency crisis seeded a new crop of Opposition dailies.[66] During the July elections of 1788, the London press was still dominated by the Government dailies subsidized through the Secret Service fund. The Treasury could count on seven papers (*Daily Advertiser, Morning Chronicle, Morning Post, Public Advertiser, Public Ledger, Times, World*) compared to just three for the Opposition (*Gazetteer, General Advertiser, Morning Herald*; Werkmeister, *London*, p. 317). But when the King went "mad" in November and the Whigs agitated for a Regency under the Prince of Wales, the picture suddenly changed. In early 1789, two of the Treasury papers—the *Morning Chronicle* and the *Morning Post*—changed sides. James Perry, a friend of Fox, bought the *Chronicle* and turned it into the Foxite paper on £300 subsidy per year (Aspinall, p. 69; Werkmeister, *London*, p. 336, *Newspaper History*, p. 166). The *Morning Post* shifted allegiances more disreputably. This libelous scandal sheet had been politically indecisive for most of its career since starting up in 1772 and had turned to the Ministry only in 1784, when infusions of Secret Service money bought its editor (Aspinall, pp. 71–72). But the old habit of scandal overpowered its new politics. Attempting a standard ploy of the netherworld of journalism, blackmail, the *Post* in late 1788 inserted an item touching upon the secret marriage of the Prince of Wales.[67] The result was that Carlton House (the shadow Court of the Prince of Wales) was forced to buy control of the paper in January 1789 and place it under Richard Brinsley Sheridan's charge (Aspinall, p. 274; Werkmeister, *Newspaper*

History, p. 36, *London*, p. 419). Meanwhile, the total number of London dailies rose, with two new Government papers (*Star, and Evening Advertiser* and *Diary*) and two additional Opposition ones (*Argus* and the "spurious" or alternate *Star*). Thus by March 1789 the Treasury still had seven dailies, but the Opposition now also controlled seven (Werkmeister, *London*, p. 317).

From this point on, the Government increasingly lost effective control of the press despite immediate efforts at repression and the later Pittite gagging laws. Harassment by taxation, libel prosecution, and Post Office interference in delivery reduced the Opposition dailies to just four in 1793: *Morning Chronicle* (with the *Star* as its evening edition), *Morning Post*, *Gazetteer*, and *Courier* (a new paper of 1792 that first supported the Whigs for venal reasons; Werkmeister, *London*, pp. 377–79; Aspinall, p. 206). Yet in circulation, the Opposition papers as a group were still a match for Government (Werkmeister, *London*, p. 377). Indeed, the *Chronicle* and *Post*, as we will see, were poised on the verge of a growth period that would see their combined sales surpass by far that of the Treasury press.

But the story of the Opposition press is not one of continuous growth. To understand the ascendancy of this press, we must pause at 1793 to observe a discontinuity in the subsidy system that had until then been the politicizing element of journalism—the element, that is, that determined the politics of papers. Relative to the Treasury system, Opposition subsidization had always been more or less haphazard.[68] But from 1793 through the end of the century, Whig subsidies lapsed almost totally. Of the four Opposition dailies, only the Foxite *Morning Chronicle* continued receiving funds (Werkmeister, *London*, pp. 336, 377–78; *Newspaper History*, p. 166). And only the *Chronicle*, therefore, was stable enough in management and politics (as well as sufficiently prudent in the face of Government prosecution) to gain steadily in editorial quality, respectability, and readership. The other Opposition papers fluctuated desperately in all these categories. The most radical of the lot, the *Courier*, wasted itself in what Lucyle Werkmeister calls "generalized abuse" and became the most vulnerable to Post Office interference (*Newspaper History*, p. 167). The *Gazetteer* retreated into moderation so extreme that it became what Werkmeister terms a "quagmire of vapidity" (*Newspaper History*, pp. 167–68). And the Sheridanite *Morning Post* maintained its historically shady character while plunging in sales to a perilous 350 copies a day in 1795.

From that point on, however, the *Morning Post* led the lost dailies out of their wilderness. Or rather, the *Post*—which now becomes central to our story—did not so much lead as swallow the flock whole. The overseer of this pitiless process of survival was Daniel Stuart, an early associate of the Sheridanite Friends of the People whose mature character was that of a "slippery" entrepreneur practiced at the art of stockjobbing (see STCE, pp. lxvii–lxviii; on the society of the Friends of the People, see Werkmeister, *Newspaper History*, pp. 72–79). After buying out the all but collapsed *Morning Post* in 1795 for £600 (Aspinall, pp. 278–80), he embarked on an opportunistic program of buying up coeval Opposition papers as well as such newcomers as the *Telegraph*.[69] In 1797 he acquired the *Gazetteer* and merged its circulation and title with the *Post*'s (renaming the latter the *Morning Post and Gazetteer*). In the same year, he similarly absorbed the *Telegraph* but suppressed its title (STCE, p. lxix n; Hindle, p. 83). Finally, in 1799 he became co-owner of the *Courier*, which, however, continued as a separate paper under the active management of his partner (STCE, p. lxxxiv; Aspinall, p. 206).[70] Partly because of these mergers, the circulation of the *Morning Post* rose steeply, from some 350 copies per day in 1795 to about 4,500 in 1803. By the time Stuart sold the *Post* in mid-1803, it had overtaken not only the leading Government papers but also the steadily gaining *Morning Chronicle*, which had a circulation of somewhere between 2,000 and 3,000 copies per day.[71]

Yet absorption of weak newspapers, of course, was clearly not the only reason for the *Post*'s spectacular growth. When it assumed the circulation of the *Telegraph* and *Gazette*, for example, the net addition to its own sales was probably only 300–450 copies a day (STCE, p. lxx n). Why its sudden popularity? One answer is that its direct competitor, the *Chronicle*, lost the public pulse by backing the Foxite doves even during the most hawkish times after 1797. But there is another way to phrase this answer that will allow us to reach the heart of our story of the Opposition press. The *Post* triumphed largely because it was the first of the new generation of Opposition papers to glimpse the true possibilities of popularity. It realized that the circulation of a modern newspaper had to depend on an economic base whose leading element was no longer Parliamentary party (whether Government or Opposition) but the vast resources of the middle-class Public—of what Coleridge in 1800 described to Stuart as "the tastes of [Lon]don Coffee house men & breakfast-table People of Quality" (*Collected Letters*, 1: 627; quoted in STCE, p. lxxi).[72] Correspondingly, the *Post* also realized that a successful paper had to advocate not just one politics versus another but *a wholly new mode of political advocacy*.

To define this mode with clarity, it may be useful to look ahead momentarily to the 1830's when Stuart's *Post* and *Courier* had both long since passed back to party control (under the Prince of Wales and the Government, respectively).[73] Because of the increase in the total press audience (and reduction of the stamp tax after 1836), the weekly and Sunday journals in these years multiplied manifold; but the ranks of the London daily papers thinned as the *Times* seized the lion's share of the expanding daily market (Asquith, pp. 99–100). It was now the *Times* that led the new journalism of "independency" (surveyed by Aspinall, pp. 369–84) by aggressively courting middle-class "public opinion" and seeking to legitimize public advocacy as no less than a full-scale ideology of journalism. What sells was what was right: a paper should hold aloof from party connection and represent only the normative or bipartisan view—a respectable *median* view that on particular issues could jump back and forth between established party views. The name for such transparty politics was "impartiality." As early as July 3, 1830, the *Times* could thus declare that control of the press by the Government (and, by implication, any party) would no longer be tolerated by a public demanding impartiality: "One single newspaper reporting, and being known to report the speeches faithfully and impartially, would soon have more sale than all the other papers so shamefully bought up" (quoted in Aspinall, p. 380).

Yet despite the success of the *Times*, we should note, the legitimacy it claimed for impartiality was not yet secure. As A. Aspinall notes, "Just because it sought accurately and faithfully to reflect the changing moods of public opinion, *The Times* was accused [by the *Quarterly Review*, January 1831] of being 'the most profligate of the London newspapers, and the most impudently inconsistent in everything except malice and mischief' " (p. 380). There was still something residually shameful, that is, about the way the *Times* deserted unprofitable party to sell out to impartiality. Such a charge can serve to return us to our proper sphere at the turn of the century because it recapitulates the origin of the journalism of impartiality: apostasy. In the late 1790's when the daily press did not yet fully know its new economic base, or—to adopt Jon Klancher's insightful approach to mass and middle-class readership in the nineteenth century—did not know how to imagine and actively shape or "make" its financially influential portion of the Public, the politics of the median view was still implicated in mere opportunism.[74] Thus the special place of the *Morning Post* in newspaper history. Traditionally venal and opportunistic, the *Post* was uniquely situated to begin the task of selling out to the new public and improvising the ideology of impartiality. All Stuart had to do was repackage opportunism.

Here we arrive upon the missing link that will allow our whole study of the *bricolage* of dialectic to evolve into applied study of Wordsworth. To reform opportunism as impartiality, the slippery Stuart needed an even more philosophically slippery propagandist. He found his man in our missing link: Coleridge, the master amphibian of test-the-waters politics. Coleridge joined the *Morning Post* in 1797 and (with several long interruptions) continued to supply the paper with leaders, political essays, poetry, and miscellania through the time of the *Post*'s sale in 1803, when he went over to the *Courier*.

Whether he was singlehandedly responsible for the *Post*'s personality and success, as he would later claim, is disputable; but it is certain that his political contributions gave the paper an élan—and probably at least some thousand more readers—that it would not otherwise have had (not to mention the other Romantics, including Southey, Lamb, and Wordsworth, that he brought into Stuart's stable).[75] Coleridge was the perfect whip for Stuart's party apart. Just as Burke articulated Opposition, so Coleridge articulated the method and beginning theory of impartiality. To study this articulation, it will be useful to turn the pages not just of the *Post* itself but of the major tool we now possess for studying Coleridge's contributions in particular: David Erdman's edition of Coleridge's *Essays on His Times in "The Morning Post" and "The Courier"* (STCE). The splendid Introduction to this collection is a fitting companion to Erdman's work on Blake. But for Coleridge, as Erdman makes clear, opposition was not true but fickle friendship. In two cycles of opportunistic apostasy punctuated by his famous recantations, Coleridge led the *Post* away from Opposition to its popular contrary: a crypto-Ministerial stand little short of outright Pittism.[76]

First there was the apostasy of Coleridge's initial season with the *Post* in 1797–98, which Erdman plots as a swing from Yea to Nay on the issue of republicanism. *Yea: Coleridge championed Opposition and French republicanism*. After a series of contributions that generally revived his "English Jacobinism" of years past (STCE, p. lix), Coleridge on January 20, 1798, brought to a point his early political stand in the *Post*: a radicalism fully in line with Opposition domestic policies and sympathy with the French cause. On this date selected by Stuart to celebrate Fox's imminent birthday, there appeared Coleridge's essay saying Yea, emphatically, to the Opposition platform of Radical Reform (STCE, p. lxxv). But even as we identify this stand, a qualification is immediately in order. For Coleridge's stand was also a standstill. As the *Post* as a whole continued unreflectively on its Opposition course, the poet's radicalism halted and began to retreat. Coleridge began to have second thoughts—qualifying his call for a Peace Cabinet in an uneasy essay of February, for example, by wishing for more effective measures against "the armies of France" (STCE, p. lxxvi).

A nexus of events in March then shaped these hesitations into his new stand. *Nay: Coleridge detested Opposition and French republicanism*. To hear the poet tell it in his "France: An Ode" (originally published in *MP* on April 16, 1798, as "The Recantation, an Ode"), the precipitating event was the news on March 19 that the French had invaded Switzerland (STCE, p. lxxix). Clearly, after all, this invasion desynonymized republicanism and liberty.[77] Yet just as clearly, the invasion was not the only factor in his recantation. In what amounts to a dev-

astating indictment of opportunism and contingent principle, Erdman notes that Coleridge's acrobatic radicalism had begun its backflip
immediately after an earlier, and nearer, incursion of liberties: the
arrest on March 1 of members of the London Corresponding Society and the United Irishmen. It was this triumph of Pitt's antiradical
campaign that forced Stuart and Coleridge to take their stand, we
might say, much as a threatened bird takes a stand: on a liberty tree
far above it all. Stuart's detailed coverage of the arrests earned him
a summons to Privy Council, with the result that the *Post* suddenly
grew silent and "independent" in its opinions (STCE, pp. lxxviii–
lxxix; see also Everest, pp. 14–15, 37). Coleridge must have suffered
only an interior inquisition akin to that Wordsworth imagines in *The
Prelude*, where he pleads "Before unjust Tribunals . . . in the place /
The holiest that I knew of, my own soul" (10.376–80). "Certainly,"
Erdman judges, the "indirect menaces" of the time were alone sufficient to bring about Coleridge's "observable change of tone" (STCE,
p. lxxix). Even in private, he now spurned Fox and Opposition: "The
Opposition & the Democrats are not only vicious—they wear the
filthy garments of vice. . . . I am no Whig, no Reformist, no Republican" (*Collected Letters*, 1: 396–97; STCE, p. lxxx).

His public metamorphosis then came after the French menace had
put the seal on indirect menaces at home. In April, he thus issued in
the *Post* his great Nay to republicanism: the recantation of the Ode
on France. "Yea," he *seems* to say to Liberty in the final stanza:

> . . . *there* I felt thee!—on that sea-cliff's verge,
>   Whose pines, scarce travelled by the breeze above,
> Had made one murmur with the distant surge!
> Yes, while I stood and gazed, my temples bare,
> And shot my being through earth, sea, and air,
>   Possessing all things with intensest love,
>   O Liberty! my spirit felt thee there.
>   (*Complete Poetical Works*, 1: 247 and *appar. crit.*)

But like blind Lear on the sea-cliff's verge, or like some ancient
mariner on the verge of feeling love for sea snakes, the poet says Yes
to natural Liberty only in the spirit of alienation from the realms of
human liberty.[78] *The* sea-verge at the time, after all, looked eastward
not with intensest love but with hate toward the expected French invasion. Natural liberty was freedom *from* the liberty-become-repres-
sion of France as well as of the land behind the poet's back: Pitt's
England. The Ode on France, we may thus say, is a poem of pure
marginality—of opposition mentality forced into a borderline stand
neither here nor there in the social world. Appropriately, perhaps,
Coleridge had already decided to cross the border and leave the whole
contest of liberty behind. Traveling with the Wordsworths to Ger-

many in 1798–99, he withdrew from the *Post* while the paper as a whole followed his course toward moderation (STCE, pp. lxxxiii–lxxxv).

When he then returned to the *Post* more than a year later, it was to enact a second and even more decisive pendulum swing from Yea to Nay. *Yea: Coleridge admired Napoleon and threw in for Opposition and peace.* Just as Napoleon in late 1799 returned to Paris from Egypt and commandeered the Directory in his Brumaire coup, so Coleridge—a month or so behind—returned to London from his private Egypt (he had just been exploring the Lakes with Wordsworth) and took the city by storm, entering into the political fray with such force that he was able to boost sales of the *Post* by some 500 copies daily in just a few months (STCE, p. xcvi n). The test issue was now Napoleon and how England should deal with him. Before actually coming to London, we know, Coleridge's admiration for the just-returned Bonaparte (still innocent of his coup) had been unbounded. As Erdman puts it, Napoleon allowed him to rekindle "the fire of old Jacobin sympathies and even Gallican sympathies" (STCE, p. lxxxvi). Thus the huzzas of his letter to Southey of October 15, 1799: "what say you of the Resurrection & Glorification of the Saviour of the East after his Tryals in the Wilderness? . . . Buonaparte—! Buonaparte! dear dear DEAR Buonaparte!" (*Collected Letters*, 1: 539; STCE, p. lxxxvi). By the time he set pen to *Post* in December 1799, however, the Saviour had become Usurper. Yet even as he excoriated Napoleon's desertion of republican principles and branded him usurper (as we had occasion to remark in Chapter 1), he said Yea to his genius. It was Coleridge who led Opposition writers in recognizing that the First Consul was sufficiently established in power for serious peace negotiations to be pursued. It was Coleridge who called upon Fox and Sheridan for leadership. And it was Coleridge who, in a series of essays from January to March 1800, worked up what Erdman summarizes as "immense respect for Napoleon and contempt for Pitt" (STCE, pp. lxxxviii–xci). By late March, the poet was prepared to bring issues to a head in a series of essays setting Napoleon face to face with Pitt. "Pitt" appeared and "Bonaparte" was scheduled. But the project died when Napoleon marched off to Marengo and Coleridge himself then withdrew from London for another long leave (STCE, pp. xcvi–xcvii).

In retrospect, the phantom "Bonaparte" seems an emblem for the ensuing hollowing out of Coleridge's Gallicism. *Nay: Coleridge detested Napoleon and threw in for Pitt and war.* After a year and a half absence (during which the Pitt ministry fell and the brief Addington ministry negotiated the preliminaries of the Peace of Amiens), Coleridge returned irregularly to the pages of the *Post* from November 1801 through the summer of 1802. At first, he resumed where he had left off—backing Fox, peace, and an Addington ministry that would be sufficiently Foxite to withstand Pittite hawkishness (STCE, pp. ci–ciii). But in September 1802, when he began writing more often for the *Post*, his views on the Peace had taken a cold-war chill—so much so, indeed, that by late 1802 he reversed himself and warmed to the resumption of war against Napoleon. In a series of celebrated essays from September on, he compared Napoleon to Caesar in a way that gave the lie to his previous assessment: Napoleon was now a provincial tyro and tyrant (STCE, p. cx). In October, he again printed in the *Post* his Ode on France (in revised form). And again he broke violently with Foxite Whiggism, denouncing Fox in his notoriously extravagant "Letters to Fox" in November. The only position left to take, it seemed, was Pittism. At the sea-cliff's verge of his present recantation, therefore, Coleridge backed Pitt and agitated for war with such intensest hatred (to vary the language of the Ode) that in retrospect he liked to think he had actually helped bring about renewed war in May 1803 (STCE, pp. cvi–cxiii).

Up to the time of the *Post*'s sale and his own imminent departure for Malta in early 1804, then, Coleridge fell *twice* from Opposition. Here we arrive upon the goal of our inquiry into the politics of journalism. For our purposes, the key point is that Coleridge's repeated apostasy was not simply a function of external circumstance—of a changing political scene whose rhythm, in syncopation with his own rhythm of periodic retreats from London, produced his two-step recantation. Rather, repeatability of change was the deep structure of his political thinking. Seen from a distance, such thinking may initially seem a kind of deliberate stockjobbing. Perhaps what is evidenced in Coleridge's changes of heart, after all, is not so much honesty as an endlessly rehearsable ploy, a device or tactics of soul-searching designed to electrify readers. Recantation, quite simply, sold newspapers. But seen close up, Coleridge's way of thinking is not credibly Machiavellian. What we read in the texture of his essays is the fact that repetitive recantation is woven into his very style as a Baconian penchant for sudden divergences regulated by a pro forma "but" or "yet."[79]

Indeed, it is precisely the recantatory—and incantatory—alterity of his Yea-but-Nays that gives Coleridge's prose in the *Post* its characteristic vitality. Consider the close weave of his March 1800 essays on Bonaparte, for example. "Bonaparte I" certainly denounces Napoleon as a vile usurper. After opening by labeling Bonaparte's action a "usurpation," it then closes upon the violent passage we observed in Chapter 1: "In his usurpation, Bonaparte stabbed his honesty in the vitals; it has perished—we admit, that it has perished—but the mausoleum, where it lies interred, is among the wonders of the world"

(STCE, pp. 207, 211). Yet the note of "wonder" in the last clause here (headed by one of Coleridge's many "buts") is a telltale. In fact, Coleridge's extreme denunciation of Napoleon is balanced in the body of the essay by a romance of Commanding Genius no less extreme: the First Consul is "a man of various talent, of commanding genius, of splendid exploit," and once more, "it is undeniable, that already his commanding genius has introduced a new tone of morality into France, and that it is now fashionable to assume the rigid and simple character of the Great Consul" (STCE, pp. 208–10). The method of such interpolations is perhaps epitomized in the following passage, where Coleridge relieves us from an otherwise relentlessly progressive train of paragraphs headed "First," "Secondly," and so forth: "These seem to us the causes, which placed Bonaparte in the Chief Consulate," he sums up, and then continues, "Of his own share in that event we have repeatedly declared our abhorrence; *but* it is required of us by truth and common justice to admit, that since then, his interest, and those of his country and of Europe, have run completely parallel" (STCE, p. 210; italics mine). Everything prior to the "but" here points the finger at the culprit; and everything after crosses the fingers, as it were, and enlists Napoleon's commanding genius in the spirit of the times.

Day by day and paragraph by paragraph, Coleridge's essays zigzag in this fashion. Or as Carl Woodring has summarized the total course of his politics: "Day after day, year after year, he looped, backtracked, redoubled, and reneged" (*Politics in English Romantic Poetry*, p. 52). How to understand such a political mutability canto? Here we need to step back from the chronological method of tracing Coleridge's apostasy to a synchronic perspective. Coleridge habitually "swung" from Yea to Nay, I suggest, because there was really no action of swinging involved at all. Rather, at every moment Coleridge faced in two directions such that the articulation of one view necessitated, as if structurally, the articulation of its opposite. Or to marry structural and diachronic views in a single perspective, we can phrase the argument in the terms of our continuing concern as follows: Coleridge's political journalism elaborates what is essentially a logic of dialectic, of an ever-moving structure of thesis and antithesis. Unity of political sentiment he may have had, as Sara Coleridge and others would later claim. But such unity was like that of Napoleon's tactics or of Opposition politics. It was a habitual method of disunity.

Erdman's overview of Coleridge's politics puts the case for such antithesis well. Commenting on Sara Coleridge's observation that "the character and conduct of Napoleon" was "the plank or bridge, whereon [her father] and the *Morning Post* crossed over from warm interest in the cause of the French nation to decided Anti-Gallicanism" (STCE, p. lxiv), Erdman writes:

In the *Morning Post* essays we see Coleridge frequently on that plank or bridge, running back and forth or pausing uncertainly in the middle. It is valid to recognise an over-all consistency in Coleridge's thinking—if we understand that the consistency is virtual or ideal, not actual; that it is his own desideratum, so that even while he speaks boldly on one side of a question he keeps a longing (or a roving) eye on the other sides of it. For example, while vigorously *opposing* a movement for Reform, "he carefully recorded his protest in favour of reform, conducted judiciously." . . . Indeed for some interpreters of Coleridge's thought, "the most striking feature . . . is its unity . . ."—perhaps because the most unexpected.

It is the unity not of a straight line but of an S-curve. (STCE, p. lxiv)

And more:

He is in truth "ever the same" in the sense that he is never single-sided or single-minded but always both Jacobin and anti-Jacobin, Radical and Tory, poet and moralist, intermingled. . . . "Recantation" is a term Coleridge uses for himself, more than once, but it is less accurate than "oscillation," a term he prefers to use for others. (STCE, p. lxv)

It was not that Coleridge changed his mind from Yea to Nay, in sum, but that he consistently said Yea *but* Nay. This was his genius: a doubling or self-divisive tactics homologous to the other provinces of practical dialectic we have surveyed. The insignia for such genius is the signature with which he closed many of his essays in the *Post*: Ἔστησε. As Coleridge wrote in a letter, " Ἔστησε signifies—*He hath stood*—which in these times of apostasy from the principles of Freedom, or of Religion in this country, & from both by the same persons [i.e., Bonaparte and followers] in France, is no unmeaning Signature" (*Collected Letters*, 2:867; STCE, pp. cv–cvi). But we may ask: what did it mean for *He hath stood* to take his stand? In essence, it meant that he slipped, slid, and desperately reversed himself in a balancing act that at last created, at great cost, a new stand. The cost was the intuition of synthesis that for Hegel intimated Absolute Knowledge but that for Coleridge characteristically inspired guilt and complicity. In moments of greatest unbalance when, as if he poised on a sea-cliff's verge within himself, he was neither here nor there, Coleridge experienced a moment of synthesis subsuming both self and enemy, both the politics he had been favoring and the politics he would soon take up.

In the most suggestive record we have of such an antithetical moment, for example, Coleridge became *as Napoleon*. The occasion was the arrival of news in May 1802 that the term of the First Consul had just been lengthened to ten years (soon to life). At this moment, Coleridge had still not returned from his second long retreat from the *Post*; nor had he yet changed his stand to the fierce anti-Bonapartism of September and after. At this moment, we may say, Coleridge did not so much take a stand as a meta-stand, an Archimedean vantage point outside the world from which to survey his own see-sawing stands in the world. Among a welter of other notebook jottings in May (some probably meant for newspaper essays), he set down what Erdman calls this "fascinated, ambivalent memorandum" representing his first response to the new Bonaparte: "A *Throne* the Δος που στω of Archimedes—Poet Bonaparte—Layer out of a World-garden—" (quoted in STCE, p. cv). In a commentary too complex to paraphrase, Erdman argues:

The Greek words ("Give me a fulcrum [and I will move the world]") evidently apply, as Kathleen Coburn observes, to Bonaparte's ambitions, but the next part of the note develops the concept of the commanding genius as poet—with a striking empathic equivalence of Bonaparte to Coleridge. A suitable gloss comes from an exercise in self-observation made by Coleridge a bit later when he was "sitting by the Eskdale side" looking at lonely mountain tarns: "O for wealth to *wood* these Tarns. . . . Bear witness for me, what thoughts I wandered about with—if ever I imagined myself a conqueror, it was always to bring peace—but mostly turned away from these thoughts to more humane & peaceable Dreams."
  What world-gardening a Coleridge-Bonaparte might have decreed! It is tempting to speculate the derivation from this Archimedean standing-place, που στῶ, of the new Coleridge signature announced three months later as a motto of non-apostasy: " Ἔστησε signifies—*He hath stood*." (STCE, p. cv)

Like some Wordsworthian "lost leader," in sum, Coleridge the Poet-Bonaparte made his *He hath stood* persona stand antithetically for Napoleon. And with perfect symmetry, the real Bonaparte in Coleridge's essay for the *Post* on September 29, 1802, became the epitome of what Poet-Bonaparte would later call the I Am of Imagination: "the great I BY ITSELF I, the AUTOCRATOR of France" (STCE, p. 331).

Yea but Nay, Yea and Nay—the circadian rhythm of Coleridge's antithetical politics continued in an endless circling of opposites that in an earlier age in England—in the Renaissance period studied by Steven Mullaney—would have been "amphibologous" or ambiguous to the point of treason. As Mullaney observes, amphibology, or rhetorical undecidability, was in a political context the very language of traitors to the state. But of course, if the amphibology of Coleridge's apostasy may be likened to treason, such treason was committed in order to escape censure for official treason in the years of Pitt's gagging laws. As Stuart's master propagandist, Coleridge made treason to the radical cause seem anti-treason, or patriotism. Or rather, and here we come to the *pièce de résistance* of his propaganda for the *Post*, there never *was* any treason, apostasy, or change of views in the first place. The dialectical imagination that made Coleridge perpetually change his views mythologized itself as an apparently perpetual *resistance* to change. In this light, the *He hath stood* byline is merely the

leading index of the wondrous web of revisionary history that Coleridge—and Stuart after him—spun throughout the *Post*. At every
fork in their political labyrinth, Coleridge and Stuart straightened
out their path in hindsight by saying, in essence, "we have ever been
the same" (see STCE, pp. lxxix, lxxxi, cvii, cxi). Thus Coleridge at
the end of the first stanza of his Ode on France:

> Yea, every thing that is and will be free!
> Bear witness for me, wheresoe'er ye be,
> With what deep worship *I have still adored*
> The spirit of divinest Liberty.
> (*Complete Poetical Works*, 1: 244;
> italics mine)

And thus Stuart in the *Post* for April 14, 1798 (the day after he received Coleridge's Ode and two days before he printed it): "are we to
be told that we have recanted our former sentiments? No, we follow
them up" (STCE, p. lxxxi).

From such revisionary or *ex Post facto* history evolved the myth
of impartiality that made the *Post* a predecessor of the later *Times*.
Consider the editorial "we" in this last statement by Stuart above.
Such a "we" has begun to shake itself loose from a partial or party
view (Burke: our "little platoon") to imagine the consensualism of
the larger, impartial Public. The link between this "we" and the
strengthening aura of impartiality in the paper in its last years under
Stuart's ownership is clear. Coleridge's leader for January 3, 1800,
for example, expresses as the paper's general credo: "It has been uniformly our creed, that in the present age of the world all extravagant
principles must be necessarily short-lived" (STCE, p. 69). Here is
an early instance of what Klancher calls the "master-sign" discourse
that in the middle-class press would soon subsume the components
of dialectical reversal (such extremes, or "absolute determiners," for
example, as "nothing, everything, every, all, none") within a persona
of grave authority ("Reading the Social Text," p. 202). Revisionary
history ("It has been uniformly our creed") marches by way of the
new "we" ("*our* creed") into the promised land of impartiality and
popular consensus ("in the present age . . . all extravagant principles
must be necessarily short-lived"). Dialectical reversal and apostasy
sink invisibly, seamlessly into a fiction of constancy.

And at last, when the day of such prescientific impartiality (to use
Thomas Kuhn's concept) had passed and the *Post* had fallen back to
partial journalism, it was Coleridge who then became one of the
earliest and shrillest voices in the mature polemics of impartiality.
As Coleridge recalled in his letters and *Biographia* of 1816, the *Morning Post* (and early *Courier*) represented the golden age of the impartial. The *Post*, he says, became "*anti-ministerial*, indeed, yet with

a very qualified approbation of the opposition, and with far greater earnestness and zeal both anti-jacobin and anti-gallican" (*Biographia*, 1: 212). Again: "the Morning Post proved a far more useful ally to the Government . . . in consequence of its being generally considered as moderately anti-ministerial. . . . The rapid and unusual increase in the sale of the Morning Post is a sufficient pledge, that genuine impartiality with a respectable portion of literary talent will secure the success of a newspaper without the aid of party or ministerial patronage" (*Biographia*, 1: 214). Or perhaps most succinctly: the *Post* was "*un*ministerial, anti-opposition, anti-jacobin, anti-gallican, anti-Napoleonic" (*Collected Letters*, 4: 639; STCE, p. lxxii). The dialectical imagination that had actually moved Coleridge to take each of these stands *in succession* becomes in retrospect an immutable principle of impartiality opposed to all party stands simultaneously. The journalism of opposition, we might say, thus ends in pure "anti"-thesis; and the mature Coleridge enrolled not in Panti- but Antisocracy, the cynical inversion of his earlier utopianism.

Finally, a tailpiece in line with the others I have appended: what is ultimately most remarkable about Coleridge's writings in the *Post* is the brilliancy of their rhetoric. It was not for nothing that Perry, the editor of the competing *Chronicle*, called Coleridge's essays "poetry in prose" (quoted in Hindle, p. 100). But we must say "brilliancy" rather than, for example, "force" because Coleridge's political rhetoric was in the final analysis like Napoleon's propaganda as viewed from England or Burke's and Fox's speeches as heard from the galleries: it was "rhetoric" in quotes. It was Coleridge, we might say, *performing* the act of taking a stand. Even as we witness the performance, something about its extremism, its pageantry of imagery, and its intricately worked improvisations of panache (characteristically punctuated with an exclamation point) makes us listen, as it were, for the knocking at the gate in *Macbeth* (in De Quincey's analysis): we are enthralled, but only in Coleridge's own spirit of suspended disbelief. Thus, for example, the gorgeous adventitiousness of the conceits in which Coleridge imagines Napoleon as a genius loci of nature much like the daemon of Wordsworth's Simplon Pass. In the "Bonaparte I" essay of March 11, 1800, for example, Napoleon "pretends to no sacredness; it is no Nile, made mysterious by the undiscoverableness of its fountainhead" (STCE, p. 209). And in the essay on "Our Future Prospects" of January 6, 1803, either Napoleon and his armies *or* the resisting Coalition powers (the metaphor is so independent that its referent is unclear) become an avalanche:

The mis-shapen mass of snow, agitated on the Alpine summit, descends at first harmless and unheeded; but accumulating, and accelerating in its progress, its track is marked by ruin and desolation. There is a limit, however, beyond which it cannot proceed. The same law that hurried it from its elevated situation, accompanies it through all the stages of its course, and conducts it, with unerring fidelity, to the spot where its impelling force is to be exhausted, and it is itself to vanish before a milder temperature. (STCE, p. 420; see also pp. cxi–cxiii)

In such conceits reminiscent of Burke's purplest prose, the journalism of opposition is at last poetic representation.

1804

There are many other cultural contexts in which the *bricolage* of dialectic constituted itself. But perhaps just these I have sketched— the art of war and the art of opposition—will serve to suggest the range of the topic and its bearing upon the riddle of apostasy that has so haunted Romantic studies. How could Wordsworth, Cole- ridge, and other liberal intellectuals of the time swing so abruptly from radicalism to Toryism? Or to cite the terms of past debate sur- veyed by Woodring: how could they swing from "romantic revolt" to Romantic "fascism" (*Politics in English Romantic Poetry*, pp. 24–48)? What we can now see is that no nonreductive solution to this prob- lem can be found unless the parameters of the conflict—Whiggish radicalism versus Pittite Toryism—are broadened. What is of inter- est is the groundless Archimedean fulcrum or Coleridgean *He hath stood* wedged undecidably within such conflict: the "versus." To stand *against* either radicalism or Pittism was to engage in an essentially new, antithetical manner of opposition—a strategy of Yea-but-Nay whose plight, in the terms of older morality, was to appear unstable apostasy.

The motive for such neo-apostasy, we can see, lay in the his- torical circumstances leading up to recantation—particularly the cir- cumstances that for formerly crypto-Gallic liberals now disallowed any straightforward narrative of the agon of nations. In popular dis- course, England combated France; Good combated Evil. But such discourse was barred to liberal intellectuals by the spectre of the Revolutionary narrative of combat. The Revolution, as we saw, had dictated its own elemental story of Liberty combating Tyranny—but in such an uncanny and interminable fashion that it became increas- ingly clear that such combat was itself the bloodiest of tyrannies. How unthinkable, then, to urge a deadly *ricorso* of Liberty's combat against Tyranny by echoing without reflection the jingoism of En- gland's combat against France. To endorse popular patriotism, the Romantics and other liberals had to *rethink* the very notion of combat, antagonism, hatred. They had to learn to hate the new Tyranny of France with equal vigilance against the tyranny lurking within their reclaimed champion of Liberty: England.

The Romantics and other intellectuals, in sum, made the narrative of contemporary history dialectical by abstracting from story-form its logical skeleton of Champion versus Enemy, thesis versus antithesis.[80] While they indeed changed their minds politically, they thus did so only by changing their very way of thinking. By occupying as their preferred ground a "versus" allowing them to criticize/sympathize with both sides, they made possible the later, more "moderate" dialecticism that Scott would dramatize on his epic canvas as wavering (in *Waverley*, 1814) and Hegel, on his equally broad canvas, as the very spirit of philosophy. We might think, after all, of Hegel's semi-fictional account of how he came to finish the *Phenomenology* all in a rush: the "composition of the book was concluded at midnight before the battle of Jena."[81] What such a statement signs in its documentably overdramatic way (as if Hegel were casting Geist as the hero in a Scott novel) is the fact that dialectical philosophy in its fullest articulation was thoroughly a creature of its times. Specifically, it was close cousin to a spirit like Edward Waverley's: a character too easily excited by changing history and so an apostate by temperament. A child of Hegel's early romantic radicalism (or at least qualified radicalism), Absolute Knowledge was first inspired by the Corsican counterpart to Scott's Highland sublime. It was one with what Hegel named Napoleon: the World Soul (*Phenomenology*, p. xx; see also R. R. Palmer, *World of the French Revolution*, pp. 248–50). But from 1807 on, Absolute Knowledge increasingly wavered as worldliness drifted rightward from soul, imperial ambition from republican freedom. When the World Soul became authoritarian and left in its wake the legacy of reaffirmed empire, Absolute Knowledge had to settle into the armchair of *The Philosophy of Right* (1821). As Harvey Gross suggests in his essay on Hegel, Beethoven, and Wordsworth (all born in 1770), Hegelian philosophy was at last the apostasy of Hegel's "youthful radical alienation." Antithesis became political accommodation, a comfortable wavering between liberty and tyranny on a par with Wordsworth's imputed "Toryism" (Gross, p. 153).

Having thus reopened the problem of Romantic apostasy in dialectical terms, we can now approach the finale—the *Eroica*—in our historical reconstruction of Wordsworth's hatred. Indeed, my earlier observation of Coleridge's "poetic" rhetoric in the *Morning Post* has already lifted the baton. What we can now observe is that, while struggling to shape his own public in the years immediately preceding 1804 (i.e., just after *Lyrical Ballads*), Wordsworth collaborated with Stuart and Coleridge in their effort to reach much the same public. He did so by writing political poems—some for the *Post*—in a lyric form able to shape liberal dialecticism into a new public persona: a double-minded "I" addressed to the bipartisan English "we." The stand of this "I" on the popular combat story of the time approximated the see-saw stand of *He hath stood* so closely that Wordsworth's prosaic poetry and Coleridge's poetic prose simply stood shoulder to shoulder on the pages of the *Post*. Wordsworth stood with the paper for the public story of England versus France. What this meant, however, was that he was forced to stand in the characteristic posture of early public advocacy: slipping and sliding. His public poems in this period are entirely composed of political second thoughts—of reversals and inversions signing the residual presence of his earlier principles within the dominant public view. In advocating the public story of England versus France, that is, Wordsworth stood not so much on "England" as in the narrow channel of the "versus." National politics became the medium for a politics of the verge that was neither fully subversive nor contained.[82] The public story of agon was transformed. It began to *shrink* into a lyric agony whose intense focus on the experience of antithesis, of mental turn itself, trained his autobiographical voice and prepared, as we will see, for *The Prelude* of 1804. To cite "September, 1802," a lyric of the period situated literally on the Channel between England and France (from Longman MS. of 1806–7):

> England! within a hollow Vale, I stood,
> And saw, while sea was calm and air was clear,
> The Coast of France, the Coast of France how near!
> Drawn almost into frightful neighbourhood.
> I shrunk, for verily the barrier flood
> Was like a Lake, or River bright and fair,
> A span of waters; yet what power is there!
> What mightiness for evil and for good!
>
> (*P2V*, p. 163 and *appar. crit.*)

As indicated by the full poem from which this octet derives, the evidence of Wordsworth's politics of the verge lies in a form of lyric especially suited to reifying turns of mind: the Miltonic (and Italianate) sonnet, which became his preferred and virtually exclusive form between May 21, 1802, and January 1804. On the former date, Dorothy read Milton's sonnets aloud, and he penned two quick imitations on the theme of Napoleon—including "I Grieved for Buonaparte" (*CMY*, p. 170). I will seek in Chapter 9 to read the sonnets of this period with attention to their full range of public and private significance. But for now it will be sufficient to isolate for study only those that were from the first manifestly political. These number some 23 through the beginning of 1804:*

* For convenience of tabulation, I standardize titles and opening lines based on the Reading Text of *P2V* (except for Sonnet 7, which does not appear in the 1807 edition and is cited from *PW*, 3: 120). In discussing the poems below, however, I will quote the earliest available version of each sonnet (with the exception that I have let texts first published in the *Morning Post*, designated *MP*, take precedence over DC MS. 38 and—in the case of a slight variant of Sonnet 1—DC MS. 41 of early 1802). *MP* texts

1. "I griev'd for Buonaparte, with a vain" *MP*
2. "Great Men have been among us; hands that penn'd"
3. "England! the time is come when thou shouldst wean"
4. "It is not to be thought of that the Flood" *MP*
5. "There is a bondage which is worse to bear"
6. "When I have borne in memory what has tamed" *MP*
7. "What if our numbers barely could defy"
8. "To a Friend, Composed Near Calais, On the Road Leading to Ardres, August 7th, 1802"
   ("Jones! when from Calais southward you and I")
9. "Calais, August, 1802" *MP*
   ("Is it a Reed that's shaken by the wind")
10. "Composed By the Sea-Side, Near Calais, August, 1802"
    ("Fair Star of Evening, Splendor of the West")
11. "To Toussaint L'Ouverture" *MP*
    ("Toussaint, the most unhappy Man of Men!")
12. "Calais, August 15th, 1802" *MP*
    ("Festivals have I seen that were not names")
13. "September 1st, 1802" *MP*
    ("We had a fellow-Passenger who came")
14. "Composed in the Valley, Near Dover, On the Day of Landing"
    ("Dear fellow-Traveller! here we are once more")
15. "September, 1802"
    ("Inland [rev. from 'England!' in Longman MS.], within a hollow vale, I stood")
16. "London, 1802"
    ("Milton! thou should'st be living at this hour")
17. "Written in London, September, 1802"
    ("O Friend! I know not which way I must look")
18. "To the Men of Kent. October, 1803"
    ("Vanguard of Liberty, Ye Men of Kent")

---

of 1802–3 may be recovered from *PW* together with the variants listed in Woof, pp. 183–85 (or from *P2V*, pp. 155–73). Texts in DC MS. 38 (probably late 1802), DC MS. 44 (Feb.–Mar. 1804), Longman MS (1806–7), and *Poems, in Two Volumes* (1807) may be recovered from *P2V*, pp. 155–73 and *appar. crit.* Where no early text is available, I quote from *PW*, 3: 109–22. On dating, see *CMY*, pp. 29–36; *P2V*, pp. 155–73 *appar. crit.*; and Woof. I have not attempted to recover the first orderings of the sonnets in DC MS. 38, DC MS. 44, and *Poems, in Two Volumes*; and have simply tabulated the sonnets in the rough chronological order found in J. Hayden. Some discussion of Wordsworth's grouping schemes will be found in Chapter 9. Sonnet 20 is the only poem in my census not eventually enrolled in "Poems Dedicated to National Independence and Liberty." Included among "Sonnets Dedicated to Liberty" from 1807–20, it was moved in 1827 to "Memorials of a Tour in Scotland, 1803." Also associated with the poems in my census is the sonnet, "On the Extinction of the Venetian Republic" (datable only to between May 21, 1802, and early Feb. 1807) and the 20-line poem, "Lines on the Expected Invasion 1803."

19. "Anticipation. October, 1803"
    ("Shout, for a mighty Victory is won!")
20. "October, 1803"
    ("Six thousand Veterans practis'd in War's game")
21. "October, 1803"
    ("One might believe that natural miseries")
22. "October, 1803"
    ("These times touch money'd Worldlings with dismay")
23. "October, 1803"
    ("When, looking on the present face of things")

The majority of this group were collected together for Coleridge in DC MS. 44 between mid-February and March 6, 1804 (*CMY*, pp. 619–22), first published in 1807 in "Sonnets Dedicated to Liberty" (*Poems, in Two Volumes*), and eventually included in "Poems Dedicated to National Independence and Liberty" (*Poetical Works*, 1849–50). The early centerpiece of the group, however, consisted of the seven sonnets marked *MP* above. Among the first poems Wordsworth himself sent to the *Morning Post*,[83] these appeared with the initials, "W. L. D." in a connected series from January to September 1803 (arabic numerals refer to my numbering in the overall group above):*

   I. (1) "I griev'd for Buonaparte, with a vain" (Jan. 29)
  II. (9) "Calais, August, 1802" (Jan. 29)
     ("Is it a Reed that's shaken by the wind")
 III. (11) "To Toussaint L'Ouverture" (Feb. 2)
     ("Toussaint, the most unhappy Man of Men!")
 IV. (13) "September 1st, 1802" (Feb. 11)
     ("We had a fellow-Passenger who came")
  V. (12) "Calais, August 15th, 1802" (Feb. 26)
     ("Festivals have I seen that were not names")
 VI. (4) "It is not to be thought of that the Flood" (Apr. 16)
VII. (6) "When I have borne in memory what has tamed" (Sept. 17)

These seven sonnets anchor the whole matrix of political sonnets at the time in a deliberately public mode of discourse, and so create the prototype for all of Wordsworth's later sequences of political poems. Indeed, they compose the poet's first such fully political discourse since the abortive *Letter to the Bishop of Llandaff* of 1793. Where the earlier essay was addressed to "My Lord" and signed "a Republi-

---

* To avoid confusion, I retain titles and first lines from my master census based on the Reading Text in *P2V*. Original titles and text may be found in Woof, pp. 184–85. The most significant differences: Sonnet II appeared in *MP* as "August, 1801"; Sonnet IV as "The Banished Negroes"; and Sonnet VII as "England." Sonnets I and II first appeared separately in the paper on Sept. 16, 1802, and Jan. 13, 1803, respectively. They were reissued on Jan. 29, 1803, to inaugurate the series proper.

can" (*Prose*, 1: 29–31), the *Morning Post* sonnets and their associates shape a new circuit of discourse eliding both Lord and Republican—both high and low, rightist and leftist. Cleaving to the social middle, they address the public in the voice of a poet now himself aggressively *of* the central public rather than of the Republican or Revolutionary People. Indeed, as announced by Stuart (who originally expected twelve poems from Wordsworth), the *Morning Post* sonnets were precisely a set of "political essays" on a par with the other editorial matter in the paper addressed to the new public: "We have been favoured with a dozen Sonnets of a Political nature, which are not only written by one of the first Poets of the age, but are among his best productions. Each forms a little Political Essay, on some recent proceeding. As we wish to publish them in connection with each other we now Reprint No. I. and No. II." (*MP*, Jan. 29, 1803; quoted in Woof, p. 155). Whether by Wordsworth's or Stuart's design, the connectivity of the serial essay was then accentuated by what seems a calculated interlacing of theme and imagery. To cite just the first few links of the open-ended sonnet corona thus produced: the first sonnet published (Sonnet 1 in my overall ordering) ends by describing the "stalk / True Power doth grow on," while the second (Sonnet 9) begins on a different stalk, "Is it a Reed that's shaken by the wind . . . ?";* this latter poem ends by calling the statesmen flattering Napoleon "feeble Heads, to slavery prone," and the next two published poems (Sonnets 11, 13) immediately take up the plight of former slaves.[84]

Addressed to the same newspaper audience that read Coleridge's essays, and coordinated into a serial discourse on a par with the multiple-part essays Coleridge sometimes wrote, the *Morning Post* sonnets (and by implication Wordsworth's other political poems of the time) can thus be read with some assurance as works of public advocacy. They not only defined an "I" able to stand for the public but also an elect "we," a true public, able to understand. But exactly what political position, premised upon what kind of public, did Wordsworth advocate? The earlier *Letter to the Bishop of Llandaff*, we observe, had opened by attacking Bishop Watson's slippery stand:

My Lord,
Reputation may not improperly be termed the moral life of man. Alluding to our natural existence, Addison, in a sublime allegory well known to your Lordship, has represented us as crossing an immense bridge, from whose surface from a variety of causes we disappear one after another, and are

---

* "Reed" is lower case in both *MP* printings according to Woof. Because of problems with the availability of *MP* in these years, I have not always been able to go back to the original issue for verification. In future, I ignore minor differences between Woof and *P2V* on the *MP* text and quote from the latter.

seen no more. Every one, who enters upon public life, has such a bridge to pass, some slip through at the very commencement of their career from thoughtlessness, others pursue their course a little longer till, misled by the phantoms of avarice and ambition, they fall victims to their delusion. Your Lordship was either seen, or supposed to be seen, continuing your way for a long time, unseduced and undismayed; but those, who now look for you, will look in vain, and it is feared you have at last fallen, through one of the numerous trap-doors, into the tide of contempt to be swept down to the ocean of oblivion. (*Prose*, 1: 31)

Ten years later, Wordsworth's sonnets are themselves an abridgement of such a stand—with the exception that his own fall into the tide of contempt now seems a fall into public patriotism. What we must observe, however, is that the poet's very process of falling into normalcy also shaped a new, fluid way of standing his ground. If Wordsworth's sonnets swim with the public tide, they also begin to swim simultaneously *against* the tide. To take one's stand was at last to exploit the antithetical to-and-fro of flux itself. Or to use the image of Blake's deceptively antithetical verse: the poet would stain the patriotic waters clear (meaning that the waters of the public were somehow both originally clear and, with incipient criticism, stained).[85]

Thesis: As befits a member of the Grasmere Volunteers (the home guard Wordsworth joined during the invasion scare in October 1803),[86] the framing argument of the political sonnets as a group is perfectly patriotic: Thou shalt hate Napoleonic France. Grief for Bonaparte in Sonnet 1 thus becomes pithy ridicule of the Consul for Life in Sonnets 9 and 12: measured by the "stalk" of true power, Napoleon is a hollow "reed." So, too, melancholy reflection upon France in general (Sonnets 2, 8, 13) escalates into increasingly militant anti-Gallicism. In Sonnets 7 and 19, for example, the English folk will rise "like one man" and fete the corpses of the French with music and glee. Nor is saber rattling the only testament of patriotism. In what we can call the Petrarchan strain of the sonnets, Francophobia gives way to an Anglophilia ardent enough to be love in all its courtly splendor: this is our "beloved Land" (Sonnet 7; *PW* version), this our joyful, blissful native England (Sonnet 14), this the "Star of my Country!" the poet says with "many heartfelt sighs" (Sonnet 10).*

---

* As I suggest in Chapter 9, consideration of dating, compositional sequence, and the order of the poems as originally published adds substantially to our understanding of these sonnets. But given the generally imprecise nature of our evidence and the complex issues involved in the poet's occasionally fictive dating and mutable thematic groupings, I have chosen for my present purposes to read the sonnets with minimal attention to chronological development. Ideally, we would need a computer-stored text that would allow ready access to Wordsworth's sonnets both horizontally (within a given manuscript or edition) and vertically (through the series of manuscripts and editions).

Antithesis: But even as we read the mounting patriotism of the sonnets, we must realize that Wordsworth's saber rattling is finally as complicated as Hamlet's in the long interregnum between his first resolve and his bloody fifth act. If Wordsworth's sonnets were a soliloquy, they would begin, "To be or not to be English." Thus while his framing argument is indeed aligned with the English public, it contains within itself a divisive counterargument dedicated to *reforming* the public. As Woodring points out generally about Wordsworth's political sonnets before 1812 (*Politics of English Romantic Poetry*, p. 119), and as Stephen Bluestone has observed about our present sonnets (in the context of the "Poems Dedicated to National Independence and Liberty"), Wordsworth is finally as hostile to the England of his day as he is to Napoleonic France. His is a "critical patriotism," Bluestone says (p. 84).

Even as the poet prepared in person and poetry to face the expected French invasion, then, he also faced the other way in Sonnets 4, 16, 17, and 22 to discipline a nation of shopkeepers.[87] We may take as representative Sonnet 4 (whose thought of British waters gains special significance when we consider that the poem first appeared placed at the top of page 3 in the *Morning Post*; page 2 contained invasion-watch accounts of French port preparations). In Sonnet 4, Wordsworth would stain the water clear through rites of purification. Condemning the pollution of the present age, he recalls the stream of British liberty to the sacramental innocence of its "first blood":

> It is not to be thought of that the Flood
> Of British freedom, which to the open Sea
> Of the world's praise from dark antiquity
> Hath flowed, "with pomp of waters, unwithstood,"
> Road by which all might come and go that would,
> And bear but freights of worth to foreign lands;
> That this most famous Stream in Bogs and Sands
> Should perish; and to evil and to good
> Be lost for ever. In our Halls is hung
> Armoury of the invincible Knights of old:
> We must live free or die, who speak the tongue
> That Shakespeare spake; the faith and morals hold
> Which Milton held. In every thing we are sprung
> Of Earth's first blood, have titles manifold.
>
> (*MP* text)

Or again, we might witness Sonnet 16, which inflects "freights of worth" above—a conceit canceled after 1827 (*P2V*, p. 166n)—to introduce Wordsworth's sharpest criticism of England at the time. In Sonnet 16 as well as other sonnets we will consider in Chapter 9, he announces a radically simplified Mosaic decalogue consisting of the single commandment: Thou shalt not be a nation of shopkeepers.

The stream of freedom bogs down in Sonnet 16 in greed, provoking
the poet to summon up his Mosaic figure, Milton:

> Milton! thou should'st be living at this hour:
> England hath need of thee: she is a fen
> Of stagnant waters: altar, sword, and pen,
> Fireside, the heroic wealth of hall and bower,
> Have forfeited their ancient English dower
> Of inward happiness. We are selfish men;
> Oh! raise us up, return to us again;
> And give us manners, virtue, freedom, power.
> Thy soul was like a Star and dwelt apart:
> Thou hadst a voice whose sound was like the sea;
> Pure as the naked heavens, majestic, free,
> So didst thee travel on life's common way,
> In chearful godliness; and yet thy heart
> The lowliest duties on itself did lay.
>
> (Longman MS. text)

Thesis and antithesis, then. In such poems of critical patriotism we
discover the deep reason the sonnet form so intrigued Wordsworth
in this period. The motive of the form is one that students of literature now accept as truism but that must have come with the force
of discovery to Wordsworth: the Italianate sonnet virtually demands
thematic opposition between octet and sestet, irrespective of subject.
The division may oppose England to France; yet just as easily it pre-
disposes the semantic field to oppose England to England. In both
Sonnets 4 and 16, the octet thus tilts against modern England while
the sestet champions the true nation of Miltonic times. By thus discriminating the goats from the sheep, the false from the true patriots,
Wordsworth carves out of the masses his ideal public—an imaginary
elect inheriting all the old honorifics of landed estate. We might call
this elect his feudal bourgeoisie. The feudal bourgeoisie (descendants
of his mythic "Statesmen") are *not* the professional and mercantile
classes of the cities and towns, but rather a middle class of rural "hall
and bower" sophisticated enough to be reading the *Morning Post*—an
imaginal class of ancient landed tenure, in other words, conflating the
auras of the provincial and cosmopolitan (or what Coleridge called
the "Coffee house" set) as well as the architecture of the barons and
the yeomen (the hall and bower, respectively).

In his political sonnets, then, the poet is as much England's devil
as advocate. Yet we would have read the devil's advocacy of these
sonnets very incompletely if we leave our argument at this point. The
Italianate sonnet, we know, is a tyrannical form. If it solicits thematic
reversal, it also encases reversal in a grid of rhyme so tight that even
the partial liberation achieved through ploys of syntax (which may
mask the fissure between octet and sestet) rarely makes the *volta* more

than pro forma, more than a convention as traditional as devil's advocacy in Church beatification. We might even say that the relation between octet and sestet is as traditional as that between Old and New Testament. The form that Petrarch used to beatify Laura (and Milton his "late espoused saint") marks a revisionism so doctrinal—in its condensation of traditional Biblical hermeneutics—that revision seems the one true vision.[88] Such revision may incorporate antithesis and sublation, but it is not by itself dialectic in the rhapsodic style of Hegel nor in the vertiginous manner of our current deconstructive hermeneutics. Wordsworth's divided stand in these years, in sum, seems at first glance to have a fixed, monumental quality. As opposed to Coleridge's "avalanching" prose essays or Ode on France (the latter Pindaric in its wild turns of thought), the sonnet form tends to freeze the antithetical moment into glacial composure—into an instance of irresistible force meeting immovable object.

But within the monument, we must see, the antithetical moment is there. To complete our reading of the political sonnets we need to see that the statuesqueness of their *volta* is only insecurely fixed; like an Archimedean fulcrum, it stands over a bottomless vortex of reversal. Consider Sonnet 3, for example, which sets up what can be called, in a deconstructive idiom, *mise en abyme*. Sonnet 3 corrects the sinful English tribe in the octet and then, at a point delayed one line into the sestet, turns about to scourge the French:

> England! the time is come when thou shouldst wean
> Thy heart from its emasculating food;
> The truth should now be better understood;
> Old things have been unsettled; we have seen
> Fair seed-time, better harvest might have been
> But for thy trespasses; and, at this day,
> If for Greece, Egypt, India, Africa,
> Aught good were destined, Thou wouldst step between.
> England! all nations in this charge agree:
> But worse, more ignorant in love and hate,
> Far, far more abject is thine Enemy:
> Therefore the wise pray for thee, though the freight
> Of thy offenses be a heavy weight:
> Oh grief! that Earth's best hopes rest all with Thee!
> (DC MS. 44 and Longman MS. text)

What should be remarked here is the curious hollowness of this sonnet. Hatred toward the French at the close is not predicated upon love of England; rather, the octet hollows out faith in England so thoroughly that it is as if the opening of the poem contained within itself the whole design of such sonnets as 4 and 16 with their opposition of England to England. Reversal at the divide between octet and sestet, that is, remembers some moment of prior reversal teaching the poet to hate his present-day England. The overall result is the sensation of a radically emptied universe. In this paradise lost, Adam may be better than Eve, but both stand in need of harsh correction.

Or again, consider what is arguably one of the most arresting of the political sonnets, Sonnet 6:

> When I have borne in memory what has tamed
> Great Nations, how ennobling thoughts depart   ·
> When Men change Swords for Ledgers, and desert
> The Student's bower for gold, some fears unnamed
> I had, my Country! am I to be blamed?
> But, when I think of Thee, and what Thou art,
> Verily, in the bottom of my heart,
> I of those fears of mine am much asham'd.
> But dearly do I prize thee: for I find
> In thee a bulwark of the cause of men;
> And I by my affection was beguiled.
> What wonder, if a Poet, now and then,
> Among the many movements of his mind,
> Felt for thee as a Lover or a Child.   (*MP* text)

Here, with the force of Wordsworth's autobiographical writing at its most urgent, monumentalism discovers itself as a process of crisis and recovery, inner fall and self-correction, much in the spirit of Coleridge's recantations.[89] Antithetical reversal marks with a "but" each movement of mind. The poet fears for England, but one line into the second quatrain reverses himself. Again, the poet is ashamed of his fears for his country, but at the sestet loves his country. The second "but" here is illogical since the poet had already reversed himself to express filial love for England. We might think of it as a sign of existential reversal, of habitually self-reversing mind.

Other sonnets also discover the antithetical moment in Wordsworth's politics—Sonnet 5, for example, which points the moral finger undecidably at France, England, or both; or again, Sonnets 18 and 20, which burden patriotism with the memory of old contests within Britain itself (the Norman invasion and Battle of Killiecrankie, respectively). But with Sonnet 6 above, we have come full circle to the autobiographical urgency we began upon in "September, 1802" (Sonnet 15), and so are prepared at last to cross the threshold to March 1804 and *The Prelude*, where the antithetical impulse heard in all the "but's" of Wordsworth's small form expands into what we must now see is the poet's largest monument to antithesis: the essential "but" that allows him to close his poem upon the spots of time and Snowdon.

The evidence at this point becomes so full that I can only recommend to the reader a perusal from early to late 1804 of the *Morning Post*, supplemented by samplings of other London periodicals (e.g., the *Times, Annual Register*) and of the immense swell of broadsheets, songs, slogans, squibs, caricatures, and other bric-a-brac of the contemporary invasion hysteria (surveyed by Ashton; Emsley, pp. 112–23; Maccunn, pp. 69–77). It is not possible, of course, to reproduce the kind of full-scale synopsis Maccunn has attempted of the imagination of Napoleon projected by such material. But certain features of popular opinion (a term I use to distinguish the full range of lower- to middle-class views from Wordsworth's more narrowly conceived "public") are especially significant. To put the case generally: what we discover in immersing ourselves in popular discourse after March 1804 is the immense desire to *discipline* Napoleon. If the story of the times was combat, in other words, the moral was lynch-mob justice.

The first event to arouse popular indignation to extravagance in 1804 occurred in March, when on Bonaparte's orders the Duke d'Enghien was kidnapped on neutral soil and then summarily executed on a slender suspicion of anti-Napoleonic conspiracy. To add fire to flame, this event appears also to have triggered the suicides in prison of General Pichegru, arrested with General Moreau for conspiracy in February, and—most maddening of all—of the Englishman, Captain Wright, implicated in an unsuccessful attempt to smuggle Georges Cadoudal back into France. To the English, these probable suicides seemed clearly "murders" (Maccunn, pp. 72–74; Sydenham, pp. 289–94; see also Ashton, pp. 229–32). Immediately after news of d'Enghien's death reached England, popular opinion followed a bipartisan, strikingly convergent strategy of defaming Napoleon. Throughout the respectable press and less respectable broadsheets, it became standard to attach an increasingly fulsome list of earlier charges to the black deed of d'Enghien's murder, thereby creating a kind of writ or summons to justice. In many cases, these lists of charges took explicitly legal form: Old Bony was a "ruffian" to be arraigned.

The *Times* charged, for example: "The treatment of the illustrious and unfortunate Duc D'ENGHIEN will, we trust, at last convince that faction in this country, who have so long been the defenders of the Corsican Ruffian, that *he was really capable of the massacre at Jaffa*, of the *poisoning of his sick and wounded soldiers*, and of *the secret assassination of* TOUSSAINT" (Apr. 16, 1804). A few days later it added Moreau to the list of victims (Apr. 20); and by the end of the year, it was able to generate a great, inclusive summation of Napoleon's outlawries: "But what has BUONAPARTE, what has the OLD MAN OF THE MOUNTAIN, to do with the law of nations? The captives of Jaffa were, unfortunately, out of the protection of the law of nations. TOUSSAINT and PICHEGRU were out of the protection of the law of nations, as well as the ELECTOR of BADEN, and the ever-to-be-lamented Duke D'ENGHIEN" (Nov. 19). Similarly, the *Morning Post* began weekly in April to accumulate crimes of the Emperor. On April 4 it charged that "there is every reason to expect" that "MOREAU, PICHEGRU, and GEORGES . . . will be treated with the same disregard to justice and humanity, as has been experienced by the unfortunate Duke D'ENGHIEN." On April 11, it continued: "The death of D'ENGHIEN seals the fate of PICHEGRU and MOREAU." And on April 18, after calling character witnesses to undermine the claim that Pichegru's death had been suicide,[90] it reported the imputation that the General had been "cruelly strangled by order of the Consular Ruffian; and in his death [is seen] a melancholy prognostic of the fate of GEORGES and MOREAU." From this point on, the *Post* progressed to a frenzied imagination of Napoleon as master criminal. It called down divine punishment, for example, to avenge the Emperor's utmost "crimes" (May 23), named Bonaparte formulaically the "poisoner of Jaffa, and the murderer of the Duke D'ENGHIEN" (Aug. 20), and rebuked him as "the Corsican robber," "Imperial highway robber," and chief of "knaves and thieves" for the seizure of papers in November from the British diplomat, Sir George Rumbold (Nov. 26, 27). The epitome of such an imagination of Napoleon as Dr. Moriarty, as it were, occurred in the *Post* for August 20, where under the headline, "MORE CRIMES OF BONAPARTE," we read a sustained essay on the Emperor's "cloud of crimes" and "black list of . . . atrocities." From such imagination in the legitimate press, at last, it was not far to the even more lurid fantasies of the broadsheets. In this underworld of the press, the trope of Napoleon as Ruffian and the device of the cumulative list of crimes took on lives of their own. Accounts of the "Plunder," "Crimes," and "Atrocities" of Bonaparte thus proliferated (Maccunn, p. 70); and broadsides were published offering "TWENTY THOUSAND POUNDS REWARD" for "NAPOLEON BONAPARTE, *alias* Jaffa Bonaparte, *alias* Opium Bonaparte, *alias* [etc.]" (Ashton, pp. 162–63).

As 1804 continued, British popular hatred for Napoleon then reached its zenith when news arrived that Bonaparte was to become Emperor, with all due pomp and circumstance. As Maccunn notes, the event had been predicted in England for years, with the result that the reality was a "*coup de théâtre*" that "naturally fell rather flat" in the popular mind (pp. 74–76).[91] Officially proposed on May 3, ratified on May 18, and reported in the English papers from the end of May on, the rise of Empire evoked both fascinated attention to the protocol of the approaching coronation and a will to demystify the theatricality of such ceremony. Demystification followed the deepest instincts of English anti-Catholicism—or more generally, since Catholicism was now identified with counterrevolution, of anti-idolatry. In both the polite and the vulgar press, ink flowed to blot out the "blasphemy" of the Emperor who would be divine. As early as July 20, the *Times* reported: "An account is given of the various acts of religion and

religious ceremony which are to take place in consequence of the elevation of BONAPARTE to the Imperial dignity. . . . When was the name
of the Supreme Being more impudently blasphemed, or his rites
more openly profaned, than by the prostitution of them in honour
of BONAPARTE, though the splendid hypocrite calls forth the blessing of Heaven, and pretends to emulate the Christian virtues!" In a
similar vein, the *Morning Post* printed letters and poems excoriating
the Emperor for his specious religiosity (e.g., in its forecast of the
coronation, May 18; in a poem, "A Coronation Ode," May 26; in a
report of Bastille Day ceremonies, July 30).[92]

When the coronation finally occurred on December 2, such anti-
idolatry came to a head. On the one hand, the English papers devoted long pages to accounts of punctilio and poise (e.g., *T*, Dec. 11,
15; *MP*, Jan. 4, 1805; *AR*, 1804: 184–88).[93] But on the other, they
also declared violent disapproval of Napoleon's self-deification. In
particular, the press singled out for special inquisition Napoleon's
summoning of a lackey Pope (see Maccunn, pp. 77–79). So indignant did the *Post* grow in reporting Napoleon's appropriation of
Holiness, for example, that it went out of its way to dramatize the
Pope's "humiliation" (e.g., in its vivid narration of the Pope's arrival in Fontainebleau, Dec. 6). Meanwhile, the broadsheets were
accompanying the polite press in lampooning Napoleon as idol and
über-Pope. Throughout the period leading to Empire, satires such as
"The New Moses or Bonaparte's Ten Commandments" delighted in
giving Napoleon a tarnished halo (Ashton, pp. 158–60).

Having charged the Ruffian in civil and then in ecclesiastical court,
the popular English imagination was then at last ready to pronounce
sentence. The sentence was for discipline of the most fundamental
sort. As recited in "The Briton's Alphabet" in the *Morning Post* for
January 28, 1804:

> A. *stands for Albion*, the Queen of the Main,
> B. *for the Britons* she boasts in her train;
> C. *for the Consul*, Invasion who drums,
> AND D. *for the* Drubbing he'll get when he comes.

But it is finally not so much to the polite press as to the Rabelaisian
riot of the broadsheet literature that we must look for the full imagination of such drubbing. Always sensitive to what Bakhtin calls the
"material bodily lower stratum" of folk imagination, the broadsheets,
handbills, squibs, caricatures, and ballads of the time gave Napoleon
his hidin', nointin', paiking, skelping, trimming, and warming (to
use Lake District parlance). As early as June 1803, for example, a
caricature by T. West titled "Britannia correcting an Unruly Boy"
shows Britannia birching Boney across her knee with a rod labeled
United Kingdom. Boney bleats, "Oh dear! Oh dear! you'll entirely de-

stroy the *Honors of the Sitting*." The disciplinarian responds: "There take that, and that, and that, and be more careful not to provoke my anger more" (Ashton, pp. 143–44). Thus rules Britannia. Similarly, the ballad "Master Boney's Hearty Welcome to England" imagines what we might call fifteen ways of cooking his goose. Each of its fifteen stanzas invents a new way to hang, draw, quarter, and otherwise butcher the culprit. The first two stanzas, for example, propose:

> Should Boney come hither, our Britons declare,
> They'd flog the dog well—you may surely guess where:
> While others have vow'd, they would hang him as high,
> As Haman the Jew—'twixt the earth and the sky.
>   Boney down, down, down, Boney down.
>
> Some say they will treat him no better than fleas,
> And 'twixt thumb and finger they'll give him a squeeze;
> Whilst some by the ears, the vile Ruffian they'll lug,
> And others will give him a good Cornish hug.
>   Boney down, &c.   (Ashton, pp. 160–62)

And if such popular literature was bloody-minded, their visual counterparts were even more so. In the best tradition of caricatural sadism, for example, a British sailor pulls Napoleon's nose while aiming a kick at his groin; and in a Gillray picture a British Volunteer raises Boney's dripping head high on a stake (Ashton, p. 171).

In this fashion, then, does Britannia make Napoleon assume the position. One further set of particulars will garnish our study of the English roasting of Napoleon.[94] As the *Times* has already made us aware, Bonaparte now usurps the previous position of Robespierre as "Old Man of the Mountain" (Nov. 19, 1804; for an earlier use in which the epithet may refer to Robespierre, see *T*, June 2, 1804). Equally suggestive for our purposes is another association probably drawn from Napoleon's Swiss campaigns. Like Coleridge comparing Bonapartism (or perhaps also Coalition resistance) to a mountain avalanche, the press of the time imagined Napoleon's rise to empire as something like an actual mountain ascent. In the *Times*, for example: "The ascent to greatness, however steep and dangerous, may entertain an active spirit with the consciousness and exercise of its own powers; but the possession of a throne has never yet been found to afford a lasting satisfaction to an ambitious mind" (June 2, 1804). One last accident may prove to be the most suggestive of all: the meteorological occurrence that signed the coronation of Napoleon on December 2 as miracle. As one spectator records:

From an early hour in the morning the weather had been exceedingly unfavourable. It was cold and rainy, and appearances seemed to indicate that the procession would be anything but agreeable to those who joined it. But, as if by the especial favour of Providence, of which so many instances are observable in the career of Napoleon, the clouds suddenly dispersed, the sky brightened up, and the multitudes who lined the streets from the Tuileries to the Cathedral, enjoyed the sight of the procession, without being, as they had anticipated, drenched by a December rain. (Quoted in Ashton, p. 246)

First broadcast in the *Moniteur* and other French papers and then picked up repeatedly in the English press, this miracle of the opening clouds was held out for conspicuous English editorial ridicule (Ashton, p. 250). The *Times* for December 15, for example, published accounts of the sun's breaking through from both the *Moniteur* and the *Bulletin de l'Europe*, and commented with a skepticism finishing in fervid anti-idolatry:

The *Moniteur* of the next day [after the coronation] had not sufficiently recovered from the effects of the pomp, grandeur, solemnity, &c. &c. to be able to understand any details of the ceremony. It merely insinuates, that the Sun miraculously penetrated through a thick fog to be present at it; a compliment which is a little diminished by a subsequent assertion, that the lamps were afterwards able to supply his place, by giving a noon-day brilliancy to the night. Then follows a disgusting hypocritical panegyric upon the union of civil and religious acts and ceremonies, the sublime representation of all that human and divine affairs could assemble to strike the mind— the venerable Apostolic virtues of the poor POPE, and the most astonishing genius of BUONAPARTE crowned by the most astonishing destiny!

With this survey of popular opinion in mind, we are prepared at last to come to the end of *The Prelude*. To do so, we need only observe that popular opinion is not "public" opinion as imagined by Wordsworth; nor is the popular hero, John Bull (or Jack Tar), the same as the poet's hero: his self. If John Bull enacts a combat story whose moral is the disciplining of Napoleon, the poet lyricizes that story so that its moral becomes antithetical autobiography—the form of ideology, we must now see, that not only corrects England along with France *but self together with Napoleon*. Bonaparte, the genius of antithetical warfare, and Wordsworth, the genius of antithetical poetry, meet across a narrow divide.

Recall the elisions of history we earlier noticed in the five-book poem of January to March 1804—particularly the passage on the "unremitting warfare" against Imagination. With reference to 1791–92, as I have suggested, the latter part of this passage may well identify the early Revolution as the agent of warfare against Imagination. But in 1804, we can now see, other agents besieged poetic Imagination as well: the nation of shopkeepers and the actual general of unremitting warfare at the time, Napoleon. Such, the poet says, "May be fit matter for another song." In what song will he resolve the agon of unremitting warfare between Imagination and the Napoleonic world?

As we have seen, the first draft for such a song consisted of the political sonnets. At their most extreme, we can now recognize, these imagine a curiously *mano a mano* relation between the poet's Imagination and Napoleon. Like Coleridge thinking himself a Poet-Bonaparte, Sonnet 23 (probably composed between October 1803 and January 1804; *P2V*, p. 170n) brings Wordsworth's "I" into sudden, startling proximity to the great Autocrator:

> When, looking on the present face of things,
> I see one Man, of Men the meanest too!
> Rais'd up to sway the World, to do, undo,
> With mighty Nations for his Underlings,
> The great events with which old story rings
> Seem vain and hollow; I find nothing great;
> Nothing is left which I can venerate;
> So that almost a doubt within me springs
> Of Providence, such emptiness at length
> Seems at the heart of all things. But, great God!
> I measure back the steps which I have trod,
> And tremble, seeing, as I do, the strength
> Of such poor Instruments, with thoughts sublime
> I tremble at the sorrow of the time.
> (DC MS. 44 and Longman MS. version)

The idolization of Napoleon, Wordsworth declares, is false providence (compare the religious imagery that also characterizes such sonnets on Napoleon as 9 and 12). It is idolatry so extreme, indeed, that for a moment he is skeptical of all that he had venerated. But then his demystifying correction of the cult of Napoleon leads to a remystifying moment of self-correction. In the name of great God he checks himself and measures back autobiographically "the steps which I have trod." It is such self-correction that at last allows him to stand as an anti-type of Napoleon: a man of "thoughts sublime" differentiated from the imperial sublime. Though it may "do" and "undo," we can say, Imagination will not be an Emperor shaping and reshaping nations.

The second draft for Wordsworth's developing song of unremitting warfare was the "Ode to Duty," which, though it removes him from the realm of explicit politics, writes large the impulse of antithetical self-correction. Composed (except for its first stanza) in early 1804 by March 6, the ode was transcribed together with the political sonnets in DC MS. 44 as follows:

> [Stern Daughter of the Voice of God!
> O Duty! if that name thou love
> Who art a Light to guide, a Rod
> To check the erring, and reprove;   [st. 1 missing in MS., but
> Thou who art victory and law   space allotted for]
> When empty terrors overawe;

From vain temptations dost set free;
From strife and from despair; a glorious ministry.]

O'er earth o'er heaven thy yoke is thrown
All Natures thy behests obey
Man only murmurs; he alone
In wilfulness rejects thy sway.   [st. 2 not in first
Him empty terrors overawe   printed version
And vain temptations are his law: or Longman MS.]
He bids his better mind be dumb;
And foresight does but breed remorse for times to come

There are who ask not [rev. from (?that)] if thine eye
Be on them; who, in love and truth,
Without misgiving do rely
Upon the genial sense of youth:
Glad Hearts! without reproach or blot;
Who do thy work, and know it not:
May joy be their's till they grow old
And if they fail do thou direct them and uphold

Serene would be our days and bright,
And happy would our nature be,
If love were an unerring light,
And joy its own security.
And bless'd are they who in the main
This holy creed do entertain
Yet even these may live to know
That they have hopes to seek, strength which elsewhere must grow

I, loving freedom, and untried;
No sport of every random gust,
Yet being to myself a guide,
Too blindly have reposed my trust:
Resolved that nothing e'er should press
Upon my present happiness,
I shoved unwelcome tasks away;
But thee I now would serve [rev. from (see[?m])] more strictly, if I
   may.

From no disturbance of my soul,
Or strong compunction in me wrought,
I supplicate for thy controul;
But in the quietness of thought:
Me this perpetual freedom tires;
I feel the weight of chance desires:
My hopes no more must change their name,
I wish for a repose that ever is the same.

Yet not the less would I throughout
Still act according to the voice
Of my own wish; and feel past doubt

That my submissiveness was choice:
Not seeking in the school of pride
For "precepts over dignified,"
Denial and restraint I prize
No farther than they breed a second will [rev. from (wish)] more
    wise.

Stern Lawgiver! yet thou dost wear
The Godhead's most benignant grace;
Nor know we any thing so fair
As is the smile upon thy face
Flowers laugh before thee on their beds;
And Fragrance in thy [rev. from (their)] footing treads;
Thou dost preserve the Stars from wrong;
And the most ancient Heavens through Thee are fresh and strong.

To humbler functions, awful Power!
I call thee: I myself commend
Unto thy guidance from this hour;
Oh! let my weakness have an end!
Give unto me, made lowly wise,
The spirit of self-sacrifice;
The confidence of reason give;
And in the light of truth thy Bondman let me live!
                    (reconstructed from *P2V*, pp. 104–7 and *appar. crit.*)

The ode begins by invoking divine Duty to correct the willfulness that suppresses "Man's" "better mind" (st. 2). But the core of the poem, of course, is not finally its critique of impersonal Man. To become Dutiful, Man must be personalized. The preparation for such personalization occurs in stanzas 3–4, which, if they seem to draw from Gray's "Eton College" ode, do so only to undermine the security of blissful ignorance. As the poet increasingly intimates at the end of stanza 4, joy is never fully "its own security." Dangers trivial and (we can guess) international await their opening. How can Man make the world more secure? The answer is that he—and first of all the poet—must correct himself *personally*. Thus the equivalent of the *volta* in the sonnets occurs at stanza 5, which suddenly foreshortens the long view of humanity into a near view of the poet's "I." In the voice of authoritative autobiography, Wordsworth confesses that "I" have been too heedless in my freedom and that "I," therefore, must experience a correction of mind. Too-free imagination must be disciplined into a personal version of Man's better mind: "quietness of thought" (st. 6). Only after this moment of self-correction can the poet then resume the voice of impersonal Man upon the "we" in stanza 8—a "we" that is one with the new public of the political sonnets. "I" and "we" compact together, and the result—in the last stanza—is the poet's personal/public return to a true "better mind."

Disciplined by the personification of divine doctrine, Duty, this better mind is not Imagination-as-god but precisely what I earlier called an ideology of logos serving higher agency. It is Imagination submitted to the new control of "confidence of reason" and "light of truth."

The final draft of Wordsworth's song of unremitting warfare is then the finale of our *Eroica* (the symphony, we remember, whose title of "Bonaparte" Beethoven tore up in 1804 when he learned Napoleon would be Emperor). This *Eroica*, of course, is the latter part of *The Prelude*. As we saw, Wordsworth after March 1804 elaborated on the theme of unremitting warfare against Imagination to write the historical sections of his poem. Then to close properly, he restructured the original plan of his conclusion so that Snowdon and the spots of time changed places. Why was this new concept of closure proper?

We can begin with the ascent of Snowdon in Book 13. Here it would be possible to draw for our emblem from the circumstances we noticed in the popular imagination of correcting Napoleon—the figure of the Old Man of the Mountain ascending a steep grade, for example, or the miracle of the opening clouds and sudden sun on coronation day. But perhaps another emblem will serve. As Emsley observes, fortifications on the model of the Martello towers at Eastbourne (his pl. 7) rose all along the Kent and Sussex coasts upon the resumption of war after the Peace of Amiens. Called "Bull-dogs" by the French, these structures stood 34 feet high and in the early years of war already numbered 79; an additional 29 were raised north of the Thames in 1810–12 (Emsley, caption to his pl. 7). Wordsworth's Snowdon, I suggest, is his Bull-dog, his mountain constructed to defend against the Old Man of the Mountain. Considered in the context of the poet's walking trip with Jones in 1791, of course, the ascent is set in Wales. But considered in the context of 1804, the real place of the mountain is on the eastern verge of Britain among the other piles of patriotism. Or rather, western and eastern verges of defense were equivalent. I have speculated elsewhere on the special political significance of the Welsh setting for Wordsworth in these years of rediscovered nationalism ("Wordsworth and Subversion"). In our present context, it is sufficient to note only that the western shores of Britain were very much *not* buffered from invasion. The first invasion scares of the war years, after all, had been prompted by the two abortive attempts in late 1796 and early 1797 to land French troops in Ireland and Wales (see Emsley, pp. 56–57). As Emsley comments, these invasion fears

help to explain why, some months later [in 1797], the people of Alfoxton [*sic*] assumed from the antics of Wordsworth and Coleridge that they were

French spies and Portland was sufficiently impressed to direct an agent to investigate. The west coast of England and Wales was the last area where the government and its military advisers had expected an invasion attempt; now men flocked to the colours of the local volunteers and the government was inundated with requests for additional protection by land and sea. (pp. 56–57)

What a historical reading of the end of *The Prelude* shows with conviction, I suggest, is that the aesthetics of closure constructed at Snowdon is one with Wordsworth's politics of patriotism. It was the volunteerism of his Mind. Here is the Snowdon experience in my selection and with my emphases:

> With forehead bent
> Earthward, *as if in opposition set*
> *Against an enemy*, I panted up
> With eager pace, and no less eager thoughts.
> Thus might we wear perhaps an hour away,
> Ascending at loose distance each from each,
> And I, as chanced, the foremost of the Band;
> When at my feet the ground appear'd to brighten,
> And with a step or two seem'd brighter still;
> Nor had I time to ask the cause of this,
> For instantly a Light upon the turf
> Fell like a flash: I look'd about, and lo!
> The Moon stood naked in the Heavens, at height
> Immense above my head, and on the shore
> I found myself of a huge sea of mist,
> Which, meek and silent, rested at my feet:
> A hundred hills their dusky backs upheaved
> All over this still Ocean, and beyond,
> Far, far beyond, the vapours shot themselves,
> In headlands, tongues, and promontory shapes,
> Into the Sea, the real Sea, that seem'd
> To dwindle, *and give up its majesty,*
> *Usurp'd upon as far as sight could reach.*
>   .   .   .
>
> A meditation rose in me that night
> Upon the lonely Mountain when the scene
> Had pass'd away, and it appear'd to me
> The perfect image of *a mighty Mind,*
> *Of one that feeds upon infinity,*
> *That is exalted by an underpresence,*
> *The sense of God, or whatsoe'er is dim*
> *Or vast in its own being,* above all
> One function of such mind had Nature there
> Exhibited by putting forth, and that
> With circumstance most awful and sublime,
> *That domination which she oftentimes*

Exerts upon the outward face of things,
So moulds them, and endues, abstracts, combines,
Or by abrupt and unhabitual influence
Doth make one object so impress itself
Upon all others, and pervade them so
That even the grossest minds must see and hear
And cannot chuse but feel.

　　　　　　.　.　.

Such minds are truly from the Deity,
For they are Powers.

　　　　　　.　.　.

　Oh! who is he that hath his whole life long
Preserved, enlarged, this freedom in himself?
For this alone is genuine Liberty.
　　　　　　　　　(13.29–119; italics mine)

　　This is Wordsworth's moment of Absolute Knowledge. As in the case of Hegel, of course, such knowledge is the knowledge of many things. But among those things, we know, is one especially charged field of objective existence that subjectivity cannot quite veil. This is the dangerously usurpatory world that the political sonnets and newspaper essays of the years leading to 1804 have prepared us to see: the world of empire. Whatever else it may be, Wordsworth's vision on the mount is the imagination of empire. Or rather, we can say that it is the imagination *not* of empire—but with a stress underscoring the overdetermined nature of the negation. As the language of *Macht* throughout Wordsworth's account of Snowdon indicates (his "politics of vision," as Abrams calls it; *Natural Supernaturalism*, pp. 371–72), Imagination is a denial of Napoleonic empire so overdetermined, detailed, and substantive that negation—as I have earlier said—becomes the positive fact. "This is my empire of majesty and genuine Liberty," we might hear the poet say, "*that* empire across the Channel is Tyranny."

　　Snowdon, then, is a vision of poetic Imagination that has "usurped" upon the world in which actual usurpers rise to power. It is the coronation of the *Poet*-Bonaparte. But what allows such usurpatory Imagination to differentiate itself from the arch-usurper, Napoleon? What permits Wordsworth, that is, to close his poem on this pinnacle with such self-assured faith in his own doctrinal rightness that he can claim, "Such minds are truly from the Deity"? (After reflecting upon Napoleon in Sonnet 23, after all, he had earlier speculated: "almost a doubt within me springs / Of Providence.") The answer is to be found in the spots of time in Book 11 (together with the sequel to Imagination Restored in Book 12). Here we arrive upon the solution to our puzzle of revisionary structure. The motive for reordering the close of *The Prelude*, I suggest, lies in the fact that only a prior moment of autobiographical self-correction can allow the Imagination to become like, but not *too* like, Napoleon. Only prior atonement for the Imagination's complicity in imperialism, that is, can justify its final ascent to empire as an act *antithetical* to Napoleonic imperialism—as an imperial restauration that is also true restoration. To cite once more from 11c at the end of the blasted hawthorn episode:

> The event
> With all the sorrow which it brought appear'd
> A chastisement; and when I call'd to mind
> That day so lately pass'd, when from the crag
> I look'd in such anxiety of hope,
> With trite reflections of morality,
> Yet in the deepest passion, I bow'd low
> To God, who thus corrected my desires.

Thus was the poet's mind corrected at the start of its overreaching desires.

Or again, to continue on to the doctrine Wordsworth placed in Book 12 probably between early October 1804 and early 1805:

> I was benighted heart and mind; but now
> On all sides day began to reappear . . .
>   .   .   .
>   Above all
> Did Nature bring again that wiser mood
> More deeply re-established in my soul,
> Which, seeing little worthy or sublime
> In what we blazon with the pompous names
> Of power and action, early tutor'd me
> To look with feelings of fraternal love
> Upon those unassuming things, that hold
> A silent station in this beauteous world.
>   .   .   .
> Ambitious virtues pleased me less, I sought
> For good in the familiar face of life
> And built thereon my hopes of good to come.
>   .   .   .
>   [I was now] prepared to find
> Ambition, folly, madness in the men
> Who thrust themselves upon this passive world
> As Rulers of the world.   (12.21–73)

In such manner does Imagination at last win its battle against what the "unremitting warfare" passage had named "blind . . . ambition obvious." To conquer the forces of conquest was to turn away from simple empire to the empire of the simple—to a light of common "day" that "*early* tutor'd" the poet to see correctly the blinding sun of imperial ambition. It was probably in December 1804, after all, that Wordsworth—in apparent reference to the miracle of the sun at Napoleon's overdramatic self-crowning—added to Book 10 the lines making France during the coronation a "sun" once splendid among "living clouds" but now "turned into a gewgaw, a machine, . . . an opera phantom" (10.935–40). Taught "early" in life to see through such worldly glory, the poet can now march along his humble rather than imperial way: the public road he walks like some tourist-messiah in the rest of Book 12. And what the way leads to is his purely pedestrian ascension atop Snowdon where, in a moment of crowning vision, the meekness that is mind without action inherits the earth of 1804.

In short, we might hear the following as the poet's essential statement in the closing books of *The Prelude*: "My public, I stand before you *already* corrected. Spots of time have *already* taught me the doctrine that makes my Imagination a mere stand-in between God and Nature. And so it is that I can now without open imperialism crown myself Poet in this, my world-cathedral at Snowdon, *my* Notre Dame in which the moon breaks through clouds to dim the revelation of that other ambitious mind across the Channel."

This, then, is how the poet's text closes, securing the contentless play of its shifters ("I"/"Mind") upon the irreversible determination of historical context. *This* Napoleonic history that underlay Imagination in its beginning is there again at its end as the very possibility of a determined "end"—of the *telos* and *arche* both into which the textual indeterminacy of lyricism points. The invisible *telos* and *arche* of contemporary history is the poem's topical referent, the *topos* that is the closing aim of all Wordsworth's pointings or deictic "this's." Such topicality grounding the spots of time is like the obscure voice that vents through clouds in the Snowdon episode: it is there and not there. It is the logos underlying the poet's ideology of logos: an invisible presence whose status as veiled or denied ground is the advent of the very consciousness of pointing in the poem: the self that lives to point into "elsewhereness."

The one great point of Wordsworth's ideology of logos, in sum, is self. But the first and last word still belong to history. For, to mark a final restitution of literary-theoretical (and deconstructive) discourse to historical study, we can note that, even in the midst of his self-correcting autobiography and revision of hidden topicality, the poet has been preempted by the Emperor. In his intriguing chapter on Napoleon as "Writer of History," George Gordon Andrews documents the fact that the Emperor was himself a practicing revisionary historian, a retrospective corrector of deeds and words. One striking example lies in the record Napoleon created of his coup of 18–19 Brumaire 1799. At the onset of the coup, he first gave a speech in the Council of Ancients that Andrews (in a later chapter) shows was badly spoken. Indeed, his own secretary, Bourrienne, records that Napoleon was incoherent. "Only the words 'brothers in arms' and the 'frankness of a soldier,' were heard," Bourrienne says, and more: "The questions of the President were presented clearly and rapidly. Nothing was more confused or more poorly expressed than the ambiguous and obscure replies of Bonaparte. He talked endlessly of 'volcanoes, secret agitations, victories, a violated Constitution'!" (quoted in Andrews, p. 145).[95] The next act then unfolded when, after storming out of the Council of Ancients, Napoleon stormed into the even more hostile Council of Five Hundred. Here, as Andrews reconstructs the scene, "As soon as he was recognized, there was a scene of wild confusion. Some deputies rushed upon him and cries of 'Armed men here?' 'Down with the dictator!' 'Outlaw him! (*Hors la loi*)' resounded through the hall. He was undoubtedly jostled about roughly" (p. 147). Only the cool intervention of his brother, Lucien Bonaparte, saved the day.

But reports in the *Moniteur* and subsequently in the English press told a different story. What we watch in this record is a gradual revision of reality allowing Napoleon to legitimize his coup as a rational and proper response to danger. By the time it appeared in the *Morning Post* and the *Times*, for example, the speech to the Council of Ancients seemed a highly polished declamation. The transcript in the *Post* begins:

Representatives of the People, you are not in a common crisis; you tread upon a volcano ready to destroy you. Yesterday Paris was in the most profound tranquillity. I have united all my brethren in arms in the execution of the measures which you have adopted.

I have given proofs of my devotion to the Republic, and the country has not had a more zealous defender than I have proved myself.—This day, however, I am surrounded with calumny, and covered with reproach and disgust. (*MP*, Nov. 19, 1799)[96]

Similarly, by the time the jostling that Napoleon received in the Council of Five Hundred appeared in print, it had grown into a hagiographic account of martyrdom. "Mystery" still shrouded events, the *Times* noted on November 18, but both the *Times* and the *Post* for November 18 and 19 nevertheless communicated reports that Napoleon had survived "assassination." Indeed, the papers eventually reported that *eighteen* assassination attempts had been thwarted in the Council of Five Hundred and that "he was twice wounded in the arm, and also in the cheek" (*T*, Nov. 19, 1799).[97]

The final act of imagination allowing Napoleon to justify his usurpation of power was the Proclamation he issued to set the record "right." I quote the full Proclamation from the *Times* of November 21 (the version in the *Post* the next day is slightly longer):

PROCLAMATION OF BUONAPARTE

On my return to Paris, I found all the Constituted Authorities split into factions, and the Constitution one half destroyed, and unable to support Liberty. All parties hastened to meet me—entrusted me with their designs —disclosed their secrets, and asked my assistance. I refused to become a party-man.

The Council of Ancients called upon me. I replied to their call. A plan of general restoration had been concerted by men whom the nation had been accustomed to behold as the defenders of liberty, equality, and property. This plan required a calm and free examination, devoid of all influence and fear. In consequence, the Council of Ancients resolved to remove the Legislative Body to *St. Cloud*, and charged me to make the necessary dispositions to maintain its independence. I thought it my duty to accept the command.

The Councils assembled at St. Cloud; the Republican troops guaranteed safety without, but assassins spread terror within. Many Deputies, armed with stilettoes and fire arms, encircled around me, menacing death.

I communicated my indignation and grief to the Council of Antients. They gave me fresh testimonies of their good will and confidence. I went to the Council of Five Hundred alone, unarmed, my head uncovered. The stillettoes which threatened the Deputies were immediately lifted against their Deliverer. Twenty assassins ran towards me, and attempted to stab me. The Grenadiers of the Legislative Body flew to my assistance, and one of the brave Grenadiers is [*sic*] struck with a stroke directed against me, which pierced his cloaths. The soldiers carried me off.

At the same moment, the cry of—"*Beyond the Law*" was heard against the *Defender of the Laws*. They pressed forward towards the President, with threats in their mouths and arms in their hands. They ordered him to pronounce me out of the reach of the law. I was informed of it, and ordered six grenadiers to rescue him. Immediately the grenadiers of the Legislative Body cleared the Hall.

The factions, intimidated, dispersed and went away. The majority returned to the Hall, heard the proposition made for the public good, deliberated, and prepared the Resolutions which were to become the new provisional law of the Republic.

Frenchmen, you will no doubt behold in this conduct the zeal of a soldier of liberty, and of a Citizen devoted to the Republic. The dispersion of the factions who oppressed the Councils have restored public order and security, and the men who were most odious have also shewn themselves the most contemptible.

(Signed) BUONAPARTE,
BERTHIER

Napoleon had returned to Paris to assume power and deliver the Republic. But what fitted him to undertake the task? Why was he the just Deliverer of the People? The answer the Proclamation gave was the intensely autobiographical statement that *I have already been accused of standing beyond the law, and have already been threatened with Caesar's punishment*. Invented by Napoleon to transform usurpation into a new doctrine of state, the Proclamation with its transumption of violence is a close analogue of Wordsworth's gibbet mast and blasted hawthorn episodes. It is Napoleon's spot of time, his autobiography dedicated to the ideological task of correcting past history as prelude to power.

PART IV

Conclusion

CHAPTER NINE

The Idea of the Memorial Tour: "Composed Upon Westminster Bridge"

To arrive upon snowdon is to finish our tour of poetic beginnings. In this tour, I have tried to reconstruct the
very possibility of poetic beginning: the ideology of originality that
emerges from, but denies, the collective agon of absence—of the
loss, dispossession, becoming—that is history. Denying the collective story of absence, I have argued, Wordsworth's poetry produces
by inversion a private lyric of presence: imagination. Imagination is
the refugee consciousness that—cut off by history from its referential ground in nation, family, and riches—crosses its mountain pass,
climbs its cloud-veiled peak, to enter a new land where collective loss
can be imagined the gain of the individual. But for such loss, what
recompense? Again those lines at the end of *The Prelude* that, in the
course of my own reading and rereading of the poem, I have found
the hardest to accept. Celebrating imagination as abundant recompense, Wordsworth apostrophizes:

> Oh! who is he that hath his whole life long
> Preserved, enlarged, this freedom in himself?
> For this alone is genuine Liberty:
> Witness, ye Solitudes! . . .   (13.117–20)

The solitary way of Adam and Eve at the end of *Paradise Lost* is bearable—if it *is* bearable—because it is both social ("hand in hand") and
directed toward the world. The solitary way of Wordsworth (until
he joins hands with Dorothy and Coleridge at the very close of the
poem) is not, I find, as easy to bear. A transport of imagination that
cherishes private freedom its "whole life long" can also appear not
liberty but something like penal transportation: a forced remove to

Solitudes that can only echo back—to abbreviate Hartman's argument—"self or nature." In the down-under of self-consciousness, the third voice of the secular trinity brooding within Wordsworth's poetry is silent: the originating absence or unholy ghost of history. The proper title of *The Prelude*, we may say, is *History Lost*.

Such has been my criticism of Wordsworth. Where Blake said that Milton was of the devil's party without knowing it, I have criticized Wordsworth's history lost by saying that the poet was of history's party without knowing it. Indeed, the precedent of Blake is prescriptive for the last movement of criticism I would now initiate. Where Blake in *Milton* then revived Milton to make him redeem his own past work, I wish to conclude my project by summoning up for my poet a similar afterlife. I wish to remember the later, imaginatively "dead" Wordsworth who, in the view I will argue here, sacrifices part of his original self—his imagination—to redeem part of history. To redeem a poet able to redeem his lost history, of course, may seem a strange task of harrowing after a series of chapters whose net result is arguably demystifying: a nailing up of the poet on the cross of the historical world that, in the act of pointing out the stigmata where political, social, and economic history have penetrated, refuses to acknowledge any of the poet's saving fictions of transcendence except in distancing quotes—as if hanging up an accusation, "This is Wordsworth, the King of the Imagination." However, there still remains a final saving fiction—no less than a counter-ideology—in the poet's corpus: his faith that transcendental imagination can at the last recollect history.[1] Illusion such recollection may be (for, certainly, the later poet is surfeit with German Ideology), but to refuse to allow this counterillusory illusion even the possibility of credence would, in my view, be to leave our task of criticism incomplete. It would be to remove the possibility that Wordsworth was his own critic.

Criticism would make it new, I have said, by opening up to view the interval of difference between a work's assumptions and other works, other assumptions. Most crucially, it opens up the interval between *then* and *now* and, in so doing, creates the essential space of the hermeneutical problem: the epochal divide between the other and the same that is the aporetic ground—the ultimate "two points" in my tour model—of historical understanding. Much of our current New Historicism is a conscious attempt to hold the gap open as long as possible in reaction against historical methods that have too forcefully interposed ideal, material, or positivist continua (a Geist or material determinant, for example). Thus in their related ways, the Foucauldian history of discontinuity, the neo-Marxist emphasis on differentiation and distantiation, and the "*Representations*-school" accent on "the impossibility of fully reconstructing and reentering the culture" of the past all pry apart the sides of the raw gap of history to prevent any too-easy credence in an interstitial "subject" able to heal the wound: spirit, consciousness, imagination, man, people, nation, humanity, and so forth.[2] As I have said about my own methodology, such new history is thus radically skeptical in its ontology but positive in its displaced locus of epistemology. It would know with precision not so much the historical other across the divide as the shape and dimensions of the divide itself together with the imprint of such impending division, or becoming, *within* the other—a palpable absence, we may say, like the track of a blade after it has left the wound.

But though we do not want a too-easy regeneration of the flesh of "humanity" in the wound or stigma of history, neither do we desire the scarring, thickening, and coarsening that endangers all the demystifying strategies of New Historicism. I refer to the potential for adversarial dogmatism that resides in all such strategies, including my own: a too inflexible and hardened preference for marks of difference. Put simply: all difference discovered between *then* and *now*, as well as all marks of difference observed within the *then* itself, threaten to become the same. Difference becomes the source of the same limited range of responses—Foucauldian laughter, wonder, shock, and, above all, irony. These responses are always just short of admitting those other affects—empathy, sympathy, identification —that, while insufficient in themselves, are nevertheless necessary to the span of understanding.[3] Or to subtract the metaphor and the language of affection I have called up in using my metaphor of wounds and stigmata: the logic of the hermeneutical circle is indeed inescapable. For historical understanding to be possible, a certain overlap or "foreknowledge" of the past within the present is necessary; and any critical method that holds the present and past (as well as the polarities within the past) too immaculately apart for fear of cross-contamination is not a possible method of critical understanding. In short, irony—the greatest of the holdovers of New Criticism and deconstruction in the New Historicism—is not by itself criticism.

How can historical criticism prevent itself from hardening into (in)difference without inventing a new Geist or material determinant to fill the breach between the other and the same, the past and the present? The answer, it seems to me, is to identify with the past in the carefully constrained sense of giving it the benefit of a doubt. If criticism observes the differences between a work's assumptions and those of other milieus (differences that allow us to see its ideology), then it should also seek—in Althusser's phrase—to discern some slight awareness of that interval of difference within the work itself as the work's "internal distantiation" (*Lenin*, p. 204). Criticism should discern not only historical difference and its forecast in the self-divisions of the past, in other words, but also the purely provisional, self-critical awareness that forms around internal differentiation as the past's own worry over the fact that it is not simply itself. Such is the past's sense of history: its own, barely emergent awareness that it is at once an ideological formation (what de Man in his work prior to the articulation of irony denominates "intent") and a state historically distanced from, in excess of, or otherwise differentiated from its formative intent.[4]

Only the surmise of a prior sense of history, it seems to me, can complete the act of critical understanding.[5] For it is precisely the ability to give the past the benefit of one's own doubt—to bracket and so make room for the possibility of previous demystification—that enables the essential overlap of foreknowledge between *then* and *now*, the work's own wrestle with historical understanding and ours. In the end, of course, it is not the discovery of prior demystification in itself that is necessary (especially since the circus-animals' desertion of a poet's self-demystification always has the potential to become a new mythology) so much as the discovery during criticism of *some* such second horizon of interpreting the poet. We need, in effect, a horizon-over-the-horizon, where the self-differentiation that is the past's sense of history and the self-differentiation that is the present's sense of history may fuse without either selves or historical worlds (bounded by the first-order horizon) also being thought to fuse.

In the criticism of Wordsworth, in sum, we require at last an overlap of horizons that will not be Romantic ideology but *anti*-Romantic ideology: an exploratory identification with the poet's own later effort to criticize the flight of imagination and recover history once more. This, perhaps, is the toughest test for any historical critic of Wordsworth and Romanticism. Are we able not only to criticize-by-difference the denial of history creative of Wordsworth's most imaginative work but also to criticize-by-identification the restitution to history responsible for his later, *dis*imaginative work? Can we recognize, in other words, that our criticism of imagination reproduces *in itself* the unimaginative flair of the poet's later work with all its dutiful remembrance of historical and institutional forms (nation, church, people) and all its reduction of imagination to occasional moments when he (and we) are surprised by joy? We can finally understand our King of the Imagination, I have suggested, only at the moment of his own forsakenness. But in that moment when his act of seeing through imagination mirrors ours, are we not also forsaken? Or to change allusions: at the moment when our Quixote, in the very fever fit of illusion, sees through fiction to mirror ourselves as critics of fiction, who would not look away?

Criticism can never end its effort to turn the windmillings of illusion into the counter-windmillings of the hermeneutical circle, of understanding. But it loses heart, grows tired, submits to the au-

thority of its own historical moment and the ideologically determined priorities that command, to take the most pertinent example,
"This book must be finished *now*." Thus it is, perhaps, that criticism
itself needs its saving fictions. I close my tour of Wordsworth's poetic
beginnings, then, upon the fiction that I merely open the book on the
poet's imaginative ending and recollection of history (though I know
I have not heart or years enough to read this book). I close upon
the many Memorial Tours, Itinerary poems, and related sequences
—including the *River Duddon* and *Ecclesiastical Sonnets*—that are the
dominant form of the later poet. Or rather (another saving fiction),
since I cannot here explore the whole of these later works, I offer
only a wild surmise of the pacific reaches.

What is the idea of the Memorial Tour, the basic unimaginative
form allowing the poet to see through imagination and remember history? An answer can be gained by marking something like
a memorial tour in our own inquiry: a turn back from *The Prelude* of 1805 to the sequence of lyric poems of 1802 that composed
what was really Wordsworth's first Memorial Tour (cf. Woodring,
Wordsworth, p. 164). The keystone of this sequence, which I will call
the "Calais Tour," was the sonnet, "Composed Upon Westminster
Bridge, Sept. 3, 1802."[6]

The Paris Diligence

Reading "Composed Upon Westminster Bridge," we know strange
déjà vu: we have been here before in such an atmosphere of radiant calm, such Claudian or picturesque repose. Yet where we have
been is not now as it was. Where the picturesque enjoyed delight,
"Westminster Bridge" stands in awe before what will become the
older poet's duty-bound version of delight, "majesty." And where
the picturesque framed delight between beauty and sublimity, "Westminster Bridge" frames majesty between "beauty" and a transformed
sublimity, "might":

> Earth has not any thing to shew more fair:
> Dull would he be of heart who could pass by
> A sight so touching in it's majesty:
> This City now doth like a garment wear
> The beauty of the morning; silent, bare,
> Ships, towers, domes, theatres, and temples lie
> Open unto the fields, and to the sky;
> All bright and glittering in the smokeless air.
> Never did sun more beautifully steep
> In his first splendor valley, rock, or hill;
> Ne'er saw I, never felt, a calm so deep!
> The river glideth at his own sweet will:

> Dear God! the very houses seem asleep;
> And all that mighty heart is lying still!
> (Longman MS. text; *P2V*, p. 147
> and *appar. crit.*)[7]

This is a poem of repose that is finally about—and of—imaginative might. What is an imagination of might? Or to use the term that is the ground and *mise en abyme* both of the recent New Historicism: what is the poetry of power?

The negative way preoccupies modern readings of the poem: the power of the poem does *not* derive from any form or content that can be determined. We notice to begin with that although "Westminster Bridge" belongs to a specific form, the sonnet, it nevertheless contains a riot of modal and generic possibilities matching the shapeless eagerness of the Revolution books in *The Prelude*. Lyric form is again transform: it is not committed to any particular form. "Westminster Bridge," we can thus say, is a love poem in the strong suit of the sonnet. But it is also, as David Ferry has pointed out with effect, an epitaph for a personified city with a stopped heart (pp. 12–14). Again, "Westminster Bridge" is a tour or locodescriptive work in the fashion of William Lisle Bowles, one of whose tour sonnets ends on the note of an actual stilled heart: "Now, far remov'd from every earthly ill, / Her woes are bury'd, and her heart is still" ("At a Convent," in *Sonnets*, p. 17).[8] Or perhaps, as Kurt Schlüter argues, the poem is both pastoral in its assimilation of the city to a garden world and apocalyptic in its hint that London resembles the brilliant New Jerusalem robed—in the words of Revelation—"as a bride adorned for her husband" ("Dear God!" Wordsworth exclaims).[9] Staying one step ahead of classification (Wordsworth assigns the sonnet form itself to the difficult and miscellaneous category of the "Idyllium" in the 1815 Preface), "Westminster Bridge" flickers perpetually on the verge of generic stability—tour poem *né* epitaph *né* love poem, and so on.

In content, too, the sonnet escapes us: the object that is the referent of its power is invisible. We can think most usefully here of object as "place." Though the poem certainly gestures toward London as its mighty place, it seems to modern eyes finally about no place at all. It is about contradiction of place—the replacement of London as referential ground by an unstable, self-canceling metamorphosis that has been variously defined: country/city, life/death, clothedness/bareness, stillness/motion, object/subject, prospect/introspect.[10] Since Wordsworth's own day, indeed, "contradiction" has seemed the poem's peculiar art. Responding to criticism of the lines showing London both robed and bare, Wordsworth answered a correspondent in 1836, "the contradiction is in the *words* only" (*Letters*, 6: 292).

The method of contradiction allowing the poem to replace London is twofold. First, Wordsworth simply misplaces the city by withholding determinate vision. Even the most graphic line, "Ships, towers, domes, theatres, and temples," resists mapping: measured against the contemporary skyline, it involves neither a clockwise nor a counterclockwise turn of the head. Nor is the view effectively centered: the central "domes" in which we might expect to see one dome in particular, St. Paul's, disperses into plural generality.[11] A strange double of the minutely detailed panoramas that were drawing crowds in the early 1800's (culminating spectacularly in Thomas Hornor's "View of London," 1828–29, complete with a dummy cutaway of St. Paul's dome inside the Regent's Park Colosseum), Wordsworth's panorama resists depicting detail.[12] If it *were* to include St. Paul's, we might say, it would veil the details as utterly as in the poet's later "St. Paul's" (1808)—a poem remarkably like "Westminster Bridge" in effect:

> It chanced
> That, while I thus was pacing, I raised up
> My heavy eyes and instantly beheld,
> Saw at a glance in that familiar spot
> A visionary scene: a length of street
> Laid open in its morning quietness,
> Deep, hollow, unobstructed, vacant, smooth,
> And white with winter's purest white, as fair,
> As fresh and spotless as he ever sheds
> On field or mountain. Moving Form was none,
> Save here and there a shadowy Passenger,
> Slow, shadowy, silent, dusky, and beyond
> And high above this winding length of street,
> This noiseless and unpeopled avenue,
> Pure, silent, solemn, beautiful, was seen
> The huge majestic Temple of St. Paul
> In awful sequestration, through a veil,
> Through its own sacred veil of falling snow.
> *(Tuft of Primroses,* p. 59)[13]

But "Westminster Bridge" not only misplaces its referential ground; it actively *dis*places it as well through figuration. It may be useful to glance by analogy to "St. Paul's." We notice that the poet misplaces vision in this poem by turning his eyes ("I raised up / My heavy eyes") upon a "visionary scene" sketched in occlusive modifiers: "Deep, hollow, unobstructed, vacant, smooth," "spotless," "Slow, shadowy, silent, dusky," "noiseless and unpeopled." The purpose of thus chanting the evacuation of London is to prepare for a counterchant of revelation near the close: "Pure, silent, solemn, beautiful." But revelation cannot occur until the entry of figuration— until, as it were, the poet snows us. By precipitating a snow "as fair, /

As fresh and spotless as [Winter] ever sheds / On field or mountain,"
he overlays London with the likeness of "field or mountain." It is
such snow of illusion that at last settles "Pure, silent, solemn, beautiful" over St. Paul's to displace it totally from London. Though no
more literally revealed than Shelley's Mont Blanc, the dome of St.
Paul's is revealed in figure. It stands behind a "sacred veil" of incipient figuration signaling that it stands *for* some otherworldly city of
God.

"Westminster Bridge" snows us in the same fashion, but with
flakes of figure so fine they are one with its very atmosphere ("All
bright and glittering in the smokeless air"). It does so by means of
what must be accounted its real achievement: a veil of *topoi* spanning
from commonplace metaphors to large-scale rhetorical commonplaces of the kind studied by Curtius.[14] "This City now doth like
a garment wear / The beauty of the morning," the poet admires,
opening his scene of figuration.[15] The metaphor is as individually
commonplace, say, as a single snowflake. Yet its personification sen-
sitizes us subsequently to even the barest presence of person—to
the aliveness of the next lines, for example, where "Ships, towers,
domes, theatres, and temples" loose their garments to lie "bare" to
the fields and sky. Metaphorics thus organizes into rhetorical *topos*:
London is the body politic. But no sooner does Wordsworth sketch
his version of Blake's *Glad Day* than a further reorganization occurs:
London becomes the *locus amoenus*. Just as the city assimilates to "field
or mountain" in "St. Paul's," so here it lies "Open unto the fields,
and to the sky." In literal terms, the poet is gazing over London
to the pleasant spot at its boundaries. Yet we notice that the line
of atmospherics then closing the octet ("All bright and glittering in
the smokeless air") refers back equipollently to either "ships, towers,
domes, theatres, and temples" *or* to "fields, and . . . sky." In his very
syntax, Wordsworth invests the pleasant spot on the margins with a
weight equivalent to the central city. Referential ground gives way in
a groundless motion toward the horizon that can only be the starting
place of invasive figure: ships, towers, domes, and so forth lie "open
unto" the fields and sky in the way a city under siege lies open to a
foreign intruder.

But as yet the displacement of London into figure is not absolute. It is up to the sestet to decide if the snow will stick. Just as at
the close of some long-drawn Homeric simile a loud "so" or "just
so" brings us back to earth with a thump, so we might now expect
Wordsworth's sonnet to return to its referential ground. It would
thus be obeying the impulse of the Miltonic sonnet, which characteristically subordinates figuration to contemporary topic or to a
dark return home.[16] (Thus the pathos of disimagination concluding
Milton's sonnet on his "late espoused Saint": "But O, as to embrace

me she inclin'd, / I wak'd, she fled, and day brought back my night.")
But though Wordsworth rounds back to darkening vistas in such
other sonnets as his wedding-day poem on "Hambleton Hills," in
"Westminster Bridge" he declines the gambit of the Homeric return.
His sestet not only confirms the metaphorics previously drafted in
the octet but reorganizes them once more into a climactic rhetorical
topos: inexpressibility. It will be useful to isolate the *ababab* closing the
poem:

> Never did sun more beautifully steep
> In his first splendor valley, rock, or hill;
> Ne'er saw I, never felt, a calm so deep!
> The river glideth at his own sweet will:
> Dear God! the very houses seem asleep;
> And all that mighty heart is lying still!

Here, while the *b* lines retouch the figures of London as landscape
and person, the *a* lines (especially the first two) frame the whole
within variations of inexpressibility. Smokeless the atmosphere may
be, but it is as if the poet has smoked his camera lens. With sweeping
indirectness, he summons up comparisons to a universality of previous experience serving to veil the view behind negation: the sunlit
calm actually before him "never" quite comes clear. Even the third *a*
line with its personification, "the very houses seem asleep," betrays
a certain awareness of inadequacy. Whatever vision prompts its observation, it is larger than this single stroke on the canvas can reveal.
So, too, the line, "The river glideth at his own sweet will," is strong
with a master's limpness of wrist. At its close, indeed, the poem then
depends on an expressive technique very like pure brushwork: an im-
pasto of punctuation. Pointing beyond the actual sense of the words,
it *exclaims* upon quiet: "a calm so deep! . . . And all that mighty heart
is lying still!"

We might recall here the inexpressibility veiling Chamonix in the
poet's 1790 letter to Dorothy: "You have undoubtedly heard of these
celebrated s[c]enes, but if you have not read of them any description
which I have here room to give you must be altogether inadequate"
(see Chapter 1). Just as *The Prelude* then at last names the inexpressible
in Simplon "Imagination!," so "Westminster Bridge" invokes at its
close a like name psychologizing its metaphorics and rhetoric of the
inexpressible. In the first *a* line of the sestet, "sun" names the original
splendor of the ineffable world. In the third *a* line, "God" is the
creative, inexpressive name. And in between nature and supernature,
the prince of inexpressibility stands confessed: "Ne'er saw *I*, never
felt . . . !" As in Caesar's asyndeton of empire ("I came, I saw, I con-
quered"), the imaginative imperialism of Wordsworth's asyndeton
marks the obliteration of the known world. Or perhaps a Keatsian

comparison will convey the right tone of discovery together with conquest. Much like the Cortez-I in "On First Looking into Chapman's Homer," Wordsworth's persona at the end of "Westminster Bridge" stares out upon pacific reaches over which he exclaims, and *claims*, "*I* see it!"[17] "I" see London as something other than it is, his poem says in essence, referring at last only to a Figure of figures, the self, as invisible *within* the frame of reference as God, the blinding sun, or—to round back to the place for which the sonnet itself is named—Westminster Bridge.[18]

In sum: indeterminacy, ambiguity, paradox. Exfoliating manifold the principle of contradiction, our modern readings of "Westminster Bridge" have concentrated on paradoxes that replace the poem's form and content with the inscrutable. We may cite here the long lineage of New Critical readings (initiated in the opening pages of Brooks's *Well Wrought Urn*, for example, or in Brooks and Warren's *Understanding Poetry*) that have appreciated the poem's paradoxical ambiguity as the promise of unity or harmony.[19] Or we can point to the extension of such readings in our newer criticism of unity fractured into difference. "Westminster Bridge" is one of the paradigms of the New Critical canon that has survived with indeterminacy intact into the deconstructive canon. Thus J. Hillis Miller, in his "The Still Heart: Poetic Form in Wordsworth" (later included in his *Linguistic Moment*), continues the thesis of ambiguity: "To follow the implications of the negatives and of the figurative language in 'Composed Upon Westminster Bridge' leads the interpreter away from an unambiguous mimetic reading toward the recognition that the poem expresses an oscillation between consciousness and nature, life and death, presence and absence, motion and stillness" (*Linguistic Moment*, p. 74). And in a recent essay, Hartman sublimes the thesis of paradox: "Rather than insisting on paradox or the cancelled presence of the opposite term [in "Westminster Bridge"], it would be better to acknowledge that contrast in Wordsworth points beyond the activity of pointing. 'Smokeless' signals, as it were, the absence of a signal" (*Unremarkable Wordsworth*, p. 208).[20]

To deManize such readings: the figuration that blinds the poem to referentiality—not only to its referent but to the very act of pointing out its referent—*is* its insight. In the New Critical readings of the poem and its successors, we may say, "Westminster Bridge" figures an inscrutable *something* or *some place* that is finally no farther away from our present reading practices than the Yale English Department from the bridgeway of High Street arch in New Haven.

But now the pivot point in my argument. In fashioning my own figuration of place here by bringing Westminster Bridge unequivocally under native spans of understanding (both of my own professional place and, in a broader sense, that of much of current criticism), I am aware of creating a certain dislocation, a disturbing wrench in orientation. Like the poem itself, after all, so much in our modern and postmodern style of interpretation transcends place in favor of universal reach that to be reminded of any particular place— especially one that is partisan, controversial or, at any rate, definitely *not* universal—seems scandalous. It is a trivialization of the universal. Yet the scandal of the particular and partisan, I believe, is of a piece with that of "Westminster Bridge" itself in its original and full context. While in one aspect the poem projects a universalism of pure figure wedding it to modern criticism, in another it also declares a shrilly localized and partisan view of history. I take an initial hint here from Charles Molesworth, who observes the poem's original suspension in a historical framework and its "republican" view of the world.[21] It is such a sense of history and of worldly power that we have elided until we see at last the mirage of a poet committed solely to figurative power.

The form and content of the poem, I assert, are *not* necessarily lost in indeterminacy, ambiguity, or paradox. Or rather, beyond the indeterminate in the poem there is also a ground of figure that extends outward into a true indeterminacy more full of paradox, contradiction, and difference than any figure can imagine: reference. As I have said, reference to history is haunted by turnings more sudden, lights more hidden, drops more wrenching than anything criticism —in its grainy snapshot of the world—has managed to shut away in the drawer of "mere" reference. If the heart is stilled at the end of "Westminster Bridge," that is because history is heartstopping.

How to refer beyond High Street arch, as it were, to "Westminster Bridge" in its own place and proper field of significance? The approach I will apply is a newer variant of the modern and postmodern criticisms of paradoxical unity and *différence*. This variant is what has become the early signature of the New Historicism (especially in Renaissance studies): the criticism of "power." A measure of discomfiture has increasingly attended the use of this term since its ascendancy.[22] The root of such embarrassment is the restrictiveness of the implicit premise that power is the most inclusive as well as "real" frame of critical inquiry. However strongly textualized, it must be said, the criticism of power does indeed draw for its unique magic— for its sense of excited novelty coupled with responsibility—from the prejudice of reality. Cultural poetics "reads" the "real," and however much it declares the realms of representation and materiality to be equivalent registers of culture, the fact remains that as received *contra* formalism it is the reality quotient or historical "matter" that gives such reading its special lure.

Yet for the most part, this lure of the real remains unthought. Except in the most literal cases, after all, power is itself an irreducibly figurative concept. The executioner who lifts the axe has power; but the monarch who commands the execution has something else—whether we call it position, tradition, law, or even God—whose connection with the axe is so mediated that the physical trope of power cannot be assumed without question as the best frame of analysis. In the end, the New Historicism focused on power has thus inevitably written only an *allegory* of reality not substantively different—as I have argued in more detail elsewhere—from the figurations of formalism. It creates so-called "paradigms" whose ability to inform us about the past is always less credible than their will to construct the past into a highly formalized pattern of unity/difference (often phrased in a vocabulary of "paradox," "ambiguity," "irony," "deferral," and so forth directly descended from New Criticism and deconstruction). To use the terms of debate in Renaissance studies, the allegory of power forms the world into a self-canceling structure of "containment"/"subversion" that is as much a depiction of our own age as of the past. Skeptical about the recovery of the past except through a hermeneutical reinvention or renascence, critics of power have turned the *bricolage* of history's material leavings into picture-perfect forms of pastness as ideal in their split vision of reality as any well-wrought—or in this case, "anamorphic"—urn. As when Greenblatt studies the fractured vision of Holbein's *The Ambassadors* (pp. 17–27), history comes to inhere in a formal paradigm not essentially different from the verbal icon. Our attention has merely shifted from the icon as a whole to the fault lines of "ambiguity," "tension," "texture," and so forth that have always been its craquelure.

Nevertheless, the approach suggested by the criticism of power can advance our present cause. Just as we have crossed throughout this book from formalism to political, social, and economic approaches via the bridgeway of a form especially capable of historicization, genre, so we can apply the residual formalism of the criticism of power—similar in kind but different in degree from the massive formalism of modern readings of "Westminster Bridge"—to the same purpose. An allegory or formal paradigm of power instinct with postmodern concerns we may create. But some allegories are more credible (function better as bases of consensual agreement about the ground of any particular figuration) than others. However limited in themselves, such allegories provide avenues from formalism to the vistas of history on the other side.

In particular, a reading of "Westminster Bridge" as originally an allegory of *national power* will be more credible, I believe, than readings developing the poet's "I"—*his* powerful allegory or Figure of figures—into what New Criticism calls the paradoxical Poem and deconstruction calls the deferred Text. Indeed, all my previous résumé of modern and postmodern readings of "Westminster Bridge" may be summed up as follows: where Wordsworth said "I," we now say "Language" (Poem, Text). "Ne'er saw I" translates: "Language (the images of the Poem, the figures or de Manian 'rhetoric' of the Text) never refers." Thus we believe that poetry—and a lyric like "Westminster Bridge" especially—should not mean but be, that the topic of texts is textuality, and that figures are about figures. Yet Nation (with Church and People), as we will see, was the figure for paradoxical unity-in-difference that at last subsumed Wordsworth's own figure of self. To read the language of his later poetry, therefore, it will be useful to hold ourselves open to a similar subsumption of our privileged subject, Language. We must open ourselves to the refugee's discovery lurking at the personal and philosophical heart of so much of our current literary theory with its comparatist roots.[23] As when settling in a new land and learning a new tongue, we must be prepared for the fact that language is not just about language. It is also about losing a nation or gaining a nation or simply belonging to a nation—to a particular people at a particular time. It is about submitting one's self to the anonymous and abject experience of crossing the boundaries—literally, the national borders—defining such ideological formations as "nation," "church," or "people." And in the end, language is about the raw elsewhereness of the sense of history: the elsewhereness of the refugee (in my paradigm) whose tongue cuts him off from the new, and of his descendant whose tongue cuts him off from the old. To speak *English*—not the King's or even Milton's English, but finally just the language of the "common" nation—was Wordsworth's refuge, his homecoming in the process of history.

As my vehicle into the history of power in "Westminster Bridge," I invoke the emblem of the Paris Diligence. The Paris Diligence was the dark historical shadow of the vehicle Wordsworth rode over Westminster Bridge at his moment of inspiration. It appears in Dorothy's journal description of the 1802 crossing like a phantom, a coach of the dead. Or in Dorothy's own favored imagery (which I have commented on in my "Autobiographical Present"), it comes like a blight upon the otherworldly purity of the day:

On Thursday morning, 29th, we arrived in London. Wm left me at the Inn—I went to bed. Etc. etc. After various troubles and disasters we left London on Saturday morning at 1/2 past 5 or 6, the 31st of July (I have forgot which). We mounted the Dover Coach at Charing Cross. It was a beautiful morning. The City, St. Paul's, with the River and a multitude of little Boats, made a most beautiful sight as we crossed Westminster Bridge. The houses were not overhung by their cloud of smoke and they were spread out endlessly, yet the sun shone so brightly with such a pure light that there was even something like the purity of one of nature's own grand spectacles. (*DWJ*, pp. 150–51)

Then there are two lines heavily erased (*DWJ*, p. 151n), and the journal continues, "We rode on chearfully now with the Paris Diligence before us, now behind."

"Westminster Bridge," I suggest, has three distinct stages of significance. *Remembering*: Imagine that the Paris coach—separated from the bridge by a heavy erasure and dogging the Wordsworths on their way to Dover and France—is the vehicle for a historical tenor in Wordsworth's poem like an impure etcetera of "various troubles and disasters." To draw once more upon my painting model: if the sonnet were a picture, the worldly concerns riding in our emblematic Diligence would be a scene of human history posted in the background like the expulsion of Adam and Eve in Fra Angelico's *Annunciation* (see Pl. 2). At the time of composition in 1802, "Westminster Bridge" was first of all one of what I propose to call Wordsworth's topical poems burdened with historical background. Its *topoi* remembered topics of collective interest centered on an uneasy axis of movement between London and Paris during the Peace of Amiens. If the poem's figurations replace London with contradiction, that is, then replaced reference and contradiction were themselves historically referenced: the poem was never about the power of London (and England) considered in itself so much as its displacement toward the power of France. English freedom and French tyranny, London and Paris, knew strange sympathy.

Forgetting: But just as the picturesque opened the background of picture space to the vanishing point by reducing *istoria* to small genre-subjects (one of which, aptly, was the cart crossing the bridge in the middle distance),[24] so Wordsworth between 1807 and about 1836 manipulated the context of his neo-picturesque poem to erase all thought of Paris Diligences and other Constable-like haywains of human business. Indeed, through an act of apocalypse so gentle we do not even notice—a kind of apocalypse in watercolors—he washed away the human population totally to open his vanishing point into ever-receding vistas of figurations unable to remember the historical referent of their groundlessness. Intolerant of the sympathy between English and French powers, the poem at last took refuge in a pure imagination of power. It liberated *topoi* from topic and became utopian.

It is this utopia, I suggest, that our modern readings of "Westminster Bridge" have recapitulated. But there is one further significance of "Westminster Bridge" and of Romanticism generally that we have not wished to recapitulate—perhaps because its impulse seems so complicit with the Victorianism (as Henry Knight Miller has studied) siring the first systematic anthologies and histories of literature (esp. pp. 68–75).

Recollecting: From 1838 on, Wordsworth remembered and forgot history all over again—but in a synoptic, anthology fashion indicative at once of memory and amnesia. In the late collections of his poetry after 1838, he "recollected" history. He juxtaposed imaginative figuration *with* historical ground, forgetting with remembering, and so allied "Westminster Bridge" and other such poems with the total act of poetic re-covery—of imaginative covering together with historical recovering—constitutive of the Memorial Tour.

It is this latter, recollective Wordsworth that enables the fulfillment of our own descendants' criticism of Wordsworth. In a moment of recovery that was decades long, the refugee poet opened himself once more to the sense of history and became the progenitor critic of his own imagination.

Remembering

We can begin remembering by studying repeating—in particular the monstrous repetition that was Wordsworth's life during the "confluence of intensities," as Irene Tayler has put it, of early 1802 (p. 123).[25] I take a page here from the twin registers of existential repetition in the first months of 1802: the poet's agonizing effort to turn the Pedlar's biography in *The Ruined Cottage* into a separate poem titled *The Pedlar* and Dorothy's record of that effort in her journal. In 1799, we know, Dorothy had transcribed in MS. D a fresh version of *The Ruined Cottage* isolating the Pedlar's biography in an addendum. Upon rereading the manuscript at the end of 1801, Wordsworth seized upon this addendum as the basis for an independent biography of the imaginative self: a *Pedlar* wholly detached from the story of Margaret (see *RC*, pp. 22–30, for textual history and content of *The Pedlar*). But in the first months of 1802, his effort to detach imagination was impeded by an immense writer's block. The structure of this block was repetition. If the writing of *The Ruined Cottage* had always been plagued by revisionism, that of *The Pedlar* carried this tendency to a pathological extreme. It made Wordsworth sick. A selection from Dorothy's record of the poem's composition and transcription (conveniently gathered by Butler in *RC*, pp. 24–25) will document the point:

> [21 December 1801] Wm sate beside me and read the Pedlar, he was in good spirits, and full of hope of what he should do with it. [*DWJ*, p. 70]
> [22 December] Wm composed a few lines of the Pedlar. [p. 71]

[23 December] William worked at The Ruined Cottage and made himself very ill. [p. 73]

[25 January 1802] William tired with composition. [p. 79]

[26 January] We sate nicely together and talked by the fire till we were both tired, for Wm wrote out part of his poem and endeavoured to alter it, and so made himself ill. I copied out the rest for him. [p. 80]

. . .

[7 February] William had had a bad night and was working at his poem. We sate by the fire and did not walk, but read the pedlar thinking it done but lo, though Wm could find fault with no one part of it—it was uninteresting and must be altered. Poor William. [p. 85]

[10 February] While I was writing out the Poem as we hope for a final writing, a letter was brought me. . . . After Molly went we read the first part of the poem and were delighted with it, but Wm afterwards got to some ugly places and went to bed tired out. [pp. 87–88]

[11 February] William sadly tired and working still at the Pedlar. [p. 88]

. . .

[16 February] He was better—had altered the pedlar. [p. 92]

[28 February] Wm very ill, employed with the pedlar. [In margin, "Disaster pedlar" added; p. 96]

[3 March] I was so unlucky as to propose to rewrite The Pedlar. Wm got to work and was worn to death. [pp. 96–97]

. . .

[8 July] William was looking at the Pedlar when I got up. He arranged it, and after tea I wrote it out—280 lines. [p. 146]

What brought *The Pedlar*'s biography of "Imagination in her growth" (*RC*, p. 343) to such an impasse of repetitive reimagining? To start with, there was the problem—both cause and effect in Dorothy's view—of sleeplessness.[26] Wordsworth in early 1802 began regularly not to sleep. More than twenty nights in the first half of 1802, especially in two spans from January 28 to February 5, and from May 24 to June 29, were given over to tossing and turning.[27] Sleeplessness is fair game for interpretation because so many of Wordsworth's poems thematize insomnia. As witnessed in the three sonnets titled "To Sleep," written between May 21 and the end of 1802 (*P2V*, pp. 140–42), nightmarish insomnia in this period signed existential repetition. "Even thus last night, and two nights more, I lay, / And could not win thee, Sleep!" one laments, capturing the essence of insomnia as recurrence. The sonnet prefaces this lament by counting sheep in a landscape of repetition:

> A flock of sheep that leisurely pass by,
> One after one; the sound of rain, and bees

> Murmuring; the fall of rivers, winds and seas,
> Smooth fields, white sheets of water, and pure sky;
> I've thought of all by turns; and still I lie
> Sleepless.   (*P2V*, pp. 140–41)*

This is a gentler version, we may say, of the bleak seriality that in "A Slumber Did My Spirit Seal" finished upon a wake over "rocks, and stones, and trees." Epitomizing such insidious wakefulness in early 1802 was the night of May 4, when Dorothy tried to lull William to sleep by reading a poem (later titled "Travelling") so repetitively that it was as much the insignia as cure of sleeplessness. "Travelling" was fixation: "I repeated verses to William while he was in bed—he was soothed and I left him. 'This is the spot' over and over again" (*DWJ*, p. 121).

There was also the problem of Coleridge, whose repeated illnesses in early 1802—cycling between bowel blockage and diarrhea—not only helped prompt Wordsworth's insomnia but seemed to Dorothy to sympathize with her brother's own sicknesses.[28] The first sustained span of sleeplessness, for example (the nights of January 28 to February 5), coincided with reception of "heart-rending" news from Coleridge (*DWJ*, p. 81). What was the meaning of Coleridge's illness to Wordsworth? Here I bring to a close the meditation on friendship that has been an undertheme of this book. Consider that literary history institutes such authorial pairs as Pope and Swift or Pound and Eliot partly as a means of explaining originality without acknowledging the "influence" of literary or cultural history. Just as the concept of friendship mediates the historical processes of family or economy, as I have argued, so at last it buffers poetic originality by mediating, and mystifying, influence. Influencing each other in nonlinear ways, literary friends bracket the historical source of creation between themselves. As the work of one friend develops, it mirrors (sometimes leads, sometimes follows) sympathetic developments in the other's work. Each friend is thus the representation to the other of the self's ability to accrue new powers. The total effect is a relationship of growing friendship that is the express form of origination.

But what if the friend—and friendship—stops developing? Then origination, unable to acknowledge other sources of influence, knows only repetition—a continual effort of reorigination.[29] The great ill at the beginning of 1802, in truth, was not that Coleridge grew physically worse but that he remained the same, in an eternally repetitive Life-in-Death registering Wordsworth's own poetic blockage. Cole-

---

* Here and in other cases where I quote from poems supplementary to my main interest in "Westminster Bridge" and the Calais Tour, as I will call it, I use the reading text of *P2V* or, failing that, *PW*, without bothering to go back to the earliest manuscripts.

ridge assumed his character as one of literature's great repeaters. Seen in this light, indeed, his famous addiction to "plagiarism" would be merely the extreme form of his lifelong predilection for repeating or plagiarizing *himself.* The published version of Coleridge's "Dejection" ode—that great poem of insomnia, blockage, and repetition— phrases such self-plagiarism as the habit of stealing "by abstruse research . . . From my own nature all the natural man" (*Complete Poetical Works*, 1: 367). After Coleridge the natural man, that is, there remained Coleridge the unnatural, sickly repetition or plagiarism of a man; and it is this remainder that is the running voice—what Barthes calls logorrhea (*S/Z*, p. 58)—of the diarrheic poet. We might remember the image of the old moon blocking the new at the beginning of the "Dejection" ode, which Coleridge read in its early form to the Wordsworths on April 21, 1802:

> For lo! the New-moon winter-bright!
> And overspread with phantom light,
> (With swimming phantom light o'erspread
> But rimmed and circled by a silver thread)
> I see the old Moon in her lap, foretelling
> The coming-on of rain and squally blast.
> (*Complete Poetical Works*, 1: 363)

The aperture of new origination is blocked by the repetition of the old. In early 1802, a purge of laxative effect was needed.

Watching over the world of sleeplessness and Coleridge's bowels was the further problem of Annette, the very muse of existential repetition. *Again* there was the problem of Annette, whom Wordsworth had known precisely ten years before, in 1792. Negotiations toward the Peace of Amiens of 1802 had cleared the way for correspondence between England and France. On the day Wordsworth began reworking *The Pedlar* (December 21, 1801), a letter suddenly arrived from Annette. After the interregnum of a monthlong visit to Eusemere, Wordsworth responded on January 26, 1802. Thereafter, six more letters arrived from Annette; one from her daughter by Wordsworth, Caroline; and one, probably related to Annette, from an unidentified "Frenchman" in London (see MM, 1: 553–55). In return, Wordsworth responded three more times, and Dorothy also wrote two letters. This correspondence, which does not survive, must have retraced in a personal idiom the negotiations toward the Peace of Amiens. Since Wordsworth had decided sometime in this period to wed Mary Hutchinson, certainly he needed to come to some final understanding with Annette. His negotiations toward a private peace occurred roughly in three stages: a span of increasing anxiety from the reception of Annette's letter of December 21, 1801, to that of her letter of March 22, 1802 (which decided the Wordsworths on visiting Annette); a span of deceptive calm from March 22 to May 21, when Wordsworth wrote his first political sonnets on Napoleon;[30] and—the occasion of "Westminster Bridge"—the span after July 9 when he and Dorothy set off to visit Annette in Calais.

Finally, *again* there was the crisis of the Lonsdale debt, which, like the problem of Annette, had last come to a head almost precisely ten years ago. Wordsworth's family had won their suit against Lonsdale in the August before Wordsworth's trip to France in 1791–92, but because the amount to be paid was left in arbitration, Lonsdale won a *de facto* stay of indefinite length (MM, 1: 169). When he died on May 24, 1802, hopes to recover the debt (now some £10,000) revived, stirring Wordsworth to excited activity. From the end of May to the beginning of July, he wrote to his brother Richard, consulted friends, and generally worried over the approach to Lonsdale's heir (see MM, 1: 558–61). The extent of his anxiety can be gauged from the tone of his letters to Richard. On June 24, he wrote with more than proper stridency to urge haste and avoidance of unseemly litigiousness: "Do write to me *immediately* at Grasmere letting me know what you mean to do: if what you purpose to do appears proper to me of course I shall be satisfied; if not, I shall then inform you in what manner I myself mean to proceed. At all events let no time be lost" (*Letters*, 1: 370). Richard returned an admonishment, with the result that William on July 3 took offense in turn: "I feel it proper to inform you that I must disapprove of the tone which pervades your second Letter. . . . You seem to speak to me as if you were speaking to a Child" (*Letters*, 1: 371).*

We can sum up by saying that while writing the biography of imagination in early 1802, Wordsworth was in the grip of Sisyphean repetition. Such existential repetition was felt as a crippling *lack* in the imaginative present, a hollowness whose superficial signs were sleeplessness and worry over Coleridge's bowels but whose deeper signs were the very epitomes of lack: the Lonsdale debt and the "widowed" Annette (then calling herself *Veuve Williams*) (MM, 1: 554; Tayler, p. 127). Here we reach the burden of our argument. Existential repetition in early 1802 discovered a constitutive lack with precisely the air of "elsewhereness" I have argued ushers in the sense of history. Indeed, elsewhereness was uncannily specific. By strange alethia, there had risen out of the Lethe of ten years past the exact spectres of personal haunt—Lonsdale and Annette—that first ushered the poet into Revolution and public history. To return to our emblem of the Paris Diligence: it is not insignificant that it was almost exactly ten years

---

* In a precise "confluence of intensities," the upsetting letter from Richard on the Lonsdale debt and a disturbing letter from Annette both arrived at Dove Cottage on the same day, July 3 (*CMY*, p. 184).

ago as well, late in 1791, that the poet landed in France on his second Continental trip, made his way to Rouen, and waited two days to board the same Paris Diligence for the capital (MM, 1: 171; *CEY*, pp. 123–25). In early 1802, Wordsworth's present had been inescapably historicized.

On July 9, 1802, then, brother and sister embarked from Grasmere to meet Annette in Calais and lay to rest at least one ghost from the time's unique blend of personal and public history. They went to Gallow Hill first to see Mary Hutchinson, continued on to London at the end of July, and departed over Westminster Bridge on July 31 for Dover and Calais. In Calais they spent a month taking long walks with Annette and her daughter by Wordsworth, Caroline. Brother and sister then sailed back to Dover at the end of August, stayed most of September in London, and returned to Gallow Hill for William's marriage to Mary on October 4. The most significant record of these months in 1802 is not Dorothy's journal, supremely reticent here about human affairs,* but the series of sonnets Wordsworth wrote while writing nothing else (cf. Heath, p. 149). We have already glanced at some of these poems in surveying the political sonnets of 1802–4 (Chapter 8). Enlarging the 1802 section of our previous census and adding "Westminster Bridge" as well as two other "personal" sonnets, we can now create a specialized census of the "Calais Tour" as follows (numbers in parentheses cross-refer to my earlier list; "*MP*" indicates sonnets first published in the *Morning Post*):[†]

---

* Focused upon details of scenery, Dorothy's brief synopsis of the month spent in Calais almost wholly avoids notice of Annette, Caroline, and general affairs in France (*DWJ*, pp. 152–53).

† This list outlines a fairly firm core of sonnets written between July 31 and Oct. 4, but has these two limitations: it does not indicate the compositional order of poems within any one bracket of dates (many of the poems cannot be assigned to a single day), and it does not show a penumbra of associated sonnets possibly of this period but not datable except roughly between May 21 and ca. late 1802 or later (for a listing, see *CMY*, pp. 29–30, 171–73). These associated works include the three sonnets "To Sleep" and a few sonnets of a pastoral nature that probably preceded the Calais Tour; it also includes some political sonnets (included in my discussion in Chapter 8) that probably followed the Tour. Inserting these latter political sonnets of unclear date among those on the same theme written ascertainably during the September stay in London would not change my argument (where it seems useful, indeed, I will call upon these associated sonnets in my discussion). I rely on Reed's assessment of dates in *CMY*, pp. 30–32, 188–96. Besides sonnets dated under the first two categories in Reed's scale of probability—"probable" and "perhaps"—I also include one "possible": "To Toussaint L'Ouverture." As before, I standardize titles and first lines in my census based on the Reading Text of *P2V*. Also as before, I quote the texts of the earliest available version (identified in parentheses in the case of long quotations) as recovered from *P2V*, *appar. crit.* (with the same exceptions indicated on pp. 428–29n above). In many cases, the earliest version derives from *MP*, DC MS. 38 (the notebook Wordsworth probably bought in Calais in Aug. or

London, July 31

"Composed Upon Westminster Bridge"

Calais, August 1–29

    A. "To a Friend, Composed Near Calais, On the Road Leading to Ardres,
        August 7th, 1802" (8)
        ("Jones! when from Calais southward you and I")

    B. "Calais, August, 1802" (9; *MP*)
        ("Is it a Reed that's shaken by the wind")

    C. "Composed By the Sea-Side, Near Calais, August, 1802" (10)
        ("Fair Star of Evening, Splendor of the West")

    D. "It is a beauteous Evening, calm and free"

    E. "To Toussaint L'Ouverture" [possibly] (11; *MP*)
        ("Toussaint, the most unhappy Man of Men!")

    F. "Calais, August 15th, 1802" (12; *MP*)
        ("Festivals have I seen that were not names")

Dover to London, August 30 to September 1

    G. "September 1st, 1802" (13; *MP*)
        ("We had a fellow-Passenger who came")

    H. "Composed in the Valley, Near Dover, On the Day of Landing" (14)
        ("Dear fellow-Traveller! here we are once more")

    I. "September, 1802" (15)
        ("Inland, within a hollow Vale, I stood")

London, September 1–22

    ["Composed Upon Westminster Bridge"]

    J. "London, 1802" (16)
        ("Milton! thou should'st be living at this hour")

    K. "Written in London, September, 1802" (17)
        ("O Friend! I know not which way I must look")

Gallow Hill to Leeming Lane, October 4

    L. "Composed After a Journey Across the Hamilton Hills, Yorkshire"
        [later spelling: "Hambleton Hills"]
        ("Ere we had reach'd the wish'd-for place, night fell")

Read together, these sonnets confirm the inference from biography that the Calais trip of 1802 was haunted by history. Haunt, indeed, conveys their exact aura. It is as if the poet were journeying to an

---

Sept. 1802 and that Dorothy used to transcribe his sonnets probably ca. late 1802 [see *P2V*, pp. xix–xx]), or DC MS. 44 of Feb.–Mar. 1804. Where manuscripts from the early 1800's are not available, I quote the Longman MS. of 1806–7 or, failing that, the first printed version in *Poems, in Two Volumes*. For further detail on the frequent changes—often slight, but sometimes significant—that Wordsworth made in the titles and texts of these sonnets through the surviving manuscripts and editions, see *P2V, appar. crit.*

underworld or hell where the "hollow" hello of a citizen seems uttered by a "dead Man" (Sonnet A);[31] where a black woman exiled
from France speaks with the "languid speech" of the not-quite-living
(Sonnet G); where the true "slaves" kneel before the tyrant as if he
were Satan in Pandemonium or a "new-born" king in a mock manger
(Sonnets B, F); and where the poet must linger among legions of the
damned who scorn his "blessed" England (Sonnet C). Only when he
returns home can he "hear and see" (Sonnet H), as if for someone
back from the dead these simple, experiential acts (the verbs have no
objects) were "perfect bliss." France is an underworld because it is
the repository of the damned *past*. Remarking little distance between
the Terror he witnessed ten years ago in 1792 and the uneasy Peace
he observes in 1802, the poet discovers that there are still the exiles
and imprisonments, still the ever-new forms of government in Paris,
and still the pomp of forced festivity.* Most tellingly, he is penetrated
by the same sharp sense of ironic reversal. Looking back from the
perspective of 1794 on his first trip to France in 1790, he had felt
mocked "under . . . a strange reverse" (*Prel.* 10.465). Looking back
from 1802, he knows the same reverse. "Another time / That was,"
he says, "when I was here twelve years ago: / The senselessness of joy
was then sublime!" (Sonnet F). The past tense here is burdened with
elsewhereness.

Embodying such strange reversal and elsewhereness is the exiled
and hauntingly silent black woman who returns from Calais with the
poet in Sonnet G. Her "gaudy" dress (variously "brilliant," "spotless," and "white-robed" in successive variants) retains its fire, and so
shows up starkly her extinguished soul. This is a shadow-version, we
may say, of *Veuve*-Annette. Aeneas-like in 1802, the poet drives dead
east over Westminster Bridge to meet the shade of his own Dido.
Only after burying her in mind can he then return to Mary, his fated
bride, and to London, *his* Rome.

Now we can turn properly to "Westminster Bridge," the Avernus gate of Wordsworth's underworld. More than anything else, I
suggest, "Westminster Bridge" served to mark the entrance and exit
of remembered history. At one moment, we look inward through
its portal to hell; and at the next, outward to a saved present. By
"moment" here I mean specifically date of composition. In a strange
dream of chronology, the sonnet has *four* separate recorded dates of
composition. The first two dates, both in 1802, anchor the poem in
the moment of history by making it simultaneously the *terminus a quo*
and *ad quem* of the Calais Tour. On the one hand, Dorothy's jour-

---

* The sense of déjà vu must have been particularly strong in Calais, we note,
because Farington, visiting Calais at virtually the same time, tells us that the town's
look and dress changed remarkably little throughout the Revolution (2: 2).

nal entry and Wordsworth's later mention to Isabella Fenwick that the poem was "Composed on the roof of a coach, on my way to France . . ." indicate that the sonnet can be dated July 31, 1802 (*PW*, 3: 431). But on the other, Wordsworth inserts in the sonnet's title the date "Sept. 3" (and the Fenwick note concludes that the poem was composed "on my way to France Sept. 1802"). The date of the poem is firmly fixed as both "on my way to France" (July 31) and "Sept. 3," roughly when the poet returned to London. One could argue that such contradiction—a temporal parallel to the "contradiction . . . in the words" the poet himself licensed—is part of Wordsworth's life-long carelessness with dates or that the sonnet may have been mentally composed, drafted, or partially begun on July 31 and not written down, revised, or completed until September 3. Alternatively, we might follow Woodring in thinking that Wordsworth's dates often instruct us only when we can "ideally" picture ourselves on the spot. I will argue that the glide from July 31 to September 3—whatever the link to the irrecoverable, actual history of composition—can best be viewed as something like a temporal slip of the tongue revealing behind one ideal conception of the poem a counterideal.[32]

Wordsworth's two conceptions of the poem in 1802 can be described in generic terms whose contradictions, which we touched upon earlier, now make some sense. On July 31 the sonnet balances between two lyric kinds, one a song of innocence, cherishing London's freedom, and the other a song of experience, mourning freedom's threatened subjection to tyranny. We can label these kinds: love poem and epitaph.

The sonnet is first of all a valediction spoken by a lover to his still-sleeping loved one—the personified city—as he departs for a land where, as he says in Sonnet C, "Men . . . do not love her." Like Blake's Beulah, London projects all Wordsworth's dearest objects of affection: not just England generally but also the "valley, rock, or hill" of the Lakes and perhaps his most focused object of affection at the time, Mary. The sonnet is a valediction in the same spirit as "A Farewell" (mostly composed late May 1802 in anticipation of the Calais trip), in which the poet bids adieu to his beloved Grasmere.[33]

But as a lover's valediction, "Westminster Bridge" is also a proleptic epitaph for loveliness about to pass away. What makes the poet's parting from his beloved city most touching, we perceive, is the defenselessness of his "now":

> Dull would he be of heart who could pass by
> A sight so touching in it's majesty:
> This City *now* doth like a garment wear
> The beauty of the morning.

Literally, of course, the poet *is* passing by (Harvey, p. 83). The essence of his "now" is its fragility, its porcelain resistance to the pressure of his eastward momentum into the sun and France—the glory of that alternative country, city, and woman. Perhaps, indeed, London's morning glory will soon be overshadowed by orient glory. Readers have noticed that the sonnet's repeated negatives ("not," "Never," "Ne'er") paradoxically evoke the dull world being nixed. The image of smokelessness, for example, raises the pall of smoke past or to come.[34] What is particularly appalling about the dullness thus summoned up by negative incantation is that its great Anarch —as intimated by the Calais Tour as a whole—is France. Hemmed round by fragile shields of negation, the English "now" foreshadows its own violation by an apocalyptic Dullness centered on France. "What is it that ye go forth to see?" the poet demands of the English fifth column in Sonnet B, and then continues in his version of *The Dunciad*:

> Lords, Lawyers, Statesmen, Squires of low degree,
> Men known, and men unknown, Sick, Lame, and Blind,
> Post forward all, like Creatures of one kind,
> With first-fruit offerings crowd to bend the knee
> In France, before the new-born Majesty.
> Thus fares it ever. Men of prostrate mind!
>
> > (*MP* version)

The sonnets in the Calais tour exactly fulfill the dark promise of the negatives in "Westminster Bridge": not an image or figure of London but it surrenders to being re-referenced upon the leaden dullness of present-day France. Wordsworth is now in "touch" with England's majestic "heart," but perhaps the pulse he feels will grow as still as that of Sonnet A, where a France once beating "like the heart of Man" at last touches the observer only with stoic impassiveness.[35] Wordsworth now views the "majesty" and "might" of England, but there is always the doppelgänger of the "new-born Majesty" and "power" of Napoleon in Sonnet B. And whereas Wordsworth now watches London's "splendor" in present tense, there is always the prospect of a time when such splendor will set. In Sonnet C, he peers westward across the Channel as England's "Splendor," "drest" in *twilight* "beauty," fades from present-tense indicative into the optative— a gloaming, fey mood twinkling between wish and command:

> > > Thou, I think,
> > *Should'st* be my Country's emblem; and *should'st* wink,
> > Bright Star! with laughter on her banners, drest
> > In thy fresh beauty.
> >
> > > (italics mine)

On the verge of embarking for France, then, Wordsworth spins a coin—to borrow Rossetti's metaphor for the sonnet form—paying tribute either to Life or to Death. As the coin spins on its delicate axis on July 31, each face highlights the luster of its twin: love makes the poet fear for a London he must weep to have, and epitaphic foreboding reinforces present love. The displacement that brings the English nation into the dark orbit of the French is well under way.

To move from July 31 to the sonnet's second date of "Sept. 3" is then to give our coin metaphor a more sinister ring. The displacement of England toward France now becomes so extreme, and in such a fashion, that the sonnet balances between love poem and something approaching a true *Dunciad*: satire. On September 3, Wordsworth imputes the subjection of English freedom not just to French tyranny but to collaboration: tyranny comes home in the dull coin of the petty bourgeois.

To begin with, September 3 marks a restoration, a glad homecoming to all that is English. The sonnet becomes epithalamial rather than valedictory, fulfilling the promise made in "A Farewell" of a return and a wedding. "Dear God!" the poet hymns in thanksgiving rather than petition, completing a spousal vow to London. Two sonnets from the Calais Tour now anticipate this spousal cheer. Sonnet D, similar to "Westminster Bridge" in lacking overt political reference, prefigures London's enduring *beauty*. Like a mirror set across the channel, the poem reflects the London to which the poet will return. Just as the "mighty heart" of things will repose in the beautiful dawn of London, so in Sonnet D a "mighty Being" wakes in the "beauteous Evening, calm and free" of Calais. And just as London's heart will lie immured in a sleeping figure, so the Calais "Being" at last comes to rest in the poet's insensate daughter Caroline:

> Dear Child! dear Girl! that walkest with me here,
> Thou dost not seem to heed these things one jot
> I see it, nor is this a grief of mine
> Thou liest in Abraham's bosom all the year;
> And worshipp'st at the Temple's inner shrine,
> God being with thee when we know it not.
>
> (MS. 44 version)

"Dear Child!" anticipates typologically the "Dear God!" of "Westminster Bridge." Even in the French wilderness, the poet is saying, he spies signs of the promised land and humanizing spirit he will reach on September 3. Sonnet D's final tercet with its allusion to Luke and the parable of the beggar dying into Abraham's bosom is surely an epitaph, but like the fingers pointing up on old tombstones, it signals the way to eternal beauty.

In the same fashion, Sonnet I (which we have already glanced at in Chapter 8) prefigures London's enduring *power*. In the parable just cited (Luke 16: 19–31), "there is a great gulf fixed" between the blessed beggar and the condemned rich man. In Sonnet I, written just after returning to England, Wordsworth watches over a version of this gulf from a Dantesque valley near Dover:

> England! within a hollow Vale, I stood,
> And saw, while sea was calm and air was clear,
> The Coast of France, the Coast of France how near!
> Drawn almost into frightful neighbourhood.
> I shrunk, for verily the barrier flood
> Was like a Lake, or River bright and fair,
> A span of waters; yet what power is there!
> (Longman MS. version) [36]

This is a boat stealing episode of adulthood. Looking back over waters he has just crossed, Wordsworth is annihilated ("I shrunk") by the sudden apparition of a France like some huge peak. "Wisdom and Spirit of the Universe!" he extols in the pause of grace after the *Prelude* episode. At Dover, he also pays homage. He recalls that the Strait of Dover, whose slenderness figures in the caesura in line 3, is blessed with protective power. "Verily," he continues, "God" (later revised to "Nature") channels strength of winds and waters to the righteous, and so makes the Strait something like a Red Sea of British naval power able to founder any French Pharaoh (see the sonnet's sestet). More than simply emphasizing truth, "verily" initiates a process of verification (as I earlier termed it), shoring up historical fact with "verily" true figures of nature able to merge all national waters in a single reservoir of *rightful* power. Verily a "Lake, or River," the Strait prefigures the Thames in "Westminster Bridge": its Samson-like power will pour on September 3 into the peaceful, Christ-like power at London's heart.

As Wordsworth rides back from Dover to arrive in London on "Sept. 3," then, he is backed by consciousness of England's beauty crowned by power. "It is a beauteous Evening, calm and free," Sonnet D opens, and "by the Soul / Only the Nations shall be great and free," Sonnet I concludes. Thus is "freedom" fully revealed—that specially English majesty accomplished in the Calais Tour by wedding power to loveliness, the sublime to the beautiful. [37] Now we know how to read the line, "The river glideth at his own sweet will," mediating in "Westminster Bridge" between initial beauty and final might. There, in the course of a river electing its own progress—electing the slow, majestic pace sounded in the word "glideth"—is the line of beauty become one with power: that muscular S-curve of liberty Wordsworth sees in the bend in the Thames just north of the bridge.

Furthermore, while "Westminster Bridge" marks the capital of earthly freedom, it itself is only a link in a continuing chain of prefiguration pointing to heavenly majesty and freedom. Specifically, the poem looks forward to the spousal verse of Sonnet L (also without explicit politics) written on Wordsworth's wedding day. As if in summation, this sonnet contains a prefigurative series within itself. Beauty and power appear in a city in the clouds, an anthology-city whose structures pretypify each other in a progression from the pagan to the Christian: "Grecian Temple, Minaret, and Bower; / And, in one part, a Minster with its Tower." The minster with its tower is the equivalent of Westminster Abbey—toward which Wordsworth rides as he returns to London and crosses the bridge westward. The unstated structure next in line, we might say, would be the immanental Temple of the New Jerusalem (Rev.: "And I saw no temple therein: for the Lord God Almighty and the Lamb are the temple of it"). Prefaces of each other, Sonnets D and I, "Westminster Bridge," and Sonnet L all at last point forward to an inner city of spirit where power and beauty will be consummated in freedom. Like the "Prospectus" to the "spousal verse" of *The Recluse*, that is, they prefigure a Spirit nursing the "heart in genuine freedom" and possessing a "metropolitan Temple in the hearts / Of mighty Poets" (*Home at Grasmere*, pp. 104–7). The Thames is a Jordan; Wordsworth crosses on September 3 with consciousness of power to marry English beauty in the temple of his heart—his own "inner shrine" in "Abraham's bosom." This is *his* majestic act of freedom, of final liberation from France.

Yet there is a second aspect of the September 3 date making the poem as poisonous as Yeats's "September 1913." September 3 places "Westminster Bridge" fully within the orbit of the dark sonnets Wordsworth began writing in London at the beginning of September —sonnets like J and K (the latter dated "September" in the title by the time of the Longman MS.), reinforced by similar works penned probably before year's end. The theme of these latter sonnets of the Calais Tour is England's self-inflicted *loss* of spiritual freedom. Like Adam watching human history in Book 11 of *Paradise Lost*—which moved the poet to tears early in 1802 (*DWJ*, p. 84)—Wordsworth surveys scenes of cursed freedom, of power wed not to beauty but to filthy lucre.[38] Suggestively, September 3 marks the tenth anniversary of the September Massacres. But the death Wordsworth now witnesses in London (as Yeats will in Ireland) kills by the slow corruption of the money changer rather than by massacre. With terrific irony, Sonnets J and K juxtapose harlot-London with the pure metropolis, or mother-city, she seems at dawn only because business has not begun. In the full light of day, they intimate, London is not a virgin mother with a pure river in her veins but "a fen / Of stagnant waters" (Sonnet J) and a superficially beautiful brook "glittering . . . In the open sunshine" (Sonnet K). London does not wear the natural beauty of the morning "like a garment," but leads an artificial life "only drest / For shew" (Sonnet K). And London does not own the dearest possession of domestic peace but is a spendthrift forfeiting the "ancient English dower / Of inward happiness" (Sonnet J) and mortgaging the "homely beauty of the good old cause" (Sonnet K).

Babylon usurps the New Jerusalem; the usurers are in the temple of the heart. It was during Wordsworth's September stay in London, after all, that Charles Lamb showed him Bartholomew Fair (*CMY*, p. 192)—that greedy desecration of a holy place where, *The Prelude* says, "Martyrs suffer'd in past time" (7.651). The Fair ran during the four days following September 3 (*Prel.*, p. 283n). What irony if the poet composed in this period his sonnet beginning, "Earth has not any thing to shew more fair"! Racked upon this kind of irony, the holy majesty of London in "Westminster Bridge" appears not a sleeping woman or bride but a virgin martyr staked out for sacrifice: "Open unto the fields, and to the sky; / All bright and glittering in the smokeless air." Smoke will rise with the business day's offering to Mammon. Indeed, we know that a cloud of irony haunts Wordsworth's actual return over Westminster Bridge to London in 1802. Dorothy's journal records that on the day of return, "It was misty and we could see nothing" (*DWJ*, p. 153). Smoked and clouded over with bitter irony, the loveliness of London's skyline will crumble as quickly as the cloud-city at the defeated close of the poet's spousal verse in Sonnet L. Watching the sky's cumulus architecture—which, together with its pendant meditation "These Words Were Utter'd in a Pensive Mood," immediately preceded "Westminster Bridge" in some editions of Wordsworth's poems (1827, 1832)—the poet feels all along that he will forget the phantom New Jerusalem because it has no earthly substance.

The invisible hand of the "nation of shopkeepers" thus ends by shaking hands with Napoleonic power. Or put another way, English freedom agrees strangely with tyranny: it contains its own petty tyranny. On "Sept. 3" even more so than "July 31," "Westminster Bridge" records a contradictory, ambiguous, and deeply ironic displacement. The most literal instance of such displacement was the flow of English visitors to Paris; but ultimately displacement widens to include the wholesale exchange of English values for those of Babylon.

The figurative "replacement" of London we earlier studied in purely formalistic terms now comes clear. "Westminster Bridge" looks out not upon a place so much as on a moral transfer of national place recorded in a precise tour of social geography (between London and Paris) and time (1802 and 1792) predictive of the Memorial Tour. A Memorial Tour is a journey that traces each present place as the intersection of whole orbits of social space and time—each *topos*, in other words, as the crossover spot of whole nations of contemporary topics. As both the *arche* and *telos* of the Calais Tour, "Westminster Bridge" was premier among the Calais Tour's *topical* poems.

We say that a poem is topical when it is about a public event of the day. Let me finish remembering by imagining a symbolic geography of topicality. *Station 1.* Observe that there is a land of events governed by political, social, and economic laws such that certain events follow others in sequence. *Station 2.* Observe that there is another land of language governed by syntax so that certain signs follow others in sequence. The two realms share a twisting boundary that we can name the historical stream.[39] (In English, of course, "history" has the felicity of denoting both the realms of active event and historiographical language.) *Station 3.* The place or topic of a topical poem is the juncture spanning events and signs, the bridge governing traffic over the river of history at one point. This topical bridge of intercourse —worlds apart from the bridge of picturesque retreat—is founded upon arches of conventionally referential meaning. It is only on a bridge thus founded, after all, that the individual actor and speaker, citizen of the lands of events and signs, can become part of the public by agreeing to cross at *this* convenient spot. It is only on the common bridge-road between events and signs shared by all manner of prosaic vehicles that an individual's communication convenes with the common language of men. The referential base is constitutive of community, of the sense stressed in the 1800 Preface to *Lyrical Ballads* of a single native society (however fractured when viewed from other historical perspectives or from other sites on the historical stream) speaking the same way about common events.

To apply such geography to our particular case: "Westminster Bridge" is a poem of commonplaces because it talks about, is referentially grounded upon, that great topic of English freedom about which everyone else was talking. We see in the poem's dawn moment an individual embracing collective freedom, talking about its constituent beauty and might by reference, and then building an ornamental architecture of commonplace figures over the referential bridge—commonplaces like the actual cupolas then on the parapet of Westminster Bridge that shelter within decoration the whole congress of workaday traffic. Or rather, commonplace figures are not ornamental at all but structural elements of reference. Wordsworth's figures are of a piece with the most basic and commonplace of all figurations (the very generalization of London as a single place, for example) constitutive of what David Simpson has called the "figuring of the real." When *topoi* and trope thus convene in the topical such that reference *is* figuration, and vice versa, *there* is the place from which the real starts.

But, of course, we must at last come back from purely symbolic geography to the actual historical lay of the land. What is public and real in any historical milieu is a highly particular ideological construct. Besides the practice of reference, there are also ideologies of reference: not just "freedom" as seen on Westminster Bridge, that is, but also Canaletto or Turner pictures of such freedom colored by ideological atmospheres, respectively, of crystalline celebration or murky conflagration (for example, in the latter's *Burning of the Houses of Parliament*, 1835).[40] As in the case of the 1832 Reform Bill, in other words, reference grounded upon the public and the real is always colored by discrimination of *who* is public and real enough to speak of (and vote for) "freedom." From any particular viewpoint, only some people know how to refer properly or "talk sense" about the public world so as to represent the real—and ideal—existence of that world.

We cannot fully understand Wordsworth's poem of public reality, then, until we discern that at its heart—whatever its assertions of timeless power, beauty, freedom—lies a principle of partisanship very much of his time. We have already studied the manner in which the poet, like Coleridge in the *Morning Post*, was attempting to invent a "public" in the years from 1802 on. We can now fully subsume this public under the ideology of *the* particular public Wordsworth increasingly believed in: *nation*. As we see in the "valley, rock, or hill" of "Westminster Bridge," England became for him no longer Lakes versus London, but Lakes-in-London. No matter that such a "true" England of mind and heart disenfranchised the England of the purse and all those whose business was the purse. To quote "Little Gidding" and a later poet who purifies the language of his tribe so severely that the tribe at last seems a single poet (with his ghosts): "History is now and England." Speaking to his own fit audience though few in "Westminster Bridge," Wordsworth also says: history is now and England. History is *this* moment and *this* place known to the righteous few where—really for the first time since his 1792 trip to France—he can come home to his nation.

My initial inquiry into poetic power can now be rephrased: what kind of power does "Westminster Bridge" have as a topical—and partisan—poem? Since topical poetry gets its start on a bridge of reference, it shares the power of its brother prose, which makes more utilitarian trips across the bridge. Topical poetry, in other words, is cognate with the discursive or prosaic power of what De Quincey—basing his analysis upon conversations with Wordsworth—called the literature of Knowledge (see W. J. B. Owen, *Wordsworth as Critic*, pp.

192–95). In Wordsworth's case, topical poetry talks *with* the nation *about* the nation's power; and insofar as "Westminster Bridge" itself has power as an act of language, that act furthers the larger power (allegory, we might say) of nationalism. Wordsworth's topical poetry, in sum, phrases with a certain additional impetus—an exclamation point or question mark, a tender affirmation or schoolmaster's rebuke—scenes of power always conceived as "out there" beyond the total control of any individual speaker. Or in the terms of the old discipline that not all our modern emphasis on the poem *qua* poem or text can fully efface: Wordsworth's topical poetry has rhetorical power. It is uttered by a particular speaker to a particular audience; and all its action of partisanship is a persuasion subordinate to more active forms of state power.

Forgetting

But now a change in argument that retraces the denial we have seen to be our poet's unique power: having remembered the moment of history in "Westminster Bridge," he forgot. Indeed, the very act of "remembering" at last eased him into a forgetfulness of history in which the ideological partisanship we discerned in his chosen topic became extreme: it shrank to the ideology of the self and its atopical, or utopian, interests.

While Wordsworth remembered history, after all, he did so in a lyric whose very idiom of personal anecdote, affection, and meditation assumed what *Lyrical Ballads* and the other lyric and proto-lyric works of the preceding years had instituted: the rhetoric of *private* memory. "We are a nation opposed to France," Wordsworth would persuade us in "Westminster Bridge" and the Calais Tour as a whole. But he chooses a rhetoric that also says, "*I* love this nation opposed to France." The developing ideology of nation, that is, knows the egotistical sublime of the self, and the consequence—to remember our argument in Chapter 8—is that a potential imperialism remains, no matter how hard the poet tries to talk his nation free of French imperialism. As long as "I" remember London with supreme—and tyrannical—affection, the topical still has the potential to become a peak vision like that at Snowdon but *without* prior correction. Viewed one way, after all, there is something predatory or conquistadorial about a poem in which a lost leader sees a depopulated city and opens, "Earth has not any thing to shew more fair." The sudden, sharp hunger of the eye expressed here is that of a raptor. Or perhaps the best comparison is not raptor but Phoenix. With just the barest change in text, we might predict, personal remembrance of things past could become remembrance of the only thing able to survive its own passing, the memorial/original self. History is now and Imagination.

In the event, Wordsworth did not have to change his text substantively to effect such an altered intonation, only his context. Beyond the moment of history in "Westminster Bridge" was a moment after history—an *exit* through the Avernus gate of his poem also affixed to a putative date of composition. In the Longman MS. and every collected edition of his poetry from the *Poems, in Two Volumes* of 1807 through the *Poetical Works* of 1836–37, Wordsworth dated his poem in its title, "Sept. 3, *1803*."[41] It is hard to believe that the poet could confuse his French trip with that to Scotland in August and September 1803—accurately dated in "Memorials of a Tour in Scotland, 1803" from *1827* on (many of the poems in this Tour were published in *1807* as "Poems Written During a Tour in Scotland," with "1803" in the title of one poem).* The major significance of "1803," I suggest, was that it was *not* 1802.

The mistake is both simple and massive. We can easily believe, of course, that the error was mere carelessness (and perhaps that Wordsworth himself had less than effective control over the tables of contents and even titles in his editions). Yet the very endurance of such carelessness in the successive editions is telling in this case. It is testimony not to any positive conclusion (which would be difficult to base on such evidence) but a negative one: by 1807 and for three decades after, Wordsworth simply no longer thought of "Westminster Bridge" and other such "personal" poems as moving in the same circle of concern as the Calais Tour. The slip in date only reinforces the more important fact that from the time of publication in 1807 onward, "Westminster Bridge" and its relatively nonpolitical companions Sonnets D and L lie scattered through the "Miscellaneous Sonnets" while the political sonnets of the Calais Tour become the "Sonnets Dedicated to Liberty" (later Part I of "Poems Dedicated to National Independence and Liberty"). Indeed, there is even the possibility that the error in dating "Westminster Bridge" is a deliberate— or at least over-assertive—mark separating the "Miscellaneous Sonnets" in Volume I of *1807* from the bulk of the succeeding "Sonnets Dedicated to Liberty" in the same volume. Nine pages in the original text divide "Westminster Bridge" from the political sonnets, and its title stands out on the contents page as the only one of the "Miscellaneous Sonnets" to bear a date. The title of "Westminster Bridge" with the year "1803" thus stands out in relief against the pronounced fixation upon "1802" in the titles of the political sonnets (with the exception of the "October, 1803" sonnets at the end, which—as I will remark upon later—would thus seem to stand in strange relation to

* For convenience, I cite editions of Wordsworth's poetry from this point on by italicized date. A census of collected editions published in the poet's lifetime may be found on p. 509 of the Appendix.

"Westminster Bridge"). To demonstrate the point as graphically as possible, I reproduce the Sonnets section of the Contents in *Poems, in Two Volumes* (P2V, pp. 60–61):[42]

Prefatory Sonnet

PART THE FIRST. MISCELLANEOUS SONNETS
  1. How sweet it is, when mother Fancy rocks
  2. Where lies the Land to which yon Ship must go?
  3. Composed after a Journey across the Hamilton Hills, Yorkshire
  4. These words were utter'd in a pensive mood
  5. To Sleep (O gentle Sleep! do they belong to thee)
  6. To Sleep (A flock of sheep that leisurely pass by)
  7. To Sleep (Fond words have oft been spoken to thee, Sleep!)
  8. With Ships the sea was sprinkled far and nigh
  9. To the River Duddon
 10. From the Italian of Michael Angelo
 11. From the Same
 12. From the Same. To the Supreme Being
 13. Written in very early Youth
 14. Composed upon Westminster Bridge, Sept. 3, 1803
 15. "Beloved Vale!" I said, "when I shall con
 16. Methought I saw the footsteps of a throne
 17. To the ———
 18. The world is too much with us; late and soon
 19. It is a beauteous Evening, calm and free
 20. To the Memory of Raisley Calvert

PART THE SECOND. SONNETS DEDICATED TO LIBERTY
  1. Composed by the Sea-side, near Calais, August, 1802
  2. Calais, August, 1802
  3. To a Friend, composed near Calais, on the Road leading to Ardres, August 7th, 1802
  4. I griev'd for Buonaparte, with a vain
  5. Calais, August 15th, 1802
  6. On the extinction of the Venetian Republic
  7. The King of Sweden
  8. To Toussaint L'Ouverture
  9. September 1st, 1802
 10. Composed in the Valley, near Dover, on the Day of landing
 11. September, 1802
 12. Thought of a Briton on the Subjugation of Switzerland
 13. Written in London, September, 1802

14. London, 1802
15. Great Men have been among us; hands that penn'd
16. It is not to be thought of that the Flood
17. When I have borne in memory what has tamed
18. October, 1803 (One might believe that natural miseries)
19. There is a bondage which is worse to bear
20. October, 1803 (These times touch money'd Worldlings with dismay)
21. England! the time is come when thou shouldst wean
22. October, 1803 (When, looking on the present face of things)
23. To the Men of Kent. October, 1803
24. October, 1803 (Six thousand Veterans practis'd in War's game)
25. Anticipation. October, 1803
26. November, 1806

The political sonnets remain linked as a riverway of topical poems. The role "Westminster Bridge" might have played in the river is filled instead by sonnets like "On the Extinction of the Venetian Republic" commemorating the glory and doom of free cities. For their part, the "Miscellaneous Sonnets" are indeed miscellaneous, blooming "singly, or in scattered knots" (to use the conceit of the "Valedictory Sonnet" composed in 1838). It becomes clear in following their shifting order from *Poems, in Two Volumes* through the late editions that "Westminster Bridge" never roots itself in any stable chronological or topical scheme.[43] Indeed, topicality itself became anathema to Wordsworth in the immediate wake of the bad reviews of the "Moods of My Own Mind" and other targets in the 1807 collection. Writing to Lady Beaumont on May 21, 1807, about the reception of *Poems, in Two Volumes*, he protests:

The things which I have taken, whether from within or without,—what have they to do with routs, dinners, morning calls, hurry from door to door, from street to street, on foot or in Carriage; with Mr. Pitt or Mr. Fox, Mr. Paul or Sir Francis Burdett, the Westminster Election or the Borough of Honiton; in a word, . . . what have they to do with endless talking about things nobody cares anything for? (*Letters*, 2: 145–46)

Moods of my mind, the poet says, are avowedly *not* topical. The letter then continues with one of Wordsworth's most severe definitions of his public fit though few:

It is an awful truth, that there neither is, nor can be, any genuine enjoyment of Poetry among nineteen out of twenty of those persons who live, or wish to live, in the broad light of the world—among those who either are, or are striving to make themselves, people of consideration in society. This is a truth, and an awful one, because to be incapable of a feeling of Poetry in my sense of the word is to be without love of human nature and reverence for God. (*Letters*, 2: 146)

What I suggest, then, is that by the time of publication in 1807, the referential ground and the power base of "Westminster Bridge" alter completely. There is now a channel, a strait of denial, separating the poem's text from the context of the political sonnets. The channel is as narrow as the single year between "1802" and "1803," but this single year at the very center of the poet's Great Decade is epochal. In *1807* the first of the "Sonnets Dedicated to Liberty" (C in the Calais Tour) still shows Wordsworth looking west from Calais to the "Fair Star of Evening" over England. But it can no longer allude to the morning aspect of that star, to freedom seen from Westminster Bridge, because Wordsworth has displaced "Westminster Bridge" out of the historical world. If previously we could view "Westminster Bridge" on "July 31"/"Sept. 3" as two points in time abutting a tour, loop, or parabolic arch of movement through social space, we must now view it as a kind of slipknot that, when manipulated, pulls the loop of the Calais Tour into itself and makes it vanish.

We revert from the historical stream, that is, to denial—to a Nile of figuration whose fount is groundless topic: in short, a spot of time. The sonnet is no longer topical because in its focus on *one* spot unrelated to adjacent spots in social space and time, it incorporates all places in itself. "*Earth* has not any thing to shew more fair," the poet begins in a statement whose "Earth" no longer allows us to see a specific place of comparison—France—in the background. "Never did sun more beautifully steep / In his first splendor," he continues, wrapping up in one breath an indeterminate reach of time between Eden and the millennium. "Westminster Bridge" becomes so time-*full* that it seems timeless. It is as if in "1803" we were reading simultaneously about 1802, 1792, 1790, Milton's time, and Biblical time without being able to distinguish which period is ground and which figure. A poem embracing all places and times indeterminately in itself, "Westminster Bridge" becomes a poem about no place and time at all. It is about utopia. One bank of the historical stream—that of actual events—recedes from view so that, if there is still a bridge extending toward it from the land of signs, the bridge no longer ends meaningfully in any public convention of reality but arches outward into an unreal and private space inaccessible to "nineteen out of twenty of those persons who live, or wish to live, in the broad light of the world." "Westminster Bridge" becomes through denial a monument of pure language, a vertical accumulation of words piling up idiosyncratically and groundlessly only on each other. "Valley, rock, or hill" thus rest not on actual ground but figuratively on "Ships, towers, domes, theatres, and temples," and the latter lie in their turn only like embroidery on a metaphorical "garment" of beauty. Or to mix metaphors thoroughly, since referential convention and the hierarchy of figurations it governs have vanished, why could it not also be said that every image in view is merely a fresh layer of snow akin to that in "St. Paul's" (or any other comparison that can be imagined)? Language is freed of what had once been its public topic: freedom. And when contact with historical context is thus lost, the thread of ornamental figures gathers into thickness as if it were itself substance, as if, in other words, the slippage in its slipknot of Ariadnean thread (to resume the deconstructive vision by allusion to J. Hillis Miller) were not itself an act of displacement referenced upon historically knowable acts of displacement—specifically, upon freedom in the Napoleonic years slipping away from England and the poet's ideal public.

What is poetic power or the Literature of Power (in De Quincey's phrase) as it now rises free of topicality? In terms summarizing Wordsworth's overall development as I have mapped it in this book: poetic power is that which emerges free from collective authority, arms itself with figurations of nature, and then at last denies its history altogether to imagine the otherworldly "freedom" of the original self. "Oh! who is he that hath his whole life long / Preserved, enlarged, this freedom in himself?" we might repeat. Or again, just before these lines in *The Prelude*: "Such minds are truly from the Deity, / For they are Powers" (13.106–7). The "I" in "Westminster Bridge" is empowered to step forth at last free of all worldly responsibility except imagination. Liberated from the thought of Annette, Caroline, the exiled black woman, the crowd of English travelers to France, Napoleon, and all the other host of lost souls memorialized in the Calais Tour, it is free to be its own powerful self, its nation of one. It is free to be a power uncommitted to any referent and so as free to change its mind about worldly commitments—about what constitutes a powerful view, city, person, or object—as any Shelleyan unacknowledged legislator of the world. As W. J. B. Owen observes in his survey of Wordsworth's usage of the term: "Among the 600-odd occasions on which Wordsworth uses the word ['power'] or its plural in his verse, all the expected contexts can no doubt be found. But there is also to be found a usage which is seemingly peculiar to Wordsworth, the use of the word without such a context stated or easily inferred—a case which provokes in the reader the questions, 'Power for what?' 'Power to do what?' and the like" (*Wordsworth as Critic*, pp. 195–96).

We can go Owen one better here. Perhaps there is no better index of the power of poetry we discover in the years following 1807 than Wordsworth's ability not only to free "power" from all worldly reference but to reground such reference wholly in the Empire of the Poet. The key text here is the "Essay, Supplementary to the Preface" of 1815, in which Wordsworth arms poetry for a long war. Poetry is a "power" exerting "pleasing bondage," he says (*Prose*, 3:62); true critics form a "dispassionate government" (3:66); Dr. Johnson was a legislator ruling his "little senate" (3:75); and Alexander and Hannibal set the pattern for true poets who must "triumph" over all opposition and imperiously *create* "the taste by which [they are] to be enjoyed" (3:67, 80). What is genius, the poet asks, "but an advance, or a conquest, made by the soul of the poet?" (3:82). The Poet indeed becomes unacknowledged legislator of the world. As the "Essay, Supplementary" phrases it climactically: "And this brings us to the point. If every great poet with whose writings men are familiar, in the highest exercise of his genius, before he can be thoroughly enjoyed, has to call forth and to communicate *power*, this service, in a still greater degree, falls upon an original writer, at his first appearance in the world" (3:82). Such is the power of originality. Wordsworth's notion of poetic power, in the end, is not a little frightening.

Recollecting

But after we have remembered and forgotten—after, that is, we have recapitulated the course of Wordsworth's early to middle poetry as traced in this book—we have yet to recollect. Here I vary upon Kenneth Johnston's insight into Wordsworthian memory in his essay on the "Intimations" ode: "Recollecting Forgetting."[44] The core statement of the ode, Johnston argues, is that the poet *remembers forgetting* immortality—a state of conscious loss different from either memory or amnesia considered separately. Applied to collective rather than personal experience, and mortality rather than immortality, such a formulation aptly describes the later Wordsworth's recovered sense of history. The later poet, we may say, is the ideologue of the post-self-conscious and post-imaginative. He is the self who *remembers* having forgotten the world and so discovers the sense of history to be his true origin of poetry. But we must not let our modern love of the prefix "post-" approximate the poet to our own criticism prematurely. Having lost absolute confidence in selfhood, Wordsworth does not enter the zone of the decentered subject that is Romantic irony or our modern analogue: postmodernism. If the poet's self is now naked of imagination, it yet comes trailing clouds of glory: ideologies of *dis*imagination celebrating the reversion of originality to national, ecclesiastical, and public authority. Not "I" but "*We* (nation, church, people) remember that I have forgotten history," the poet says, submitting his sense of history to that of the tribe. Or again, "We all know what I have denied, what I have imagined." The voice of the older poet is a voice blurred by multitudes.

Such is what I propose to call Wordsworth's later poetry of recollection. Where the poetry of denial once formed itself in lyric,

the poetry of recollection formed itself at a higher level of organization in collected editions that gathered lyrics into sequences-within-
sequences. Huddled with the masses not only of other selves—past,
present, and future—but of the entirety of its topical concerns, the
"I" submitted fully to the "we." Like Eliot proclaiming himself clas-
sicist, royalist, and Anglo-Catholic, we may say, Wordsworth at last
confessed himself conventional. And, though to a lesser degree than
Eliot, he also became a critic of imagination.

The fourth date of composition underlying "Westminster Bridge"
is "Sept. 3, *1802*," which Wordsworth first entered informally in his
sonnet's title in the densely annotated copy of *1836–37* he used to prepare future revisions (*P2V*, p. 147 *appar. crit.*)[45] and then—with gradually increasing fidelity—in the printed titles of the ensuing principal
editions: *1838*, *1840*, and *1845*.[46] What this restoration of the sonnet's
date indexes, I suggest, is that for the later poet "Westminster Bridge"
and the intensely private lyricism it had come to express after 1807
finally returned to the world of the public and topical. It did so because of a much larger change in the poet's overall conception of his
work. In the years between 1807 and 1838, Wordsworth wholly rethought the very act of collecting his poetry. He developed a theory
of collection, we might name it, and the outcome of this theory was
that it was no longer possible to think of any one unit of lyrics—the
"Miscellaneous Sonnets," for example—as separate from any other
unit however foreign in theme or treatment. The poetry of self and
of topic recollected each other.

To trace the genesis of this theory of collection, we can return momentarily to 1807 and the earliest era of Wordsworthian collection.[47]
What we should now realize is that "Westminster Bridge" and the
poetry of private vision from the first had *some* necessary relation to
the topical poems—even if that relation was only beginning to be
thought. If the loud "1803" of "Westminster Bridge" in the contents
of *1807* creates a channel dividing the poem from the "1802" of the
succeeding "Sonnets Dedicated to Liberty," "1803" must nevertheless
still touch down somewhere in the public world. Thus the sonnet
touches uncannily upon the sonnets dated "October, 1803" at the
very close of the political poems. The gravity well of public history
is too strong to escape entirely: all the lyric satellites of private vision must collect around the public mass in some manner of orbit,
some arc of separation that is also a confession of attraction. Or again,
consider once more the May 21, 1807, letter to Lady Beaumont in
which Wordsworth aggressively rejects topicality. Defending himself
against a detractor of his poems of eccentric privacy (such as "Moods
of My Own Mind"), the poet is at last forced to argue that at least
some of his poems do gravitate around weighty topics. Imagining a
discourse with his critic, he writes:

there is one thing which must strike you at once if you will only read these poems,—that those to Liberty, at least, have a connection with, or a bearing upon, each other, and therefore, if individually they want weight, perhaps, as a Body, they may not be so deficient, at least this ought to induce you to suspend your judgement, and qualify it so far as to allow that the writer aims at least at comprehensiveness. But dropping this, I would boldly say at once, that these Sonnets, while they each fix the attention upon some important sentiment separately considered, do at the same time collectively make a Poem on the subject of civil Liberty and national independence, which, either for simplicity of style or grandeur of moral sentiment, is alas! likely to have few parallels in the Poetry of the present day. (*Letters*, 2: 147)

We can underscore the terms "connection," "comprehensiveness," and "collectively" here. Even as early as 1807, Wordsworth was not simply collecting his poems but beginning to work out a theory of collection able to gather moods of his own mind and topical poetry into a single comprehensiveness.

After *1807*, the comprehensiveness of Wordsworth's theory of collection steadily increased—not only in *1815*, whose classification of poems has attracted the most attention, but also in each successive, substantively new collected edition: *1820, 1827, 1832, 1836–37, (1838*, consisting only of the sonnets), *1845*, and *1849–50*. As studies of *1815* by James Scoggins, Frances Ferguson, Gene Ruoff, Judith Herman, Donald Ross, Jr., and others demonstrate, it is clear that Wordsworth's early interest lay in the controversial connection between the poems of Affection, Fancy, Imagination, and Sentiment and Reflection and secondly in his overall scheme of developmental psycho-biography (the progression from "Poems Referring to the Period of Childhood" through "Poems Referring to the Period of Old Age" and "Epitaphs and Elegiac Poems"). Looking through *1815* to the succeeding editions, however, we can discriminate a crucial shift in attention. The possibility of this shift lay in an indeterminate, barely organized middle zone in *1815* between the poems of childhood and faculty psychology, on the one hand, and those of old age and death, on the other—a zone of raw topicality, as it might be called, in which the connection between private moments and public topics ("Miscellaneous Sonnets" and "Sonnets Dedicated to Liberty," respectively) remains unthought except insofar as both bottom out at last in natural "place" ("Poems on the Naming of Places," "Inscriptions"). We can isolate this middle zone in the contents of *1815* by indenting as follows:

> Poems Referring to the Period of Childhood
> Juvenile Pieces
> Poems Founded on the Affections
> Poems of the Fancy

Poems of the Imagination
Poems Proceeding from Sentiment and Reflection
    Miscellaneous Sonnets
    Sonnets Dedicated to Liberty
    Poems on the Naming of Places
    Inscriptions
Poems Referring to the Period of Old Age
Epitaphs and Elegiac Poems
Ode.—Intimations, &c. [later subsumed in "Epitaphs
    and Elegiac Poems"]

After *1815*, Wordsworth articulated his theory of collection by expanding and reorganizing this middle zone. The most efficient way to suggest the scope of this reworking is to display in one view the contents lists of the principal collected editions from *1820* on (omitting the 1838 collection of just sonnets); see Appendix.

Given the complexity of Wordsworth's constant reshufflings, of course, no one explanation can claim to be exclusive. With Occam's razor in mind, however, I suggest that the simplest and clearest explanation of the poet's changes is as follows. The categories that open the psychobiographical scheme from "Poems Referring to the Period of Childhood" through "Poems of the Imagination" remain unchanged (except for the occasional inclusion of "Poems on the Naming of Places" and "Inscriptions"). But a divide opens at this point between "Poems of the Imagination" and "Poems of Sentiment and Reflection" such that these two categories now frame the middle zone of topicality. Within this zone, a massive reorganization takes place. "Poems on the Naming of Places" and "Inscriptions" are spun outward so that by *1849–50* they flank the middle zone. In their stead, a new category arises to "place" the "Miscellaneous Sonnets" and the "Sonnets Dedicated to Liberty" (together with such narrative poems as "The White Doe of Rylstone") on common ground. This category is the Memorial Tour proper: the Memorials of a Tour in Scotland, on the Continent, in Italy, and in the Summer of 1833. The ultimate version of such Tours, perhaps, is "The River Duddon" or "Ecclesiastical Sketches"—the latter the *magnum opus* of Memorial Tours in which Wordsworth applies his form of peripatetic meditation to the places and events of public history. Finally, the original psychobiography resumes, but with a new willingness to accommodate the topical: "Poems of Sentiment and Reflection" point the way not only to old age and death but to categories of topical interest ending in *public* death ("Sonnets Dedicated to Liberty and Order" and "Sonnets Upon the Punishment of Death"). The whole scheme then resolves at last into *The Excursion*, which, conceived one way, is Wordsworth's largest—indeed, interminable—Memorial Tour.

The net effect of the reorganization was that the middle zone of private and public concerns became increasingly sure ground for a poet concerned to walk through life attentive to both realms. Not natural place ("Poems on the Naming of Places," "Inscriptions") but *commonplace* in the Memorial Tours—meditations upon place compounded of lyricism and topicality—now ensured that there was indeed continuity between, for example, "Miscellaneous Sonnets" and "Sonnets Dedicated to Liberty"; ensured, that is, that there was *one* road to walk among all the private and public moments of life. The continuity or common ground thus guaranteed by the Memorial Tour, as Peter Manning and Stuart Peterfreund show in their studies of the later poetry, was discontinuous, serial, or decentered in structure. Yet decentering in this case *was* the poet's new center: a pendulum of perspective that was neither private nor public but precisely the to-and-fro interchange between the two.[48] It was such to-and-fro rhythm, we may say, that at last allowed Wordsworth fully to collect himself in all senses of the word. Even in the face of the most topical issues, he now stayed collected, reposed. We might instance here the sonnet on "The Jung-Frau and the Fall of the Rhine Near Schaffhausen," whose place at the intersection of aesthetic and political concerns Theresa Kelley has insightfully studied ("Wordsworth and the Rhinefall," pp. 73–74). Originally published in 1822 in both the individual issues of *Memorials of a Tour on the Continent, 1820,* and *Ecclesiastical Sketches* (see Wise), the sonnet is in one sense about the loss of repose:

> The Virgin-Mountain, wearing like a Queen
> A brilliant crown of everlasting snow,
> Sheds ruin from her sides; and men below
> Wonder that aught of aspect so serene
> Can link with desolation. Smooth and green,
> And seeming, at a little distance, slow,
> The waters of the Rhine; but on they go
> Fretting and whitening, keener and more keen;
> Till madness seizes on the whole wide Flood,
> Turned to a fearful Thing whose nostrils breathe
> Blasts of tempestuous smoke—wherewith he tries
> To hide himself, but only magnifies;
> And doth in more conspicuous torment writhe,
> Deafening the region in his ireful mood.
> (*PW*, 3: 382–83)

Yet the final effect of the sonnet in "Ecclesiastical Sketches" was a new sort of repose. Called in the title an "Illustration," the sonnet arrives like a momentary respite from history between two explicitly topical poems, "Gunpowder Plot" and "Troubles of Charles the First." In the ultimate Memorial Tour of "Ecclesiastical Sonnets," lyric vision comforts public concern; and, conversely, public concern makes lyric vision responsible. The two repose together.

When Wordsworth in the editions from *1838* on changed the date of "Westminster Bridge" to "1802," then, we should see in the background a long-developing change in his thought knitting together the private and public. Ultimately, what "1802" and innumerable other clues in the themes, language, titles, dates, and organization of the later works signal is that the project of the later poet, as Ross has argued, was to imagine "a general or collective biography of the early nineteenth century"—a biography, that is, not of the poet himself or even of his mind so much as of the public concerns that everyman has on his mind in his middle zone of maturity (p. 134; see also pp. 137–38).[49] With the affixing of "1802" in the title of "Westminster Bridge," in sum, private utopia and public topic collected together in a relation preparing the poet to be the Laureate, a national poet. We might listen, for example, to the Advertisement Wordsworth inserted at the head of his collected sonnets (*1838*): "My admiration of some of the Sonnets of Milton, first tempted me to write in that form. The fact is not mentioned from a notion that it will be deemed of any importance by the reader, but merely as a public acknowledgement of one of the innumerable obligations, which, as a Poet and a Man, I am under to our great fellow-countryman." The Poet is a Man influenced not so much by Milton, the poet, as by his "fellow-countryman." Or again, we might listen to the headnote to the 1816 *Thanksgiving Ode* (afterwards included in "Sonnets Dedicated to National Independence and Liberty"): "Every man deserving the name of Briton adds his voice to the chorus which extols the exploits of his countrymen, with a consciousness, at times overpowering the effort, that they transcend all praise" (*PW*, 3: 463). Wordsworth would be the Vox Populi.

I close by turning back to Molesworth's fine essay on "Westminster Bridge." Molesworth argues that both in its occasion and in its internal structure, "Westminster Bridge" is a poem of temporal "suspension," of a moment, that is, withdrawn from quotidian existence. Such suspension can be felt either "as a seam, experienced as difference related to over-riding sameness, or apprehended as a rending, a fissure" (p. 267). The sonnet either displays a moment of splendor emerging from the continuum of the historical past, in other words, or reveals through the gap it makes in the quotidian a wholly other, separate world as mythic as Eden. Molesworth concludes that "Westminster Bridge" is a seam-experience stitching together present and past times (p. 273). What I have argued in this chapter adds a further stitch in time. "Westminster Bridge" is a poem that originated as a seam in history, a remembrance of the public and the past. It became a fissure forgetting the historical past in favor of otherworldly utopia.

But at last, as in the case of some of the poet's literally stitched manuscripts, the sonnet of remembering and of forgetting, the sonnet of the national poet and of the lyric self, gathered together in the same folio. The power of originality and the power of national, ecclesiastical, and popular authority stood collected.

Doubtless such rapprochement between self and history was a fragile construct, as dependent for its integrity upon ideology (tradition, solidarity, a particular vision of democracy) as the constructs it subsumed. But it is sufficient to end our criticism here. The act of recollection by which self and history drew together, I venture, was the poet's own implicit criticism of himself. Collected side by side with history, Wordsworth's imagination at last knew its place. Phrased critically: imagination was put in its place. This is the foreknowledge we have had to discover or, at a minimum, surmise in order to complete our own criticism.

This book has been about the elsewhereness of history, the gap in present being where the self stands in exchange with an absence or infinitude urgent with the ghosts of past selves, past presents, whole other worlds. Infinite absence can wear many names, many ideological vestments or ideas of history doomed always to be after-the-fact. Originating in a sense of alienated sourcehood that in its very moment of discovery—like the Nile flowing from undiscovered sources—evacuates the notions of sourcehood and origination, an idea of history, it seems, can only emerge with a certain air of unreality. The moment when an individual—poet or critic—seeks to explain the reality of absent history, or first recognizes the existence of such a reality in need of historical account, is also the moment when he discovers that he cannot by himself originate a fully sufficient explanation. The very forms of his explanation are unreal. They evade the agon, the raw story of contest between the same and the other, the here and the not-here, the present and the past. Poet's description and critic's account, poet's lyric and critic's schema: all these forms cover as much as they recover. In the end, they romanticize.

How, then, to know history as real?

The largest, most capacious theme of Wordsworth's lifework, I believe, fits that of the nineteenth century generally: realizing the sense of history as an ideology or philosophy explaining away originating absence. Within the envelope of this theme belong the traditional constructs of Wordsworth criticism—nature, time, self, mind—as well as those other figures of capable imagination, or perhaps of disimagination, we are only beginning to know how to read: nation, church, people. Wordsworth's career begins with tour works such as *An Evening Walk* and *Descriptive Sketches* and ends, after tracing the ideological lineage of nature, time, self, mind, nation, church, and people, in that remarkable series of later tour forms: the many Memorial Tours and their cognates. These latter works are the poet's accommodation with the sense of history: they are the form in which history's infinite absence collects to create a massively finished and yet ever-increasing facsimile of reality. Though Wordsworth's poetry moves in a field of absence that repays dialectical and deconstructive study, his mind is in the end one of the most nondialectical and re-constructive we know. At the last, he turns back the Hegelian move-ment toward philosophy so that mind literally, rather than mentally, tours in the world. The Memorial Tour is Wordsworth's version of the Lukácsian novel: his form adjusting self-consciousness to social reality.[50]

To explore more fully Wordsworth's later realizations of history—and thus the disinvestment of his imagination—would be to extend Hartman's apocalyptic approach with power intact to the full corpus of the poems. The true apocalypse, I have said, will come when history rends the veil of nature to face the self directly, when the sense of history and imagination thus become one, and nature, the mediating figure, is no more. Let me now add that there is an even more devastating apocalypse to come when history will rend the veil of imagination itself to leave at last only a confrontation with history akin to tautology. Not the divine "I am that I am," but "*We* are that we are." Or perhaps the tense should be altered: "We are that we were." This is Wordsworth's apocalypse of unimagination leaving us only with the Laureateship of collective reality, of the profound mundane.

In lieu of a full-scale examination of the many Memorial Tours and related forms in the later works recording this unimaginative apocalypse, I offer just a snapshot from the first sustained attempt to reimagine the landscape of Europe after Waterloo, the "Memorials of a Tour on the Continent, 1820":

THE COLUMN INTENDED BY BUONAPARTE FOR
A TRIUMPHAL EDIFICE IN MILAN, NOW LYING
BY THE WAY-SIDE IN THE SIMPLON PASS

AMBITION—following down this far-famed slope
Her Pioneer, the snow-dissolving Sun,
While clarions prate of kingdoms to be won—
Perchance, in future ages, here may stop;
Taught to mistrust her flattering horoscope
By admonition from this prostrate Stone!
Memento uninscribed of Pride o'erthrown;
Vanity's hieroglyphic; a choice trope
In Fortune's rhetoric. Daughter of the Rock,
Rest where thy course was stayed by Power divine!
The Soul transported sees, from hint of thine,

Crimes which the great Avenger's hand provoke,
Hears combats whistling o'er the ensanguined heath:
What groans! what shrieks! what quietness in death!

(PW, 3: 189)

Let this sonnet be a hieroglyphic for the later Wordsworth, an icon
for the layered monument through whose encrusted ideologies of nation, church, and people appears, if we penetrate deeply enough, the
moving agon of the sense of history in its original power. The quatrains are themselves absolute pieces of rhetoric, attempts by a poet,
in the pride of his own ambition, to suppress Napoleon's Ozyman-
dian ambition with a sheer artillery of tropes lifted whole from the
literary tradition of the "character" and turned into political ideology fused with religious faith. The "Daughter of the Rock"—blank,
uninscribed—is a piece of potent nothingness, a gap in everyday
being as potentially "usurpatory" as the summit of Mont Blanc or the
gap of experience discovered in Simplon Pass in *The Prelude*. It is an
epitaph whose object is still to be recollected and thought into an idea
of history. The older poet, his ideologies ready to the tongue, rushes
in too quickly, we feel, to inscribe that blankness with his hieroglyphics; we miss the pause and bewilderment that occurs in Book 6
of *The Prelude* before the poet, at the end of the Gondo Gorge passage, can write hieroglyphics into the gap: "Characters of the great
Apocalypse, / The types and symbols of Eternity, / Of first and last,
and midst, and without end." But penetrate deeply enough under
the rhetorical ambition and hardened ideology of the sonnet—to the
couplet—and we can recognize the original sense of history, inchoate, terrifying, and brutal, underlying Wordsworth's poetry: not the
fully formed hieroglyphic, but the inarticulate sense of significance
not yet present; not statement, but mutilated half-questions, half-
exclamations through whose pointings of horror protrudes history:
"What groans! what shrieks! what quietness in death!"

Epilogue

So now you have spent eight years—a long march—writing this study. We would put to you the most important question we can conceive: have you believed in what you were saying all this time?[*]

I have. After I discovered what I was saying, after the first few exploratory attempts, I did believe, and more so with each piece in place. There were many moments of falling off, and they are recorded here in spots of contrivance or mere bridgework. But in the main, I believe this work to be true.

Yet it is your very belief we find disturbing. You have said that literature is historical in origin, and you have amassed historical context from whatever sources were available to you or that you had time to accomplish in order to make yourself credible. And on the whole, you believe that you have succeeded, that armies of context allow you to translate yourself from literature into history, from present into past, from yourself into someone other. Yet consider the events in your own life in these past eight years—even the most joyful, frightening, or purposeful among them. Choose the most significant one—shall it be your marriage? your advancement in career?—and try to determine how that event reflects itself in your writing. Can you do so with certainty even in your own mind?

I confess I cannot. This is why a portion of my method, as I say, is skeptical. When drawing the link between Napoleon and the Simplon Pass, for example, I take as much care as possible to set up a "ladder of

---

[*] Among other precedents for this Epilogue, should any be required: Hartman's "The Interpreter: A Self-Analysis," the Conclusion to Foucault's *Archaeology of Knowledge*, and the Epilogue to a work that, in the latter stages of writing this book, I have come increasingly to admire, Greenblatt's *Renaissance Self-Fashioning*.

certainty." No one can know the differential relation between history and literature, or any other register of mind, with full certainty. This is why, after all, I say "I believe." I treat not of certainty but of credibility.

And yet we do not believe you, somehow, when you say that you are content with credibility short of certainty. There is a certain driven quality about your amassing of material, not to mention the interpretive use to which you put it, that confesses you a fanatic. You add the extra fact to the already sufficient fact; and then you push your interpretation toward the extreme verge of probable truth. We believe you, in your heart, to desire certainty. And we thus believe you to be lying when you formulate history as "elsewhereness." You would penetrate through the veil of elsewhereness to know what is really there.

I believe I do have a certain desire to recover what I know rationally cannot be recovered: the actual stuff of the past.

You are still sparing yourself. Is it not true that the "facts" you have perused in your researches have often moved you more than any literature—least of all that of your chosen poet—could ever do? We have seen you reading books of "facts" with all your skeptical guard down, alive to the materiality of the past in a way you are not alive to literature even in your most imaginative moment. Does not that mention of desperate serving girls hiding their dead babies in chests in Chapter 6, for example, stop you each time you reread your work in the way certain lines of "The Vanity of Human Wishes" stopped Johnson and made him—we can barely think it—burst into tears? Can you explain this rationally even to yourself, let alone to others?

You embarrass me.

You embarrass yourself. There is the faintest unmistakable taint of transcendence about your whole project. It is not enough that religion spills into imagination. You must spill imagination into history. You are a believer in history, and literature is only your testament. Can you say this is untruth?

It is not the whole of the truth. But it is part of it. I do believe in history.

And now we come to the heart of your deception. Can you honestly say that what you mean by history is distinguishable from what your poet meant by imagination? Can you even say that history, for you, is different from autobiography?

I do not know what you mean.

Do not be disingenuous. Critic, we criticize you in the way that recidivists were "criticized" in that other revolution of culture you would rather not think about in that land of your parents' origin. We criticize you for being the romanticizer of your own elsewhereness. Has not Wordsworth's sense of history, emergent from the French Revolution, merely served as the medium for your own sense of history, emergent from a different revolution—a history and a world for which you have no other means of expression?

I deny that this is a significant truth.

But you do not deny that it is a truth?

The truth is not that simple. You have told a nice story to link my personal milieu (and not even mine, but my parents'!) to my study. But there are other stories. I have been teaching the Age of Johnson throughout these years of writing, for example. Perhaps that alone accounts for my love of material truth.

Do not hide behind the good Doctor.

My students, then, whose blend of native intelligence and non-intelligence has held me closer to literal truth than I might otherwise have stayed.

Do not hide behind your students.

The deep truth is imageless.

Do not hide behind him either.

Then must I stand alone?

You are not that original. If you have denied motives for writing as you have written—whether or not the particular motives we assign you or you assign yourself are the true ones—you merely stand confessed as one of many. That is what you cannot abide. That is what you must deny: that conventionality is deep as your soul.

I am wordless.

No, you have much more to deny, whole books to write.

Appendix

~⊙~

Contents Lists of Principal Editions of Wordsworth's Poems from 1820 to 1849–50

To allow the main contours of Wordsworth's classifications to appear clearly through the sequence of principal editions, some simplifications have been made in compiling the following contents lists. Only the main categories on the contents pages of the original editions, excluding entries for Wordsworth's prose essays, are listed. Such major poems as *Descriptive Sketches*, *The Waggoner*, *Peter Bell*, and the "Intimations" ode are subsumed within the primary categories to which they are appended, even though typographical separation or full capitalization in the contents sometimes indicates that these poems should be regarded as constituting their own category or semi-independent coda. As in the contents list for *1815* in Chapter 9, I indent the unstable section of the listings that is my special concern in tracing the poet's evolving "theory of collection."

Following these listings is a full census of collected editions published in the poet's lifetime, with bibliographic information.

1820 Poems Referring to Childhood and Early Youth
   Juvenile Pieces
   Poems Founded on the Affections
   Poems of Fancy
   Poems of the Imagination
    The White Doe of Rylstone
    The Prioress's Tale
    Miscellaneous Sonnets
    Sonnets Dedicated to Liberty
    The River Duddon, A Series of Sonnets
   Poems of Sentiment and Reflection
   Poems on the Naming of Places

Inscriptions
Poems Referring to the Period of Old Age
Epitaphs and Elegiac Poems

1827   Poems Referring to the Period of Childhood
Juvenile Pieces
Poems Founded on the Affections
Poems of the Fancy
Poems of the Imagination
    Miscellaneous Sonnets
    Memorials of a Tour in Scotland, 1803
    Memorial of a Tour in Scotland, 1814
    Poems on the Naming of Places
    Inscriptions
    Sonnets Dedicated to Liberty
    Memorials of a Tour on the Continent, 1820
    Ecclesiastical Sketches
    The White Doe of Rylstone
    The Prioress's Tale
    The River Duddon
Poems of Sentiment and Reflection
Poems Referring to the Period of Old Age
Epitaphs and Elegiac Poems
The Excursion

1832   Poems Referring to the Period of Childhood
Juvenile Pieces
Poems Founded on the Affections
Poems of the Fancy
Poems on the Naming of Places
Inscriptions
The Prioress's Tale
Poems of the Imagination
    Miscellaneous Sonnets
    Memorials of a Tour in Scotland, 1803
    Memorials of a Tour in Scotland, 1814
    Sonnets Dedicated to Liberty
    Memorials of a Tour on the Continent
    The River Duddon
    The White Doe of Rylstone
    Ecclesiastical Sketches
Poems of Sentiment and Reflection
Poems Referring to the Period of Old Age

The following is a census of collected editions published in Wordsworth's lifetime, including also the partial collections of *Poems, in Two Volumes* and the *Sonnets* of 1838 (because of their relevance to my discussion of the sonnets in Chapters 8 and 9), but excluding other selected or specialized editions as well as the unauthorized Paris collected edition of 1828 and the American collected editions. For more bibliographical information on these collections (as well as the other editions) and for a sense of the relation between the principal issues and their reissues, see the fuller census of lifetime printings in *P2V*, pp. 57–58; see also Healey, Wise. In making my argument in Chapter 9, I have consulted all collected editions except for *1843, 1846,* and *1849a,* to which I did not have access.

1807. Poems, in Two Volumes. 2 vols. London, 1807.

1815. Poems by William Wordsworth: Including "Lyrical Ballads," and the Miscellaneous Pieces of the Author. With Additional Poems, a New Preface, and a Supplementary Essay. 2 vols. London, 1815.

1820. The Miscellaneous Poems of William Wordsworth. 4 vols. London, 1820.

1827. Poetical Works of William Wordsworth. 5 vols. London, 1827.

1832. Poetical Works of William Wordsworth. A New Edition. 4 vols. London, 1832.

1836–37. Poetical Works of William Wordsworth. A New Edition. 6 vols. London, 1836–37.

1838. The Sonnets of William Wordsworth. Collected in One Volume, with a Few Additional Ones, Now First Published. London, 1838.

1840. Poetical Works of William Wordsworth. A New Edition. 6 vols. London, 1840. (Reissue of *1836–37,* with alterations)

1841. Poetical Works of William Wordsworth. A New Edition. 6 vols. London, 1841. (Reissue of *1836–37,* with alterations)

1843. Poetical Works of William Wordsworth. A New Edition. 6 vols. London, 1843. (Reissue of *1836–37,* with alterations)

1845. Poems of William Wordsworth, D. C. L., Poet Laureate, Etc. Etc. A New Edition. London, 1845.

1846. Poetical Works of William Wordsworth, D. C. L., Poet Laureate, Honorary Member of the Royal Society of Edinburgh, and of the Royal Irish Academy, Etc. Etc. A New and Revised Edition. 7 vols. London, 1846. (Reissue of *1836–37,* with alterations and incorporating *Poems, Chiefly of Early and Late Years,* 1842)

1847. Poems of William Wordsworth, D. C. L., Poet Laureate, Etc. Etc. A New Edition. London, 1847. (Reissue of *1845,* with alterations)

1849. Poetical Works of William Wordsworth, D. C. L., Poet Laureate, Honorary Member of the Royal Society of Edinburgh, and of the Royal Irish Academy, Etc., Etc. A New and Revised Edition. 7 vols. London, 1849. (Reissue of *1846,* with alterations)

1849a. Poems of William Wordsworth, D. C. L., Poet Laureate, Etc. Etc. London, 1849. (Reissue of *1845,* with alterations)

1849–50. Poetical Works of William Wordsworth, D. C. L., Poet Laureate, Etc. Etc. A New Edition. 6 vols. London, 1849–50.

Reference Matter

Notes

1. Bruce's long-awaited work appeared in 1790 in time for the *European Magazine* to review it in its issues from May through August (with many excerpts including the passage I quote). But it is unlikely that Wordsworth read Bruce or the reviews before he embarked in July of the same year on his Continental tour, which I will compare to Bruce's journey. Charles Norton Coe does not mention Bruce in his *Wordsworth and the Literature of Travel*, and there is no direct evidence that Wordsworth read Bruce before working on the 1805 *Prelude*. We surmise that Wordsworth at least knew of the *Travels* by this time, however, because he and Dorothy visited "the residence of the famous traveller Bruce" during their 1803 tour of Scotland (*Journals of Dorothy Wordsworth*, ed. Selincourt, 1: 364–65). The first direct mention of the *Travels* occurs in a letter from Dorothy to Lady Beaumont on January 24, 1807, which mentions Coleridge's recommendation of the 1804 edition and petitions, "If you purchase it we should be very glad to have the reading of it" (*Letters*, 2: 129). The 1790 first edition of the *Travels* was later among Wordsworth's books at Rydal Mount (Shaver and Shaver, p. 36).

2. *WP*, esp. pp. 31–69. I should also mention Thomas Weiskel's work, which, through its phrasing of the Imagination in Simplon Pass as amnesia, resistance, and rejection, has particularly guided my description of Imagination as denial (pp. 202–3).

3. Hartman's description of the poet's "turn" of mind in Simplon Pass models itself on a Pauline, Augustinian, or "mystic" conversion (*WP*, p. 33) whose external manifestation as pilgrimage is directly contrasted to the experience of the revolutionary in 1790 France (p. 56). My insistence upon "turn" as worldly tour implies in part that being a pilgrim in 1790 does not distinguish Wordsworth from the thousands of French *fédérés* journey-

ing to and from the Fete of Federation; cf. Ozouf: "*La Fédération en prend son caractère singulier d'être plus et moins qu'un pèlerinage*" (p. 71).

Since Hartman's book is the landmark work in Wordsworth studies, it may be useful at the start to chart my intended navigation relative to it. A bare paraphrase of Hartman's argument might run as follows: in the beginning, there is a radical of consciousness whose very condition of being is its effort to emerge as self-consciousness. Emergence involves a dialectic between "apocalypse," in which the self moves toward imaginative independence from nature, and "humanization," in which the self restores nature to primacy through the "myth" that nature guided mind beyond itself in the first place. The final outcome is "humanized imagination," reached by 1805 in the Simplon Pass and Snowdon episodes: a consciousness aware of self as the "borderer" subsuming both the powers of mind and nature. Such imagination may be called humanized because nature is the common medium through which mind allies itself to everyday human existence (esp. p. 140).

Yet, of course, such a bare reading of Hartman misses his book's very pulse: the tremendous pathos with which it watches over, as if over a dead body, the empiricist component in the dialectic of self—the return to nature. Hartman is never more moving than when describing this return, and it soon becomes clear that his dialectic was never a balance but a master-slave relation of apocalypse to humanization, respectively, in which the traitorous slave binds the master. For Hartman, nature is Wordsworth's tragic flaw, and the return to nature his Prometheus bound. Apocalyptic imagination appears in a cloak of connotation—"apocalyptic vigor" and bravery in the face of "dangers," for example—dramatizing its heroic priority as the origin of phenomena (pp. 61, xiii). By contrast, humanizing nature is "pedantically faithful" (p. 39), an "avoidance of apocalypse" (p. 61), an "evaded recognition" (p. 61), an effort to "retard" or "beguile" (p. 147), a "displacement" (p. 257), and a "flight" (p. 293) by which Wordsworth "dooms himself" (p. 187). If apocalypse is phenomenal, in other words, humanization can only be epiphenomenal "myth" (p. 135), "superstition" (p. 330), or "illusion" (p. 330).

In sum, Hartman's argument consists not only of an analytic—the dialectic explaining Wordsworth's development up to about 1805—but of a genuinely critical act: the shaping of that analytic into a sort of divine tragedy in which the poet's guiding Virgil, nature, misleads him. But there is no innate reason why the analytic should privilege apocalypse. Blake, to whom Hartman consistently alludes, is one demon behind such twist of dialectic. The real demon is Hegel—or, perhaps, a Paulinized Hegel. The terms "Akedah" and "Apocalypse," after all, are not ideologically neutral: they contain in seed the entire teleology by which the Old Testament opens out into the New, or—in the Pauline vision to which Hartman sometimes refers (pp. 50, 56)—the "natural" man (*psychikos*) into the "spiritual" (*pneumatikos*). And as Abraham opens out into Paul, so Paul at last opens out into Hegel, whose method deeply, and sometimes explicitly, underlies Hartman's turn of mind. As Hartman implies in his Critical Bibliography for the chapter "Via Naturaliter Negativa," his attempt to unite two strands of criticism, one for which Wordsworth is the poet of nature and the other for which he is the poet of consciousness opposed to nature, proceeds "in a genuinely dialectical manner" (p. 349). The precedent Hartman endorses for such an approach is Hegel's—as opposed, for example, to Heidegger's (see *WP*, p. 366 n. 3 on the latter). Arguing the movement of the soul in *The Borderers* "toward individuation, or from a morality based on 'nature' to one based on the autonomous self" (p. 129), he adds in a note: "This transition is studied exhaustively in Hegel's *The Phenomenology of Mind* . . . (especially the chapters on lordship and bondage, and stoicism, skepticism, and the unhappy consciousness); it also has affinities with sections Hegel wrote with the cataclysm of the French Revolution in mind, such as 'Reason as Lawgiver' and 'Reason as a Test of Laws'" (p. 369 n. 26).

Hegel's work balances the mind's effort to "annul and transcend" reality against its contrary dispersion into reality "as an object" (Hegel, *Phenomenology*, p. 86) and so predicts Hartman's dialectic of apocalypse and humanization. But it weights that balance teleologically such that originating consciousness points inexorably to terminating self-consciousness. In this field of idealism, dialectic cannot but privilege the mastery of pure mind over objectivity. Thus the overall process of Hegelian dialectic is progress: the world-mind transforms reality into ideologies or philosophies, and then climbs the peak of self-consciousness when it reviews and subsumes philosophies so as to project itself, at last, as the world-mind direct. With this dynamo powering his method, Hartman cannot avoid viewing Wordsworth's return to nature as tragic—not unless the poetry after 1805 or so is made to vanish. Wordsworth's Snowdon-consciousness is aware of itself as the totality of the mind-nature dialectic and so measures up to Hegel's epiphanic Absolute Knowledge. But the "late" poetry after this peak from 1805 to the 1814 *Excursion* then appears a fall because post–self-consciousness is unimaginable in the Hegelian method. It is the tragedy of post–self-consciousness that casts its long shadow over the early corpus.

My own book is meant to place consciousness and nature alike in history. Only a historicization of dialectic, I argue most fully in Chapter 8, can deploy what Hartman calls the Hegelian "affinities" between consciousness and the French Revolution (together with other cultural phenomena) in such a way that the power of the apocalyptic reading can be extended integrally into the whole of Wordsworth's corpus. The alpha and omega of Wordsworth's apocalypse, I believe, is the recognition that history was there before, and will be there after, the agony of consciousness.

4. The best work on the 1790 tour is now Donald E. Hayden's, which appeared too late for me to make full use of it. In grasping the details and total shape of the 1790 trip, I am indebted primarily to Havens, pp. 418–34; MM, 1: 128–149; and *CEY*, pp. 97–115. D. Hayden (*passim*) and Havens (pp. 420–23) include maps of the trip.

5. I have written elsewhere on the problem of linear repetition ("Toward a Theory of Common Sense") and have noted that my mediate guide is Continental thought on repetition, most notably the work of Derrida, and my primary immediate guide, J. Hillis Miller ("Ariadne's Thread" and *Fiction*). I should add in my current context a secondary—but more specific —immediate guidance: Stuart Peterfreund's fascinating "Seriality and Cen-

tered Structure in Wordsworth's Later Poetry." In the view I express here, the seriality of the later poetry is built into the structure of tour experience itself.

6. On other travel literature that may have guided Wordsworth's trip, see MM, 1: 128, 135; D. Hayden, pp. 103–7; *DS*, p. 5.

7. Describing "the steep horrid roughness of the Wood" and "the gentle calmness of the flood," Denham observes, "Such huge extreams when Nature doth unite, / Wonder from thence results, from thence delight" (p. 79).

8. Bowles explains the melancholy cast of his sonnets in his 1800 Preface by saying: "They who know [the author], know the occasions of [his poems] to have been real; to the publick he might only mention the sudden death of a deserving young woman" (p. vii).

9. On Wordsworth's 1790 letter in the context of the picturesque, see Heffernan, *Wordsworth's Theory*, pp. 17–18; Spector, pp. 92–93.

10. Coxe's attention to Swiss history is too extensive to be fully documented; an example of his commentary, matched by a note on the post-Revolutionary situation, is Letter 17 as published in an 1812 edition. Here, description of the 1444 battle between the Swiss and French near Basel is compared to the French-instigated revolution in Basel leading ultimately to the Helvetic Republic (pp. 697–700, 697n).

11. I follow the lead of Weiskel, pp. 150–51 and *passim*, in allowing myself to be influenced here by Lacan, whose mirror paradigm and concept of the imaginary hold out enormous potential for extending psychoanalytic study of Wordsworth beyond the elementary Freud. In Lacan's terms, Wordsworth's nature becomes a mirror rejecting the order of the "symbolic" in favor of the "imaginary." The "imaginary" is epitomized in the moment the infant first identifies itself with its image in the mirror/mother of objective existence without awareness of difference (the self "out there" becomes a more definite version of the uncoordinated subject standing before the mirror). The specular, external "self," in other words, is not known to be merely a signifier and so subordinate to a collective convention of signification, to history. By contrast, the symbolic, in Lacan's generalization of the Oedipal crux, is the realm in which acceptance of a collective authority (named the Father, or Law) demonstrates to the subject standing before the mirror that his external image is indeed a signifier like all other social selves, enrolled in a system over which individuals have little control. The self sees itself in history, and knows that the "I" it enacts "out there" is alienated by convention from the true subject who does the enacting. In Book 6 it is not so much that Wordsworth has not yet glimpsed the collective authority of history as that he denies it, represses it behind an "imaginary" mirror/mother of nature, a one-way mark, veil, or boundary. I draw generally upon *Ecrits*, but with special reference to pp. 1–7. Lemaire's *Jacques Lacan* has been especially helpful in elucidating Lacan's difficult writing.

12. I originally wrote this chapter before the advent of the New Historicism and before I read Stephen Greenblatt's excellent *Renaissance Self-Fashioning*. Any discussion of Holbein's *Ambassadors* in a literary or cultural studies context must now take account of Greenblatt's suggestive use of this picture, which he reproduces on his cover and applies as a crucial para-

digm (esp. pp. 17–27). Greenblatt's focus is on the disruptive and estranging power of the anamorphic skull in the foreground: "To see the large death's-head requires a . . . radical abandonment of what we take to be 'normal' vision; we must throw the entire painting out of perspective in order to bring into perspective what our usual mode of perception cannot comprehend" (p. 19). A curious fact is that in teaching the painting in my British Studies course over the years, I have noticed that students seeing the painting in a slide presentation consistently and immediately identify the skull without any prompting or desire to look at the painting from the side (unless this is suggested to them) or real surprise ("That's a memento mori, isn't it?" is a stock response). Does Holbein's picture appear less tricky to modern viewers accustomed to inventive video techniques, or was the picture ever as radically unsettling as Greenblatt suggests? The whole issue of what constitutes the "trickiness" of trick pictures in any age is of interest. Besides the approaches of Arnheim or Gombrich, it would be useful to inquire into the social, political, and economic determinations of trickiness. When and for what reasons, for example, did Machiavellian *virtù* acquire its modern connotations of political trickiness so that viewers of statecraft on television news, a sort of modern *Ambassadors*, now often *look* for signs of cosmetic and other trickiness?

13. See Baker, pp. 113–43.

14. Paulson has studied the representational structure of contemporary British reactions to the Revolution in his *Representations of Revolution*. I was able to read early sections of Paulson's manuscript—including the chapter that previously appeared as "Burke's Sublime and the Representation of Revolution," in Perez Zagorin, ed., *Culture and Politics from Puritanism to the Enlightenment* (Berkeley, Calif., 1980)—in time to make use of it in the following discussion. Paulson's work here and elsewhere has particularly made me aware of the richness in the verbal/visual seam. I regret that Lynn Hunt's *Politics, Culture, and Class in the French Revolution*, with its suggestive discussion of the rhetoric, symbolism, and imagery of revolution, did not appear in time for me to draw upon it in the argument below.

15. See Herbert (p. 71 and accompanying illustration). See also Paulson on David (*Representations*, pp. 28–36, 260). The oath motif of upraised arms was standard in the Revolution's visual representation of itself, appearing also, for example, on the medal commemorating the Federation (see the design in Sagnac and Robiquet, p. 230).

16. For the congruence between the towers of the Bastille and dances in the round, see the illustrations in Hampson, *French Revolution*, pp. 72–73. For the Bastille as an open-air dance hall, see the illustration in Henderson, p. 144. Contemporary engravings of the July 14 Fete on the Champ-de-Mars are plentiful; for ones displaying the dance-like military evolutions, see Hampson, *French Revolution*, p. 86; Henderson, p. 141. See also Henderson, p. 142, for a contemporary report of the circles formed by cavorting soldiers at the Champ-de-Mars. For a view of Federation in the Arras square, with its central altar resembling that at the Paris fete, see the engraving in DHotel, p. 197.

17. I abbreviate considerably the conclusions in Ozouf's chapter, "*La fête et l'espace,*" pp. 149–87.

18. *Collection Complète des Tableaux Historiques de la Révolution Française,* 1:

155. The narrations of the Paris Fete of Federation and preceding events in this work and in Sagnac and Robiquet, pp. 222–34, are particularly full and vivid.

19. "*Celui qui s'élève, on l'abaissera; / Et qui s'abaisse, on l'élèvera*" (Sagnac and Robiquet, p. 224). On the festivity coupled with "contained violence" of the preparations for the Paris Fete, see Ozouf's chapter on "*La fête de la Fédération: le modèle et les réalités.*"

20. See the reproduction of *The Tree of Freedom, 1789* on the cover of Burke, *Reflections* (O'Brien edition).

21. Such collective imagination was not imaginary in Lacan's sense because Revolutionary propaganda was not innocent of awareness that the Fete was a grand signifier rather than uncontaminated reality. From the first, the Revolution's under-narrative of verbalization was grounded in historical process, in an Oedipal rather than pre-Oedipal struggle to destroy the fathering conventions, fetes, decorums, and art works of the *ancien régime* so that the collective Law behind society could be renamed "People" instead of "Father/King." As seen in the time's prodigious experiments in costumes, personal names, names of streets, and so forth, the Revolution took place in the sphere of the historically activated signifier rather than that of the referential sign identified timelessly with reality. Until the 1803 legislation regulating the explosion of names, for example, one named oneself Betterave, Raisin, or Tournesol (Garaud and Szramkiewicz, p. 16) not in naive imagination of man as nature but in rejection of the oppressive past and its restrictions binding names to place, class, and religion. (On naming and renaming, see Robiquet, pp. 55–64; and Garaud and Szramkiewicz, pp. 9–19. See also Paulson, *Representations*, pp. 15–16.)

22. Schneider, pp. 165–66. Schneider notes Wordsworth's particular attention to the description of beehive society in the fourth *Georgic*.

23. Paulson remarks with regard to Constable, "It is well . . . to remember the political dimension of the georgic poem: the symbol of regeneration becomes the rusted sword or the soldier's rotting corpse turned up by the plough, and civil war always casts a shadow over harvest" (*Literary Landscape*, p. 131). My understanding of the historical implications of georgic is greatly enriched by Wilkinson.

24. Coleridge's criticism of the line, "Descending from the mountain to make sport," helps confirm that there is some instability in the text here: "This line I would omit; as it clearly carries on the metaphor of the Lion, and yet is contradictory to the idea of a 'tamed' Lion. 'to make sport' *etc.* is here at once the proof of his having been 'tamed' and the object of his 'descending from the mountains,' which appear incompatible" (quoted in *Prel.*, pp. 276–77n). Wordsworth's Lion is only insecurely tame.

25. As Reed notes, there is a slight possibility that 6c was "composed," if not actually written, in 1799, the date given upon publication of the passage as "The Simplon Pass" in 1845. But other evidence makes it much more likely that 6c was composed with 6a and 6b in 1804 (*CEY*, pp. 31, 261 and n). Hartman uses the 1799 date for 6c in *WP*, pp. 48, 63.

26. Gates studies Wordsworth's use of rivers as images of history in "Wordsworth and the Course of History." Partly under the guidance of R. G. Collingwood, she also speaks of the historical imagination in "The Prelude and the Development of Wordsworth's Historical Imagination," but

her approach is to make historical imagination a secondary faculty, in addition to "apocalyptic imagination."

27. Turner's *Snowstorm: Hannibal and His Army Crossing the Alps*, exhibited in 1812, provides an analogue of the combined mimesis and effacement of Napoleon I indicate here. Napoleon is nowhere to be seen in Turner's celebrated landscape of human diminishment—no more so than Hannibal himself. But as Lynn R. Matteson shows, such invisibility is not simple absence. Relevant are Turner's earlier sketches on the Hannibal theme and the link between *Hannibal and His Army Crossing the Alps* and ancient British, as well as contemporary French, history (made more pointed, perhaps, by Turner's private viewing of David's *Napoleon at the St. Bernard Pass* in Paris in 1802, coupled with general British interest in the 1809 uprising against Napoleon in the Tyrolean Alps; Matteson, esp. pp. 393–96). These factors allow us to posit—i.e., to hypothesize and further confirm or disprove—the absence of Napoleon with a precision we usually reserve for positive fact. The absence of the Emperor known as the contemporary Hannibal may be firm enough, indeed, to shape the very landscape: imperial absence is the vortex, or revolution, that is Turner's totalitarian vision of nature. With assured relevance, then, we see in *Hannibal and His Army Crossing the Alps* the fact that the man who would cross nature—in more than one sense—is definitively *not* there. He has been crossed out. (On the link between Turner's painting and Napoleon, see also Lindsay, p. 118; Butlin and Joll, p. 89; Kroeber, "Experience as History," p. 329; and Heffernan, *Re-Creation*, p. 85. Heffernan compares Rousseau's account of his Alpine passage, which invokes Hannibal, with Wordsworth's account of Simplon; Heffernan's comments about the intimations of history at Simplon—specifically the history of Hannibal's crossing—are consonant with my own views; *Re-Creation*, pp. 65–67.)

28. See, for example, Ashton, pp. 5–11 and *passim*.

29. Contemporary accounts of Napoleon and the Napoleonic years will be cited when used; I have also benefited from modern accounts, the two most helpful for my purposes being those by Sydenham and D. Chandler.

30. Since publishing an early version of this chapter in 1984, I have discovered Mary Jacobus's excellent 1983 essay, " 'That Great Stage Where Senators Perform': *Macbeth* and the Politics of Romantic Theater." In arguing the "dangerous theatricality of the imagination," Jacobus anticipates many of the points I make in the following discussion about Wordsworth's use of Macbeth, including the linkage between Macbeth and the concept of usurpation (p. 356) and between Macbeth and Robespierre (p. 363).

31. On political differences in British attitudes toward Napoleon after the usurpation, see Maccunn.

32. The 1802 volume of *AR* appeared in 1803. For the usage of "usurper" and "usurpation" in *T* in 1804, see the issues of Apr. 16 and 20; May 30; June 2; Nov. 19. (The Nov. 19 issue brands Napoleon a "usurper" five times within the space of a single column.) On the image of Napoleon in English periodicals of 1804, the year of his coronation as Emperor, see also Chapter 8 below.

33. On the troops at Simplon, see D. Chandler, p. 276 and p. 168 map; also Thiers, p. 214. *AR* for 1800 (published 1801) gives a brief contemporary notice of the movement through Simplon (1800: 190). Bonaparte had

originally designed his main crossings for Simplon and Mount St. Gotthard (D. Chandler, p. 274). For an appreciation of the strategic concerns that caused him to shift his emphasis from these two most northern passes, see Thiers, pp. 201–2. Simplon was one of the passes Napoleon continued to hold after his crossing in order to secure his avenues of retreat (Thiers, pp. 211, 221). Convenient maps of the campaign may be found in D. Chandler, pp. 168, 272–73; Sydenham, p. 245. There is also one other intriguing resemblance between Napoleon's and Wordsworth's crossings that I have not pursued. This is the extent to which Napoleon at Great St. Bernard was precisely a tourist. Besides the breaking down of the artillery, the most famous episodes from the crossing in nineteenth-century lore concerned Napoleon's conversations with his native guide and with the monks at the hospice in Great St. Bernard. See, for example, the highly novelistic rendering of Napoleon and his guide in Abbott, p. 320.

34. According to *AR*, 1800: 192. But D. Chandler notes that the Fort, though essentially bypassed, held out until June (p. 280).

35. Abbott's 1855 biography of Napoleon shows the influence of Romanticism even more strikingly. Relating the superhuman devotion and love of the cannoneers for their guns in the Great St. Bernard pass, Abbott writes: "It was the genius of Napoleon which thus penetrated these mysterious depths of the human soul, and called to his aid those mighty energies. 'It is nothing but imagination,' said one once to Napoleon. '*Nothing but imagination!*' he rejoined. '*Imagination rules the world*'" (p. 318).

CHAPTER TWO

1. For Simpson's specific focus on Hartman's *Wordsworth's Poetry*, which prepared "the way for the deconstructionist enterprise" (Simpson's main target in his essay), see "Criticism," pp. 69–70. Simpson's recent *Wordsworth's Historical Imagination* and "Literary Criticism and the Return to 'History'" are also highly relevant to my enterprise in this book, but appeared too late for me to use them alongside his other works (see my forthcoming review essay on *Wordsworth's Historical Imagination* and the New Historicism in Romantic studies for a fuller appreciation).

2. As Kenneth Johnston has argued, the challenge Wordsworth faced in *The Prelude* was the *linked* irruption of Revolution and Imagination (*Wordsworth and "The Recluse,"* p. 115). "The reconciliation of these two forces," Johnston comments, "was for Wordsworth a task equal in magnitude to the composition of all the individual lines" of the poem (p. 119). I regret that in writing this book I was not able to read Johnston's expansively conceived and meticulously argued *Wordsworth and "The Recluse"* in time to make a difference. Through the vagaries of compositional history, the chapters of my book (1, 7–8) that would have gained the most from Johnston's work were among the earliest pieces written. At one stage, I entertained the ambition of going back and (as has proved practicable in the case of smaller recent works) revising to take detailed account of Johnston—particularly of his acute and sustained scrutiny of the tense relations between mind and history in Wordsworth. But the press of life has awakened me to the reality of the present, unsatisfactory *über*-note. A reader with the endurance to read in one

view Johnston's book and my own would benefit from considering at least the following pairings: (1) the overall argument of my work and Johnston's commentary that "the philosophy informing *The Recluse* shifts, during the three main stages of its active compositional existence . . . , from an initial phase in which human mental consciousness is presented in strongly ambivalent tension with its socio-physical contexts . . . ; through a dialectically contrary stage in which, in the form of the artist's creative imagination, it acts as if radically independent of material limitation . . . ; to a tertiary compromise between acts of mind and their necessary containment and conservation in the social, educational, and religious institutions of human civilization" (p. 15); (2) my Chapter 1 and Johnston's discussions of Book VI of *The Prelude*; (3) my Chapter 7 and Johnston's views on the Pedlar and *The Ruined Cottage*; (4) my Chapter 8 and Johnston's commentary on the Revolution books in *The Prelude*; and (5) my section on verbal "shifters" in *The Prelude* (also Chapter 8) and Johnston's discussion of the rhetorical reversals set in motion by the "Was it for this?" lead-in to the same poem (pp. 62–65).

On apocalyptic imagination and Simplon, see also Abrams, "English Romanticism," pp. 108–10. Bloom, "The Internalization of Quest-Romance," pp. 19–20, is also relevant to the internalized apocalypse of history I have studied in Simplon.

3. Marianne Dekoven's essay "History as Suppressed Referent in Modernist Fiction" is congruent with my thesis (partly because Fredric Jameson is a common influence). Her conclusion is especially resonant: "The complex, powerful techniques of figuration available to modernist fiction writers allowed them simultaneously to turn away from the devastating facts of modern history—a gesture of survival as well as of denial—and at the same time to render those facts with greater power than direct representation would give. Because they simultaneously muffle and assert the historical referent, these fictions make us experience it as an unassimilable, subterranean dissonance, denying us any illusion of clarity, mastery, or resolution. Any content that insists on remaining unclear, unmastered, unresolved is far more troubling, persistently troubling, and therefore powerful, than that which can be understood, assimilated, explained—it stays with us, undermining complacency, demanding attention. In the very act of suppressing history, these modernist fictions make it subversive" (pp. 150–51). Dekoven's view of modernist time will also be relevant to my project: "The actual depredations of contemporary history are eternalized as the universal depredations of Time" (p. 150). I might also mention here Peter Brooks's study of Stendhal's *The Red and the Black* in his *Reading for the Plot*: "But if politics is the indelible tracer dye in the social and narrative codes of the novel, the very force of the political dynamic is matched by the intensity with which it is repressed. For to admit to the force of the political is to sanction a process of change, of temporal slippage and movement forward —of history, in fact—whereas the codes of the Restoration are all overtly predicated on temporal analepsis, a re-creation within history of an ahistorical past, a facsimile Ancien Régime that rigorously excludes the possibility of change, of revolution" (p. 70). Also congruent with my approach is James Chandler's emphasis upon the strategies of "disguise, distortion, and dislocation" by which Wordsworth "veiled" the Burkean "second nature"

in his poetry (pp. xviii–xxii) and Morse Peckham's suggestive work on Romanticism and history as "inaccessibility" (esp. pp. 40–66). (Weiskel, as previously stated in n. 2 to Chapter 1, is relevant as well to the "negative" approach to Wordsworth.) For Marxist discussions of the negative presence of history in literature, see below.

4. See n. 3 to Chapter 1 on Hartman's model of mystic pilgrimage. A fuller account of the connection between Simplon and the conversion experience would begin by grounding Wordsworth's poem in the tradition of confessional literature; see Richard E. Brantley, *Wordsworth's "Natural Methodism,"* and Frank McConnell, *The Confessional Imagination.* See also Chapter 8 below on the exegetical dimension of autobiography.

5. Joseph Fouché and Pierre-Gaspard ("Anaxagoras") Chaumette, in their capacity as Convention deputies-at-large, propagated the extremist de-Christianizing movement in Paris and the provinces in 1793. The movement began in the Nièvre (on the Loire just southeast of the Orléans region in which Wordsworth summered in 1792) when Fouché enacted a series of antisacral decrees in September and October, including the one that ordered the raising of this widely known motto over area cemeteries. Chaumette, with whom Carlyle associates the "Eternal Sleep" motto (2:293), then helped Hébert spread many of the antisacral ideas to other provinces and to Paris, where, *EM* for Nov. 1793 notes, the motto was also raised. See also Soboul, pp. 346–49; Hampson, *Social History,* pp. 202–5.

6. Simpson's excellent *Wordsworth and the Figurings of the Real* is consonant with the overall view of Wordsworth I suggest here. The sense of history, as I sketch it, involves a mode of antithetical reference to the real that subsumes figuration. In Simpson's terms: for Wordsworth there is first a discovery of figuration and of the self as maker of figures that appropriates history for Imagination. But in the later poetry there is a contrary effort to surrender private or subjective figuration back to the consensual "Real." Indeed, the socialization, or what I will call "collection," of the self's figures alongside conventional figurations *composes* the Real. While figuration is a denial of collective reality, in short, it is also in the end a deep acknowledgment that reality *is* historicized figuration. I should also mention R. F. Storch's "The Politics of the Imagination," whose fundamental argument that "the very concept of imagination becomes otiose unless it means an access of knowledge through the engagement with historical reality" (pp. 449–50) proceeds partly through a comparison of Coleridge's thought with dialectic. Storch's view of the philosophical idealism and "faith, vision, aestheticism" (pp. 450–51) that finally turn Coleridge's imagination away from history is consonant with my notion of Wordsworth's denial—with the exception that the deep "ambivalence" Storch sees in such a turn (p. 456) seems to me a necessary part of the sense of history itself. Denial of history, whether through figuration or ideal abstraction, is part of the process of knowing history.

7. In my paper on "The Power of Formalism: The New Historicism." I also discuss the New Historicism briefly in Chapter 9, but since I was well into this book before the movement became widely known after about 1983, I have not been able to address its underlying assumptions as centrally or in a manner as integrated throughout with my argument as I would like.

Speaking broadly, my own stance toward the New Historicism is akin to my view of formalism proper: I am both implicated and critical. Though I cannot summarize my paper on the subject here, I should say that the formalism of power appears to me at once the insight and the blindness of the method. By "insight and blindness" I advert not only to the deep congruence between the New Historicism—especially in the practice of Stephen Greenblatt or Louis Montrose—with de Manian deconstruction (together with underlying sediments of New Criticism) but to the *Romantic* paradigms that undergird so much of formalist and deconstructive theory itself. One missing ingredient in the still under-theorized work of the New Historicism is a recognition of the extent to which it participates in what McGann calls Romantic ideology. The blindness and insight of the method, it may be said, is its Romanticization of the Renaissance (more fully: its freight of nineteenth- and twentieth-century critical assumptions generally). In the work of Greenblatt or Montrose, which I read with admiration, this freight of nineteenth- and twentieth-century preoccupations both insistently comes to the fore in a thematized manner and is quickly shunted aside. The preoccupation with May 1968 or 1970 (more fully: the conflicted role of the intellect in the sequence of revolutions from 1789 on) is what underlies the formal abstractions of "ambiguity," "subversion," and so forth that allow the method (as I intimate below) to differentiate itself as a modernity separate from—but also equivocally authorized by—the Renaissance. The New Historicism, in part, is a romanticized wish for the renaissance of intellect. The measure of my own implication is that I have not myself been able in this book to manifest my cargo of modernity fully. Though I make an attempt in my theoretical discussions, I recognize that I at last point—and only point—to a ship about to come in on the far horizon. Witness, for example, the modern/postmodern metaphor of refugee consciousness that at times haunts this book. Like the Epilogue to Greenblatt's *Renaissance Self-Fashioning*, my own Epilogue will be an attempt to make restitution to the desires and resistances that combine to quarantine my ship of modernity, my own fugitivism of intellect, on the horizon.

8. Highly relevant to the issues I raise here is Philippe Carrard's intriguing study of the quotation mark and its postmodern assumptions in *Annales*-style history after the late 1960's. It may be noted here, with a wry nod to my editors, that the major stylistic problem I wrestled with in reviewing the copy editing of this book was the overuse of quotation marks, which I have since attempted to purge. Should we speak of Wordsworth's nature, for example, or of "nature"? And if we choose the latter option to highlight the constructed nature of the concept (see Carrard on this issue), should we also pursue the practice to its reductio ad absurdum by placing "Wordsworth" himself in destabilizing quotation marks when addressing the construction of his "self"? The answer to these questions hinges upon the degree of our own self-reflexivity as critics: to what degree should we advertise our own implication in or detachment from our object of study?

9. Recall the anxiety of verification Wordsworth experiences in his Paris hotel room, where he needs to "feel and touch" the September Massacres, "a substantial dread" (10.66). The impact of history, we might say, is precisely that it resists such direct sensory verification and so—as we will see—

demands the invention of new means of verification. Ultimately, time will descend upon Wordsworth like a deus ex machina to reconceptualize the haunting absence of history, making it an "unimaginable touch of Time" ("Mutability") more acceptable to consciousness. (In his essay, "A Touching Compulsion," Hartman has used a psychoanalytic context to compare the poet's urge to touch with reality testing; see p. 350.) Regarding the ambivalence in history that allows it to extend in time or social space, cf. Claudio Guillén: "The historical imagination cannot be defined by the degree to which it is retrospective, past-oriented, memory-bound. It issues just as genuinely from a human being's commitment to his own time, from his involvement in the 'life' around him—the lives, the processes, and the durations that envelop his own" (p. 175). In purely practical terms as well, historical time always overlaps to some extent with social space. In Wordsworth's day, for example, news of events in France or any other locale was always already "historical" in time because the traversal of space by mail took many days (about four to seven days from Paris to the London *Times* in 1792 and 1793). To notice such interdependence between historical time and space is to foreshadow my argument in Part II: as I will suggest, the *philosophical* construct of time is always after-the-fact. It is always consequent to historical experience with its less distinct, everyday notions of time.

10. For Carlyle's flame picture and his evocation of the difficulties of perceiving history, see *French Revolution*, 2: 324–30.

11. See also Jameson, *Political Unconsciousness*, p. 35. As Jameson points out, Althusser uses the concept of absent cause both to criticize Hegelian "expressive causality" (in which cause is always an essence or telos distinct from its phenomenal effects) and to prepare for his own notion of a causality immanent throughout the whole structure of social effects. I use the term absent cause without its critical import here because the transmission of telos (put religiously, the sense of anagogy) will be one of my subjects of study. "History," in this sense, recalls the older historiography according to which human events make sense only when seen to be caused by a logos always hidden within, beyond, or outside human sense. Also informing my thought on denial are other Marxist discussions of history as negative cause. See my use of Macherey below.

12. By "disturbance of ontology" in the Continental context, I mean in particular the clash between idealism and positivism in the middle to late nineteenth century that led to the conciliatory philosophies of history of Dilthey, Collingwood, and others. In the context of British thought, I use the concept of disturbed ontology as shorthand for the late seventeenth- and eighteenth-century hollowing out of the Chain of Being universe with its ordered realities grounded upon a prime mover. Insecurity of faith in being became displaced into the empiricist effort to verify the relation between being and knowing.

It is regrettable that Romantics criticism has in general made so little use of the neo-idealist (or, from the standpoint of early nineteenth-century idealism itself, neo-realist) historiography of Dilthey and Collingwood (esp. Dilthey, pp. 83–112; Collingwood, *Idea of History*, pp. 205–49, 282–302). The effort of both philosophers to embed the mind in historical experience and vice versa could provide a bridgeway between criticism that cherishes

Romantic imagination and criticism that foregrounds the cultural embeddedness of such imagination. Indeed, the potential reconciling of history
and Romantic literature suggested by Dilthey and Collingwood is so striking and full that I can attempt no more than an advertisement. Dilthey's
vision of the *geistige Welt* characterized by its ambience of *Zusammenhang* (or
connectivity) could usefully gloss the "One Life" as well as look forward
to the Russian Formalist notion of "motive" (the principle of connection
in a work) together with its later structuralist elaborations. Collingwood's
rethinking of historical knowledge as the "re-enactment of past thought in
the historian's mind" could similarly gloss Romantic memory. And for both
Dilthey and Collingwood, the crux of philosophy of history lies in a principle of imaginative understanding—a *Verstehen* (Dilthey) or "historical imagination" (Collingwood) sufficiently close to what we mean by Romantic
imagination that it finally issues in autobiography. Thus Dilthey emphasizes
the act of thinking individual lives in autobiography and biography, and
Collingwood not only focuses on acts of imaginative construction modeled
on autobiography and the novel but at last wrote his own celebrated *Autobiography*. (I am much aided in my reading of Dilthey by Michael Ermarth's
highly informative *Wilhelm Dilthey: The Critique of Historical Reason*. For an
approximation of Dilthey's *Verstehen* to "historical imagination" see H. P.
Rickman's Introduction in Dilthey, pp. 43–50. It is instructive that though
Dilthey conceived *Verstehen* to be rooted in the world, it has often been
thought to consist in a mysteriously intuitive flash of insight; see Ermarth,
pp. 241–42, and Rickman's Introduction in Dilthey, p. 40.)

13. On skepticism and deconstruction, see Goodheart.

14. Levinson's excellent overview of recent historicist approaches to the
Romantics in the Introduction to her *Wordsworth's Great Period Poems* is highly
consonant with the method I sketch here in my own terms. Especially apropos is her discussion of "a theory of negative allegory," pp. 8–13.

A fascinating inversion of my intended method of studying denied posi-
tivisms may be found in Erdman's "The Man Who Was Not Napoleon"
together with his subsequent retraction, "Oops! My Misprision!" Where
I study the overdetermined absence of Napoleon, for example, Erdman
studies such absence in positivistic form as the man who was not Napoleon:
"Wordsworth's radical military friend, John Oswald—a man so visible to
his contemporaries that he was mistaken for Napoleon" ("The Man," p. 93).
The relation of denial I sketch between Wordsworth and Napoleon, in other
words, is for Erdman a relation of sympathy with a flesh-and-blood Not-
Napoleon—a sympathy so strong that Erdman speculates the poet might
have been involved in Oswald's plan for a cross-channel attack on London
in autumn 1792. Yet there is a clear excess of negativity in the research necessary for such an argument that Erdman's positive method cannot accommodate. Not only is there no evidence of Wordsworth's enlistment in the
assassination plan (if I read Erdman's "conjecture" correctly, "The Man,"
p. 95), but the effort to implicate the poet by "looking under the carpet of
official history to find 'classified' records" of Oswald ("The Man," p. 93) as
well as generally to trace radicals who use incognitos, "rarely write down
their proposals," and "when they do . . . write in cipher" ("Oops!", p. 202)
begins insidiously to undermine the very feeling of positivity that is the goal

of positive demonstration. In the end, Erdman in "Oops!" confesses that he misapplied a passage in *The Prelude* that he had relied upon to authorize his speculation of Wordsworth's involvement (*Prel.* 10.188–96). My own instincts are entirely consonant with Erdman's in seeking to refer the poetry to historical event (even to the extent of stressing the usefulness of the military context in Chapter 8); and despite my best efforts in gathering, applying, and double-checking facts, it would be unrealistic for me to expect always to be correct. In terms of factual validity, after all, Erdman's book on Blake long ago helped set the standard for historically oriented literary study. But by emphasizing poetry's *denial* of fact, I hope to work with, rather than against, the grain of negativity Erdman encounters. Wordsworth's implication in historical event is a conspiracy that is to be proved by the force of his *not* seeming to be implicated. "Not me!" he says, going incognito under the cipher of Imagination.

15. I include the Russian Formalists here despite their predominant focus on the literary partly to indicate that the genealogy of the notion of cultural context is interwoven with the total fabric of formal and structural thought and partly because the Formalists, together with Propp, were sufficiently interested in the folktale to make literature and popular culture bedfellows. (An example is Shklovsky's interest in erotic tales in "Art as Technique.") Under the gun of ideological scrutiny, of course, the Formalists in their later works increasingly addressed the integration—or potential compatibility—of literary issues and cultural context; see Erlich, pp. 110–39. For the Formalist usage of motive and motif, see Eichenbaum, pp. 119–22; Shklovsky, "Sterne's *Tristram Shandy*," esp. p. 40; and Tomashevsky, esp. pp. 78–87. See also Propp's related usage of "move" in chap. 9 of *Morphology of the Folktale*. Tomashevsky's explanation of motive is especially useful: "The system of motifs comprising the theme of a given work must show some kind of artistic unity. If the individual motifs, or a complex of motifs, are not sufficiently suited to the work, if the reader feels that the relationship between certain complexes of motifs and the work itself is obscure, then that complex is said to be superfluous. If all the parts of the work are badly suited to one another, the work is *incoherent*. That is why the introduction of each separate motif or complex of motifs must be *motivated*. The network of devices justifying the introduction of individual motifs or of groups of motifs is called *motivation*" (p. 78). Tynjanov's development of such notions as "network of devices" into a structural concept touching upon social conventions (for example, in "On Literary Evolution") demonstrates the firm connection between later Russian Formalism and the culturally oriented structuralism that Lévi-Strauss, Barthes (in *Mythologies* or in the "cultural codes" of *S/Z*), and Foucault have since deployed. (I also use "motif" in Chapter 3 in its art-historical sense, which, by way of Wölfflin, may have influenced the Russian Formalists; see Eichenbaum, p. 104, and Erlich, pp. 59–60, 274, on the Formalists and Wölfflin.)

16. William Keach's paper on "Arbitrary Power: Romanticism and the Politics of Language," presented Oct. 11, 1986, at Northwestern University has greatly aided my thought during the late stages of revision on this chapter. Keach's excellent discussion of the political and other torsions in the

Saussurean concept of the arbitrary—together with the anticipations of such torsions in the work of writers from Locke through the Romantics—set me to applying the concepts of the arbitrary and the determinate to the problem of reference. Especially suggestive for my discussion below is Keach's consideration (informed by the work of Tony Bennett and Jonathan Culler) of Saussure's views on the historical determination of language. Also relevant is Keach's discussion of Emile Benveniste's critique of Saussure. Benveniste, Keach notes, finds in Saussure a surreptitious grounding of arbitrary signification on referential reality.

17. The symmetrical opposition of the concepts "free" and "determined" represents my attempt to simplify the more complex web of contradiction Keach uncovers. In fact, "arbitrary" may be seen to involve a circle rather than simple binarism of connotation: on the one hand, it implies determination, supervision, and rule; on the other, as Keach shows, it implies an order of willfulness, voluntariness, and capriciousness that in eighteenth-century usage *rounds back* to the notion of determined rule again through the additional concept of *tyrannical* capriciousness.

18. In more elaborate form, this schema might be visualized as something like Lévi-Strauss's "totemic operator" (*Savage Mind*, p. 152), which he describes as follows: "The whole set thus constitutes a sort of conceptual apparatus which filters unity through multiplicity, multiplicity through unity, diversity through identity, and identity through diversity. Endowed with a theoretically unlimited extension on its median level it contracts (or expands) into pure comprehension at its two extreme vertices, but in symmetrically reverse forms, and not without undergoing a sort of torsion" (*Savage Mind*, p. 153). However, the linear simplicity of my schema and the more complex but equally geometrical crystal of Lévi-Strauss's operator are perhaps deceptive. In fact, the determined but also free operation of cultural structure—especially at its median level between "reality" and "truth" —might best be thought of as an improvisation founded on, but divergent from, strict regularity (it is what I term "arabesque" below). In my paper on the "Power of Formalism: The New Historicism," I discuss more generally the dual paradigms of what I call the "governing line" and the "disturbed array" in current cultural studies.

19. As Ermarth points out, pp. 334–38, it is often charged that Dilthey's notion of world-views is relativist. My use of the Saussurean "arbitrary" to define the inner dialectic of his world-views is meant to harness this charge usefully. World-views are as relative and arbitrary as language, and thus just as determinate as well.

20. It would be inviting to consider in more depth the complex parallel between Dilthey and Saussure. In this quote, the exact nature of the parallel would depend on how we read Dilthey's view of the relationship between the comparative philology of the earlier nineteenth century and the new historicization of language associated with the Neogrammarians after the 1870's. The qualification of the comparatist perspective effected by the latter movement directly anticipated Saussure. See Saussure, pp. 1–5; Culler, *Ferdinand de Saussure*, pp. 65–85.

21. Tomashevsky, pp. 84–87, discusses defamiliarization and motivation.

22. For a useful introduction to the *Annales* school and history of mentalities as well as such practitioners of history of mentalities outside the *Annales* circle as Ariès and Foucault, see Hutton.

23. Braudel's view of the differential relation of structures is conflicted and problematic. On the one hand, he recognizes that allowing for various levels of temporal structure can lead to the dispersed structures of such sociologists as Georges Gurvitch. But on the other, he desires a "historian's" vision of unified time binding all the structures together (see pp. 47–50). The result is the fractured uniformity of a statement such as the following: "A structural social crisis should be equally possible to locate in time, and through it. We should be able to place it exactly, both in itself and even more in relation to the movement of associated structures. What is profoundly interesting to the historian is the way these movements cross one another, and how they interact, and how they break up: all things which can be recorded only in relation to the uniform time of historians, which can stand as a general measure of all these phenomena, and not in relation to the multiform time of social reality, which can stand only as the individual measure of each of these phenomena separately" (p. 49). See also Hall, pp. 114–18, on this subject.

24. For convenience I have centered my discussion of Foucault's theory on the *Archaeology*, in which he achieves a measure of panopticism in regard to his earlier work. But other parts of his corpus would serve just as well. Particularly useful to my work is the exposition of genealogical method in "Nietzsche, Genealogy, History"—e.g.: "the historical sense can evade metaphysics and become a privileged instrument of genealogy if it refuses the certainty of absolutes. Given this, it corresponds to the acuity of a glance that distinguishes, separates, and disperses, that is capable of liberating divergence and marginal elements—the kind of dissociating view that is capable of decomposing itself, capable of shattering the unity of man's being through which it was thought that he could extend his sovereignty to the events of his past" (pp. 152–53).

25. McGann addresses the problem of referentiality in his "Introduction: A Point of Reference," where he argues a thesis of reference as difference: "What art 'imitates,' then, what it 'has reference to,' is [the] totality of human changes in all its diverse and particular manifestations. Since the totality neither is nor ever can be *conceptually* completed, however, art works must always intersect with it at a differential. That is to say, art must establish its referential systems—including its reference to the totality—in the forms of dynamic particulars which at once gesture toward the place of these particulars in the ceaseless process of totalization, and also assert their freedom within the process. Such freedom is relational, and it illustrates a key element in the maintenance of the process of dynamic totalization: that the particulars which are to count in art, the particular acts, events, circumstances, details, and so forth, along with the textualizations through which they are constituted, are those which in fact *make (and/or have made) a difference*—particulars which will be seen to have been (and to be still) positively engaged in processes of change. . . . The reader's attention will be drawn, via such details, to the socially located tensions and contradictions, as well as the responses to such things, which poetry imitates and partici-

pates in. In art and poetry these particulars always appear as *incommensurates*: details, persons, events, which the work's own (reflected) conceptual formulas and ideologies must admit, but which they cannot wholly account for" (pp. 13–14). See also McGann's discussion of the determined and determinative in this essay (p. 14) as well as his commentary in *Romantic Ideology* on the way Romantic poems "occlude and disguise" historical reference through a tissue of "erasures and displacements" (pp. 82, 85). A particularly resonant phrase occurs on p. 90 of *Romantic Ideology*: "For Wordsworth's poem does not actually transcend the evils it is haunted by, it merely occupies them at the level of consciousness." Like an occupying army, we may say, the poetry vanquishes historical reference only to occupy the same land with all its tensions.

D. Simpson's discussion of referentiality in his recent work is also consonant with mine. In "Criticism" he asserts that it is precisely the formal discontinuities and disjunctions of Wordsworth's poetry that allow it to refer to historical contexts that are themselves discontinuous (pp. 53–54). A "poem cannot refer to a world that is not itself subject to the same problems of projection and displacement that effect the construction (creative) and elucidation (critical) of the poem's language," he argues (p. 73). The method by which poetry does refer to such discontinuous context is negative. It is the "*silence* of the poem on certain questions" (p. 58), its emptiness of felt historical weight (p. 59), and the seemingly indeterminate "contest of significations" in its language that communicate historical context's own polemical contests and collisions (p. 67). Put another way: it is the play of language that exhibits historicity and "definite referentiality" (p. 59). See also Simpson's discussion of the "articulateness in . . . inconclusiveness" or the "aesthetics and ethics of indeterminacy" in Wordsworth's poetry ("What Bothered Charles Lamb," pp. 591, 607, and *passim*).

My own emphasis is on the referentiality not of Wordsworth's occlusions, erasures, or displacements so much as on his denials. In avoiding for the most part the vocabulary of displacement, that is, I intend a difference in connotation. Displacement suggests a little too much *glissade* for my purposes—a little too much of arbitrarily free indirection and not enough of stubbornly determined and overdetermined opposition. By "denial" I mean to charge the notion of displacement with as much agon, contestation, and affective weight as possible. As I will argue, it is such agon, manifested through what McGann calls incommensurates and I will call phenomenal spots of history, that first issues on the level of generic form as *narrative*. The historicity of Wordsworth's poetry is best observed in its effort then to gentle agon by transforming or repudiating narrative. In this regard, the Romanticist I myself feel the closest affiliation with is Levinson, whose work agrees with mine both in its texture and in the felt connotation it often imparts to poetry's displacements. In her chapter on the "Intimations" Ode, for example, Levinson phrases displacement as "repudiation" and "refusal" (*Wordsworth's Great Period Poems*, pp. 81–83). It would be tempting to stage as chorus here Faulkner's Ike McCaslin, whose usage of "repudiation" in the episode of the genealogical ledger in *Go Down, Moses* (pp. 255–73) evokes exactly the agonized denial of history I seek to define. Indeed, Levinson's explanation of poetic displacement in her chapter on "Michael" draws upon the same Biblical aura of historicity and denied historicity that Faulkner mines. Much of what I mean by denial may be read in the transumed *Akedah*—that great narrative of Abraham's agon and its elision through figure and paradox—that she isolates at the heart of the ideological substitutions in "Michael" (*Wordsworth's Great Period Poems*, pp. 58–79). Generalizing the paradigm to fit *The Prelude*, we may say that Wordsworth binds his younger or Isaac-self to history through the action of memory and then, in a rigor of poetic ritual, releases that self from history. An angel of prophetic Imagination comes at the moment of imminent sacrifice during the Revolution in Book 10 and commands: Lay not thine hand upon him. A ram is offered up instead, and the name of the ram, as we will witness in Chapter 8, is Robespierre (together with more loved stand-ins: the poet's old schoolteacher and Coleridge). Such is the story of historical bind and substitutive release that is Wordsworth's Genesis. (Hartman, of course, first offered up the episode of the *Akedah* in a different manner as the paradigm for Wordsworth's avoidance of apocalyptic Imagination, *WP*, pp. 225–26.)

26. Eagleton's comment in *Criticism*, p. 72, is instructive here: history enters a text "as a presence determined and distorted by its measurable absences. This is not to say that the real history is present in the text but in disguised form. . . . It is rather that history is 'present' in the text in the form of a *double-absence*. The text takes as its object, not the real, but certain significations by which the real lives itself—significations which are themselves the product of its partial abolition. . . . For the text presents itself to us less as historical than as a sportive flight from history, a reversal and resistance of history, a momentarily liberated zone in which the exigencies of the real seem to evaporate, an enclave of freedom enclosed within the realm of necessity. We know that such freedom is largely illusory—that the text is *governed*; but it is not illusory merely in the sense of being a false perception of our own. The text's illusion of freedom is part of its very nature—an effect of its peculiarly *overdetermined* relation to historical reality."

27. Cf. Jameson's concept of the "logic of content" (*Marxism and Form*, pp. 327–40). Much excellent work has been done recently on Wordsworth and the mutations of genre by Clifford Siskin ("Romantic Genre," "The Un-Kind Imagination"), Stuart Peterfreund ("*The Prelude*: Wordsworth's Metamorphic Epic"), and Mary Jacobus ("The Law of/and Gender"). I will draw upon these works especially in Part III. Also pertinent is Jay Clayton's excellent discussion of the conflict of narrative and lyric modes in Wordsworth in *Romantic Vision and the Novel*, as well as June Howard's *Form and History in American Literary Naturalism*. In a statement with which I very much agree, Howard writes: "Genre becomes a concept uniquely capable of revealing the interrelations of ideological discourses, cultural practices, and social institutions" (p. 10). Of course, there are many levels of form upon which to base our analytic, ranging from the deployment of Wordsworth's consonants and vowels through his diction, syntax, figures, and higher orders of style. Morse Peckham's comment is apt here: history, he speculates, is inaccessible except through linguistic artifact and, therefore, "it seems reasonable to assert that history is a rhetorical mode, that is, a linguistic overdetermination" (pp. 59–60). While I do not eschew study of overdetermined style at a level of minuteness akin to Freud's thought on

puns, I mean to subordinate the whole series of lesser stylistic devices (or, more precisely, the structure of such devices) to consideration of modes and genres. The issue of how we can "know" such modes and genres, indeed, is precisely parallel to that of how we can know historical contexts. Though I cannot here sketch in full a theory of generic manifestation, it may be useful to indicate that my notion of such manifestation is not directly referential. It is not adequate to say that certain generic indexes (title, metrical or stanzaic form, type of diction, etc.) refer us to the relevant context of generic expectations. Such an explanation leads to an infinite regress because the next question would be: how do we recognize certain details in the text as belonging to the class—that is, genre—of genre-indicators? (See Derrida, "Law of Genre," pp. 59–62.) Only a method of negative reference, it seems to me, can account for genre manifestation. Like the phenomenal spots of history I have postulated (for example, a ruined cottage), certain textual details stand as markers of genre because there is a certain negativity in them, an awareness that they do not belong wholly to the plane of the text but rather to a collision of other contexts of generic expectation in the background (contexts that were themselves originally understood without evidence and solely upon the basis of authority in the manner that a book of poetry placed in a student's hands is "poetic"). The markers that indicate genre, in other words, are constituted by instability in the overall field of genres (cf. my discussion of georgic in Chapter 1). Fowler's definition of genre as quintessentially transformative or dynamic is especially suggestive in this regard (pp. 18, 23, and *passim*). Of course, in explaining Wordsworth's sense of history on the basis of his sense of genre and then explaining the sense of genre by analogy to the sense of history, I depend at last on a notion of explanation as hermeneutic circle. It is never the case that we can ground the sense of history absolutely on a sense of genre or some other modality of knowledge.

28. In this brief view of logic, I draw from Allendoerfer and Oakley; Brennan; and Cohen and Nagel. "A = a" is my improvisation upon the symbolic logic notation "∃x" ("there exists the category specified").

29. White's most directly relevant work is his collection of essays, *The Content of the Form*, which appeared too late for me to make use of it. I have found very helpful, however, "The Value of Narrativity in the Representation of Reality" (which appeared in essay form previous to its inclusion in *The Content of the Form*), *Tropics of Discourse*, and White's sustained exploration of narrative in *Metahistory*. Nevertheless, I look less to White and more in the direction of post-Althusserian Marxism for help in understanding the generic structure of the sense of history. The reason is that I find White's efforts to ground the tropes of historical understanding less useful for my purposes than efforts theorizing the absence of ground itself. The difference is one of emphasis: there is a certain massive stability in White's fourfold tropological scheme that suggests to the reader that there may *be* a positivity, a ground to the whole structure. In a passage that is both indeterminate in its questings and evocative of trust in the more determinate sciences, White poses the question: "Are the tropes intrinsic to natural language? And if so, do they function to provide models of representation and explanation within any field of study not yet raised to the status of a genu-

ine science? Further: is what we mean by 'science' simply a field of study in which one or the other of the tropes has achieved the status of paradigm for the linguistic protocol in which the scientist is constrained to formulate his questions and encode his answers to them? These questions must await the further researches of psychologists and linguists into the generative aspect of language and speech. But it does seem possible to me that what we mean by 'interpretation' can be clarified significantly by further analysis of the modalities of speech in which a given field of perception is rendered provisionally comprehensible by being 'seized' in language" (*Tropics*, p. 74). What comes to the fore in such a passage is a tremendous desire or nostalgia for foundation akin to Newton's for absolute space and time, Einstein's for a connection between microcosmic and macrocosmic phenomena, or Braudel's for uniformity of time (see Chapter 2, n. 23 above). Discourse hovers on the brink of being thought a "natural language."

30. On Collingwood's approximation of historical imagination to the act of writing a novel, see *Idea of History*, pp. 242–46.

31. This question, which is also my epigraph, derives from Robert Penn Warren's "A Conversation with Cleanth Brooks," p. 7. The "Conversation" may best be thought of as a cross between Platonic dialogue and New Journalism. According to Warren, it is the composite and edited result of many conversations between himself and Brooks (L. P. Simpson, pp. 1–2).

BEFORE TIME

1. See especially Lindenberger, *On Wordsworth's "Prelude,"* pp. 131–204; Salvesen, pp. 1–45; Stelzig, *All Shades of Consciousness*, pp. 13–53. For other recent studies of Wordsworthian time, see Baker; Beer, *Wordsworth in Time*, pp. 29–52; and Durrant, pp. 61–86. I have written on the problem of Wordsworthian time from a different perspective in my "On the Autobiographical Present"; see esp. pp. 115–16, 134 n. 4.

2. Poulet, however, also points out that in the Christian Middle Ages corporeal time, which was subject to succession due to a defect in matter (p. 4), and spiritual time were related in an overall stepped tier of "*durations*, ranked one above another" (p. 7).

3. This notion of everyday time as timing is suggested by Foxe's speculations on common sense (pp. 231–32, 261).

4. *An Evening Walk* thus directly anticipates the 1790 letter detailing the picturesqueness of the poet's first Continental trip. See *CEY*, pp. 309–12, and *EW*, pp. 7–8, however, on the difficulty of assigning a *terminus ad quem* for the composition of *An Evening Walk*. In fact, *An Evening Walk* and the 1790 letter may be considered to be at least partially contemporaneous, since Wordsworth probably continued revising the poem up until the time of publication in 1793.

CHAPTER THREE

1. Beatty (*Wordsworth*, pp. 11–28) and Selincourt (*PW*, 1: 320–24) adduce the debt of *An Evening Walk* to John Brown's *Letter to Lord Lyttelton* describ-

ing the Vale of Keswick (first published in 1767 in Newcastle, then popularized when reprinted in London as a note to Dalton's 1768 edition of his *A Descriptive Poem Addressed to Two Ladies at Their Return from Viewing the Mines Near Whitehaven* as well as in the 1774 edition of Hutchinson and the 1780 edition of West; see Hussey, pp. 97–98; Salvesen, p. 53; *Prose*, 2: 400–401n); Gray's journal of his 1769 Lakes tour (first published by William Mason in his *Memoirs of the Life and Writings of Mr. Gray* in 1775); William Hutchinson's *Excursion to the Lakes in Westmoreland and Cumberland* (first published 1774); Thomas West's *Guide to the Lakes* (first published 1778); William Gilpin's *Observations* on the Lakes (first published 1786; cited hereafter as *Lakes*) as well as *Observations* on the Highlands of Scotland (first published 1789); and James Clarke's *Survey of the Lakes* (first published 1787), as well as locodescriptive and georgic poets both British and French. See also Salvesen, p. 53 and notes. For further bibliographical information on the picturesque writers and theorists cited in this chapter, see the notes in Hipple. On editions used in this chapter, see References and n. 6 below.

The evidence of Wordsworth's correspondence shows that he had certainly read Gray's journal of the Lakes by 1794 (*Letters*, 1: 115) and owned Gilpin's *Lakes* and *Observations* of the Highlands of Scotland before 1796 (the latter works, he twice stresses, were particularly expensive; *Letters*, 1: 170, 227). As *An Evening Walk* itself directly attests, he had also read Clarke (ll. 175–90 and Wordsworth's note). The library at Rydal Mount offers later evidence of the importance to Wordsworth of the picturesque tourists and surveyors of the Lakes. The library included the poems of Gray with Mason's memoirs (1776 edition); Gilpin's *Lakes* (1st ed. of 1786 and 2d ed. of 1788); Clarke's *Survey* (2d ed., 1789); West's *Guide* (9th ed., 1807); John Housman's *A Descriptive Tour and Guide to the Lakes, Caves, Mountains . . . in Cumberland, Westmoreland, Lancashire, and a Part of the West Riding of Yorkshire* (2d ed., 1802); and Joseph Nicolson and Richard Burn's *The History and Antiquities of the Counties of Westmorland and Cumberland* (1777 edition)—see the listings in Shaver and Shaver, *Wordsworth's Library*. Also relevant in the library: Gilpin's *Observations On the River Wye* (2d ed., 1789); Thomas Dudley Fosbroke's *The Wye Tour; or, Gilpin on the Wye, with Picturesque Additions* (3d ed., 1826); and Richard Payne Knight's *An Analytical Inquiry into the Principles of Taste* (3d ed., 1806). (The copy of Knight is interesting because, though owned by Coleridge, it bears extensive annotations—mostly of an abusive kind— in Wordsworth's hand; see Shearer. The annotations are longer and much more involved than Wordsworth's characteristic marginalia, and are also evidently Coleridgean in voice and thought. As Julian Lindsay has speculated, they may have been made at the suggestion of, or by dictation from, Coleridge while the latter was incapacitated.) Other books on the Lakes that may have influenced Wordsworth's poem, including pictorial works, will be cited below.

2. Hussey, p. 4, dates the overall period of the picturesque as roughly 1730 to 1830. For our purposes, however, it will make sense to shift this century-window back somewhat to view the hundred years leading up to the conclusion of Wordsworth's great decade and his *Guide* to the Lakes. I will speak of three overlapping periods of the picturesque: the early pictur-

esque from the 1710's through the 1760's (bracketed by the age of Shaftesbury and Pope at one end and of Capability Brown at the other); the high picturesque from about 1770 on in tour literature, the visual arts, and gardening; and, as a special zone within the latter period, the climax of picturesque theory from about 1792 to 1810. The theoretical climax arrived with the publication of Gilpin's *Three Essays* of 1792, Uvedale Price's *An Essay on the Picturesque* of 1794 (later the first volume in the 1810 edition of his *Essays*), Richard Payne Knight's *The Landscape* of 1794 (which Dorothy Wordsworth tells us she was reading in 1800; *DWJ*, p. 31), and Humphry Repton's *A Letter to Uvedale Price* of 1794. It continued through the various stages of the Price-Knight-Repton controversy after 1794 (discussed later in this chapter). And it lasted until about the time of Knight's 1805 *An Analytical Inquiry into the Principles of Taste* or the 1810 edition of Price's *Essays* (now expanded to three volumes). It can be argued that the high picturesque up to the publication of *An Evening Walk* in 1793 (and even slightly later in the case of the revisions to the poem I discuss in Chapter 5) directly influenced Wordsworth. But only an argument of parallel can be made with regard to the contemporaneous peak of picturesque theory after 1792 or 1794. I will thus read these latter theoretical works as commentaries upon the earlier body of picturesque literature and as parallels of *An Evening Walk*. In general, my aim is not so much to argue strict influence between particular picturesque texts and Wordsworth's work (though I will include such argument) but a more substantial and illuminating influence exerted by the picturesque context as a whole. It is to the frictions, transitions, and elisions within this context that we must look to account for the peculiar quality of repose that the picturesque communicated to *An Evening Walk*.

3. Studies of *An Evening Walk* or of Wordsworth's early descriptive verse have generally approached it in either a picturesque or locodescriptive context. Picturesque: see, for example, Heffernan, *Wordsworth's Theory*, pp. 19–20; Watson, *Picturesque*, pp. 65–72; Ramsey, pp. 376–78, 386–89. Locodescriptive or topographical: see Hartman, *WP*, p. 90; Sheats, pp. 49–50. (For contemporary reviews that saw *An Evening Walk* as picturesque, see *EW*, p. 303).

4. James A. W. Heffernan and Karl Kroeber have recently published books on Romantic poetry and art that appeared after I completed this chapter. Heffernan's *The Re-Creation of Landscape* discusses the displacement of history in Romantic poetry and pictures (pp. 54–102) and other topics pertinent to my present interest: for example, Claude's *Hagar and the Angel* in relation to Constable's *Dedham Vale* (pp. 26–29, 100, 105–6), atmosphere (pp. 143–54, 170–81), and reflective waters (pp. 201–24). His title is also suggestive in relation to my own emphasis on the theme of creation and recreation in Claude. Kroeber's *British Romantic Art* discusses history in its insightful argument about the nationalism or "natural patriotism" of the picturesque (pp. 82–104). As my Chapter 8 below will show, I also share Kroeber's interest in applying military theory to Romanticism; see his discussion of Karl von Clausewitz, pp. 105–16.

5. Appleton's inclination in his innovative study is to define the viewer of landscape as an individual *animal* whose experience of "prospect," "hazard," or "refuge" landscapes may be understood in behavioristic terms as an

instinctual response to sign-stimuli in the habitat (p. 69). "Habitat theory," he concludes in a statement of method, "thus asserts that the relationship between the human observer and the perceived environment is basically the same as the relationship of a creature to its habitat" (pp. 69–70). Impelled by the need to explain the connection between Wordsworth's earlier pictur-esque and his later poetry—and, it must be admitted, by different expecta-tions about what constitutes an adequate explanation of human response— my own inclination is to see the viewer of landscape as neither an individual nor animal, but as a *citizen*.

6. A word may be in order here on editions of picturesque works used in this chapter. Because my argument is not limited to strict influence (see n. 2 to this chapter above), I have in general tried to select as my base text the contemporary edition that allows the fullest access to picturesque prac-tice and theory (whether through expansion, revision, or addition of notes and illustrations). Thus, for example, I cite primarily from the 2d ed. of Hutchinson, 1776; the 2d ed. of Knight's *The Landscape*, 1795; and Price's 1810 *Essays*. (In some cases, my base text is also the edition Wordsworth himself cited or owned—for example, the 1789 edition of Clarke. In a few such instances, the text has the extra authority of being the first edition—as in the instance of Gilpin's *Lakes*, 1786.) Where there is a significant differ-ence between the text I quote and earlier editions or the edition Wordsworth used, I will when possible point out the divergence. I should perhaps add, finally, that the literature of the picturesque is itself a little too picturesque to be regulated by any completely consistent bibliographical policy. Limita-tions in my library resources have also in some places contributed to leaving my Palladian dream of bibliography in delightful ruins. Ideally, the *appar. crit.* to this chapter would track for all texts the fullest contemporary edition, the first edition, and Wordsworth's edition. But to apply to bibliography the lament of Johnson: "these were the dreams of a poet doomed at last to wake a lexicographer."

7. Messmann notes Knight's frequent use of sexual analogies (p. 109). Relevant also is the fact that Knight's first publication was the infamous *An Account of the Remains of the Worship of Priapus* (1786). On the work and the reaction it generated, see Messmann, pp. 42–53.

8. The fact that the primary sense of "embattl'd" here may be architec-tural does not change my meaning.

9. As psychologized by Price and Knight, "roughness" was then nervous "irritation" (e.g., Price, *Essays*, 1: 115; Knight, *Landscape*, pp. 20n, 22n).

10. Clarke, whose *Survey of the Lakes* attends throughout to the history of Border violence, similarly refers repeatedly to "violent" winds and falls (e.g., pp. xxxix, xl, 28). Knight is more moderate, but calls "irritation" sometimes "violent" (*Landscape*, p. 20n).

11. As it first appeared in 1794, the last sentence of this extract reads: "A mind in such a state is like a pure and tranquil lake, the slightest impulse on whose surface excites a correspondent motion in its waters, which gently expand themselves on every side" (quoted in Russell, p. 422). Cf. John Brown's poem on night at Keswick, which first appeared in 1776 and should be distinguished from his prose *Letter* on the same locale (see *Prose*, 2: 400–401). Wordsworth quoted the poem in his *Guide* (*Prose*, 2: 193):

Now sunk the sun, now twilight sunk, and night
Rode in her zenith; not a passing breeze
Sigh'd to the grove, which in the midnight air
Stood motionless, and in the peaceful floods
Inverted hung: for now the billows slept
Along the shore, nor heav'd the deep; but spread
A shining mirror to the moon's pale orb,
Which, dim and waning, o'er the shadowy cliffs,
The solemn woods, and spiry mountain tops,
Her glimmering faintness threw: now every eye,
Oppress'd with toil, was drown'd in deep repose. . . .

12. West, pp. 15–16, gives instructions on the use of the Claude glass.

13. Martin Price, in his "Picturesque Moment," pp. 260–61, has formulated the "picturicity" of the picturesque as "the dissociation of visual, pictorial, or generally aesthetic elements from other values in contemplating a scene. This is, in effect, a restriction placed late upon the picturesque and its full import depends upon the values that are observed to be excluded." Later in his essay, M. Price defines picturesque "form" more dynamically than I do here: "[The picturesque] seeks a tension between the disorderly or irrelevant and the perfected form. Its favorite scenes are those in which form emerges only with study or is at the point of dissolution" (p. 277). My stress on the static repose or arrest of picturesque form in part prepares for the contrasting study of the "trembling" of the "locodescriptive moment" later in this chapter.

14. A thorough inquiry into this aspect of art history would need to study not just Claude's repose, which I use to stand generally for seventeenth-century School of Rome "classicism," but also Gaspard Dughet Poussin's compositional balance or harmony and the earlier composure of the Carraccis. (Nicolas Poussin, of course, is also relevant, but his now lesser known brother-in-law Gaspard was much more famous in the eighteenth century; see Sutton, pp. 13–14. Though the distinction between the two was not firm, most references to "Poussin" at the time celebrated Gaspard. The Poussin in Beaumont's collection, however, was by N. Poussin; Shackford, p. 13.) The broader implications of Classicism as a movement are touched on later in this chapter.

15. See also Reynolds on the "quietness and repose" of Claude (p. 70).

16. Color reproductions of *Hagar and the Angel* may be found in M. Wilson, p. 95; Bicknell, p. 84. Claude's painting probably conflates the first, primarily J-strand version in Genesis with the following E-strand version. In the former, Hagar is carrying the unborn Ishmael when she encounters the angel by a fountain. In the latter, Ishmael, now a child, accompanies Hagar into the wilderness. Succumbing to nearly fatal thirst, he is abandoned by his weeping mother "under one of the shrubs . . . a good way off" and is saved only when the angel reveals to Hagar "a well of water." Claude's omission of Ishmael and inclusion of the barely discernible dark spring or pool at the lower right could thus draw from both stories. Other details also indicate a conflation. While the morning light from the left (Röthlisberger, 1: 269) possibly specifies the E-strand, in which Abraham expels mother and son "early in the morning," the Annunciation-iconography of the fig-

ures, which I discuss below, also indicates the J-strand, in which Hagar has not yet borne Ishmael.

17. Shackford, p. 13, notes that there is some confusion in contemporary sources about whether the painting Beaumont always carried with him was *Hagar and the Angel* or Claude's *Narcissus and Echo*.

18. On Constable and *Hagar and the Angel*, see Röthlisberger, 1: 269; Heffernan, *Re-Creation*, esp. pp. 26–29. On Beaumont's collection and Wordsworth's familiarity with it, see Shackford, pp. 13–14. Wordsworth expressed an interest in seeing Beaumont's collection in the latter's company in 1804 (*Letters*, 1: 517) and certainly saw *Hagar and the Angel* in 1806 when he became in effect a houseguest at Beaumont's Grosvenor Square residence (*CMY*, p. 317). Wordsworth's general education in pictures began under the informal tutelage of Beaumont in 1804 (see Shackford, pp. 16–18).

19. Röthlisberger argues: "Contrary to common belief, Claude's figures are not simply an embellishment, nor are they *a posteriori*; rather, the subject is the primordial element, from which the entire composition is conceived and by which it has to be understood. All of Claude's pictures contain figures, and they provide the key to the meaning of the landscapes" (1: 23). I leave to one side Röthlisberger's accompanying mention that Claude, especially in his earlier works, sometimes employed figure painters (1: 15; see also Russell, pp. 77–78). This seems to be permissible because what will be most important in my analysis is precisely the *conventionality* upon which Claude begins his imagination of *istoria* and its cultural assumptions. The sharing of authoritative images, as we will see, is part of his theme. In any case, the overall authenticity of Claude's pictures is clear, since unlike other successful artists of the time he employed no workshop (Russell, pp. 49–50).

20. *Istoria*: the term from Renaissance Italy "originally used for narrative pictures of state, for which the Bible and classical mythology provided the ideal repertory of subjects" (J. Burke, p. 91). The broader term is *historia*, which is applicable to both verbal narrative and history painting. On *historia*, see especially Stephen G. Nichols, Jr., *Romanesque Signs*. Though it deals with a period before my primary span of interest, Nichols's work is highly relevant in its emphasis on *historia* as a literary and artistic hermeneutics of *translatio*, "by which the multiplicity of events in the world could be shown to be part of divine intentionality" (p. 9). *Historia*, Nichols observes about the early medieval milieu, "did not seek to describe events as they *were*, but to transform them into texts paralleling those of Scripture and theology in order to complete the dialectic of Revelation. For Scripture was veiled truth; it could only be understood . . . with effort, an effort to separate the imperfect reflections of the sensible world from the Truth. *Historia* was now to become an ancillary to the hermeneutics of the Logos, helping people to understand it and how it related to their world" (p. 9).

21. On Claude's quietism and exclusion of both "lascivious" and "violent" themes even from Ovidean subjects, see Russell, pp. 57–58. Russell's additional observation (p. 85) that Claude seems not to have been touched by the Stoic philosophy then current among artists such as Poussin or Salvator suggests that we will need to explain his quietism by other than purely classical means (see my discussion of Claude's quietist response to Counter-Reformation below). On Annunciation patterns, see Baxandall, pp. 51–56. Four patterns illustrated the story as told in Luke: *Conturbatio*

(disquiet), *Cogitatio* (reflection), *Interrogatio* (inquiry), and *Humiliatio* (submission). A fifth pattern of *Annunziata* pictures illustrated the condition of *Meritatio* (merit) in which Mary remains after the departure of Gabriel.

22. The other frequent stance of the angel is demonstrated in the Domenico *Annunciation* discussed below; see Pl. 7. The hands of the Virgin, we may note, also cross in the associated but separate category of *Meritatio* pictures, where she appears alone after her colloquy with Gabriel (Baxandall, p. 55; see, for example, Antonello da Messina's *Virgin Annunciate* in Baxandall, his pl. 50).

23. The whole notion of *translatio* as developed by Nichols in his study of *historia* is suggestive in this context: "*translatio* was a metaphoric process whereby one construct assumed the symbolic signification of another considered greater than itself. For example, when Charlemagne sought to renew the Roman Empire, he built his capital at Aix-la-Chapelle as an acknowledged *translatio* of Rome and Jerusalem, calling it a 'Second Rome, a New Jerusalem' " (p. 20). Literal and metaphorical at once in their displacement of divinity into secular culture, Claude's journeys are images precisely of *translatio*.

24. A catalog of journey pictures in Claude's work would also include his famous seaport or embarkation scenes. Various examples of journey subjects: *Seaport with the Embarkation of Ulysses from the Phaeacians, Landscape with the Landing of Aeneas in Latium, Landscape with the Voyage of Jacob, Coast View with the Embarkation of St. Paul, Seaport with the Embarkation of St. Ursala*, and —as we will see—the many Flights into Egypt and Rests on the Flight into Egypt.

25. See Grabar, pp. 112–46, for discussion of the iconography of Trinitarian and Incarnational dogma.

26. On the place of icons in the church, see Weitzmann et al., p. 7 and *passim*; Weitzmann, pp. 11–13; Cavarnos, pp. 22–29. On the mobility of icons, see Weitzmann et al., pp. 7, 63, 140, 148–50.

27. Grabar, p. 131, comments: "The Christian image-makers placed the Annunciation and the Visitation side by side as two parallel images of the same theme of conception, the second being added—in conformity with common iconographic tradition—to show the first witness to Christ's conception."

28. The drawing in *Liber Veritatis* associated with this painting, *Landscape with the Rest on the Flight into Egypt*, is No. 88. Röthlisberger, 1:268, notes that this Flight was in turn based on *Landscape with the Finding of Moses (Liber Veritatis*, No. 47).

29. E.g., Piero di Cosimo, *The Visitation* (reproduced in Baxandall, his pl. 38). My generalization about journeys, of course, will only serve for some purposes. A more comprehensive description would need to distinguish between types of journeys and accommodate exceptions to architecturally closed space.

30. Cf. such British portraits of "absorption" in the eighteenth century as Reynolds's *Offie Palmer Reading "Clarissa"* (1771) and *Joseph Baretti* (1774) or Wordsworth's own depiction in *The Prelude* of Ann Tyson sleeping with her head on a Bible (4.207–21).

31. A notable example of the dominance of allegorical exegesis in

Claude's time appears in Giovanni Fabrini's edition and annotation of *The Aeneid* (Russell, p. 86).

32. Alberti's treatise *On Painting* formulates the theory of pointing and other gestures in history-painting: "In an *istoria* I like to see someone who admonishes and points out to us what is happening there; or beckons with his hand to see. . . . Thus whatever the painted persons do among themselves or with the beholder, all is pointed toward ornamenting or teaching the *istoria*" (p. 78).

33. The precedent for such allegorical interpretation of the Hagar story, we may note, is authoritative. In Gal. 4: 21–31, Paul allegorizes the bondswoman Hagar as Mt. Sinai and the rule of Law, and argues that Christians must instead embrace the freewoman Sarah, whose law is faith. Moreover, Philo at the beginning of systematic allegorical thought (see n. 35 to this chapter) then also interpreted the Hagar episode allegorically (Sandmel, pp. 18–19; Winston, p. 37).

34. For a wholly secular version of the tableau with boat and onlooker, see *Liber Veritatis*, No. 130. In general, it is instructive to compare Wordsworth's pointer-figures, messengers, or other hermeneuticians of imagination with their counterparts in history-painting. The greatest pointers in Wordsworth's poetry are like the Pedlar in *The Ruined Cottage*: in countering the literal or deictic pointings of such figures as the peasant who directs the poet downwards in Simplon Pass, they point *through* the literal immediately to the anagogical—to such seemingly pointless images as that of a sunflower or spear-grass plant (see my discussion of the Pedlar "pointing" to vegetable images in Chapter 7). Whereas in Claude's *istoria* we see a literal point and then, along another axis in the perspective system, a plurality of figurative points (a mode of multiple perspective preserved in Blake's single, twofold, threefold and fourfold visions; Blake, pp. 816–18), in Wordsworth we see either the Coleridgean translucence of or—in times of spiritual darkness— the *eclipse* of the eternal behind the literal. *Istoria* in Wordsworth, in other words, is either the disappearance (in my terms, the denial) of the literal or the obstruction imposed by the literal, seldom a coexistence of the figural *with* the literal. Thus, for example, the literal view of Mont Blanc in Book 6 of *The Prelude* must cancel, rather than coincide with, a living thought that nevermore could be. Much of Wordsworth's later poetry, as I will point out in Chapter 9, involves learning to place the topical and the imaginative, the literal and the figural, side by side once more in a "collected" view. Thus will an older mode of *istoria*, more ample in its visual options, be restored.

35. By referring specifically to Logos as it appears in post-Philonic allegorical thought, I emphasize its older character as the *intermediary* agency between God's understanding and man's. By contrast, the tendency in recent literary criticism has been simply to collapse the distinctions made by Philo, Clement, and Origen and identify the logocentric indiscriminately with the absolute. As an intermediary agency, Logos was what allowed the communication of the ideal to the material, the general to the specific, the invisible to the visible, and the Word to the verbal—where these relations were complexly subordinated to each other such that, to take the most relevant example, for Philo the visible or synoptic manifestation of God's ideas was prior to verbal representation. (In the universe, he argued, Logos rep-

resents the "archetypal ideas from which the intelligible world was framed, and the visible objects which are the copies and likenesses of those ideas. With man in one form it resides within, in the other it passes out from him in utterance"; quoted in Winston, p. 17.) Logos in the Philonic understanding was thus quintessentially allegorical or, in our modern terminology, intertextual: it was at once the Author and the writing, an agency participating in the absolute and merely the interlinear translation of the absolute. (See Chapter 8, where I develop the notion of the intermediary Logos further to address Wordsworth's mature notion of Imagination.) On Philo and Logos, see Winston, pp. 15–25, 43–58; Sandmel, pp. 94–101; González, pp. 43–44; Berchman, pp. 27–53. On allegorical thought in the logological tradition of Philo, Clement, and Origen, see Sandmel, pp. 17–28; González, pp. 191–233; Berchman, pp. 55–164. On Philo's emphasis on the visual in particular, see Berchman, esp. p. 49: "For Philo the Logos is the image (*eikôn*) of God, who is its archetype, and itself (the Logos) is the archetype to all other things, which are its images."

36. On inverted perspective, see Osborne, pp. 846–47, 857.

37. See Cavarnos, pp. 43–44. I make no attempt to account for the diversity and complexity of iconic style, particularly the tension between *apatheia* and "emotionalism" (for which see Weitzmann et al., pp. 23–24; Weitzmann, pp. 20–21).

38. Attendant upon such typology, of course, was a morality—specifically the thesis of Original Sin redeemed by the virtues of Virginity and the second Adam. Fifteenth-century Italian exegesis thus not only articulated Mary's Virginity as an expressive scale of "disquiet," "reflection," "inquiry," and "submission," but launched on the basis of these attitudes explicit exercises on the "laudable" virtues of "prudence," "modesty," "humility," and so forth (see Baxandall, pp. 51–55).

39. Russell, p. 208, has noted the common occurrence of bridges in Claude's works and the prevalence of the motif in the work of such influences upon Claude as Paul Bril. Bridges in the work of Domenichino and Jacques Callot also come to mind. See also Holcomb, p. 50: "A broad, level bridge composed of a series of arches spanning a river in the mid-to-remote distance of a landscape was regarded as the most typical furnishing of Claude's art in early nineteenth-century England." Holcomb, p. 50 and her n. 45, observes Turner's *Bridge in the Middle Distance* and his use of the Claudian motif elsewhere.

40. The vanishing or "centric" point was crucial to Albertian construction but not rationalized until Claude's time in Desargue's Theorem of 1636 (Osborne, pp. 843, 850).

41. Nichols writes: "The narrative mechanism for *translatio* may also be understood via the analogy Eriugena made with the mixing of air and sunlight: the literal element to be transformed by the symbolic one is like the air which provided the vehicle for revealing the light, not perceptible in itself" (p. 21). In these terms, the immanental revelation of light that is Claude's atmosphere continues the *translatio* of his journey theme.

42. In artistic usage, "local color" is a function of the color constancy effect by which a viewer tends to see objects in their normalized or "natural" color (as remembered in common daylight illumination) irrespective of

their actual color under existent lighting conditions. Thus "a neutrally grey road surface illuminated by sunlight falling through green foliage may be violet; but its local colour remains grey" (Osborne, p. 261). In general, as Osborne notes, fidelity to local color in painting argues an object-oriented perception, whereas fidelity to actual color indicates concentration upon lighting and atmosphere.

43. Gilbert's whole discussion, pp. 211–16, of the displacement of subject by atmosphere in *The Tempest* is useful. In arguing the relation of the picturesque to Claude, I have also found very suggestive Gilbert's general thesis on the interpenetration of "Subject and Not-Subject" pictures in the Italian Renaissance.

44. By the beginning of the eighteenth century in Britain, works such as Chambers's *Cyclopedia* (1727–38) defined "repose" wholly in atmospheric terms as "assemblages of light and shade"—or, alternatively, as a "harmony" of "masses" rooted in Poussin's more purely compositional approach to setting (see *OED*, s.v. "repose"). Bringing such Claudian atmosphere home as English "haziness," Gilpin later described it as follows: "it corrects the glare of colours—it softens the harshness of lines; and above all, it throws over the face of landscape that harmonizing tint, which blends the whole into unity, and repose" (*Lakes*, 1: 11).

45. E.g., *Pastoral Landscape* (*Liber Veritatis*, No. 52); discussed in Röthlisberger, 1: 187–89. See also Röthlisberger, 1: 39, on the forgetting of Claude's subjects. Such forgetting was made possible by a lack of resistance on the part of the artist himself. Unlike Poussin, a *pictor philosophus* who left extensive writings on his views of art, philosophy, history, and so forth, Claude was virtually silent (Russell, pp. 54, 81). In speaking of the picturesque as a "forgetting," I am guided by Spector's thesis about picturesque "mirror imagery": "Picturesque reflection imagery is significant because of its omissions. Reflecting waters are not seen as dark shadows of heaven; here are no deceitful crystal floods waiting to snare self-loving Narcissi; here are no souls tempted by their reflections on the sea of hyle, . . . here are no emblems of *vanitas*. . . . What is present . . . is an attempt to see the world in purely aesthetic terms, without the mediation of traditional associations. Originally the Picturesque was an integral part of the Enlightenment's attempt to see the world without the distorting mirrors of Romance, Religion, or Superstition" (p. 91).

46. Diagonal recession, as Russell has observed (p. 71), was Claude's own early hallmark under the influence of such Northern landscapists as Bril, and survived as an alternative even after he had solved the problem of straight recession. A *Pastoral Landscape* such as the one in the Yale University Art Gallery (*Liber Veritatis*, No. 116), for example, simply realigns Claude's characteristic picture of repose—complete with shepherds, boat, bridge, and off-center villa—along the diagonal; and even *Hagar and the Angel* interpolates a suggestion of slant recession in its body of water.

47. On the Claudean inspiration of this painting, see Hayes, 2: 350. Another especially suggestive instance in a Wordsworthian context is the double-diagonal recession in Rubens's *Landscape with Chateau Steen*, which Beaumont acquired in 1803 (Greaves, p. 57). For an analysis of the painting particularly concerned with its diagonals, see Vergara, pp. 99–135. Gains-

borough's own use of double-diagonal composition can be seen in a work such as *Wooded Landscape with Figures, Bridge, Donkeys, Distant Buildings and Mountain* (Hayes, 2: his pl. 83), where the two diagonal recessions are indexed by crossed-diagonal pointers so elaborate—the donkey with its head crossed over the back of another donkey, the forked trunk at the right—that they suggest a virtually conscious twisting of space around the Claudean bridge in the middle distance.

48. As we noticed earlier, Claude also shifts his subject group to the side in *Hagar and the Angel*. The difference is that in the Claude a straight recession is still accessible; in the Gainsborough, such recession from the vantage of the peasant is closed off by the sidescreen of trees.

49. The relationship between visual blockages in a picture and stationary human figures is an interesting one. In Barrell's terms, we might say that a matted clump of bush, a stump, or a cow are not only visual blockages but markers of all the inert or slow objects in the landscape whose natural state of rest competes directly with human rest. The repose of a stump or other obstruction demands the labor of the human; cows must be driven. Appleton's vocabulary of prospect and refuge landscapes would also provide a means of studying the relation between human figures and visual blockages. (I should add that in thus speculating on blockages and diagonal recessions, I am conscious of a debt to Paulson, who during the writing of his *Literary Landscape* imparted much to me in the routine course of our teaching and administrative duties in the Yale British Studies Program.)

50. As shown by Gilpin's extensive discussion of the aesthetics of horses, cows, and sheep as seen in landscape (in the second volume of *Lakes*), the picturesque made cattle functional parts of the view. In Pl. 8, for example, the cow in the middle distance allows Gainsborough to "bridge" the several distances in much the same compositional manner as Claude's actual bridges. As Hayes notes, 2: 350, "the lack of relationship between the foreground and middleground is masked by the cow and sheep." Such use of cattle to regulate or define the distance planes, we may note, is consistent throughout Gainsborough's landscapes. For another especially clear instance, see *Wooded Landscape with Figures in a Country Cart Followed by Two Peasants Passing Over a Rocky Mound, Peasant with Donkeys, and Shepherd and Sheep* (Hayes, 2: his pl. 118). See also *River Landscape with Rustic Lovers, Mounted Herdsman Driving Cattle and Sheep Over a Bridge and Ruined Castle* (together with its studies), where cows and sheep crossing the bridge conflate the motifs of cattle and bridge (Hayes, 2: his pl. 128). For another artist's use of cattle to define the middle distance, see John Glover's *Landscape with Cattle* (G. Reynolds, *Victoria and Albert Museum British Water-Colours*, his pl. 20). Here the silhouetted cows in the middle distance appear almost as if they might be arches of a bridge. Claude himself, of course, anticipated the English use of cattle for compositional purposes in such works as *Pastoral Landscape* (my Pl. 4). Here, the grouping of cattle serves to regulate the foreground plane in a manner paralleling the bridge's regulation of the middle plane.

51. Examples, with convenient sources in which they are illustrated: Gilpin, *Landscape with River and a Bridge* (Murdoch, cat. no. 10); Wilson, *The Great Bridge Over the Taafe* (Grigson, p. 51); Farington, *The Waterfall at Rydal*,

Ambleside (see below and Pl. 11); Sandby, *Pont y Pair over the River Conway Above Llanrwst in the County of Denbigh* (Herrmann, his pl. 35b); Hearne, *A Scene Near Keswick* (Thomas, p. 189); Cotman, *A Study of Trees* (*British Watercolors*, cat. no. 17); Towne, *A View of Exeter* (*British Watercolors*, cat. no. 87); Abbott, *Pastoral Landscape* (*English Watercolours*, pl. 17); Varley, *Dolgelly, N. Wales* (G. Reynolds, *An Introduction*, his pl. 23); Beaumont, *A Bridge Over a Stream* (Thomas, p. 70). The catalog of the "bridge in the middle distance" swells even further if we include pictures of the "urban picturesque"—e.g., Farington, *The Ouse Bridge, York* (Wilton, his pl. 59); Girtin, *The Rue St. Denis, Paris* (Wilton, his pl. 75). Also noteworthy are pictures of arches in the middle distance—e.g., Girtin, *Entrance to the Porte Chapelle, Compiègne* (*British Watercolors*, cat. no. 43); Henry Edridge Ara, *Furness Abbey* (Thomas, p. 155).

I am much aided by Holcomb's notice of the emphasis on bridges in British art in the eighteenth and early nineteenth centuries (pp. 50–55). But her reading of bridges as quasi-literary "symbols" (particularly of hope) in the Romantic era depends on what may perhaps be a too well-formed notion of symbol akin to older allegory. If, as I argue, bridges in the eighteenth century were primarily "formal" in significance, then the beginning of trans-formal symbol in the Romantic vision of bridges would logically be formlessness. Very relevant here is John Dixon Hunt's argument that Turner uses arched bridges to frame *nothing* within the arch—an especially potent formlessness forcing the viewer "to participate by seeking to understand the area beyond the arches of a bridge or, where the bridge itself is absent, spaces still instinct with all the mystery of precisely located but imprecisely registered ambiance" ("Wondrous Deep," p. 143). Turner, in Hunt's view, thus adapts "picturesque forms for sublime ends" (p. 142).

52. A fuller study would here need to take account of differences in media. To look from Claude's paintings to his much more "various" drawings in *Liber Veritatis*, for example, is to spy the picturesque in seed. Noyes, p. 11, has cited the conclusion of Elizabeth Manwaring that Italian ideal landscape was propagated in England primarily through such works as Richard Earlham's reproduction (in etching and mezzotint) of the *Liber Veritatis*.

53. As in another drawing Hearne made of the footbridge at Downton, where the background is all foliage, *The Teme at Downton, Herefordshire* (Murdoch, cat. no. 11); or as in John Sell Cotman's *The Scotchman's Stone on the Greta*, where the composition is virtually all rock (Grigson, p. 83).

54. For reproductions, see n. 51 to this chapter.

55. On Knight's architectural tastes, see Messmann, pp. 17, 76–77. The irregularities of the house in our plate are made especially meaningful by comparison with the mansion in the matching illustration of the un-picturesque in *The Landscape*.

56. Ramsey, pp. 383–84, observes the diminutive place of figures in *An Evening Walk* itself. For an expansive view of the changing relation of figures to landscape, see J. Hunt, *Figures*. See also Wesling on Wordsworth and the "peopling" of landscape (pp. 59–92). In general, Wesling's subtle questioning of the "adequacy" of landscape for a full social vision is consonant with my own approach to the picturesque. But rather than argue that "landscape

is landscape because it is finally other, inhuman," and thus needs the compensation of a meditative and ultimately ethical approach to nature (p. 75), I will argue that landscape is from the first constituted by sedimented layers of human culture. It is the recognition, or denial, of these bedrock layers that determines the course of Wordsworth's poetry in the years succeeding his early descriptive verse. On "association" in the picturesque, see Knight, *Analytical Inquiry*, Part II, "Of the Association of Ideas"; and Messmann, pp. 112–16.

57. Wordsworth could have read the note quoted in West's *Guide to the Lakes* (Sheats, p. 51; see also Watson, *Picturesque*, pp. 68–69).

58. Whereas West gives equal emphasis to Rydal Upper Falls in the section where he quotes Mason's note on the Lower Falls, Gilpin singles out the latter for "particular notice" (*Lakes*, 1: 161).

59. It is difficult to tell whether "its wild waves repose" in l. 74 refers literally to the waters in the basin or figuratively to the patterns of foliage reflected on the waters. Wordsworth partially corrects the problem in the 1836 version of the poem, where the lines, "While thick above the rill the branches close, / In rocky basin its wild waves repose" (*EW*, p. 39), supply "rill" as an adequate, if not fully pleasing, referent for "its." But in the 1793 poem, the syntax swirling around "its wild waves repose" is so undecidable that the phrase becomes an impressionistic vision—a splotch of texture like a Monet water lily—left floating above literal reference. In the experience of reading, four unsatisfactory possibilities suggest themselves: "its" refers the wild waves to (1) "rill" in l. 71 (though this would require ignoring the semicolon), (2) "branches" in l. 73 (necessitating an agreement problem), (3) "dark-brown bason" in l. 74 (making "its" egregiously unnecessary), (4) or "Inverted shrubs, and moss" in l. 75 (involving both an agreement problem and a total breakdown of syntax once we reach the verb "cling" in l. 76). The last possibility seems on its surface the weakest (though there is certainly a strong tendency to be fooled in this manner while reading from line to line); but in fact picturesque tradition gives it extra cogency. As in Brown's *Letter* on Keswick, where "islands, fields, woods, rocks, and mountains, are seen inverted and floating" on the surface of a mirror-like lake (quoted in Spector, p. 88), inverted reflections were a standard picturesque motif. Moreover, it appears unlikely that there were any literally inverted shrubs at Rydal Lower Falls: none of the many contemporary depictions of Rydal Lower Falls I have seen includes any shrub or bush that could be called inverted (though the Wright of Derby painting does show inclining shrubs); nor does the foliage around the present Falls suggest inversion. As Gilpin demonstrates in his description of the wood that "hangs over" the rocks of the Falls, and as West confirms in his description of "shrubs" that "hang on the rocks" and "hanging woods" in the area nearby (pp. 79, 81), the normal picturesque idiom for foliage that inclines to any degree or stands over a precipice is "hanging." At the point of repose in l. 74, the poem's syntax itself simply comes to rest: like Monet's water lilies, it floats above literal reference to reflect, gather, focus, highlight, or otherwise express the total atmosphere of the scene.

60. On the influence of the picturesque on the *Guide*, see Heffernan, *Wordsworth's Theory*, pp. 18–19; Spector, p. 101; and Bicknell, pp. 11–15, 27.

Because the *Guide* occurs after the period of my primary interest in this book, I will as much as possible simplify its complex textual history in my citations. Unless otherwise noted, I cite from the 1835 version that Owen and Smyser print as their main text in *Prose*, vol. 2. Where it seems useful, however, I will also cite as "1810 *Guide*" or *Select Views* the earliest version as preserved in the text and *appar. crit.* of the 1835, or, in the case of the highly divergent second section of the 1810, as separately printed in *Prose*, vol. 2, under the title "Select Views." The unpublished manuscripts associated with Wordsworth's early efforts to transform and expand the 1810 will be cited under Owen and Smyser's titles of "An Unpublished Tour" and "The Sublime and the Beautiful." For further guidance through the tangled texts of the *Guide*, see *Prose*, 2: 123–49.

61. Under the rubric philosophical "meaning" I conflate for present purposes the notion of "ideas" in history of ideas and that of Geist in the subject-object dialectic of post-Hegelian thought. The conflation is useful in discussing the genesis of formalism from its nineteenth-century background. From about the 1930's on, however, history of ideas and dialectical thought diverged as the former (e.g., in the work of Lovejoy) increasingly drew upon the scientific model of knowledge for its study of "unit-ideas." The same model, we know, was also shaping early Anglo-American formalism (e.g., in the work of Ransom).

62. In history of art terms, New Criticism may be conceived as the subtraction of all "iconological" study to leave an exclusive "stylistics." But there is a chronological twist. Where formalism was aggressively new in relation to iconology-like history of ideas in the field of literary study, the reverse was true for art history: stylistics was turn-of-the-century while iconology was the newer trend roughly simultaneous with the ascendancy of the New Criticism. (See Podro for a history of art-theory that is sensitive to the duel between the aesthetic and contextual approaches to art and broader than my Wölfflin-Panofsky framework permits.) It would be intriguing to study the reasons for the out-of-step development of literary and artistic study, which may underlie what is now often felt to be the incommensurability, and sometimes general lack of sympathy, between mainstream art historians and literary critics. (Especially suggestive is the divide in attitude toward the artistic object that accompanied the divergence in methodology: literary criticism increasingly appreciated the ownerless "text" free of its social and historical context, while art history and curatorship increasingly appreciated the value of specifically owned artifacts authorized by origin and provenance. It may be that there is a rough formula for artistic value into which each discipline must variously factor the ownerless aesthetics of style, on the one hand, and the authority of ownership or historical lineage, on the other. Style plus authority equals value. Cf. Stallknecht on the ownership of aesthetic enjoyment, quoted in n. 68 to Chapter 7.) Suppressing the chronological problem, we can chart a comparative model of modern art and literary interpretation (see table, p. 546) where the base reference for the comparison is traditional hermeneutics (cf. Panofsky's "synoptical table" of art interpretation, pp. 40–41).

63. Hartman, *WP*, pp. 90–101; Sheats, pp. 49–59, esp. 53ff.; Ramsey, esp. pp. 376, 385–89. Christopher Hussey's general study of the picturesque

TABLE TO NOTE 62
Comparative Model of Art-Historical and Literary Interpretation

	Traditional hermeneutics	Iconology (Panofsky)[a]	Stylistics (Wölfflin)[b]	New Criticism
Matter (*rem*)	Canon of forms	Motifs	Motifs	Iconic forms
Interpretation (*verba*)	Literal, moral, typological themes	Iconography (motifs with themes)	Style ("modes of representation" or schemata)	Imagery
Authority (*doxa*)	Doctrinal tradition	Literary convention and world-view	Natural laws of perception and *Zeitgeist*	Organic unity
Meaning (*logos*)	Anagogy	Idea or Geist ("essential tendencies of the human mind . . . expressed by specific themes and concepts")	Mood (expression)	Ambiguity, paradox, tension, irony

[a] *Meaning*, pp. 26–54; for the terms and concepts in this column, see esp. pp. 28–29, 35–39.

[b] Except for "mood" and "expression" from *Renaissance*, p. 77, terms in this column are from *Principles*, esp. pp. 6, 9–17.

may be seen to anticipate such an approach in its definition of the picturesque, as "a long phase in the aesthetic relation of man to nature" during which art "shifted its appeal from the reason to the imagination" as "a prelude to romanticism" (p. 4).

64. If we were to follow such an approach further, we would at this point need to complete one major task remaining to investigation of the poem's style: the systematic correlation of verbal form with pictorial motif. To what extent, for example, is the couplet analogous to the planimetrically defined, symmetrical, closed space of Albertian construction? And to what extent do the stylistic aberrations cataloged by Leguois (inversions, suspensions, elisions, etc.) function to ventilate the couplet in the way of atmosphere? (See Ramsey, pp. 381–82, on Wordsworth's use of modifiers in *An Evening Walk* to create "entangled relationships.")

65. See Grabar's thesis, pp. 7–30, that the earliest Christian images emerged only under the creed of the sign—i.e., as "image-signs" with other than descriptive value.

66. Contrast Steven Mullaney's very different concept of cultural "rehearsal," according to which a culture enacts/consumes the unfamiliar instead of the strictly familiar or doctrinal ("Strange Things").

67. Cf. Russell: "It seems, moreover, that Claude's very concept of nature owes a great deal to the philosophy of the Roman Church. Almost without exception, the world of his paintings is one in which order and tranquillity prevail, where men and animals perform no labor but rather exist peacefully in beautiful pastoral settings which are blessed with always clement weather" (p. 57).

68. Discussing the French divergence from the mainstream of Counter-Reformation and Roman art, Huyghe, p. 338, notes that Claude and Poussin "turned their backs on rhetorical painting and returned to poetical painting." (Huyghe's reference is to Nicolas Poussin. The Poussin I invoke here and elsewhere to discuss Classicism is Gaspard Dughet, the essential Poussin for the picturesque; see n. 14 to this chapter.)

69. A specialized inquiry into this topic would here need to trace the descent of British landscape aesthetics through the seventeenth century with its contests between old religious forms and Puritan reform (see J. Turner, p. 55 and *passim*).

70. Contrast, for example, Francis Towne's angled view of Rydal Upper Falls from a clifftop (reproduced in Bicknell, p. 183), or Hutchinson's description of his clifftop view of another falls near Ambleside (pp. 182–84; see also West, pp. 78–79). All the pictures I have seen of Rydal Lower Falls show the same frontal view. Besides ones already mentioned, these include Towne's watercolor of the Falls (reproduced in Bicknell, p. 183), Julius Caesar Ibbetson's *Rydal Waterfall* (reproduced in B. Nicolson, 1: 93), Constable's sketch (Yale Center for British Art Photograph Archive), William Banks's engraving in his *Views of the Lakes*, the engraving on the half-title page of Blanchard's guide, and the engraving after G. Pickering in Rose's guide. Pickering's picture is especially interesting because it shows two hunters on the cliffs overlooking the Falls. The presumption is that only those in a proprietary relation to the estate can themselves enter the view (as seen from the summer house) to observe the falls from an oblique angle; unauthorized viewers in the position of the hunters would be akin to poachers.

71. See also the photograph in *Discovery*, p. 114, which shows the Lower Falls through the window of the summer house in 1984. For contemporary and nineteenth-century accounts of access to the two falls, see West, p. 80; Gell, pp. 9–10; Farington, Nov. 3, 1801 (1: 339); *Black's Picturesque Guide*, p. 14; Blanchard, p. 32; Baedeker, p. 391; Baddeley, p. 70; Rose, pp. 36–37. See also Lofthouse, p. 121. Baddeley's guide indicates that tourists could in 1895 view the Lower Falls from a bridge as well (p. 70). On Rydal Hall and its summer houses, see Royal Commission, pp. 201–2; Nicolson and Burn, 1: 174. My special thanks to Frederick Badger, who, during a trip to the Lakes in May 1987 for his study project at Eastern Connecticut State University, very kindly offered to take photographs for me of the Lower Falls and summer house.

72. Rose, p. 37, quotes one visitor's response to the dramatic effect of the summer house: "The approach to [the Falls] is through a narrow glen, till you come to a little thatched summer-house, standing on the banks of the Rothay, and which, from the date upon one of the window-shutters, would seem to have been erected in the year 1617. On entering the room of the summer-house, the view of the cascade bursts at once upon the eye. The suddenness and velocity of the impressions which the mind receives, defy every attempt to describe the effect produced on the spectator. The momentary effect is electrical."

73. On the contemporary habit of dioramic and panoramic vision, see Chapters 5 and 9. For an ironic counterpoint to the dioramic effect of Rydal Lower Falls, see Wordsworth's later derision of an over-theatricalized

scene in "Effusion in the Pleasure-Ground on the Banks of the Bran, Near Dunkeld." The poem is prefaced by a headnote excerpted from Dorothy Wordsworth's journal of their 1803 tour of Scotland: "The waterfall, by a loud roaring, warned us when we must expect it. We were first, however, conducted into a small apartment, where the Gardener desired us to look at a picture of Ossian, which, while he was telling the history of the young Artist who executed the work, disappeared, parting in the middle—flying asunder as by the touch of magic—and lo! we are at the entrance of a splendid apartment, which was almost dizzy and alive with waterfalls, that tumbled in all directions; the great cascade, opposite the window, which faced us, being reflected in innumerable mirrors upon the ceiling and against the walls" (*PW*, 3: 102). Dorothy continues in her journal: "We both laughed heartily" (Selincourt edition, 1: 359).

74. I take my general inspiration in this section from Williams, pp. 120–41; J. Turner, pp. 116–85; and Barrell.

75. Cf. Williams, p. 124: "It was that kind of confidence, to make Nature move to an arranged design, that was the real invention of the landlords. And we cannot then separate their decorative from their productive arts; this new self-conscious observer was very specifically the self-conscious owner." Also J. Turner, pp. 38–39: "Property and the orderly countryside are the same thing. In the composition of landscape practicality and aesthetics are allowed to melt together" (see, in addition, p. 141). In the 1793 edition of Blackstone's *Commentaries on the Laws of England*, we may note, the institution of property was thoroughly naturalized: a revision refers to "that law of property, which nature herself has written upon the hearts of all mankind" (quoted in Hay, "Property," p. 19).

76. Cf. the more influential *posse comitatus* raised by William Clavell, High Sheriff of Dorset, at about the same time. The plan was publicized by William Morton Pitt in *Thoughts on the Defence of these Kingdoms and the Raising of the Posse Comitatus* (1798). See Emsley, pp. 72–73.

77. Wordsworth's discussion of social history in his *Guide* (*Prose*, 2: 198–201) makes it clear that "enclosing" had, by tradition, a restricted meaning in the Lakes. Wordsworth uses the term to refer to the walling or hedging off of very small tenements of land first around individual homesteads, then on the mountain sides, and at last, after the mid-seventeenth century, in the meadows and lower grounds. Large-scale enclosures of the sort we commonly associate with the social history of the eighteenth century occurred essentially in a massive burst from about 1793 to 1816, when Cumberland, for instance, saw the enclosure of some 200,000 acres (*LC2*, p. 4).

78. See J. Turner, p. 165, on the sheer number of occupational activities "censored from the ideal landscape."

79. Barrell, p. 21, qualifies that the artistic tradition of working laborers "does not of course always mean that they must never be shown at rest . . . but it does prescribe the terms on which they may relax—in the evening, after a hard day's work; after the harvest, on their way to the ritual feast; during the harvest, at meal-breaks, but never far from the hooks and scythes which indicate that they are resting only for a moment." Barrell's whole thesis about the rules governing the size, lighting, and placement of working figures in the landscape bears upon my study of repose.

80. Cf. Wordsworth on the same mines and their connection with the pencil (*Prose*, 2: 347–48). Both Gilpin (*Lakes*, 1: 205–6) and Wordsworth were aware that the mines had been the site of spectacular struggles over property rights and their encroachment (by such means as tunneling slantwise from adjoining property). The "injurious" productivity of the pencil that Wordsworth mentions may thus be seen to be a sort of realized trope for actual misappropriation of local landscape. Wordsworth says, "It seems not improbable that a material which the Reader is daily holding in his hand in the familiar shape of a Pencil may have contributed to produce . . . local injuries in this remote part of the island." See *Prose*, 2: 450n, for other contemporary treatments of the Borrowdale lead mines.

81. On the investment of labor and capital needed to enclose land, see Darby, pp. 24–25.

82. Cf. Williams, p. 124: "The mathematical grids of the enclosure awards, with their straight hedges and straight roads, are contemporary with the natural curves and scatterings of the park scenery. And yet they are related parts of the same process—superficially opposed in taste but only because in the one case the land is being organised for production . . . while in the other case it is being organised for consumption—the view, the ordered proprietary repose, the prospect." See also J. Turner, pp. 126–29.

83. Though I cite the 1810 *Guide* here, I quote for convenience from the 1835 edition (the two versions differ only by a word in this passage). In the 1810, the passage occurs at the close of Section I; in subsequent editions, Section I became part of the main essay of the *Guide* and was itself broken into what descends to us in the 1835 as Sections I, II, and III.

84. On the word "station" and Wordsworth's use of it, see Fink, pp. 132, 125–26; Heffernan, *Wordsworth's Theory*, p. 19.

85. My thanks to Linda Colley of the Yale History Department for steering me to the Webbs when I was first researching this section.

86. Sir Daniel and two later William Flemings were Sheriffs of Cumberland (*DNB*, 7: 275; *Complete Baronetage*, 4: 192–93). On Gilpin's promotion of a new poorhouse, see *DNB*, 7: 1263. For an appreciation of Burn's *Justice of the Peace*, see Webb, 1: 354.

87. See Webb, 1: 15–32. Appointed annually by the Justices from a list of "substantial" householders, the officers of the parish also answered to the Vestry of their parish, which, as the Webbs have pointed out, tended to be restricted to an "oligarchy" of leading farmers occupying land in the parish (Webb, 1: 42–60).

88. See also Darby, pp. 72–75 and, concerning turnpikes in the Lake District and North, pp. 155, 201. A convenient map of roads in the Lakes c. 1777 may be found in Nicolson and Burn (frontispieces in both volumes).

89. As Owen and Smyser note in their commentary on the *Guide* (*Prose*, 2: 406, 443, and *passim*), Clarke's *Survey* often informs Wordsworth's *Guide* and its associated manuscripts; see also T. Kelley, "Economics," p. 24.

90. My notion of the in-and-out flux of Romantic conversation poems is informed by Abrams, "Structure and Style." On Wordsworth's use of clouds and other atmospheric phenomena as images of liberty, see Woodring, "On Liberty."

91. It would be intriguing to study Wordsworth's vision from the top

of Lancaster Castle in relation to two other panoramic visions he associates with the area. After describing his vision, he goes on in "An Unpublished Tour" to mention a peasant who, upon entering the courts of justice in the Castle, "passed with a deliberate step into the centre of it, & having looked around took off his hat in sign of reverence that unequivocally expressed the awe with which his mind was stricken" (*Prose*, 2: 292). In the first of the "Sonnets Upon the Punishment of Death," titled "Suggested by the View of Lancaster Castle (On the Road from the South)," the poet then later pictures thousands of prisoners weeping as they reach a "bare eminence" and "cast / Their first look" on the Castle (*PW*, 4: 135). The overview of freedom we witness in Wordsworth's own panorama from the top of the Castle is thus flanked by lower and interior panoramas of discipline.

92. Cf. Barrell's thesis that the unstated rules of pictorial composition required that laborers in a view be stationed at precise distances as if they could only occupy certain zones (pp. 21–22, 134–64). Indeed, we can resume our own pictorial paradigm by noting that Claude's *Hagar and the Angel*, and more broadly the tripartite picture space learned from the Renaissance, was implicit with disciplinary structure. It is as if Wordsworth's view at Lancaster Castle simply projected a painting like *Hagar and the Angel* in 360 degrees: multiple versions of the exiled Hagar fill the foreground while innumerable recessions promise freedom in the background. A wraparound version of the bridge in the middle distance then negotiates foreground and background to create the total picture of repose. This bridge is the castle wall. "There is a counterpoise . . . in the majesty of the building," Wordsworth says, finding his point of repose. So pictorial is such repose that he then proceeds to an aesthetic critique of the paintings inside the castle (*Prose*, 2: 291–92). (Similarly, West used the castle and its environs to usher in precisely the Classical pictorial experience. Just before describing the area, he recommended beginning a Lakes tour at Lancaster because "by this course the lakes lie in an order more pleasing to the eye. . . . The change of scenes is from what is pleasing, to what is surprising, from the delicate and elegant touches of Claude to the noble scenes of Poussin, and, from these, to the stupendous romantic ideas of Salvator Rosa"; pp. 13–14. As Owen and Smyser note, *Prose*, 2: 436n, Wordsworth immediately goes on to allude to this passage from West in his "Unpublished Tour," *Prose*, 2: 293.)

93. Unfortunately, I was not able to benefit from John Bender's work on prison design and narrative consciousness in time for this book. Bender's basic thesis in *Imagining the Penitentiary*—which I have had a chance to peruse in manuscript form—would provide a useful means of plotting the overall transition I follow in this book from picturesque vision (especially in its panoramic or panoptic form) to narrative and post-narrative visions. Bender's argument concerning the priority of narrative structures to such actual cultural structures as prison designs is consonant with my emphasis on underlying narrativity. (A section of Bender's book previously appeared as "The Novel and the Rise of the Penitentiary: Narrative and Ideology in Defoe, Gay, Hogarth, and Fielding," *Stanford Literature Review* 1 [1984]: 55–84.)

94. J. Turner's comments on violence are also apropos to my general thesis in this part of my book. Turner, p. 189, writes: "The demonstra-

tion of the historicity of 'Nature,' and its covertly propagandist use, is the backbone of my work; indeed I extend the analysis to show how the political concept 'Violence' is made to work simultaneously as an inversion of Nature and as a part of it."

95. Pevsner is more politically specific than de Wolfe, who speaks generally of English democratization and individualism. Only after the Whigs rose to complete dominance with Walpole, we may note, could "free" landscape then be championed by Pope and a Tory ideology now itself in opposition. I use the suggestions of Pevsner and de Wolfe despite Hipple's dismissal: "But really, the appeal to the British constitution is a mere rhetorical trick, whether it appears in Knight, in Price, or in Repton. . . . To stress [the assimilation of politics to aesthetics in their work] is to equivocate with terms and to distort picturesque theory" (pp. 241–42). Hipple's argument, it seems to me, holds only so long as we accept a highly bounded, *a priori* notion of "picturesque theory," believe that such a theory is to be tested purely in its own frame, and presume that "rhetoric" somehow has less ontological status than "aesthetics" or "theory." As is corroborated by the general tone of Hipple's book, in other words, his project may be called "philosophical" in the high sense of respecting a sort of Platonic *Republic* of aesthetics outside actual society and its marketplace of sophistry. But the daemon of philosophy, as it was for Plato, is precisely the rhetorical trick— the simile, analogy, grand myth—without which philosophy itself would be tongue-tied. Where Plato had the simile of the Cave, directed outward from an interior social landscape to a sunny prospect of philosophy, the picturesque writers had what we will see to be repeated recourse to political similes directed inversely from aesthetic prospects back into social truth.

96. Cf. Watson, *Picturesque*, pp. 15–16; de Wolfe, p. 356. On the political significance of Richmond Gardens, see Colton. On Richmond, Stowe, and other English gardens versus French gardening, see Wiebenson, pp. 23–38.

97. A particularly convenient guide to the political history I sketch here from the restricted perspective of party politics may be found in A. Beattie.

98. For a convenient visualization and summary of the makeup of the eighteenth-century House of Commons, see J. Owen, pp. 105–7. Besides the politicians associated with the leading political families or parties, the House consisted of Court and Treasury placemen who depended upon the King and tended for security of office to distance themselves from individual politicians, and "independents" or "non-dependents," who differed from the politicians "in that they were essentially back benchers," and from the Court and Treasury corps "in that they relied upon the Crown neither for their incomes nor their parliamentary seats" (J. Owen, pp. 106–7).

99. E.g., remarks by P. J. Grosley in his 1770 guide to London and in G. L. LeRouge's *Détails des nouveaux jardins à la mode* (both quoted in Wiebenson, pp. 31, 37).

100. Paulson, *Representations*, p. 150, has remarked on Price's tour with Fox.

101. Indeed, Repton goes on to justify planting belts of trees around an estate as a method of ensuring a happy medium of privacy and "liberty" for the owner, pp. 14–15; see also Hipple, p. 242. Hipple, p. 241, discusses Repton's analogy to the Constitution and Price's rejoinder to it.

102. Wordsworth in his *Guide*, for example, speaks in conventional terms when he depicts a civil war or riot of vegetation: "what shall we say to whole acres of artificial shrubbery and exotic trees among rocks and dashing torrents, with their own wild wood in sight—where we have the whole contents of the nurseryman's catalogue jumbled together—colour at war with colour, and form with form?—among the most peaceful subjects of Nature's kingdom, everywhere discord, distraction, and bewilderment!" (*Prose*, 2: 219).

103. Compare, for example, Fox's speech of February 18, 1793, with Knight's note. Fox denounces the prosecution of a war that made it "not easy for the French to know with what we would be satisfied, nor to discover on what terms our amity . . . could be cultivated. . . . How could we hope the French, who were thus wantonly insulted, to expect that anything would be considered as satisfactory, or any pledge a sufficient security?" (in Joll, p. 43). Knight, *Landscape*, p. 96n, argues: "the present war, as it has been hitherto conducted, is exactly calculated to produce this effect [causing the French to fight more ferociously]; and consequently to cooperate with the views of the sanguinary rulers of Paris, who excited it. By not avowing their intentions, the allied powers with-hold all security from the well-disposed among the French, as to what may be the consequence of their success."

104. As Emsley, pp. 65–66, observes, the *Anti-Jacobin* was started in 1797 on the inspiration of George Canning, Under-Secretary at the Foreign Office, and with occasional contributions by Pitt, Grenville, and Jenkinson. Its designedly short run had a wide readership.

105. My thanks to Liz Bohls of Stanford University, who corresponded with me regarding her own intriguing work on the place of the picturesque in Radcliffe's *Mysteries of Udolpho* and who took the time to read my chapter carefully. I owe some improvements in this section to her suggestion.

106. Ozouf reproduces in juxtaposition these two plates in her own work (her pls. 6, 7).

107. See also Gilpin's extended play on sound, echoes, and "music" (*Lakes*, 2: 59–63); and Clarke's notice of echoes, sounds, and voices (pp. 26, 73). Clarke, p. 125, observes as well the echoes of falls at Rydal. Surprisingly, the theme of sound could appear in picturesque art as well, as in Paul Sandby's *Music by Moonlight* (reproduced in *Art of Paul Sandby*, p. 89).

108. Watson, *Picturesque*, p. 71, and Ramsey, p. 384, have remarked upon the anomalous presence of the Female Beggar episode. See also Wesling, pp. 14–15, who comments that *An Evening Walk* includes social commentary "only in digressions from description" similar to those of Thomson and Cowper.

109. Averill, p. 65, writes about "Summer," ll. 1223–29, "It is as if the girl's death causes the heavens to seem sublimer, brighter, clearer, purer. The contemplation of suffering gives to experience an intensity and awesomeness it has previously lacked." In general, Averill's reading of this episode and of Wordsworth's Female Beggar is perceptive and sensitive. I build upon it in this discussion.

110. I choose this term not only because so many locodescriptive mo-

ments describe actual edges but because it invokes Hartman's similar study of a scene in *An Evening Walk*: "Strange contrasts . . . between headlong motion and quiet pasturing, make one uncertain as to whether the powers in this magic mountain are ordinary, or whether they are near to overwhelming ordinary perception. Wordsworth's edgy point of view (on the edge between a natural and a supernatural perspective) is intensified" (*WP*, pp. 95–96).

111. Wordsworth's footnote to l. 173 in *An Evening Walk* refers to "Summer" together with John Scott's *Critical Essays* (London, 1785). As shown by Averill, p. 64, and Sheats, pp. 53–54, Scott—whom Wordsworth read at Cambridge—not only discusses the Celadon and Amelia episode in particular but also, in the section touched upon in Wordsworth's note, a later passage from "Summer." Averill notices as well Wordsworth's later remark in the "Essay, Supplementary": "In any well-used copy of the Seasons the book generally opens of itself with the rhapsody on love [in "Spring"], or with one of the stories (perhaps Damon and Musidora)"; *Prose*, 3:74. As I indicate below, Damon and Musidora from "Summer" is also relevant to *An Evening Walk*.

112. It should be emphasized that the extra-descriptive truth documented in Wordsworth's footnote on Stanemoor was not reality but "realism"—i.e., a different convention. Averill's footnote on p. 66 draws upon J. Wordsworth to highlight the divergence of the poet's realism from reality: "As Jonathan Wordsworth has pointed out, the creation of the frozen family episode c. 1788 antedated the actual deaths on Stanemoor (of three men!) by some six years, suggesting that Wordsworth was 'trying to disguise its merely sentimental origin' (*The Music of Humanity*, p. 52). Moreover, the poet perhaps knew from his reading that Scott had praised Thomson for sometimes being 'happy enough to bring real facts in example' in treating pathetic episodes."

113. It is instructive to set such later Wordsworthian waters as the "still water" of memory over which the poet "hangs down-bending from . . . a slow-moving Boat" in *The Prelude* (4.247–68) or the "calm Lake" of the drowned man in the same poem (5.450–81) beside the locodescriptive tradition of still pools. Wordsworth's later waters betray a glimpse, however atavistic, of the locodescriptive moment. They tremble with refracted story. Thus the still water of memory over which the poet hangs is strangely crossed with "motions . . . sent he knows not whence"—tremblings indicative of the passage's function as an epic simile refracting the basic post-Miltonic story of the poem in which it is embedded: it remembers the past paradise—and prefigures the paradise lost—of the poet's life story (the "perplex'd" and self-crossed motion of images in the waters foreshadows the "heady thoughts jostling each other" and "strange rendezvous" of mind the poet next confesses as his "inner falling-off"; *Prel.* 4.270–73, 346). Just so, the calm lake of the drowned man is a palimpsest for submerged story. First there is the "plain Tale" of the drowned man's discarded clothes with its terrifying climax; then there is the gentling of that tale into a vision from "Fairy Land, the Forests of Romance"; finally there is the subsidence of all story, however romantic, beneath "A dignity, a smoothness, like the works /

Of Grecian Art, and purest Poesy." The locodescriptive moment, as we will see, is implicit with the possibility not only of time but ultimately of a spot of time.

114. Lest the superstitious flinch away from tragedy I indicate here seem too extravagant, I should add that some of the most affecting moments in picturesque literature are those in which the author sees the descriptive world suddenly penetrated by a tragic story of personal significance and therefore in need of reconstruction. Whether achieved through figuration or some other means, this reconstruction must be virtually ritualistic or superstitious in effect. I have in mind particularly the following moment in Hutchinson's *Excursion*, pp. 25–26: "In order to examine this fortress [Brough] with greater attention, I revisited it the succeeding year.—When I attempt to give a reason for my second visit to the Lakes, and beating the same road again, my eyes swim with tears, and my heart-rending sorrow is renewed to me with all its energy, for the inestimable loss I have sustained since my first excursion, in my fellow-traveller, my draughtsman, my friend, my second self, my *Brother*;—his virtues were too excellent to be detained from Heaven;—he departed in the flower of youth, amidst all the fire of genius, in the twenty-third year of his age.—Plate IV.—With him the unfinished draughts of those remarkable views were lost;—to recover them, though imperfectly, from my great inferiority in that art, I again visited the objects of his admiration, I repassed his lines, trod his steps, and with a melancholy degree of satisfaction viewed the scenes, which were then become to me solemn memorials of him who was not." It is clear that landscape here is equivalent with a step-by-step ritual of memorialization as suffused with superstition (or rather, the religiosity we saw the picturesque descended from) as a pilgrimage. Ritual gentles Hutchinson's personal tragedy (his buried epyllion), and the aesthetic artifacts such ritual leaves behind include a literary style of figuration or trope akin to pastoral elegy (we might almost hear a "Lycidas" or "Adonais" in Hutchinson's clichéd lament for the "flower of youth" who could not be "detained from Heaven") and a pictorial style with something like pastoral elegy's effect of supernatural restoration. The abrupt positioning of "Plate IV" in the above passage makes it in essence a nix or charm. Blocking off the swell of grief, the charm introduces in the following sentence a transformed mood of melancholy and solemn repose. (It would also be possible to consider locodescription and its affiliates in this light by looking, for example, to Collins's ode on Thomson or Bowles's sonnets; on the latter, see n. 8 to Chapter 1.)

115. Craquelure, we may note, is an especially English effect. Osborne defines it as "the network of small cracks which appears on a painting when in the course of time the pigment or varnish has become brittle. This was so notorious with some English masters, such as Reynolds, who glazed their work with bitumen to give it a glowing effect, that it was known in France as *craquelure anglaise* (p. 289).

116. If "pale steam" enwraps a "glaring hill," for example, the hill is nevertheless visible at the same time. And while we see in detail the "twinkling tail and glancing ear" of the deer at noon, we observe simultaneously and with equal precision the straining necks of the horses far above in their mountain enclosure. The stylistic corollary of such simultaneity

is Wordsworth's shaggy, undercoordinated verse—the radical inversion of sentence order and excessive interpolation of subordinate clauses that Leguois has cataloged, for example (*Early Life*, pp. 133–35). The fantastic idea behind such style, I suggest, is that it makes no difference whether a sentence is read from beginning to end, end to beginning, or even from the middle outwards: all things possible to be described are *already* coordinated in a simultaneous action. Take, for example, these difficult lines in the noon-piece: "And shades of deep embattl'd clouds were seen / Spotting the northern cliffs with lights between; / Gazing the tempting shades to them deny'd, / When stood the shorten'd herds amid' the tide." It is clear from punctuation that the clause beginning with "gazing" modifies the way the herds stood; but punctuation is a lost cause in this poem, and it is impossible to read these lines without first wanting to attach the gaze to the actions of the "deep embattl'd clouds." Distinct actions merge in a single moment.

117. Averill's use of the phrase "proto–*Evening Walk*" applies to materials prior to work on the actual poem and thus previous to the partial early version of *An Evening Walk* gathered in DC MS. 7. For convenience, however, I include the latter under the designation.

118. Siskin's perceptive essay on "The Vale of Esthwaite" and "Wordsworth's Gothic Endeavor" is apropos—particularly his thesis that "Wordsworth's gothicism evolved formally towards the creation of a narrative device capable of subordinating sensational episodes of 'visionary woe' to a comprehensive developmental scheme anchored by memory to the landscape" (p. 167). For Siskin, "sensational episodes of 'visionary woe'" are to a "developmental scheme anchored . . . to the landscape" in this formula as Fancy, the supernatural, and the super-tragical are to Nature, realism, and novelistic credibility (see *passim*). However, this alignment of oppositions creates a coordinate system primarily adapted to explaining Wordsworth's work in the late 1790's (the intended goal of Siskin's essay). Since the explanatory goal in this part of my book is earlier, we will need to notice that after "The Vale of Esthwaite" but before the onset of the Great Decade, the coordinates were quite different. "Sensational episodes" or the "tragic super-tragic" found their own assertively "realistic" and "natural" referent counter to the realism and naturalism of the novelistic norm. Antithetical to any notion of Fancy or of the visionary mind, this referent was the Reason of the French Revolution (whose early stage might be called a political "juvenilia" demonstrating lack of formal control over the story of the People). It was the Revolution that guaranteed sensationalism as fact.

119. On the import of the *oeil de la surveillance*, see Mathiez, p. 122. Leith, pp. 108–9, discusses the place of the Eye in the panoply of Republican allegory.

CHAPTER FOUR

1. A rudimentary calendar of the most famous Revolutionary *journées* and other violences extending from the period I concentrate upon through the high Terror would include the following: the Storming of the Tuileries (Aug. 10, 1792), the September Massacres (Sept. 2–6, 1792), the execution of Louis (Jan. 21, 1793), the assassination of Marat (July 13, 1793), the exe-

cution of Marie Antoinette (Oct. 16, 1793), the massacres at Lyons, Nantes, and other centers of the Vendéan revolt (fall–winter 1793), the execution of the Girondin leaders (Oct. 31, 1793), the execution of the Hébertist extremists (Mar. 24, 1794), the execution of the Dantonists (Apr. 5, 1794), and the denunciation and execution of Robespierre ("9–10 Thermidor": July 27–28, 1794). As previously noted, the period of the Storming of the Tuileries and September Massacres is sometimes referred to as the "first" or "popular" Terror (Soboul, pp. 262, 385). The September Massacres, one of my key paradigms, occurred when the Paris crowd, with the cooperation of the jailors, methodically killed and mutilated priests and other imprisoned "aristocrats." A most devastating narration of these events occurs in Carlyle's *The French Revolution*, especially in its horrified fascination with the mutilation of the Princess Lamballe. (Cf. Robert M. Maniquis, "Who Ate the Princesse de Lamballe's Heart?—Cannibalism and Revolution." Maniquis's paper, which I heard after the completion of this book, is relevant to my general concern with violence.) Spring and summer 1793 then saw the preparation of the institutions necessary for the second or official Terror. Strengthened and centralized, these institutions oversaw the high Terror from 1793 to June and July 1794—the latter month and a half of which, just before the Thermidorian reaction, was the "Great Terror." Convenient guides to the events and the terms I make use of in this chapter include the following: (A) Glossaries of Revolutionary terms: Rudé, *Crowd in the French Revolution*, pp. 253–57; Rudé, *Revolutionary Europe*, pp. 324–28. (B) Chronologies: Roberts, pp. 166–72; Sydenham, pp. 310–22. (C) Conversion table for dates in Revolutionary calendar: Lyons, pp. 239–40. (D) Maps of Revolutionary Paris, France, and Europe: Rudé, *Revolutionary Europe*, pp. 302–11. (E) Bibliographies and bibliographical essays designed for scholars working in English: Roberts, pp. 160–65; Lefebvre, *French Revolution*, 2: 363–95; Soboul, pp. 615–17. The best general purpose guide to the Revolution is *DSFR*, which excerpts chronologically from primary documents and includes helpful headnotes and bibliographies.

2. For the sake of clarity, I make two key simplifications in this chapter. *Perspective*: in the case of Wordsworth, the two perspectives upon the Revolution I study—the "English" and "French"—should really be at least three. The "French" view, of course, is a grand simplification. In my effort to locate the interpretive action of the Revolution in a differential of language between the English and French, I understress a related differential between the rightist and the radical presses in France. Excellent materials for studying the latter divide may be found in Popkin and in Censer. In regard to Wordsworth, it would be possible to narrow the field of study by exploring just the difference between the Paris radical press and the rightist or moderate language of politics the poet encountered in Orléans and Blois during 1792. Relevant here would be the language of the Vallons, Michel Beaupuy, and the officers with whom he quartered; of the newspapers he would have had access to; and of the "Friends of the Constitution," whose meetings he attended in Blois (see *CEY*, pp. 127ff.; MM, 1: 174–202). In practice, however, I have not found this line of inquiry practicable because of a paucity of materials available to me and, with regard to periodicals or other contemporary political literature, the uncertainty about what, if any-

thing, the poet read other than—as he himself regrets in a letter to William Mathews from Blois—the departmental "annals" available in a "petty provincial town" (*Letters*, 1: 77). The letter to Mathews, indeed, suggests that, with the exception of the Apr. 2 murder of General Theobald Dillon by his troops, Wordsworth felt cut off from national events during the Blois period: "You will naturally expect that writing from a country agitated by the storms of a revolution, my Letter should not be confined merely to us and our friends. But the truth is that in London you have perhaps a better opportunity of being informed of the general concerns of france" (*Letters*, 1: 77). (One other simplification along these lines may be mentioned. I have also not sought to supplement my samples of general political language in English and French periodicals with the idiom of the subculture of English and other radicals personally known to Wordsworth—an area of inquiry in which David Erdman has been working.) *Wordsworth's movements*: my quick summary here of Wordsworth's itinerary during the Revolution streamlines a very complex problem in biographical research. There are two areas of mystery especially relevant to a study of the poet's relation to violence. First, it is unclear whether he was in Orléans or Paris during the September Massacres (*CEY*, p. 135n). The memory of the Massacres in *Prel.* 10.64–67 is ambiguous on this score. Indeed, *The Prelude* suggests a strange mix of proximity to the Massacres (which the poet "felt and touch'd . . . a substantial dread") and distance, as if he had only read about them in a book ("The rest was conjured up from tragic fictions"). It thus seems best to think of Wordsworth in transition *toward* the Parisian center of violence during its first high-water mark of violence. (As Moorman points out, Orléans was itself tainted by massacre on Sept. 4 when prisoners held for trial in the city were moved to Versailles and consequently slaughtered. Also, the city witnessed "some riots and one or two murders" later in September [MM, 1: 201; for more details see Bimbenet, 5: 1174–1205]. On the whole, however, Orléans and the nearby Loire region were remarkably free of violence during the Revolution, as confirmed by the statistical maps of Revolutionary disturbances and executions in Greer.) Secondly, there is also the famous uncertainty about whether Wordsworth made a quick trip back to Paris in Oct. 1793 to witness the execution of Gorsas. Reed thinks the trip probable (*CEY*, p. 147). Since the event in any case postdates the period at the heart of my chapter (late 1792 to mid-1793), I leave it out of consideration.

3. I regret very much that I did not read Hunt's *Politics, Culture, and Class in the French Revolution* in time to use it in this chapter (a draft of which was completed in 1984). I have added a notice of *Politics, Culture, and Class* at this point, however, because of the close bearing it has on my themes and because it brings to a culmination the lineage of work on the French Revolution inspired by Furet's emphasis on language and discourse. The lack of Hunt in this chapter will in part be compensated for by the grounding of my overall approach in Furet as a common antecedent. Hunt's suggestive argument throughout her part on "The Poetics of Power" (with chapters on "The Rhetoric of Revolution," "Symbolic Forms of Political Power," and "The Imagery of Radicalism") is apropos to my discussion—especially to my section on "Paris" rather than that on London newspapers. I have not in most cases, however, attempted to interpolate after-the-fact references

below. Still, it may be useful to indicate one central congruency: Hunt's generic analysis of the Revolution as comedy/romance/tragedy (pp. 34–38) and my own work in this chapter and in Chapter 8. Hunt draws upon Northrop Frye for her understanding of narrative genres, whereas I draw upon other theoreticians of narrative. The particular understanding of narrative, and specifically of tragedy, I offer is thus different. (The Revolutionary obsession with conspiracy discussed by Hunt on pp. 38–44 is also relevant to the notion of narrative/political "plotting" I develop on the basis of prior work on conspiracy by Furet and by Cobb.)

4. Kelly, p. 4, summarizes some of the main currents in recent historiography of the Revolution responsible for the elevation of the paradigm of "language": the influence of "theories of semiotics, language, and symbolization"; the introduction of "structural and depersonalized interpretations"; and the effort "to recover the French Revolution as, par excellence, a sequence of political action represented by styles or traditions of political rhetoric." The leading figure in such historiography is clearly Furet, whose work strongly marks that of Kelly and Huet. It is Furet who uses most fully the explanatory paradigm of the depersonalized or collective *langue* of Revolution (esp. pp. 46, 48–49); and it is Furet who anchors what would otherwise be a purely modern theoretical construct in historical fact by concentrating on the causal role of depersonalized "opinion" in the Revolution (esp. pp. 38–39, 48, 50). "Opinion" is the endless, authorless *parole* whose deep *langue* is the structure of the Revolutionary conflict of discourses. Cobb's work ranks with Furet's in breadth of application, and outdoes it on the score of compelling, localized work with the facts of Revolutionary political and social history. Though Cobb's *Police* and *Reactions* really belong in a class by themselves (British rather than French in methodological style; practical rather than theoretical; and supremely heterogeneous rather than systematic), they also witness a fascination for "language" (esp. *Police*, pp. 49–52, 77–78, 87–88, 91, 193, 199, 246–49, 332 n. B, 363 n. K, 365 n. N). Indeed, it is one of Cobb's central theses that violence in the Revolution was first and foremost a *verbal* phenomenon, a way of talking. (I am grateful to Suzanne Desan of the University of Wisconsin, Madison, for the chance to talk about Cobb with a specialist in the field.) See also Paulson on the Revolution as an action of linguistic "renaming" (*Representations*, p. 15).

5. See, for example, Furet's thoughts about "narrative" (p. 18) and his vocabulary of the "theatre" and "centre stage" (pp. 46, 49). Huet's work is a sustained comparative reading of Revolutionary justice and Revolutionary theater, especially the trial of Louis and the plays written about Marat. (I am grateful to Carl Woodring for first pointing me to Huet.)

6. It would have been useful to include in our sample another Opposition paper that will be important in my argument in Chapter 8, the *Morning Post*. But the *Morning Post* is now almost wholly missing for 1792 (Werkmeister, *London*, p. 349). Werkmeister's studies, *The London Daily Press, 1772–1792* and *A Newspaper History of England, 1792–93* are a superb resource for study of the period covered by this chapter. For an overview of the London press in these years, see esp. *London*, pp. 317–79, and *Newspaper*, pp. 19–44.

7. Cf. "Inspector" in *MC*, Sept. 1, 1792: "I deny that any Government was ever changed without some bloodshed and much distraction."

8. Special care must be taken in using *The Annual Register* for the 1790's. After the transfer of the *Register* from the control of Burke and Dodsley (following the appearance of the volume for 1790 in 1793), publication of the volume for any particular year in the 1790's sometimes occurred with a lag of as much as seven years. Thus the volumes for 1792 and 1793 were not published until 1799.

9. I give page citations for the weekly and monthly press; dates alone will serve for the daily press because of the small number of pages and the fact that conventions of layout at the time (massive pages of miscellaneous material) would in any case make page citations difficult to use without additional column citations.

10. Such emphasis upon the "uncivilized" nature of the French, it should be noted, was especially pronounced given the prior reputation of the French for polished civility (cf. Paulson, *Representations*, p. 43). Relevant here is what might be called the *topos* of "drawing-room" criticism of the Revolution—the commonplace in the magazines that the Revolution was simply in bad taste. The Revolution, indeed, was the very inversion of Gallic good taste. As a letter in *GM* snidely points out, now the English could see what had always underlain the "politeness and delicacy" of that "fawning set of people" (July 1792, p. 645). For a broader study of the logic underlying arguments of "taste," see my "Toward a Theory of Common Sense."

11. In general, Gombrich's thesis complements Paulson's study of the way representation of the Revolution produces such centrifugal spin-offs from the classical as the sublime, the grotesque, the picturesque, and so forth.

12. The very assumption that the English language of violence was one of referential truth, it may be added, confirmed its classificatory function. The Culture/Nature divide was clearly cognate with the divide between conceptual language itself and such "bestial" or "savage" utterances—to draw upon images in our montage—as *ça ira* chanted around a fire. Language that refers to such a purely performative language of "nature" on a separate plane of being thus enacts classificatory difference in its very method.

13. Burke's scientific analogies for revolution in his *Reflections* epitomize an English language of violence structured according to what Foucault calls a "classical" *episteme*. Drawing numerous metaphors from contemporary chemistry and physics, Burke imagines the Revolution to be an experiment in which explosive violence breaks the human compound into constituent elements—gases or sometimes precipitates—assignable on a sort of periodic table of society (e.g., the "wild *gas*" metaphor on p. 90). But such a paradigm could not account for what the Romantics would call "organic" change, irreducible to shifting configurations of unchanging elements. Burke thus cannot fathom social "experiments" in which human nature appears to alter in its very atoms. Considering the abolition of religious "superstition" in France, for example, he is incredulous: "To destroy any power, growing wild from the rank productive force of the human mind, is almost tantamount, in the moral world, to the destruction of the apparently active properties of bodies in the material. It would be like the

attempt to destroy . . . the expansive force of fixed air in nitre, or the power of steam, or of electricity, or of magnetism" (p. 268).

14. This chapter is necessarily only a partial exploration of the complicity between narrative and violence. What has made the limitations of my project especially apparent to me is the body of provocative interdisciplinary work on violence that has emerged quite recently. My argument could have gained much, for example, from a reading of Elaine Scarry's *The Body in Pain*. Most of all, I regret that I put this chapter to bed before having the occasion to hear Richard Sennett's three talks on "The Aesthetics of Violence" ("Narrative and Violence," "Strategic Play," and "Sacrifice and Terror"), delivered from work-in-progress at Yale University, Mar. 31 to Apr. 14, 1986. Though set in a "modern" context, Sennett's searching, wide-ranging inquiry could have much facilitated my efforts to embed my particular concerns in a larger field of speculation. Particularly apropos to my overall project is Sennett's post-Girardian thesis that "sacred" narratives once imagined violence in such a way as to bond community but that modern secular narratives disrupt this original social function. In this light, the French Revolution is a key precedent for the transition from sacred to secular narratives of violence. Also apt in the context of my chapters on "Violence and Time" is Sennett's observation that narratives of violence achieve their power through the "destruction of the logos of time." With regard to my present study of "radicals of violence," cf. Sennett's contention that certain kinds of narratives distance the spectator from the victims of violence so "entertainingly" that the result is "pseudo-speciation" (i.e., the invention of a sub-species of humans designed for pain).

15. See *Reflections*, pp. 92 and 156, for other examples. Paine, as Paulson observes, early on recognized Burke's theatricality (*Representations*, p. 79).

16. Cf. Lindenberger, *Historical Drama*, pp. 141–46, on the way in which the theatrical way of seeing history—epitomized in historical dramas—projected "hierarchies" and models for ascending them. My emphasis upon the relation between history and tragic narrative in this chapter owes much to Lindenberger's study. Reading *Historical Drama* prior to Huet's *Rehearsing the Revolution* and Farrell's *Revolution as Tragedy* is especially useful.

17. It is intriguing to note that the high water mark of English and French enchantment with the "savages" of the Pacific occurred immediately prior to the onset of the French Revolution in 1789. As Bernard Smith observes in his *European Vision and the South Pacific*, widespread interest in Captain Cook's voyages prompted the Theatre Royal, Covent Garden, to stage John O'Keefe's *Omai: or a Trip Round the World* with Philip de Loutherbourg's costumes and scenery in 1785–86. The spectacular extravaganza was so successful that it ran 50 times its first season and was revived for shortened runs in the fall of 1786 as well as spring of 1788. Moreover, it inspired *le Théâtre de l'Ambigu-Comique* in Paris to mount an equally successful pantomime titled *La Mort du Capitaine Cook* in October 1788—a production that Covent Garden then in turn staged in an English version the year following (B. Smith, pp. 114–19). Smith's general argument concerns the manner in which Europe and the English first saw the Tahitians and other natives of the Pacific as Noble Savages—that is, as masked versions of classical heroic man (e.g., the Greeks) assimilable to Western culture without disturbance.

But by the early nineteenth century—in the period, we might note, just after the Revolutionary wars—such enthusiasm for the Noble Savage had altered into a compound view of the Pacific peoples as either ignoble or "romantic" savages (on the latter, see B. Smith, pp. 317–32).

18. Here, as throughout this chapter, my analysis is also informed by Girard. In the present instance, see Girard's chapter on the "monstrous double"—e.g., p. 158: "In a tragedy the reciprocal relationship between the characters is real, but it is the sum of nonreciprocal moments. The antagonists never occupy the same positions at the same time, to be sure; but they occupy these positions in succession. There is never anything on one side of the system that cannot be found on the other side, provided we wait long enough. The quicker the rhythm of reprisals, the shorter the wait. The faster the blows rain down, the clearer it becomes that there is no difference between those who strike the blows and those who receive them. On both sides everything is equal; not only the desire, the violence, the strategy, but also the alternation of victory and defeat, of exaltation and despair." A reading of Girard's thesis on the "monstrous double" together with Kelly's *Victims, Authority, and Terror* is useful. Kelly's whole work is devoted to the study of a special type of "victim" necessary to the French Revolution: the aristocratic revolutionary who espoused the new ideals but "embodied in their persons hereditary and institutional mentalities and visions of a political outcome offensive to the [Jacobin] Republic of Virtue" (p. 23).

19. In the light of Girard's thesis, it is instructive that "vengeance" was often taken to be the most basic or inclusive of all Revolutionary rationales. In a splendid piece of fiction, the correspondent for the *Morning Chronicle* records a collective "interview" with the French mob after the September Massacres as follows: "If I ask of the people, as I have often done, their reason, they answer, 'How can we march to the frontiers and leave behind us such a host of acknowledged foes, who will, when Paris is unprotected by us, be set at liberty by those without, with whom the City is filled, but at whom we cannot strike, because they are concealed or unknown, and who will, especially if success attend the German arms, not only point out to the enemy our wives and children, but in conjunction with the criminals also released join in the plunder? Of their murderous intentions we are too well convinced without any individual provocation, the sword is now drawn to be sheathed on no terms, but the extirpation of the enemy or ourselves. As the National Assembly, with the Courts of Judicature, have taken three weeks to condemn three criminals, our country will be lost, if we wait their decisions on the one hand, or if we leave behind us such a determined, acknowledged band of conspirators, and criminals, on the other. No, let us discriminate as much as possible, but let us strike at the guilty for this moment without pity. This example which we know and feel to be just, will deter the cowards who are concealed, and who will fear too much our returning vengeance to hazard any attempt against ourselves and the country, whilst we are marching to meet the invaders' " (Sept. 10, 1792). Here, "vengeance" is the summary of all the previous rationale. It may be noted that this correspondent—perhaps because of the general sympathies of the *Morning Chronicle*—makes an unusual effort to put words of reason in the mouths of the "savages." A similar effort to explain the actions of

the "mob" as rationally as possible underlies Rudé's valuable works, *The Crowd in the French Revolution* and *The Crowd in History*. The latter work, for example, stresses "the remarkable single-mindedness and discriminating purposefulness of crowds, even those whose actions appear to be the most spontaneous" (p. 253). For a criticism of the notion of "Popular Thought" and of Rudé's work as somehow too rational and "respectable," see Cobb, *Police*, pp. 89, 206.

20. For the paranoia of "plot" in Revolutionary France (including the hysteria of "prison plots" and "food plots"), see Furet, pp. 54–55; Cobb, *Police*, pp. 8–13, 288–90. On the "myth" of secret societies at the time, see Paulson, *Representations*, p. 40.

21. Or again, the fomenting of factions or of a divisive "plot" in a foreign nation could justify the intervention by an aggressive nation on behalf of one party or the other. As applied *mutatis mutandis* by France in its annexation of Switzerland in 1797 and after, such strategy modernized the old ploy of "dividing and conquering."

22. No better record exists of the English and European misunderstanding of the Revolutionary war than the war dispatches in the 1790's, which concentrated on traditional movements of troop columns and materiel while ignoring the reorganization of the French army as an *amalgame*, or mass movement blending old line troops and new recruits, professionals and amateurs (Rudé, *Revolutionary Europe*, p. 206; R. R. Palmer, *Twelve*, pp. 339–40). The result of the reorganization was formally unthinkable in a war tradition that had lost the means to apprehend the "barbaric": an *organized* "savagery" or *militant* "nature."

23. "Civiliz'd war!—How strangely pair'd appear / These words in pensive Rumination's ear! / Civiliz'd war!" (p. 249). In general, the binary of "savage" and "civilized" is one of the key structures in Fawcett's thought. For the documentable influence that Fawcett exerted upon Wordsworth, see Beatty's highly informative introduction to *The Art of War*.

24. Burke spoke of "merciless savages" and "barbarians" with "hands red with . . . blood" (*AR*, 1793: 20), we can notice, primarily to establish the "vertical" difference between French and English examples of insurrection. The French nation "was *sui generis*," he says, "and bore no analogy to any other. . . . It therefore did not follow that we ought to recognize it, merely because different powers in Europe had recognized the republic of England, under Oliver Cromwell" (*AR*, 1793: 20).

25. The English press was consistently fascinated by silence at moments of violence. It was commonplace, for example, to remark the "silence" preceding Louis's execution. An "anonymous historian of the revolution in France" reports in the *Annual Register* (1793: 219): "A melancholy gloom and awful silence . . . superseded the native gaiety of the French capital, during the last days of the king's life, as if some horrid calamity was presaged by its inhabitants: while bodies of armed men patroled the metropolis, the suppressed sighs and the restrained lamentations that were every where observed, encouraged the belief that a fair appeal to the people would, at least, have saved the devoted king from the horrid and unmerited fate which he so soon suffered." Other episodes of "silence" include the "solemn stillness" that affected the spectators when Louis arrived to be tried and the "silence"

with which he at first submitted to the proceedings (*AR*, 1793: 195); the "dumbness" of Malesherbes after communicating to Louis the death sentence (*AR*, 1793: 219); and the "profound silence" of Marat's funeral procession as well as the "most profound silence" of Charlotte Corday's execution (*T*, July 30, 1793). The pendant to the "silence" prefacing the execution of Louis, finally, is the sublime muteness of Marie Antoinette when meeting her end: "The procession lasted near an hour and a half; during this whole time no murmur, no sign of indignation, anger or complaint, escaped her; she looked round her with a calm and dignified air" (*Observer*, Oct. 11, 1793; quoted in Miliband, p. 7). A fuller study of "silence" in the Revolution would measure the English sensitivity to muteness against that of the French themselves, who could also remark "silence" but organized it in a way that made it part of Revolutionary discourse. See the "silence" in Kelly's schematic representation of the "Progress of the Revolution" (p. 20). See also Huet, pp. 7, 14, 41, 43, on codes of "silence" in the legislation, trial process, and theater of the Revolution. Frederick Brown's study of the "speechless tradition" in the illegitimate or censored theater preceding the Revolution shows that the French had long practiced organizing pantomimic silence into an effective discourse (pp. 41–82).

26. Hernadi, "The Erotics of Retrospection"; Punter, "1789: The Sex of Revolution"; Jameson, *Political Unconscious*, pp. 65–68, 151–84; P. Brooks, *Reading for the Plot*, pp. 37–61.

27. Couthon's paralysis in 1792–93 has been diagnosed as meningitis; but Couthon himself thought it due to sexual excess (R. R. Palmer, *Twelve*, pp. 13–14). On Sade, see the Chronology in Sade, p. 100.

28. See Cobb, *Police*, pp. 234–39, for detailed information about prostitution during the Revolution.

29. My model of literary desire grows out of a cooperative reading of recent theoreticians of desire together with Lindenberger's chapter on the sense of "reality" in historical drama (*Historical Drama*, pp. 1–29). Of course, a deeper look into the problem of literary desire in line with my broader discussion of reference in Chapter 2 would need to investigate the dependence of "empirical" or independently verifiable fact itself on prior structures of shared fiction or consensual belief. It would also be useful to return to the repressive "epic similes" of fictionality I discussed in Chapter 3 to add a further dimension to the model of literature as desire. If desire opens up the space between "fact" and "fiction," then *repression* of desire closes the space to subordinate fiction to the sense of absolute factual reality. Punter, in his provocative study of English reactions to the Revolution, has underscored Isaac Kramnick's thesis that Burke, for example, saw Jacobinism as a perpetual fantasy of sexual desire—of rape and aphrodisiacal frenzy (cited in Punter, p. 202). To reaffirm fact as opposed to fiction, Burke and other guardians of the English "boundary," as Punter calls them, had to represent "resistance and protection" in the face of desire (pp. 203–4)—i.e., repression. Repression is the device by which the escape from fact to fiction across what I have called the "atrium of literariness" can become an inverse commitment of fiction to fact—of what would otherwise be the merely fanciful rhetoric or epic similes of Burke's "purple passages," for example, to fundamental truth (see Punter, p. 204; see also Punter's broader statement on

the repressive uses of fiction-making during the French Revolution, p. 210). The French, I go on to suggest, had a method of resubmitting consensual fiction to fact even more brutal than Burke's verbal *energia*: actual violence. Violence, which the English saw merely as an extension of savage desire, was the repressive aspect of Revolution responsible for constituting official fact (i.e., "natural" and "just" fact) from fiction.

30. On the *Bande d'Orgères*, see Cobb, *Reactions*, pp. 180–211. The gang was on the rise during Wordsworth's stay in the area, and reached its zenith during the famine crisis of 1795 (*Reactions*, p. 195). Its sphere of operations was centered just north of Orléans.

31. I refer to Bergson's self-conflicted effort to adjust the violence of laughter to social purposes at the end of his essay on "Laughter." In a passage on the "natural" justice of laughing that may also be applied to the ideology of "naturally" violent humor in the French Revolution, Bergson writes: "Laughter is, above all, a corrective. Being intended to humiliate, it must make a painful impression on the person against whom it is directed. By laughter, society avenges itself for the liberties taken with it. . . . But it does not therefore follow that laughter always hits the mark or is invariably inspired by sentiments of kindness or even of justice. To be certain of always hitting the mark, it would have to proceed from an act of reflection. Now laughter is simply the result of a mechanism set up in us by nature or, what is almost the same thing, by our long acquaintance with social life. It goes off spontaneously and returns tit for tat. It has no time to look where it hits. Laughter punishes certain failings somewhat as disease punishes certain forms of excess, striking down some who are innocent and sparing some who are guilty, aiming at a general result and incapable of dealing separately with each individual case. And so it is with everything that comes to pass by natural means instead of happening by conscious reflection" (pp. 187–88).

32. I have tried to be as selective as possible in culling examples from my dossier on "sacrifice," which in fact threatened to be bottomless. There are also such visual representations as the picture in Henderson, p. 244, showing the French preparing to sacrifice husbands, children, jewels to the country.

33. The Convention decreed "Terror" the "order of the day" on Sept. 5, 1793 (*DSFR*, p. 479) and instituted the provisional government of Terror via the Declaration on Revolutionary Government of Oct. 10, the so-called "Constitution of the Terror" of Dec. 4, and the various decrees of the Economic Terror (*DSFR*, pp. 479–506). The Revolutionary Tribunal, Watch Committees, and Committee of Public Safety had already been formed earlier in 1793, and were thus in place ready to be radicalized toward the close of the year (*DSFR*, pp. 409–14, 423–25).

34. Even literal war could be conceived as "sacrifice" if considered in an "inward" context. Marat writes on Mar. 9, 1793: "I hear at this very time that Miranda's advance guard has been sacrificed by the treachery of the generals" (*Le Journal de la République française*; quoted in Gilchrist and Murray, p. 221).

35. Kelly, pp. 18–23. I conflate and improvise upon elements in Kelly's two schemas (his figs. 1 and 2).

36. In keeping with my earlier discussion of desire, we may also say that

Nature is what converts a sentence such as "war demands sacrifice" into the reality-oriented equivalent: "war *needs* sacrifice" (and vice versa).

37. It may be noted that I have reversed the directionality of the three-fold pictorial model of historical representation I introduced in sketch form in Chapter 1 (where in Wordsworth's 1790 tour "history marks the background, nature stands in the middle ground, and the real foreground stages the tourist himself, or 'I' of description"). The model remains the same; but my vantage point has changed. My initial perspective in Chapter 1 was that of the "Egotistical" self (as Wordsworth named it in his 1790 letter) in the act of looking through the mediation/deflection of descriptive nature into the "weather" of historical background. From this present chapter on, however, I position myself in historical action itself, and look with reverse gaze through nature into the new background constituted by the previous foreground. It is this latter, new background that is now the weather. Weather is an "atmosphere" first occupied by the collective ideology (anagogy, in the older terminology) of justice, but eventually productive of Wordsworth's personalized ideologies of self-righteousness: time, self, Imagination.

Besides bringing my viewpoint closer to that of historical action, an additional advantage of reversing the pictorial field in this manner is that it allows us to calibrate the relation of the self to history more accurately. Whereas in Chapter 1 it appeared that the self or tourist's "I" stood *in* the picture (on the foreground), the eventual reappearance of the "I" in the ideological background clarifies that there must be another, unaccounted-for identity—ill-defined, preconscious, pre-egotistical—standing at an apparent remove from the picture looking in. This is the identity that looks through foreground history and middle-ground nature to a background "I" enacting the *idea* or ideology of itself. "There *I* am in history!" the spectator-identity declares. In essence, my picture of history may thus be considered a three-dimensional version of Lacan's mirror paradigm of subjectivity (see n. 11 to Chapter 1). The pre-egotistical identity looks into the picture of history to see and denominate its social self ("I") standing in history, and precisely in this act first knows itself as the true subject *able* to see and denominate a social self in history. After all, as I have said elsewhere, it is precisely the recognition that "I am like all others" (i.e., a social self) that simultaneously provokes the profound discovery that "I am myself" ("Toward a Theory of Common Sense," p. 194).

But one last elaboration: we must also acknowledge that at the moment the subject sees its social self in history and so comes to "true" self-knowledge, that is the moment of infinite regress when there appears at the margins of knowledge a yet more removed spectator-subject—as yet unidentified and unformed—peering into an *expanded* picture space now including both the original spectator subject and its denominated "I." Ultimately, that is, there is no "true" subject at a stable perceptual remove from the historical picture: the instant the subject knows its true self as a consequence of seeing its social self ("I") clearly in history, that is the instant it has lost sight of the overall historical picture—in which there are no subjects except as defined from the viewpoint of other subjects; and in which we can never distinguish between watching the action and being part of an action (if nothing else, of "watching") that some other watcher or Watch Committee surveys. History or "elsewhereness," as I have called it, *is* otherness; and a theory of subject that seeks to domesticate otherness completely would lose sight of such essential differentiation. If this notion of infinite regress seems too deconstructive, I can only repeat with variation my earlier suggestion in Chapter 2: what deconstruction discovers in exploring endless regress, deferral, trace-structure, and so forth is the space of history: the unclosable, many-layered picture in which meaning recedes into other meaning, identity into refugee-identity, along an infinite perspective toward the vanishing point.

38. The *Public Advertiser* (Aug. 16, 1792) reports on a lynching on the day of the Storming of the Tuileries: "A scene of terrible confusion ensued: The unfortunate victims underwent a sort of mock trial, were convicted, and execution immediately followed." *T* (Sept. 10, 1792) quotes from a French report of the September Massacres: "In the different prisons, the mob formed a tribunal consisting of twelve persons; after examining the jailor's book, and asking different questions, the judges placed their hands upon the head of the prisoner, and said, 'Do you think that in our consciences we can release this gentleman?'—This word *release* was his condemnation. When they answered *yes*, the accused person, apparently set at liberty, was immediately dashed upon the pikes of the surrounding people."

39. The link between legitimacy and theatricality will be part of my concern in Chapter 6, where I read *The Borderers* as a trial.

40. Cf. Huet, p. 56, on Revolutionary justice as a "language" constantly spoken in the name of a phantom People.

41. It is instructive to read Farrell, p. 29, while keeping in view our schema of the Revolutionary "ideology of combat": "The literature before us . . . forms one of the classic nineteenth-century meditations on the problem of alienation. The dialectical dancers are trapped between isomorphic sociopolitical forces that, like a pair of reflecting mirrors, swallow up all the space between them. What the dancers find is that they are existentially missing in action. Tragedy is their claim to being, a spectacle of significant form thrown up between the mirrors which endows the dancers with gravity." My argument is that the dancers in the fire here, always purging and yet never purged, cannot remain poised in unscorched moderation between the deadly fires (not just bright mirrors) of the Revolution itself (except insofar as politics was simply unimportant to the participant—as in the case of Cobb's examples of Frenchmen wholly oblivious to the occurrence of the Revolution; *Reactions*, pp. 132–42). Farrell's "moderates" would be precisely the monstrous doubles (to use Girard's term) that the Revolution delighted to sacrifice or "victimize" (in the language of Kelly's study) in order to mark turning points in its progress.

42. I am grateful to Herbert Lindenberger for helping me identify the precise precedent of Corday's self-dramatizing tragic composure. As Lindenberger puts it: "Corday was more Corneillian than Racinian . . . and her tyrannicide is a typical Corneille tragic action" (private communication). Lindenberger also notes that Corday not only came from Corneille's native province, but was descended from his sister (see also Mathiez, p. 343).

43. To complete my subthesis of the "humor" of Revolutionary violence would require at this point reading the *Times* report of the executioner slap-

ping Corday's face ("twice on the cheek!!") together with the passage that Mehlman, p. 9, quotes from Marx's *The Eighteenth Brumaire of Louis Bonaparte*: "Hegel remarks somewhere that all great events and historical personages occur, as it were, twice. He forgot to add: the first time as tragedy, the second as farce." The relation between the two reversible pairs, history/repetition and tragedy/laughter (all expressed in the form of revolution) is powerful. But it is also problematic. Here is Bergson on the metonymical repetitiousness of laughter: "Many a comic form, that cannot be explained by itself, can indeed only be understood from its resemblance to another, which only makes us laugh by reason of its relationship with a third, and so on indefinitely. . . . What can be the driving force, the strange impulse which causes the comic to glide thus from image to image, farther and farther away from the starting-point, until it is broken up and lost in infinitely remote analogies? But what is that force which divides and subdivides the branches of a tree into smaller boughs and its roots into radicles? An inexorable law dooms every living energy, during the brief interval allotted to it in time, to cover the widest possible extent in space" ("Laughter," p. 102). We can add our own questions to this litany. What determines whether repetition on the historical scene is taken tragically or comically? If historical repetition is innately "farce," that is, why did no one laugh when, in a fit of ultimate slapstick, the executioner slapped Corday's face twice? (Surely such caricatural excess would have been giggled at elsewhere in a Revolution not fastidious at laughing its head off over repetitious violences—not just one cooked mother, for example, but also all her daughters followed by a group of priests.) Or again, if comedy is by nature repetitious, why does Bergson's tone in the above passage—especially as it comes to the "inexorable law" that "dooms every living energy"—become so unmistakably tragic? In a perfect enactment of Bergson's thesis about the "mechanisation" of persons involved in humor, Corday's head falls—*plop*—from the guillotine. Such would be a perfect example of the force dividing the branches of the tree or the inexorable law dooming every living energy to cover the widest extent in space. Yet in the very effort to make a weak stab at humor here (my onomatopoeic *plop* above), we sense we have done injury. Our laughter is itself forced and doomed.

Phrased in terms of the comic universe, the "elsewhereness" of history takes on new meaning: a full acceptance of the sense of history, we may say, requires the ability to laugh at the dismembered, the exiled, the dead, the doomed, and all those other disappeared ones in the human version of the madly repetitive "Chinese encyclopaedia" of dogs Foucault "laughs" at expansively in his Preface to *The Order of Things*. Perhaps, therefore, it is not the case that the *commedia dell'arte* of laughter is merely an early prologue to the tragic response to historical agony. Perhaps it is just the reverse: tragedy, with its demand that all repetition be unity, is the stunted and early form of an expanded ability to laugh—of a laughter transcending the ordinary giggling that tragedy, in its own defense, *calls* laughter. (I deal with the concept of irony—one exit from our current impasse between agony and laughter—in Chapter 6. There we will see that the hidden term in the problem of tragic/comic response to repetitive violence is a strange doppelgänger of disaffected irony: affection or emotion.)

44. Sundays, we may note, were *not* a popular time for crowd events and disturbances in England. M. Harrison shows that few such events occurred on the customary "domestic" Sunday, whereas "outdoor" Monday attracted many such events (pp. 157–60).

45. Perhaps the closest English analogue to this sentence, with its syntactical and ideological subordination of the *ancien régime* to the awakening of consciousness, is Blake's prophecy of 1794, *Europe*: "Then Enitharmon woke, nor knew that she had slept; / And eighteen hundred years were fled" (p. 243). It may be said that the entire plot of this poem, which terminates "eighteen hundred years" of history upon a fiery sunrise of awakening, is Blake's attempt to reinvent the calendar.

46. Ozouf approaches Revolutionary temporality as an *action* structured around the functions of beginning, distributing, remembering, and ending. It would be instructive to think of the locodescriptive moment (and, indeed, of the descriptive mode in general) along similar lines. Conceived as an action, the locodescriptive interface between narration and description occurs when acts of beginning or ending (originally narrative in assumption) are reified into a static distribution or organization of space (thus creating in the "middle" of beginning and end the descriptive firmament). The trace-act of temporality that maintains the connection between narrative and description is then "remembering." As when Celadon turns into a funerary statue in Thomson (see Chapter 3), the descriptive landscape is dotted over by monuments commemorating the fact that the middle of things is haunted by beginnings and endings. In short, if narrative action is quintessentially a verb form akin to Ozouf's *commencer*, *distribuer*, *commémorer*, and *finir*, then the descriptive world is not so much a noun as a participial or gerund construction. It is the world of "trembling."

47. Cf. L. Hunt's discussion of the colossus at this fourth station, which she approximates to the Hercules imagery of the Revolution (pp. 96–98 and her pl. 13). Hunt writes: "David orchestrated a festival that aimed at nothing less than a review of the Revolution's development. It was a morality play with a set of striking allegorical messages" (p. 96).

CHAPTER FIVE

1. In moving quickly from France back to Wordsworth, and from a "duration in the history of peoples" to poetic time, I elide an intermediate realm of investigation that could allow the construction of a more ample causeway back across the Channel. This realm is the connection between Revolutionary time and the general English sense of political time as studied in J. G. A. Pocock's expansively conceived "Modes of Political and Historical Time in Early Eighteenth-Century England." Especially suggestive in our context is Pocock's consideration of the opposition in English historical temporality between contingency and continuity, and between an eschatological/millennial view of time and a Burkean, traditionary, or customary time. What Pocock's argument allows us to surmise is that there was an uncanny link of similarity/difference between the Revolutionary and English notions of historical time. The Revolution also conceived a time of customary continuity, which it told as its version of Burkean "prejudice" passed

on from generation to generation: *grievance.* Particularly telling in this regard were the massive lists of grievances, or *cahiers de doléances* (almost sixty
thousand of which still survive), collected during the electoral campaign
for the Estates General in 1789 (see Soboul, pp. 125–26). But the history
of continuous and enduring grievance added up to what English historical
time suppressed: a millennial new beginning. Time, as we saw in the last
chapter, began over again; and on the other side of the millennial divide—
as if through a looking glass—the enduring grievances of the past became
the equally enduring freedoms of the future. The French, in sum, were in
the paradoxical position of making tradition eschatological and convention
inventive: they customized custom. Paradox of this sort, as Pocock suggests at the end of his essay, would lead ultimately to the dialectical mode
of thought that the English skirted: "A liberal interpretation of the constitution, of the relations between virtue and commerce, and of the relations
between personality, polity and economy, ensured that England did not develop a dialectical historicism based on the need to maintain consciousness
of a self being constantly transformed into its antithesis" (pp. 100–101).

2. Cf. Paulson, *Representations*, p. 270: "The political books, in short,
have a powerful effect on the final spots of time, showing the relationship
on a poetic level between the killing of the king and of Robespierre and
the death of Wordsworth's own father." See also *Representations*, p. 259. The
concept of the spot of time and of the *journée*, we can thus say, are equivalent at a deep level. Both celebrate a place in time (e.g., Penrith Beacon,
Bastille) where a signal violence freed the People/Imagination. But as I go
on to argue in Part III, the history feted on Wordsworth's spots of time
at last includes the English social scene as well as Revolutionary politics.
(For a recent political reading of the spots of time, see J. Chandler's provocative thesis that Wordsworth's spots stage a "discipline" instinct with
the anti-Revolutionary traditionalism of Burkean prejudice, pp. 184–215. I
draw upon J. Chandler's argument more fully in Chapter 8.)

3. By saying that Revolutionary ideology was "premised" upon nature's
transparency to history, I do not mean that ideology can ever fully realize such a premise and reveal historical agon in total transparency. Rather,
it at once reveals and masks. As I suggested in my introduction to Part II
("Before Time"), any *idea* of time must be to some extent an "explanation,
mitigation, and denial" of underlying history. "Explanation, mitigation,
and denial" indicates that the ability of ideology to reveal history lies along a
sliding scale of varying opacity (a scale that no single interpreter, embedded
in his own opacities of history and ideology, can read with certainty). This
is one reason why, as I suggested earlier (see esp. n. 25 to Chapter 2), it
is useful to distinguish "displacement" from "denial." Though we cannot
know with certainty the distortion that past ideology imposes upon its history, nevertheless it seems sensible to think there *is* a difference in quality
(and perhaps degree) between collective and poetic distortions. Collective
ideology *displaces* historical agon; and the *glissade* such displacement connotes, as I earlier termed it, exactly indicates the broad, imprecise, careless,
and often contradictory manner in which popular ideology functions. The
ideology of the Revolution, after all, was not too much disturbed if its
raw underlying agony erupted back into direct vision and so necessitated

a further, inconsistent reworking of ideology. By contrast, poetic ideology (specifically, Wordsworth's idea of time) is more carefully constructed, more concentrated, more effective in screening agon, and so also—like a fine optical instrument—more fragile. It is an overdetermined displacement: a denial.

4. The order of events in the first part of the 1790 tour is particularly important for the purposes of this chapter. As the maps in Havens, pp. 420–23, and D. Hayden, pp. 16, 22, 28, 32, 40, make clear, Wordsworth and Jones first traversed France and then began what I earlier called the 1790b leg of their trip by crossing into the Savoy (the zone at the intersection of France, Switzerland, and Italy then ruled by independent dukes). After visiting the Grande Chartreuse, Chambéry, and other sites in the Savoy, Wordsworth and Jones crossed the Rhone into Switzerland and walked the length of Lake Geneva along its northern bank to Martigny. At this point, they detoured back into the Savoy to visit Chamonix and Mont Blanc. Retracing the route of the detour back into Switzerland, they then continued up the Rhone toward Simplon and all the rest of their Swiss and northern Italian itinerary. With the exception of the northern bank of Lake Geneva, then, all the French and Savoyard sights of the 1790 tour preceded the poet's experiences in Switzerland.

5. We can put this thesis in the specific terms of Chapter 3 as follows. In order to comprehend the agonic plot of the Revolution, Wordsworth's description had to cede part of the space of "form" back to *istoria*. Description, that is, had to provide a David-like stage of action upon which to restage the old narratives underlying form with emphasis on the agonic *Conturbatio* that precedes the *Humiliatio* of "repose." In Wordsworth's later aesthetics, the staging ground for stories of *Conturbatio* in his own life will be the "sublime." But not yet able to enlist the full resources of the sublime (see n. 16 to this chapter), the poet in the period we are considering must compensate for the diminished narrative stage of the picturesque by adding a new stage of action invisible in space: time. (Under the aspect of "a sense of duration," indeed, the concept of time at last helps Wordsworth define the sublime in his unfinished essay on "The Sublime and Beautiful" of 1811–12; *Prose*, 2: 351.)

6. According to one in a series of articles on the Monastery in *EM* for 1791: "Their Order is very severe. The Monks wear nothing but flannel next their skins; never lie on any thing but straw beds; use no sheets; eat no flesh even in illness; dine alone except on Sundays and Holidays; never speak to each other in the Cloister, and only once a week elsewhere. . . . [The General's] dress and way of life were full as hard as the common Monks" (May 1791, p. 343). The same article continues: "The good Monks were so terrified by the distant successes of the King of Prussia, in the Seven Years War, that they applied for and obtained a small body of soldiers to protect their retreat. Under a rock, in a sort of cavern, are some wooden barracks for the soldiery, which the Government lend them in time of war" (May 1791, p. 344). It is instructive to read Wordsworth's Grande Chartreuse excursus in the 1850 *Prelude* together with the many poems, inscriptions, and visitor-album entries dedicated to the monastery (which hosted some ten thousand tourists and three to four thousand pilgrims each year; *EM*,

May 1791, p. 343). Selections from this literature, which shares much of Wordsworth's somber sublimity, appear in *EM*, Apr. 1791, p. 285; Sept. 1791, pp. 168ff.

7. It is instructive to note that the temporal instability at this point in the poem gave Wordsworth trouble in his later attempts at revision. In his Introduction to *DS*, Eric Birdsall notices that in the Wellesley Quarto the line, "Ev'n now I sigh at hoary Chartreuse' doom," is altered in pencil to cancel the "Ev'n now"—a change then reproduced in the 1815 edition (*DS*, pp. 15–16).

8. See the presumed miniature portrait of Annette in Legouis, *William Wordsworth and Annette Vallon* (frontispiece).

9. "Blessing the Torrent," pp. 201 and 203 n. 17. Hartman suggests that Wordsworth may actually have been thinking of the name Devil's Bridge when inventing this bridge in *Descriptive Sketches*, "though what is actually described is a wooden covered bridge and not the famous stone bridge of that name in the Viamala region." The later poem that Hartman makes the centerpiece of his essay is "To the Torrent at the Devil's Bridge, North Wales, 1824."

10. Beatty, *Wordsworth*, p. 47n. On the general influence Ramond's translation and expansion of Coxe had upon *Descriptive Sketches*, see ibid., pp. 33–35.

11. In a note, Wordsworth acknowledges the influence of Ramond here (*DS*, p. 84n). Beatty's gloss is instructive: "The passage in Ramond to which Wordsworth refers is a long and interesting one. . . . It is rather exactly summarized by Wordsworth. Both authors make it clear that while the Swiss peasant does not live in the golden age, he represents that age of uncorrupted hearts more nearly than any other man; and both had the earnest hope that the French Revolution would 'beget that golden age again'" (*Wordsworth*, p. 53n).

12. It is possible that Wordsworth's typification of the Swiss mountaineers owes much to Charlotte Smith's "The Peasant of the Alps," which appeared in *EM*, July 1791, pp. 72–73, soon before Wordsworth visited Smith in Brighton on his way to France (*CEY*, p. 123). As Reed notes, we know that he possibly read and copied other poems of Smith at this time (*CEY*, p. 123 and n).

13. Wordsworth's note to l. 631 makes it clear that he is thinking of the Swiss mercenaries: "The effect of the famous air called in French Ranz des Vaches upon the Swiss troops removed from their native country is well known, as also the injunction of not playing it . . . before the regiments of that nation, in the service of France and Holland" (*DS*, p. 100n).

14. Sheats comments about the poem: "A suddenly elevated sense of the justice, power, and benevolence of natural law reflects ideas common to Rousseau, d'Holbach, and other pre-revolutionary political theorists, ideas that were 'on every tongue' in the France of 1792" (pp. 62–63).

15. I have adopted Selincourt's "cannon sound" in l. 776 (*PW*, 1:88) rather than the "cannon found" in *DS*.

16. A reading of Theresa Kelley's fine essay on "Wordsworth and the Rhinefall" together with my argument here would be instructive. As Kelley notes, Wordsworth first visited the Fall of the Rhine near Schaffhausen on

his 1790 tour and then returned to the site in 1820. "For Wordsworth," she suggests, "it became in the intervening years a *locus* or gathering place in his art, politics, and aesthetics" (p. 61). Specifically, Kelley argues that Wordsworth gradually learned to fit such sites as the Rhinefall into an aesthetics of the sublime able to accommodate his mature anti-Gallic politics. Kelley's essay indicates how we could extend our own argument of aesthetics and politics into the later works. I argue here that the picturesque of 1790 deforms under the stress of the poet's early politics to yield a "*locus* or gathering place" of meanings in *time*—i.e., a spot of time. Rethought as the "sense of duration," as I earlier suggested (in n. 5 to this chapter), such time then joins "individuality of form" and the "sense of power" to constitute the poet's mature aesthetics of the sublime (*Prose*, 2: 351). By the time of the 1820 counterpart of the 1790 tour, Kelley shows, it is this aesthetics that takes over for the picturesque in providing a thought medium for politics.

17. The poem, however, descends to us in the fair copy in DC MS. 10, dating probably from spring 1794. As evidenced by the missing stanzas at the end of Gill's Reading Text, a few of the pages were torn out of the manuscript.

18. Sheats, p. 91, comments: "Each negative statement names an image that the traveler seeks, but denies its objective existence. Imagery imitates desire, and syntax the force with which the object-world denies that desire."

19. Paul Kelley has documented the echoes of Rousseau in the first two stanzas of *Salisbury Plain*.

20. On dating the *Letter*, see *Prose*, 1: 20–21, and *CEY*, p. 142. Reed opts for the later period in June or just after.

21. Other endorsements of the principle of necessity in the *Letter* include the following passages: "But, above all, these men lament that any combination of circumstances should have rendered it necessary or advisable to veil for a moment the statues [*sic*] of the laws" (*Prose*, 1: 33); "This apparent contradiction between the principles of liberty and the march of revolutions, this spirit of jealousy, of severity, of disquietude, of vexation . . . must of necessity confuse the ideas of morality" (1: 34); "It is the province of education . . . to soften this ferocity of character proceeding from a necessary suspension of the mild and social virtues" (1: 34); "Even the clergy were conscious of such necessity" (1: 34); "The end of government cannot be attained without authorising some members of the society to command, and, of course, without imposing on the rest the necessity of obedience" (1: 42); "this necessity is attached to a struggle for Liberty" (1: 49). As I noted in Chapter 4, such rationalizations of violence were commonplace among liberal correspondents of the *Morning Chronicle*. See also Wüscher, p. 40, on the occurrence of "necessity" in the *Letter*. In general, Wüscher's analysis of the *Letter* is excellent.

22. For a résumé of the debate over Godwin's influence on the *Letter*, see *Prose*, 1: 23–24 and 23n. Early to mid-1795, as Reed says, "may be counted [the period of Wordsworth's] firmest adherence to the doctrines of William Godwin" (*CEY*, p. 163). Wordsworth visited repeatedly with Godwin in London from Feb. to Aug. (and saw him again in 1796 and 1797) (*CEY*, pp. 164–66, 182–83, 211).

23. "During a period of revolution, enquiry, and all those patient specu-

lations to which mankind are indebted for their greatest improvements, are suspended. Such speculations demand a period of security and permanence; they can scarcely be pursued when men cannot foresee what shall happen tomorrow, and the most astonishing vicissitudes are affairs of perpetual recurrence" (*Political Justice*, p. 271).

24. The sacrifice concept undergirds Wordsworth's *Letter*. To begin with, "sacrifice" is as deeply ingrained in the poet's vocabulary (e.g., *Prose*, 1: 39, 45) as the idiom of "self-sacrifice" he later remembers speaking with Beaupuy in 1792 (*Prel.* 9.394). More importantly, the allusion to Racine shows that the poetics of sacrifice is part of the bedrock argument of violence in the *Letter*. In the Appendix to the sermon provoking Wordsworth, Bishop Watson had depicted the execution of Louis on Jan. 21, 1793 as the defilement of an altar: "I fly with terror and abhorrence even from the altar of Liberty. . . . My heart sinks within me when I see it streaming with the blood of the Monarch himself" (quoted in *EM*, Feb. 1793, p. 111; see *Prose*, 1: 52n). Wordsworth, however, deems such defilement necessary. After quoting Watson's passage on the "altar of Liberty," he launches upon the justification of violence by stern necessity quoted above (*Prose*, 1: 33). The justification capitalizes upon a brilliant appropriation of Racine's *Athalie* in the sentence immediately preceding the *Letter*'s quotation of Watson— a revisionary appropriation serving to resacralize Watson's bloody altar of liberty as the site of legitimate sacrifice. In Racine's play, the High Priest of the Temple of Jerusalem had raised the young Joash from infancy without letting him know that he was the descendant of David and thus the rightful king (whose line the tyrannical queen, Athalie, had wanted extinguished). The High Priest, in Act I, Scene ii, expresses a wish that Wordsworth, in a footnote to his allusion, quotes in the original: "Now we must have upon the throne a man / Who one day will remember that God's priests, / Out of the dark oblivion of the grave, / At God's command, restored him to his place / Lighting anew the vanished light of David" (*Athalie*, p. 167; *Prose*, 1: 33n). By *negating* this wish in his allusion, Wordsworth strikes a blow at once against monarchy, religion, and his version of a "high priest": Watson. Leading up to his justification of violence, he thus writes: "In France royalty is no more . . . and I flatter myself I am not alone, even in this *kingdom*, when I wish that it may please the almighty neither by the hands of his priests nor his nobles (I allude to a striking passage of Racine) to raise his posterity to the rank of his ancestors and reillume the torch of extinguished David" (*Prose*, 1: 33). Louis becomes the extinguished David, and Louis's young son a Joash, whom Wordsworth would keep uncrowned within his version of the Jerusalem Temple—the "Temple" prison in Paris that still held Marie Antoinette and her son (and was so recently the scene of Louis's widely reported acts of devoutness before his execution; see, for example, *AR*, 1793: 222–24). Nor does the application of Racine in the *Letter* end here. "The conclusion of the same speech [in *Athalie*] applies so strongly to the present period that I cannot forbear transcribing it," Wordsworth finishes in his footnote. He then quotes in the original: "Be pleased, O God, be pleased to pour upon / The Queen and her ungodly minister [*sur Mathan et sur elle*] / That spirit of confusion and of blindness / That ever ushers in the fall of princes" (*Athalie*, p. 168; *Prose*, 1: 33n). At this point, we notice, he reads

Racine correctly: Marie Antoinette is a new Athalie and must also be denounced. Putting Wordsworth's perverse and correct applications of Racine together (i.e., his denunciations of Louis/David and of Marie Antoinette/Athalie, respectively), we see that *all* monarchs, whatever their legitimacy, must now be extinguished. Or to phrase this tenet in terms of the single most pervasive and powerful concept of *Athalie*, all monarchy must be *sacrificed* for the good of the people. The leading function of the priests in *Athalie* is sacrifice; Joash fears he will be "offered up as a burnt-sacrifice / To turn away the anger of the Lord" (*Athalie*, p. 195); and the very Temple of Jerusalem is identified as the site of Abraham's near-sacrifice of Isaac. Assimilating this quintessential drama of sacrifice to his *Letter*, Wordsworth thus becomes something like a Corday of the left: a devotee of *hallowed* violence. As we saw in our montage of sacrifice in Chapter 4, Corday came to Paris with the avowed purpose of "sacrificing" Marat in roughly the same period Wordsworth was writing his letter.

25. See also the argument concerning "general" versus "particular" representation later in the *Letter*. These two principles, Wordsworth says, "must war with each other, till one of them is extinguished. It was so in France" (*Prose*, 1: 41).

26. The resemblance between the last stanza of the poem and the fourth stage in David's fete is strong enough to suggest that the poet may have read in Wales about the fete before writing the end of his poem, or that the end of the poem was informed by knowledge of the event gained on his possible third trip to France sometime in early October (and perhaps slightly earlier; see *CEY*, p. 147 and n.). The evidence, however, is too insecure to allow for more than speculation along either of these lines.

27. For a contrasting, more thoroughly non-violent reading of the last "herculean" stanza in the poem, see Gillcrist.

28. Regarding l. 379 in the Vagrant's tale, "And oft, robbed of my perfect mind," Gill cites W. J. B. Owen's notice of the allusion to *Lear* IV.vii: "I fear I am not in my perfect mind" (*SP*, p. 33n).

29. Drawing upon the concept of "repetition-compulsion," Clayton has called such repetition the "conservative impulse" or "turning back" in narrative that opposes a tale's forward-moving necessity (p. 153).

30. For Miller's meditation upon the "shell" in the Arab-Quixote dream, see his *The Linguistic Moment*, pp. 67, 95–99 (in a chapter on Wordsworth originally published in 1972 as two separate essays: "The Still Heart: Poetic Form in Wordsworth" and "The Stone and the Shell: The Problem of Poetic Form in Wordsworth"). For Miller's unraveling of the "labyrinthine" narrative "line," see his 1978 essay on "Ariadne's Thread." His *Fiction and Repetition*, of course, is also relevant.

31. The poem, of course, is written in Spenserian stanzas. For a study of the implications of Spenserian form in the poem, see Schulman. Well informed about political and social background, Schulman's essay is a valuable addition to the criticism of *Salisbury Plain*. Part of Schulman's thesis is that "it is important to see that Wordsworth's use of the Spenserian mode in a poem like this—contemporary, socially advanced, anti-war—is a repudiation of the antiquarian sensibility that had, up to now, cherished and pro-

moted the appreciation of Spenser. *Salisbury Plain*, taut and bitter, repudiates
. . . dreamy and escapist medievalism" (p. 225). I argue that Wordsworth's
Spenserianism, if no longer dreamy, is nightmarish. It can only be "contemporary" in an allegorical, displaced manner. Cf. Hartman on the Spenserian
stanza in the poem (*WP*, p. 125).

32. For convenience, I cite Caesar's work and other classical sources
from Kendrick wherever possible. Kendrick brings together the classical
passages on the Druids in translation and reproduces the originals in his Appendix. Caesar's comment here, we may note, was often echoed in Wordsworth's time. In his *Observations on the Western Parts of England*, pp. 87–88, for
example, Gilpin cites the comment with relevance specifically to Salisbury
Plain: "It is probable also, (as Caesar tells us the Druid discipline was carried
originally into Gaul, from Britain, which was the great source of Druid-
learning), that Salisbury Plain might have been a scene of great antiquity
many years before the time of Caesar."

33. It is unclear whether this event occurred in the Wales tour of 1791
or 1793—the latter, of course, precisely the goal of the trip across Salisbury
Plain that occasioned our present poem (see *CEY*, pp. 316–17). The record
of the incident, in Wordsworth's letter to George Huntly Gordon of May
14, 1829, is worth quoting in full: "Five and thirty years ago I passed a
few days in one of [Montgomeryshire's] most retired vallies at the house
of a Mr Thomas . . . where an event took place so characteristic of the
Cambro Britons that I will venture upon a recital of it. I was introduced
to Mr Thomas by my old friend and fellow Pedestrian among the Alps,
Robert Jones. . . . One day we sat down une partie quarrée at the Squire's
Table, himself at the head; the Parson of the Parish, a bulky broad-faced
man between 50 and 60 at the foot and Jones and I opposite each other.
I must observe that 'the Man of God' had not unprofessionally been employed most part of the morning in bottling the Squire's 'Cwrrw', anglisé
strong Ale, this had redden'd his visage (we will suppose by the fumes)
but I sat at table not apprehending mischief. The conversation proceeded
with the cheerfulness good appetite, and good cheer, naturally inspire—the
Topic—the powers of the Welsh Language. 'They are marvellous,' said the
revd Taffy. 'Your English is not to be compared especially in conciseness,
we can often express in one word what you can scarcely do in a long sentence.' 'That,' said I, 'is indeed wonderful be so kind as to favor me with
an instance?' 'That I will' he answered. 'You know perhaps the word Tad?'
'Yes.' 'What does it mean?' 'Father' I replied. 'Well,' stammer'd the Priest in
triumph, 'Tad and Father there you have it'—on hearing this odd illustration of his confused notions I could not help smiling on my friend opposite;
whereupon, the incensed Welshman rose from his chair and brandished over
me a huge sharp pointed carving knife. I held up my arm in a defensive attitude; judge of the consternation of the Squire, the dismay of my friend, and
my own astonishment not unmixed with fear whilst he stood threat[e]ning
me in this manner and heaping on my poor English head every reproachful
epithet which his scanty knowledge of our language could supply to lungs
almost stifled with rage. 'You vile Saxon!' I recollect was one of his terms,
'To come here and insult me an ancient Briton on my own territory!' At last

his wrath subsided 'et me servavit Apollo' " (*Letters*, 5: 77–79). Remembering our subargument about the "humor" of violence in France in Chapter 4, we may ask: why is the Ancient Briton so funny?

34. Coleridge, of course, used this phrase to describe *The Faerie Queene* (quoted in Spenser, p. 580).

35. As the poet records in his fragmentary poem beginning, "How sweet the walk along the woody steep" (summer 1793) and his later Advertisement to *Guilt and Sorrow*. See *CEY*, p. 144.

36. For other examples of the interest in poetry about Druids and Bards in the periodicals of the time, see *GM*, Sept. 1792, pp. 790–91; May 1793, pp. 434–35; *EM*, Sept. 1791, pp. 225–26; Oct. 1791, pp. 303–4. See Piggott, pp. 169–71 for other examples.

37. As Beatty first noted, the story of Jarvis Matchem might have been the source of the Sailor's story in *Adventures* (see *SP*, pp. 307–10). On John Walford (and Wordsworth's "Robert Walford"), see *SP*, pp. 11–12.

38. Cf. "Sage Beneath the Spreading Oak," chap. 8 in A. L. Owen. As the works of Diodorus Siculus and Strabo claimed shortly after Caesar, the Druids even intervened to halt war (quoted in Kendrick, pp. 82–83). On "hard" versus "soft" primitivism and the two distinct traditions in writings about the Druids, see Piggott, pp. 92–103 and *passim*. As Piggott notes, the two traditions can also be named after their classical contexts as the "Posidonian" and the "Alexandrian" (corresponding roughly to what I call the "savage" and the "mandarin," respectively). Though later literature made some attempt to link the two traditions of Druidism via the overlapping concept of the Bard (who abstained from war but sang of it), the conflict remained essentially unresolved. In the eighteenth century, "Druid" could thus denote either a "gentle Spirit" such as Thomson in Collins's ode or a bloody savage. On Druids in English literature, see A. L. Owen, pp. 158–68; Piggott, pp. 131–64 and *passim*. A. L. Owen, p. 163, observes, "It is surprising to find that Wordsworth, who was much interested in the Druids, was particularly fascinated by their sacrifices."

39. Throughout his *History of the County of Cumberland*, Hutchinson expresses an interest in the legislative and judicial function of the Druids. "One of the chief attributes of the Deity, venerated and insisted on by the druids," Hutchinson thus says, "was *justice*; the maxims of justice made great part of their precepts, which was natural and proper, as they held a double function, being both priests and judges.—Their executions, therefore, were sacrifices made to justice . . . *at once an act of religion, and an execution of the law*" (1: 249). For other passages stressing Druidical justice in Hutchinson's work, see 1: 5, 7, 251.

40. While Chatterton associates Stonehenge with Druidical sacrifice in "The Battle of Hastings I," the second version of this poem—which I refer to here—alters the myth so that the Druids are purged from the scene entirely. See Taylor on Chatterton's use of Stonehenge and Hengist's slaughter of the British (Chatterton, *Complete Works*, 2: 830–32). For the original Monmouth legend, itself derived from Nennius, *Historia Brittonum*, see Monmouth, pp. 164–66, 164n, 196. On the Monmouth legend generally, see Kendrick, pp. 4–7. Hutchinson, *Cumberland*, 1: 234, excerpts the legend.

41. "Savagery" is a key motif in Fawcett's poem—e.g., pp. 243, 247 (see

also n. 23 to Chapter 4 of this book). On the relation between Fawcett's work and *Adventures on Salisbury Plain*, see Gill, "Wordsworth's Poetry of Protest," pp. 61–62.

42. Cf. Welsford, p. 19: "Salisbury Plain is not just a desolate tract of England, it is the 'illimitable waste' of historic time down which marches the unfortunate human race, some of them for some of the time a little happy and a little civilized, most of them for most of the time tormented with disease and war and poverty—and what is to be the end?" See also Schulman, p. 224: "the traveler on the moor moves back through time as he journeys onward, first to an 'antique castle' (l. 78) surrounded with 'strange marks of mighty arms of former days' (l. 76)." Also, p. 228: "Wordsworth's continual pressure backward into time achieves only a dismal stasis, precisely because it takes its characters out of the present, the only time when *we* can know them. . . . And this historical debris, this burden of reminiscence and the antiquarian, only weakens the poet's swagger at the end of the poem when he calls upon his readers to 'uptear' the Bastilles of oppression."

43. The beacon on an eminence, of course, is not identified in the text as Penrith Beacon. But M. Osborn's argument that the play's ostensible setting in the Solway Plain really masks the area around Penrith (including the tree just mentioned) is very convincing. R. Osborn notes that the scene at the beacon is reminiscent of Gilpin's description of Penrith Beacon and that "alone among writers on the district, Wordsworth calls Penrith Beacon the Border Beacon" (*B*, p. 202n).

44. In Fig. 4 I pare down the complexity of Wordsworth's compositional history to isolate some of the major works of the period. The idea for a visual flowchart of this kind derives from an early attempt I made during preparatory work for this book to plot the whole course of Wordsworth's compositional history (using the best available dates) on a series of large wallboards. The resulting diorama of dates and compositional facts (which, by an irony of fate, has since been lost along the way of the geographical moves complicating my own compositional history) suggested two lessons: (1) the need for a visual representation to complement our current, elaborately detailed chronologies with all their repetitions, syncopations, overlaps, local mysteries, and strange loops, and (2) the ultimately labyrinthine contradiction or dream's navel (to use Freud's concept) of any chronology sufficiently detailed to suggest the texture of life. See Lévi-Strauss on the logical problem of "chronology" (*Savage Mind*, pp. 258–62). See also Reed on the subject, *CEY*, pp. 1–6.

45. I assign *Adventures on Salisbury Plain* to 1795 for convenience of reference. Wordsworth probably revised *Salisbury Plain* into *Adventures* in late 1795, but the surviving manuscript of the latter work in DC MS. 16 dates from a few years later (see *CEY*, pp. 333–36; *SP*, pp. 9–12).

46. On the Druid stones, see Wordsworth's footnote, *EW*, p. 50, as well as Beatty, *Wordsworth*, p. 19n. Beatty (p. 20n) identifies "the lonely beacon" as Penrith Beacon.

47. That it is useful to extend the "sacrificial" implications of the fire at Broughton to that at Penrith is further attested to by the fact that sacrifice is also a prime concern elsewhere in 1794. See my discussion below of Wordsworth's allusion to the sacrificial ritual in Horace's ode on Blandusia. The

relation of the "fen" (and what Wordsworth also calls the "rising" meadows) to the "mossy mound" is ambiguous; I have for convenience conflated the two as identical burial sites (distinguishing the mound from the fen would make no difference in my argument). The "mound" that thus disgorges a "horseman skeleton of giant mould," of course, is not specifically designated as Celtic. However, the image of gigantism does indicate that the legendary pedigree of the horseman in Wordsworth's imagination can be traced back ultimately to the ancient Britons. Penrith, we may note, was famous for putatively "Druid" sites—though Wordsworth did not see the most celebrated of these, "Long Meg," until the winter of 1820–21 (*Prose*, 2: 404). Tenth-century stones named the Giant's Grave and Giant's Thumb are also in the area. A more thorough investigation of the pedigree of Wordsworth's horseman would need to dig archaeologically back through successive layers of Norse and Roman history to the Celtics. (The area of Penrith is dotted with remains of all three cultures.) An aid to such research into the multileveled legends informing Wordsworth's work (both here and elsewhere) would be the icon of the horse. As Ralph Whitlock documents, giant horse carvings are a traditional part of English folklore (*Folklore*, pp. 32–35). Some have not only a datable (usually relatively modern) history but also a legendary history. In British imagination generally, the icon of the horse often serves to mark a social or historical interface. Just as the horse in Stubbs's paintings, for example, is a central subject that also situates the margin between the higher-class owners and the lower-class stable workers (the latter often included in the picture), so the horse in folklore seems to situate the margin between Celtic and later times. Whitlock's work on ghost tales of the Salisbury Plain area (*Folklore*, e.g., pp. 122–25) and the wildlife of the environs (*Salisbury Plain*, e.g., pp. 84–87) are also helpful in reading Wordsworth's description of landscape in the *Salisbury Plain* period.

48. Cf. Sheats's discussion of *1794*: "Instead of affirming the purgative violence of political revolution, . . . [Wordsworth] now looks to the power of an active and progressive nature that itself tends toward the ends of the revolution. . . . The barbaric rites of primitive man have become a wreath of smoke, and the abbey, monument of a tyrannic superstition, is humbled and partly concealed by its natural recess. . . . War, pain and violent confrontation of any kind are consigned to the past or the earth, or are shielded or reduced by mediating agencies. A 'mountain shepherd' shelters from the noontime sun behind a 'mossy mound' in which slayer and slain, the relics of the border wars, lie buried" (pp. 96–97).

49. For modern readers, this has characteristically meant that the original Revolutionary story underlying Wordsworth's work is displaced into the allegory for another story of agony with a more private function: the Oedipus plot.

50. These works may be seen conveniently in Markham, pp. 82–83, 88–89.

51. In an effort to reproduce the sensation of standing inside something like a panorama, I recently visited one of the few remaining camera obscuras in the United States at Garden of the Gods in Colorado Springs. The experience was enlightening specifically in regard to the relationship of panoramic vision to the "self." In this instance, a lens mounted above the darkened

chamber of the camera obscura cast a wide-angle view of the surrounding scenery on a concave surface the size of a large table; as the lens swiveled, the entire 360° of the scene appeared by turns in rotation on the viewing surface. The salient feature of the experience, however, was the competition among the viewers (a dozen or so) for the perfect spot from which to see the panorama. In the camera obscura, there was only one perfect spot; and the spot moved around the viewing surface (requiring the viewer not only to establish a vantage point but actively to maintain it). In a panorama like those of the late eighteenth century, there would have been more favorable spots (from which to view specially interesting sights and perspective recessions); nevertheless, the experience must at times have been like trying to push past competitors to see the pandas at today's zoos. The panorama is the vision of and for the self.

52. The original manuscript of this book included at this point a longer exegesis of "Tintern Abbey." I have retracted this section and substituted a much more cursory sketch because I cannot do it better than it has been done—with specificity, verve, cunning, and relentlessness—by the critics who have recently read the poem in its historical relations and whom I cite in the discussion that follows. Nevertheless, I felt it important to indicate where I stand on this poem. Even though "Tintern Abbey" has become a commonplace of the historicist approach to Romanticism, such commonplace—as demonstrated in the supple yet forthright work of Levinson, for example—is far from being exhausted in cliché. My own view of the poem, as expressed briefly in the following discussion, is consonant with McGann's or Levinson's attempt to see not so much historical reference in the text as the historical groundedness or determinateness of the lack of reference itself.

53. In considering "Tintern Abbey" as a battleground between those readers who historicize poetry and those who—to vary upon de Man— argue not so much the resistance to theory as its intriguing doppelgänger, a resistance to history, I am indebted to conversations about "Tintern Abbey" and its historicizing readers with Paul Fry of Yale University and Donald Pearce of University of California, Santa Barbara, among others. It was in these discussions that the lineaments of the conflict came clear to me. I should emphasize as well that in establishing my three questions above, I am eliding a controversy internal to the historicizing approach to the poem. This controversy regards whether Wordsworth displaces political engagement or (as Brinkley intimates) attempts a version of political engagement. At stake is what seems to me the next domain of inquiry for cultural and historical approaches to literature generally: the relationship between "historical," "social," and "political" aspects of discourse. At present, these terms tend to flit across the surface of historicizing criticism in such a way as to establish a blurred confusion between notions of passive and of active engagement in cultural process. The relation between approaches to literature that stress "the politics of . . ." and those that emphasize "the history in . . . ," for example, is unclear. The opening sentence of Johnston's essay on "Tintern Abbey" expresses the same problem with regard to the "social": "Wordsworth's ['Tintern Abbey'] is not usually considered a political poem, but if we shift from 'political' to 'social,' and thence to the still more gen-

eral 'moral,' we find ourselves on familiar grounds of interpretation" (p. 6). The leading edge of historicizing criticism, it seems to me, now involves rethinking the relationship between such terms—a process that can only occur on the basis of a deeper rethinking of the relation in any era between "representation" and "action" (as mediated through our own modern ways of relating these concepts). What is it in a particular culture that determines some actions (e.g., writing poetry) to be considered less active in their representational engagement/disengagement with historical and social issues than other representational actions known to be political (e.g., forming a "seditious" club)? In the terms of my operative concept in this book: "denial" connotes a more *active* form of passive representation than "displacement." But how to measure and define such action?

LYRIC AND EMPIRE

1. Recall, for example, the "mind" we saw Wordsworth insert after first mentioning the Grison Gypsy in *Descriptive Sketches* in Chapter 5. The whole issue of the genesis of the Romantic "I" from Sensibility personification is intriguing (as I take up below). A literary-historical approach to the problem might begin by studying the unstable personality of the "I" in eighteenth-century georgic, particularly in Thomson's *The Seasons* and Cowper's *The Task*.

2. Using Hartman's argument in "Milton's Counterplot," it would be possible here to extend the notion of epic similes I developed in Part II. Epic similes embedded within description, I suggested, were signs of a repressed narrative. The name of such repression will at last be the Romantic self. Whereas the mysterious similes in *Paradise Lost* point us out of the Devilish plot to what Hartman calls the "imperturbability" of divine supervision, such epic similes as that of "mind" in *Descriptive Sketches* ultimately point us away from the older anagogy to a precise analogue of Milton's Satan: a Romantic self under whose supervision, as we will see, all plot or mythos becomes internalized.

3. Relevant here, of course, is Coleridge's title for Wordsworth: "*Spectator ab extra*" (*Table Talk*, July 21, 1832). See Lindenberger on this concept in his chapter on "Visionary Aloofness" (*On Wordsworth's "Prelude,"* pp. 205–31); the section "Skirting Tragedy" is especially helpful in my present context—e.g., "Wordsworth's theory of tragedy is perhaps not so far removed from Aristotle's as one might think: the *katharsis* which for Aristotle occurred within the audience as a result of the tragic events enacted on the stage, for Wordsworth becomes a process . . . enacted within the poet himself" (p. 225).

CHAPTER SIX

1. In frequency of mention, justice is one of the most important concepts in the play (see, for example, I.i.240, iii.147; II.i.54, iii.16, 199, 386, 396, 418; III.v.24, 136). Wüscher observes, " 'Justice' and words related to it are frequently used in *The Borderers*, but in the majority of cases the terms stand for outrageous injustice" (p. 68). As I will go on to suggest, one way to

read *The Borderers* is simply to make a short glossary of its most recurrent words. There is a stuttering quality about the play, a tendency to stumble over such charmed words as "justice," "friend," or "love" again and again. The very reverse of Freudian slips of the tongue, such words are notable for their immense resistance to slippage.

2. The symbolism that attaches Matilda to Herbert's scrip will become in *The Ruined Cottage* the symbolism of a "bond of brotherhood" between laborer and tool (which I study in Chapter 7). Pointing to the handmade belt upon which Mortimer has hung the scrip he took from her father, Matilda says: "I see you love me still— / The labours of my hand are still your joy. / Bethink you of that hour when on your shoulder . . . I hung this belt" (III. v. 162–65).

3. As I argue with respect to peddling in Chapter 7, we often undervalue the significance of the occupations Wordsworth gives his characters. The upsurge in crimes by veterans would help explain the dangerous side of such characters as the Sailor in *Adventures* and the Discharged Soldier in *The Prelude*.

4. Part of the difficulty in measuring Wordsworth's criminal poetry against criminal history with precision is that while there are studies of historical crime in England as a whole, as well as close studies of crime in such areas as Surrey, Sussex, Staffordshire, and London, no detailed study exists (to my knowledge) of the Lakes and Dorset. Moreover, the nineteenth-century evidence that does exist for the Lakes—which, as M. Osborn shows, grounds Wordsworth's picture of the Border—would seem to strengthen my argument for a mismatch between the poet's criminal interest and actual criminality (if we assume that the nineteenth century tells us something about earlier traditionary levels of crime). As noted in *LC2*, the Lakes were not only one of the least policed areas of England, with extremely low serious crime and misdemeanor rates, but also *known* at the time to be so (pp. 99, 148). Regarding the biographical evidence: the fact that the mid-1790's represent Wordsworth's strongest contact with Godwin and Godwinism allows us to make some inferences about the source of his criminal interest (cf. the intellectual-history approach I suggest below; see Chapter 5 on Wordsworth and Godwin). Moreover, the poet's biography at this point is supported by a degree of day-by-day documentation—with the diaries of Godwin and of Joseph Gill, for example, fulfilling in minimal fashion the corroborative role of Dorothy Wordsworth's journals in later years (see *CEY* on the years 1795–96). Nevertheless, Wordsworth was so mobile in this decade—and, as usual, his writings often so difficult to pin down chronologically—that the problems of biographical interpretation are compounded. Gordon Wordsworth's deliberate destruction in 1931 of the majority of *A Somersetshire Tragedy*—the inception of which is otherwise biographically rooted—compounds the difficulty (see J. Wordsworth, "A Wordsworth Tragedy"). If the play had survived, we would have text, biographical occasion, *and* specific historical crime—a complete experiment, as it were, allowing us to draw a baseline for measuring the relation between the poetry and historical criminality.

5. Many more references could be adduced here, but Godwin's imagination of criminality in *Caleb Williams* and Schiller's in *The Robbers* (which

probably directly influenced *The Borderers*) are perhaps most relevant. See *B*, p. 28; Storch, "Wordsworth's *The Borderers*," p. 344.

6. Alan Bewell's insightful "Wordsworth's Primal Scene," which traces the far-reaching effects of the story behind *A Somersetshire Tragedy* on the poet's work, can usefully be read together with this chapter. My search for a deeper social agony behind Wordsworth's criminal interest in these years parallels the basic direction of Bewell's inquiry—e.g., p. 321: the story that first prompted *A Somersetshire Tragedy* "increasingly takes on the character of an originary myth or 'primal scene' in the development of the human mind —a universal story of violence and crime that precedes and makes possible human memory and language." In describing Wordsworth's underlying agony later in this chapter as that of a "primal scene family," I am in part influenced by Bewell.

7. Since completing the draft of this book, I had the opportunity to trade manuscripts and to discuss *The Borderers* and other matters with Reeve Parker. I was thus able to read his exciting and substantial "Reading Wordsworth's Power: Narrative and Usurpation in *The Borderers*" (which has since appeared in print). Though we developed our projects independently, Parker and I agree on many points, the most important of which include a concern with the problem of illegitimacy (see also n. 9 to this chapter) and a perception of the uncanny affiliation between Matilda's family history and the fraudulent version of that history staged by Rivers for a too-credulous Mortimer. Parker's discussion of this affiliation is particularly penetrating (see esp. pp. 309–11). The deepest (though less specific) correspondence between Parker's essay and my own work concerns narrative and its relation to the concept of self. More recently, I have benefited from reading in manuscript Julie Carlson's forthcoming "An Active Imagination." Carlson's essay, together with the project of which it is part, has made me aware of the larger implications of Romantic drama (see n. 100 to this chapter).

8. We cannot engage here, of course, upon a full discussion of Coleridge's poem. Especially striking in our present context, however, is the fact that the moment of poetic emancipation arrives immediately after the mention of Lamb's "strange calamity": "Ah! slowly sink / Behind the western ridge, thou glorious Sun!" the poet begins in the expansive movement of the poem. Also suggestive are contextual factors: Coleridge's emphasis upon strange mothers in other poems in the period of "This Lime-Tree Bower" (e.g., "The Foster-Mother's Tale," the dead mother in "Christabel"); and his 1797 autobiographical letters to Thomas Poole centered on his relation to his mother (especially the letter of Oct. 16, 1797, on the childhood incident in which he ran away from his mother after she had prevented him, in a strange variance of the Lamb catastrophe, from stabbing his brother). Of course, Coleridge's wife had just become a mother in 1796, probably accounting for the fact that she was boiling the milk that then spilled on his foot and made him—as if he were some foot-injured Oedipus—start his poem of sublimated tragedy. (On Coleridge, "Christabel," and the Mother, see Schapiro, pp. 61–92; see also McFarland, pp. 114–21.)

9. In meditating the deep interrelation between illegitimacy, criminality, family, theatricality, and the imaginative or autobiographical self in this chapter, I am crucially aided by Mary Jacobus's provocative recent work,

including "The Law Of/And Gender," " 'That Great Stage Where Senators Perform,' " and " 'Splitting the Race of Men / In Twain.' " On illegitimacy and the conception of autobiography, see esp. "The Law Of/And Gender." " 'That Great Stage,' " pp. 383–87, touches directly upon *The Borderers*. Though I read it unfortunately only when well into the writing of this chapter, Michael Ragussis's excellent essay on *The Scarlet Letter* has also helped give final shape to my argument. Ragussis deals centrally with the connection between family discourse, criminality, the theatricalization or outward projection needed to discriminate criminality, and the self: "Fiction understands that the most radical name we bestow upon the self, the name that in fact logically follows from 'author' and 'subject,' is 'the criminal.' The idea of the criminal stems from the false differences the self ascribes to another, the way the self writes him off: we mark him clearly so that we can safely stay away from him. But he is . . . the other side of myself. . . . By showing the family as a tangle of crimes where kindred and enemy often change places, Hawthorne shows how criminal and victim are one, with each member of the family on both sides of the border of crime. In this light the way in which we typically define the self merges with the discourse of the family: the reified self is the subject-author-criminal-father" (p. 881).

10. Another anticipation of "The Thorn" occurs in the Rough Notebook drafts for the play, where at one point a Pilgrim (originally Matilda's mother in the Prose Synopsis for act III; *B*, p. 48) fixates upon a grave and exclaims: "Hah! 'tis an infant's grave. I once had infants—" (*B*, p. 50).

11. On the use of Shakespeare in the play, see W. J. B. Owen, "*The Borderers* and the Aesthetics of Drama."

12. I do not suggest that Mortimer and Matilda are actually at the point of marriage (though see V.iii.185). In fact, they are probably still a few years too young as measured against the eighteenth-century norm (though there is no reason, of course, that literary convention in the manner of *Romeo and Juliet* could not drop the nuptial age). The evidence Stone surveys indicates that in the middle and lower classes men married in their late twenties and women in their middle twenties. (Evidence of age at marriage in the Lakes, which I discuss below, generally supports these findings.) Vann, however, argues that age of marriage was declining in the late eighteenth century, rather than rising as Stone suggests (p. 311).

13. Rivers, we may note, has all along been attempting to interest Mortimer in this salacious version of reality with hardly a nibble. In I.i.197–266, he begins to hint at a conspiracy between Herbert and Clifford. At the end of the scene he implies that the voluptuary Clifford had been at Herbert's door. There then follows this exchange between Rivers and Mortimer:

RIVERS: And yet I now remember
   That when your praise was warm upon my tongue,
And I began to tell how you had rescued
A maiden from the ruffian violence
Of this same Clifford, Herbert grew impatient
And would not hear me—
MORTIMER: No, it cannot be—
   I dare not trust myself with such a thought—

> Yet whence this strong aversion? You are a man
> Not used to rash conjectures—

On the one hand, Mortimer begins to follow up on Rivers's lead, and his phrasing—"I dare not trust myself with such a thought"—might suggest that in I.i it is the pimping and prostitution charge that is from the first "Enough!" Yet he immediately drops the thought, and his following thought—"Yet whence this strong aversion?"—only apparently indicates a strong aversion on his own part to pimping and prostitution. As made clear in the conversation earlier in the scene (I.i.202, 226), "aversion" refers instead to Herbert's distaste for Mortimer. Throughout the play, Mortimer's response to Rivers's main charge is curiously muffled.

14. Cf. the opening of the essay Wordsworth prefaced to the Early Version. In sketching the character of Rivers, Wordsworth presents a ruling-passion analysis: "His master passions are pride and the love of distinction" (*B*, p. 62).

15. Though Wordsworth's prefatory essay to the play deploys baroque involutions of moral logic to press Rivers into contemporaneity, in sum, the latter is finally as much an unreconstructed throwback as Dr. Johnson's favorite Savage, also the author of a work titled *The Wanderer*. Not inaptly named, Richard Savage in Johnson's *Life of Savage* is essentially a throwback to an earlier shame-culture. Unable to fit himself properly into polite society, unable to respect the normal divisions of the day, unable to grasp the principle of handling money, he is without origin in the present (i.e., without parentage). His illegitimacy lies in the fact that his true origin is the past.

16. Wordsworth's initial conception of *The Borderers* thus parallels Godwin's conception of *Caleb Williams*. Godwin began by setting down "hints" for his novel beginning with the third section, then the second, and finally the first (*Caleb Williams*, p. x). A symptom of Wordsworth's backward conception is that he himself recognized that act I of the finished play only partly prepared for the following action. It did not go back far enough in sketching the background circumstances and motivations of the story. Commenting on the act in 1842, Wordsworth wrote: "my only fear was that the *action* was too far advanced in it" (*LY*, p. 1122).

17. Though positioned earlier than the "Drafts for the Deception" in the Rough Notebook, the drafts for I.iii.115–56 with their inclusion of the Beggar are probably of later date. In writing the *Ur-Borderers*, Wordsworth worked from the front to the back of the Notebook and then—using available blank spaces—in reverse toward the front once more. Thus he entered "Drafts for the Deception" on pp. 38^v–42^v of the Notebook and then the draft for I.iii.115–56 on pp. 31^r–33^r (see *B*, pp. 13–14, 300). It is intriguing that the draft of the Beggar's lie is more explicit at its crux than the finished scene. After the equivalent of I.iii.139 in the Early Version, in which Mortimer exclaims upon Matilda's newly discovered parentage and asks the Beggar "are you Herbert's wife?", the draft continues with the Beggar responding, "Ay mine and I was at the Christening of her" (the next line is then crossed out: "And he shall never rob me of the money"; *B*, p. 329).

18. Moorman observes that the young Wordsworth and other boys

boarded by the Tysons at Hawkshead (and later at Colthouse) must have been "almost like foster-children" (MM, 1: 29).

19. Just as it is useful to read Boswell's journals or the Farington diary with attention to seating arrangements at table, so it is instructive to peruse *CEY* and *CMY* with attention to a single mundane concern: how would we, if we were master or mistress of the house, sleep everyone? Such a question (which the use of floorplans, I have found, makes successful in the classroom) reveals quite a bit about the difference between older and more recent notions of the inner form of the family. As Moorman says about the early years at Dove Cottage: "At all times one or other of the Hutchinson sisters, or Coleridge, was to be found there on visits long or short, so that, as Dorothy said, they were sometimes 'crammed edge-full' " (MM, 1: 460). The logistics of sleeping the family are even more suggestive, as we will see, if we consider the floorplans and average resident population of a Lakes yeoman cottage, which, unlike Dove Cottage, was not partitioned on the top floor.

20. Of course, communication with Annette was interrupted by the Revolutionary Wars until just before the Peace of Amiens in 1802, when correspondence resumed and a visit could be arranged (see Chapter 9). On the letters Wordsworth received from Annette at the end of 1801 and beginning of 1802 and the troubled involvement of the Vallons in Royalist counterrevolution, see MM, 1: 553–55, and Legouis, *William Wordsworth and Annette Vallon*, pp. 39–56.

21. For genealogical tables of the Wordsworth family in its relation to the Robinson, Myers, Monkhouse, Hutchinson, and Cookson families, see *Letters*, 1: 694–97. It must be said right away, however, that the materials for studying the family history of the Wordsworth milieu have for the most part not been amassed. Besides C. Roy Hudleston's account of Anne Crackanthorpe (Wordsworth's great-aunt) and Chester L. Shaver's of the Griffith family, I have not found much in the way of sustained research into the families tangent to Wordsworth's own. (A recent exception is Stella Colwell's intriguing *Tracing Your Family Tree*, a "how-to" introduction to genealogy that provides a research and resource guide for studying the family histories of the Wordsworths, the Christians [of mutiny-on-the-*Bounty* fame], and the Greens, whose tragic deaths in 1808 both Dorothy and William Wordsworth wrote about.) I am aware of at least three areas in this context ripe for primary research: the family histories of the Penrith clan and of the Hutchinsons; Wordsworth's architectural history (i.e., a sociological study of the succession of houses he lived in, virtually all of which from Cockermouth on far exceeded the norms even of the relatively well-to-do yeomanry; on the latter, see below); and a medical history of the Lakes, to provide a base against which to measure the important familial discourse of "sickness" in the inner documents of the Wordsworth clan—its journals, letters to Coleridge, etc. (cf. my comments on Dorothy's vision of sickness as community in "On the Autobiographical Present," p. 133). To study the social history of the Wordsworth family, in sum, we need access not only to the genealogy but to the practice of familiarity—i.e., to the shape of domestic space and the patterns of shared activity, discourse, and even contagion within such space that together created the habit of community.

22. On the relative numbers of freeholders and customary tenants among the yeomen, see Searle, p. 110. In the late eighteenth century customary tenants held about two-thirds of all Lake manorial tenures.

The primary focus in the historical literature on the rural middle class is on the yeoman (also variously classified as "statesman," hill-farmer, and dalesman). Despite the distinction between yeoman and leaseholder, however, it has seemed to me sensible to include both groups of occupiers in establishing a rough count of the rural middle class. This is because the difference between the two, while sometimes substantial, was also often extremely blurred by economic and social mobility. First, many of the yeoman class themselves became leaseholders through losing their estates, being forced by primogeniture to leave their family's holding (see my discussion below), or becoming wealthy enough to lease land in addition to their proper holding (G. P. Jones, "Decline," pp. 213–14). Secondly, yeoman "ownership" (a complex system of postfeudal obligations spanning from freeholding to varieties of manorial tenancy) was itself not necessarily de jure or de facto more secure than leaseholding (G. P. Jones, "Decline," pp. 205–7; Marshall, *Old Lakeland*, p. 34). As attested to by extremely high rates of change in tenancy, yeoman landholding was characterized by a restless mobility both voluntary and imposed: *contra* the Wordsworthian myth of the "statesman," holdings thus often stayed in the family only one or two generations (G. P. Jones, "Decline," pp. 209–10; Marshall, *Old Lakeland*, p. 37). Inversely, leaseholders could sometimes maintain a semipermanent relation to the land rivaling that of the yeomen; though most leaseholders in Cumberland, for example, held leases of 7 years or less, some had terms of 9, 14, or 21 years (*LC1*, pp. 229–30). Finally, leaseholders could at times be more well-to-do than yeomen, materially and socially. In material terms, they were as a group more advanced and efficient farmers, with the result that they could make higher profits despite paying regular rents (*LC1*, p. 238). (The yeoman's manorial fines, heriots, and other forms of duty were themselves sometimes as onerous as rent; see esp. Searle; also Marshall, "Domestic Economy," p. 214; G. P. Jones, "Decline," pp. 205–6.) In social terms, as Bouch and Jones argue, "it was not inevitable that [leaseholders], even when they displaced yeoman families of long standing, should take a less active, benevolent and intelligent interest in the affairs of the parish and neighbourhood" (*LC1*, p. 238). Moreover, it may well be that leaseholders also began to claim the honorific of "yeoman." Paralleling his thesis about "statesmen" (for which see below), Marshall in *LC2*, p. 112, argues that "yeoman" became increasingly a "status-word" without direct bearing on particular kinds of ownership. On the whole, therefore, I denominate a single category of owner-occupiers whose stratifications— designated simply "upper," "middle," and "lower" peasantry by Marshall ("Agrarian Wealth")—do not necessarily correspond to fixed distinctions between the traditional yeomen and the leaseholders with less traditional status. In any case, the problem of yeoman versus leaseholder is less prominent in the later eighteenth century than in the nineteenth (from which the majority of our statistics derive). As I discuss below, the yeomen were probably still preponderant over leaseholders until after the beginning of the new century; it was their economy and society that set the tone for a middle class that included both yeomen and leaseholders.

23. Holdings under 100 acres accounted for some 60 (Cumberland) to 70 (Westmorland) percent of all farms in the Lakes in 1851 (*LC2*, p. 60 and table 3.1a on p. 61). If we expand the notion of "small farm" to include holdings up to 300 acres, then at least 91–93 percent of all farms in the Lakes fell into this class in 1851 (*LC2*, tables 3.1a and 3.1b on p. 61). In this same year, farms under 100 acres accounted for only about 22 percent of English farms generally (*LC2*, table 3.1a). An estimate of 1766 (possibly exaggerated) suggests that some 10,000 occupiers held estates worth less than £100 a year in Cumberland alone (*LC1*, p. 229). The 1851 census lists only a total of 4,889 farms in Cumberland (*LC2*, table 3.1a). I discuss below the "decline of the yeomanry" that may have accounted for some of the out-migration and amalgamation of land between the late eighteenth and mid to late nineteenth century.

24. I discuss the economics of Lakeland yeomanry, including the effects of the troubles of the 1790's, more fully in Chapter 7. Outstanding historical research into yeoman savings and credit transactions in the Lakes, increasing standards of material comfort, entry into the land, commodity, and money markets, and varying levels of wealth may be found in Marshall, "Agrarian Wealth," "Domestic Economy," *Old Lakeland*, pp. 32–60, and *LC2, passim*; G. P. Jones, "Some Sources" and "Decline"; and Searle. It should also be noted that while much of the yeomanry passed into self-sufficiency and beyond, a large pool near the lower boundary of the class had to compete desperately for land holdings numbering far fewer than the number of self-proclaimed "farmers" (*LC2*, pp. 59–60, documents this point dramatically). As regards the osmosis in social standing between the upper yeomanry and the lower gentry, see G. P. Jones, "Decline," pp. 207–8. Also relevant is the aspiration of upper yeomanry toward the honorific of "Statesman," which I discuss below.

I should stress that my purpose in describing the rural "middle class" of the Lakes is differential—i.e., to establish the site of the group on the basis of its differences from other contemporary groups. I do not mean to assimilate the class directly to our own dominant social class. The distinction between the rural middle class of the eighteenth-century Lakes and our own suburban or urban middle class is not simply that the standard of comfort has since risen (see Marshall on the yeoman resistance to increased "comfort" in his "Agrarian Wealth" and *Old Lakeland*, esp. p. 45) but that subtle inversions and transformations have occurred. It thus appears paradoxical, for example, that Lakeland yeomanry in the eighteenth century lived in a subsistence economy and yet also saved earnings in a fashion without modern compare (see esp. Marshall, "Domestic Economy," p. 207). By the 1870's, as Marshall shows, the arrival of "*bourgeois* settlers" in the region (including both lesser squires and what we would today call the middle class) began to make up for the earlier lack of a social level intervening between the great landlords and the yeomen (*LC2*, pp. 113–20). Applied to this later period, "middle class" would acquire a different, or at least more various, referent.

25. As has become increasingly clear to historians of the Lakes, the celebrated decline in freeholders and customary tenant-right occupiers cannot be ascertained with statistical evidence for the period prior to the mid-nineteenth century (see, for example, *LC2*, pp. 6–7, 112–13; G. P. Jones,

"Decline," p. 212). This raises questions about how the "decline" in numbers was figured in the estimation of such authors as Wordsworth. *LC1*, p. 237, cites with some caution Wordsworth's own estimate that the number of freeholders dropped by half between 1770 and 1820. Relevant is Marshall's argument that "yeoman" became in part only an honorific (see n. 22 to this chapter). The implication is that the "decline" in the yeomanry "does not necessarily indicate a decimation of owner-occupiers, but may also suggest a change of emphasis in the use of a title" (*LC2*, p. 112).

26. *LC1* cites Arthur Young's findings here to argue that the labor requirement of yeoman farmers was relatively small. But this evaluation holds only if the basis of comparison is the rapid rise in the number of Lakes laborers in the nineteenth century. I have evaluated these findings as indicating a "substantial" number of laborers because my standard of comparison is both national (the much lower percentages of laborers in other parts of England) and domestic (the numbers of kin in the yeoman household).

27. For average numbers of rural Lakeland family members (kin) in the late eighteenth century, I speculate on the basis of figures for 1821 (*LC1*, p. 320; see also Laslett, *Household*, table 4.15 on p. 154, which gives the figure of 5.7 members in yeoman households in England generally from 1574 to 1821). Rural families in these figures, we may note, come closer to being one-a-household than urban ones (though we will see that "family" did not mean precisely the close-knit nuclear unit we conceive today). Earlier statistics for the general population in a variety of Lakes locations may also be found in Wall (though these data are difficult to interpret and to use for our purposes). For a view of the proportion of laborers to the related family members from the middle of the nineteenth century on, see *LC2*, p. 249. Parity between kin and laborers increasingly became the norm as the nineteenth century proceeded—even given the fact that the data also reflect an increasing number of large farms with many more laborers than tradition allowed for. As *LC2* puts it, the farmhouses of the area sheltered "not only large families . . . but strikingly large teams of labourers" (p. 5).

28. Later variations are described at the end of this chapter. Brunskill, "Small House," provides a chronology and percentage breakdown of the various kinds of small houses in the table facing his p. 161. On the Lakeland small house, see also Brunskill, *Vernacular*, pp. 17, 50–65; *LC1*, pp. 108–15; Marshall, *Old Lakeland*, pp. 32–44; Barley, pp. 233–38. I am grateful to Dr. Brunskill for his personal aid in acquiring a reproduction of the drawing he made for the cottage in my Fig. 6.

29. John Housman records in his *A Topographical Description of Cumberland, Westmorland, Lancashire and a Part of the West Riding of Yorkshire* (1800): "The farmer labours in the fields together with his family and servants, and eats at the same table" (quoted in *LC1*, p. 229). See also *LC1*, p. 245; Gough, p. 11; Brunskill, "Small House," p. 163. On the tradition of "general-purpose" rooms in Europe as a whole, see Ariès, *Centuries*, pp. 394–98.

30. Gough's work is an excellent resource for study of daily life in the eighteenth-century Lakes. Though neither full nor scientific, his series of letters on manners, clothes, houses, furniture, food, games and entertainments, literacy, and roads show a keen eye for the social use of space, materials, and utensils.

31. As we will see, Gough's anxiety in the early nineteenth century was simultaneous with a massive rise in English, and especially Lakes, bastardy. For similar fears about promiscuity in laborers' cottages in the nineteenth century, see Ford, p. 36.

32. I am much indebted to Patricia Fumerton for instruction on the history of fosterage. On the extensiveness and cross-class nature of fosterage, see also Stone, *Family*, pp. 107–8, 167, 375; Mitterauer and Sieder, p. 61.

33. Brunskill, *Vernacular*, p. 66, also suggests that laborers' cottages began to proliferate only well into the eighteenth century, because there would have been relatively few hired laborers prior to this time. I am inclined to follow Marshall's suggestion of a higher number of earlier cottages because there is some evidence (as I discussed earlier) that the hired agricultural labor force in the Lakes was already substantial before its rapid increase in our period. However, I am not competent to judge the "quality" of the lack of earlier evidence—i.e., whether the lack can credibly conceal a large number of cottages torn down or decayed beyond recovery. It would be useful if architectural historians of the Lakes could provide guidance on how structures characteristically decay under climatic and social forces. On the "myth" of the cottage at odds with reality, see Burnett, pp. 30–32. See also Ford for a survey of Victorian literary imaginations of the English cottage.

34. In order to suggest the range of family experience in the Lakes, I have so far stressed the difference between the urban-professional and the rural-agricultural family—the former extending itself by taking in stem or lateral blood relations and the latter by taking in "servants." However, a more comprehensive survey of family history in the Lakes would also have to stress the similarities between urban and rural, and professional and agricultural families. Each took on some of the distinctive traits of the other. The full "family" of a rural yeoman before the later eighteenth century thus probably consisted not only of the conjugal unit and its servants but also what Marshall argues was a wide network of kin in the surrounding area and sometimes in another house on the same estate (*Old Lakeland*, pp. 49–51). Inversely, the full "family" of a townsman of the middle and even laboring class often consisted not only of inhouse or crosstown networks of kin (see Michael Anderson's study of families in nineteenth-century Lancashire) but of lodgers and—if the family was sufficiently well-to-do—of servants. Data for 1821, for example, show that while the number of immediate family members in Lakeland urban households was smaller than in rural households, the number of families per housing unit was higher (*LC1*, pp. 320–21). This meant that urban families consistently took on lodgers (*LC1*, p. 321)—a circumstance made telling by the fact that earlier surveys in the late eighteenth and early nineteenth centuries often simply counted all boarded lodgers as part of the "family" (Wall, pp. 160–67). Despite distinctive differences, in sum, the patterns of rural and urban family experience were broadly similar: in both cases, the conjugal unit cohabited or otherwise associated closely with extra-nuclear elements, both kin and non-kin.

35. See Shorter, p. 205; Stone, *Family*, pp. 23–26; Mitterauer and Sieder, pp. 28–29; Flandrin, pp. 3, 50–92. The general point made by these family historians is that figures for household "size" do not adequately account for such other defining traits of "family" as overall social, temporal, or

emotional structure. Flandrin's critical use of Laslett is particularly full and detailed.

36. For clarity I use Stone's figures here even though in this instance he draws upon a study of seventeenth-century France. An approximate corroboration of these figures for England may be found in Laslett's more complex data based upon nineteen communities from 1599 to 1811 ("Parental Deprivation," table 2 on p. 13). Out of all orphaned children, 20 percent lived with remarried parents and 3.3 percent lived with persons other than parents or stepparents (some of whom must have been uncles or aunts). About 23 percent, or one-fourth, in other words, lived in what Stone calls "hybrid" families. It should be noted, however, that the one-fourth figure probably considerably understates the case. First, most of the rest of the orphans in Laslett's study lived not in "hybrid" families but either with their widowed mother who had not remarried (52 percent) or with their widowed father in the same circumstance (24 percent). Yet in such situations, some form of hybridization probably entered the picture because many of the children would necessarily have been cared for in part by other kin and strangers. The young Wordsworths, for example, could be classified as living with their widowed father, with maternal kin, *and* with the unrelated Tysons. Second, a small percentage of children in Laslett's findings lived in even more complexly hybrid situations with their stepfather only or with *two* stepparents. Finally, as we will see, children born out of wedlock in late eighteenth-century England (and especially in the Lakes) add a further tier of complex family forms to be accounted for. Bastardy is in part a kind of parental deprivation. To Laslett's categories we would also need to add a category for pseudo-orphans—i.e., illegitimate children—living with never-married mothers, with maternal grandparents, or, when abandoned, with strangers.

37. A reading of Ariès on scholastic life and the family helps illuminate the entire social matrix of Wordsworth's Hawkshead years—the years during which, for example, he would wait by a blasted hawthorn for the horses that would take him home for school vacation. Indeed, the usefulness of Ariès for Wordsworth scholarship is that he allows us to see the interest not just in such already privileged moments as the blasted-hawthorn spot of time but in a tremendous backlog of biographical detail that has so far remained inert, awaiting interpretive application. I refer in particular to all the ledger- and account-records we now possess of money spent on the young Wordsworths at school, their to-and-fro round of visits between various homes and Hawkshead, and so forth. The following details from the amassed material in T. W. Thompson's *Wordsworth's Hawkshead*, for example, become of interest when we realize that they reveal a complex circulation, transference, and sharing of custodianship articulated by means of small funds shuttled from parent or kin to school: "John Wordsworth of Cockermouth, attorney-at-law . . . notes in his private memorandum book that his sons Richard and William went to Hawkshead School at Whitsuntide 1779, Mr. Cookson paying the entrance fee; and that in December 1779, he himself paid Hugh Tyson £10. 10s. 0d. for 'half a Year's Board from Entry,' and a further 10s. 6d. for half a year's washing, these payments being for the two boys" (p. 32; see also *CEY*, p. 47 and n.).

38. The debate has recently been joined, however, about the true affec-

tive tone of households previous to our period. Steven Ozment attacks the thesis of Ariès and Stone that in the past "little genuine affection existed" between "husband and wife or between parents and children" (Ozment, p. 2; see also p. 177).

39. As Mitterauer has put it in regard to the European family: "Those family functions that remain today relate to a fairly clearly defined group of persons. On the other hand, the greater number of functions performed by members of the family of the past resulted in a strongly differentiated interaction between them because of the various tasks allotted to them, and therefore in the more or less close integration of these individuals into the household community. With the reduction of family functions went a reduction in the types of familial role. The relative homogeneity of modern family forms contrasts with the multiplicity of roles in historical families" (Mitterauer and Sieder, p. 19; see also pp. 71–90). My variation upon this argument is that the greater differentiation of functions in past families also allowed the family to be penetrated by a greater number of social functions. To be part of a Lakeland yeoman's "family" or household, that is, was to be part of a work, play, property-holding, child-raising, youth-training, storytelling unit (and so forth) that intersected integrally with village or settlement-wide activities. The most telling documentation of this fact is to be found in Marshall's count of the sheer number of "Satterthwaites," "Braithwaites," and so forth in certain Lake District areas. Quite literally, the family in such cases *was* the community; and the family's functions were entirely continuous (through such customs as mutual-aid "boon ploughs" and "boon clippings") with the overall functioning of the settlement (Marshall, *Old Lakeland*, pp. 49–50). For an excellent overview of the way family groups worked within the total operation of Lakeland settlements, see *Old Lakeland*, pp. 51–60.

40. Family life at Penrith appears to have approximated what Stone calls the "patriarchal" or authoritarian predecessor of the nuclear family. As Moorman puts it, Wordsworth's grandparents and his Uncle Kit "were not sympathetic towards the aspirations of high-spirited children: the atmosphere was one of respectability and decorum without culture or good nature among the 'grown-ups'; hence William, who had, as he afterwards admitted, 'a stiff, moody and violent temper,' was pretty often in collision with authority" (MM, 1: 13). See also MM, 1: 19. On the tradition of the close attachment between English brothers and sisters, which has special bearing in Wordsworth's case, see Stone, *Family*, p. 115. In the sixteenth and seventeenth centuries (and to some extent the eighteenth), Stone suggests, "the brother-sister relationship was often the closest in the family."

41. See also Hahn on Joseph in the Mérode Triptych (c. 1425–35) and the early canonization of the nuclear family. See also Flandrin on the presence of other extra-nuclear members in the Holy Family as conceived in the seventeenth through nineteenth centuries (p. 8).

42. It should be clear, of course, that I view Stone's work from the vantage of a literary discipline that has not been predominantly positivist for some decades. From the social historian's viewpoint, however, Stone can appear to be not positivist *enough*. See, for example, Vann's review of Stone's *Family*, which also goes on to critique Stone's theoretical content.

43. Stone's characteristic method is to treat each class as its own "mode"

of behavior unconnected to other modes. The result is a rigid typology (of class, of dominant causes, and often also of quantity and quality of evidence) whose most marked effect is the quarantining of the poor and propertyless —almost as an afterthought—in a small paragraph or subsection usually at the end of an argument. See, for example, *Family*, pp. 25, 92, 149, 255–56, 297, 393, 470–78. It is clear, of course, that such a typology respects perceptions of class in large part native to the times under study. But it is questionable to make received perception the unexamined premise for a method of explanation dedicated to accounting, in the last analysis, precisely for contemporary perceptions of the family. What drops out of the picture, as I argue here, is the explanatory power not of the class concept in itself but of the differentials in class perception that create and sustain the concept in the first place.

44. A subject on which Stone has speculated entertainingly, even suggesting that it was a factor contributing to nationalist expansion (*Family*, pp. 52–54).

45. I refer particularly to the controversy that has arisen over Shorter's claim that the rise in illegitimacy was due to a freeing of sexuality. See, for example, Fairchilds, also Meteyard. See also the cultural and economic causes Stone suggests for the rise in illegitimate sexuality, *Family*, pp. 622–48.

46. On the saturnalia of the hiring fairs, see Stone, *Family*, p. 640. On bundling, see Shorter, pp. 102–4; Stone, *Family*, pp. 605–7; and for the Lakes, see *LC2*, p. 160. In his *Letter to the Bishop of Llandaff*, Wordsworth shows some concern over "promiscuous intercourse" and bastardy among the poor. He wishes "that the miseries entailed upon the marriage of those who are not rich will no longer tempt the bulk of mankind to fly to that promiscuous intercourse to which they are impelled by the instincts of nature, and the dreadful satisfaction of escaping the prospect of infants, sad fruit of such intercourse, whom they are unable to support" (*Prose*, 1: 43).

47. On the fact that the rise in illegitimacy was especially a phenomenon of the laboring poor, see Stone, *Family*, pp. 9, 473, 611, 637–38, 643, 645–48. For the concern in the nineteenth century about the promiscuity specifically of the Lakes farm laborers, see *LC2*, p. 82.

48. I should emphasize that the difference I draw between the poor and the yeomanry in terms of bastardy and infanticide rates is not an absolute, since it appears that yeomen also sired bastards (*LC2*, p. 82) and perhaps sometimes killed their children. For the present, however, I stress the difference in degree (for which see Stone's view of the treatment of children in poor families; *Family*, pp. 473–76). Later I will reverse the emphasis.

49. The 1624 statute that first gave infanticide legal definition ("An Acte to prevent the murthering of Bastard children") did so, as it were, catachrestically by identifying murder with a more documentable action. As Wrightson reports, "The act argued that 'many lewd Women that have been delivered of Bastard Children, to avoyd their shame and to escape Punishment, doe secretlie bury or conceale the Death of their Children and after if the Child be found dead the said Women do Alleadge that the said Childe was borne dead; whereas it falleth out sometymes (although hardlie is it to be proved) that the said Child or Children were murthered by the said

Women their lewd Mothers or by their assent or procurement.' To rectify this situation, the act laid down that any mother of a bastard who concealed its death was to be presumed guilty of murder unless she could prove by the oath of one witness that the child had been born dead" (p. 11). Strictly conceived, then, the crime became the concealment of a dead child. As J. M. Beattie puts it, "It was an offence unique in English law, for the usual presumption of innocence was entirely disregarded" (p. 84). The statute was repealed in 1803 (Wrightson, p. 20, n. 15).

50. As Stone notes, of course, not all the children involved were bastards: "Although many of this growing mass of abandoned children were illegitimate, a majority seem to have been legitimate children of couples who were financially unable to support them. Abandonment of infants was thus a product partly of rising rates of bastardy, but still more of a deepening economic crisis for the very poor" (*Family*, p. 476).

51. J. M. Beattie reports the case of a domestic servant who in 1679 "had concealed her pregnancy by 'wearing loose garments.' When she was delivered she cried out in the night but answered all enquiries by saying that she had an ache. A child was found hidden in her box the next morning. It had been strangled, and she was convicted" (p. 111, n. 14). See also the seventeenth-century case of Elizabeth Terrey, charged with placing her infant in a wooden chest and allowing it to die. She was found innocent because the child was proven to be stillborn (Wrightson, p. 15). Regarding domestic servants of the late seventeenth and eighteenth centuries, J. M. Beattie comments: "A large number of those accused of infanticide were women for whom pregnancy and motherhood posed serious threats to their livelihood and indeed, to their survival—domestic servants, for example. It is hardly surprising that many of the women accused in Surrey and a majority of those tried at the Old Bailey were domestic servants, for women in service were, on the one hand, most commonly in their early child-bearing years and on the other, in close and constant contact with men. . . . In addition, of course, a domestic servant was especially threatened by pregnancy, for apart from the ruinous blow it gave her character, it meant dismissal. . . . Indeed, the pregnancy itself put her at risk and most of the women who came before the Surrey courts . . . had apparently managed to conceal their condition. Their children had been born unaided and under appalling conditions, in garrets, outhouses, and under stairs" (p. 84).

52. This case from the early English milieu ended in acquittal for all parties. A later example is the case of Cuthbert Mason, who fathered a bastard upon Elizabeth Bradell in 1626 and, with the consent of both the mother and her sister, put the infant out to a vagrant beggar nurse in cold weather (Wrightson, pp. 16–17). The central fact to emerge from such instances is that in a life crowded with fellow servants, family members, and others, infanticide and such associated acts as concealment of pregnancy became almost inevitably social events that a household as a whole had to consent tacitly to or reject (see J. M. Beattie, p. 84). Wrightson reports on the infanticide indictment against a woman known as "Dennis" Presland, for example: "She was a servant at Elsenham Hall who succeeded in concealing her pregnancy until 1 December 1645, when she took to her bed 'very sick.' She seems to have miscarried her child and further attempted to

conceal the fact from three fellow servants, who nonetheless deposed before a justice three weeks later that 'they doe veryly beeleeve that shee was delivered of a Chylde wch they are induced unto for that they did see sum matter or burthen wch came from her body and wraped in a sheete where she lay wch did signifie soe much unto them, And they do Judge by what they sawe that shee was gone wth child about a quarter of a yeare and noe more.' 'Dennis' later that night burned the remains in the kitchen fire" (p. 14).

53. I improvise here upon what Stone has called the "indifferent and exploitative mode" of relations between parents and children in poor families (*Family*, pp. 470–78)—a mode that retained in relatively unchanged form what he takes to be the general tone of affective relations in older society (on the latter, see *Family*, pp. 93–114; see also Shorter, pp. 54–78). But see Ozment, as mentioned in n. 38 to this chapter.

54. As Darton observes, Watts's work prompted commentators to publish point-by-point exegeses and was recited by generations of schoolchildren in periodic compulsory performances. It was in common use until well into the nineteenth century (Darton, pp. 108–11). Stone notes that Watts's poems sold "some eight million copies between 1775 and 1850" (*Family*, p. 252). Read against the backdrop of a developing children's literature, the most striking and lasting innovation of the *Divine Songs* was the "middle-classing" of a genre originally rooted, as in Bunyan's *Divine Emblems* (originally *A Book for Boys and Girls: or, Country Rhymes for Children*; 1686), in a rural and peasant milieu. Probably modeled directly on Bunyan (A. P. Davis, pp. 76–77), Watts's work adds to a universe of characteristically rustic props specifically middle-class and upwardly mobile furniture. Watts addresses children who live in a world of cozy beds ("The Sluggard") and fancy clothes ("Against Pride in Cloaths"), and who need to be protected from thieves, beggars, and evil company. More crucially, Watts adds to the Puritan code of values a bourgeois code of social manners. Thus such poems as "Love Between Brothers and Sisters," "Against Quarrelling and Fighting," and "Against Evil Company" teach an etiquette of family love, conduct, and language. A fuller study of Watts's influence would go on to trace his impact on such writers of children's books at the end of the eighteenth century as Mrs. Barbauld (*Hymns in Prose for Children*, 1781), Mary Wollstonecraft (*Original Stories from Real Life*, 1788), and—in an extended sense of "children's book"—Blake (see Pinto).

55. Especially apropos among Barbauld's popular prose hymns are such instances as the third, which depicts the tender solicitude of a child's parents in order to prepare for the analogy of God as the "parent's Parent," or the eighth, which discusses the nuclear family before going on to consider village, kingdom, and world.

56. I should add, of course, that Wollstonecraft's view of familial relations was not *just* nuclear. A more complex reading of the inflection she gives the nuclear ethos would need to address both the biographical context of her children's works—the documentable "Real Life" underlying the *Original Stories*, for example—and her later life and other works. At a minimum, we would need to read her severe views in the *Vindication of the Rights of Woman* (1792) upon the two mainstays of the nuclear family: love between husband and wife and parental affection.

57. As T. W. Thompson points out, pp. 232–33, there is some uncertainty about just how infamous, concerted, or petty the Castlehows were in their criminality. One writer, whom Thompson believes exaggerates, considered them a band of robbers who used their houses "as rendezvous for sheep-stealing forays, and possibly for actual highway robberies" (quoted in Thompson, p. 232). Thompson also notes that it is possible Wordsworth wrote some of his earliest verses on the escape of Jonathan Castlehow (p. 233).

58. I am aided in seeing the pathos and autobiographical resonance of Gainsborough's drawing by a talk given on "Thomas Gainsborough and 'Real Views from Nature'" by Duncan Robinson, Director of the Yale Center for British Art. For the social meaning of Gainsborough's genre pictures, including *Cottage Door with Children Playing* with its version of a woodman passing by an extended family, see Barrell, pp. 35–88.

59. When later versions of "Robert" and "Margaret" reappear in *The Ruined Cottage*, as we will see in Chapter 7, they occupy a cottage whose ruin leaves just "four clay walls"—a closer approximation to a laborer's "one up and one down" residence (see the lower set of drawings in Brunskill, *Vernacular*, p. 70). Even as their cottage shrinks, however, their social status climbs to yeoman or artisan level.

60. During late revision of this section of my chapter, I benefited from correspondence with William Jewett of Yale University on Robert in *The Borderers*.

61. See n. 7 to this chapter for the relationship between the following discussion and Parker's "Reading Wordsworth's Power," which may profitably be read in parallel at this point. My discussion of the family dynamics in the play has expanded somewhat in late revision, particularly in regard to the structural nature of illegitimate "exchange" that makes it cognate with incest. I have not, however, attempted to assimilate Parker's penetrating analyses in these revisions, though his discussion of "the problematic way Matilda displaces the mother in her father's arms" (p. 309) would certainly be relevant. (Cf. also Parker, p. 310, on the homology between the Beggar with her infant and Matilda's perished mother and brother; and pp. 327–28 n. 18 on the Pilgrim/Mother of the *Ur-Borderers*.)

62. For an analogue to my structuring of the family form and its narrative transformations in *The Borderers*, see Jan B. Gordon's excellent essay on the family and Hardy. Gordon's diagrams on pp. 383 and 385 helped me to conceive the visualization in Fig. 7.

63. For convenience, I name Clifford a "father" in the Beggar's composite family even though his parentage of Matilda can only be speculated upon. "Clifford" is thus generic in my usage for *some* illegitimate lover prior to the Beggar's marriage to Gilfrid. The internal logic of her lie, as I earlier discussed, would in all probability make this lover Matilda's natural father.

64. Though I have not developed the mother-son relationship in my analysis, it is potentially one of the most interesting in the play. The infant son, we notice, is a blind spot for all the characters. Mortimer and Rivers hardly seem to glance at it; and even the Beggar herself seems to treat it like an object to be carried around and spoken *about* rather than *to*. The son is a *tabula rasa* and, as such, marks the site of future rewritings of the family

form. Most obviously, the son is the role Mortimer adopts symbolically in his conflict with Herbert. Within the play itself, however, the blank site of the son is reserved primarily for Herbert. As we will see, Herbert is reimagined as a child to be killed by exposure. The Beggar's infanticidal dreams are prophetic.

65. By using such terms as "commodification" to describe the primal stock exchange of the middle-class family, I do not mean to be derogatory. What lies in the background here is a deep sympathy in popular culture between the forms of market transaction and the newer, still-forming "possessiveness" of the nuclear family. Stone recounts the striking case of divorce among the poor and middle class in the eighteenth century by written contract or sometimes "wife-sale," a recidivist custom modeled on cattle selling in which the husband led his wife to market by a halter and "sold" her to a prearranged buyer (*Family*, pp. 40–41). Such customs, which might remind us of the "primitive" transactions in wives and gifts studied by the anthropologists (see, for example, Lévi-Strauss on the exchange of women, in *Elementary Structures*, pp. 52–68), suggest that the transition from the older "household," or family-as-production-unit, to the nuclear family required the cooptation—and then *repression*—of existing idioms of economic imagination. Though the "partners" in the new-style, companionate marriage would be "possessive" of each other, therefore, they could not admit that possessiveness was in origin indistinguishable from the kind of ownership exhibited in divorce by wife-sale—the anathema of the nuclear ideal, it seems, in every way.

66. I am highly influenced here by Searle, whose study provides a concrete way to address the issue of feudalism in the Lakes. See esp. pp. 108–9, where Searle fits the abstract Marxist formulation of feudalism specifically to the eighteenth-century Lakes with its continuing high proportion of land held by customary tenure.

67. I am thinking, of course, of II.i in *Richard II*, where in his "demi-paradise" speech Gaunt remonstrates Richard for "leasing out" England. Richard answers after Gaunt's death by confiscating his property, leaving the latter's son Bolingbroke—as Bolingbroke says in III.i.25—no "imprese" or "sign." As regards Burke, it is difficult to overstate the importance of the property/money distinction in the *Reflections*. It is against the backdrop of the French "revolution in property" (p. 216) with its creation of paper money ("Issue *assignats*," Burke mocks in a superb chant of irony; pp. 359–60) that the contract metaphor in the *Reflections* takes shape. "Society is indeed a contract," Burke begins in his sustained definition of the concept, but immediately qualifies that such contract is more than a matter of mere trade, of some petty "partnership agreement in a trade of pepper and coffee, callico or tobacco, or some other such low concern" (p. 194). Rather, the contractual partnership that constitutes the state extends across all trades and through all time. Indeed, "it becomes a partnership . . . between those who are living, those who are dead, and those who are to be born" (pp. 194–95). In essence, such a partnership is not a transaction in capital so much as an inheritance of property—a concept that Burke throughout the *Reflections* weds to the concept of family. Thus the sustained conceit of the state as *paterfamilias* by which he introduces the "contract" definition (p. 194). Thus

also his "mortmain" conceit earlier in the work: "Whatever advantages are obtained by a state . . . are locked fast as in a sort of family settlement; grasped as in a kind of mortmain for ever" (p. 120). And again, thus his conflation of the metaphors of inheritance and of *paterfamilias*: "In this choice of inheritance we have given to our frame of polity the image of a relation in blood; binding up the constitution of our country with our dearest domestic ties; adopting our fundamental laws into the bosom of our family affections; keeping inseparable, and cherishing with the warmth of all their combined and mutually reflected charities, our state, our hearths, our sepulchres, and our altars" (p. 120). Ultimately, the difference for Burke between property that is inheritable and property that is rendered an anonymous value convertible with money (the *assignat* was secured upon Church property) lay in the matter of identity. Though property may be "assigned" identity by state fiat, such identity free of the impress of inheritance is not true identity. Imagining himself a peasant faced with a new breed of unnoble landlords, Burke exclaims: "You have sent down our old aristocratic landlords in no other character, and with no other title, but that of exactors under your authority. Have you endeavoured to make these your rent-gatherers respectable to us? No. You have sent them to us with their arms reversed, their shields broken, their impresses defaced. . . . They are strangers to us. . . . Physically they may be the same men; though we are not quite sure of that, on your new philosophic doctrines of personal identity" (pp. 347–48). Wordsworth's letter to Fox (quoted at the close of this chapter) parallels Burke's vision of political inheritance as "the image of a relation in blood." Just as Burke relates property and propriety to "affection," so Wordsworth weds "affection" to inheritable "proprietorship."

68. J. Wordsworth recounts in "A Wordsworth Tragedy": "It is difficult to say precisely what features of the story would have appealed to Wordsworth. . . . [W. L.] Nichols [in his *The Quantocks and Their Associations*, 2d ed., 1891] refers enigmatically to 'the incident of the shilling' which 'occurred just as Wordsworth has described it.' It was apparently this incident which more than anything led to Walford's conviction. His alibi was that he had given his wife a shilling to go and buy some cider, and that she had been robbed and murdered on the way. On being shown her body, [Thomas] Poole records, he asked: 'if he might search her pocket for the shilling he gave her . . . which he did, but found no shilling; on which he insinuated, that some one might have robbed and murdered her. He was asked what money he had last night: he said, "six shillings," which he received for his wages. He then showed five shillings, the other he said he had given his wife.' Later, when his bloodstained clothing was found, there was a single shilling in the pocket of his breeches. He had had the presence of mind to take it from the corpse, but had failed to throw it away."

69. On "recognition" in the misrecognized family, see Ragussis on the chapter titled "The Recognition" in *The Scarlet Letter* (Ragussis, pp. 864–66).

70. In thinking about the relation between magic and luck, I am guided by Frye on romance "luck" in *Secular Scripture*, pp. 67–68. Exhibits in the Romantic psychologization of magic would include not only Heathcliff at the close of the novel but, as we will see, Mortimer seeing strange dust and a ghost staff in act V.

71. Since I use Frye only as a starting point, I have not attempted to apply the full complexity of his thought on irony—especially with regard to the phased mergence of tragedy with irony (see *Anatomy*, pp. 236–38). As I perceive it, the ironization of tragedy for Wordsworth is not just a phase of generic development but the problematization of tragedy—a problematization whose implications for the handling of narrative and tone extend from *The Borderers* through such following tragedies *manqué* as *The Ruined Cottage*.

72. On the close relationship between drama and the courtroom trial, see Lindenberger, *Historical Drama*, pp. 21–22, and Sokol. See also Huet on the "theatricality" of the trial of Louis. In the following staging of the play's action as courtroom drama, I have not tried to be precise to the point of following the exact sequence of a trial. It has seemed to make sense, for example, to open with defense rather than prosecution because Mortimer's basic disposition is overdefensiveness. Like some of the defendants who acted as their own counsel in the Scottish sedition trials of 1793 and 1794, defense of the family in the play is characterized by being always slightly inappropriate—too early or late, too vigorous or dispirited, and so forth. Indeed, a reading of the harsh sedition trials especially of Scotland in 1793 to 1794 is excellent background for understanding the courtroom universes of Wordsworth or Godwin. Compare, for example, Caleb's speeches of self-defense in Godwin's novel and Thomas Muir's similarly spirited, and futile, speech of self-defense (quoted in Cockburn, 1: 174–75).

73. Osborn compares this passage to *Macbeth*, I.vii.54–59, and also to a passage in Schiller's *The Robbers* (*B*, p. 188n).

74. Or at least, infanticide was the only analogue for trial-by-waste that Wordsworth knew about when first composing *The Borderers*. In 1798—after first drafting the play (but before the Early Version manuscript)—he read Samuel Hearne's *A Journey from Prince of Wales's Fort in Hudson's Bay to Northern Ocean 1769–1772* (1795) and consequently wrote "The Complaint of a Forsaken Indian Woman." As he learned from Hearne, the Indians exposed their old (*PW*, 2: 474–75n).

75. A major advance in this field was marked by McFarland's chapter on "The Symbiosis of Coleridge and Wordsworth" in his *Romanticism*, pp. 56–103. I have not managed fully to assimilate McFarland's argument in the following argument, however, because of a significant difference in explanatory paradigm. McFarland describes the friendship between Wordsworth and Coleridge by means of three paradigms: "symbiosis," "gravitational pull" or "influence" (pp. 84, 86, 90), and gender relationship (e.g., "[Coleridge's] relationship to Wordsworth . . . is as a feminine principle to its masculine counterpart"; p. 65). Of these three, only the first is truly operative. Its special function in McFarland's context is not so much explanatory precision (the concept of "symbiotic dependence" is very general) as the capacity to ally the whole inquiry with the host metaphor of biological organism. The dark doppelgänger of "symbiosis" in the universe of the poet-as-organism is "disease." McFarland's chapter on symbiosis thus leads into the succeeding chapter on "Coleridge's Anxiety," which evolves a full theory of psychological dependence from the biographical facts of Coleridge's "disease" (pp. 104–36). My own concerns, however, are oriented toward the social rather than biological or psychological. While it is possi-

ble to develop disease into a paradigm for social interaction (as in the Dove Cottage "community of contagion" I sketch in my "On the Autobiographical Present," p. 133), the purposes of a broader inquiry into the historical conditions of friendship would seem to be better served by a more flexible and commonly accessible model. It is for this reason that I will turn in the following pages to rhetorical and semiotic resources to label the friendship between Wordsworth and Coleridge not a "symbiosis" but a "metonymy."

During the writing of this chapter, I had occasion to attend a Wordsworth–Coleridge Association session at a Modern Language Association convention that also advanced this issue. The session (Dec. 29, 1985) was on "The Fictions of Friendship: Wordsworth's 'Coleridge' and Coleridge's 'Wordsworth,'" and featured talks by Eugene Stelzig ("'Coleridge' in *The Prelude*: Wordsworth's Fiction of Alterity"), William Galperin ("'Wordsworth' in the *Biographia*"), Linda Marie Brooks ("Coleridge's 'Wordsworthian' Persona in the *Biographia*"), and Linda Palumbo ("Fictions of 'Coleridge' in Wordsworth's *The River Duddon*"). Since this was also the MLA convention that featured three sessions on Romantic women (plus a session on sexuality and literature in the late eighteenth century), I was prompted to think that there are two aspects of the problem of friendship that I have neglected in my concern with male bonding in Romantic poetry. One is friendship between the sexes (e.g., Dorothy and Coleridge); and the other is friendship between women (e.g., Dorothy and Mary). For a particularly telling piece of evidence regarding gender and friendship, see Dorothy's letter to Jane Pollard in 1793, which near its end rises to the following crescendo of friendship: "Ah! Jane! I never thought of the cold when he [William] was with me. I am as heretical as yourself in my opinions concerning Love and Friendship; I am very sure that Love will never bind me closer to any human Being than Friendship binds me to you my earliest female Friend, and to William my earliest and my dearest Male Friend" (*Letters*, 1: 96). Localized and class-sensitive research into the relation between male fraternity and female sorority in the period would be needed before a full theory of gender and friendship could be developed. A question to initiate research might be: which friend, male or female, is best tolerated by the nuclear family? Exhibits such as Dr. Johnson in Mrs. Thrale's family, Coleridge in Wordsworth's, or Dorothy in Mary Wordsworth's come to mind. Family/friendly relations in the Shelley or Byron circles would also provide rich material.

76. Also known as the "Rock of Names," this memorial was unfortunately destroyed in the making of a new road to Thirlmere (MM, 1: 551). We thus do not know the precise arrangement of the initials. It is intriguing, however, that the inscription of the rock probably occurred in three stages: first the carving of "M. H." and "S. H.," then the addition by Coleridge of "S. T. C." and "D. W.," and finally the addition (also by Coleridge) of "W. W." and "J. W." (*CMY*, pp. 143, 162, 166–67, 167n). What we witness is Coleridge gradually carving himself and Dorothy into the Wordsworth family as intermediaries between the eminently bachelor or marriageable members of the circle (the women "M. H." and "S. H.," on the one hand, and the men "W. W." and "J. W.," on the other). Coleridge and Dorothy, that is, are "friends" embedded at the core of nascent conjugal families.

William and Mary, of course, would marry later in 1802; and John and Sara were at least structurally cognate to William and Mary even if they were not, as Coleridge fantasized, intended for each other (see Ketcham on our knowledge of the relation between John and Sara in *The Letters of John Wordsworth*, pp. 35–36). It is also intriguing, of course, that the carving of friendship and nascent family into stone in early 1802 belies a radical instability in both friendship and family: the intervention of Annette Vallon and William's illegitimate child Caroline (whom he and Dorothy would soon visit in France in 1802 prior to his marriage to Mary). On Sara's Rock, or the Rock of Names, see also the Introduction and p. 82n in Betz's edition of Wordsworth's *Benjamin the Waggoner*.

77. The rhetorical or semiotic approach holds special promise for studying the mark family history leaves in literature. Galperin's excellent essay on "desynonymization" plays upon the complex coupling of similitude and differentiation in the relation between Coleridge and Wordsworth, and also touches upon the concept of metonymy. "Coleridge's representation of Wordsworth in the *Biographia Literaria*," Galperin says, "enables the former to represent himself not only as a defender of Wordsworth but metonymically as the defense: as one whose claims are founded on an ideal of which he, rather than the defendant, is the more accurate representative" (p. 515). Besides Galperin, there is also Ragussis's essay on family discourse in *The Scarlet Letter*. Pursuing a line of inquiry initiated by Roman Jakobson's essay, "Shifters, Verbal Categories, and the Russian Verb," Ragussis argues that titles such as "father," "husband," or "child" are linguistic shifters in a deep family "discourse" functioning to relativize the identity of family members, each of whom may have more than one title (pp. 874, 887 n. 5). What such lines of inquiry indicate, as Ragussis's application of Jakobson anticipates and Galperin's references to Paul de Man confirm, is that there is a useful deconstructive approach to family and friendship. Such an approach centered on "absence," or the lack of a centered discourse in human relations, reveals that the entire tonality of deconstruction—superficially preoccupied with the ideology of play and the idiom of violence (as I consider in my essay on Christopher Smart and the ethics of literary history)—communicates with a deeper tonality of the most traditional pathos. As I will argue below, absence in the family is a matter of "love."

78. I build here upon the analysis of tropes as revivified and transformed by Jakobson's work on language and aphasia. In traditional rhetoric, "metonymy" is a trope of "misnaming" that substitutes "cause for effect or effect for cause, proper name for one of its qualities or vice versa" (Lanham, p. 67). A standard example is the "action of the crown," where "crown" misnames "king." The influence of Jakobson's work has been to subordinate analysis by cause/effect and class/member (or whole/part) to a broadly conceived notion of "syntagmatic" or contiguous association. Jonathan Culler's visual paradigm is most succinct: "in 'George has been chasing that skirt' the skirt and the girl are related as parts of a notional or visual whole; in other instances cause can stand for effect or vice versa because both are parts of a single process" (*Structuralist Poetics*, p. 181). One part of a conceptual field, that is, substitutes for a contiguous part to which it bears no "metaphorical" resemblance. Robert Scholes's explanation is also useful for our purposes:

"metaphorical substitution is based on a likeness or *analogy* between the literal word and its metaphorical replacement (as when we substitute *den* or *burrow* for *hut*), while metonymical substitution is based on an *association* between the literal word and its substitute. Things which are logically related by cause and effect (*poverty* and *hut*) or whole and part (*hut* and *thatch*), as well as things that are habitually found together in familiar contexts (*hut* and *peasant*), are all in metonymic relationship to one another" (p. 20). In my argument, a "friend" is precisely an associate "habitually found together" with family members in a "familiar context." The "liking" between friend and family member is thus qualitatively different from the metaphorical "analogy" or "likeness" of family resemblance.

A fuller study of the "rhetoric" of friendship could usefully soften the qualitative difference between metaphor and metonymy in the structuralist analysis. In practice, we know, the difference between metaphorical resemblance and metonymical contiguity is not always easy to maintain. A speculation about where such "practice" comes from might begin with the chapter on "The Prose of the World" in Foucault's *The Order of Things*. In the Chain-of-Being universe, Foucault argues, there were originally *four* ways to relate objects or beings: convenience, emulation, analogy, and sympathy. It may well be, I suggest, that metonymy in the structuralist acceptation *begins* in convenience (where two objects are "convenient" or contiguous to each other in space) but leans into emulation and other modes of resemblance freed of the need for physical propinquity. Inversely, it may be that metaphor (and family resemblance) is a mode of relation that begins in sympathy (a quasi-magical Sameness causing objects to assimilate each other homeopathically) but shades down the scale toward mere convenience. Qualitative difference would thus become quantitative. A "crown," that is, is never simply just a "convenience" of the "king"; it is also a piece of fetishistic magic "sympathetic" with the very essence of kingship. Crowning, after all, *makes* kings. The advantage of such an analysis of metonymy and metaphor is that it would clarify that the interest in any one term lies precisely in the middle zone where it overlaps or clashes with the other. In the uncrowning scene of *Richard II*, for example, which is the real metonymy (marginal attribute) and which the metaphor (sympathetic agent) of divine "kingship," Richard or his crown?

79. The sense of banishment from paradise is also very strong in another notebook entry mentioned by Moorman. Under one of his name-game experiments linking his own name to those of the Wordsworth ensemble, Coleridge adds the couplet: "O blessed Flock! I the sole scabbed Sheep! / And even me they love, awake, asleep" (quoted in MM, 2: 85n).

80. The great exhibit here, of course, is the estrangement between Coleridge and Wordsworth from 1810 on. The gossip that was the immediate trigger of the alienation is revealing in its language. As Coleridge records in a letter of 1812, Montagu reported a conversation he had with Wordsworth as follows: "Nay, but Wordsworth has *commissioned* me to tell you, first that he has no hope of you," next that Coleridge has been "an ABSOLUTE NUISANCE in the family" (MM, 2: 198).

81. On indolence versus industry, see Chapter 7. On Dorothy and sickness, see my "Autobiographical Present," p. 133.

82. Stone observes that "friend" in the sixteenth and seventeenth centuries was a nonspecific term that could apply to many kinds of social relationship. This was especially so when the word was plural: "Used in the plural, as 'my friends,' the word before the eighteenth century always meant no more than 'my advisors, associates and backers.' This category often indicated a relative, particularly a parent or an uncle by blood or marriage. But it could also include a member of the household, such as a steward, chaplain or tutor; or a neighbour; or a political associate sharing a common party affiliation; or a person of high status and influence" (*Family*, p. 97).

83. The political meaning of "fraternal" should not be forgotten here (cf. Wüscher, pp. 73–75). There is also a further context of investigation that I have not pursued. We know that the young Wordsworth boarded with Ann Tyson in the hamlet of Colthouse (where the Tysons moved in 1782 or 1783; *CEY*, p. 54) just outside Hawkshead proper, and that this was the site of a Quaker settlement in whose meeting-house Wordsworth occasionally worshiped (MM, 1: 29). "What I chiefly recollect," Wordsworth later said, "is that they were always telling God Almighty of His attributes, rather than seeking spiritual communion with Him for themselves" (quoted in MM, 1: 29). It would be useful to study together the possible impact of Godwinian "benevolence" and of religious "friendliness" upon *The Borderers*.

84. As K. E. Smith has noted, that is, love tangles "with other, incompatible emotions in a way that mirrors the darkening of the action as a whole" (p. 100). With regard to the exemplification of complicated love that follows here, cf. Smith, pp. 100–101.

85. Works that are especially relevant here include McFarland's introduction on "Fragmented Modalities and the Criteria of Romanticism" in his *Romanticism*; de Man, "The Rhetoric of Temporality" (in *Blindness*); Mellor (esp. the chapter on "The Paradigm of Romantic Irony"); and David Simpson, *Irony and Authority*.

86. Not only did Wordsworth later make this passage the epigraph to *The White Doe of Rylstone* (composed 1807–8), but he also redacted it in *Guilt and Sorrow*—the 1842 revision of *Salisbury Plain*—in order to send his Sailor to his fate "prepared / For act and suffering" (*SP*, pp. 279–81). It is clear that the binary of action and suffering became for Wordsworth a critical formula on a par with such other binaries as the "terror and beauty" of locodescriptive tradition.

87. Highly relevant to my speculations below upon the copula in Wordsworth and Coleridge is the chapter on "The Copula" in Ward's intriguing recent book, which I read too late to integrate into this chapter alongside my use of Ferguson. A rhetorical reading of Wordsworth would do well to read Ward together with Ferguson under the aspect of the broader de Manian wedding of Romanticism to rhetorical method.

88. I am not ambitious here of sustaining a precise rhetorical analysis of "affection." However, it does seem that such an ambition—drawing, for example, not only upon Ferguson but also upon Murray—could be fruitful. Most of the figures of speech I cite here have in common the fact that they are disorders in agreement, case, conjunction, word order, or some other dimension of syntax. Similarly, as we have seen, metonymy is a figure of speech dependent upon a disordered relation between a cause and its effect,

a class and its member, or a whole and its part. This leads to a conclusion with deep implications for the study of the rhetoric of identity in Wordsworth. An identity that is metaphorically unified or "organic" can only be spoken if, by contrast with metonymy, it "agrees" in case, number, or gender. A disagreement in the first category here would alienate "subject" from "object"; a disagreement in the second would produce disorders of "symbolism" in Coleridge's sense of the general and the particular; and a disagreement in the last (in the "sex" of Imagination or Fancy, for example) would generate disturbances in gender relations.

89. We might also note the residual personification in Coleridge's conversation poems of the 1790's—renovations of Sensibility in which "Nature," "Love," "Beauty" and so forth exert their gentle ministries. Witness, for example, the muted Sensibility in "This Lime-Tree Bower My Prison," 1797: "Henceforth I shall know / That Nature ne'er deserts the wise and pure; / No plot so narrow, be but Nature there, / No waste so vacant, but may well employ / Each faculty of sense, and keep the heart / Awake to Love and Beauty!"

90. On the persistence of Sensibility personification in Romantic poetry, contrary to Wordsworth's apparent rejection of the device, see Abrams, *Mirror and the Lamp*, pp. 55, 289–97.

91. Cf. Wüscher, p. 74: "In *The Borderers* the mental torture as a result of the crime against brotherhood is yet more pronounced."

92. We might compare here Yorick's feelings for the caged bird and the captive in Sterne's *A Sentimental Journey* (the ultimate "cage" in the work being the Bastille).

93. I am much aided in reading this passage with its hysterics of imaginary torture by Bewell's essay, "A 'Word Scarce Said'" (a draft of which I had the opportunity to read prior to its publication). Bewell focuses on episodes of female "hysteria" in Wordsworth's poetry as they descend from —and demystify—an older tradition of witchcraft. Wordsworth's project of writing a genealogy of the imagination, Bewell argues, thus involves in part a regrounding of magical in medical discourse, witches in hysterics, and thus the opening of a theater in which to think about imagination: hysteria was a disease of the imagination, and in Wordsworth's handling was the empirical mediation necessary to a psychologization and poeticization of imagination. In the course of making his argument, Bewell examines "The Three Graves" among other poems. His comment upon "Goody Blake and Harry Gill" is especially relevant to my present concerns and my following discussion of *Peter Bell*: "Harry's disease manifests a double relation. It is an *accusation*. . . . Yet it is also a form of *punishment*, and thus reflects, at the level of his body, the inceptive stages of *conscience* and *guilt*, the sense that he has violated the primitive law of charity. . . . Like Peter Bell's sympathy, guilt and charity seem to come from the outside, but are, in fact, products of the mind's terrified recoil from the sublime threat of its own projections and conjurations" (p. 372).

94. It seems clear that there is a tradition here. Both Peter Bell and Crabbe's Peter Grimes most resemble "Grimes" in *Caleb Williams*—a character that Godwin portrays in a memorably written passage as subhuman (p. 47).

95. Wüscher, pp. 66–67n, quotes the following condemnation of the

"bleeding-heart" Lakers and other contemporary poets in the *Edinburgh Review* for Oct. 1802: "[These poets express for] all sorts of vice and profligacy in the lower orders of society . . . virtuous horror, and . . . tender compassion. While the existence of these offences overpowers them with grief and confusion, they never permit themselves to feel the smallest indignation or dislike towards the offenders. The present vicious constitution of society alone is responsible for all these enormities: the poor sinners are but the helpless victims or instruments of its disorders, and could not possibly have avoided the errors into which they have been betrayed. Though they can bear with crimes, therefore, they cannot reconcile themselves to punishments; and have an unconquerable antipathy to prisons, gibbets, and houses of correction, as engines of oppression, and instruments of atrocious injustice."

96. For a synopsis of the Godwinian reading of the play, see Sharrock, p. 170n; Thorslev, pp. 85–88; Priestman, p. 56.

97. Cf. Ragussis, pp. 879–80: "the self is familial, . . . it contains the genealogical trace or blood-guilt of its ancestry. . . . The family member, then, is not only the person found on the border of another in his present family relations; he is also the person who is a 'residuum' or 'diluted repetition' or 'vestige' [cited from Hawthorne] of the ancestors that went before him. This is what it means to be a daughter or son, all one's life." Also relevant is McFarland's thesis about the relation of Wordsworth's self to the "significant group" (pp. 137–215). Wordsworth's "egotistical sublime," McFarland argues, defined itself within the field of an "intensified" sense of human relationship—an intensification whose realization lay in the "significant group" of loved ones (most tellingly, the family; p. 172). "For the significant group might most simply be defined as that society the loss of any member of which attacks the participant's sense of his own being. Furthermore, the significant group is composed exactly of those people, the loving of whom and then the loss of whom tested Wordsworth's stoic fortitude throughout his life" (pp. 168–69). My own argument takes McFarland's thesis to its logical extreme: the sense of self is *only* an internalization of the "significant group"; and such a group is no more than a formation of loss. Finally, I should mention an argument congruent with McFarland's in Friedman's groundbreaking *Making of a Tory Humanist*. Friedman's work is significant, I believe, not so much for its superstructure of Freudian and Marxist theory as for its infrastructure: the kind of historical documentation it brings to Wordsworth studies. By introducing me to *LC1*, for example, it has made a major contribution to my own work. Ultimately, however, I find myself at odds with Friedman because of a difference in approach and because of new evidence. The basic argument of *Making of a Tory Humanist* is that there is an *a priori* dialectic of selfhood in Wordsworth (an "oscillation" between the "princely" and the "contracted" ego), and that the poetry and prose record the process by which such ego sought to secure itself within a "stabilizing and enclosing social community" much like McFarland's "significant group" (pp. 2–3). Specifically, Wordsworth's ego sought to alleviate its internal tensions by securing itself within a Lakes community characterized by the "patriarchal" "nuclear family" and a traditional climate of affection (esp. pp. 143–45). On the matter of approach, I have chosen to

trace the self to the historical situation rather than the relevance of a particular historical situation to the *a priori* self. As regards evidence: Friedman's work is currently difficult to use because, through no fault of its own, its historical material has since been largely superseded. This is true in the fields of demography and family history (Friedman's primary source is the early Laslett of *The World We Have Lost*, 1965) as well as in the more specific province of Lakes economics and social history (his main source, *LC1*, has been much amplified by *LC2* and many excellent essays by J. D. Marshall and others). The combined evidence now available depicts a very different Lakes community in which "affection" is not a given. Stone's work on family history, for example, shows that the patriarchal nuclear family was not identical with the more affectionate "closed domesticated nuclear family." And the supplementary evidence of the Lake District historians suggests that the term "nuclear" comes nowhere near describing the family life of yeomen or laborers. Thus even if we accept Friedman's thesis that a particular kind of *a priori* self seeks out "traditional" community, we would now need to explore how the *actual* community of the times determined such a search—and, implicitly, the motivating self—in the first place.

98. "Where is the body?" is a reductive way of phrasing the question debated in an exchange between J. Hillis Miller and M. H. Abrams (Eaves and Fischer, pp. 111–82). Taking "A Slumber Did My Spirit Seal" as their pretext, and the issue of deconstruction as their context, the two antagonists duel over the nature of reference.

99. Since my argument here is merely a vehicle, I am content to leave it suggestive. In fact, however, I believe that the congruence between the Lucy poems and infanticide could be developed much more fully. Crucially, such a development would only use the concept of reference (of poems "about" child death) as a point of embarkation. The real power in such an analysis would lie in a second-stage inquiry into the congruence between *poetic language* and infanticide. DeMause's thesis of "projective" and "reversal" reactions in the attitudes of parents toward children is relevant here (pp. 6–7). It may well be that to expose a child to nature or to "expose" it in poetry to the general reader is in each case to project the wishes and will of the adult upon the child to such a degree that there *is* no child. Though this is only one way to put it, it may be said that there are no children in Wordsworth's poetry. The social facts only make such barrenness more intense: "legitimate" and "original" poetry is hostile to illegitimate children of unspeakable origin. It either kills them or encrypts them within safeguarding ideologies of legitimacy (as in the case of Wordsworth's poem on his own bastard daughter, "It Is a Beauteous Evening, Calm and Free").

100. This was written before the full-scale performance of the Early Version of *The Borderers* at Yale University, Nov. 12–15, 1987. The reviews of the production directed by Murray Biggs are still coming in, including an actual review-article by Julie Carlson (whose book-in-progress concerns the politics of Romantic drama as a whole). In my own estimation (based on the performance of Nov. 13), the production discovers some surprising points about the play considered as performance. In fact, "philosophical drama" is not necessarily incommensurable with "action" (in the dual sense of the active and actable). The long philosophical speeches and other set pieces

of the play—including not just Rivers's discourses, for example, but also Mortimer's final speech—were arresting in their intensity. Carlson's essay, "An Active Imagination: Coleridge and the Politics of Dramatic Reform," addresses the interface between imagination and action in sustained fashion. I have lately benefited much from discussions with Carlson, whose overall strategy of taking Romantic theater (often labeled "closet drama") as the central paradigm for studying the interrelations of imaginal and political "action" is intriguing. My own most current interests—formed in the process of revising, editing, and reflecting upon this book—are similar, if different in focus and materials. In my "Wordsworth and Subversion" (and also "Power of Formalism"), I have begun thinking about the history and theory of literary "action." Literary action *qua* action (rather than as an expression of subjectivity) may well be the blind side of cultural criticism to date, whose primary insight has been into the ideology of the subject or the representation of self-fashioning.

101. These changes were characteristic especially of the period from 1750 to 1840 (Brunskill, "Small House," table facing p. 161), and were accompanied by the transformation of the ground-floor "bower" into a "parlour" and the moving of the front door to the center of the living unit (to create the so-called "double-fronted" cottage). On the larger houses of the Lakes, see Brunskill, "Large House." For the literary use of the "closet" in a work relevant to *The Borderers*, see *Caleb Williams*, where Godwin tells us that the fatal "trunk" that so fascinates Caleb lies in "a closet or small apartment which was separated from the library by a narrow gallery" (p. 7).

102. It is clear that invention was necessary to style the yeomanry "statesmen." Though commonly accepted as indigenous, the term was in fact a neologism, as Marshall has shown, imported at the turn of the century from elsewhere in England in great part through the efforts of Wordsworth himself. "Statesman" was signed only on very rare occasions in the late-eighteenth-century Lakes by socially ambitious farmers anxious for what amounted to a middle-class "title" on a par with "Mr." or "Gentleman" (Marshall, "Statesmen," pp. 254–56). Such use of "Statesman" was first popularized "romantically," as Marshall puts it, by John Housman in his highly successful *Topographical Description* of the Lakes (1800). Only after Wordsworth then lent additional authority to the term did it at last come fully into its own as the "traditional" title of the Lakes yeomanry (Marshall, "Statesmen," pp. 262–65). The overriding function of the neologism Wordsworth boosted, in sum, was legitimation. No matter the actual home-life of the class; no matter even that a significant portion of the yeomanry never respected the permanent attachment to ancestral land that Wordsworth assumes (G. P. Jones, "Decline," pp. 209–10; Oosterveen; see also Friedman, p. 146): "statesmen" came to stand in the poet's eyes for the "traditional" respectability of the guardians of the home hearth. The direct application of the 1801 letter is to "Michael" and "The Brothers," which Wordsworth recommends to Fox. But the indirect application we can make is just as telling. The true ancestry of the "statesmen" lies in *The Borderers* and associated works of the mid-1790's. It was only after overcoming doubt about the legitimacy of the rural middle class in these works—and particularly as manifested in the family—that Wordsworth could then with restored confidence dub the yeomen, mythically, "statesmen."

As an addendum, perhaps we can here finally set to rest the assumption that Wordsworth must have known the realities of Lakes society because he lived there. Such an assumption is contradicted by more recent historians and natives. Marshall comments wryly: "As for the argument that Wordsworth 'knew' what he was writing about by virtue of direct experience, nobody who has ever studied the Lakeland yeomanry in detail, or who has even lived in a Lakeland village, would imagine that his peasants were all cast in the mould of Michael!" ("Statesmen," p. 265). Marshall also adduces as witness Jay, whose study of Wordsworth at Colthouse, p. 7, in its turn cites the opinion of a contemporary local Medical Officer (Alexander Craig Gibson) with "a more down-to-earth relationship with the dalesmen."

CHAPTER SEVEN

1. See C. C. Clarke, esp. pp. 26–39. Clarke's identification of the "perplexity" or "paradox" in Wordsworth's notion of imagery has aided me in isolating the "image" as the best entry into my problem. Cf. Lindenberger on "images of interaction" (*On Wordsworth's "Prelude,"* pp. 69–98). Also helpful have been Hodgson's analysis of "iconic" or One-Life "symbolism" in *The Ruined Cottage* (pp. xv, xx–xxi, 19–28) and Marsh's book on Wordsworth's imagery.

2. C. Day Lewis confirms the extent to which credit was given to the Romantics as the originators of "imagery" at the time of the New Criticism (pp. 18, 59). It is beyond the scope of this chapter, of course, to study the full intervening lineage of "imagery" in its Symbolist and Imagist inflections. On the general "Romanticism" of New Criticism, see Foster's strong argument (esp. pp. 30–44).

3. Esp. the chapter on "Symbols and Relationships" (*Music of Humanity*, pp. 102–20) and the examination of Wordsworth's own idea of "imagery" (pp. 204–10). In general, the overlapping terms "image" and "symbol" lie deeply embedded in J. Wordsworth's reading (e.g., pp. 20, 52, 124, 125, 128–29, 139, 144, 192). The congruence of Romantic and New Critical imagery similarly informs C. C. Clarke's work, which studies the "image" with consistent help from Wimsatt's *Verbal Icon* (*Romantic Paradox*, pp. 50, 53, 60). Also telling in our context is Welsford's *Salisbury Plain*, which reads the "imagery" of "symbolic pattern" in *The Ruined Cottage*, in its form as *Excursion*, Book 1 (pp. 80–83).

4. In discussing the "value-property" of the icon, Ransom is making use of Charles W. Morris's semantic theory. Cf. Tate's 1941 essay, "Literature as Knowledge" (*Collected Essays*, pp. 16–48) and Wimsatt's definition of "icon" in the headnote to *Verbal Icon*. Considering Wordsworth, Ransom later speaks of the icon as the "concrete" ("William Wordsworth," p. 503).

5. The first pair of terms are the signatures of Ransom; the next pair, of Brooks; and the final pair, of Tate and William Empson, respectively.

6. I can only suggest here that the study of Romantic imagery in its historical emergence cannot be separated from that of the New Criticism in its conflicted response to the modern emergence of industrial economy and urban pluralism. With regard to economic issues, a fertile research agenda would be to compare Wordsworth's agrarian nostalgia for yeoman "inde-

pendence" in the Lakes (see my argument below) with Southern Agrarianism. To transplant to the American South Wordsworth's "spear-grass" and the industrial cash-exchange economy that ruins yeoman independence would be to arrive upon the plight of "cash-crop" farming in the South of the early twentieth century. As Stewart puts it in his excellent history of the Fugitive and Agrarian movements: "Whether they owned their places or worked for others, most [farmers] raised 'cash crops' such as cotton and tobacco, which they could not consume themselves. Since these crops had only exchange value, the farmer's well-being depended wholly on the market, now at a very low point. . . . The long growing season kept him short of cash and forced him to go into debt to the banks and supply merchant or to trade his labor for goods under the sharecropping system" (p. 93). This passage could be read in parallel with my analysis of the "economy of debt" in the Lakes below (as applied not to crops but to wool). The spear-grass signing the Lakeland yeoman's ruin, as it were, is Wordsworth's sublimation of a crop like tobacco or cotton. None of these crops can be eaten. None, that is, has any wholly independent value-property; all must be valued through negotiations with the economic other in which cash and debt are two faces of the same coin. In response to an industrial economy that depended on methods of credit financing, Wordsworth and the New Critics both sublimated the signs of debt and made them icons of a restored, self-sufficient, and purely imaginary system of value. Both saw precious "images" even in the midst of ruin, greed, desperation, disenfranchisement, and the other indicators of economic change.

As regards the response of the New Criticism to the fracturing of traditional society and the development of mass culture, Stewart's book can be conveniently supplemented by L. P. Simpson's Introduction in *Possibilities of Order*, which quotes Brooks's fear that the "present" is "merely a collection of sensations, or at best, unrelated images" (p. xviii), to argue that the New Critics—especially those belonging to the Vanderbilt Fugitive group and the Agrarian movement of the 1920's and 1930's—had to invent a "technique of inclusion" by which to unify the pluralistic self-image of modernity. As Simpson says, the central theme of Brooks's criticism is "the contemplation of the drama of the quest, among the disorders of history, for the true order of the human community; as this quest reveals itself . . . in works of the literary imagination" (p. xix). Fittingly, Simpson's Introduction leads into Warren's "Conversation" with Brooks, which is really a Platonic dialogue, a new *Republic* moving from literary criticism to an overall critique of history and community. The dialogue concludes with a Myth not of Er but of Humanity: "[Brooks:] I do think that the study of history is essential, but I think that the study of literature is essential too. For, with all of their differences, the subject matter is basically the same. [Warren:] The human being regarded in his humanity. Is that right? [Brooks:] Yes" (Warren, p. 124).

Sharing in the New Critical turn against urban pluralism is Tate's fear of "mass language" in his seminal "Tension in Poetry" (*Collected Essays*, pp. 75–76) and C. Day Lewis's fear of "Broken Images" (pp. 111–34). Lewis (pp. 50–51, 99, 117) and Kermode (p. 145) are aware of the historical motive compelling poets and critics to see "unity" in imagery. Historical motive, we can speculate, underlies New Criticism's preoccupation with tradition as well: if modern imagery yields no unity, then perhaps unity must be hypothesized diachronically, as the moveable feast of intellectual community that is "tradition" in Eliot's sense. See especially Tate's "What Is a Traditional Society?" (*Collected Essays*, pp. 294–304).

7. Hartman's understanding of "humanization" in *The Ruined Cottage* as the principle of mediation between self and Nature is the most analytically strict to date (*WP*, pp. 135–40).

8. On the poem as a "new conception of the narrative-poem" devoid of action and dramatizing instead the play of perspective between the Pedlar and Poet, see J. Wordsworth, *Music of Humanity*, pp. 84, 87–101; see also Clayton, p. 105, and P. Cohen. On the "drama" of perspective specifically, see Leavis, "Wordsworth: The Creative Conditions," esp. p. 333; Parker, " 'Finer Distance,' " pp. 90, 95, 103; and Macdonell ("Place of the Device"). On the poem as "tragedy," however, see Averill, pp. 55–61, 82, 116–41; and Pirie, pp. 51–73.

9. See Macdonell, "Place of the Device," on the opening passage and its "difference in visions" (p. 431).

10. On Margaret's final vision, see Jacobus, *Tradition and Experiment*, p. 176.

11. On the relation between the "dreaming man" and the Pedlar, see J. Wordsworth, *Music of Humanity*, p. 100; Parker, " 'Finer Distance,' " p. 96; Hodgson, pp. 20–24.

12. Welsford observes the sun imagery in the poem (pp. 81–82). On the Pedlar's "eyes" (in his character as the Wanderer), see Hartman, *WP*, p. 304.

13. See C. C. Clarke on Wordsworthian imagery and "depth" (pp. 69–73).

14. I simplify the "supertext" for my purposes by omitting mention of one other key addition, the "momentary trance" in which the Pedlar thinks Margaret is "destined to awake / To human life or something very near" (*RC*, p. 241). I have also made no attempt to distinguish between the several (sometimes repetitive) stages of drafts in the supertext or to consider the issue of whether the revisions of the Pedlar's biography antedate or follow the "moral addendum" (see Butler's Introduction). It is a sad testament to the power of the Cornell Wordsworth editions that every critic must now set an arbitrary "event horizon" beneath which he has not the human endurance to descend.

15. In grafting "heliotrope" to the concepts of "trope" and "sun," of course, I am indebted to Derrida's "White Mythology." An excellent teaching exercise for advanced students may be constructed by assigning *The Ruined Cottage*, MS. B, together with "White Mythology."

16. I am inspired by Heidegger's work with the concept of "equipment" or tools (pp. 97–122).

17. Cf. J. Wordsworth's observation that Robert "cannot love because [he has] lost the occupation that gave emotional as well as financial stability, [Margaret] cannot work because her love is unfulfilled" (*Music of Humanity*, p. 249). For a detailed study of the relation between the industrialization of labor and the structure of the family, see Smelser, chaps. 9–10.

18. In conceiving the affiliative resemblance of imagery as "convenience" and sympathy, of course, I am influenced by Foucault's overall analysis of

universal tropology or the "prose of the world" (*Order of Things*, pp. 17–45). A fuller use of this analysis might also elucidate the heliotropology of *The Ruined Cottage* through the other two terms or "turns" in Foucault's self-completing cycle: emulation and analogy. Between the most literal order of resemblance (convenience) and the most magical (sympathy), Wordsworth's poem inserts a displacement whose tropical structure turns upon an emulation (of nature for humanity) founded upon analogy (between humanity as a relation of labor and nature as a relation of vision). The convenient proximity of spear-grass to a ruin can thus augur the sympathy of spear-grass for Margaret if a Metaphysical conceit (compounded of equal parts Donnean metaphor and analogy) is interposed.

19. J. Wordsworth, *Music of Humanity*, pp. 145–47, and P. Cohen, p. 190, also discuss the essay. I should add that the design of this chapter, which studies Romantic imagery within the matrix of "close reading," requires that I privilege such seminal New Critics as Brooks. The turn of thought by which New Critical method recognizes the potential inhumanity of Wordsworthian humanity can also be documented from the work of Wordsworth specialists. Ferry is most famous and sweeping on this point (pp. 51–53). With regard to the possible inhumanity specifically of *The Ruined Cottage*, the Pedlar, and his imagistic solution to human suffering, see Perkins, pp. 115–16; Parker, " 'Finer Distance,' " p. 110; Sheats, p. 178; P. Cohen, pp. 192, 196; Averill, p. 55; Pirie, pp. 82–86.

20. At the beginning of his entertaining prosecution of the poem, De Quincey imagines asking the Pedlar, "Pray, amongst your other experiments, did you ever try the effect of a guinea?" (p. 305).

21. The tic of "richness" in Brooks's critical vocabulary is most obvious in Warren, "Conversation," e.g., pp. 15, 23, 28, 33, 39, 44. Brooks's teaching device of the "tariff walls" of criticism and his encouragement to students that they allow a regulated "free trade" between criticisms is also telling ("Conversation," pp. 40–41). The following references from studies in the New Critical mode, while far from comprehensive, are sufficient to document how firmly "richness" and its partners control modern literary appreciation: Tate, pp. 82, 83, 84; Empson, pp. 3, 5, 29, 36–37, 46, 49, 101, 106, 236; C. Day Lewis, pp. 35, 51, 62, 79, 95, 104; Wimsatt, pp. 82, 91, 109, 116, and, most centrally, the discussion of "poetic value," pp. 98, 235–51. Emblematic of such modern appreciation is Tuve's placement of "rich" at the head of her catalog of nineteenth-century valorizations of imagery: "rich, graphic, brilliant, colorful, exuberant, decorative, concrete, picturesque, precise, robust, full-blooded" (p. 5). Tuve's study clues us to the fact that a full assay of New Critical "richness" would have to trace its alloy with the Metaphysical imagery of "gold" and "coin" (as in the coin Donne flips in the first stanza of "The Canonization").

22. Cf. Heinzelman on the economics of the dictum that poetry should not "mean" but "be" (*Economics of the Imagination*, p. 162).

23. I regret that Shoaf's study did not appear in time for me to assimilate it fully. His analysis of the economics of reference in light of the theology of the Image provides a prolegomenon to what I only touch upon in this chapter: the insistent nostalgia of faith that makes both the Romantic "image" and New Critical "icon" chalices for what T. E. Hulme called "spilt reli-

gion." Particularly apropos as well is Shoaf's study of the narcissistic image —within whose endless hall of mirrors reference is lost—as a danger to be overcome by an act of faith patterned either after Dante's transcendental self-imaging or Chaucer's other-imaging. It is the complex sin and salvation of the Pedlar (as well as of Wordsworth's "egotistical sublime" in general) to be caught perpetually in a flirtation with narcissism, in the unstable vector or dialectic between the Dantesque and the Chaucerian.

Also relevant are works that have appeared in the burgeoning field of economic approaches to Romanticism and Wordsworth since I wrote this chapter. Highly consonant with my chapter, for example, is Levinson's essay on "Spiritual Economics" in "Michael" (now chap. 2 in her *Wordsworth's Great Period Poems*), which not only addresses centrally the issue of symbolic as opposed to material value but touches upon one of my subthemes: the value-laden relationship of Wordsworth's characters to artifacts and utensils. Levinson's introduction of the Akedah analogy in discussing the spiritualization of economy also extends the religious direction of inquiry. Other works that I have lately had a chance to consult include Gary Harrison's dissertation on the discourse of poverty in Wordsworth, Mark Schoenfield's unpublished essay on the theory of property in *The Excursion*, Susan Eilenberg's essays on "Michael," and the papers by Lee Erickson, Charles Rzepka, John Hodgson, Kurt Heinzelman, and Raimonda Modiano in the sessions on "The Value of Romanticism" at the MLA convention in San Francisco, Dec. 28, 1987 (the sessions also included papers on broader or less directly related issues of criticism and value by Robert M. Ryan, Kim Blank, and Herbert Lindenberger).

24. For Nicole Oresme's false etymology assimilating "economics" to the "icon," see Shoaf, pp. 168–69, 191.

25. Cf. McGann's brief treatment of the poem with its conclusion that " 'The Ruined Cottage' is an exemplary case of what commentators mean when they speak of the 'displacement' that occurs in a Romantic poem" (*Romantic Ideology*, pp. 82–85).

26. There is intriguing but incomplete evidence to suggest that the link between the textile and text trades is more than simply poetic metaphor. Initiating research into book subscription lists in eighteenth-century Britain, Laslett and the Cambridge Group for the History of Population and Social Structure reported that by far the largest (and, by inference, most literate) group of book owners in their Scottish examples were weavers. In one extensive list, for example, 31 percent of subscribers were weavers; in another, 41 percent were weavers (Laslett, "Scottish Weavers"). As Laslett notes, shoemakers were "a very bad second" to weavers despite having the reputation of being "the best read and the most independent in outlook of the craftsmen of earlier times" (p. 10). It is uncertain, however, whether the conclusions drawn from these select cases can be safely generalized.

27. For the effect of bad harvests and the war on national economy from 1790 to 1801, see Gayer, pp. 7–57. For data on harvests and prices specifically of the Northwest, see Booth, pp. 87–91.

28. Textiles and clothmaking ranked behind only leathercrafts in the nonagricultural occupations of Hawkshead (Marshall, "Agrarian Wealth," p. 515). On John Martin, see T. W. Thompson, pp. 206–7.

29. Moreover, it would have been hard to imagine a cotton weaver *un-employed* before the first setbacks in 1799 foreboding the end of cotton hand-looming's "golden age" from 1788 to 1803. Bouch and Jones trace the arrival of the cotton industry in the Lakes (*LC1*, pp. 266–68). On the traditional strength of the Lakes in coarse woolens or "cottons," see *LC1*, pp. 134–36, 263. On the boom and crash in cotton handlooming, see Bythell; see also Smelser, pp. 129–57.

30. On the Northern household system specifically in the Lakes, see *LC1*, pp. 132–41, 143–44, 236. A more general sketch of the Northern "domestic" system may be found in Lipson, pp. 69–93. The terms "household" and "domestic" appear to be somewhat plastic in economic history. "Domestic" indicates that work was done in the home as opposed to factory. By "household domestic" system, I mean to distinguish the Northern form of the domestic system from the Bristol-area form. Lipson suggests calling the Northern system—which was akin in spirit, if not organization, to the older guild system—a "primitive" form of the Bristol-area system (p. 69n). Of course, the Northern and Bristol-area systems overlapped to some degree (see *LC1*, p. 143). Marshall and Davies-Shiel provide a useful, step-by-step description of the whole process of Northern textile production (p. 19).

31. Bouch and Jones observe the "independence of the weaver" and suggest its somewhat mythic or "illusory" nature (*LC1*, p. 143). See also Lipson, p. xlv. E. P. Thompson gives the best reading of the ideology of weaving "independence" as it reached its tragic complication in the early nineteenth century (pp. 271–74).

32. Marshall, "Agrarian Wealth," esp. pp. 510–11, 514, 518–20. See also Marshall, *Old Lakeland*, pp. 41–48, and "Domestic Economy"; G. P. Jones, "Some Sources," pp. 282–92; and Searle, p. 117. The probate inventory was "a list of movable personal goods, credits, and debts compiled under oath by the friends and neighbors (appraisers or apprisers) of a person newly deceased, as a central part of the process of proving a will" ("Agrarian Wealth," p. 506).

33. The probate inventories show lists of debts in "tiny sums" owed by weavers to spinners for yarn (Marshall, "Agrarian Wealth," p. 514). Also see Lipson for the "method of credit" in the textile trade that was "one of the reasons for the survival of the domestic system" in the North (p. 79). On the small size of many loans among the Lakeland yeomanry in general, see Marshall, "Domestic Economy," p. 217.

34. Marshall comments on the problem of what the probate inventories leave out of consideration ("Agrarian Wealth," pp. 505, 507; "Domestic Economy," p. 191).

35. On the textile industry of the West Country or Bristol area, see Lipson, pp. 11–54; and on the way the putting-out system resembled the wage system, Lipson, esp. p. 31.

36. Robert's residency in the Lakes is bolstered in the poem's later versions, where Wordsworth sets the Poet's childhood meetings with the Pedlar in Hawkshead (beginning in MS. D; *RC*, p. 327). Supposing the Poet to be the same age as Wordsworth himself, these meetings may be imagined to occur in the mid to late 1780's, precisely at the outset of Robert's troubles ("some ten years gone"). Since the Pedlar is relatively settled in Hawkshead

during the Poet's childhood, Wordsworth probably conceived Robert as living nearby and certainly in the North within a few days' walk.

37. Nearby Alfoxden, site of the early 1798 work on MS. B, was also set amid countryside covered with furze (gorse) (*DWJ*, pp. 5, 10).

38. As emphasized by Wordsworth himself in MS. E, where he alters "flax" to "hemp" and adds that Margaret "gain'd / By spinning hemp, a pittance for herself" (*RC*, p. 440; see J. Wordsworth, *Music of Humanity*, pp. 24–25). Working ten or eleven hours a day, a flax spinner of the time earned what one contemporary observer remarked was the "very inconsiderable" sum of four pence (*LC1*, pp. 242–43). See also Marshall, "Domestic Economy," p. 195.

39. E. P. Thompson charts this crossover with characteristic force and clarity: "We may simplify the experiences of the years 1780–1830 if we say that they saw the merging of [most types of weavers] into a group, whose status was greatly debased—that of the proletarian outworker, who worked in his own home, sometimes owned and sometimes rented his loom, and who wove up the yarn to the specifications of the factor or agent of a mill or of some middleman" (p. 271).

40. Individual case studies of yeomen or merchants in the Lakes allow us to gain a feel for the degree to which the economy of "independence" was saturated by small debt transactions whose enabling climate of trust could be threatened during a depression. G. P. Jones, for example, records the case of Abraham Dent of Kirby Stephen, an eighteenth-century shopkeeper, brewer, wine seller, and merchant hosier: "Being a prudent merchant he kept a record of purchases by customers who did not pay cash down, the entries being crossed out when payment was made, which sometimes happened on market day. The time taken to clear the account was often only a week or two but in some cases was a year or longer. Dent as a rule needed time to settle with the suppliers of the goods he sold and was ordinarily allowed six or seven months. He discharged his obligation by paying the suppliers' agents or representatives when they called in Kirkby Stephen or occasionally when he himself called on the supplier" ("Some Sources," p. 291).

41. I return to the revisionary work of early 1802 in Chapter 9. Parker observes, "As entry after entry in Dorothy's journal for that winter [of 1801–2] shows, no other project was more sustained or more likely to induce in [William] the weariness and physical illness that most distressed her" (" 'Finer Distance,' " p. 107n).

42. With regard to the repetitiousness of the Poet's continually "baffled" toil, Manning's intriguing analysis of the poem clues us that one way to understand such labor would be to psychoanalyze it ("Wordsworth, Margaret, and the Pedlar"). What compulsion, we might ask, creates a neurosis recapitulating the theme of repetitive labor in the poet's repetitive *compositional* labor? (See also Chapter 9, where I resume the theme of compositional repetition in early 1802.) As in my "On the Autobiographical Present," however, I choose here to read repetition compulsion within a context of actual rather than dream work: repetition at the stitch-by-stitch level is the root act of labor.

43. After the initial drafting of this chapter, I had the opportunity to

share the podium with Chris R. Vanden Bossche in the Modern Language Association convention session on "English Romanticism and the French Revolution" (Dec. 28, 1983) and, subsequently, to exchange manuscripts and read his excellent, fuller treatment of Carlyle and the Revolution. Some of Vanden Bossche's concerns are congruent with mine at this point, especially his effort to trace the development of Carlyle's "personal mythology" or ideology of career writing. Also relevant to my overall interests is Vanden Bossche's argument that Carlyle's search for the proper genre (epic as opposed to the novel) was driven by the interaction of his careerist and historiographical imaginations. In Wordsworth's case, the interweaving of political, social, and what I have termed vocational imaginations led away from Carlylean epic to lyric, and from Hero to self.

44. Many of the details of Wordsworth's finances in the period of *The Ruined Cottage* (as well as later years) are admirably collected in Douglas's 1948 essay on "Wordsworth as Business Man," which I unfortunately did not discover until after attempting the following narration of the poet's cash flow. (Thanks to Charles Rzepka for bringing Douglas to my attention.) I have been able to add some of Douglas's observations below. Ultimately, however, the effort to recover for myself the close weave of the poet's finances by reading the letters supplemented by factual works published since 1948 (e.g., MM, *CEY*) has proved beneficial. It has allowed me to isolate the anxiety of debt, as it may be called, at the center of Wordsworth's vocational imagination in the mid to late 1790's. Such anxiety may be taken to be the ground of what in Douglas appears only as the possibly "usurious" nature of the poet's early investment strategy (see esp. pp. 628–30). In general, Douglas's essentially static picture of Wordsworth as "a shrewd and practical man" (p. 641) perhaps undervalues the illusoriness, ignorance, anxiety, contradiction, and just plain messiness of the poet's financial aspirations, particularly in his early years. Much of this messiness is socially significant, since it arises from Wordsworth's complex feelings of lordship/bondage with regard to his older brother on matters of finance. In this light, the whole premise of taking Wordsworth to be the shrewd manager of his own finances may be questioned: "Wordsworth" as middle manager was enmeshed in the whole network of imaginal and actual economics regulated by the firm of his family (with its higher managers and lower dependents).

45. As Johnston points out in his highly informative "Philanthropy or Treason?" (which extends his previous treatment of the topic in "The Politics of 'Tintern Abbey'"), a liberal-radical journal named *The Philanthropist* ran for eleven months in 1795–96. Johnston's case for Wordsworth's personal involvement rests upon sophisticated management of circumstantial evidence both in regard to the poet's milieu in 1795 and to the likeness between his 1794 plans for the journal and the texts of the actual *Philanthropist*. In its aggregate, the case is very plausible even if not wholly provable on positive grounds. More instructive than the issue of positive conviction, however, is the manner in which Johnston supplements the standards of positive proof with an assortment of evidentiary strategies whose sum is an implicit criticism of purely positive historical knowledge. We might consider, for example, the following passage: "the difficulty of proving Wordsworth's authorship, or partial authorship, of these and other parts of *The*

Philanthropist is part and parcel of the hypothesis which makes his involvement in the enterprise plausible. Proving it requires that we abandon the convenient fiction of single, or even unitary, authorship. Wordsworth is certainly not a consistent sum of political opinions and literary options in 1795 (if he ever was), and neither is *The Philanthropist*" ("Philanthropy or Treason?" p. 393). Read one way, such argument acknowledges that there is no "smoking gun" of incontrovertible authorship (as Johnston phrases it; p. 403). But read another way, it goes far toward discovering that any positive "fact" of literary authorship, intention, or textual expression is knowable only insofar as it assumes certain conventional or consensual notions about the nature of authority. To argue assertively on the basis of seemingly nonpositive evidence is thus ultimately to premise a different notion of literary or cultural authority—of authority, for example, as plurality.

In this light, Johnston's approach collaborates to some degree with the reading of silence, denial, displacement, or negative evidence generally in the work not only of myself but of McGann, Levinson, D. Simpson, and others. Contrary to M. H. Abrams's recent trenchant attack on such evidentiary technique ("On Reading Wordsworth's *Lyrical Ballads*"), the silence or lack of positive evidence is *not* necessarily irrelevant. *Argumentum e silentio* may indeed appear at the level of the unitary individual as silence. But in certain contexts shaped by the collective or conflicted voices of a culture whose sum expression *is* the silence or subjection of individuals (as in the instance of the Pittite sedition and treason laws of 1795), silence speaks loudly. To take Johnston's instance, the silent anonymity of Wordsworth as individual may bespeak the multiple authorship of *The Philanthropist*.

Seen in a long view, the evidence of contextually charged silence is what our newer historicist methods have inherited from the original nineteenth-century historicism through the intermediary of structural thought. Historicism had sought to identify the silent anonymity (or, what is the same, the too noisy Heroism) of the individual as the mob, People, or nation; structural thought reconceived silence as marked negativity or differentiation, and the mob as *langue*; and our newer methods of cultural criticism complete the circle to read the dialogic mob back into the maw of *langue*. Abrams's whole assault upon the hermeneutics of silence, in sum, is wrong because founded on a mishearing of silence. There may be true silence in the physical universe; but in culture, there is never silence—only that which *is silenced* by loudly competitive or censorious voices; and it is the relation of difference between the silenced and the silencing that the newer modes of historicism address. (Also bearing upon these issues is my recent "Wordsworth and Subversion, 1793–1804," which addresses "silence" in a concrete historical context.)

In the following discussion, I have not fully committed myself to Johnston's most recent development of his thesis (in "Philanthropy or Treason?") because to do so would have involved too much revision of existing copy. To accept Johnston's argument as plausible would require only that my later discussion of Wordsworth's first true encounter with the ethos of "industrious" writing apply to a date slightly before 1797. Most relevant in this context is Johnston's emphasis that if Wordsworth did become involved in *The Philanthropist* of 1795–96, he did so in great part because "he had dodged, muffed, or refused every other vocational opportunity . . . since graduating from university." "Wordsworth went to London to *work*," Johnston writes ("Philanthropy or Treason?" p. 385).

46. On the relation between friendship and political patronage in nineteenth-century England, see Bourne, p. 79. A useful analogue of Wordsworth's early vocational imagination is Byron's as traced by Heinzelman ("Byron's Poetry of Politics"). Esp. suggestive for my argument is Heinzelman's observation that "while a minor . . . Byron was not living in debt so much as he was living on credit, the collateral for which was literally himself and his future prospects, and his creditors were often the very 'friends' who nominally comprised the original audience for his poetry" (p. 365).

47. Even when he then again thought of joining Mathews as a London correspondent in late 1794, Wordsworth was still picturing Grub Street as a sort of unapproachable Miltonic Chaos. It is a "mightly [*sic*] gulph which has swallowed up so many, of talents and attainments infinitely superior to my own" (*Letters*, 1: 135).

48. As Dorothy recorded in a letter of September 1795, the initial plan was to invest the legacy at 9 percent on good security. Added to the £50 per year Basil Montagu was supposed to pay the Wordsworths for raising his son, this interest would have been enough both to support William in his endeavors and to start an insurance policy securing Dorothy's own independence (*Letters*, 1: 147). The legacy was at last securely invested in government bonds at 3 percent in December of 1798 (MM, 1: 270; *CEY*, p. 259).

49. Montagu was slightly better at paying the premium of £7/10/6 on the insurance policy Wordsworth took out on his life in 1796 (*CEY*, pp. 186, 205, 208, 246; see my notice of this policy below). As Douglas points out (pp. 629–30), this premium in effect added to the already high interest that Montagu paid for his original £300 loan and brought the entire transaction closer to being usurious. Whatever the ultimate wisdom of substituting an insurance policy (to be paid for by the debtor himself) in lieu of security for an annuity, the practice was not unique to Wordsworth. Doris Langley Moore, in her *Lord Byron: Accounts Rendered* (New York, 1974), observes: "The consequence [of Byron's profligacy as a minor] was that he could not produce the interest on the loans his mother had raised for him, and he was borrowing afresh. To run up debts while still a minor was a costly and intricate operation. One of Byron's ways of doing it was to undertake to pay annuities, when he came of age, to persons whose capital was secured by an insurance on his life effected by some other party at his expense. The premiums fell due relentlessly at moments of greatest inconvenience" (quoted in Heinzelman, "Byron's Poetry of Politics," p. 365).

50. Heinzelman discusses the mention of Calvert in *The Prelude* and observes that the legacy "released the imaginative endowments of the poet's words" (*Economics of the Imagination*, p. 199).

51. Selincourt thought that the preamble referred specifically to the move to Racedown (*Prel.*, pp. 245–46n). But the later move to Grasmere now seems the more likely referent (*CMY*, pp. 628–29). For my purposes, however, the walks of 1795 and 1799 are alike in that both pace out the measure of freedom granted by the Calvert legacy, which began arriving in 1795 but was finally paid in full only in 1798.

52. The benevolence of Wordsworth's 10 percent loans to Montagu and Douglas, we can now note, was from the first complicated by the spectre of usury. W. Douglas notes that "annuities of the sort Wordsworth bought from Montagu were known as devices by which money could be loaned on bad security at usurious interest. Twenty years earlier they had been condemned by a parliamentary committee, which had moreover brought in a bill that regularized the interest rate at figures far below what Montagu paid" (p. 628; see also pp. 629–30).

53. In linguistics, "as in the study of political economy, one is dealing with the notion of *value*. In both cases, we have a *system of equivalence between things belonging to different orders*. In one case, work and wages; in the other case, signification and signal" (Saussure, p. 80). See Heinzelman on this passage (*Economics of the Imagination*, pp. 9–10), as well as on the modern divorce in meaning between "work" and "labor" (pp. 146–47).

54. Additional perspective on *The Oeconomist* may be gained by viewing it in the context of the contemporary literature and economics of agrarianism (on the latter, see MacLean).

55. For the role of weavers in the riots, see Booth, p. 99. On food riots at the time generally, see Hammond and Hammond, pp. 96–98; and E. P. Thompson, pp. 64–68, 143.

56. In his study of "Dearth, Famine and the Common People, 1793–1818," Cobb pays special attention to the role of black marketeers and other illegitimate speculators in the French Revolution (*Police*, pp. 213–324; esp. pp. 244, 301, 304).

57. Gupta, p. 8. Gupta's study (as well as Ray's, which I refer to later) centers on the black market of India. For theoretical studies of the black market inspired by the situation in Europe after the Second World War, see Boulding and also Plumptre.

58. The importance of the issue to the Lakes can be gauged from the fact that the single speech Sir Michael Le Fleming made in the House of Commons prior to 1790 was an address supporting the ban on peddlers (Valentine, p. 527). Le Fleming's view of wandering packmen thus paralleled his harsh view of such wandering trespassers of property as Wordsworth and Coleridge (see Chapter 3).

59. *Journals of the House of Commons* 40 (1785) and 41 (1786). For petitions from the Lakes, see 40: 1018, 1030–31; and 41: 337, 470. For others, see 40: 1007–8, 1017–18, 1020, 1026, 1039–40, 1042, 1042, 1052, 1059 (repeated page numbers represent separate petitions). My quotes are drawn from, in order of citation, 40: 1031, 1059, 1031; 41: 337. Many of the petitions repeat parts of others verbatim, thus indicating a fairly high level of national organization.

60. *Journals of the House of Commons* 40 (1785). For petitions from the Lakes, see 40: 1091, 1091. For others, see 40: 1078, 1090, 1091–92, 1109, 1114, 1114, 1117–18, 1118, 1120–21, 1124, 1137–38. My quotes are drawn from, in order of citation, 40: 1117, 1078, 1091, 1090, 1109, 1091, 1091, 1109. Again, many of the petitions repeat parts of others.

61. If I read the complex revisions correctly, these lines were entered interlinearly in 1801–2 over 1799 material in MS. D and then subsequently deleted with vertical pencil strokes.

62. Marx's comment on imagery is suggestive: "Being the external, com-

mon medium and faculty for turning an image into reality and reality into a mere image, . . . money transforms the real essential powers of man and nature into what are merely abstract conceits and therefore imperfections —into tormenting chimeras—just as it transforms real imperfections and chimeras—essential powers which are really impotent, which exist only in the mind of the individual—into real powers and faculties" (*The Economic and Philosophic Manuscripts of 1844*, ed. Dirk J. Struick, trans. Martin Milligan [New York, 1964], p. 169; quoted in Shell, pp. 41–42).

63. See Hartman, "Voice of the Shuttle," and Shell's chapter, "The Golden Fleece and the Voice of the Shuttle: Economy in Literary Theory."

64. See also Heinzelman on Blake's Guinea-Sun (*Economics of the Imagination*, pp. 120–21).

65. Very relevant to my concerns here and throughout my discussion of Wordsworth's imagery is W. J. T. Mitchell's *Iconology: Image, Text, Ideology*, which appeared subsequent to the writing of this chapter. Mitchell's general approach of investigating the ideological and cultural forces shaping the perceived relation between images and words—as well as many of his particular insights—greatly extend and expand upon my focus on peddling poetry. Esp. apropos are Mitchell's excellent chapters on the politics and ideology of the image in Lessing, Burke, and Marx. Also relevant to my present, brief speculations about evaluation are Barbara Herrnstein Smith's essays on literary value—to which I must also make belated reference (thanks to Michael Warner of Northwestern University for bringing Smith's work in this field to my attention). See esp. her "Contingencies of Value," which includes a section on "The Economics of Literary and Aesthetic Value." The entire notion of literary value—as it is presently being reevaluated at the level of both economic and philosophical speculation—is undergoing a renascence. I have recently attempted to give some notice of this by organizing the Wordsworth-Coleridge Association sessions for the 1987 MLA convention on "The Value of Romanticism I: Wordsworth, Coleridge, and Romantic Money" and "The Value of Romanticism II: Romanticism and Evaluation."

66. Apologies to Marjorie Levinson for enrolling her as negotiator at this point between myself and McGann, who in his supportive and also searching criticism of my manuscript found the following discussion—particularly the section on the gift of poetry—not sufficiently antithetical to the mystique of poetic genius. I have tried to respond by adding these comments on evaluation, which in effect place quotation marks around the discussion to come. What follows is meant to be appreciative to the point that the values of the poetry are allowed to express themselves. From that point on the "switch-and-bait" con of criticism I outlined as my application of antithetical criticism should be seen to take over: the gift of poetry must be viewed with a measure of ironic depreciation; but there is a following stage of re-appreciation when we realize that the theory of the gift (and the denial of economy it implies) is itself built into actual economic thought. Just as economy is a primary poetics of the imagination, that is, so it is also the primary poetics of the gift. As the gift anthropologists and theoreticians tell us, the coexistence of market and gift-exchange mechanisms in societies at times makes their relation undecidable and even their definition indis-

tinguishable (thanks to Patricia Fumerton for help on gift theory). Even in market economies, the notion of the gift can thus be both an ideological and a practical presence (e.g., in the complex interrelation between philanthropy and the corporate tax structure, between holiday bonuses and labor relations, or, to take an example nearer to home, even between the network of dedications, recommendations, and acknowledgments bonding the academic community and the advancement and review processes that embed such community within the larger economy). For me to acknowledge a debt to Levinson, whose book is in turn "for" McGann, is thus inevitably to ravel criticism itself into the complexly interwoven fabric of gift and market ideologies that includes Wordsworth's own texts. To unravel Wordsworth's theory of the gift depreciatively, then, is inauthentic unless we appreciate that our very act of unraveling is supported by extensions of that theory elsewhere. Put most intuitively: the trade of criticism may demystify a poet who thinks himself gifted, but—as anyone who has written or asked for an academic recommendation knows—such trade itself depends on the interrelated ideals of the "gifted critic" (who deserves recommendations) and the "giving" critic (who writes recommendations and deserves thanks). Ultimately, perhaps, it is as useful to criticize criticism by the standards of gifted poetry (i.e., the clichéd view that gifted critics are failed poets) as to criticize poetry by the standards of critical insight.

67. Cf. Shoaf: "When we *communicate*, we are sharing the *wealth* and the *gifts* of language; in the word itself, we confront how language is a kind of wealth. But this wealth is more than and other than coin: with coin I *possess* wealth; with language I *share* wealth" (p. 33).

68. On the influence of the One Life on the Pedlar's biography, see J. Wordsworth, *Music of Humanity*, pp. 184–215 and *passim*; Hodgson, pp. 19–28; and Watson, *Wordsworth's Vital Soul*, p. 83. I owe the idea of a link between the One Life and economy particularly to David Simpson, who in his *Wordsworth and the Figurings of the Real*, pp. 132–69, studies the relation between economy and the problem of the "many and the one"; and also to Stallknecht's discussion of the One Life as a question of proprietorship: "imagination belongs as much to the object seen as to the eye that sees"; mental life "is often enriched by objects which seem to possess it. . . . It is perhaps our greatest spiritual limitation that we consider thoughts and feelings to be a species of private property. . . . Do I own *my* enjoyment of El Greco?" (pp. 74–75). On the relation between Coleridge's own vision of the One Life and the rich "luxury" of the "image," see his "Reflections on Entering into Active Life" in *The Monthly Magazine* (October 1796): from atop a mountain, Coleridge exclaims, "It seem'd like Omnipresence! God, methought, / Had built him there a temple! The whole world / Was *imag'd* in its vast circumference. / No wish profan'd my overwhelmed heart: / Blest hour! it was a luxury—*to be*!" (quoted in J. Wordsworth, *Music of Humanity*, p. 193). We might also think of the imagery of One Life in "This Lime-Tree Bower My Prison" (July 1797): "richlier burn, ye clouds!"

69. An analogue of the economics of the One Life is that of the Heraclitean flux: "All things are an equal exchange for fire and fire for all things, as goods are for gold and gold for goods" (quoted in Shell, p. 52).

70. Cf. Georg Simmel: "the strange coalescing, abstraction, and antici-

pation of ownership of property, which constitutes the meaning of money, is like aesthetic pleasure in permitting consciousness a free play, a portentous extension into an unresisting medium, and the incorporation of all possibilities without violation or deterioration by reality" (*Philosophie des Geldes*, quoted in Shell, p. 8).

71. I am indebted to Patricia Fumerton for aid on the theory of gifts. See her "Exchanging Gifts: The Elizabethan Currency of Children and Poetry."

72. There is strong documentation linking the raven's nest episode (*Prel.* 1: 333–50) in particular to the idea of theft. As T. W. Thompson recounts, Wordsworth was one of the group of Hawkshead boys who climbed a crag to take eggs from a raven's nest in 1782 (as dated in *CEY*, p. 55). When one of their number became caught in the crag, it was Frank Castlehow and his son Jonathan who came to the rescue (Thompson, pp. 211–14, 222). As we saw in Chapter 6, the Castlehows were petty thieves of some local notoriety.

CHAPTER EIGHT

1. Lacan's essay may usefully be read alongside Derrida's "The Law of Genre," which is Jacobus's inspiration in her "The Law Of/And Gender."

2. I choose this term partly under the guidance of Collingwood's *The Idea of History*. For Collingwood historical thinking involves "reenacting" history—i.e., reexperiencing past thought in present consciousness—as a prelude to knowing or thinking about history (pp. 282–302; see also n. 12 to Chapter 2). The spatial characteristic of enactive history—its refusal to let historian and reader stay at a distance from the subject—can thus be rephrased temporally as an insistence upon making the past present. A case in point is the curious time sense of the Revolution books. While Wordsworth clearly presents experience in the past tense, he simultaneously undercuts the sense of pastness (like Carlyle narrating *The French Revolution* in present tense) by inserting wedges of presentness: "And now the strength of Britain was put forth" (10.229); "Now had I other business" (10.249); "Domestic carnage now fill'd all the year" (10.329).

3. In comparing the Revolution books of *The Prelude* with Book 3 of *The Excursion*, Lindenberger finds that the former are "dramatic" and "immediate" in their presentation of mental struggle, while the latter displays emotions and attitudes that seem "to reecho only as reconsidered passion, recollected in perhaps too rigidly imposed a tranquillity" (*On Wordsworth's "Prelude*," p. 260). I have benefited from Lindenberger's chapter on "The Non-Visionary Books" as a whole, and from its discussion of the unique features of Wordsworth's historical consciousness in France within the context of the poet's overall social vision. What Lindenberger calls "dramatic," I have called "enactive."

4. We might be reminded here of the Druids in *Salisbury Plain* pointing from the ground to the stars, or perhaps of the "image of tranquillity" upon which the Pedlar reflects in *The Ruined Cottage*.

5. My development of the historical consciousness implied by the epitaph is influenced by several works on Wordsworth and epitaphic poetry beginning with Bernhardt-Kabisch's essays and Hartman's "Wordsworth,

Inscriptions, and Romantic Nature Poetry." Hartman traces the link between the poet's work and the inscription that "points to" rather than "evokes" the landscape (p. 221). Ferguson, p. 33, further suggests that the poet makes the epitaph the "epitome of poetic language" and creates "a kind of power vacuum within words themselves, so that they can only 'speak of something that is gone.' " And Fry, p. 433, argues that for Wordsworth (and Byron) the epitaphic mode accomplishes the "burial of voice"; it is the "gravesite" of "sublime" communication. Conceived as epitaph, these readers thus suggest, poetic language remains inevitably removed from its buried subject; it can only point stiffly and briefly to a once "living" portion of experience that has vanished. As a historical tool, it constitutes an elaborately ritualized way of *not* presenting the immediacy of the past, of resigning the speaker and hearer (communing over the carved inscription) to the fact that the subject of their thoughts and feelings must remain sealed in silent memory. Whereas enactive history strives to make the historian proximate to and contemporary with his subject, epitaphic history—as I will go on to argue—resigns him to being distant from and posterior to historical "life." Or, rather, if enactive history brings the past into the present, epitaphic history effects precisely the reverse: it displaces even the living present into the undisturbed past.

6. We may instance here a moment near the close of the third "Essay upon Epitaphs" where Wordsworth interrupts his mode of critical discourse for a meditation upon the barest epitaph possible: "In an obscure corner of a Country Church-yard I once espied, half-overgrown with Hemlock and Nettles, a very small Stone laid upon the ground, bearing nothing more than the name of the Deceased with the date of birth and death, importing that it was an Infant which had been born one day and died the following. I know not how far the Reader may be in sympathy with me, but more awful thoughts of rights conferred, of hopes awakened, of remembrances stealing away or vanishing were imparted to my mind by that Inscription there before my eyes than by any other that it has ever been my lot to meet with upon a Tomb-stone" (*Prose*, 2: 93).

7. Spivak discusses Wordsworth's transformation of the Revolution into a literary-historical and "iconic" text in her intriguing essay on "Sex and History" in the closing books of *The Prelude*.

8. Compare Wordsworth's experience and vocabulary with Gibbon's upon entering Rome: "My temper is not very susceptible of enthusiasm, and the enthusiasm which I do not feel I have ever scorned to affect. But at the distance of twenty five years I can neither forget nor express the strong emotions which agitated my mind as I first approached and entered the *eternal* City. After a sleepless night I trod with a lofty step the ruins of the Forum; each memorable spot where Romulus *stood*, or Tully spoke, or Caesar fell was at once present to my eye; and several days of intoxication were lost or enjoyed before I could descend to a cool and minute investigation" (p. 134).

9. For information about the painting, the convent, and the "liberation" of Le Brun's work from the Carmelites during the Revolution, see Jouin, pp. 493–94; *Charles Le Brun*, pp. 43, 67; Eriau, pp. 97–99 and *passim*; and *Inventaire Général*, 1: 22–23, 2: 18, 38. The painting was taken from the con-

vent in late 1792 first to the Petits Augustins and then to the *Musée central des arts* in early 1793.

10. Recusant priests imprisoned at the Carmelite convent, we may note, were among the most prominent victims of the pike during the September Massacres. The *Times* for Sept. 10, 1792, reports: "The number of Clergy found in the Carmelite Convent was about 220. They were handed out of the prison door two by two into the *Rue Vaugerard*, where their throats were cut. Their bodies were fixed on pikes and exhibited to the wretched victims who were next to suffer. The mangled bodies of others are piled against the houses in the streets." See also Mathiez, p. 181, and Lenotre.

11. Burke's analysis of beauty, indeed, stressed fairness of hue and curvature of line, and was equally applicable to landscapes and women (*Sublime and Beautiful*, esp. pp. 114–17). Boulton in his Introduction to that work, p. lxxv, cites those who have noticed the "femininity" of Burke's concept of beauty. See Burke's passage on p. 115 on the "beautiful woman." Regarding "Baroque": the *OED* traces the usage of the term from the mid-nineteenth century. The specifically Baroque air of Le Brun's painting must be seen by Wordsworth as a complexity of "beauty" and—as we will see below— "sublimity."

12. For British reproductions of Le Brun's illustrations of the passions contemporary with Wordsworth, see *Heads Representing the Various Passions* and *Elements of Drawing*. Among other signal differences between Rapture and Sadness is the fact that in the latter, the head is literally "dejected," or faced downwards. On *Le Repas chez Simon*, see *Charles Le Brun*, p. 47; Jouin, pp. 470–71; and Eriau, p. 95.

13. My thinking on the aesthetics of revolution was spurred on by Paulson's wide-ranging talk, "Burke's Sublime and the Representation of Revolution," at Stanford University, January 19, 1978. The paper has since appeared in Perez Zagorin, ed., *Culture and Politics from Puritanism to the Enlightenment* (Berkeley, Calif., 1980) and in revised form in Paulson, *Representations*. Focusing on Burke amid other figures, Paulson follows the use of vegetable, sexual, and other imagery to depict the Revolution's violent release of energy and then relates such imagery to Burke's own concept of the sublime. As Paulson suggests, "Burke's solution to the confrontation with this unthinkable phenomenon, the French Revolution . . . was to fit it into the framework of aesthetic categories he had worked out himself thirty years before" (*Representations*, p. 68). He then sketches a psychological model of response to the Revolution based on the sexual dynamics of the sublime. For another suggestive study of the aesthetics of history, see Kroeber, "Romantic Historicism." For Kroeber, a signal feature of Romanticism is "a dialectical engagement with confusingly open-ended experiences," an effort to represent "sublime" historical subjects that the writer or artist already knows "cannot be represented" (p. 164).

14. The painting hung in Beaumont's collection, and Wordsworth probably saw it in 1806 when he also first saw Claude's *Hagar and the Angel* (see n. 18 to Chapter 3).

15. Telling evidence of Wordsworth's increasing mastery of aesthetic categories—especially of the sublime—may be found in the letter to Coleridge of Mar. 6, 1804, in which Dorothy recounts her brother's discovery

of the "slip" farther up the rill at Rydal Lower Falls: "William found it out by himself—it is a little slip of the River above Rydale that makes the *famous* waterfalls—about two hundred yards in length, it is high up towards the mountains where one would not have expected any trees to be, and down it tumbles among Rocks and trees, trees of all shapes, elegant Birches, and ancient oaks, that have grown as tall as the storms would let them, and are now decaying away, their naked Branches like shattered lances, or the whole tree like a thing hacked away and dismantled, as William says to impale malefactors upon. . . . With these are green hollies, and junipers, a little waterfall, endless, endless waterbreaks—now a rock starting forward, now an old tree enough to look at for hours, and then the whole seen in a long prospect. It is a miniature of all that can be conceived of savage and grand about a river, with a great deal of the beautiful. William says that whatever Salvator might desire could there be found. He longed for Sir George Beaumont, but if it is not seen in winter it would be nothing" (*Letters*, 1: 449). What is clear here is that the picturesque "miniature" of the Falls and its environs, which we saw in Chapter 3, is being reanalyzed by brother and sister (under the tutelary spirit of Beaumont) to fit the schema of the beautiful and of the Salvatorean "savage and grand."

16. See *Charles Le Brun*, p. 67; and Eriau, pp. 98–99. It is improbable that Le Brun actually depicted La Vallière, whom he did not meet until later and who, in any case, was a child at the time of the painting's composition. For more information on La Vallière, her infamous seduction by the king, and the sensational ceremony in which she took the veil, see Lair, esp. pp. 60–86, 306–28; and Wolf, pp. 290–304.

17. It would be interesting to take the purely pictorial aspect of the problem to its logical end. We can speculate that in order truly to paint the agon of revolution, in which sublimity and beauty combat, an artist would need to utilize some compositional framework expressive of struggle. Rectilinear stasis on the model of Hubert Robert's picture of the storming of the Bastille would not be adequate (a point I owe to William Pressly, formerly of the History of Art department, Yale University, with whom I co-taught a course on the Age of Revolution). Neither would straight-line recession serve, whether of the direct or diagonal variety. Rather, we would need at least a double-diagonal model able to create a binary composition (as in Rubens's *Chateau Steen* or, with the diagonals transposed onto the vertical plane as a gigantic "X," in Martin's *The Deluge*). Or we would need to follow Turner's lead in choosing an orbicular scheme (evident in Martin's *Deluge* as well) framing color antagonism.

18. See Woodring's thesis, *Politics in English Romantic Poetry*, p. 49 and *passim*, that Wordsworth and other Romantics faced a dilemma posed "by discrepancies between the intellectual principles underlying [their] first political assents and [their] romantic intuitions of organic wholeness made apparent by the creative, unifying imagination."

19. Since the appearance of this portion of my argument in earlier form, J. Chandler, pp. 203–6, has published excellent commentary on the Beaupuy segment of Book 9. Also relevant to my following discussion is Paulson's fuller consideration of the relation between gothic fiction and the French Revolution (*Representations*, pp. 215–47), which appeared too late for

me to make use of it here. Since the topic of the gothic is only a small part of my argument in this chapter, I have not attempted to go back and reinforce my discussion with Paulson's insights. Particularly relevant would be his discussion of *Caleb Williams* and—by way of *Frankenstein*—of the monstrous.

20. In identifying Wordsworth's allusions and literary references, I am guided throughout by Selincourt's notes in *Prel.* (supplemented by WAG and Maxwell's notes in his edition of *The Prelude*). Here, for purposes of comparison, Selincourt cites passages from *The Faerie Queene* depicting Una and Hellenore (*Prel.*, p. 294). But Hellenore (*Faerie Queene*, 3.10) seems an unlikely candidate because she is certainly not an "unhappy Thrall."

21. As Selincourt notes, Wordsworth was mistaken that Beaupuy died in the Vendée. In fact, he was only wounded and did not die until the battle of the Elz in 1796 (*Prel.*, p. 293).

22. I deal here with the Vaudracour and Julia segment by linking literary form to historical allegory. An alternative would be to link the historical allegory to the biographical relationship between Wordsworth and Annette Vallon, for which see Erdman, "Wordsworth as Heartsworth."

23. In the 1850 poem, Wordsworth relates the Vaudracour and Julia episode more closely to the Revolution, but then does not tell the full tale.

24. See Jacobus, "'That Great Stage,'" p. 363, on the link between Robespierre and Macbeth in *The Prelude*.

25. On Burke's similar use of Milton in condemning the Jacobin Hell, see Paulson, *Representations*, pp. 66–71.

26. Selincourt identifies the Miltonic echoes here in his note to lines 479–86 (*Prel.*, p. 303).

27. This epitaph, which still exists in the graveyard at Cartmel Priory, varies Gray's lines only slightly. The "Elegy" closes: "No farther seek his merits to disclose, / Or draw his frailties from their dread abode, / (There they alike in trembling hope repose) / The Bosom of his Father and his God." In quoting the tombstone, I have not normalized capitalization or punctuation (cf. *Prel.*, p. 303).

28. On common measure ($a^4 b^3 a^4 b^3$), see Deutsch, pp. 34–35. Needless to say, I am arguing very broadly here in situating Wordsworth's lyricism at the intersection of Classical and Hebraic forms. The simplification, however, has the advantage of allowing his early lyricism to be seen as cognate with that of other lyrical hermeneutics—as it might be called—designed to reinterpret the Classical in the light of the Hebraic. Christopher Smart's negotiation between the Psalms and Horace's Odes in his translations is a case in point (see my "Christopher Smart's 'Uncommunicated Letters'").

29. In this list, it is useful to read Ode as mediational between Hymn and Elegy. Song and Ballad may then be read as the popular or lay forms of the structure: Hymn ← Ode → Elegy. This is why the ode-like turns and counterturns of a poem like "Tintern Abbey" seem to the poet perfectly assimilable to the rest of the *Lyrical Ballads*. The strophe, antistrophe, and epode of ode in the high style—so well suited to modulating the transition between what I have called the elegiac and the hymnal—become separate voices in the low-style ballads (in the manner Bialostosky calls Wordsworth's "dialogism"; see esp. pp. 105–59): first there is the turn of the narrator's voice, then the counterturn of encounter with another, often

vulgar voice, and finally the epode-like "stand" of a narrator left at rest. It is in this manner, for example, that the narrator's elegiac mood at the opening of "Resolution and Independence" (1802) modulates through the intervention of the Leech-gatherer's voice into the hymnal strain in the final stanza (cf. Bialostosky's treatment of the poem at the close of his chapter on "Dialogic Personal Anecdotes," pp. 148–59).

30. We can notice that in the Preface of 1815 Wordsworth assigns epitaph and sonnet, along with locodescription and the epistle, to his fourth category, the "Idyllium." Appended after the first three categories of narrative, drama, and lyric, epitaph and sonnet must thus be presumed to denote lyricism of a special kind. Recalling our earlier discussion of locodescription and georgic as mediational forms (in Chapters 1 and 3), we can speculate that epitaph and sonnet for Wordsworth are also mediational in function. They are not just lyrics but transformational lyrics designed to organize, reverse, or otherwise adjust the relations between the narrative, dramatic, and lyric. Wordsworth's sonnet form, as we will see, thus serves to subordinate narrative history to lyric or personal history.

31. My reading of the shell's song as pan-lyric—or perhaps a panic of lyric—is indebted to Miller's reading of the shell as containing "the original and originating Word, source of all language, which is yet no word because it holds all words undistinguished within it" (*Linguistic Moment*, p. 67).

32. There is much more to my historicization of Bloom's theory of poetry than can be explored in my present context. It would be useful, for example, to read Bloom's system of swerves in relation to the process of faction formation in the Revolution. My discussion below of Opposition politics is also apropos. For such a "strong" poet-among-politicians as Burke, to take a stand was to swerve.

33. For a fuller study of *apophrades* or metalepsis in rhetorical tradition, see Hollander, pp. 133–49. Hollander stresses the fact that the term has had an exceptionally tangled history.

34. With J. Chandler's book in mind, we may think here of the contract between the living and dead in Burke's *Reflections*.

35. Cf. J. Chandler's reading of the romantic "bright spot" in the context of Wordsworth's spots of time (pp. 205–6).

36. On repetition in *The Prelude*, see Lindenberger, *On Wordsworth's "Prelude,"* pp. 188–97. Throughout this section of my chapter dealing with Books 9–10 in *The Prelude*, I am indebted to Lindenberger for much early encouragement and advice. See "The Poetry of Revolution" in *On Wordsworth's "Prelude"* (pp. 252–70) for a sustained discussion of the Revolution books consonant with mine.

37. An explication of the somewhat mysterious notion of "humanization" in Hartman could take its start here. In fully acculturated form, perhaps, nature's humanization of the Imagination is identical with doctrine as well as *doxa*—i.e., with the indoctrination of mind in shared opinion.

38. I have elsewhere speculated on the nature of autobiography using the approach of Olney and others. My discussion of the exegetics of autobiography, indeed, is related to the opening argument of my "On the Autobiographical Present," pp. 115–16. In particular, the formulation, "God is that I am," is a variation of my earlier formulation, "I sin therefore I am."

39. I have discussed the estranged autobiography of Paul in 2 Cor. 12: 1–7 in my "Christopher Smart's 'Uncommunicated Letters.'" In his *Jubilate Agno* Smart varies Paul's story of the man who heard unspeakable words.

40. It was Lindenberger who first mentioned to me that Hegel's philosophy can usefully be read as autobiography.

41. Eagleton's phrasing of the problem is very acute: "Criticism is not a passage from text to reader: its task is not to redouble the text's self-understanding, to collude with its object in a conspiracy of eloquence. Its task is to show the text as it cannot know itself, to manifest those conditions of its making (inscribed in its very letter) about which it is necessarily silent. It is not just that the text knows some things and not others; it is rather that its very self-knowledge is the construction of a self-oblivion" (*Criticism*, p. 43).

42. This line of thought first occurred to me after reading the description of a course given by Shira Wolosky at Yale in 1981–82 on "The Christian Logos and the Hebraic Word." The *ricorso* between the histories of theology and of criticism I suggest here, of course, would need further development to make it fully useful. At stake is the relation between deconstruction and skepticism posed by Goodheart as well as by Altizer et al. In the framework of the *ricorso* I posit, the skepticism of deconstruction is a moment within the process of theology.

43. See, for example, Hartman, "Christopher Smart's *Magnificat*," in which the care-ful reading of the poet is also in part a reading of Derridaean deconstruction.

44. To be fair, I should reiterate what I have written elsewhere ("Christopher Smart's 'Uncommunicated Letters'"): part of the Anglo-American misapprehension of deconstruction stems from the fact that the deep ethics of the method—mediated through Rousseau and Nietzsche—are simply too removed from the grasp of Johnsonian, Arnoldian, and Eliotic literary ethics. But deconstruction has not contributed enough toward closing this divide. Miller's recent essay on "The Search for Grounds in Literary Study," for example, both takes up the problem seriously and exacerbates the divide between Anglo-American and Continental understandings when, in pursuit of a polemical point *contra* Goodheart, it claims for Arnold the status of "a nihilist writer through and through, nihilist in the precise sense in which Nietzsche or Heidegger defines the term: as a specifically historical designation of the moment within the development of Western metaphysics when the highest values devalue themselves and come to nothing as their transcendent base dissolves" (p. 28). What is needed to elucidate the ethical or evaluative underthought of deconstruction to Anglo-American perception, perhaps, is a deconstructive reading of Johnson, Arnold, and Eliot to match the amplitude of Derrida's readings, for example, of Rousseau and Plato.

45. E.g., see Miller on "oddness" in *Fiction and Repetition*, p. 18; also my "Christopher Smart's 'Uncommunicated Letters,'" pp. 139–40.

46. I am indebted for my terminology here—and for many provocative and sensitive discussions in the past on these and other issues—to John Guillory. On the relation between Eliotic orthodoxy and New Critical paradoxy, see Guillory's essay.

47. I regret that Chandler's important work did not appear until much of

my overall argument and interpretive apparatus in this book was already in place. The result is that the following discussion addresses his deep concerns and assumptions only imprecisely. In particular, a full effort to read my argument together with Chandler's would need to solve the relationship between Burkean prejudice and what I have called denial.

48. For our purposes, the controversy between J. Wordsworth and Reed over how certainly to read the "fifth book" in MS. w as the intended conclusion of the five-book poem is a subsidiary issue. What needs to be explained —whatever its precise place in the transition from the five-book to the thirteen-book plan—is the reordering of elements the "fifth book" required.

49. It is not possible to date with exactness the final writing and assembly stages of the poem relative to the great trauma of February 1805: John's death (see WAG, p. 520). If the decision to assemble Books 11 and 13 in their present order was in fact finalized after February, then the possibility exists that the shipwreck of John is cognate with the crowning of Napoleon (to which I turn below) in instigating the transposition of the spots of time and Snowdon. Both John's death and Napoleon's rise discipline the imagination. To study the correction learned after the shipwreck together with that learned upon the final foundering of Wordsworth's hopes for the Revolution would require—in my framework—adding the family context addressed in Chapter 6 to my current political considerations. Hatred for Napoleon, we may say, was the end of political fraternity; and the personal realization of such broken faith was what Wordsworth in his letter on John's death called the breaking of the set (*Letters*, 1: 540).

50. MacGillivray remarks about the five-book poem that it "was to be about a poet's education, by nature and by books, down to the end of his formal education" (p. 112). Crisis in the longer poem, we may say, was then constituted as graduation from *Bildungsroman*.

51. If I follow correctly the details of textual history presented by J. Wordsworth ("Five-Book *Prelude*"), WAG, and *CMY*, it is unclear when the verses on fealty to the mind (11.266–74) entered the full poem in 1804. Another revision of 1804 may also be noticed here (although the evidence for interpretation seems so slight that I have left it alone): as WAG points out, the "fructifying" virtue of the spots of time in the "Two-Part *Prelude*" becomes "vivifying" at an intermediate stage of composition in 1804 (Selincourt retains "vivifying" in *Prel.*). But "vivifying" is then corrected in manuscript to "renovating," retained in WAG (p. 8n and p. 428n). WAG suggests that the revision "loses the implication that the mind becomes creative" (p. 8n).

52. I am aware that such a reading of Wordsworth is potentially reductive. It partakes of the "depreciation" of the poem that Barthes accounts to his own reading of "proairetic" kernel sentences in Balzac (*S/Z*, p. 104) and that to some extent threatens the entire structuralist (and Russian Formalist) enterprise of parsing narrative. When a narrative is emptied to produce a predicative relation between shifters (its subjects and objects), what remains but an inert form like some paradigm sentence in a grammar book? The answer may be suggested by quoting the opening of the Third Meditation of Descartes: "Now I shall close my eyes, I shall stop my ears, I shall disregard my senses, I shall even efface from my mind all the images of corporeal

things; or at least, since that can hardly be done, I shall consider them vain and false. By thus dealing only with myself and considering what is included in me, I shall try to make myself, little by little, better known and more familiar to myself" (p. 91). If emptying out Wordsworth's poem to its elementary shifters and their interrelationship is a reduction, it is also an intensification—an effort to isolate within the narrative of self the meditation that is the work of *cogito* ("A meditation rose in me that night / Upon the lonely Mountain when the scene / Had pass'd away"; *Prel.* 13.66–68). Just as the Cartesian *cogito* refers to "myself," so the Wordsworthian "I" refers to "mind." And in both cases, the clean symmetry of the shift in reference is disturbed by an asymmetrical shift outside the system: neither "corporeal things" nor history can finally be "effaced from my mind." It is the embeddedness of one set of shifts in *The Prelude* (those of self-meditation) within another (those of historical denial) that will interest us. It is such extra-meditational shifting that constitutes Jakobson's "context," to which I refer below.

53. The impersonality of Mind in Book 13, we may note, is reinforced by the odd "they's" and "he's" of Wordsworth's third-person omniscience (e.g., "Oh! who is he that hath his whole life long / Preserved, enlarged, this freedom in himself"; 13.117–18). I should also clarify that my isolation of a "decisive close" on "impersonal Mind" in Book 13 is a simplification. A fuller study would need to read the complex network of shiftings in the "acknowledgments" section of Book 13 following Snowdon (beginning l. 204). After shifting his attention to Dorothy, Coleridge, and Calvert, and then adopting the voice of a great, symphonic "we" ("Prophets of Nature, we to them will speak"; 13.435), the poet once more shifts to the impersonal for his finale: "the mind of man becomes / A thousand times more beautiful than the earth . . . as it is itself / Of substance and of fabric more divine" (13.439–45).

54. By adverting to this term, I emphasize not only the fragmentary and unsystematic nature of such thinking but also its historical indebtedness: the fact that *bricolage* depends upon the *found* and the *material*—i.e., pre-ideational (see Lévi-Strauss, *Savage Mind*, pp. 16–22). On "Spy Nozy," see MM, 1: 331; *CEY*, pp. 204–5; Roe. As Moorman notes, "Coleridge's account of how the spy [sent by the Home Office] used to lie behind the sanddunes by the shore listening to him and Wordsworth discoursing about 'Spy Nozy' (Spinoza) and drawing conclusions therefrom that they were referring to him and his 'Bardolph nose,' is hardly credible." As we will see, however, Coleridge's elaboration upon the extravagances of public suspicion were not far from the mark. Interpretation by paranoia, as it might be called, turned the shores of Britain into a Pynchonesque Zone. A day-by-day reading of the *Morning Post* in early to middle 1804, for example, shows that the invasion fear at its peak produced innumerable "false alarms" and needless mobilizations of Volunteer regiments.

55. Napoleon's Grand Tactics were so integral with his broader, strategic philosophy that the two followed the same overall plan dependent on the enveloping movement. I choose to center my examination on Grand Tactics because it is the threshold of action where strategy becomes visible to the actors of hand-to-hand tactics.

56. A maxim from General Lloyd's *L'introduction à l'histoire de la guerre en*

1756 that Napoleon often repeats in his *Correspondance* (D. Chandler, pp. 179, 1128n).

57. As Liddell-Hart notes, the sense of Napoleon's "point" has been disputed. It seems most logical to military historians that he meant by "point" not the enemy's strongest concentration but his weak "joint" (pp. 109–10).

58. On the Romantic Moment, see Salm, Jackson, Neubauer.

59. See Scarry, pp. 7–9, on the "embodiment" of armies. On the formations of the Luftwaffe and RAF, see J. E. Johnson, pp. 89–90, 101–2.

60. The trope of politics as war runs right through our period from beginning to end. A. Beattie, p. 73, thus cites Lord Abingdon in a speech of Mar. 19, 1788, on the East India Declaratory Bill: "And how shall we account for this? has the devil got into the herd of swine? . . . Or is it that some great political general, putting himself at the head of a scouting party of his own, is so manoeuvring between the two grand armies of Whigs and Tories, as to be ready to join either whenever the strongest of the two shall afford him the opportunity of doing so?"

61. See, for example, the report on the endless evolutions of French factions in *MC* for Oct. 20, 1792, and *T* for June 1, 1793. The *MC* piece (which we glanced at in Chapter 4) quotes its Paris correspondent: "It is not in France as with you, parties have not taken consistency. Men are not arranged under distinct standards upon specific principles. There is no steady phalanx acting upon fundamental doctrines, and attached to each other by habits of affection and confidence. On the contrary, all is fortuitous —their arguments and disunions are both transitory—they rally upon measures, and not upon maxims; and therefore, though there may be lines, they are by no means parallels." My point is that the politics of English Opposition certainly were *not* that of the "steady phalanx." Such reporting assumes a virtually Classic geometry of Parliament at odds with the criss-crossing lines of actual politics at the time.

62. The other way to view such shifts, of course, is to see them not as apostasy but as loyalty to a deeper principle. In Burke's historiography, therefore, new-found conservatism is prejudice in favor of the old and English. And in Fox's case, his anti-Pitt measures may be taken as evidence of apparent constancy—well after the fashion—to the cause of French Liberty.

63. On "personality" as a category of historical understanding in this period, see Barnes.

64. See, for example, my discussion of the "radicals" of "savagery," "cannibalism," "parricide," etc., in Chapter 4. On metaphor and topicality, see Chapter 9.

65. The *Times*, for example, reported on the astonishment caused by Burke as follows: "It had, [Mr. Burke said], been stated, that nineteen assassins had come from France. These were seven more than were sufficient to murder all the Royal Family. . . . Some thousand daggers were bespoke at Birmingham; how many of these were to be sent abroad and how many used for home consumption he could not tell. Here Mr. Burke astonished the House by drawing a long dagger, branding it in his hand, and then throwing it violently on the floor. There said he is French fraternity for you. This a dagger made exactly according to the directions given to the Gentlemen at Birmingham" (Dec. 24, 1792).

66. I concentrate here just on the daily press in this period—a simplifi-

cation based on the facts that Wordsworth read only the *Morning Post* and that the great proliferation of weekly journals did not in any case occur until the first several decades of the nineteenth century, as mentioned below. A note on my sources in this study of the daily press may be in order. In general, Werkmeister and STCE provide the most full, up-to-date, and trustworthy information. Aspinall's survey, which Werkmeister recommends highly (*Newspaper History*, p. 490), provides much primary documentation, but in certain instances its information needs to be corrected or supplemented by more recent research. Hindle's history of the *Morning Post*, which Werkmeister also approves (*Newspaper History*, p. 490), is highly useful for our specific purposes. However, its too-rosy picture of the *Post*'s beginnings suggests that we cannot take it on complete trust. Where there is contradiction on dates or other matters in the sources I cite, Werkmeister and STCE should be assumed to take precedence.

67. On the prevalence at the time of financing by blackmail and its opposite, "puffing," see Werkmeister, *Newspaper History*, pp. 20–21.

68. On the ability of Treasury both to finance and to regulate newspapers, see Werkmeister, *London*, p. 318, *Newspaper History*, p. 31.

69. Stuart had already absorbed the Government *World* in 1794 (STCE, p. lxix n). Also, before buying out the *Post*, he was listed as the *Post*'s printer (STCE, p. lxix).

70. Werkmeister, as Erdman reports in STCE, pp. lxix–lxx n, finds that Stuart may have earlier acquired shares in the *Courier* when he bought the *Telegraph*.

71. Data interpreted from STCE, pp. lxx n, xcvi n, civ n; and Hindle, p. 82, show a continual growth curve in the circulation of the *Post* as follows: 350 copies per day in 1795; 1,000 (perhaps more) in 1798; 1,500 in 1799; 2,000 in 1800; 2,400 in 1801; 3,300 in 1802; 4,500 (perhaps less) in 1803. At the end of this period, important competitors registered the following circulation figures: *Morning Herald*, 2,400 copies per day in 1802; *Times*, 2,240 in 1802; *Morning Chronicle*, 1,650 in 1802 and 2,000–3,000 in 1803. (Hindle puts the circulation of the *Post* for 1797 and 1798 at 1,000 and 2,000, respectively, but may be inflating his figures. I have adjusted these figures downward in the entry for 1798 to be consistent with later figures. Hindle's figure of 4,500 for 1803 may also be inflated. All other figures are from STCE, which for some years gives circulations for various seasons. Where there is a choice, I have set down a rounded-off representative average.) As Asquith and other historians of the press in this period note, readership was much larger than these circulation figures indicate. Between 10 and 30 people probably read each paper sold (Asquith, p. 101).

72. It is useful to keep in mind the distinction between such a middle-class "Public" and the less polite mass readership that fueled the rise of the popular press in the early nineteenth century. See Klancher's works for the difference.

73. See Aspinall, pp. 88–89, 206; STCE, pp. lxxi, cxviii. Aspinall notes that T. G. Street, editor and co-owner of the *Courier*, was in the pay of the Treasury without Stuart's knowledge.

74. It may be useful to think, in Kuhn's terms, of impartiality coming to be as the prescientific version of our modern paradigm of journalism. There

is a suggestive congruence between Kuhn's notion of audience (a cohesive scientific community) and Klancher's of a much more inchoate nineteenth-century Public. In writing an article, both the scientist and the journalist must imagine an audience validating their methods: the "objective" method of the former and the "impartial" method of the latter. But the massive, internally rifted, and changing audience of the nineteenth-century journalist was always merely a congeries of partial views—with the result that journalistic objectivity was always less than fully scientific. To anthropologize Kuhn: it was always poised between the *bricoleur*'s and the engineer's points of view. Like *bricolage* in Lévi-Strauss's formulation, such prescientific journalism was perpetually open to the charge of opportunism, of merely picking up whatever was most ready to hand.

75. As Erdman notes, Coleridge later persistently magnified his own impact on the *Post* and the national scene. Yet even discounting such amplification, Erdman concludes that Coleridge's stamp on the personality of the paper was decisive. In this regard, a single political essay or poem counted for much more than the impersonal reports and listings that made up the bulk of any paper of the time (STCE, pp. lxxii–lxxiii). Certainly the rise in circulation from less than 1,500 to 2,000 after Coleridge resumed writing for the *Post* in late 1799 impressed Stuart (STCE, p. xcvi n). On Coleridge's connections with the other Romantic contributors to Stuart's newspapers, see Hindle, pp. 71–72.

76. Other studies relevant to Coleridge's art of political apostasy, equivocation, dialectic, and audience-making include the special section edited by Woodring on "Coleridge: The Politics of the Imagination" in *Studies in Romanticism* 21 (1982), 447–74, with essays by Christensen, Fisher, Modiano ("Metaphysical Debate"), and Storch ("Politics of the Imagination"); see also Reiman; and Everest, pp. 97–145. On politics in Coleridge's works generally, see Woodring, *Politics in the Poetry of Coleridge*.

77. As in Chapter 6, I am indebted to William Galperin for suggesting the usefulness of this Coleridgean concept.

78. As Everest puts it, this stanza displaces Coleridge's political vision into "a personal, elemental unity with nature" (p. 38); see also Woodring on the poem, *Politics in the Poetry of Coleridge*, pp. 180–87.

79. For example, see the many "buts" in Bacon's essay, "Of Truth."

80. As was the case in Chapter 4, I am indebted here to K. Burke's chapter on "Myth, Poetry, and Philosophy."

81. From a letter to Schelling, quoted in Hegel, *Phenomenology*, p. 27. As Baillie points out in his introduction, Hegel's account of the finishing of the *Phenomenology* is most probably a "fanciful" reconstruction based on hindsight of the fall of Jena (pp. 27–29).

82. I use the terms "subversion"/"containment" in acknowledgment of one of the key problems addressed by the New Historicism. See my essays, "The Power of Formalism" and "Wordsworth and Subversion."

83. Wordsworth's previous poems in the *Post* had mostly been sent in by Coleridge or lifted from *Lyrical Ballads* by Stuart (Woof, pp. 150–55).

84. To continue: the sad woman "like a Lady gay" in the fourth published sonnet (no. 13) ushers in the sadly "gay" festivities of Napoleon's birthday in the next sonnet in the series (no. 12). The "pomps and games"

of these festivities then find their echo in the "pomp of waters" of the succeeding "It is not to be thought of that the flood" (no. 4). And finally, this latter sonnet's ringing affirmation of England's "titles manifold" links up with Wordsworth's fears for the "ennobling thoughts" and prowess of past history at the beginning of the last of the sonnet corona, "When I have borne in memory what has tamed" (no. 6; titled "England" in *MP*). It is difficult to say whether this corona effect was designed with full deliberateness and, if so, by whom. On the basis of the abnormally tight interlacing of themes, language, and imagery here, coupled with the fact (to be demonstrated in Chapter 9) that Wordsworth generally took care in ordering his sonnets, I would hazard that the poet had more, rather than less, control of the matter.

85. I allude, of course, to the famously unclear sense of the verses from the "Introduction" to the *Songs of Innocence*: "And I made a rural pen, / And I stain'd the water clear."

86. I cite Wordsworth's joining up here as a sign of "patriotism." However, it should be noted that the entire matter of the Volunteer system during the invasion scare needs fuller examination before we can truly interpret what it meant for Wordsworth to join (and Coleridge not to; see STCE, p. cxxi). Emsley points out that the Volunteer corps was an easy out from the regular draft and that the entire system was implicated in a controversy over inefficiency, corruption, and class prejudice, with William Cobbett charging that men "volunteered" to escape both the regular military ballots and "low company" (pp. 102–6). Particularly relevant is the fact that the *Morning Post* throughout 1804 carried on a sustained examination of the volunteer system (with many long essays on the subject in the first months of the year).

87. For the sensitivity of the English to Napoleon's slur upon the "nation of shopkeepers," see, for example, *MP*, Jan. 3, 1804: "We have been ridiculed by France, as *une Nation boutiquiere*."

88. I will speculate further in Chapter 9 regarding the religious argument of Wordsworth's sonnets. Bluestone's perception of the poet's religious intonations in his political sonnets is acute: "The implied notion that England is a saving remnant among nations carries with it the corollary that the duty of a poet who aspires to the role of national prophet . . . is twofold: to justify the sense of national election and to point out as forcefully as possible the faults of the elect" (p. 85).

89. Self-consciousness in the *MP* version of line 8 ("I of those fears of mine am much asham'd") is doubly insistent compared to later versions. By 1807, the poem subtracts the redundancy, "of mine," to read: "Of those unfilial fears I am ashamed" (*P2V*, p. 167).

90. "The account of the event here given," the *Post* said, "is . . . considered by the General's friends in London as extremely doubtful." On Apr. 20 the *Post* cited medical testimony as well: "The opinion of most medical Gentlemen is, that General PICHEGRU could not have put himself to death in the manner described in the *Moniteur*."

91. In 1804 itself, we observe, the *Morning Post* serves notice of Napoleon's imperial intent as early as Apr. 18. And both the *Post* and the *Times* at first expected the coronation to occur much earlier than December.

92. As *AR* 1804 summed up: "Had his vanity and presumption prompted

him, in imitation of some of the heroes of antiquity, to claim to be recognised of divine origin, he would probably have experienced no resistance on the part of the [French] nation" (p. 165). Since *AR* 1804 was not published until 1806, I use it in this section merely to supplement the daily press with a slightly longer view of 1804.

93. As regards the actual coronation ceremony itself, the *Morning Post*—which was only able to print a belated report—was clearly scooped by the *Times* and other papers. But the *Post* elaborates so fully on the events leading up to the coronation and on the fetes accompanying the main event that it certainly communicated the main point upon which the English press agreed: the idolatrous pomp and circumstance of the new Emperor.

94. I should stress that the circumstances I adduce below derive from the *Times* and not from the *Post*, which seems not to have noticed them. I use the circumstances, therefore, in a supplementary or emblematic manner. Of course, it is not inconceivable that Wordsworth could have heard these details of the coronation ceremony from sources other than the *Post*. Indeed, as we will later see, the lines on Napoleon's coronation added (probably in December 1804) to *The Prelude*, Book 10, seem to allude directly to the sun breaking through clouds over the Emperor.

95. A fuller historical treatment of the Brumaire speeches would also need to address the issue of probable revisionism in Bourrienne's memoirs; see A. Palmer, pp. 55–56.

96. Bourrienne tells us, "All the speeches which have been prepared since the event for Bonaparte are different" (quoted in Andrews, p. 145).

97. Bourrienne (as well as eyewitnesses on the scene) tells us that nothing of the kind occurred: all the talk "about assaults and poignards, is pure invention" (quoted in Andrews, p. 151).

CHAPTER NINE

1. My concept of "counter-ideology" here applies with variation J. Chandler's useful discrimination of Wordsworth's "ideology against ideology" (pp. 216–34). To counter the ideology not just of the Ideologues but at last of Imagination itself is to qualify the very idea of "ideology." A consonance may also be remarked between the notion of criticism I sketch below, which posits Wordsworth's own counter-Romantic ideology or self-criticism, and many elements in McGann's development of Heine's thought (as well as of the thought of Uhland, Chamisso, and Della Volpe); see *Romantic Ideology*, esp. pp. 31–39, 49–56, 147–52. Though I am not knowledgeable enough about the works and times of McGann's chosen critical preceptors to assess properly the degree of overlap (and of differences in emphasis) between his core statement in *Romantic Ideology* and my own concluding statement, certainly such passages as the following could be set in parallel with my discussion addressed to Wordsworth criticism: "The fact is—and Heine's essay [*The Romantic School*] shows itself fully alive to this matter—that important cultural phenomena subject themselves to criticism at all times. To the degree that a later critical assessment cannot emulate the initial self-criticism which significant cultural products call out or generate, to that degree the later criticism has been consumed by its own ideology" (*Romantic Ideology*,

p. 36). Also: "Heine's method is profoundly critical largely because it is so systematically self-critical and exploratory. He views his subject from a distance which permits him to analyze and judge his materials, but at the same time that distance gives his subject matter the power to qualify his critical judgments. Thus Heine's sardonic comments on the German School's use of Romantic Irony succeed to a moment of sympathetic understanding and conclude in a typical gesture of reversal" (p. 39). Finally: "To the extent that Heine's essay is a critical . . . work, its own polemical distortions lay it open to the critique of the actual poetical works it presumes to judge. . . . Heine's essay, however, actively generates and responds to its own polemical moves, so that the practise of the essay institutes a critique on itself. To the extent that this takes place, the essay functions toward its own ideas as a work of art. . . . This aspect of the essay seems to me one of its most important features so far as the literary critic is concerned, for it reminds us that if the critic lays art under the microscope, a mordant eye returns his quizzing gaze" (pp. 151–52).

2. For the terms "differentiation" and "distantiation" see Chapter 2. "*Representations*-school" is an admittedly inadequate synecdoche for one branch of the current New Historicism—the branch identified most visibly with American Renaissance studies. The quote on the impossibility of reentering past culture is from Greenblatt, *Renaissance Self-Fashioning*, p. 5. We might also adduce the moderate skepticism of Montrose's hermeneutics—e.g.: "In brief, to speak today of an historical criticism must be to recognize that not only the poet but also the critic exists in history; that the texts of each are inscriptions of history; and that our comprehension, representation, interpretation of the texts of the past always proceeds by a mixture of estrangement and appropriation, as a reciprocal conditioning of the Renaissance text and our text of the Renaissance" ("Renaissance Literary Studies and the Subject of History," p. 8). Both the Greenblatt and Montrose works cited here focus historical interpretation upon the problem of the "subject."

A general word may be in order regarding the relation between this book and the New Historicism (which I discuss further below). As earlier indicated (in n. 7 to Chapter 2), I began this work in 1979–80 before the advent of a recognizably New Historicist method. I have therefore not been able to engage with the method as centrally or fully as I would have liked—in the manner in which I have engaged with the deep assumptions of New Criticism and deconstruction, for example. In this concluding chapter (an early version of which was written in 1981), I have attempted only to provide some avenues of communication—both of similarity and difference—between New Historicism as a whole and my own work. For a fuller critical reflection upon the New Historicism, see my "The Power of Formalism," "Wordsworth and Subversion," and review essay on David Simpson's *Wordsworth's Historical Imagination: The Poetry of Displacement* and the New Historicism in Romanticism.

3. I should clarify that by "Foucauldian" here I mean only that affective side of Foucault that has proved most reproducible: the celebrated "laughter that shattered," for example, that initiates *The Order of Things* (p. xv). Foucault himself, of course, is much wider in affective range. Broad effects of sympathy or empathy wash through his works (and Greenblatt's) in a manner a Romanticist might be tempted to name after his own field.

4. I develop freely from de Man's formal definition of intentionality in his "Form and Intent in the American New Criticism" (*Blindness*, pp. 20–35). The whole of this essay is suggestive when applied to the problem of historical and cultural interpretation.

5. The application of "surmise" to "Westminster Bridge" has as many echoes for me as the Miltonic "jocund" had for Wordsworth (as in *Prel.* 10.14). In my case, not so much Milton as Hartman: especially the latter's meditation in *WP*, p. 11, on the ability of surmise to "revive in us the capacity for the virtual, a trembling of the imagined on the brink of the real, a sustained inner freedom in the face of death, disbelief, and fact." See *WP*, pp. 9–13, on the Romantic "lyric of surmise." See also the section on "Wordsworth (1): Star and Surmise" in Hartman's "Reflections on the Evening Star," which associates the term with "Westminster Bridge" (pp. 95–97). On the specifically Keatsian aspect of my surmise, see below.

6. I cite here the date finally assigned to the sonnet's title from c. 1838 on. See below for discussion of dating.

7. "Westminster Bridge" is one of the sonnets first published in *Poems, in Two Volumes* (1807) that does not appear in DC MS. 38 or DC MS. 44. We have no manuscript for the poem earlier than the Longman MS. of 1806–7 serving as printer's copy for the 1807 edition. I have used the earlier stratum in the Longman MS. as my base text (quoting the earlier wording, that is, even when a subsequently printed revision was entered in the MS. itself). I have not, however, attempted to recover the nonverbal variants recorded in *P2V*, p. 463, even though some of the variants (e.g., the capitalization of nouns and addition or omission of exclamation points) are potentially significant. A few key revisions in the textual history of the sonnet may be noticed: "Heart" in line 2 of the Longman MS. was revised in the MS. to the "soul" of the 1807 publication. The only revision after the 1807 edition is a variant of 1836 in which ll. 4–6 read: "The city now doth on her forehead wear / The glorious crown of morning; silent, bare, / Ships, towers," etc. (*P2V*, p. 147 *appar. crit.*). The sonnet first appeared in the Longman MS. and 1807 edition with the date in its title, "Sept. 3, 1803"; for discussion of this date, see below.

8. As Abrams observes, the Bowles sonnets influencing Coleridge and, subsequently, Wordsworth first appeared in 1789 ("Structure," pp. 212–17). The biographical circumstances of these sonnets—written on a tour that included a trip from Dover to Ostend when, as Bowles says in his Preface, he suffered "depression of spirits" connected with the "sudden death of a deserving young woman"—parallel in interesting ways the biographical occasion of "Westminster Bridge." As we will see, Wordsworth's "deserving young woman"—Annette—had not died.

9. I improvise slightly upon Schlüter, who makes the comparison to the city of the Apocalypse, but alludes specifically to the white-robed martyrs of Rev. 6: 11; 7: 9–17.

10. Constituting virtually an anthology of New Critical method, scholarship on this sonnet has centered on the "paradox," "irony," "surprise," and "tension" that ensues when both terms of such contradictions coexist on the poem's canvas. I have culled my catalog of contradictions from many sources, including C. Brooks, *Well Wrought Urn*, pp. 5–7; C. Davis; Garrison; Harvey; Holland; Leavis, "Imagery and Movement"; Sucksmith; and

Van Doren, pp. 55–58. Arguing against Brooks, Hartung stresses the "harmony" rather than the paradox of the sonnet, but in doing so only completes the New Critical analysis of the poem by balancing the method's privileging of ironic tension, ambiguity, paradox, and so on with its simultaneous insistence upon "unity," "harmony," "fusion," or "resolved stresses." On the extension of the New Critical meditation upon "Westminster Bridge" into deconstruction, see my citations from Hartman and Miller below.

11. The poem's odd blend of pictorial insistence and graphic unclarity has often been discussed. Part of the reason it has been such a canonical icon for applied New Criticism, indeed, may well be that it is a test case of the appreciation of "imagery." Cleanth Brooks writes: "The attempt to make a case for the poem in terms of the brilliance of its images also quickly breaks down: the student searches for graphic details in vain. . . . We get a blurred impression—points of roofs and pinnacles along the skyline, all twinkling in the morning light" (*Well Wrought Urn*, p. 5). See also L. Johnson, p. 107; Swanson, p. 13. In the early stages of writing this chapter, I took the pictorial approach to the poem one step further by attempting unsuccessfully to map the line, "Ships, towers," etc., against obvious features on contemporary maps and surveys of London. Wordsworth confuses what could have been the simplest possibility: a counterclockwise, or upriver, turn of the head starting at the shipyards. Since this early episode of literal-mindedness, a 1985 exhibit of panoramic views of London and other British towns at the Yale Center for British Art (cataloged in R. Hyde) has convinced me that literal-mindedness is indeed called for to bring out the extravagant reticence of the poem. Views of the contemporary skyline (e.g., R. Hyde, pp. 133, 151) demonstrate how difficult it would have been from Westminster Bridge *not* to single out St. Paul's as clearly the most dominant—if not the only—"dome." The general plurality of Wordsworth's line—or, put another way, the demand for formal symmetry in his language—subdues the actual landmark. Indeed, "domes" may be taken to be the central disruption in the poet's field of disturbed vision. Though "ships" lie close beside "theatres, and temples" on the map, it is important for metrical (and, as we will see, symbolic) reasons to place "domes" in the middle of the line. (On panorama views of London, see also Altick, pp. 128–210, and my discussion below.)

12. For details and illustrations of Hornor's extravagant panorama in the Colosseum, see Altick, pp. 141–62; R. Hyde, pp. 141–45. In general, see Altick, pp. 128–210, and R. Hyde, pp. 128–49, for graphic confirmation of the fact that the 360° panorama and its affiliate forms are undoubtedly one of the contexts in which we should read "Westminster Bridge." Some panoramas, indeed, took Westminster Bridge either as their vantage point or subject (e.g., R. Hyde, p. 135). We might recall here the panorama of 1794 we viewed earlier in Barker's rotunda at Leicester Square (Pl. 18). "Westminster Bridge" is a fitting reprise of the argument of panoramic vision I broached at the close of Chapter 5 because it is exactly like this rotunda. On the one hand, we have the choice to restrict ourselves to the relatively small, high viewing compartment of New Critical and—as we will see—deconstructive readings of the poem. Here, the contradictoriness of a city robed in figures seems transcendence: contradiction is a perpetual veiling and unveiling of tropes situating an interface of reality/otherworldliness akin to

Revelation or, in the negative apocalypse of deconstruction, *mise en abyme*. But on the other hand, it is also possible to descend the staircase into the poem's more capacious compartment to see an analogue of Barker's Grand Fleet picture: a scene of topography-cum-topicality locating the dialectics of transcendence within the larger field of historical experience.

It is instructive, indeed, to follow up on our notice in Chapter 5 of the increasingly historical emphasis of actual panoramas in London and Paris during the Napoleonic wars. As Altick shows, panoramic artists in London exploited the rising interest in large history-paintings to concentrate on such topical subjects as the fleet at Spithead sailing to escape the burning warship *Boyne*, the siege of Acre, the battles of Agincourt, Alexandria, and Lodi, the crossing of the Alps at Mount St. Gotthard, Napoleon's expected invasion fleet, and so forth (pp. 134–36). Meanwhile, panoramas in Paris also followed the footsteps of current history. As Hemmings documents (pp. 146–49) and p. 321 n. 11; see also Altick, p. 135n), the initial two panoramas in Paris were built by James Thayer, an American who acquired the rights for the idea from an associate of Barker. In 1800, Thayer's first exhibits wedded topographical and topical interests by showing Paris and Toulon during the latter's evacuation by the British. Later French panoramas were even more historical and ideological: celebrating battles and other high points of the Napoleonic years (Hemmings, p. 146), they rehearsed the popular eye in the totalitarian vision of imperialism.

To descend from New Critical or deconstructive visions of the poem-as-mystery to a larger view of "Westminster Bridge," I will argue, is to open our eyes to a full panorama of historical consciousness cognate with such actual panoramas of history. As we will see, the "staircase" we must walk down (as if from the top of Barker's rotunda) to reach the historical ground is the Calais Tour of sonnets.

13. Though the poem was left untitled by Wordsworth, I have, for ease of reference, retained Selincourt's designation (*PW*, 4: 374). I have not attempted to take account of revisions of the poem, evidence of which is reproduced by Kishel in *Tuft of Primroses*. St. Paul's, we may note, was also one of Coleridge's favorite objects of demonstration (see, for example, *Biographia*, 1: 111; 2: 62–63).

14. As Frank J. Warnke points out, the relation between metaphorics and *topoi* in Curtius's acceptation is indeed a span of complex continuity rather than clear difference (*Princeton Encyclopedia*, p. 989).

15. In the spirit of Hartman's "A Touching Compulsion," we might speculate on the latent metaphorics of touching sight in line 3 or, probing deeper, even the dull heart of line 2. But I open simply upon lines 4–5, where metaphors snow down.

16. I generalize on the basis only of the English sonnets in Milton's middle and later years.

17. I introduce the present allusion to Keats less because it is necessary (the argument stands or falls without it) than because I should like to think this chapter stands in fraternity with Levinson's beautiful, historicizing essay on the "Chapman's Homer" sonnet, delivered at the MLA convention in Chicago, 1985. After delivering a paper on the New Historicism recently, I was asked what a New Historicist study would select as its per-

fect primary text. The answer, I thought, would be a text that on its surface bore the least possible affiliation with history in its everyday sense: a poem, that is, as smooth of history as an effaced coin. Though starting from different directions, both Levinson and I have arrived at the coin of the Romantic sonnet, in which we would like to see tokens of the original face and date. (See also Levinson's recent essay "The New Historicism," which centers on Wordsworth's sonnet "The World Is Too Much With Us.")

18. For the paradigm of the blinding sun, I am indebted in particular to J. Hillis Miller's paper "Graphic and Verbal."

19. As I observe in my catalog of New Critical studies in n. 10 to this chapter, Hartung's essay is the most extreme in appreciating the "harmony" of the sonnet, but even New Critical readings that have stressed ambiguity, paradox, or tension—as in the case of New Criticism generally—open out at last into philosophies of unity. On the uncanny relation between ambiguity and unity in the New Criticism, see de Man, *Blindness*, p. 28.

20. This chapter stands in what might be called a correspondent relation with Hartman's "The Unremarkable Poet" in his *Unremarkable Wordsworth*. My own treatment of the poem was delivered in a very much earlier form at the Yale Center for British Art in March 1981, on which occasion Hartman was the respondent (initiating a vigorous, memorable discussion). Subsequently, I read his "Unremarkable Poet" in manuscript and have drawn upon it here.

21. I return to Molesworth's fine essay below. In a similar vein, Beach, pp. 64–71, has read the poem as an exemplary record of both social and private experience. See also Curtis's *Wordsworth's Experiments*, which, though it focuses mainly on the poems of early to mid-1802, provides a useful study of this "crisis" year in Wordsworth's art and life. Heath, pp. 147–53, is also excellent on the personal and political milieu of "Westminster Bridge" and the Calais Tour. (Very relevant as well is Judith W. Page's intriguing essay, which, though it does not discuss "Westminster Bridge," does address the complications of "public and private concerns" in the Calais sonnets. The essay appeared too late for me to do more than notice it here in galley-proof revisions.)

22. Regarding the specific problem of "power," I have benefited much from conversation with Patricia Fumerton and Jonathan Freedman (see the latter's review essay on an application of "power" to American literature).

23. The same may be said for the intranational displacement, from "Old South" to "New South," or South to North, at the root of the New Criticism. My refugee paradigm, that is, could be developed to take account of "fugitivism" and its sequalia.

24. In picturesque and topographical pictures, the motif of the cart or wagon crossing a bridge belongs to the more general category of bridge-crossings by pedestrians, packhorses, cattle, and so forth. Examples of carts on bridges include: Thomas Girtin's *The Old Bridge in Devon* (Morris, her pl. 57); Michael Angelo Rooker's *The Cast Iron Bridge Near Coalbrookdale* and *Newport on the Usk, Monmouthshire, With Bridge and Castle* (shown in Conner, pp. 38, 159); and Paul Sandby's *Old Welsh Bridge at Shewsbury* and *Pont-y-Pair Over the River Conway Above Llanrwst in the County of Denbigh* (pls. 88 and 98 in *Art of Paul Sandby*). Wordsworth's poem conflates the motif of passers-

by on a bridge (whether on foot or mounted) with that of the stationary observer: on Westminster Bridge, he both passes and is halted in vision.

25. On the "poetry of crisis" in this period, see also Curtis and Heath. I have elsewhere studied the climate of existential repetition that worried Dorothy in this same season ("On the Autobiographical Present," esp. pp. 121–33).

26. The concept of causality will be of limited usefulness here, not only because of the impossibility of verification, but because Dorothy's evidence insistently entangles causality in nonlinear relations of homeopathic sympathy and parallelism. Insomnia and sickness, for example, are at once causes, effects, and expressions of William's writing problems.

27. References to William's sleeplessness in early 1802 occur in *DWJ* under the entries for Jan. 28, 29, 31; Feb. 1, 3, 6; Mar. 14; May 4, 15, 24, 25; June 4, 7, 9, 11, 13, 15, 19, 20, 21, 25, 30; July 6. Other nights of insomnia may also be inferred from Dorothy's occasional mentions of William having slept especially late or "better" than previously. The string of sleepless nights in June leading up to the Calais Tour in July is remarkable.

28. On the representational properties of sickness in Dorothy's journal, see the conclusion of my "On the Autobiographical Present."

29. In a more frustrated sense than Brisman develops in *Romantic Origins*.

30. A fuller study of 1802 on the order of Curtis's would need to consider here not just *The Pedlar* of Jan.–Mar. and what I will call the Calais Tour of sonnets in the summer but also the intervening lyrics of Mar.–July. The entire period of Mar.–July, with its deceptive calm and utter lyricism, is of the highest interest when considered as the zone of mediation between blocked imagination on the one hand (*The Pedlar*) and the sense of history on the other (the Calais Tour).

31. And where, in versions from 1827 on, summer must be figured as winter (*P2V*, p. 157 *appar. crit.*).

32. Selincourt calls the poem an example of Wordsworth's "untrustworthiness" in dating, though he suggests the possibility that it was "inspired and drafted on July 31, 1802, and rewritten on Sept. 3" (*PW*, 3: 431). For the theory of Wordsworth's ideal dating, see Woodring, *Wordsworth*, pp. 168–69. My interpretation is crafted not to exclude specifically either Selincourt's or Woodring's, although there is one assumption—that if there was a textual change between July 31 and Sept. 3, it was not so substantive as to alter the effect of the poem—and one proviso—that the matter of dates is not "proof" of anything in itself but only a key to further evidence, internal and external.

33. Cf. L. Johnson, who associates the pastoralized view of London in "Westminster Bridge" with the later "Departure From the Vale of Grasmere. August, 1803" (pp. 105–6).

34. On the subject of the negative in "Westminster Bridge," see especially J. H. Miller, *Linguistic Moment*, pp. 70–72. Miller, p. 76, also calls the poem "the epitaph for a dead city."

35. Versions of Sonnet A after 1827, we can note, introduce a figure of "touching" akin to that in "Westminster Bridge." "Despair" at the end "Touches me not" (*P2V*, p. 157 *appar. crit.*).

36. "England!" is the earlier, more palpably public opening in the Long-

man MS. The word was revised to "Inland" in the MS. itself, and appears as such in *Poems, in Two Volumes* in 1807 (*P2V*, p. 163 *appar. crit.*).

37. Woodring, *Wordsworth*, p. 166, observes that for Wordsworth the "openness to heaven" in "Westminster Bridge" is "the essence of liberty and independence."

38. Groom, p. 60, suggests: "If 'Sept. 3rd, 1802' is the correct date for the composition of 'Westminster Bridge,' it looks as if he was now recalling his feelings of 31 July on the way to France in their relation to his task of reviving the 'plain living and high thinking' of the past."

39. Again, we may refer to Gates's essay, "Wordsworth and the Course of History," for Wordsworth's metaphor of the historical stream.

40. A spectacular study in contrasting pictorial and ideological views may be gained by juxtaposing Canaletto's *Westminster Bridge, London, with the Lord Mayor's Procession on the Thames* (in the Yale Center for British Art) with Turner's *Burning of the Houses of Parliament*. Francis Sheppard opens his *London 1808–1870: The Infernal Wen* by quoting Wordsworth's "Westminster Bridge" and then recovering the changes in view from the bridge in the Victorian era. In a passage that goes far toward filling in the transition between Canaletto's world and Turner's post–Reform-Bill apocalypse, Sheppard writes: "within the space of only two generations [after "Westminster Bridge"] the view from the bridge . . . had changed greatly. The air had become laden with the smoke of steam vessels, gasworks and the furnaces of a host of industrial establishments, and the snort and hiss of railway locomotives at the new terminus at Waterloo Station could constantly be heard. Downstream the noble prospect towards the City and the dome of St. Paul's had been ruthlessly sundered by the brick and iron of Charing Cross railway bridge. Beneath Westminster Bridge itself still flowed the perennial river, no longer gliding 'at his own sweet will,' but controlled and restricted by the great granite wall of the Victoria Embankment. . . . Nothing within sight lay 'open unto the fields,' and even the sooty parapet of Westminster Bridge itself was new—iron in place of stone" (pp. xv–xvi).

41. In most editions from *1807* through *1836–37*, "Sept. 3, 1803" appears in the title of "Westminster Bridge" both on the contents page and above the actual sonnet. The exceptions are *1815* and *1820*, in which the contents pages vary slightly in dating strategy but in which the title in the text remains the same (see discussion below). On editions consulted, see Appendix.

42. The point applies with variation to the contents page of later collected editions up through *1836–37*. In *1815* and *1820*, where "Miscellaneous Sonnets" lead immediately to "Sonnets Dedicated to Liberty," Wordsworth employed a columnar dating device for the contents (instead of "Sept. 3, 1803," for example, we read "1803" under the column for "Composed" and/ or "1807" under the column for "Published"). *1815* is anomalous among all the collected editions because its contents list only the date of first publication for both "Westminster Bridge" and the succeeding political sonnets. *1820*, however, restores "1803" to the former as well as compositional dates for the latter. From *1827* through the important, oft-reissued *1836–37*, Wordsworth then returned "Sept. 3, 1803" to "Westminster Bridge" in the contents and interposed between "Miscellaneous Sonnets" and "Sonnets Dedicated to Liberty" the "Memorials of a Tour in Scotland, 1803" and

"Memorials of a Tour in Scotland, 1814" (in *1827* "Poems on the Naming of Places" and "Inscriptions" also intervene). In these latter editions, the first of the political sonnets (and often others) is dated "1802," and the intervening Memorial Tours are themselves strongly dated in their titles. For a census of collected editions, see Appendix.

43. Various readers have viewed the "Miscellaneous Sonnets" as finally collected in *1849–50* as a unified text. Edward Dowden, for example, outlines in part the group's "happy ordering" (an outline included in Hutchinson's edition of Wordsworth's *Poetical Works*, pp. 703–4); and L. Johnson, pp. 63–88, studies the group's organization around a "garden" theme linking the poems with those on gardens in the poet's other sonnets. But if we contrast the evolution of the "Miscellaneous Sonnets" with that of the political sonnets, it becomes clear that the unity of the former differs both in degree and kind from that of the latter. In the years from 1802 to 1804, the poet seems not really to have distinguished between the miscellaneous and the political sonnets. Reed reproduces the order of some of the lists and copies of poems transcribed by the poet, his sister, and his wife between late 1802 and early 1804 (*CMY*, pp. 617–22). Though the evidence is uncertain (and "Westminster Bridge" is lacking in these early MSS.), it appears that in the *oeuvre* as conceived at least through DC MS. 38, the political sonnets stood indiscriminately within the "garden" of miscellaneous sonnets. But in DC MS. 44 of Feb. to early Mar. 1804 (as newly reconstructed by Curtis in *P2V*, Appendix 1), in the 1806 manuscript rescension (see *P2V*, pp. 6–11), and in *1807*, the two groups of sonnets diverged and from this period onward assumed strikingly different developmental patterns. The "Sonnets Dedicated to Liberty" were from the start a relatively stable unit whose order and constitution survived virtually unchanged into the later editions: they became Part 1 of the *1849–50* "Poems Dedicated to National Independence and Liberty." The "Miscellaneous Sonnets," on the other hand, not only did not stabilize between DC MS. 44 and *1807* (see *P2V*, p. 708) but thereafter continued changing in order and constitution, establishing transient units of context. Here, for example, are the sonnets flanking "Westminster Bridge" in the principal editions from *1807* on: "Sonnet, Written at Evening" and "'Beloved Vale!' I said, 'When I Shall Con" (*1807*); "Written in Very Early Youth" and "Pelion and Ossa Flourish Side by Side" (*1815, 1820*); "These Words Were Uttered as in Pensive Mood" and "Oxford, May 30, 1820" (*1827, 1832*); "Gordale" and "Oxford, May 30, 1820" (*1836–37, 1838, 1849*); "Gordale" and "Conclusion: To———" (*1845, 1849–50*). While one could say that "Westminster Bridge" stood among sonnets all generally associated with the countryside, it is evident on close inspection that its placement after the Hambleton Hills sonnets or at the conclusion of a section of the "Miscellaneous Sonnets" varied its contextual meaning substantially. The "Miscellaneous Sonnets" represent not so much an order as a lifelong search for order. This is why they cannot be studied from *1849–50* alone as the political sonnets have been successfully studied by Johnson, pp. 39–62; or Bluestone. (See Fraistat for an informative recent study of the principles underlying Romantic collections and arrangements of poetry.)

44. Johnston, in his turn, builds his essay on top of Stuart Sperry's.

45. I call this a "fourth" date even though we earlier considered "Sept. 3"

in the implicit context of 1802 because the poet's explicit change of "1803" to "1802" makes a marked difference. *P2V* cites the annotated copy of *1836–37*, now in the Royal Library at Windsor, as MS. 1836/45. As Darbishire observes in her selective reproduction of the text (which unfortunately does not afford a glimpse of either "Westminster Bridge" or of the contents pages), Wordsworth used this copy of *1836–37* as working copy for the revisions that appeared in *1838*, *1840*, and *1845* (*Some Variants*, p. ix). Revisions for *1838* and *1840* were entered primarily in the hand of Wordsworth's clerk, John Carter. But it seems safe to assume that a change in date could only have come at the instigation of the poet (especially since Carter's special province was punctuation; *Some Variants*, p. ix). Revisions for the important *1845*—the source of two subsequent reissues—appear in the poet's own hand or in those of his wife Mary or daughter Dora (*Some Variants*, p. ix).

46. While *1838* dates the sonnet "1802" in the body of its text, it omits date entirely from the title in the contents—a striking absence given the bold dating of the next two sonnets in the contents, both titled "Oxford, May 30, 1820." Similarly, while *1840* titles the poem "1802" in its text, it retains the old "1803" in the contents (a pattern later repeated in *1841* and the seven-volume *1849*). Not until *1845* was the metamorphosis in both the text and the contents listings complete. The canonical edition of *1849–50* then transmitted "Sept. 3, 1802" to future editions.

47. Of the many studies that address Wordsworth's collections, arrangements, and sonnet sequences (some of which I cite in this chapter and elsewhere), four that I am aware of merit special mention with regard to a general theory and history of Wordsworthian collection: Fraistat's recent *The Poem and the Book: Interpreting Collections of Romantic Poetry*; Curtis's "Introduction" to *P2V*, esp. pp. 35–39; Peterfreund's "Seriality and Centered Structure"; and Manning's "Wordsworth's *Yarrow Revisited* and the Shape of a Period." My speculations here are consonant particularly with Manning's paper, which is part of his project of reconceiving the later Wordsworth. As Manning puts it (manuscript version courtesy of the author): "The tension between an historical understanding, placing experience, private and cultural, in a demarcated chronological sequence, and an essentialist apprehension which stands free of time . . . recurs throughout the [*Yarrow Revisited*] volume" and models the tour form in general as "the quintessential genre of the late Wordsworth."

48. See Manning, "Wordsworth's *Yarrow Revisited*," and Peterfreund, "Seriality and Centered Structure." My terminology here is also reminiscent of the section on "The Public and Private Centers of the Sonnets to Liberty" in L. Johnson.

49. Ross studies *1815* but extrapolates his conclusions to include the general design of the later editions.

50. A fruitful exercise is to read Hartman's *WP* together with Lukács's *The Theory of the Novel*—for example, p. 54: "Only when a subject, far removed from all life and from the empirical which is necessarily posited together with life, becomes enthroned in the pure heights of essence, when it has become nothing but the carrier of the transcendental synthesis, can it contain all the conditions for totality within its own structure and transform

its own limitations into the frontiers of the world. But such a subject cannot write an epic: the epic *is* life, immanence, the empirical." Wordsworth could not write *The Recluse*, we can speculate, because he did not know that it had to be a novel, the second home of epic. Wordsworth's later *Recluse* is to be found in the substitute novel of his tours.

References

Frequently cited works are listed, with full bibliographic information, in Abbreviations, pp. xi–xiii. Collected editions of Wordsworth's poetry published in his lifetime can be found on p. 509 of the Appendix.

Abbott, John S. C. *The History of Napoleon Bonaparte*. New edition, vol 2. New York, 1883.

Abrams, M. H. "English Romanticism: The Spirit of the Age." In Harold Bloom, ed., *Romanticism and Consciousness: Essays in Criticism*. New York, 1970.

———. *The Mirror and the Lamp: Romantic Theory and the Critical Tradition*. New York, 1958.

———. *Natural Supernaturalism: Tradition and Revolution in Romantic Literature*. New York, 1971.

———. "On Reading Wordsworth's *Lyrical Ballads*." Paper presented at the Yale University conference on "Wordsworth and the Borders of Romanticism," Nov. 14, 1987.

———. "Structure and Style in the Greater Romantic Lyric." In Harold Bloom, ed., *Romanticism and Consciousness: Essays in Criticism*. New York, 1970.

Alberti, Leon Battista. *On Painting*. Rev. ed. Trans. John R. Spencer. New Haven, Conn., 1966.

Allendoerfer, Carl B., and Cletus O. Oakley. *Principles of Mathematics*, 3d ed. New York, 1969.

Althusser, Louis. *Lenin and Philosophy and Other Essays*. Trans. Ben Brewster. London, 1971.

Althusser, Louis, and Etienne Balibar. *Reading Capital*. Trans. Ben Brewster. London, 1970.

Altick, Richard D. *The Shows of London*. Cambridge, Mass., 1978.

Altizer, Thomas J. J., et al. *Deconstruction and Theology*. New York, 1982.

Anderson, Michael. *Family Structure in Nineteenth-Century Lancashire*. Cambridge, Eng., 1971.

Andrews, George Gordon. *Napoleon in Review*. New York, 1939.

Appleton, Jay. *The Experience of Landscape*. Chichester, Eng., 1975.

Ariès, Philippe. *Centuries of Childhood: A Social History of Family Life*. Trans. Robert Baldick. New York, 1962.

———. *The Hour of Our Death*. Trans. Helen Weaver. New York, 1981.

———. *Western Attitudes Toward Death: From the Middle Ages to the Present*. Trans. Patricia M. Ranum. The Johns Hopkins Symposia in Comparative History. Baltimore, Md., 1974.

Aristotle. *The Poetics*. In *On Poetry and Style: Aristotle*. Trans. G. M. A. Grube. Indianapolis, 1958.

The Art of Paul Sandby. Introduction and catalog entries by Bruce Robertson. New Haven, Conn., 1985.

Ashton, John. *English Caricature and Satire on Napoleon I*. 1888. Rpt. New York, 1968.

Aspinall, A. *Politics and the Press, c. 1780–1850*. London, 1949.

Asquith, Ivon. "The Structure, Ownership and Control of the Press, 1780–1855." In George Boyce, James Curran, and Pauline Wingate, eds., *Newspaper History from the Seventeenth Century to the Present Day*. London, 1978.

Auerbach, Erich. *Mimesis: The Representation of Reality in Western Literature*. Trans. William R. Trask. Princeton, N.J., 1953.

St. Augustine. *Confessions*. Trans. R. S. Pine-Coffin. Harmondsworth, Eng., 1961.

Averill, James H. *Wordsworth and the Poetry of Human Suffering*. Ithaca, N.Y., 1980.

Bacon, Sir Francis. "Of Truth." In Arthur Johnston, ed., *Francis Bacon*. New York, 1965.

Baddeley, M. J. B. *The English Lake District*. Thorough Guide Series. 7th ed. rev. London, 1895.

Baedeker, Karl. *Great Britain*. Leipzig, 1887.

Baker, Jeffrey. *Time and Mind in Wordsworth's Poetry*. Detroit, 1980.

Bakhtin, Mikhail. *Rabelais and His World*. Trans. Hélène Iswolsky. Bloomington, Ind., 1984.

Banks, William. *Views of the Lakes*. Windermere, n.d.

Barbauld, Anna Laetitia. *Hymns in Prose for Children*. 4th ed. Norwich, Conn., 1786.

Barley, M. W. *The English Farmhouse and Cottage*. London, 1961.

Barnes, M. J. *Politics and Personality, 1760–1827: A Selection of Articles from "History Today."* Edinburgh, 1967.

Barrell, John. *The Dark Side of the Landscape: The Rural Poor in English Painting 1730–1840*. Cambridge, Eng., 1980.

Barthes, Roland. *Mythologies*. Trans. Annette Lavers. New York, 1972.

———. *S/Z*. Trans. Richard Miller. New York, 1974.

Baxandall, Michael. *Painting and Experience in Fifteenth Century Italy: A Primer in the Social History of Pictorial Style*. London, 1972.

Bazin, Germain. *Baroque and Rococo*. Trans. Jonathan Griffin. New York, 1964.

Beach, Joseph Warren. *A Romantic View of Poetry; Being Lectures Given at the Johns Hopkins University on the Percy Turnbull Memorial Foundation in Nov. 1941*. Minneapolis, 1944.

Beattie, Alan, ed. *English Party Politics*. Vol. 1. London, 1970.

Beattie, J. M. "The Criminality of Women in Eighteenth-Century England." *Journal of Social History* 8 (Summer 1975): 80–116.

Beatty, Arthur. "Joseph Fawcett: The Art of War: Its Relation to the Early Development of William Wordsworth." *University of Wisconsin Studies in Language and Literature* 2 (Sept. 1918): 224–69.

———. *Wordsworth: Representative Poems*. Garden City, N.J., 1937.

Beer, John. *Wordsworth and the Human Heart*. New York, 1978.

———. *Wordsworth in Time*. London, 1979.

Bender, John. *Imagining the Penitentiary: Fiction and the Architecture of Mind in Eighteenth-Century England*. Chicago, 1987.

Bennett, Tony. *Formalism and Marxism*. New Accents. London, 1979.

Bentham, Jeremy. *The Works of Jeremy Bentham*. Vol. 4. Edinburgh, 1843.

Berchman, Robert M. *From Philo to Origen: Middle Platonism in Transition*. Brown Judaic Studies, No. 69. Chico, Calif., 1984.

Bergson, Henri. "Laughter." In Wylie Sypher, ed., *Comedy: An Essay on Comedy, George Meredith; Laughter, Henri Bergson*. Garden City, N.Y., 1956.

———. *Time and Free Will: An Essay on the Immediate Data of Consciousness*. Trans. F. L. Pogson. 1910. Rpt. New York, 1960.

Bernhardt-Kabisch, Ernest. "The Epitaph and the Romantic Poets: A Survey." *Huntington Library Quarterly* 30 (1967): 113–46.

———. "Wordsworth: The Monumental Poet." *Philological Quarterly* 44 (1965): 503–18.

Bewell, Alan. "A 'Word Scarce Said': Hysteria and Witchcraft in Wordsworth's 'Experimental' Poetry of 1797–1798." *ELH* 53 (1986): 357–90. In Bewell, *Wordsworth and the Enlightenment: Nature, Man, and Society in the Experimental Poetry*. New Haven, Conn., 1989.

———. "Wordsworth's Primal Scene: Retrospective Tales of Idiots, Wild Children, and Savages." *ELH* 50 (1983): 321–46.

Bialostosky, Don H. *Making Tales: The Poetics of Wordsworth's Narrative Experiments*. Chicago, 1984.

Bicknell, Peter, ed. *The Illustrated Wordsworth's Guide to the Lakes*. New York, 1984.

Bimbenet, Eugène. *Histoire de la Ville d'Orléans*. Vol. 5. Orléans, 1888.

Black's Picturesque Guide to the English Lakes. Edinburgh, 1841.

Blake, William. *Complete Writings*. Ed. Geoffrey Keynes. London, 1966.

Blanchard, E. L. *Adams' Illustrated Guide to The English Lakes*. London, 1855.

Bloom, Harold. *The Anxiety of Influence: A Theory of Poetry*. London, 1973.

———. "The Internalization of Quest-Romance." In Bloom, ed., *Romanticism and Consciousness: Essays in Criticism*. New York, 1970.

Bluestone, Stephen. "On Wordsworth's Political Sonnets of 1802–1803." *Rackham Literary Studies* 2 (1972): 79–86.

Booth, Alan. "Food Riots in the North-West of England 1790–1801." *Past and Present* 77 (1977): 84–107.

Boswell, James. *Life of Johnson*. Ed. R. W. Chapman. World's Classics. Oxford, 1980.

Boulding, K. E. "A Note on the Theory of the Black Market." *Canadian Journal of Economics and Political Science* 13 (1947): 115–18.

Bourne, J. M. *Patronage and Society in Nineteenth-Century England.* London, 1986.

Bowles, William Lisle. *Sonnets and Other Poems and the Spirit of Discovery.* 1800–1804. Rpt. ed. Donald H. Reiman. New York, 1978.

Bragg, Melvyn. *Land of the Lakes.* New York, 1983.

Brantley, Richard E. *Wordsworth's "Natural Methodism."* New Haven, Conn., 1975.

Braudel, Fernand. *On History.* Trans. Sarah Matthews. Chicago, 1980.

Brennan, Joseph Gerard. *A Handbook of Logic.* New York, 1957.

Brinkley, Robert A. "Vagrant and Hermit: Milton and the Politics of 'Tintern Abbey.' " *The Wordsworth Circle* 16 (1985): 126–33.

Brisman, Leslie. *Romantic Origins.* Ithaca, N.Y., 1978.

British Watercolors, 1750–1850, A Loan Exhibition from the Victoria and Albert Museum. Washington, D.C., 1966.

Brooks, Cleanth. "The Uses of Literature." In Brooks, *A Shaping Joy: Studies in the Writer's Craft.* London, 1971.

———. *The Well Wrought Urn: Studies in the Structure of Poetry.* New York, 1947, 1975.

———. "Wordsworth and Human Suffering: Notes on Two Early Poems." In Frederick W. Hilles and Harold Bloom, eds., *From Sensibility to Romanticism: Essays Presented to Frederick A. Pottle.* New York, 1965.

Brooks, Cleanth, and Robert Penn Warren. *Understanding Poetry.* 3d ed. New York, 1960.

Brooks, Linda Marie. "Coleridge's 'Wordsworthian' Persona in the *Biographia.*" Paper presented at the Modern Language Association convention, Chicago, Dec. 29, 1985.

Brooks, Peter. *The Melodramatic Imagination: Balzac, Henry James, Melodrama, and the Mode of Excess.* New Haven, Conn., 1976.

———. *Reading for the Plot: Design and Intention in Narrative.* New York, 1984.

Brown, Frederick. *Theater and Revolution: The Culture of the French Stage.* New York, 1980.

Brown, John. *Letter to Lord Lyttleton.* Newcastle, Eng., 1767.

Bruce, James. *Travels to Discover the Source of the Nile, in Years 1768, 1769, 1770, 1771, 1772, and 1773.* 5 vols. Edinburgh, 1790.

Brunskill, R. W. "The Development of the Large House in the Eden Valley, 1350–1840." *Transactions of the Cumberland and Westmorland Antiquarian and Archaeological Society,* n.s. 57 (1958): 72–96.

———. "The Development of the Small House in the Eden Valley from 1650 to 1840." *Transactions of the Cumberland and Westmorland Antiquarian and Archaeological Society,* n.s. 53 (1954): 160–89.

———. *Vernacular Architecture of the Lake Counties: A Field Handbook.* London, 1974.

Burch, Thomas K. "Some Demographic Determinants of Average Household Size: An Analytic Approach." In Peter Laslett, ed., with Richard Wall, *Household and Family in Past Time.* Cambridge, Eng., 1972.

Burke, Edmund. *A Letter from the Right Honourable Edmund Burke to a Noble Lord, on the Attacks Made upon Him and His Pension, in the House of Lords, by* the Duke of Bedford and the Earl of Lauderdale, Early in the Present Sessions of Parliament. London, 1796.

————. *A Philosophical Enquiry into the Origin of Our Ideas of the Sublime and Beautiful*. Ed. James T. Boulton. Notre Dame, Ind., 1958. Rpt. 1968.

————. *Reflections on the Revolution in France*. Ed. Conor Cruise O'Brien. Harmondsworth, Eng., 1969.

Burke, Joseph. *English Art, 1714–1800*. Oxford History of English Art. Oxford, 1976.

Burke, Kenneth. *Language as Symbolic Action: Essays on Life, Literature, and Method*. Berkeley, Calif., 1966.

Burn, Richard. *The History of the Poor Laws: With Observations*. London, 1764.

————. *The Justice of the Peace, and Parish Officer*. 2 vols. London, 1755.

Burnett, John. *A Social History of Housing, 1815–1970*. Newton Abbot, Eng., 1978.

Butler, James A. "Wordsworth, Cottle, and the *Lyrical Ballads*: Five Letters, 1797–1800." *JEGP* 75 (1976): 139–53.

Butlin, Martin, and Evelyn Joll. *The Paintings of J. M. W. Turner*. Rev. ed. New Haven, Conn., 1984.

Bythell, Duncan. "The Hand-Loom Weavers in the English Cotton Industry During the Industrial Revolution: Some Problems." *Economic History Review*, 2d series, 17 (1964): 339–53.

Carlson, Julie. "An Active Imagination: Coleridge and the Politics of Dramatic Reform." Forthcoming in *Modern Philology*.

Carlyle, Thomas. *The French Revolution*. 2 vols. London, 1906.

Carrard, Philippe. "The New History and the Discourse of the Tentative: Le Roy Ladurie's Quotation Marks." *Clio* 15 (1985): 1–14.

Cavarnos, Constantine. *Orthodox Iconography*. Belmont, Mass., 1977.

Caws, Mary Ann. *The Eye in the Text: Essays on Perception, Mannerist to Modern*. Princeton Essays on the Arts, no. 11. Princeton, N.J., 1981.

Celoria, Francis. "Chatterton, Wordsworth and Stonehenge." *Notes and Queries*, n.s. 23 (1976): 103–4.

Censer, Jack Richard. *Prelude to Power: The Parisian Radical Press, 1789–1791*. Baltimore, Md., 1976.

Chandler, David G. *The Campaigns of Napoleon*. New York, 1966.

Chandler, James K. *Wordsworth's Second Nature: A Study of the Poetry and Politics*. Chicago, 1984.

Chapin, Chester F. *Personification in Eighteenth-Century English Poetry*. New York, 1955.

Charles Le Brun, 1619–1690: Peintre et dessinateur. Versailles, 1963.

Chatterton, Thomas. *The Complete Works of Thomas Chatterton: A Bicentenary Edition*. Ed. Donald S. Taylor with Benjamin B. Hoover. Vol. 2. Oxford, 1971.

————. *Poems, Supposed to Have Been Written at Bristol, By Thomas Rowley, 1777*. Facsimile rpt. Menston, Eng., 1969.

Christensen, Jerome. "Once an Apostate Always an Apostate." *Studies in Romanticism* 21 (1982): 461–64.

Clarke, C. C. *Romantic Paradox: An Essay on the Poetry of Wordsworth*. London, 1962.

Clarke, James. *A Survey of the Lakes of Cumberland, Westmorland, and Lan-*

cashire: Together With An Account, Historical, Topographical, and Descriptive, of the Adjacent Country. To Which Is Added, A Sketch of the Border Laws and Customs. 2d ed. London, 1789.

Claude. See Lorrain, Claude.

Clayton, Jay. *Romantic Vision and the Novel.* Cambridge, Eng., 1987.

Cobb, Richard. *The Police and the People: French Popular Protest, 1789–1820.* Oxford, 1970.

———. *Reactions to the French Revolution.* London, 1972.

Cockburn, Henry. *An Examination of the Trials for Sedition Which Have Hitherto Occurred in Scotland.* 2 vols. 1888. Rpt. New York, 1970.

Coe, Charles Norton. *Wordsworth and the Literature of Travel.* New York, 1953.

Cohen, Morris R., and Ernest Nagel. *An Introduction to Logic and Scientific Method.* New York, 1934.

Cohen, Philip. "Narrative and Persuasion in *The Ruined Cottage.*" *Journal of Narrative Technique* 8 (1978): 185–99.

Coleridge, Samuel Taylor. *Biographia Literaria, or Biographical Sketches of My Literary Life and Opinions.* 2 vols. Ed. James Engell and W. Jackson Bate. Collected Works of Samuel Taylor Coleridge, no. 7. Princeton, N.J., 1983.

———. *Collected Letters of Samuel Taylor Coleridge.* Ed. Earl Leslie Griggs. Vols. 1, 2, 4. Oxford, 1956–59.

———. *The Complete Poetical Works of Samuel Taylor Coleridge.* Ed. Ernest Hartley Coleridge. Vol. 1. Oxford, 1912.

———. *Lay Sermons.* Ed. R. J. White. The Collected Works of Samuel Taylor Coleridge, no. 6. Princeton, N.J., 1972.

———. *Specimens of the Table Talk of Samuel Taylor Coleridge.* Ed. H. N. Coleridge. Edinburgh, 1836.

Collection Complete des Tableaux Historiques de la Révolution Française. Vol. 1. Paris, 1798.

Collingwood, R. G. *An Autobiography.* London, 1939.

———. *The Idea of History.* 1946. Rpt. Oxford, 1977.

Collins, William. *Odes on Several Descriptive and Allegoric Subjects.* In Roger Lonsdale, ed., *The Poems of Thomas Gray, William Collins, Oliver Goldsmith.* London, 1969.

Colton, Judith. "Merlin's Cave and Queen Caroline: Garden Art as Political Propaganda." *Eighteenth-Century Studies* 10 (1976): 1–20.

Colwell, Stella. *Tracing Your Family Tree.* London, 1984.

Complete Baronetage. Ed. G. E. C. Vol. 4. Exeter, Eng., 1904.

Connelly, Owen. *Blundering to Glory: Napoleon's Military Campaigns.* Wilmington, Del., 1987.

Conner, Patrick. *Michael Angelo Rooker, 1746–1801.* London, 1984.

Cook, Chris, and John Stevenson. *Longman Atlas of Modern British History: A Visual Guide to British Society and Politics 1700–1970.* London, 1978.

Coxe, William. *Travels in Switzerland, and in the Country of the Grisons: In a Series of Letters to William Melmoth, Esq.* In *A General Collection of the Best and Most Interesting Voyages and Travels, in All Parts of the World.* Vol. 5. Ed. John Pinkerton. Philadelphia, 1812.

Culler, Jonathan. *Ferdinand de Saussure.* Rev. ed. Ithaca, N.Y., 1986.

———. *Structuralist Poetics: Structuralism, Linguistics and the Study of Literature.* Ithaca, N.Y., 1975.

Curtis, Jared R. *Wordsworth's Experiments with Tradition: The Lyric Poems of 1802, With Texts of the Poems Based on Early Manuscripts.* Ithaca, N.Y., 1971.

Curtius, Ernst Robert. *European Literature and the Latin Middle Ages.* Trans. Willard R. Trask. Princeton, N.J., 1953.

Danto, Arthur C. *Narration and Knowledge.* New York, 1985.

Darbishire, Helen, ed. *Some Variants in Wordsworth's Text in the Volumes of 1836–7 in the King's Library.* Oxford, 1949.

Darby, H. C., ed. *A New Historical Geography of England After 1600.* Cambridge, Eng., 1976.

Darton, F. J. Harvey. *Children's Books in England: Five Centuries of Social Life.* 3d ed. Rev. by Brian Alderson. Cambridge, Eng., 1982.

Davis, Arthur P. *Isaac Watts: His Life and Works.* New York, 1943.

Davis, Charles G. "The Structure of Wordsworth's Sonnet 'Composed Upon Westminster Bridge.'" *English* 19 (Spring 1970): 18–21.

Davis, Robert Con. "The Structure of the Picturesque: Dorothy Wordsworth's Journals." *The Wordsworth Circle* 9 (1978): 45–49.

Dekoven, Marianne. "History as Suppressed Referent in Modernist Fiction." *ELH* 51 (1984): 137–52.

de Man, Paul. *Blindness and Insight: Essays in the Rhetoric of Contemporary Criticism.* 2d ed. rev. Minneapolis, 1983.

———. "Intentional Structure of the Romantic Image." In de Man, *The Rhetoric of Romanticism.* New York, 1984.

DeMause, Lloyd. "The Evolution of Childhood." In deMause, ed., *The History of Childhood.* New York, 1974.

Denham, John. *The Poetical Works of Sir John Denham.* Ed. Theodore Howard Banks, Jr. New Haven, Conn., 1928.

Denny, Don. *The Annunciation From the Right, From Early Christian Times to the Sixteenth Century.* New York, 1977.

De Quincey, Thomas. *Collected Writings.* New and enlarged ed. Vol. 11: *Literary Theory and Criticism.* Ed. David Masson. Edinburgh, 1890.

Derrida, Jacques. "The Law of Genre." Trans. Avital Ronell. In W. J. T. Mitchell, ed., *On Narrative.* Chicago, 1981.

———. *Positions.* Trans. Alan Bass. Chicago, 1981.

———. "White Mythology: Metaphor in the Text of Philosophy." Trans. F. C. T. Moore. *New Literary History* 6 (1974): 5–74.

Descartes, René. *Discourse on Method and Meditations.* Trans. Laurence J. Lafleur. Indianapolis, 1960.

Deutsch, Babette. *Poetry Handbook: A Dictionary of Terms.* Rev. and enlarged ed. New York, 1962.

de Wolfe, I. "Townscape: A Plea for English Visual Philosophy Founded on the True Rock of Sir Uvedale Price." *Architectural Review* 106 (1949): 354–74.

DHotel, Yves. *Joseph Le Bon, ou Arras sous la Terreur: Essai sur la Psychose Révolutionnaire.* Paris, 1934.

Dilthey, Wilhelm. *Pattern and Meaning in History: Thoughts on History and Society.* Trans. and ed. H. P. Rickman. 1961. Rpt. New York, 1962.

The Discovery of the Lake District: A Northern Arcadia and Its Uses. London, 1984.

Donne, John. *The Complete Poetry of John Donne.* Ed. John T. Shawcross. Garden City, N.Y., 1967.

Douglas, Wallace W. "Wordsworth as Business Man." *PMLA* 63 (1948): 625–41.

Drayton, Michael. *The Poly-Olbion; A Chorographicall Description of Great Britain*. 1889–90. Rpt. New York, 1970.

Durrant, Geoffrey. *Wordsworth and the Great System: A Study of Wordsworth's Poetic Universe*. Cambridge, Eng., 1970.

Eagleton, Terry. *Criticism and Ideology: A Study in Marxist Literary Theory*. London, 1978.

———. *Marxism and Literary Criticism*. Berkeley, Calif., 1976.

Eaves, Morris, and Michael Fischer, eds. *Romanticism and Contemporary Criticism*. Ithaca, N.Y., 1986.

Eichenbaum, Boris. "The Theory of the 'Formal Method.'" In *Russian Formalist Criticism: Four Essays*. Trans. Lee T. Lemon and Marion J. Reis. Lincoln, Nebr., 1965.

Eilenberg, Susan. "'Michael,' 'Christabel,' and the Poetry of Possession." *Criticism* 30 (1988): 205–24.

———. "Wordsworth's 'Michael': The Poetry of Property." *Essays in Literature* 15 (1988): 13–25.

The Elements of Drawing in All its Branches. Perth, Scotland, 1802.

Eliot, T. S. *Four Quartets*. New York, 1943.

Empson, William. *Seven Types of Ambiguity*. New York, 1947.

Emsley, Clive. *British Society and the French Wars, 1793–1815*. Totowa, N.J., 1979.

English Watercolours in the Collection of C. F. J. Beausire. Liverpool, 1970.

Erdman, David V. *Blake, Prophet Against Empire: A Poet's Interpretation of the History of His Own Times*. Rev. ed. Garden City, N.Y., 1969.

———. "The Man Who Was Not Napoleon." *The Wordsworth Circle* 12 (1981): 92–96.

———. "Oops! My Misprision." *The Wordsworth Circle* 13 (1982): 201–2.

———. "Wordsworth as Heartsworth; or, Was Regicide the Prophetic Ground of Those 'Moral Questions'?" In Donald H. Reiman, Michael C. Jaye, and Betty T. Bennett, eds., with Doucet Deven Fischer and Ricki B. Herzfeld, *The Evidence of the Imagination: Studies of Interactions Between Life and Art in English Romantic Literature*. New York, 1978.

Eriau, J.-B. *L'Ancien Carmel du Faubourg Saint-Jacques (1604–1792)*. Paris, 1929.

Erickson, Lee. "The Egoism of Authorship: Wordsworth's Poetic Career." Paper presented at the Modern Language Association convention, San Francisco, Dec. 28, 1987.

Erlich, Victor. *Russian Formalism: History—Doctrine*. 3d ed. New Haven, Conn., 1981.

Ermarth, Michael. *Wilhelm Dilthey: The Critique of Historical Reason*. Chicago, 1978.

Everest, Kelvin. *Coleridge's Secret Ministry: The Context of the Conversation Poems 1795–1798*. Hassocks, Eng., 1979.

Fairchilds, Cissie. "Female Sexual Attitudes and the Rise of Illegitimacy: A Case Study." *Journal of Interdisciplinary History* 8 (1978): 627–67.

Farington, Joseph. *The Farington Diary*. Ed. James Grieg. Vols. 1 (3d ed.), 2, 4. New York, 1923–24.

Farrell, John P. *Revolution as Tragedy: The Dilemma of the Moderate from Scott to Arnold*. Ithaca, N.Y., 1980.

Faulkner, William. *Go Down, Moses*. New York, 1973.

Fawcett, Joseph. *The Art of War*. In Arthur Beatty, "Joseph Fawcett: The Art of War: Its Relation to the Early Development of William Wordsworth." *University of Wisconsin Studies in Language and Literature* 2 (Sept. 1918): 224–69.

Ferguson, Frances. *Wordsworth: Language as Counter-Spirit*. New Haven, Conn., 1977.

Ferry, David. *The Limits of Mortality: An Essay on Wordsworth's Major Poems*. Middletown, Conn., 1959.

Fink, Z. S., ed. *The Early Wordsworthian Milieu: A Notebook of Christopher Wordsworth with a Few Entries by William Wordsworth*. Oxford, 1958.

Fischer, Michael. "Morality and History in Coleridge's Political Theory." *Studies in Romanticism* 21 (1982): 457–60.

Flandrin, Jean-Louis. *Families in Former Times: Kinship, Household and Sexuality*. Trans. Richard Southern. Themes in the Social Sciences. Cambridge, Eng., 1979.

Fletcher, Angus. *Allegory: The Theory of a Symbolic Mode*. Ithaca, N.Y., 1964.

Foord, Archibald S. *His Majesty's Opposition, 1714–1830*. Oxford, 1964.

Ford, George H. "Felicitous Space: The Cottage Controversy." In U. C. Knoepflmacher and G. B. Tennyson, eds., *Nature and the Victorian Imagination*. Berkeley, Calif., 1977.

Foster, Richard. *The New Romantics: A Reappraisal of the New Criticism*. 1962. Rpt. Port Washington, N.Y., 1973.

Foucault, Michel. *The Archaeology of Knowledge*. Trans. A. M. Sheridan Smith. New York, 1972.

———. *Discipline and Punish: The Birth of the Prison*. Trans. Alan Sheridan. New York, 1979.

———. "Nietzsche, Genealogy, History." In Foucault, *Language, Counter-Memory, Practice: Selected Essays and Interviews*. Trans. Donald F. Bouchard and Sherry Simon. Ed. Donald F. Bouchard. Ithaca, N.Y., 1977.

———. *The Order of Things: An Archaeology of the Human Sciences*. New York, 1973.

Fowler, Alistair. *The Kinds of Literature: An Introduction to the Theory of Genres and Modes*. Cambridge, Mass., 1982.

Fox, Charles James. *Speeches During the French Revolutionary War Period*. Ed. Irene Cooper Willis. London, 1924.

Foxe, Arthur N. *The Common Sense from Heraclitus to Peirce: The Sources, Substance, and Possibilities of the Common Sense*. New York, 1962.

Fraistat, Neil. *The Poem and the Book: Interpreting Collections of Romantic Poetry*. Chapel Hill, N.C., 1985.

Freedman, Jonathan. Review of Carren Kaston's *Imagination and Desire in the Novels of Henry James* and Mark Seltzer's *Henry James and the Art of Power*. *New England Quarterly* 59 (1985): 323–30.

Freud, Sigmund. *The Interpretation of Dreams*. Trans. and ed. James Strachey. New York, 1965.

———. "The 'Uncanny.' " In Freud, *On Creativity and the Unconscious: Papers on the Psychology of Art, Literature, Love, Religion*. Ed. Benjamin Nelson. New York, 1958.

Fried, Michael. *Absorption and Theatricality: Painting and Beholder in the Age of Diderot*. Berkeley, Calif., 1980.

Friedman, Michael H. *The Making of a Tory Humanist: William Wordsworth and the Idea of Community*. New York, 1979.

Fry, Paul H. "The Absent Dead: Wordsworth, Byron, and the Epitaph." *Studies in Romanticism* 17 (1978): 413–33.

Frye, Northrop. *Anatomy of Criticism: Four Essays*. Princeton, N.J., 1957.

———. *The Secular Scripture: A Study of the Structure of Romance*. Cambridge, Mass., 1976.

Fumerton, Patricia. "Exchanging Gifts: The Elizabethan Currency of Children and Poetry." *ELH* 53 (1986): 241–78.

———. " 'Secret' Arts: Elizabethan Miniatures and Sonnets." *Representations* 15 (Summer 1986): 57–97.

Furet, François. *Interpreting the French Revolution*. Trans. Elborg Forster. Cambridge, Eng., 1981. (First published in French as *Penser la Révolution Française*. Paris, 1978.)

Furet, François, and Denis Richet. *La Révolution: des états généraux au 9 Thermidor*. Paris, 1965.

Fussell, G. E. *The English Rural Labourer: His Home, Furniture, Clothing and Food from Tudor to Victorian Times*. London, 1949.

Galperin, William. " 'Wordsworth' in the *Biographia*." Paper presented at the Modern Language Association convention, Chicago, Dec. 29, 1985. Since published in revised form as " 'Desynonymizing' the Self in Wordsworth and Coleridge." *Studies in Romanticism* 26 (1987): 513–26.

Garaud, Marcel, and Romuald Szramkiewicz. *La Révolution Française et la Famille*. Paris, 1978.

Garrison, Joseph M., Jr. "Knowledge and Beauty in Wordsworth's 'Composed Upon Westminster Bridge.' " *Research Studies* 40 (1972): 46–47.

Garrod, H. W. *Wordsworth: Lectures and Essays*. 2d ed., enlarged. Oxford, 1927.

Gates, Barbara T. "The Prelude and the Development of Wordsworth's Historical Imagination." *Etudes Anglaises* 30 (1977): 169–78.

———. "Wordsworth and the Course of History." *Research Studies* 44 (1976): 199–207.

Gayer, Arthur D., W. W. Rostow, Anna Jacobson Schwartz, with Isaiah Frank. *The Growth and Fluctuation of the British Economy, 1790–1850: An Historical, Statistical, and Theoretical Study of Britain's Economic Development*. Vol. 1. 1953. Rpt. Hassocks, Eng., 1975.

Gell, William. *A Tour in the Lakes Made in 1797*. Ed. William Rollinson. Newcastle upon Tyne, 1968.

Gibbon, Edward. *Memoirs of My Life*. Ed. Georges A. Bonnard. New York, 1969.

Gilbert, Creighton. "On Subject and Not-Subject in Italian Renaissance Pictures." *Art Bulletin* 34 (1952): 202–16.

Gilchrist, J., and W. J. Murray. *The Press in the French Revolution: A Selection of Documents Taken from the Press of the Revolution for the Years 1789–1794*. New York, 1971.

Gill, Stephen C. " 'Adventures on Salisbury Plain' and Wordsworth's Poetry of Protest 1795–97." *Studies in Romanticism* 11 (1972): 48–65.

Gillcrist, T. J. "Spenser and Reason in the Conclusion of 'Salisbury Plain.' " *English Language Notes* 7 (1969): 11–18.

Gilpin, William. *Observations on Several Parts of Great Britain, Particularly the High-lands of Scotland, Relative Chiefly to Picturesque Beauty, Made in the Year 1776*. 3d ed. 2 vols. London, 1808.

———. *Observations on the Western Parts of England*. 1798. Rpt. Richmond, Eng., 1973.

———. *Remarks on Forest Scenery, and Other Woodland Views (Relative Chiefly to Picturesque Beauty). Illustrated by the Scenes of New-Forest in Hampshire*. Vol. 2. London, 1791.

———. *Three Essays: On Picturesque Beauty; On Picturesque Travel; and On Sketching Landscape: To Which is Added a Poem, On Landscape Painting*. 2d ed. London, 1794.

Girard, René. *Violence and the Sacred*. Trans. Patrick Gregory. Baltimore, Md., 1977.

Godwin, William. *Caleb Williams*. Ed. David McCracken. New York, 1977.

———. *Enquiry Concerning Political Justice and Its Influence on Modern Morals and Happiness*. Ed. Isaac Kramnick. Harmondsworth, Eng., 1976.

Gombrich, E. H. *Norm and Form: Studies in the Art of the Renaissance*. London, 1966.

González, Justo L. *A History of Christian Thought*. Vol. 1: *From the Beginnings to the Council of Chalcedon*. Nashville, 1970.

Goodheart, Eugene. *The Skeptic Disposition in Contemporary Criticism*. Princeton, N.J., 1984.

Gordon, Jan B. "Origins, History, and the Reconstitution of Family: Tess' Journey." *ELH* 43 (1976): 366–88.

[Gough, John.] *The Manners and Customs of Westmorland, and the Adjoining Parts of Cumberland, Lancashire, and Yorkshire, in the Former Part of the Eighteenth Century; Described in a Series of Letters*. First pub. in *Kendal Chronicle*, 1812. Rpt. Kendal, 1827.

Grabar, André. *Christian Iconography: A Study of Its Origins*. Bollingen Series XXXV.10. Princeton, N.J., 1968.

Gray, Thomas. Journal of Lakes tour, in *Correspondence of Thomas Gray*. Ed. Paget Toynbee and Leonard Whibley. Vol. 3: *1766–1771*. Oxford, 1935.

———. *The Poems of Thomas Gray, William Collins, Oliver Goldsmith*. Ed. Roger Lonsdale. New York, 1969.

Greaves, Margaret. *Regency Patron: Sir George Beaumont*. London, 1966.

Greenblatt, Stephen. *Renaissance Self-Fashioning: From More to Shakespeare*. Chicago, 1980.

Greer, Donald. *The Incidence of the Terror During the French Revolution: A Statistical Interpretation*. Cambridge, Mass., 1935.

Grigson, Geoffrey. *Britain Observed: The Landscape Through Artists' Eyes*. London, 1975.

Groom, Bernard. *The Unity of Wordsworth's Poetry*. New York, 1966.

Gross, Harvey. "Hegel, Beethoven, Wordsworth: 1770–1970." *American Scholar* 40 (1970–71): 142–56.

Guillén, Claudio. *Literature as System: Essays Toward the Theory of Literary History*. Princeton, N.J., 1971.

Guillory, John. "The Ideology of Canon-Formation: T. S. Eliot and Cleanth Brooks." *Critical Inquiry* 10 (1983): 173–98.

Gupta, Sanjeev. *Black Market Exchange Rates. Kieler Studien, Institut für Welt-wirtschaft an der Universität Kiel,* no. 167. Tubingen, 1981.

Hahn, Cynthia. " 'Joseph Will Perfect, Mary Enlighten and Jesus Save Thee': The Holy Family as Marriage Model in the Mérode Triptych." *The Art Bulletin* 68 (1986): 54–66.

Hair, P. E. H. "Deaths from Violence in Britain: A Tentative Secular Survey." *Population Studies* 25 (1971): 5–24.

Hall, John R. "The Time of History and the History of Times." *History and Theory* 19 (1980): 113–31.

Hammond, J. L., and Barbara Hammond. *The Village Labourer, 1760–1832: A Study in the Government of England Before the Reform Bill.* 1911. Rpt. New York, 1970.

Hampshire, Jean. "Daniel Fleming, Industrious Squire of Rydal." *Cumbria: Lakeland and the Borders* 16 (1966–67): 592–95.

Hampson, Norman. *The French Revolution: A Concise History.* London, 1975.

——— . *A Social History of the French Revolution.* Toronto, 1963.

Hanawalt, Barbara A. "Childrearing Among the Lower Classes of Late Medieval England." *Journal of Interdisciplinary History* 8 (1977): 1–22.

Harper, George McLean. *William Wordsworth: His Life, Works and Influence.* Vol. 1. London, 1916.

Harrison, Gary Lee. "Wordsworth and the Itinerant Poor: The Discourse on Poverty." Ph.D. diss., Stanford University, 1987.

Harrison, Mark. "The Ordering of the Urban Environment: Time, Work and the Occurrence of Crowds 1790–1835." *Past and Present* 110 (Feb. 1986): 134–68.

Hartman, Geoffrey H. "Blessing the Torrent: On Wordsworth's Later Style." *PMLA* 93 (1978): 196–204.

——— . "Christopher Smart's *Magnificat*: Toward a Theory of Representation." In Hartman, *The Fate of Reading and Other Essays.* Chicago, 1975.

——— . "The Interpreter: A Self-Analysis." In Hartman, *The Fate of Reading and Other Essays.* Chicago, 1975.

——— . "Milton's Counterplot." In Arthur E. Barker, ed., *Milton: Modern Essays in Criticism.* London, 1965.

——— . "Reflections on the Evening Star: Akenside to Coleridge." In Hartman, ed., *New Perspectives on Coleridge and Wordsworth: Selected Papers from the English Institute.* New York, 1972.

——— . "A Touching Compulsion: Wordsworth and the Problem of Literary Representation." *Georgia Review* 31 (1977): 345–61.

——— . *The Unremarkable Wordsworth.* Minneapolis, 1987.

——— . "The Voice of the Shuttle: Language from the Point of View of Literature." In Hartman, *Beyond Formalism: Literary Essays 1958–70.* New Haven, Conn., 1970.

——— . "Wordsworth, Inscriptions, and Romantic Nature Poetry." In Hartman, *Beyond Formalism: Literary Essays 1958–70.* New Haven, Conn., 1970.

Hartt, Frederick. *History of Italian Renaissance Art: Painting, Sculpture, Architecture.* 2d ed. New York, 1979.

Hartung, Charles V. "Wordsworth on Westminster Bridge: Paradox or Harmony?" *College English* 13 (1952): 201–3.

Harvey, G. M. "The Design of Wordsworth's Sonnets." *Ariel* 6 (July 1975): 78–90.

Havens, Raymond Dexter. *The Mind of a Poet: A Study of Wordsworth's Thought with Particular Reference to "The Prelude."* Vol. 2: *"The Prelude," A Commentary*. Baltimore, Md., 1941.

Hay, Douglas. "Property, Authority and the Criminal Law." In Douglas Hay et al., eds., *Albion's Fatal Tree: Crime and Society in Eighteenth-Century England*. New York, 1975.

——— . "War, Dearth and Theft in the Eighteenth Century: The Record of the English Courts." *Past and Present* 95 (1982): 117–60.

Hayden, Donald E. *Wordsworth's Walking Tour of 1790*. Tulsa, Okla., 1983.

Hayden, John O., ed. *William Wordsworth: The Poems*. Vol. 1. The English Poets. New Haven, Conn., 1981.

Hayes, John. *The Landscape Paintings of Thomas Gainsborough: A Critical Text and Catalogue Raisonné*. 2 vols. Ithaca, N.Y., 1982.

Hazlitt, William. *The Life of Napoleon Buonaparte*. Vol. 2. Philadelphia, 1875.

Heads Representing the Various Passions of the Soul; as They Are Expressed in the Human Countenance: Drawn by that Great Master Mons. Le Brun. London, 1794.

Healey, George Harris. *The Cornell Wordsworth Collection: A Catalogue of Books and Manuscripts Presented to the University by Mr. Victor Emanuel, Cornell 1919*. Ithaca, 1957.

Heath, William. *Wordsworth and Coleridge: A Study of Their Literary Relations in 1801–1802*. Oxford, 1970.

Heffernan, James A. W. *The Re-Creation of Landscape: A Study of Wordsworth, Coleridge, Constable, and Turner*. Hanover, N.H., 1985.

——— . *Wordsworth's Theory of Poetry: The Transforming Imagination*. Ithaca, N.Y., 1969.

Hegel, G. W. F. *Hegel's Philosophy of Right*. Trans. T. M. Knox. Oxford, 1942.

——— . *The Phenomenology of Mind*. Trans. J. B. Baillie. 1910. Rpt. New York, 1967.

Heidegger, Martin. *Being and Time*. Trans. John Macquarrie and Edward Robinson. New York, 1962.

Heinzelman, Kurt. "Byron's Poetry of Politics: The Economic Basis of the 'Poetical Character.'" *Texas Studies in Literature and Language* 23 (1981): 361–88.

——— . *The Economics of the Imagination*. Amherst, Mass., 1980.

——— . "Wordsworth as Developer: Romantic Real Estate." Paper presented at the Modern Language Association convention, San Francisco, Dec. 28, 1987.

Hemmings, F. W. J. *Culture and Society in France, 1789–1848*. Leicester, Eng., 1987.

Henderson, Ernest F. *Symbol and Satire in the French Revolution*. New York, 1912.

Herbert, Robert L. *David, "Brutus," and the French Revolution: An Essay in Art and Politics*. Art in Context. London, 1972.

Herman, Judith B. "The Poet as Editor: Wordsworth's Edition of 1815." *The Wordsworth Circle* 9 (1978): 82–87.

Hernadi, Paul. "The Erotics of Retrospection: Historytelling, Audience Response, and the Strategies of Desire." *New Literary History* 12 (1981): 243–52.

Herrmann, Luke. *British Landscape Painting of the Eighteenth Century*. London, 1973.

Hiller, Geoffrey G. " 'Sacred Bards' and 'Wise Druides': Drayton and His Archetype of the Poet." *ELH* 51 (1984): 1–15.

Himmelfarb, Gertrude. "The Haunted House of Jeremy Bentham." In Richard Herr and Harold T. Parker, eds., *Ideas in History: Essays Presented to Louis Gottschalk by His Former Students*. Durham, N.C., 1965.

Hindle, Wilfrid. *The Morning Post, 1772–1937: Portrait of a Newspaper*. London, 1937.

Hipple, Walter John, Jr. *The Beautiful, the Sublime, and the Picturesque in Eighteenth-Century British Aesthetic Theory*. Carbondale, Ill., 1957.

Hirsch, E. D., Jr. *Validity in Interpretation*. New Haven, Conn., 1976.

Hodgson, John A. " 'Simon Lee': The Conditions of Revolution." Paper presented at the Modern Language Association convention, San Francisco, Dec. 28, 1987.

———. *Wordsworth's Philosophical Poetry, 1787–1814*. Lincoln, Nebr., 1980.

Holcomb, Adele M. "The Bridge in the Middle Distance: Symbolic Elements in Romantic Landscape." *Art Quarterly* 37 (1974): 31–58.

Holland, Patrick. "The Two Contrasts of Wordsworth's 'Westminster Bridge' Sonnet." *The Wordsworth Circle* 8 (1977): 32–34.

Hollander, John. *The Figure of Echo: A Mode of Allusion in Milton and After*. Berkeley, Calif., 1981.

Howard, June. *Form and History in American Literary Naturalism*. Chapel Hill, N.C., 1985.

Hudleston, C. Roy. "Ann Crackanthorpe: Wordsworth's Great-Aunt." *Transactions of the Cumberland and Westmorland Antiquarian and Archaeological Society*, n.s. 60 (1960): 135–55.

Huet, Marie-Hélène. *Rehearsing the Revolution: The Staging of Marat's Death, 1793–1797*. Trans. Robert Hurley. Berkeley, Calif., 1982.

Hunt, John Dixon. *The Figure in the Landscape: Poetry, Painting, and Gardening During the Eighteenth Century*. Baltimore, Md., 1976.

———. "Wondrous Deep and Dark: Turner and the Sublime." *Georgia Review* 30 (1976): 139–64.

Hunt, Lynn. *Politics, Culture, and Class in the French Revolution*. Berkeley, Calif., 1984.

Hussey, Christopher. *The Picturesque: Studies in a Point of View*. London, 1967.

Hutchinson, William. *An Excursion to the Lakes in Westmoreland and Cumberland; With a Tour Through Part of the Northern Counties, In the Years 1773 and 1774*. London, 1776.

———. *The History of the County of Cumberland*. Vol. 1. 1794–97. Rpt. East Ardsley, Eng., 1974.

Hutton, Patrick H. "The History of Mentalities: The New Map of Cultural History." *History and Theory* 20 (1981): 237–59.

Huyghe, René. *Art and Mankind: Larousse Encyclopedia of Renaissance and Baroque Art*. Ed. René Huyghe. New York, 1964.

Hyde, Lewis. *The Gift: Imagination and the Erotic Life of Property*. New York, 1979.

Hyde, Ralph. *Gilded Scenes and Shining Prospects: Panoramic Views of British Towns, 1575–1900*. New Haven, Conn., 1985.

Inventaire Général des Richesses d'Art de la France, Archives de Musée des Monuments Français. Vol. 1. Paris, 1883. Vol. 2. Paris, 1886.

Jackson, Richard. "The Romantic Metaphysics of Time." *Studies in Romanticism* 19 (1980): 19–30.

Jacobus, Mary. "The Law Of/And Gender: Genre Theory and *The Prelude*." *Diacritics* 14 (Winter 1984): 47–57.

———. " 'Splitting the Race of Men / In Twain': Prostitution and *The Prelude*." Paper presented at the Modern Language Association convention, Chicago, Dec. 28, 1985.

———. " 'That Great Stage Where Senators Perform': *Macbeth* and the Politics of Romantic Theater." *Studies in Romanticism* 22 (1983): 353–87.

———. *Tradition and Experiment in Wordsworth's "Lyrical Ballads" (1798)*. Oxford, 1976.

Jakobson, Roman. "Closing Statement: Linguistics and Poetics." In Thomas A. Sebeok, ed., *Style in Language*. Cambridge, Mass., 1960.

———. "Shifters, Verbal Categories, and the Russian Verb." In Jakobson, *Selected Writings*. Vol. 2: *Word and Language*. The Hague, 1971.

———. "Two Aspects of Language and Two Types of Aphasia Disturbances." In Roman Jakobson and Morris Halle, *Fundamentals of Language*. 2d ed. The Hague, 1971.

Jameson, Fredric. *Marxism and Form: Twentieth-Century Dialectical Theories of Literature*. Princeton, N.J., 1971.

———. *The Political Unconscious: Narrative as a Socially Symbolic Act*. Ithaca, N.Y., 1981.

Jay, Eileen. *Wordsworth at Colthouse: An Account of the Poet's Boyhood Years Spent in the Remote Lakeland Hamlet of Colthouse*. Kendal, Eng., 1970.

Jefferson, Samuel. *The History and Antiquities of Cumberland: With Biographical Notices and Memoirs*. Vol. 1. Carlisle, Eng., 1840.

Johnson, J. E. *The Story of Air Fighting*. Previously published as *Full Circle*. Expanded ed. New York, 1986.

Johnson, Lee M. *Wordsworth and the Sonnet*. Anglistica no. 19. Copenhagen, 1973.

Johnson, Samuel. *Life of Savage*. In Frank Brady and W. K. Wimsatt, eds., *Samuel Johnson: Selected Poetry and Prose*. Berkeley, Calif., 1977.

Johnston, Kenneth R. "Philanthropy or Treason? Wordsworth as 'Active Partisan.' " *Studies in Romanticism* 25 (1986): 371–409.

———. "The Politics of 'Tintern Abbey.' " *The Wordsworth Circle* 14 (1983): 6–14.

———. "Recollecting Forgetting: Forcing Paradox to the Limit in the 'Intimations Ode.' " *The Wordsworth Circle* 2 (1971): 59–64.

———. *Wordsworth and "The Recluse."* New Haven, Conn., 1984.

Joll, James, ed. *Britain and Europe: Pitt to Churchill, 1793–1940*. 1950. Rpt. London, 1967.

Jones, G. P. "The Decline of the Yeomanry in the Lake Counties." *Transactions of the Cumberland and Westmorland Antiquarian and Archaeological Society*, n.s. 62 (1962): 198–223.

———. "Some Sources of Loans and Credit in Cumbria Before the Rise of Banks." *Transactions of the Cumberland and Westmorland Antiquarian and Archaeological Society*, n.s. 75 (1975): 275–92.

Jones, R. Ben. *Napoleon: Man and Myth*. London, 1977.

Jouin, Henry. *Charles Le Brun et les arts sous Louis XIV: Le premier peintre sa vie, son oeuvre, ses écrits, ses contemporains, son influence d'après le manuscrit de Nivelon et de nombreuses pièces inédites*. Paris, 1889.

Journals of the House of Commons. Vols. 40 (1785) and 41 (1786).

Keach, William. "Arbitrary Power: Romanticism and the Politics of Language." Paper presented at the conference on "English Romanticism: Recent Trends in Criticism," Northwestern University, Oct. 11, 1986.

Kelley, Donald R. *Historians and the Law in Postrevolutionary France*. Princeton, N.J., 1984.

Kelley, Paul. "Rousseau's 'Discourse on the Origins of Inequality' and Wordsworth's 'Salisbury Plain.'" *Notes and Queries*, n.s. 24 (1977): 323.

Kelley, Theresa M. "The Economics of the Heart: Wordsworth's Sublime and Beautiful." *Romanticism Past and Present* 5 (1981): 15–32.

———. "Wordsworth and the Rhinefall." *Studies in Romanticism* 23 (1984): 61–79.

Kelly, George Armstrong. *Victims, Authority, and Terror: The Parallel Deaths of d'Orléans, Custine, Bailly, and Malesherbes*. Chapel Hill, N.C., 1982.

Kendrick, Thomas Downing. *The Druids: A Study in Keltic Prehistory*. 1927. Rpt. New York, 1966.

Kermode, Frank. *Romantic Image*. London, 1957.

Kern, Stephen. "Explosive Intimacy: Psychodynamics of the Victorian Family." *History of Childhood Quarterly* 1 (1974): 437–61.

Klancher, Jon P. "From 'Crowd' to 'Audience': The Making of an English Mass Readership in the Nineteenth Century." *ELH* 50 (1983): 155–73.

———. "Reading the Social Text: Power, Signs, and Audience in Early Nineteenth-Century Prose." *Studies in Romanticism* 23 (1984): 183–204.

Knight, Richard Payne. *An Account of the Remains of the Worship of Priapus, Lately Existing at Isernia, in the Kingdom of Naples: In Two Letters; One from Sir William Hamilton, K. B. . . . to Sir Joseph Banks, bart., . . . and the Other from a Person Residing at Isernia: to Which is Added, a Discourse on the Worship of Priapus, and Its Connexion with the Mystic Theology of the Ancients*. London, 1786.

———. *An Analytical Inquiry into the Principles of Taste*. London, 1805.

———. *The Landscape, A Didactic Poem. In Three Books*. London, 1794.

———. *The Landscape, A Didactic Poem. In Three Books*. 2d ed. 1795. Rpt. Westmead, Farnborough, Hants., Eng., 1972.

———. *A Monody on the Death of the Right Honourable Charles James Fox*. London, 1806–7.

———. *The Progress of Civil Society: A Didactic Poem, in Six Books*. London, 1796.

Kramnick, Isaac, ed. *Edmund Burke*. Great Lives Observed. Englewood Cliffs, N.J., 1974.

Kroeber, Karl. *British Romantic Art*. Berkeley, Calif., 1986.

———. "Experience As History: Shelley's Venice, Turner's Carthage." *ELH* 41 (1974): 321–39.

———. "Romantic Historicism: The Temporal Sublime." In Karl Kroeber and William Walling, eds., *Images of Romanticism: Verbal and Visual Affinities*. New Haven, Conn., 1978.

———. *Romantic Landscape Vision: Constable and Wordsworth*. Madison, Wis., 1975.

Kuhn, Thomas S. *The Structure of Scientific Revolutions*. 2d ed. International Encyclopedia of Unified Science, vol. 2, no. 2. Chicago, 1970.

Kussmaul, K. S. "The Ambiguous Mobility of Farm Servants." *Economic History Review*, 2d series, 34 (1981): 222–35.

Lacan, Jacques. *Ecrits*. Trans. Alan Sheridan. New York, 1977.

———. "Of Structure as an Inmixing of an Otherness Prerequisite to Any Subject Whatever." In Richard Macksey and Eugenio Donato, eds., *The Structuralist Controversy: The Languages of Criticism and the Sciences of Man*. Baltimore, Md., 1970.

Lair, Jules. *Louise de La Vallière and the Early Life of Louis XIV*. 3d ed. Trans. Ethel Colburn Mayne. London, 1881.

Lanham, Richard A. *A Handlist of Rhetorical Terms: A Guide for Students of English Literature*. Berkeley, Calif., 1968.

Laslett, Peter. "Parental Deprivation in the Past: A Note on the History of Orphans in England." *Local Population Studies* 13 (Autumn 1974): 11–18.

———. "Scottish Weavers, Cobblers and Miners Who Bought Books in the 1750's." *Local Population Studies* 3 (Autumn 1969): 7–15.

Laslett, Peter, ed., with Richard Wall. *Household and Family in Past Time: Comparative Studies in the Size and Structure of the Domestic Group Over the Last Three Centuries in England, France, Serbia, Japan and Colonial North America, with Further Materials from Western Europe*. Cambridge, Eng., 1972.

Laslett, Peter, and Karla Oosterveen, "Long-Term Trends in Bastardy in England: A Study of the Illegitimacy Figures in the Parish Registers and in the Reports of the Registrar General, 1561–1960." *Population Studies* 27 (1973): 255–86.

Leavis, F. R. "Imagery and Movement: Notes in the Analysis of Poetry." *Scrutiny* 13 (1945–46): 119–34.

———. "Wordsworth: The Creative Conditions." In Reuben A. Brower, ed., *Twentieth-Century Literature in Retrospect*. Harvard English Studies, 2. Cambridge, Mass., 1971.

Lefebvre, Georges. *The French Revolution: From 1793 to 1799*. Vol. 2. Trans. John Hall Stewart, James Friguglietti. London, 1964.

———. *The Great Fear of 1789: Rural Panic in Revolutionary France*. Trans. Joan White. Princeton, N.J., 1982.

Legouis, Emile. *The Early Life of William Wordsworth, 1770–1798: A Study of "The Prelude."* Trans. J. W. Matthews. 1897. Rpt. with additional appendix, London, 1932.

———. *William Wordsworth and Annette Vallon*. Rev. and enlarged ed. Hamden, Conn., 1967.

Leith, James A. *The Idea of Art as Propaganda in France, 1750–1799: A Study in the History of Ideas*. Univ. of Toronto Romance Series, no. 8. Toronto, 1965.

Lemaire, Anika. *Jacques Lacan*. Trans. David Macey. London, 1977.

Lenotre, G. *The September Massacres: Accounts of Personal Experiences Written by Some of the Few Survivors of the Terrible Days of September 2nd and 3rd, 1792, Together With a Series of Hitherto Unpublished Police Reports*. London, n. d.

Levinson, Marjorie. "The New Historicism: What's in a Name?" Paper presented at the conference on "Romanticism, Politics, and the New Historicism: In Honor of Carl Woodring," University of California, Los Angeles, Nov. 14, 1986. Expanded MS. courtesy of author.

———. "A New Prospect on 'Chapman's Homer.'" Paper presented at the Modern Language Association convention, Chicago, Dec. 30, 1985.

———. *The Romantic Fragment Poem: A Critique of a Form*. Chapel Hill, N.C., 1986.

———. *Wordsworth's Great Period Poems: Four Essays*. Cambridge, Eng., 1986.

Lévi-Strauss, Claude. *The Elementary Structures of Kinship*. Rev. ed. Trans. James Harle Bell, John Richard von Sturmer, and Rodney Needham. Ed. Rodney Needham. Boston, 1969.

———. *The Savage Mind*. Chicago, 1966.

Lewis, C. Day. *The Poetic Image*. 1947. Rpt. Los Angeles, 1984.

Lewis, C. S. *A Preface to Paradise Lost*. London, 1942.

Liddell-Hart, B. H. *The Strategy of Indirect Approach*. Enlarged ed. London, 1946.

Lindenberger, Herbert. *Historical Drama: The Relation of Literature and Reality*. Chicago, 1975.

———. *On Wordsworth's "Prelude."* Princeton, N.J., 1963.

Lindsay, Jack. *J. M. W. Turner: His Life and Work*. London, 1966.

Lindsay, Julian Ira. "A Note on the Marginalia." *Huntington Library Quarterly* 1 (1937): 95–99.

Lipson, E. *The Economic History of England*. Vol. 2: *The Age of Mercantilism*. 5th ed. London, 1948.

Liu, Alan. "Christopher Smart's 'Uncommunicated Letters': Translation and the Ethics of Literary History." *Boundary 2* 14, Nos. 1–2 (Fall 1985/Winter 1986): 115–46.

———. "On the Autobiographical Present: Dorothy Wordsworth's *Grasmere Journals*." *Criticism* 26 (1984): 115–37.

———. "The Power of Formalism: The New Historicism." Paper presented at the conference on "Romanticism, Politics, and the New Historicism: In Honor of Carl Woodring," University of California, Los Angeles, Nov. 14, 1986.

———. Review of David Simpson, *Wordsworth's Historical Imagination: The Poetry of Displacement*. Forthcoming in *The Wordsworth Circle*.

———. "Toward a Theory of Common Sense: Beckford's *Vathek* and Johnson's *Rasselas*." *Texas Studies in Literature and Language* 26 (1984): 183–217.

———. "Wordsworth and Subversion, 1793–1804." Paper presented at the conference on "Wordsworth and the Borders of Romanticism," Yale University, Nov. 15, 1987, and the Modern Language Association convention, San Francisco, Dec. 28, 1987. Forthcoming in *Yale Journal of Criticism*, No. 2 (Spring 1989).

Lofthouse, Jessica. *The Curious Traveller Through Lakeland: Historic Ways North from Kendal and Cartmel to Keswick and Penrith*. London, 1973.

Lonsdale, Roger, ed. *The Poems of Thomas Gray, William Collins, Oliver Goldsmith*. London, 1969.

Lorrain, Claude. *Liber Veritatis*. In Michael Kitson, *Claude Lorrain: Liber Veritatis*. London, 1978.

Lukács, Georg. *The Theory of the Novel: A Historico-Philosophical Essay on the Forms of Great Epic Literature*. Trans. Anna Bostock. Cambridge, Mass., 1971.

Lyons, Martyn. *France Under the Directory*. Cambridge, Eng., 1975.

McConnell, Frank D. *The Confessional Imagination: A Reading of Wordsworth's "Prelude."* Baltimore, Md., 1974.

Maccunn, F. J. *The Contemporary English View of Napoleon.* London, 1914.

Macdonell, Diane C. "The Place of the Device of Expectation, or 'Seeing Through a Medium,' in Book I of *The Excursion.*" *Studies in Romanticism* 18 (1979): 427–51.

McFarland, Thomas. *Romanticism and the Forms of Ruin: Wordsworth, Coleridge, and Modalities of Fragmentation.* Princeton, N.J., 1981.

McGann, Jerome J. "Introduction: A Point of Reference." In McGann, ed., *Historical Studies and Literary Criticism.* Madison, Wisc., 1985.

———. *The Romantic Ideology: A Critical Investigation.* Chicago, 1983.

MacGillivray, J. R. "The Three Forms of *The Prelude,* 1798–1805." In W. J. Harvey and Richard Gravil, eds., *Wordsworth, "The Prelude": A Casebook.* London, 1972.

McGrath, William J. *Freud's Discovery of Psychoanalysis: The Politics of Hysteria.* Ithaca, N.Y., 1986.

Macherey, Pierre. *A Theory of Literary Production.* Trans. Geoffrey Wall. London, 1978.

MacLean, Kenneth. *Agrarian Age: A Background for Wordsworth.* Yale Studies in English, no. 115. New Haven, Conn., 1950.

Mallarmé, Stéphane. "The Book: A Spiritual Instrument." In *Mallarmé: Selected Prose Poems, Essays, and Letters.* Trans. Bradford Cook. Baltimore, Md., 1956.

Maniquis, Robert M. "Who Ate the Princess de Lamballe's Heart?—Cannibalism and Revolution." Paper presented at the conference on "Romanticism, Politics, and the New Historicism: In Honor of Carl Woodring," University of California, Los Angeles, Nov. 14, 1986.

Manley, Lawrence. "Concepts of Convention and Models of Critical Discourse." *New Literary History* 13 (1981): 31–52.

Manning, Peter J. "Wordsworth, Margaret, and the Pedlar." *Studies in Romanticism* 15 (1976): 195–220.

———. "Wordsworth's *Yarrow Revisited* and the Shape of a Period." Paper presented at the Modern Language Association convention, New York, Dec. 29, 1986.

Markham, Felix. *The Bonapartes.* New York, 1975.

Marsh, Florence. *Wordsworth's Imagery: A Study in Poetic Vision.* 1952. Rpt. Hamden, Conn., 1963.

Marshall, J. D. "Agrarian Wealth and Social Structure in Pre-Industrial Cumbria." *The Economic History Review,* 2d series 33 (1980): 503–21.

———. "The Domestic Economy of the Lakeland Yeoman, 1660–1749." *Transactions of the Cumberland and Westmorland Antiquarian and Archaeological Society,* n.s. 73 (1973): 190–219.

———. "Kendal in the Late Seventeenth and Eighteenth Centuries." *Transactions of the Cumberland and Westmorland Antiquarian and Archaeological Society,* n.s. 75 (1975): 188–257.

———. *Old Lakeland: Some Cumbrian Social History.* Newton Abbot, Eng., 1971.

———. "'Statesmen' in Cumbria: The Vicissitudes of an Expression." *Transactions of the Cumberland and Westmorland Antiquarian and Archaeological Society,* n.s. 72 (1972): 248–73.

Marshall, J. D., and M. Davies-Shiel. *The Lake District at Work: Past and Present*. Newton Abbot, Eng., 1971.

Mathiez, Albert. *The French Revolution*. Trans. Catherine Alison Phillips. New York, 1964.

Matteson, Lynn R. "The Poetics and Politics of Alpine Passage: Turner's *Snowstorm: Hannibal and His Army Crossing the Alps*." *Art Bulletin* 62 (1980): 385–98.

Mauss, Marcel. *The Gift: Forms and Functions of Exchange in Archaic Societies*. Trans. Ian Cunnison. New York, 1967.

Maxwell, J. C. "Wordsworth and the Subjugation of Switzerland." *Modern Language Review* 65 (1970): 16–18.

Meerloo, Joost A. M. "The Time Sense in Psychiatry." In J. T. Fraser, ed., *The Voices of Time: A Cooperative Survey of Man's Views of Time as Expressed by the Sciences and by the Humanities*. 2d ed. Amherst, Mass., 1981.

Mehlman, Jeffrey. *Revolution and Repetition: Marx/Hugo/Balzac*. Berkeley, Calif., 1977.

Melchior-Bonnet, Bernardine. *La Révolution 1789–1799*. Paris, 1984.

Mellor, Anne K. *English Romantic Irony*. Cambridge, Mass., 1980.

Messmann, Frank J. *Richard Payne Knight: The Twilight of Virtuosity*. Studies in English Literature, vol. 89. The Hague, 1974.

Meteyard, Belinda. "Illegitimacy and Marriage in Eighteenth-Century England." *Journal of Interdisciplinary History* 10 (1980): 479–89.

Metzger, Lore. "Coleridge in Sicily: A Pastoral Interlude in *The Prelude*." *Genre* 11 (1978): 63–81.

Miliband, Marion, ed. *The Observer of the Nineteenth Century, 1791–1901: A Selection*. London, 1966.

Miller, Henry Knight. "The 'Whig Interpretation' of Literary History." *Eighteenth-Century Studies* 6 (1972–73): 60–84.

Miller, J. Hillis. "Ariadne's Thread: Repetition and the Narrative Line." In Mario J. Valdés and Owen J. Miller, eds., *Interpretation of Narrative*. Toronto, 1978.

———. *Fiction and Repetition: Seven English Novels*. Cambridge, Mass., 1982.

———. "Graphic and Verbal: Turner to Phiz." Paper presented at the Yale Center for British Art, Mar. 31, 1980.

———. *The Linguistic Moment: From Wordsworth to Stevens*. Princeton, N.J., 1985.

———. "The Search for Grounds in Literary Study." In Robert Con Davis and Ronald Schleifer, eds., *Rhetoric and Form: Deconstruction at Yale*. Norman, Okla., 1985.

———. "The Still Heart: Poetic Form in Wordsworth." *New Literary History* 2 (1971): 297–310. Included in *Linguistic Moment*.

Millward, Roy, and Adrian Robinson. *The Lake District*. London, 1970.

Milton, John. *John Milton: Complete Poems and Major Prose*. Ed. Merritt Y. Hughes. Indianapolis, 1957.

Mink, Louis O. "Change and Causality in the History of Ideas." *Eighteenth-Century Studies* 2 (1968): 7–25.

Mitchell, Charles. "Benjamin West's 'Death of General Wolfe' and the Popular History Piece." *Journal of the Warburg and Courtauld Institutes* 7 (1944): 20–33.

Mitchell, W. J. T. *Iconology: Image, Text, Ideology*. Chicago, 1986.

Mitterauer, Michael, and Reinhard Sieder. *The European Family: Patriarchy to Partnership from the Middle Ages to the Present*. Trans. Karla Oosterveen and Manfred Hörzinger. Chicago, 1982.

Modiano, Raimonda. "Coleridge and Wordsworth: The Ethics of Gift Exchange and Literary Ownership." Paper presented at the Modern Language Association convention, San Francisco, Dec. 28, 1987.

———. "Metaphysical Debate in Coleridge's Political Theory." *Studies in Romanticism* 21 (1982): 465–74.

Molesworth, Charles. "Wordsworth's 'Westminster Bridge' Sonnet: The Republican Structure of Time and Perception." *Clio* 6 (1977): 261–73.

Monmouth, Geoffrey of. *The History of the Kings of Britain*. Trans. Lewis Thorpe. Harmondsworth, Eng., 1966.

Montrose, Louis. "Renaissance Literary Studies and the Subject of History." *English Literary Renaissance* 16 (1986): 5–12.

Moorman, Mary. "Wordsworth and His Children." In Jonathan Wordsworth, ed., with Beth Darlington, *Bicentenary Wordsworth Studies in Memory of John Alban Finch*. Ithaca, N.Y., 1970.

Morris, Susan. *Thomas Girtin, 1775–1802*. New Haven, Conn., 1986.

Mullaney, Steven. "Lying Like Truth: Riddle, Representation and Treason in Renaissance England." *ELH* 47 (1980): 32–47.

———. "Strange Things, Gross Terms, Curious Customs: The Rehearsal of Cultures in the Late Renaissance." *Representations* 3 (Summer 1983): 40–67.

Murdoch, John. *Forty-Two British Watercolours from the Victoria and Albert Museum*. London, 1977.

Murray, Roger N. *Wordsworth's Style: Figures and Themes in the "Lyrical Ballads" of 1800*. Lincoln, Nebr., 1967.

Murrin, Michael. *The Veil of Allegory: Some Notes Toward a Theory of Allegorical Rhetoric in the English Renaissance*. Chicago, 1969.

Musson, A. E. *The Growth of British Industry*. London, 1978.

Neubauer, John. "The Mines of Falun: Temporal Fortunes of a Romantic Myth of Time." *Studies in Romanticism* 19 (1980): 475–95.

Nichols, Stephen G., Jr. *Romanesque Signs: Early Medieval Narrative and Iconography*. New Haven, Conn., 1983.

Nicolson, Benedict. *Joseph Wright of Derby: Painter of Light*. Vol. 1. London, 1968.

Nicolson, Joseph, and Richard Burn. *The History and Antiquities of the Counties of Westmorland and Cumberland*. Vol. 1. London, 1777.

Noyes, Russell. *Wordsworth and the Art of Landscape*. Indiana Univ. Humanities Series, no. 65. Bloomington, Ind., 1968.

The Oeconomist, or, Englishman's Magazine. (Only 2 vols. published.) Newcastle upon Tyne, 1 (1798) and 2 (1799).

Olney, James. "Some Versions of Memory / Some Versions of *Bios*: The Ontology of Autobiography." In Olney, ed., *Autobiography: Essays Theoretical and Critical*. Princeton, N.J., 1980.

Oosterveen, Karla. "Hawkshead (Lancs.) Mobility (Geographical and Occupational) as Shown by the Reconstitution of the Parish from the Registers, 1585–1840." *Local Population Studies* 12 (Spring 1974): 38–41.

Osborn, Marijane. "Wordsworth's 'Borderers' and the Landscape of Penrith." *Transactions of the Cumberland and Westmorland Antiquarian and Archaeological Society*, n.s. 76 (1976): 144–58.

Osborne, Harold, ed. *The Oxford Companion to Art*. Oxford, 1970.

Owen, A. L. *The Famous Druids: A Survey of Three Centuries of English Literature on the Druids*. Oxford, 1962.

Owen, John B. *The Eighteenth Century, 1714–1815*. New York, 1976.

Owen, W. J. B. "*The Borderers* and the Aesthetics of Drama." *The Wordsworth Circle* 6 (1975): 227–39.

———. *Wordsworth as Critic*. Toronto, 1969.

Ozment, Steven. *When Fathers Ruled: Family Life in Reformation Europe*. Studies in Cultural History. Cambridge, Mass., 1983.

Ozouf, Mona. *La fête révolutionnaire, 1789–1799*. Paris, 1976.

Page, Judith W. "'The weight of too much liberty': Genre and Gender in Wordsworth's Calais Sonnets." *Criticism* 30 (1988): 189–203.

Palmer, Alan. *An Encyclopaedia of Napoleon's Europe*. New York, 1984.

Palmer, R. R. *Twelve Who Ruled: The Committee of Public Safety During the Terror*. Princeton, N.J., 1941.

———. *The World of the French Revolution*. New York, 1972.

Palumbo, Linda. "Fictions of 'Coleridge' in Wordsworth's *The River Duddon*." Paper presented at the Modern Language Association convention, Chicago, Dec. 29, 1985.

Panofsky, Erwin. *Meaning in the Visual Arts*. 1955. Rpt. Chicago, 1982.

Parker, Reeve. "'Finer Distance': The Narrative Art of Wordsworth's 'The Wanderer.'" *ELH* 39 (1972): 87–111.

———. "Reading Wordsworth's Power: Narrative and Usurpation in *The Borderers*." *ELH* 54 (1987): 299–331.

Paulson, Ronald. *Literary Landscape: Turner and Constable*. New Haven, Conn., 1982.

———. *Representations of Revolution (1789–1820)*. New Haven, Conn., 1983.

Peckham, Morse. *Romanticism and Behavior*. Vol. 2 of *Collected Essays*. Columbia, S.C., 1976.

Perkins, David. *Wordsworth and the Poetry of Sincerity*. Cambridge, Mass., 1964.

Peterfreund, Stuart. "*The Prelude*: Wordsworth's Metamorphic Epic." *Genre* 14 (1981): 441–72.

———. "Seriality and Centered Structure in Wordsworth's Later Poetry." Paper presented at Modern Language Association convention, New York, Dec. 28, 1981.

Pevsner, Nikolaus. *The Englishness of English Art*. 1956. Rpt. Harmondsworth, Eng., 1976.

———. "The Genesis of the Picturesque." *Architectural Review* 96 (1944): 139–46.

Piaget, Jean. "Time Perception in Children." In J. T. Fraser, ed., *The Voices of Time: A Cooperative Survey of Man's Views of Time as Expressed by the Sciences and by the Humanities*. Amherst, Mass., 1981.

Piggott, Stuart. *The Druids*. Ancient Peoples and Places, no. 63. London, 1968.

Pinto, V. de S. "Isaac Watts and William Blake." *Review of English Studies* 20 (1944): 214–23.

Pirie, David B. *William Wordsworth: The Poetry of Grandeur and of Tenderness*. London, 1982.

Pitt, William. *The War Speeches of William Pitt the Younger*. Ed. R. Coupland. Oxford, 1915.

Plumptre, A. F. W. "The Theory of the Black Market: Further Considerations." *Canadian Journal of Economics and Political Science* 13 (1947): 280–82.

Pocock, J. G. A. "Modes of Political and Historical Time in Early Eighteenth-Century England." In Ronald C. Rosbottom, ed., *Studies in Eighteenth-Century Culture* 5 (1976): 87–102.

Podro, Michael. *The Critical Historians of Art*. New Haven, Conn., 1982.

Pollin, Burton R. "Permutations of Names in *The Borderers*, or Hints of Godwin, Charles Lloyd, and a Real Renegade." *The Wordsworth Circle* 4 (1973): 31–35.

Pope, Alexander. *The Poems of Alexander Pope*. Ed. John Butt. New Haven, Conn., 1963.

Popkin, Jeremy D. *The Right-Wing Press in France, 1792–1800*. Chapel Hill, N.C., 1980.

Poster, Mark. *Critical Theory of the Family*. New York, 1978.

Poulet, Georges. *Studies in Human Time*. Trans. Elliott Coleman. Baltimore, Md., 1956.

Price, Martin. "The Picturesque Moment." In Frederick W. Hilles and Harold Bloom, eds., *From Sensibility to Romanticism: Essays Presented to Frederick A. Pottle*. New York, 1965.

Price, Uvedale. *Essays on the Picturesque, As Compared with the Sublime and the Beautiful; and, on the Use of Studying Pictures, for the Purpose of Improving Real Landscape*. 3 vols. London, 1810.

———. *Thoughts on the Defence of Property. Addressed to the County of Hereford in Particular; and to the Kingdom at Large*. Hereford, Eng., 1797.

Priestman, Donald G. "*The Borderers*: Wordsworth's Addenda to Godwin." *University of Toronto Quarterly* 44 (1974): 56–65.

Princeton Encyclopedia of Poetry and Poetics. Eds. Alex Preminger, Frank J. Warnke, and O. B. Hardison, Jr. Enlarged ed. Princeton, N.J., 1974.

Propp, Vladímir. *Morphology of the Folktale*. 2d ed. Trans. Laurence Scott. Ed. Louis A. Wagner. Austin, Tex., 1968.

Public Advertiser. London, 1792.

Punter, David. "1789: The Sex of Revolution." *Criticism* 24 (1982): 201–17.

Racine, Jean. *Athalie*. In *Jean Racine: Four Greek Plays: Andromache—Iphigenia—Phaedra—Athaliah*. Trans. and ed. R. C. Knight. Cambridge, Eng., 1982.

Ragussis, Michael. "Family Discourse and Fiction in *The Scarlet Letter*." *ELH* 49 (1982): 863–88.

Ramm, H. G., R. W. McDowall, and Eric Mercer. *Shielings and Bastles*. London, 1970.

Ramsey, Jonathan. "Seeing and Perceiving in Wordsworth's *An Evening Walk*." *Modern Language Quarterly* 36 (1975): 376–89.

Ransom, John Crowe. *The New Criticism*. Norfolk, Conn., 1941.

———. "William Wordsworth: Notes Toward an Understanding of Poetry." *Kenyon Review* 12 (1950): 498–519.

Ray, S. K. *Economics of the Black Market*. Boulder, Colo., 1981.

Reiman, Donald H. "Coleridge and the Art of Equivocation." *Studies in Romanticism* 25 (1986): 325–50.

Repton, Humphry. *Letter to Mr. Price.* In Uvedale Price, *Essays on the Picturesque,* vol. 3. London, 1810.

Reynolds, Graham. *An Introduction to English Water-Colour Painting.* London, 1950.

———. *Victoria and Albert Museum British Water-Colours.* London, 1968.

Reynolds, Sir Joshua. *Discourses on Art.* Ed. Robert R. Wark. 1959. Rpt. New Haven, Conn., 1975.

Ricoeur, Paul. *Time and Narrative.* Vol. 1. Chicago, 1984.

Roberts, J. M. *The French Revolution.* Oxford, 1978.

Robinson, Duncan. "Thomas Gainsborough and 'Real Views from Nature.'" Paper presented at the Yale Center for British Art, Mar. 6, 1984.

Robiquet, Jean. *Daily Life in the French Revolution.* Trans. James Kirkup. London, 1964.

Roe, Nicholas. "Who Was Spy Nozy?" *The Wordsworth Circle* 15 (1984): 46–50.

Rose, Thomas. *Westmorland, Cumberland, Durham, and Northumberland, Illustrated, From Original Drawings by Thomas Allom, &c. with Historical and Topographical Descriptions.* London, 1833.

Rosmarin, Adena. *The Power of Genre.* Minneapolis, 1985.

Ross, Donald, Jr. "Poems 'Bound Each to Each' in the 1815 Edition of Wordsworth." *The Wordsworth Circle* 12 (1981): 133–40.

Röthlisberger, Marcel. *Claude Lorrain: The Paintings.* 2 vols. New Haven, Conn., 1961.

Royal Commission on Historical Monuments, England. *An Inventory of the Historical Monuments in Westmorland.* London, 1936.

Rudé, George. *The Crowd in the French Revolution.* Oxford, 1959.

———. *The Crowd in History: A Study of Popular Disturbances in France and England, 1730–1848.* Rev. ed. London, 1981.

———. *Revolutionary Europe, 1783–1815.* 1964. Rpt. New York, 1975.

Ruoff, Gene W. "Critical Explications of Wordsworth's 1815 Categorization, with Some Animadversions on Binaristic Commentary." *The Wordsworth Circle* 9 (1978): 75–82.

Russell, H. Diane. *Claude Lorrain, 1600–1682.* Washington, D.C., 1982.

Rzepka, Charles J. "A Gift That Complicates Employ: Poetry and Poverty in 'Resolution and Independence.'" Paper presented at the Modern Language Association convention, San Francisco, Dec. 28, 1987.

Sade, Marquis de. *The Marquis de Sade: The Complete Justine, Philosophy in the Bedroom, and Other Writings.* Trans. Richard Seaver and Austryn Wainhouse. New York, 1966.

Sagnac, Philippe, and Jean Robiquet. *La Révolution de 1789.* Vol. 1. Paris, 1934.

Salerno, Luigi. *Salvator Rosa.* [Italy], 1963.

Salm, Peter. "Pinpoint of Eternity: The Sufficient Moment in Literature." In Harold E. Pagliaro, ed., *Studies in Eighteenth-Century Culture* 3 ("Racism in the Eighteenth Century," 1973): 49–65.

Salvesen, Christopher. *The Landscape of Memory: A Study of Wordsworth's Poetry.* Lincoln, Nebr., 1965.

Salzmann, Christian G. *Elements of Morality, for the Use of Children; with an Introductory Address to Parents.* 3 vols. Trans. Mary Wollstonecraft. 3d ed. London, 1792.

Sandmel, Samuel. *Philo of Alexandria: An Introduction.* New York, 1979.

Saussure, Ferdinand de. *Course in General Linguistics.* Trans. Roy Harris. Ed. Charles Bally and Albert Sechehaye, with Albert Riedlinger. La Salle, Ill., 1986.

Scarry, Elaine. "Injury and the Structure of War." *Representations* 10 (Spring 1985): 1–51. Included in expanded form in *The Body in Pain: The Making and Unmaking of the World.* New York, 1985.

Schapiro, Barbara A. *The Romantic Mother: Narcissistic Patterns in Romantic Poetry.* Baltimore, Md., 1983.

Schlüter, Kurt. "Wieder einmal 'Upon Westminster Bridge.'" *Literatur in Wissenschaft und Unterricht* 12 (1979): 202–5.

Schneider, Ben Ross, Jr. *Wordsworth's Cambridge Education.* Cambridge, Eng., 1957.

Schoenfield, Mark. "An Incursion into a Theory of Property: Wordsworth's *Excursion.*" Unpub. MS., courtesy of the author.

Scholes, Robert. *Structuralism in Literature: An Introduction.* New Haven, Conn., 1974.

Schorske, Carl E. *Fin-de-Siècle Vienna: Politics and Culture.* New York, 1980.

Schulman, Samuel E. "Wordsworth's Salisbury Plain Poems and Their Spenserian Motives." *JEGP* 84 (1985): 221–42.

Schur, Owen. "Developments and Transformations of Pastoral Melancholy in Some Poems of Keats, Tennyson, and Hardy." Ph.D. diss., Yale University, 1985.

Scoggins, James. *Imagination and Fancy: Complementary Modes in the Poetry of Wordsworth.* Lincoln, Nebr., 1966.

Scott, Sir Walter. *The Life of Napoleon Buonaparte, Emperor of the French, with a Preliminary View of the French Revolution.* Vol. 1. Exeter, Eng., 1843.

———. *Waverley.* London, 1906.

Searle, C. E. "Custom, Class Conflict and Agrarian Capitalism: The Cumbrian Customary Economy in the Eighteenth Century." *Past and Present* 110 (Feb. 1986): 106–33.

Sennett, Richard. "The Aesthetics of Violence: Narrative and Violence; Strategic Play; Sacrifice and Terror." Three papers presented at the Whitney Humanities Center, Yale University, Mar. 31 to Apr. 14, 1986.

Shackford, Martha Hale. *Wordsworth's Interest in Painters and Pictures.* Wellesley, Mass., 1945.

Shakespeare, William. *The Riverside Shakespeare.* Ed. G. Blakemore Evans et al. Boston, 1974.

Sharrock, Roger. "*The Borderers*: Wordsworth on the Moral Frontier." *Durham University Journal,* n.s. 25 (1964): 170–83.

Shaver, Chester L. "The Griffith Family: Wordsworth's Kinsmen." *Transactions of the Cumberland and Westmorland Antiquarian and Archaeological Society,* n.s. 63 (1963): 199–230.

Shaver, Chester L., and Alice C. Shaver. *Wordsworth's Library: A Catalogue.* New York, 1979.

Shearer, Edna Aston. "Wordsworth and Coleridge Marginalia in a Copy of Richard Payne Knight's *Analytical Inquiry into the Principles of Taste.*" *Huntington Library Quarterly* 1 (1937): 63–94.

Sheats, Paul D. *The Making of Wordsworth's Poetry, 1785–1798.* Cambridge, Mass., 1973.

Shell, Marc. *The Economy of Literature.* Baltimore, Md., 1978.

Sheppard, Francis. *History of London: London 1808–1870: The Infernal Wen.* Berkeley, Calif., 1971.

Shklovsky, Victor. "Art as Technique." In *Russian Formalist Criticism: Four Essays.* Trans. Lee T. Lemon and Marion J. Reis. Lincoln, Nebr., 1965.

———. "Sterne's *Tristram Shandy*: Stylistic Commentary." In *Russian Formalist Criticism: Four Essays.* Trans. Lee T. Lemon and Marion J. Reis. Lincoln, Nebr., 1965.

Shoaf, R. A. *Dante, Chaucer, and the Currency of the Word: Money, Images, and Reference in Late Medieval Poetry.* Norman, Okla., 1983.

Shorter, Edward. *The Making of the Modern Family.* New York, 1975.

Sieburg, Friedrich. *La France de la Royauté à la Nation, 1789–1848.* Stuttgart, 1963.

Simpson, David. "Criticism, Politics, and Style in Wordsworth's Poetry." *Critical Inquiry* 11 (1984): 52–81.

———. *Irony and Authority in Romantic Poetry.* London, 1979.

———. "Literary Criticism and the Return to 'History.'" *Critical Inquiry* 14 (1988): 721–47.

———. "What Bothered Charles Lamb About Poor Susan?" *Studies in English Literature* 26 (1986): 589–612.

———. *Wordsworth and the Figurings of the Real.* Atlantic Highlands, N.J., 1982.

———. *Wordsworth's Historical Imagination: The Poetry of Displacement.* New York, 1987.

Simpson, Lewis P., ed. *The Possibilities of Order: Cleanth Brooks and His Work.* Baton Rouge, La., 1976.

Siskin, Clifford. "Romantic Genre: Lyric Form and Revisionary Behavior in Wordsworth." *Genre* 16 (1983): 137–55.

———. "The Un-Kind Imagination: Reformulating Romanticism." Paper presented at the Modern Language Association convention, New York, Dec. 29, 1983.

———. "Wordsworth's Gothic Endeavor: From *Esthwaite* to the Great Decade." *The Wordsworth Circle* 10 (1979): 161–73.

Smelser, Neil J. *Social Change in the Industrial Revolution: An Application of Theory to the Lancashire Cotton Industry, 1770–1840.* London, 1959.

Smith, Adam. *An Inquiry into the Nature and Causes of the Wealth of Nations.* Ed. Edwin Cannan. Vol. 1. Chicago, 1976.

Smith, Barbara Herrnstein. "Contingencies of Value." *Critical Inquiry* 10 (1983): 1–35.

———. "Fixed Marks and Variable Constancies: A Parable of Literary Value." *Poetics Today* 1 (1979), Nos. 1–2, 7–22.

Smith, Bernard. *European Vision and the South Pacific.* 2d ed. New Haven, Conn., 1985.

Smith, K. E. "Love in *The Borderers.*" *Durham University Journal*, n.s. 43 (1981): 97–102.

Soboul, Albert. *The French Revolution, 1787–1799: From the Storming of the Bastille to Napoleon.* Trans. Alan Forrest and Colin Jones. New York, 1975.

Sokol, Ronald P. "The Political Trial: Courtroom as Stage, History as Critic." *New Literary History* 2 (1971): 495–516.

Spector, Stephen J. "Wordsworth's Mirror Imagery and the Picturesque Tradition." *ELH* 44 (1977): 85–107.

Spenser, Edmund. *Edmund Spenser's Poetry: Authoritative Texts, Criticism.* 2d ed. Ed. Hugh Maclean. Norton Critical Edition. New York, 1982.

Sperry, Stuart M., Jr. "From 'Tintern Abbey' to the 'Intimations Ode': Wordsworth and the Function of Memory." *The Wordsworth Circle* 1 (1970): 40–49.

Spivak, Gayatri Chakravorty. "Sex and History in *The Prelude* (1805): Books Nine to Thirteen." *Texas Studies in Literature and Language* 23 (1981): 324–60.

Stallknecht, Newton P. *Strange Seas of Thought: Studies in William Wordsworth's Philosophy of Man and Nature.* Bloomington, Ind., 1958.

Stelzig, Eugene L. *All Shades of Consciousness: Wordsworth's Poetry and the Self in Time.* Studies in English Literature, vol. 102. The Hague, 1975.

———. "'Coleridge' in *The Prelude*: Wordsworth's Fiction of Alterity." Paper presented at the Modern Language Association convention, Chicago, Dec. 29, 1985.

Sterne, Laurence. *A Sentimental Journey Through France and Italy.* Ed. Graham Petrie. Harmondsworth, Eng., 1967.

Stewart, John L. *The Burden of Time, The Fugitives and Agrarians: The Nashville Groups of the 1920's and 1930's, and the Writing of John Crowe Ransom, Allen Tate, and Robert Penn Warren.* Princeton, N.J., 1965.

Stone, Lawrence. *The Family, Sex and Marriage in England 1500–1800.* New York, 1977.

———. *The Past and the Present.* London, 1981.

Storch, R. F. "The Politics of the Imagination." *Studies in Romanticism* 21 (1982): 448–56.

———. "Wordsworth's *The Borderers*: The Poet as Anthropologist." *ELH* 36 (1969): 340–60.

Sucksmith, Harvey Peter. "Ultimate Affirmation: A Critical Analysis of Wordsworth's Sonnet, 'Composed Upon Westminster Bridge,' and the Image of the City in *The Prelude.*" *Yearbook of English Studies* 6 (1976): 113–19.

Sutherland, L. Stuart. "Edmund Burke and the First Rockingham Ministry." *English Historical Review* 47 (1932): 46–72.

Sutton, Denys, ed. *An Italian Sketchbook by Richard Wilson R.A.* London, 1968.

Swanson, Donald R. "Wordsworth's Sonnets." *CEA Critic* 30 (1968), no. 5: 12–13.

Sydenham, M. J. *The First French Republic, 1792–1804.* London, 1974.

Tate, Allen. *Collected Essays.* Denver, Colo., 1959.

Tayler, Irene. "By Peculiar Grace: Wordsworth in 1802." In Donald H. Reiman, Michael C. Jaye, and Betty T. Bennett, eds., with Doucet Devin Fischer and Ricki B. Herzfeld, *The Evidence of the Imagination: Studies of Interactions Between Life and Art in English Romantic Literature.* New York, 1978.

Thiers, M. A. *History of the Consulate and the Empire of France Under Napoleon, Forming a Sequel to "The History of the French Revolution."* Trans. D. Forbes Campbell. Vol. 1. London, 1845.

Thomas, Denis, with Ian Bennett. *The Price Guide to English Watercolours, 1750–1900.* Woodbridge, Eng., 1971.

Thompson, E. P. *The Making of the English Working Class.* New York, 1963.

Thompson, T. W. *Wordsworth's Hawkshead.* Ed. Robert Woof. London, 1970.

Thomson, James. *"The Seasons" and "The Castle of Indolence."* Ed. James Sambrook. Oxford, 1972.

Thorslev, Peter L., Jr. "Wordsworth's *Borderers* and the Romantic Villain-Hero." *Studies in Romanticism* 5 (1966): 84–103.

Tilly, Louise A. "The Food Riot as a Form of Political Conflict in France." *Journal of Interdisciplinary History* 2 (1971): 23–57.

Tomashevsky, Boris. "Thematics." In *Russian Formalist Criticism: Four Essays.* Trans. Lee T. Lemon and Marion J. Reis. Lincoln, Nebr., 1965.

Trigg, Joseph Wilson. *Origen: The Bible and Philosophy in the Third-Century Church.* Atlanta, 1983.

Turner, J. M. W. *Liber Studiorum.* In Alexander J. Finberg, *The History of Turner's "Liber Studiorum" with a New Catalogue Raisonné.* London, 1924.

Turner, James. *The Politics of Landscape: Rural Scenery and Society in English Poetry 1630–1660.* Oxford, 1979.

Tuve, Rosemond. *Elizabethan and Metaphysical Imagery: Renaissance Poetic and Twentieth-Century Critics.* Chicago, 1947.

Tynjanov, Jurij. "On Literary Evolution." Trans. C. A. Luplow. In Ladislav Matejka and Krystyna Pomorska, eds., *Readings in Russian Poetics: Formalist and Structuralist Views.* Cambridge, Mass., 1971.

Valentine, Alan. *The British Establishment, 1760–1784: An Eighteenth-Century Biographical Dictionary.* Vol. 2. Norman, Okla., 1970.

Vanden Bossche, Chris R. "Instituting Literature: Carlyle, Career, and Genre." MS. courtesy of the author. Published in revised form as "Carlyle, Career, and Genre," *The Arnoldian: A Review of Mid-Victorian Culture* 13 (1986): 28–43.

Van Doren, Mark. *Introduction to Poetry.* New York, 1951.

Vann, Richard T. Review of Lawrence Stone's *The Family, Sex and Marriage in England, 1500–1800. Journal of Family History* 4 (1979): 308–15.

Vergara, Lisa. *Rubens and the Poetics of Landscape.* New Haven, Conn., 1982.

Virgil. *The Georgics.* Trans. C. Day Lewis. New York, 1947.

Wall, Richard. "Mean Household Size in England from Printed Sources." In Peter Laslett, ed., with Richard Wall, *Household and Family in Past Time.* Cambridge, Eng., 1972.

The Wanderer. Trans. E. Talbot Donaldson. In *The Norton Anthology of English Literature,* 5th ed. Vol. 1. Ed. M. H. Abrams et al. New York, 1986.

Ward, J. P. *Wordsworth's Language of Men.* Brighton, Eng., 1984.

Warren, Robert Penn. "A Conversation with Cleanth Brooks." In Lewis P. Simpson, ed., *The Possibilities of Order: Cleanth Brooks and His Work.* Baton Rouge, La., 1976.

Watson, J. R. *Picturesque Landscape and English Romantic Poetry.* London, 1970.

———. *Wordsworth's Vital Soul: The Sacred and Profane in Wordsworth's Poetry.* Atlantic Highlands, N.J., 1982.

Watt, Ian. *The Rise of the Novel: Studies in Defoe, Richardson and Fielding.* Berkeley, Calif., 1957.

Watts, Isaac. *Divine Songs Attempted in Easy Language For the Use of Children.* London, 1781.

Webb, Sidney, and Beatrice Webb. *English Local Government: From the Revolution to the Municipal Corporations Act.* Vol. 1: *The Parish and the County.* London, 1906. Vol. 4: *Statutory Authorities for Special Purposes.* London, 1922.

Webster, Mary. *Francis Wheatley.* London, 1970.

Weiskel, Thomas. *The Romantic Sublime: Studies in the Structure and Psychology of Transcendence.* Baltimore, Md., 1976.

Weitzmann, Kurt. *The Icon: Holy Images, Sixth to Fourteenth Century.* London, 1978.

Weitzmann, Kurt, Manolis Chatzidakis, and Svetozar Radojcic. *Icons.* New York, 1980.

Wellek, René, and Austin Warren. *Theory of Literature.* 3d ed. New York, 1970.

Welsford, Enid. *Salisbury Plain: A Study in the Development of Wordsworth's Mind and Art.* Oxford, 1966.

Werkmeister, Lucyle. *The London Daily Press, 1772–1792.* Lincoln, Nebr., 1963.

———. *A Newspaper History of England, 1792–1793.* Lincoln, Nebr., 1967.

Wesling, Donald. *Wordsworth and the Adequacy of Landscape.* London, 1970.

West, Thomas. *A Guide to the Lakes: Dedicated to the Lovers of Landscape Studies, and to All Who Have Visited, or Intend to Visit the Lakes in Cumberland, Westmorland, and Lancashire.* London, 1778.

Wheaton, Robert, and Tamara K. Hareven, eds. *Family and Sexuality in French History.* Philadelphia, 1980.

Whellan, William. *The History and Topography of the Counties of Cumberland and Westmoreland, Comprising Their Ancient and Modern History, A General View of Their Physical Character, Trade, Commerce, Manufactures, Agricultural Condition, Statistics, Etc., Etc.* Pontrefract, Eng., 1860.

White, Hayden. *The Content of the Form: Narrative Discourse and Historical Representation.* Baltimore, Md., 1987.

———. *Metahistory: The Historical Imagination in Nineteenth-Century Europe.* Baltimore, Md., 1973.

———. *Tropics of Discourse: Essays in Cultural Criticism.* Baltimore, Md., 1978.

———. "The Value of Narrativity in the Representation of Reality." In W. J. T. Mitchell, ed., *On Narrative.* Chicago, 1981.

Whitlock, Ralph. *The Folklore of Wiltshire.* London, 1976.

———. *Salisbury Plain.* London, 1955.

Wiebenson, Dora. *The Picturesque Garden in France.* Princeton, N.J., 1978.

Wildi, Max. "Wordsworth and the Simplon Pass." *English Studies* 40 (1959): 224–32.

Wilkinson, L. P. *The Georgics of Virgil: A Critical Survey.* Cambridge, Eng., 1969.

Williams, Raymond. *The Country and the City.* New York, 1973.

Wilson, Michael. *The National Gallery, London.* New York, 1983.

Wilton, Andrew. *British Watercolours, 1750 to 1850*. Oxford, 1977.

Wimsatt, W. K., Jr. *The Verbal Icon: Studies in the Meaning of Poetry*. Lexington, Ky., 1954.

Winstanley, D. A. *Lord Chatham and the Whig Opposition*. Cambridge, Eng., 1912.

Winston, David. *Logos and Mystical Theology in Philo of Alexandria*. Cincinnati, Ohio, 1985.

Wise, Thomas J. *A Bibliography of the Writings in Prose and Verse of William Wordsworth*. London, 1916.

Wolf, John B. *Louis XIV*. New York, 1968.

Wölfflin, Heinrich. *Kunstgeschichtliche Grundbegriffe: das Problem der Stilentwicklung in der neueren Kunst*. 5th ed. Munich, 1921.

——— . *Principles of Art History: The Problem of the Development of Style in Later Art*. Trans. M. D. Hottinger. 1932. Rpt. New York, 1950.

——— . *Renaissance and Baroque*. Trans. Kathrin Simon. Ithaca, N.Y., 1966.

Wollstonecraft, Mary. *Original Stories from Real Life; With Conversations, Calculated to Regulate the Affections, and Form the Mind to Truth and Goodness*. London, 1791.

——— . *A Vindication of the Rights of Woman*. Ed. Miriam Brody Kramnick. Harmondsworth, Eng., 1975.

Woodring, Carl. "On Liberty in the Poetry of Wordsworth." *PMLA* 70 (1955): 1033–48.

——— . *Politics in English Romantic Poetry*. Cambridge, Mass., 1970.

——— . *Politics in the Poetry of Coleridge*. Madison, Wis., 1961.

——— . *Wordsworth*. Riverside Studies in Literature. Cambridge, Mass., 1968.

Woof, R. S. "Wordsworth's Poetry and Stuart's Newspapers: 1797–1803." *Studies in Bibliography* 15 (1962): 149–89.

Wordsworth, Dorothy. *Journals of Dorothy Wordsworth*. Ed. Ernest de Selincourt. 2 vols. 1941. Rpt. Hamden, Conn., 1970.

Wordsworth, John. *The Letters of John Wordsworth*. Ed. Carl H. Ketcham. Ithaca, N.Y., 1969.

Wordsworth, Jonathan. "The Five-Book *Prelude* of Early Spring 1804." *JEGP* 76 (1977): 1–25.

——— . *The Music of Humanity: A Critical Study of Wordsworth's "Ruined Cottage."* London, 1969.

——— . *William Wordsworth: The Borders of Vision*. New York, 1982.

——— . "A Wordsworth Tragedy." *TLS*, July 21, 1966, p. 642.

Wordsworth, William. *Benjamin the Waggoner*. Ed. Paul F. Betz. The Cornell Wordsworth. Ithaca, N.Y., 1981.

——— . *"Home at Grasmere," Part First, Book First of "The Recluse."* Ed. Beth Darlington. The Cornell Wordsworth. Ithaca, N.Y., 1977.

——— . *The Love Letters of William and Mary Wordsworth*. Ed. Beth Darlington. Ithaca, N.Y., 1981.

——— . *Poetical Works*. Ed. Thomas Hutchinson. Rev. by Ernest de Selincourt. London, 1936.

——— . *The Prelude: A Parallel Text*. Ed. J. C. Maxwell. Harmondsworth, Eng., 1971.

————. *The Tuft of Primroses with Other Late Poems for "The Recluse."* Ed. Joseph F. Kishel. The Cornell Wordsworth. Ithaca, N.Y., 1986.

Wrightson, Keith. "Infanticide in Earlier Seventeenth-Century England." *Local Population Studies* 15 (Autumn 1975): 10–22.

Wrigley, E. A., and R. S. Schofield. "English Population History from Family Reconstitution: Summary Results 1600–1799." *Population Studies* 37 (1983): 157–84.

Wüscher, Hermann J. *Liberty, Equality, and Fraternity in Wordsworth: 1791–1800.* Studia Anglistica Upsaliensia, no. 39. Uppsala, 1980.

Index

In this index an "f" after a number indicates a separate reference on the next page, and an "ff" indicates separate references on the next two pages. A continuous discussion over two or more pages is indicated by a span of page numbers, e.g., "pp. 57–58." *Passim* is used for a cluster of references in close but not consecutive sequence, with at most three pages intervening. References to works are included under the author's or artist's name, though most works mentioned in the notes, as well as the majority of secondary or critical works throughout, are indicated only by the author's name. British daily newspapers are those of London except where otherwise identified. Works without attribution are Wordsworth's. Unless otherwise noted, "*Prelude*" subsumes all versions. "*Guide*" here subsumes all versions of *A Guide Through the District of the Lakes*, as well as the satellite work "An Unpublished Tour."

Library of Congress Cataloging-in-Publication Data

Liu, Alan, 1953–
   Wordsworth, the sense of history.

   Bibliography: p.
   Includes index.
   1. Wordsworth, William, 1770–1850—Knowledge—History.
2. History in literature.   I. Title.
PR5892.H5L5   1989   821'.7   88-28382
ISBN 0-8047-1373-1 (alk. paper)